A History of Science, Magic and Belief is an exploration of the origins of modern society through the culture of the middle ages and early modern period. By examining the intertwined paths of three different systems for interpreting the world, it seeks to create a narrative which culminates in the birth of modernity. It looks at the tensions and boundaries between science and magic throughout the middle ages and how they were affected by elite efforts to rationalize society, often through religion. The witch-crazes of the sixteenth and seventeenth century are seen as a pivotal point, and the emergence from these into social peace is deemed possible due to the Scientific Revolution and the politics of the early modern state.

This book is unique in drawing together the histories of science, magic and religion. It is thus an ideal book for those studying any or all of these topics, and with its broad time frame, it is also suitable for students of the history of Europe or Western civilization in general.

Steven P. Marrone is Professor of History at Tufts University, USA.

A History of Science, Magic and Belief

From Medieval to Early Modern Europe

STEVEN P. MARRONE

Professor of History, Tufts University, USA

 palgrave

First published 2015 by
PALGRAVE

Palgrave in the UK is an imprint of Macmillan Publishers Limited, registered in England, company number 785998, of 4 Crinan Street, London N1 9XW

Palgrave Macmillan in the US is a division of St Martin's Press LLC, 175 Fifth Avenue, New York, NY 10010.

Palgrave is the global imprint of the above companies and is represented throughout the world.

Palgrave® and Macmillan® are registered trademarks in the United States, the United Kingdom, Europe and other countries

ISBN: 978–1–137–02977–5 hardback
ISBN: 978–1–137–02976–8 paperback

This book is printed on paper suitable for recycling and made from fully managed and sustained forest sources. Logging, pulping and manufacturing processes are expected to conform to the environmental regulations of the country of origin.

A catalogue record for this book is available from the British Library.

A catalog record for this book is available from the Library of Congress.

Printed and bound in the UK by The Lavenham Press Ltd, Suffolk.

MIX
Paper from
responsible sources
FSC
www.fsc.org
FSC® C010693

To Jean

Contents

Introduction

Ask most people in what period the European witchcraze occurred, and the reply will be "the Middle Ages." Ask when the Scientific Revolution happened, and the answer is "modern times" or perhaps "the early modern period." Yet, as any historian of Europe will tell you, the two phenomena date to more or less the same time. At the very least, they greatly overlap. The witch persecutions reached their height in Europe during the sixteenth and seventeenth centuries, while the Scientific Revolution hails back to the late sixteenth to early eighteenth century. The commonplace confusion about their dating is surely due to the fact that the witchcraze is often taken as a sign of the ending of an era – premodern or medieval – and the Scientific Revolution is held even among historians to be a harbinger of the modern world. But of course that would not necessarily mean they were not simultaneous. In fact, both arose from a single process of broad change sweeping through Europe for a much longer period, a process which together they capped and to a great degree brought to an end.

The fundamental thesis of this book is that the period from the twelfth through the late seventeenth and early eighteenth centuries must be taken as an historical unit susceptible to a narrative giving it a clear beginning and a distinct end, the latter following a social crisis whose resolution brought the period to a close and signaled the start of modernity. The job will be to lay out that thesis in detail and provide evidence for its validity. This book works the way most histories do, by presenting the story on which the thesis depends. In this case the story is complex. It binds together three threads of historical change. And what makes this binding possible is the fact that the three threads are causally interdependent. Each can be explained, in the end, only with reference to the dynamics of the other two.

The first thread has to do with science. Its story begins and ends with processes of change. In the twelfth and thirteenth centuries learned culture in western Europe was subject to the transformative injection of new modes of reasoning associated with what the thirteenth century came to know as "science." Accompanying these modes was a vast reservoir of hitherto unknown material, stored and developed in an antique past and a more recent Islamic Middle Ages and spanning a variety of disciplines, the most important of which, for the present study, is natural philosophy or natural science. Yet by the late sixteenth century this scientific current of thought was beginning to shift directions, inaugurating a second period of rapid transformation. This second time of volatility is associated with the Scientific Revolution, stretching up to the first half of the eighteenth century.

It culminated in a new regime in thinking that we designate as "modern" and take as marking the advent of another era. Along the path from the twelfth to the seventeenth century there was, moreover, a secondary story concerning magic. For as we shall see, the emergence of a scientific model in the twelfth and thirteenth centuries entailed the introduction as well of learned magic. The fortunes of this magic were tied to science, at least until the seventeenth century. Again, the Scientific Revolution marked a change. Learned magic and science separated, and the latter dismissed the former as both untruthful and irrelevant.

With the second thread of importance to this book we enter a broader social domain. Here the story involves the interaction between the elite and the rest of the people. It begins with what can only be called the cultural spin-off of the scientific mode of thinking described earlier. For with the new science there arose a novel idea of the social order. As we shall see, this new attitude entailed a commitment to "rationalizing" culture, ultimately to "rationalizing" society itself. The cultural sphere in which such efforts played themselves out was largely that of religious and spiritual matters. Once more magic works its way into our sights, though it is now the magic of the populace at large. As tensions mounted from elite efforts to intervene in and change popular culture, a breaking point was reached. The upshot was the convulsions of the witchcraze of the sixteenth and seventeenth centuries. Again the resolution of the crisis saw a transition to a new cultural norm associated with modernity. And that meant the withdrawal of the elite from aggressive intervention into the people's cultural world. The end of the witchcraft prosecutions ushered in a relative indifference, lasting for several centuries, of the elite toward the culture of those below.

Our third and final thread engages institutions of social and political control. One should think of this as the material correlative to the issues of cultural interaction manifested by the second thread. Most prominent in this regard is the emergence of centralized government, specifically the premodern state at the level of both the nation and the city. Yet of equal interest is the centralization that took place with the church, entailing the rise of an increasingly monarchical papacy. As such governing entities developed, their earliest relationship to the populace came in the juridical sphere. Here we see the emergence of an inquisitorial or investigative mode of operation, with the signal instance being the foundation of a loosely organized medieval inquisition. One ideological side to this judicial strand touches again on the theme of witchcraft, where we are witness to the rise of a comprehensive stereotype of the witch that fueled the sixteenth- and seventeenth-century persecutions of alleged witches. As with the first two historical threads, this one draws to a close in the seventeenth and early eighteenth centuries in another transformation. The early modern nation state both regularized relations between governing elite and the people and, largely as a result, terminated the social paroxysms of witchcraft prosecution. What made this relative pacification of the social landscape possible was the adoption of a new ideology of state. And with modern European politics, a different historical narrative begins.

None of these three threads has been marked out by a distinct historiographical tradition in the scholarly literature. But of course each of them arises out of a
body of scholarship spread across the general fields of cultural and social history,
and so it is worth looking at some of this work if only to situate the present book
in the context of recent and current historical discussion. Here it is useful to
elaborate on the three themes presented in the title: science, magic and belief. So
far as concerns the history of science, the early twentieth century saw the beginnings of an effort to locate the rise of an intellectual atmosphere in which the
natural sciences, long familiar in the cultural world of Arabic and Hebrew scholarly traditions, were welcomed into the Latin west. Charles Homer Haskins had
already completed his investigations into the early history of medieval science
when, in 1927, he published his famous work titled *The Renaissance of the Twelfth
Century*, designating the 1100s as the time of an awakening in many intellectual and cultural fields, including that of natural science.[1] Later in the twentieth
century Marie-Dominique Chenu added his voice to the chorus of those hailing
the twelfth century as pivotal in this establishment of science in western Europe.[2]
Emphasizing a borrowing from an unbroken scientific tradition in the eastern
Mediterranean, Chenu characterized the development more precisely as the Latin
discovery of the idea of "nature," a rule-bound system in the external world,
susceptible to investigation by a logic-oriented and systematizing mind. Work
on the twelfth century has thenceforth proceeded apace, with a deepening of
the appreciation of a body of scientific learning directed toward nature, nowhere
more plainly evident than in the writing of Andreas Speer.[3] Meanwhile attention
has begun to be focused on the thirteenth century as witnessing a second stage
in the elaboration of a scientific paradigm in general, whether applied to nature
or not. My own work on the erection of a formal model for knowledge that
could be considered scientific, starting with the early-thirteenth-century efforts
of two scholastics, William of Auvergne and Robert Grosseteste, provides a suitable example.[4]

Of course, the idea of a scientific recommencement in the west in the late
sixteenth and the seventeenth centuries has an even older pedigree. This period
of the so-called Scientific Revolution was seen even in its own day as marking a
break with the scientific traditions of the Middle Ages, impelled by a new vision
of the cosmos, an understanding of mechanics as fundamental to change in the
natural world and a conviction that scientific knowledge must be based in systematic procedures of experiment. The 1950s witnessed the flowering of attempts by
historians of science to paint a general picture of dramatic transformation in all
fields of natural science in those centuries of early modern Europe. Among the
most prominent efforts were works by two titans of twentieth-century history
of science, George Sarton and Alexandre Koyré. In two works, both appearing
in 1957, they established what can be considered the classic view of the early
modern Scientific Revolution.[5] And in that same year was published one of the
most influential renditions of the way such scientific reorientation came about
in Thomas Kuhn's *The Copernican Revolution*.[6] Here was an explanation of change

in science that was inextricably related to other, and broader, alterations in the social world.

Interestingly enough, the historiographical literature on the Scientific Revolution also provided an avenue toward the second of the themes, the scholarly engagement with which furnishes a context for the investigations of this book – that is, magic. Already in 1957, the date of the three aforementioned works on science, Paolo Rossi was turning his efforts to disentangling the threads of the new natural science and the older learned magic with his *Francesco Bacone. Dalla magia alla scienza*.[7] And while Rossi was mainly interested in separating the strands of natural science and magic, within little over two decades Charles Webster was admonishing his readers on how a complete break between the traditions of learned magic and the new paths of natural science ran afoul of the actual interconnectedness of the two themes in the period of the Scientific Revolution.[8] Webster argued that what we call magic held a purchase on the minds of scientific innovators up through the late seventeenth century and indeed prompted some of the insights we associate with revolutionary advance. Meanwhile Betty Jo Teeter Dobbs was drawing attention to the formidable place that alchemy, both theory and practice, held in the thought of that paragon of the new science, Isaac Newton himself.[9]

The door having been opened, other scholars pressed in to investigate the magical disciplines feeding into some of revolutionary science's most telling innovations. In the past few decades, the study of alchemy on its own terms has matured enormously, yielding a growing awareness that early modern chemistry and the experimental procedures accompanying it developed quite directly out of the alchemical past, in contrast to the analysis by means of the mixture of elements associated with the preceding scholastic tradition but also partly independent of the new reliance on a mechanical hypothesis. The works of William Newman and Lawrence Principe have made the most significant advances in this regard.[10] They have succeeded in totally recasting our understanding of modern chemistry's relation to the traditions that preceded it.

While this foray into magic's ambivalent role in the classic Scientific Revolution of the late sixteenth to early eighteenth centuries was taking place, there were also efforts to place the development of the new science and the activities of its promoters in the broader context of society as a whole. Indeed, the origins of such investigations go back at least to the late 1930s. Robert Merton's *Science, Technology and Society in Seventeenth-Century England* represented an audacious attempt to link the new currents in science to the rise of an entrepreneurial and calculating milieu in the business-oriented sector of the early modern world, especially in England.[11] Since Merton's time the field has broadened and the attention to it steadily increased. A major advance was marked by the appearance in 1985 of Steven Shapin and Simon Schaffer's *Leviathan and the Air-Pump*, a subtle analysis of the interconnections between scientific circles, even some of the substance of innovations in natural science, and a much broader element of the elite population, influenced among other things by the rise of the early modern state, than Merton had ever envisioned.[12]

As for the traditions of magic in the high Middle Ages and early modern Europe in the period just preceding the Scientific Revolution, the scholarly territory was initially mapped out by Lynn Thorndike in his monumental *A History of Magic and Experimental Science*, the first volume of which was published in 1923.[13] Research on the subject was slower in picking up momentum than had been the case for seventeenth-century science, but by the 1950s and 1960s major studies had begun to appear, particularly on learned magic in the Renaissance. D.P. Walker and Allen Debus, for example, made substantial contributions in those decades.[14] Perhaps even more important for future work were the efforts of Frances Yates, which extended into the seventeenth century and eventually linked up with the steps noted earlier to sort out the ways that magic factored into, or contrasted with, advances in the direction of the revolutionary new science.[15] More recently great strides have been made in the understanding of currents of learned magic going back further into the Middle Ages, while trailblazing work, such as that of William Eamon in *Science and the Secrets of Nature*, has added greatly to our knowledge by linking medieval magic to that of the period targeted decades earlier by Walker and Debus.[16]

The third general theme mentioned in the title of this book is belief. Although the religious beliefs of the populace will be one of the subjects addressed in the chapters that follow, for the present bibliographical purposes let us turn to belief as represented in witchcraft, both attitudes toward it and efforts to prosecute those connected to it, and focus on the historiography of the period of the great witch hunts and beyond.[17] During much of the twentieth century the standard interpretation of the witchcraft phenomenon depended on the accounting set forth in 1921 by Margaret Murray in her famous *The Witch-Cult in Western Europe*.[18] According to Murray, the witches hunted down in the sixteenth and seventeenth centuries were the adherents to an ancient fertility cult native to all of Europe and which had lain more or less unnoticed for nearly a thousand years among the people, the illiterate classes.[19] Only in late medieval and early modern times did the Christian authorities take it upon themselves to exterminate this rival religion. There resulted the great "witch hunt," which largely succeeded in attaining its goal.

After more than three decades of dominance Murray's position was finally discredited among scholars specializing in the history of witchcraft, though it still seems to be common outside of academic circles. What replaced it was a view of witchcraft that saw it, particularly as characterized by the courts of the witch hunt, as largely an ideological construct manufactured by the literate elite, most especially by members of the clergy. Norman Cohn, in his *Europe's Inner Demons*, managed the most searing indictment of Murray.[20] And he, along with Richard Kieckhefer, advanced a persuasive argument that the cultic aspects of witchcraft were attributes invented in a stereotype that took hold among the elite in the mid-fifteenth century and that was, in courtroom procedures, laid over more authentically popular concerns about common sorcery.[21] At the same time that Cohn and Kieckhefer were presenting their interpretation, these popular concerns were also the subject of scholarly inquiry. Adopting a more anthropological approach, Alan Macfarlane and Keith Thomas saw in the historical sources evidence that at the level of the people at large accusations of witchcraft provided vehicles for giving vent to social tensions.[22] Moreover other scholars, Christina Larner perhaps most prominently of all, drew attention to the politics of the early modern state. For Larner it was the state, intent on asserting its hegemony, that used witchcraft prosecutions as an expression of the legitimacy of its authority and as a means of social control.[23]

More recently, there have been efforts to reread the documents of the witchcraft trials and the mass of demonological literature that accompanied them with an eye more to their coherence as testimony to broadly held social assumptions of their time. Pathbreaking in this regard has been Stuart Clark's *Thinking with Demons*, which appeared in 1997.[24] Euan Cameron has somewhat broadened the scope by drawing in superstition as well in his *Enchanted Europe* of 2010.[25] Both of these works focused on the understanding of social elites. So perhaps Robin Briggs's work, which looks at the way ideas and patterns of behavior associated with witchcraft and its stigmatization were accommodated more widely throughout society as a whole, should be seen as adding a complementary point of view.[26] Attempts have also emerged to investigate the presence ideas about witchcraft maintained in European society in the centuries after the great period of the witch hunts was over. For it is now understood that the decriminalization of witchcraft did not mean that elites would not continue to be concerned with charges of witchcraft among the populace or that the lower ranks of society were absolutely free of the inner tensions that the notion of witchcraft often served to reveal. Signal here has been the volume authored by Marijke Gijswijt-Hofstra, Brian Levack and Roy Porter on *Witchcraft and Magic in Europe. The Eighteenth and Nineteenth Centuries*.[27] And some studies have taken the investigative theme all the way up to the twentieth century. Here the work of Owen Davies stands out.[28]

The present study is grounded in all this work and naturally most strongly affected by the more recent endeavors. Further bibliographical debts will be laid out in greater detail in the chapters that follow. However, let me take a moment here before we begin to present the general structure of the analysis chapter by chapter. If we return to the three historical threads introduced at the beginning of this chapter, it should be said that this book takes it as established by the research that these three threads follow along a unitary historical track. In all three we find a convergence in the high Middle Ages on a new paradigm, whether it be a new model for knowledge, a new recipe for social action or a new sort of governing institution. The inevitable transformation required to accommodate the new paradigm inaugurates in all three a period of ideological and institutional activity engaging both elites and the populace. Eventually there arises a crisis disruptive of the patterns of social interaction the new paradigms had introduced. And as these crises are resolved, novel modes of thought and social interchange emerge marking an end to our story and the commencement of another narrative.

The task at hand now is to interweave these threads into the fabric of an historical account stretching from the twelfth to the beginning of the eighteenth century. To lay the groundwork it will be necessary in both the first and the second chapters to look back at the preceding years, in the first chapter all the way to late Antiquity. Chapter 1, after laying down two typologies for the relationship among science, magic and religion, thus begins by examining the term "magic" as it was used in the early centuries of the Roman Empire. It extends its coverage to Augustine in the late fourth and early fifth centuries, by which time the word "superstition" had also come into play. The argument is then advanced that for most of the early Middle Ages both the meaning and the employment of the word "magic" were much reduced, limited by and large to referring disdainfully to what were known as the superstitions of the people. Beginning in the twelfth century, however, the atmosphere changed dramatically with the introduction among the literate elite of the natural sciences from the Greek, Arabic and Hebrew traditions. Along with science came learned magic, which thus after many centuries of absence reappears as an element of elite culture. The chapter ends by investigating the response to this new learned magic in the twelfth and early thirteenth centuries.

Chapter 2 starts out, again after a theoretical discussion of the notion of popular religion, by returning to the early Middle Ages, this time for an extended survey of the beliefs of the populace at large insofar as they reflected what clerical elites would have regarded as superstition. The topic is broken down into four large pieces, each representing a different aspect of popular culture. They are: first, witchcraft; second, measures for healing; third, superstition in the narrow sense of paganizing practice or belief; and finally, what can only be called folklore. Here we find material that will be of special relevance later when in Chapter 5 we come to the witch trials of the fifteenth through seventeenth centuries. The analysis then shifts to the "rationalization" of religion, both attempts by the elite to impose a rationalization on the beliefs of common folk and efforts by the people to rationalize their own system of belief. After a theoretical excursus on the notion of "rationalization," the chapter goes over the people's rationalization, leading to the rise of popular heresy by the early twelfth century, and repressive efforts from above to enforce a rationalization more in line with the doctrine of the official church, including the foundation of a papal inquisition in the early thirteenth century.

Chapters 3 and 4 comprise the fulcrum on which the whole book is balanced. They deal with the crucial developments of the thirteenth century and part of the fourteenth as well. It was in those years that clerical elites established a standard for the ideological assault on learned magic, one that would eventually be borrowed for the attack on popular magic and superstition mounted in the centuries of the witchcraze. Chapter 3 sets up the grounds for the consensus that would be reached by the end of the thirteenth century that learned magic represented a danger demanding a concerted repressive response. It begins by connecting up with the discussion at the very end of Chapter 1, when by the early thirteenth century learned magic was beginning to come into its own in western Europe. After a short recapitulation of the ideas of Michael Scot, it examines the sometimes alarmed survey of magical practices by one of the first learned clerics to be familiar with the magical arts as they had emerged by this critical moment in their development, the scholar, theologian and bishop of Paris, William of Auvergne. The rest of the chapter is devoted to close analysis of four texts or textual traditions that can be dated to the thirteenth century and reveal just how far learned magic had become available in detail for those interested in it and perhaps willing to put it into practice. These four are the *Ars notoria*, the *Liber iuratus Honorii*, *Picatrix* and the *Speculum astronomiae*.

Chapter 4 chronicles the response that the new literature on magic and the interest it aroused engendered. Attention first turns to Thomas Aquinas, who can stand as representative of a position adopted increasingly by the end of the thirteenth century among those clerics who saw themselves as official defenders of the faith against the rising tide of magic. Thomas's stance was that all magic was diabolical and that any attempt to put magic into practice implicated the practitioner in a sacrilegious pact with demonic spirits. The chapter then analyzes the thoughts of Roger Bacon, a cleric who was sympathetic to some of the new magic and tried to mount a defense of it. The defense failed, and after a return to the typologies relating science, magic and religion in order to draw in the contributions of Marcel Mauss, the chapter finishes with a discussion of how, over the course of the fourteenth century, the position on magic formulated by those like Thomas Aquinas was woven into the business of juridical practice, particularly that of the church and especially the inquisition. Chronicled first is the long battle to establish the practice of learned magic as heresy, followed by a reading of two fourteenth-century handbooks for inquisitors that set the seal on learned magic's fate at court.

Chapter 5 deals with the witch trials. Harking back to material from Chapter 2 on both popular beliefs and superstitions and efforts by the church to regulate attitudes of the people toward religion, the chapter sets out to narrate the story whereby in the first half of the fifteenth century, in the foothills of the western Alps, a series of trials transferred the juridical posture toward learned magic laid out in the preceding chapter to the beliefs and practices of the common people. Four works are examined as testament to this transition. By the middle of the fifteenth century were established not only the presumption that among the people there existed a crime, worthy of being labeled heresy, that constituted the practice of witchcraft but also an understanding of the details of which this crime consisted that we associate with the classic stereotype of the witch. With the juridical paradigm available, the witch trials ensued. The rest of the chapter is devoted to describing how the stereotype spread and then analyzing the historiography of the witch trials for a number of themes important for the argument of this book.

With Chapter 6 we continue examination of the witch trials but also return to the theme of learned magic and eventually of natural science, too. The chapter begins by looking at a revival of learned magic in the late fifteenth and sixteenth centuries. Surveyed are the magical works of three leading lights of learned magic's resurgence: Marsilio Ficino, Giambattista Della Porta and Heinrich Cornelius Agrippa. It is noted that their thought did little to affect the course of the contemporary witchcraze but that it did to some degree influence the rise of the classical science of the Scientific Revolution of the seventeenth century. Returning to the witch trials, the chapter then considers the way the witchcraze wound down. Treated first is a growing juridical skepticism regarding the ability to hold a fair trial about witchcraft, perhaps the most important early factor countering the prosecution of witches. But then attention is given to the mechanical philosophy of the new sciences of the Scientific Revolution. The focus is on Robert Boyle, and then René Descartes, and the point is that their views about the mechanical nature of operations in the natural world leave little room for magic, much less witchcraft. That lesson is driven home with a glance at the ideas of Thomas Hobbes. After an excursus on Max Weber's idea of the disenchantment of society, the chapter continues on magic by noting how, despite the fact that magic was progressively banished from the learned milieu by the new, mechanical sciences, it still managed to transfer to the latter some of its substance. A review of the historiographical themes introduced at the end of the preceding chapter permits speculation on how those same themes were woven into the decline of the witchcraze. The chapter finishes by going back to politics, in this case political ideology. The argument is presented that novel political ideologies – represented in the thought of Thomas Hobbes and John Locke – arose in the latter part of the seventeenth century, and these set the seal on magic's decline and the growing tendency on the part of the elite to ignore charges of witchcraft. By this point we have arrived at the threshold of the modern European world.

It is time now to get to the business of laying out the narrative sketched out in this quick synopsis of the chapters. The way may sometimes seem meandering, and it is surely complex. In order to keep the overarching argument in sight, I ask the reader to keep the three threads of broad historical change continually in mind. On my part, I will try with introductory summaries and conclusions to provide a roadmap to the journey we shall cover. With luck I shall succeed in weaving a tapestry depicting the sometimes tumultuous world out of which modern Europe arose.

1

Superstition, Science and Magic, 200 BCE–1200 CE

In 1921, Margaret Murray set the terms for everyday discourse about European witchcraft with the publication of her celebrated work, *The Witch-Cult in Western Europe*.[1] So far as concerns Europe and North America, the commonplace view of witches and witchcraft derives directly from the arguments Murray laid out in her book. To put it more precisely, what Murray initiated in 1921 was the rise to dominance, originally among historians wanting to explain the phenomenon of the witch-hunt of the fifteenth through the seventeenth centuries but then broadly throughout society whenever attention turned to witchcraft and witch belief, of a particular vision of magic and its relation to the traditions of the common folk.

This vision, which both accounts for a social phenomenon and identifies its ideological complexion, is one that I confront among my students every time I teach my course "Science, Magic and Society." It begins with the premise that witchcraft, which most of us take today as either the stuff of fairy tales or the mythology behind the childhood caprices played out at Halloween – but which a number of young women and men in contemporary Great Britain and America seek to reconstitute as the basis for an authentic religion designated by the name of "Wicca" – was at the time of the European witch-hunt a ubiquitous and concrete presence in everyday life.[2] That means that the object of the persecutions of the witch trials of early modern Europe was a social reality, actually to be found among the populace and, allowance made for exaggeration and defamation, approximated by the descriptions recorded as evidence during the trials. Just as important is the assumption that the behavior described was determined by a set of ideas and values that should at bottom be thought of as religious. The target of the witch trials can, in short, honestly be characterized as none other than "the religious beliefs and ritual of the people known in late mediaeval times as 'Witches.'"[3]

To be more historically exact, these beliefs and ritual consisted – so goes the standard account – at the time of the witch trials in the subterranean but still surviving elements of the primitive and pre-Christian religion of the people of Europe's north and northwest. Technically speaking, as Murray explained, such remnants fell under the rubric of "ritual witchcraft." But the label she preferred to use for them was the "Dianic cult."[4] By Murray's reading of the historical record, it was a confession whose practice among the populace had continued unbroken from antiquity.

> The evidence proves that underlying the Christian religion was a cult practised by many classes of the community, chiefly, however, by the more ignorant or those in the less thickly inhabited parts of the country. It can be traced back to pre-Christian times, and appears to be the ancient religion of Western Europe... [I]t was a definite religion with beliefs, ritual, and organization as highly developed as that of any other cult in the world.[5]

No wonder the authorities of early modern Europe, when they realized what they were up against, reacted with mass trials followed by public burnings of those who were convicted. In her somewhat more sensationalized publication of 1931, *The God of the Witches*, Murray laid out her claims most clearly. The witch trials and their more rationalistic follow-up in the enlightened contempt for witch belief in early modern Europe came down to the eradication of Christianity's only serious competitor in Europe after the conversion of Rome.

> [T]he Christian Church was... engaged in crushing out the remains of Paganism and was reinforced in this action by the medical profession, who recognized in the witches their most dangerous rivals in the economic field... Religion and medical science united against the witches, and when the law could no longer be enforced against them, they were vilified in every way that human tongue or pen could invent.[6]

What remained after Murray for the vision I have in mind to emerge in its entirety was for this explanation of the witch trials and understanding of their object to be associated with almost everything that could be described as magical in the culture of medieval and early modern Europe. For Murray herself, the magic of charms and spells, which she thought of as rampant throughout the world and present in practically every age, were to be kept separate from the witchcraft involved in her account. In technical terms, those magical practices and beliefs were to be labeled "operative witchcraft," in opposition to the "ritual witchcraft" at play in her "Dianic cult."[7] Yet gradually this distinction was eroded. Instead, the witchcraft that Murray saw as targeted by the trials and limited to the practice of a religious cult was interwoven with beliefs and behaviors among the populace of early modern Europe ranging from the kinds of sorcery Murray had in mind with her charms and spells to what might be thought of as simple superstitions and all the specifically "marvelous" elements of folkloric tradition. It has become typical to consider this whole domain of European culture as a manifestation of witchcraft and witch belief in the broadest sense. From this perspective, the witchcraft of early modern Europe and the practices and beliefs associated with it can be taken as effectively equivalent to popular magic. Or perhaps it would be better to say, witchcraft in early modern times should be seen as simply one aspect of magic in the cultural traditions of the people of Europe.

Magic, science and religion

The subject of this book, of course, is neither Murray's witchcraft as pagan cult nor the broader category of magic as a formative element of popular culture. It is true that witchcraft and magic, even the magic of just the people, are among the themes that the book will deal with, but the focus of what follows will fall on an historical object at once broader than either witchcraft or magic yet also more restrictively defined. My intention in this and subsequent chapters is to explore the crossroads where several pathways of both the culture of the populace and the culture of the dominant elite of medieval and early modern Europe ran together and then diverged. Among the ingredients of the cultural object that will emerge, several will come under the rubric of magic and others will land us on the issue of witchcraft and the social tension with which it was almost always associated. But magic as I see it, and witchcraft, too, will often have less to do with the religious life of simple, ordinary folk and more with a type of knowledge. At the same time, magic will also refer to a practice and along with witchcraft find its place among the customs of a social group, though not exactly religious rite.

To begin the examination, let me return for a moment to Murray, or rather to her intellectual precursors and their ideological competitors. For with Murray and the argument she advances, we find ourselves face to face with two important constituents of culture: magic and religion. For reasons that will soon become apparent, I want to add a third, which Murray does not address head on but which was certainly present to her thoughts, betrayed by the reference to professional medicine in the quotation given earlier.[8] This third cultural constituent is science, which along with the other two makes up a triad that anthropologists have long studied together. We have thus science, magic and religion. For the moment I want to concern myself with the similarities that bind these three and the differences that hold them apart. My purpose will be to sharpen our notion of them so as to allow us to use them as analytical tools in the investigation that follows.

Over 40 years have passed since Norman Cohn drew our attention, in his path-blazing *Europe's Inner Demons*, to the fact that the source for Murray's scholarly view, and the inspiration for her understanding of witchcraft – thus, I would add, for the general approach toward magic that her writings eventually provoked – was the renowned Scottish classicist and anthropologist James George Frazer.[9] Frazer's *Golden Bough*, which first appeared in two volumes in 1890, introduced educated Europeans to the idea of magic as the ancient religion of the populace of Europe, or rather of the lower classes in all periods throughout the world. One need only read Frazer's impassioned rhetoric on the subject of this omnipresent confession and practice to understand how it was that Murray and nearly all enlightened men and women of her day were seized with the conviction that the historical religion of the people was precisely magic:

> [W]hen we have penetrated through these differences [of contemporary religions], which affect mainly the intelligent and thoughtful part of the community, we shall find underlying them all a solid stratum of intellectual agreement among the dull, the weak, the ignorant and the superstitious, who constitute, unfortunately, the vast majority of mankind...It is beneath our feet – and not very far beneath them – here in Europe at the present day, and it crops up on the surface...wherever the advent of a higher civilisation has not crushed it under ground. This universal faith, this truly Catholic creed, is a belief in the efficacy of magic.[10]

In these sentences we find Murray reduced to the essential: magic as popular religion.

Still, when we pay close attention to what Frazer says about the character of magic, we quickly realize that in his opinion magic in its purity was not expressly religious and not even to be thought of as genuinely analogous to religion in the strict sense of the word. It was instead a cultural article of an entirely different sort. Frazer admitted that loosely speaking magic was sometimes taken as appealing to the workings of spirits or beings higher than mankind. To the extent that this loose usage was accepted, it was therefore permissible to think of magic as encompassing both animism – the way we usually refer to what he called "the view of the world as pervaded by spiritual forces" – and a notion of a completely non-animate web of processes that Frazer associated with what he called "sympathetic magic."[11] Yet to be technically correct animism was to be excluded from the principles implicated in magical thought. And in the end, animism alone linked magic to religion. It was religion, in Frazer's eyes, that pointed to the complex of ideas and practices making reference to spirits and higher animate powers and working to propitiate them or engage their aid, not magic in any proper sense.[12] The semantic overlap between the two terms had arisen out of understandable circumstances, but the anthropologist needed constantly to correct for the resultant imprecision and keep them theoretically apart. As Frazer insisted, the "stage [in the development of culture]...in which magic is confused with religion, is not...the earliest of all, having been preceded by a still earlier stage in which magic existed alone."[13] The evolution of animism out of sympathetic magic, and of religion proper out of animism after the magical had been left behind, was a fact of history, but in philosophical terms it constituted an accident.[14]

In Frazer's opinion, magic, strictly speaking, had to be regarded as analogous not to religion but rather to science. The first and the last of these, magic and science, but not religion, looked upon external reality as comprised of a system of invariable processes that could be known and sometimes manipulated but never changed or vitiated. Both concerned themselves with rules and laws of operation instead of the supplications, sacrifices, subterfuges or commands characteristic of religious act. Frazer imagined the charm or spell as the paradigmatic magical operation. In casting a spell, the magician considered himself to be quite mechanically calling into play invariable processes of the world whereby particular objects bring about determinate effects. In almost all cases, the processes depended on either of two rules of the behavior of inanimate things, according to the first of which like produces like and according to the second, two things, once put into contact, continue to operate on each other even after they have been separated by a distance. Frazer called these the "Law of Similarity" and the "Law of Contact or Contagion," and he considered them, from the point of view of the magician, just as worthy of being characterized as natural as were, from the scientist's perspective, any of science's laws of nature.[15] Indeed, as he insisted, the "fundamental [conception of magic] is identical with that of modern science; underlying the whole system is a faith, implicit but real and firm, in the order and uniformity of nature."[16]

Frazer even believed that, from an historical point of view, magic was the progenitor of science, as he put it "the mother of freedom and truth."[17] Hence science arose even more organically out of magic than had animism, which followed upon magic, as we have seen, only by commixture with religion.[18] Magic was thus formally indistinguishable from science by Frazer's estimation. In a word, magic and science each represented a form of knowledge, whether it be applied as practice or approached theoretically as speculation pure and simple. Both even took pains to render their calculations of real laws and operations as precise as possible.[19] What separated the two as Frazer understood them was not a formality but rather a material condition of the knowledge each set forth. For Frazer, this material divergence hinged upon the truth. Magic was incapable of producing truth; science destined always to reject the false. And that was all that made them different. To Frazer's eyes, magic was just plain "spurious science" or "bastard art." By nature and by inclination it aspired always to become scientific, but by its inevitable failure and consequent declension into error it remained forever science's "bastard sister."[20]

Yet Frazer's point of view would not stand uncontested. Imposing voices arose to insist that magic bore no real affinity to science. They claimed that just the opposite was the case. As Murray herself had always assumed, the true blood line ran from magic to religion. I would guess that this perspective predominates today, even in academic circles. One version of it that has exercised exceptional influence, particularly in the United States, was offered by the Polish-English anthropologist Bronislaw Malinowski several decades after Frazer had first introduced his own position. Like Frazer before him, Malinowski believed that considerable theoretical profit was to be won by examining the relation among the three anthropological categories I began with earlier, a relation he referred to as "the three-cornered constellation of magic, religion and science."[21] But as Malinowski conceived of things, the fundamental divide among the arts and practices cultivated by humanity throughout its long cultural history ran between magic – eventually magic augmented by religion – and science, not, as Frazer had maintained, between the pair magic-science and religion.

For Malinowski, science was the very type for the category of knowledge. What made knowledge knowledge was, indeed, that it comprised a cognitive artifact reliant upon what he liked to think of as a "scientific attitude."[22] And this attitude consisted in an uncompromising orientation toward experience guided by the analytical power of reason. Moreover, every member of humanity, from the first *homo sapiens* to the contemporary laboratory technician, possessed both the capability and the desire to extract from his or her experience, with the aid of reason, an intellectual product that could be described as either strictly scientific or at least furnishing the basis for a knowledge that might in time be transformed into science. Even societies conventionally labeled "savage" or "primitive" thus regularly generated what might be thought of as an epistemic treasury, reposited in arts and crafts such as agriculture, hunting and navigation, that had to be entered onto the scientific side of the cultural ledger. Otherwise, no such society would be able to survive in a world that was, after all, real and determinate but not without effort respondent to human needs. Malinowski's language betrays no hesitation in this regard:

> Can we regard primitive knowledge, which, as we found, is both empirical and rational, as a rudimentary stage of science, or is it not at all related to it? If by science be understood a body of rules and conceptions, based on experience and derived from it by logical inference, embodied in material achievements and in a fixed form of tradition … then there is no doubt that even the lowest savage communities have the beginnings of science.[23]

It is clear from all this that Malinowski's notion of science was not dissimilar to Frazer's. Just like Frazer, Malinowski held that requisite for science was belief in what Frazer had called "the order and uniformity of nature."[24] His own words stand as eloquent testimony to the fact: "[A] moment's reflection is sufficient to show that no art or craft however primitive could have been invented or maintained … without the careful observation of natural process and a firm belief in its regularity."[25] Furthermore, since both Frazer and Malinowski were convinced that a regularly operating nature corresponded to actual conditions in the real world, science invariably led toward the truth. To that degree, Malinowski was willing to second Frazer's contention that what separated science from magic was that the latter was ineluctably cut off from truthfulness. What he did not accept was that magic, itself, ever actually aspired to be true knowledge. To be sure, Malinowski was prepared to admit, magic was "directed toward the attainment of practical aims," just like the scientific arts, and it was "governed by a theory, by a system of principles," which lent it the same rule-oriented physiognomy as science. His words explicitly conceded the point: "[W]ith Sir James Frazer, we can appropriately call magic a pseudo-science."[26] But for Malinowski, the similarity ended with appearances. Magic was not, like science, committed to uncovering authentic regularities in the external world drawing upon experience guided by reason. Instead, magic began precisely where the scientific enterprise failed, where the limits of knowledge were surpassed by what remained of the ungovernable and as yet uncomprehended forces of the real, external world.[27] Again, in Malinowski's words:

> Science...is based on...experience won in man's struggle with nature for his subsistence and safety...Magic is based on specific experience of emotional states in which man observes not nature but himself...Science is founded on the conviction that experience, effort, and reason are valid; magic on the belief that hope cannot fail nor desire ever deceive.[28]

Thus, it was on the other side of his basic cultural divide, contrasted in all but illusory appearances with authentic knowledge and at bottom opposed to it, that Malinowski located magic. Here it stood accompanied by what he might have called, to mimic Frazer's terminology, its *real* sister, which was for him religion. The pair magic-religion served for Malinowski to designate the reservoir of culture not derived from experience of the external world and not subject to the laws of reason – hence, neither empirical nor rational. Both paid homage to mankind's hopes and aspirations, and they drew upon emotions and intuitions, not hard-won lessons of practical success, to set the parameters for action and behavior. Though in a broad sense we might call the cognitive element of what they provided a form of knowledge, they did not contribute to knowledge in any authentic sense. Neither magic nor religion embodied science, held out any promise of yielding scientific truth, or were driven by anything approximating the "scientific attitude." They were to be regarded, therefore, less as having a cognitive content than as fulfilling the function – and we must remember that for a functionalist like Malinowski, identifying function was the most basic tool for separating a culture into its parts – of pacifying the emotions in times of crisis and stress, irremediable regret and disappointment.[29]

To put it in simplest terms, Malinowski held that magic and religion were separated from science or knowledge by an opposition hailing back nearly to the origin of humanity. This opposition was that, already a commonplace in anthropological literature by Malinowski's day, between the sacred and the profane. Science owed its very existence to the real demands of reproduction and survival, assigned by practical necessity to the domain of the profane. Magic and religion, on the other hand, withdrew from external reality to an inner psychic and emotional core, upon which all cultures erected the less matter-of-fact domain of the sacred.[30] To this domain, for instance, were assigned all ritual observances and taboos. Much like Frazer, Malinowski viewed magic as for the most part concerned with this marvelous realm insofar as it was filled with inanimate but supernatural forces, religion generally with the same as inhabited by "beings, spirits, ghosts, dead ancestors, or gods."[31] Still, he did not regard recourse to spirits and animistic beliefs as in essence alien to magic or deviating from its proper character, as Frazer had. Instead, he located the fundamental divergence between magic and religion in the question of intention or ends. Magic always employed its techniques with an eye to accomplishing a specific goal, and this goal, whether the attainment of a desire or the infliction of an injury, lay outside magic itself. In contrast, religion eschewed any particular goal – especially a goal separate from religion itself – but rather prescribed for its followers practices simply affirming the value of its fundamental beliefs. Religious acts were done for the sake of having religious observances performed. Or as Malinowski put it, religion represented "a body of self-contained acts being themselves the fulfillment of their purpose."[32] To exemplify the difference, he compared a rite intended to ward off death in childbirth with a ceremony celebrating a birth. While the former directed a technique toward accomplishing an end, the latter offered a means to no end other than itself.[33]

We thus find ourselves with two competing ways of casting the relationship among science, magic and religion. According to the first, the model for which I have found in Frazer, magic and science occupy two extremes along the same cultural axis. That axis is constituted by knowledge, which can take the form of pure theory or be applied as practice. In either case, what differentiates the extremes is nothing that can be determined by examining their form or function but rather a judgment that must be made about them with regard to the cognitive attribute denoted by the term "truth." Both being kinds of knowledge, both aspire to being true. Yet only science approaches the truth, while magic continually veers away from it. Situated in fundamental contrast to either science or magic is religion, an aspect of culture that is not primarily cognitive and does not present itself for interrogation about how close it comes to either falsehood or truth. Instead, religion is composed of a set of beliefs and practices that regulate mankind's posture relative to a world of higher spirits, most importantly divine but sometimes also evil, and allow each person to find a place in the moral order of good and bad.

The second way of approaching the same three categories, drawn from Malinowski, leads to a different configuration. Now it is magic and religion that are situated along the same axis, in this instance constituted by the cultural domain of the sacred. What distinguishes these two is not the degree to which they realize a single attribute to which they both aspire but instead their modus operandi. Magic works to an end presented to it from outside; religion exists solely for itself. In any case, since both fall within the realm of the sacred, both carry a certain moral weight, although religion alone is normative in the fullest sense of the word. In this scheme, it is science that is set apart, opposed to the other two as the perfect type of knowledge and valuable only to the degree it can prove itself to be true. There is no question here of setting moral norms. Moreover both these conditions for science hold – the possibility of producing knowledge in conformity to the truth and the irrelevance of ethical norms – precisely because science limits itself to the domain of the profane.

Roman Antiquity

Let us turn at last to our own historical subject. We can start with the society of Rome, the Mediterranean world and western Europe in the days of the empire and what is today called late Antiquity. That takes us, of course, outside the chronological boundaries laid out in the title of this book. But a glance at the ancient cultural milieu allows us to establish a base for our narrative, an ideological standard either from which the culture of medieval Europe – where our real investigative interest begins – can be said to diverge or to which it can be held to conform. A quick look is enough to convince us that in this Roman society and at that time both of the taxonomies or conceptual schemas presented just above were operative, at least among the educated classes, whose opinions are the only ones to have survived for us in the textual sources.

It goes practically without saying that there was learning, "science" in the lexicon of either Frazer or Malinowski, though even most Roman intellectuals were not concerned to separate out from other cognitive forms a body of knowledge distinguished by strict criteria for establishing the truth. Thus *"scientia"* was rarely used with the special force its cognate, "science," carries in the modern world, and that set the conditions for what both Frazer and Malinowski considered scientific. But that is of little importance to us right now. Both Frazer and Malinowski permitted the category "scientific" to embrace the much wider realm of all knowledge that could plausibly be considered true. In this latter sense, science and knowledge ran together, designated by all the derivatives of the verb *"scio,"* to know, from which we take as well our more restrictive modern "science." By this broad meaning, "science" according to either of our two taxonomies was a part of the Roman cultural firmament.

More instructive is the question of whether distinct categories of magic and religion were recognized, and if so, how each was understood. If we look to the term "magic" alone, it existed in the form of the Latin root, *"magia,"* source, again, of the modern English word. But the semantics of the term were largely fixed by the meaning of its linguistic parent *"magus,"* a word of much greater currency in the Roman world and greater relevance to our concerns. Although we possess a literal modern English equivalent, "magus," singular of "magi," loosely speaking, the Latin original may also be translated as "magician." But just producing one or the other of these two English proxies either begs the question or obscures what the Romans took the *magus* to be. As any cultivated Roman could explain, *"magus"* transliterated the Persian word for the priests of that ancient land. Appuleius, the North-African writer of the second century who was much interested in such matters, put it succinctly to his readers: "I read in the writings of many authorities that *'magus'* in the language of the Persians is what in our language we call 'priest.'"[34] Magicians of this sort were those whom the author of the Gospel of Matthew claimed had predicted the birth of Jesus – the *"Magi ab Oriente"* – and come to seek him in Jerusalem, far from their home.[35] If we restrict ourselves to "magician" taken in precisely this way, then "magic," as the Romans conceived of it, conformed to the Malinowskian paradigm and fell along the same axis as religion.

Of course, as most modern readers of Matthew take for granted, the Magi who were looking for Jesus were also wise men, instructed in the art of gazing at the stars to read a meaning bearing on objects and events in the world here below. The priests of the Persians were therefore not simply practitioners of sacred rites but also hieratic adepts of special arts of learning associated with the exotic wisdom of the East. They may have been priests, but what raised them to their office and distinguished them in particular was the knowledge they had obtained and that they guarded for the rest of society. It was "*magus*" according to this estimation of its significance that Cicero had in mind when, two centuries before Appuleius in his *De divinatione*, he related the story of the *magi* who interpreted for the Persian king Cyrus a strange dream he had had of the sun at his feet. In Cicero's words, the *magi* were a special kind of learned man found in the old days in the Persian realm.[36] If magicians of this sort were the key to "magic," then the latter plainly constituted a type of learning, indeed just the proto-scientific learning Frazer was imagining when he balanced magic and science on a single scale.

It is important to add, however, that among the Romans as indeed already among the Greeks, the magic associated with such a body of knowledge was commonly viewed as something much less benign than the wisdom Cicero or the author of the Gospel of Matthew had in mind. The Persian *Magi* knew how to read dreams or look to the stars in order to unlock the significance of events of the day as well as peer into the future. But a *magus* one might encounter on the streets of Rome was more likely someone who knew things that could be turned to more mundane purposes, such as casting a spell or finding lost objects and maybe even treasures. Such practices were frequently feared. The emperor Valens I, to take a spectacular instance, having discovered a plot against his life in which magicians had been enlisted to deploy their special art, brought the full force of Roman criminal law down upon the presumed assailants, charging them with high treason. As the historian Edward Peters reminds us, it would not be long before "anyone convicted of being a *magus* was to be burned alive."[37] We would call the practitioners of arts like these sorcerers and enchanters. For the Roman populace, the preferred term was *maleficus* or *malefica*. Both the Theodosian Code of 438 and Justinian's *Codex* from a century later, just at the point where they turn to formal condemnation of the *magi*, take the time to inform us that the common people referred to the same as *malefici*.[38] Drawn from the classical Latin adjective for "evil-doing" or "wicked," occasionally employed as a substantive along the same lines to designate an "evil-doer" or "criminal," this word would later become standard Latin for what most historians today would translate as "witch." That is not a suitable English equivalent for what we are dealing with here. If Bernadette Filotas is right, it was just at the time of the Christianization of the Empire that the noun *maleficus* took on this early and mainly popular link to sorcery pure and simple.[39]

Perhaps it should come as no surprise that so far as the relationship between "magic" and "religion" is concerned, a look at the word "*superstitio*" – in English, "superstition" – has as much to tell us as does inspection of *magi* and its derivatives. Here, one must pay especially careful heed to the historical variability of the term's meaning. Denise Grodzynski has laid out a three-fold developmental schema that appears in broad strokes to comport quite nicely with the textual evidence. According to this account, the earliest usage of *"superstitio"* among the Romans, evident already by the third century BCE, was to designate the bare practice of divination – that is, vatic predicting of the future. In this sense, *"superstitiosus"* – superstitious person – was the same as *"hariolus,"* Latin for soothsayer. Plautus, for instance, in the second century BCE, could refer to a young slave known for her ability to prophesy what was to come as "aut superstitiosa aut hariola."[40] To this extent, superstition was a variety of what Romans at the time considered magical practice, understood along the lines of the Frazerian paradigm.

Yet by the first century BCE this early application was being pushed aside by a second that located superstition instead with reference to religion. Cicero, among others, turned to *"superstitio"* to designate what might be called "religion gone bad." In his *De deorum natura* he explained: "Our forebears separated 'superstition' expressly from 'religion.'"[41] What made superstition different from religion was that it involved an attitude toward the gods grounded in excessive fear, hence provoking unseemly or inadequate reverence.[42] Again Cicero from the same work: "The claims of such people undermine not only superstition, in which we find a worthless fear of the gods, but also religion, which is marked by pious worship of the same."[43] It was but a short step from this understanding to the view of superstition as any purportedly religious practice exceeding the bounds of propriety, especially if executed with immoderate anxiety or scrupulousness.[44] The second-century writer Aulus Gellius, quoted Nigidius Figulus, a contemporary of Cicero's, as evidence for the correctness of this latter usage: "They used to call someone 'religious' who wrapped himself up in an excessive and superstitious [practice of] religion, for such behavior was considered a vice."[45] Some Romans even explained the etymology of the word according to this meaning by pointing to the prefix "*super*," taken in this case with the radical "*status*," or "standing," to indicate the inclination to go *beyond* what religion could reasonably be said to require.[46]

The second century CE saw this second meaning itself superseded. Grodzynski hypothesizes that the resultant third appreciation of superstition was connected to a growing fear within the establishment that non-Roman cults increasingly prevalent among the populace were beginning to pose a danger to traditional society.[47] In response, *superstitio* slipped into being employed not to censure excessive or irrational recourse to religious rites but instead to stigmatize, in Grodzynski's words, "the religion of others" – that is, religious practice or belief that deviated from a presumed Roman norm. Pliny the Younger, for example, in the second century, thought of superstition in these terms.[48] The religious heritage of any marginal group or one considered socially inferior was liable to be attacked henceforth as superstitious.[49] Christianity naturally fell into this camp before it was protected and then favored by the state. And once Christians rose to influence and eventually authority they turned the tables on the old Roman elite, berating the beliefs and practices of the venerable tradition of Cicero and Pliny as themselves a variety of superstition. There was apparently an intermediate stage in which Christian belief and the cult of the old Roman state could both be considered "religion" and neither "superstitious." The orthodox Christian emperor Valentinian I in 371 condoned the public divinatory rituals known in Latin as the *haruspicina* – which of course by the original, pre-first-century-BCE meaning of the word would qualify as a form of superstition – as authentically belonging to "*religio.*"[50] Yet already before Constantine's conversion, at the beginning of the very same century in which Valentinian issued his pronouncement, the Christian apologist Lactantius was insisting that "those who honor many gods, all [to be sure] false, are superstitious, while we, who kneel before the one true God, are the [authentically] religious."[51] Or as he put it in an even more lapidary phrase: "Religion is the cult of the true God, superstition that of the false."[52]

In all this talk of superstition, we still see, of course, both approaches to the relationship among the general categories magic, science and religion – that of Frazer and that of Malinowski. The word "superstition" supplied an equivocal, hence mediating term. At times it pointed to an ancient art or wisdom, a semantic content signified as well by the word "magic" and construed in the Frazerian sense as a species of knowledge. At other times it signified either a diminished variant of religion or something like an anti-religion itself. Here perhaps the category of magic was only rarely explicit in the mind of Romans, up through the fourth century, when referring to superstition, but ritual practices that smacked of magic according to Malinowski's scheme – Valentinian's *haruspicina*, for instance – hovered in the air.

Augustine

It was in the fifth century that we see the extraordinary phenomenon of the two taxonomies becoming confused, perhaps actually collapsing into one. And it is antique Christianity's most influential Latin spokesperson who first reveals to us that such a conflation could take place. Augustine, in his treatise *De doctrina christiana*, which he worked on episodically over the final three decades of his life, the first three of the fifth century, denounced magic in all its forms. Yet it is clear that he conceived of the object of his attack – magic – as simultaneously a species of knowledge, erroneously reputed by many to be not only valid but also elevated and even wise, and a kind of ritual or practice competing with religion and degrading the religious life. His choice of term for the broader rubric under which magic as both false knowledge and false religion fell was "superstition" – *superstitio*. As his words make plain, he thought of superstition mainly according to the third and latest Roman usage – current, of course, in his time – as the "religion" of those who did not accept the way of Christianity.

There are two sorts of learning revealed even in the practices of the pagans. One concerns those things that have been instituted by humans, the other things recognized as having been already long cultivated or divinely instituted. Of the learning concerning things instituted by humans, part is superstitious, part not.[53]

The text then continues by explaining exactly what constituted the kind of learning designated as superstitious:

"Superstitious" is whatever has been instituted by humans pertaining to the making or worshipping of idols, or to the worshipping of a creature or any part of creation as if it were God, or to the taking consultation with demons or drawing up of contracts expressly arranged and agreed upon with them such as we see in the undertakings associated with the magical arts.[54]

What then follows is a listing of all the types of activity Augustine considered as belonging to these arts of magic.[55] First of course were the practices taught in the books of soothsayers ("*haruspicum et augurum libri*"), of venerable tradition in Rome, and as we have seen identified as superstition according to its most primitive meaning but as late as the days of Valentinian accepted as part of the state religion. Second came "all the amulets and remedies that [true] medicine condemns, whether they involve incantations, or various written marks which [their purveyors] call 'characters,' or the hanging and tying up of certain [special] objects and somehow even making them dance." Next, and in some sense most importantly, were included the operations of astrologers, who, Augustine commented, were known by the learned name "*genethliaci*," because they paid special heed to the birth dates of their clients, but who in popular speech were called "*mathematici*." It would seem that Augustine had a particularly acute distaste for this specific aspect of magic, for while he only briefly illustrated the other types introduced in the text, to the art of reading the stars he devoted several pages of invective accompanied by an attempt to demonstrate how its claims to predict the future flew in the face of reason. But not to be omitted were also, and not least, a host of what Augustine regarded as utterly inane practices that could be observed daily on the streets of any Roman city. Examples he gave included taking a particular precaution if a part of one's body suddenly twitched or taking another if, while walking with a friend, one found the way forward inadvertently bisected by a wayward stone or dog or child. Here we find the class of superstitions as most of us think of them today.

One can see that every one of these types of magic depended on or was constituted by a body of knowledge of utility for the conduct of daily life. Each sort was therefore magical according to the Frazerian schema whereby "magic" competed with "science" to provide a store of valuable lore. Yet what ultimately determined their magical nature, to Augustine's way of seeing things, was the fact that together they comprised both functionally and formally a subclass of the category of false religion, the paradigmatic instances of which were idolatry and the worship of many gods. To that extent each of these types was a manifestation of "magic" as Malinowski conceived of it, vying with "religion" for top honors in the realm of the sacred. It was Augustine's genius – or perhaps it was just an understanding he borrowed from the intellectual conventions of his day – that made possible the connection between the two ways of approaching the matter. And it did so by introducing the notion of a contract with demons and insisting that even the most trivial instance of magical observance necessarily implied a recourse to demons dependent at least tacitly on an idolatrous agreement with them.[56] Augustine summed up his case with the warning that magic, idolatry, pagan ritual were all variants on the same thing – that is, false religion – and as such were to be strictly avoided and their promoters repudiated by every Christian. "Therefore all the practitioners of this sort of vain and noxious superstition, and the contracts, as one might call them, resting on a treacherous and deceitful alliance arising from the disastrous trafficking of humans with demons, must by any Christian be entirely rejected and shunned."[57]

Early Middle Ages

With the complete triumph of Christianity in the elite world of learned Roman culture, already foreseeable in Augustine's day and fully accomplished within a century of his death, the Augustinian understanding of magic became not only dominant for the educated classes but also effectively exclusive of all others. By an irony of history, ultimately dependent on the radical decline of the political and economic eminence of Roman Empire as one moves into the sixth and seventh centuries and what is usually thought of as the world of early medieval Europe, this same dominance also gradually led to a diminution of magic's profile in the ideological inventory of the Christian intelligentsia. On the one hand, the phenomenon I have in mind can be described as the virtual exorcism of magic from the world of learning. Peter Brown has urged us to remember that much of the early success of Christianity had to do with its ability to present itself, already in the Gospels, as a powerful counter-force to dangerous magic, an agent for exorcising the maleficent currents seen as rife in the spiritual atmosphere of late antiquity.[58] A community in which Christianity was established at the very top of the social and political pyramid would leave virtually no room for any but Christian religious ritual while at the same time squeezing out all of those "magical" usages which, under the Augustinian construal of "superstition," had had so long a life in classical culture.[59] Such a development would have held especially true among the clergy, who, in the centuries of the empire's dissolution in its western half, increasingly monopolized literacy and literate knowledge. As an indication of official strictures in this regard, Edward Peters has pointed to the decrees of a fourth-century synod held at Laodicea, calling for the deposition of any cleric who practiced magic or astrology, or even consented to making amulets.[60] Elite circles of late Rome and the early Middle Ages adopted an official policy of zero tolerance for everything falling under the Augustinian rubric "superstitious."

On the other hand, however, one can conceive of the same process as a progressive impoverishment of the "scientific" heritage, including its magical components, of Latin culture in the post-Roman west. After Augustine, and surely after the Ostrogothic enlightenment embodied by scholars such as Boethius and Cassiodorus at the court of Theodoric in late-fifth and early-sixth-century Italy, learning in letters, increasingly the provenance of those exercising a religious role in society, restricted itself more and more to matters useful to religious ritual and understanding or to the intellectual issues they raised. In what we call the early Middle Ages, literate discourse came to depend almost exclusively on education in the linguistic arts, specifically grammar and rhetoric, and to manifest itself in the genres of history (including hagiography), liturgy and penitential regulation, Biblical commentary and homiletics. Philosophy, especially natural philosophy in which antique magic of the Frazerian sort had found a learned home, was reduced to a minimum, exception made for enough geometry to sustain building and construction and the astronomy required to calculate the calendar of the church. The result was the same as with the more premeditated hieratic exorcism of the social and cultural spheres: magic as much evaporated as withdrew into the shadows.

That is not to say that it entirely disappeared. Valerie Flint has reminded us of the learned magic that continued to circulate in western Europe even after the so-called fall of Rome. Most conspicuous were the seductive pair, divination and astrology. Given divination's rooting in Roman rituals of state, is it any wonder that among the canons believed to come from the papacy of Gregory III and possibly dating to 731 can be found a condemnation of all people having recourse to "augures" or "harioli" or taking care to look for the auspicious signs (auspicia) before making a departure?[61] The frequency alone of early medieval ecclesiastical warnings against soothsaying and soothsayers indicates that more is in play here than mere repetition of an Augustinian commonplace.[62] Even Christianity could not turn the elite from its desire to receive from clairvoyants information about what the future would hold. With regard to astrology, Flint argues convincingly against the prevalent scholarly assumption that before the ninth or tenth century there was little literate interest in it – which would mean little interest in it at all – in the medieval west. Indeed she would see in those same centuries between Augustine and Gerbert of Aurillac not just continued knowledge of and recourse to astrological practice but even an intensification of learned fascination with it.[63] In addition to finding explicit references to astrology among the writings of such as Eligius in the seventh century and Aldhelm and Bede in the eighth, she also shows that for much of this early medieval period, soothsaying and augury were not cleanly divided from horoscopy in the learned lexicon.[64] Thus much of the evidence for widespread divinatory practices can likewise be taken as a sign that astrology continued to have its adherents as well.

All the same, one can be forgiven – in light of the dramatically contrasting circumstances we find in the high and later medieval periods – for concluding that, broadly speaking, magic, whether in the form of non-Christian ritual or that of wisdom from the ancients, receded in importance as a cultural item among learned circles in the early Middle Ages. The same is not true with respect to the largely non-literate culture of the populace at large. From the point of view of the people, whether peasants or even many in the non-clerical elite, it is probable that there was very little change from the period before. The nature of the evidence for the contents of this lay and popular culture – that is, both its paucity and its near-total clerical origin – makes any assertion in this regard diffi-cult, though as we shall see in Chapter 2 not impossible to produce. Concerning just the perspective of the literate elite, however, we are much better informed. And that at present is all that is important. Penitentials, church canons and sermons abound in condemnation of magic as practiced among common men and women. Here, the full force of the Augustinian attitude toward "*superstitio*" bore down as a warning, perhaps even a verdict of guilt, delivered by the clerical elite against the people ostensibly under its care. Magical practices as well as non-Christian belief and ritual in general were thought to be incessantly threat-ening to draw the allegiance of the majority of the population away from the church.

Given the disdain those with Latin letters held for the culture of the popu-lace – the lore and learning of the *illiterati* or the *rustici* – the result was that from the point of view of the elite, the magic recognized as most evident in the world and against which one was called upon to inveigh increasingly bore very little of the character of wisdom or knowledge along the lines Frazer had proposed in his conception of the "magical" as competitor to "science." The references to magic found in the Latin sources from this period carry much more the semantic weight of vulgar, irrational and forbidden religious practice. Of course, in the Augustinian lexicon, the word "superstition" covered magic in all its forms, but it did so insofar as it pointed primarily to the "magical" framed according to such ritualistic, anti-religious dimensions. It is hardly surprising, therefore, that we find few instances where the subject is identified by means of the cognates of Latin "*magia*." Far more common are animadversions against superstition and superstitious usage. It is tempting, in fact, to think of magic as envisioned by the elite of these centuries as evoking almost entirely the interpretative scheme I have associated with Malinowski. In short, discussion of magic in those early medieval years revolved nearly exclusively around the practices of the people, and it targeted those practices just to the extent that they could be conceived of as anti-Christian, hence expressly to the degree that they could be linked up with paganism.[65]

I believe that these are precisely the cultural circumstances we see reflected in the famous text eventually to be known as the "Canon Episcopi." Around the year 900, sometime abbot Regino of Prüm included among the precepts of canon law he was collecting in his *Libri de synodalibus causis et disciplinis ecclesiasticis* a ruling often thereafter assumed to stem from a fourth-century Council of Ancyra but almost surely originating in Carolingian ecclesiastical legislation of the century preceding its appearance in Regino's work. Although the text as presented by Regino and as it was transmitted practically unchanged through later compilations until reaching its classic form in Gratian's *Decretum* appears to be an undifferentiated whole, in fact it consists of two quite separate parts, each probably derivative of a different canonical source – that is, distinct synodal acts or clerical pronouncements. Only the first part concerns us now. It begins with a statement of both its target and its practical goal: "Bishops and their ministers should strive with all their power to eradicate fully from their parishes the pernicious and wicked art of sorcery, which was invented by the devil."[66] The precise words the canon employs to designate the activity it wants to prohibit – in Latin, "*sortilega et malefica ars*" – leave no doubt about the object intended. It is sorcery in either of the two traditional senses of magic as practiced by soothsayers (*sortilegi*) or by enchanters (*malefici*). By employing both adjectives the authors manage to embrace the ancient pagan terminology regarding divination as well as the late Roman, perhaps specifically Christian vocabulary for combined divination and casting spells. The latter, it will be remembered, was summed up in that portentous word *maleficus*, which was eventually to become standard in Latin for what modern historians think of as the "witch."[67]

It is possible to conceive of the magical target of the canon as a form of practical knowledge, falling expressly into the category of magic as conceived in Frazerian terms. But if we attend to what follows the first line in the text, we see that driving the prohibition, and surely characterizing the paradigm for "magic" the authors are invoking, is the notion of semi-religious and fundamentally anti-Christian ritual – that is, magic along Malinowskian lines. The steps the bishops and their officers are directed to adopt in order to effect the eradication they are called upon to accomplish are unambiguous: "If they find any man or woman given over to this sort of depravity, they are to expel him or her from those same parishes, [making clear how the person has already been] foully disgraced [by his or her own acts]."[68] In short, the remedy and the punishment were identical: banishment from the community. And the grounds for both alarm and penalty were that the suspects had shown themselves to have abandoned the Christian faith. Drawing from the biblical book of Titus, the canon quotes the Apostle Paul's command that a heretic be shunned after a first and second warning. As Paul suggested, it continues, the heretic's crime is to have allowed himself to be subverted.[69] In the case of the sorcerer, moreover, the subversion comes directly at a devil's instigation, the fact of which the text establishes by explaining that anyone who seeks the diabolical assistance implicated in all acts of sorcery necessarily turns his back on God and acceptable Christian usage.[70] There can be no mistaking the recourse here to Augustine's idea of magic as part of a larger and irreligious submission to spirits and spiritual practices inimical to God. Sorcery is to be hated because it constitutes false religion. Only when all sorcery has been banished can Christ's church and its people be considered clean.

The twelfth century

Such were the ideological and cultural conditions attached to the understanding of magic that prevailed, with minimal exception, in the medieval west practically through the eleventh century. By the twelfth century, however, a dramatic change was under way. It was then that the learned in the Latin world began to turn for inspiration to the cultures of the Arabic-, Hebrew- and Greek-speaking east, or by way of these intermediaries to Greek antiquity. Marie-Dominique Chenu has said that around the end of the eleventh century, the beginning of the twelfth, western medieval Europeans rediscovered "nature." That marked for him the age of a Hellenistic renaissance (with a small "r").[71] With regard to my own field of research, centered more on ways of knowing or philosophy of knowledge, the same set of transformations can be characterized as the rediscovery of "science," or what would eventually become "science" as it was spoken of one hundred years later.[72] In either case, the upshot was that for the first time since antiquity in the Latin west, the literate elite – first clerics but gradually laypeople as well – began to take interest in a kind of learning ordered by the principles of formal argumentation and often directed to the pursuit of knowledge in itself, not necessarily tied to either liturgical or simply practical ends.

Important for our present purposes is the fact that this rediscovered learning carried with it magic in expressly the form that had practically disappeared in the west during the early Middle Ages. It was thus precisely at this point in the history of Latin Europe that we see reintroduced into the culture of the learned elites magic considered as part of the couplet magic-science. And with the return of magic conceived of as a kind of knowledge competing with science, the literate cultural world of the medieval west was reconfigured to such an extent that historians can once again, after giving their attention to centuries for which this is not the case, apply the analytical scheme I derived a while ago from Frazer. From this simple cultural transformation the most radical effects were eventually to be multiplied and transmitted throughout high-medieval society.

For the emergence in the twelfth century of a class of Latin intellectuals dedicated not to the modes of thought traditional to the western church in the central Middle Ages but rather to Arab, Greek and Hebrew philosophy and logical argumentation entailed almost by necessity the emergence as well of the learned magician. The first signs of the novel development appeared, not surprisingly, in southern Europe, on the border between Latin and Arabic cultural spheres. Spain proved to be an especially propitious foyer for the transmission and progressive domestication of the new types of investigation, caught up as it was from at least the mid-eleventh century in the sporadic but ever accumulating encroachments of Christian rule into Islamic territory commonly referred to as the Reconquista. By the twelfth century the Spanish Christian kingdoms had established themselves as clearing houses for cultural exchange among the intellectual elites of east and west. Toledo, wrested from the Muslims in 1085 and soon turned into the capital of the kingdom of Castile, was only the most prominent among a number of Spanish cities where translations were made into Latin of Arabic – and by way of Arabic, also originally Greek – works of philosophy and what we would call natural science.

Probably only shortly after 1150, the archdeacon of Cuellar, Dominicus Gundissalinus (in the vernacular, Domingo Gonsalvo), active for much of his life while resident in Toledo, produced a guide to the vast body of secular studies made accessible with the addition of the new resources from the Arab and Greek world, his *De divisione philosophiae* or *On the Division of Philosophy*.[73] Immediately after the introduction, he turned to one of the most exciting of the new fields of learning, surely among the least familiar at the time to the Latin west, which he, himself, placed under the rubric "natural science" (*scientia naturalis*).

> Among the sciences, some are universal and others particular, the universal ones being so designated because numerous other sciences are contained under them. By this reckoning, natural science is [a] universal [science], because eight sciences are contained within it. They are the science of medicine, the science of judgments, the science of necromancy following the rules of physics, the science of images, the science of agriculture, the science of navigation, the science of mirrors, [and] the science of alchemy, which is the science about converting things into other species. And these eight are [all] types of natural science.[74]

Gundissalinus was not reaching for originality in producing his list. Instead, his words were lifted almost verbatim from an Arabic text of the great Muslim philosopher of tenth-century Damascus, Al-Farabi, translated into Latin probably in Toledo at just this time, possibly by Gundissalinus himself, under the title *The Origin of the Sciences* (*De ortu scientiarum*).[75] Indeed, Gundissalinus's *On the Division of Philosophy* drew as well upon another of Al-Farabi's works, itself rendered into Latin at about the same time – in this case assuredly by Gundissalinus – in a half-translation, half-commentary entitled *De scientiis*.[76] What is important is that sciences appear in Gundissalinus's listing that must be associated with the traditions of magic in the antique and Islamic worlds, no matter which of the two approaches to "magic" one opts for. First we see the science of judgments, equivalent to what we today would call astrology, often in past centuries known as judicial astrology or judicial astronomy insofar as it consulted the movements and position of the stars and planets in order to issue judgments, or predictions, about what would happen in the world here below. Next comes the science of necromancy, originally the art of divination reliant upon conversing with the spirits of the dead but here made more restrictive by the addition of the Al-Farabian gloss Latinized as "*secundum physicam*." It is likely that Al-Farabi, or Gundissalinus, or both, had in mind operations going beyond divination and involving manipulations that by the thirteenth century would be identified with something called "natural magic."[77] There follow the science of images, not further clarified but surely related to an art of the same name with magical overtones about which much more will be said later, that of alchemy, unquestionably magical from at least a modern point of view, and the science of mirrors, frequently associated with other magical arts in subsequent centuries. With the exception perhaps of astrology, none of these had been objects of curiosity among the learned in the Latin world in the preceding medieval tradition, many of them not even imagined as areas of investigation or practice. Now here they were trotted forth as identifiable fields of knowledge with pedigrees reaching far back in time and accorded the respect of venerated disciplines like medicine or agronomy.

It was not long before the same view had penetrated into northern Europe. By then the association of the new fields with the previously vilified territory of magic had become even more explicit, and a consciously apologetic strategy adopted to counter the negative reaction of long-standing cultural norms. Daniel of Morley was an Englishman several decades younger than Gundissalinus who, almost surely during the years when the latter was still active, traveled to Spain in search of the wisdom of the Arabs, which he had found sorely lacking both in England and across the Channel at the rising French center of learning, Paris. He returned, probably having spent time in Toledo, armed with a knowledge of the intriguing disciplines only recently introduced and anxious to disseminate them among his peers. In his *Liber de naturis inferiorum et superiorum* or *Philosophia*, written ostensibly at the request of a potential patron, the bishop of Norwich, he sang the praises of the judicial art of the stars and proclaimed his disdain for anyone who would criticize it on the grounds of a presumably suspect genealogy.

> Those who deny the power and efficacy of the motions of the stars reveal themselves subject to so impudent a madness as to impugn the findings of a science even before they have studied its teachings. For many bear a hatred for astronomy (*astronomia*) solely because of its name. Yet if they were to consider its great dignity and utility, they would not impugn it except [maybe] out of envy.[78]

That Daniel intended the term "*astronomia*" to evoke more what we would call astrology than the non-predictive study of the heavens associated with our word "astronomy" is obvious from the terms of the utility for which he commended the science. That he regarded astrological learning as at least loosely bound to a range of scholarly arts that either applied the lessons of horoscopy to further practical ends or were in some way dependent on a similar judicial but also traditionally magical manipulation of the secrets of nature becomes clear in the passage that immediately follows.

> Concerning the dignity of this science, we find – as the sages of old have told us – that it is divided into eight parts. They are the science of judgments, the science of medicine, the science of necromancy *secundum physicam*, the science of agriculture, the science of illusions, the science of alchemy, which is the

science of the transformation of metals into other kinds, the science of images, which has been passed down to us by the great and universal *Book of Venus* composed by Thoz the Greek, and the science of mirrors. This [last] science is more fruitful and comprehensive than the others, as Aristotle makes clear in his *Book of Burning Glasses.*[79]

Evident right away, of course, is that Daniel has here simply repeated the listing of disciplines provided centuries earlier by Al-Farabi and introduced into Latin learning by such as Gundissalinus. The tone of the list, however, has been rendered still more exotic by the fact that the overarching rubric has changed now from "natural science" to the "science of the stars," and its already magical cast given even more uncompromising expression by the substitution in Daniel's list of "science of illusions" for the more staid "navigation science" of Al-Farabi and Gundissalinus. Assuming, as we should, that Daniel was speaking for at least a scattering of others in the intellectual elite of his time, it is plain how far the cultural atmosphere had by the late twelfth century altered from just one hundred years before. Magic, once spurned, had been welcomed; once disdainfully relegated to the precincts of illiterate behavior, it had been installed among the very highest of the literate disciplines. Would it not appear that some learned minds in the west had returned to an ideological posture not just predating central medieval sensibilities as evidenced in the Canon Episcopi but somehow even free of the monolithic approach to magic, superstition and false religion triumphant in lettered circles since the days of Augustine?

Such being the state of affairs, it is hardly surprising that many educated observers, including a good number in the schools in which the new learning with its openness to magic had begun to spread, reacted with disapproval and occasionally alarm. Beyond the negativity common to every case, the responses divided themselves into two groups of different character. Exemplary of one sort of counterassault is the *Didascalicon*, subtitled *On the Study of Letters* (*De studio legendi*), composed around 1120 by the Parisian canon regular Hugh of St. Victor. The work constitutes an introduction to the learned disciplines, especially in demand at a time when, as we have seen, the syllabus of arts and sciences had expanded so rapidly. Although there is no reason to think that Hugh was himself any more than vaguely acquainted with the details – indeed many of his words were drawn from the standard authorities Augustine and Isidore of Seville – he was plainly aware of the growing body of literature drawn from the Arabs and the Greeks concerning the areas of study we have been dealing with, those likely to raise the suspicions of anyone with a traditional scholarly cast of mind. At the very end of his treatise, he briefly set them out in order before his reader under the general heading of magic (*magica*).

The sorts of learning Hugh had in mind as magical were just those we would associate with soothsaying, casting judgments, in the technical sense already noted in Gundissalinus and Daniel of Morely, and what I have called sorcery – more truly novel subjects such as alchemy or the science of images having apparently escaped his notice. As he explained, all together these varieties of knowledge fell into five major divisions comprehending the whole of the magical art. First was what he called *"mantice,"* a term derived, as he realized, from the Greek for "divination." Next came "vain mathematics" (*mathematica vana*), drawn from the established Latin usage already seen in Augustine above and embracing what might be considered astrology and related "judicial" disciplines. There followed fortune-telling (*sortilegia*), sorcery (again designated with a Latin plural: *maleficia*) and illusions (*praestigia*).[80]

For *"mantice"* or divination Hugh recognized five principal sorts.[81] Necromancy, the etymology of which he acknowledged as prefixing the Greek word for "dead" to the term *"mantice"* just introduced, he understood to be the art of gathering information from the spirits of the dead. To Hugh's eyes the process required the shedding of human blood, which demons drank in return for their assistance in moving the process along. The other four sorts were less spectacular, and they depended on the skillful manipulation of the elements: earth, water, air and fire. They were geomancy, hydromancy, aeromancy and pyromancy. *"Mathematica,"* the specifically "judicial" arts, he divided into three kinds. The first two involved what we would take as more properly sub-varieties of divination. *"Aruspicina,"* already encountered earlier in relation to Valentinian I and translatable with the English term "haruspicy," designated the ancient practice of telling the future by reading the entrails of sacrificed animals.[82] Though inaccurate in his etymology, Hugh appreciated the fundamentals of the practice well enough.[83] Augury (*"augurium"*), which Hugh conflated with "auspicy" (*"auspicium"*), entailed reading the future in the flight of birds or – and this, he said, marked off "augury" in the strict sense – in the sounds of their warbling. Only the last of the three concerned what Augustine would have thought of as a "mathematical" art, which Hugh denominated with the precise term *"horoscopia"* or horoscopy. Commenting that this branch of knowledge could also be dubbed *"constellatio,"* Hugh characterized it as "seeking the fate of humankind in the stars." With a nod again to Augustine, he added that those in this discipline who specialized in making predictions based on the date of birth were known as *"genethliaci,"* among whom should be counted the *magi* referred to in the Gospels.

The next three major types could not be further subdivided. *"Sortilegia,"* which I have translated with the general word "fortune-telling" – no more than a colloquial synonym for "divination" or "soothsaying" – Hugh narrowed more specifically to prediction by means of casting lots. Those who practiced it were called by the name *"sortilegi."* Sorcery, for whose practitioners Hugh employed the noun preferred on the street in Latin antiquity, *"malefici,"* he indicated simply by providing several prominent examples. Sorcerers, Hugh explained, cast spells (*"incantationes"*), fashioned amulets (*"ligaturae"*) or made use of any of innumerable other "execrable" objects deployed in this art. The fact that to express the latter Hugh turned to the Latin term *"remedia"* – in English, remedies – would seem to indicate that to his mind one of the primary functions of the practice was curative. In any case, he made it clear that both the motivation for and at least a necessary ingredient of the power of performing the requisite acts derived from demons. It was a discipline from which only wicked things (*"nefanda"*) could be expected. Last, there was the art of illusion. Once more Hugh apparently assumed his readers needed little in the way of commentary to know what he meant. He did, however, bother to remark that in the course of accomplishing their goal the deluders effected changes in the surrounding reality by which the sensory powers of the victims were deceived. In the end, here, too, demons were somehow implicated, for Hugh attributed the changes he was speaking about to the workings of a "demonic art."[84]

In unequivocal terms, Hugh denounced every one of the varieties of magic he presented. His indictment was absolute and to the point.

> Magic is not a part of philosophy but rather stands outside it, making false claims [to our attention]. It is [indeed] the master of all iniquity and evil, lying about the truth and truly injuring [our] souls. It seduces [people] from divine religion, promotes the cult of demons, instigates the corruption of morals and propels the minds of its followers to every wickedness and impiety.[85]

If we pay careful heed to Hugh's words, we can see that he is here advancing against the magical arts two distinct though not contradictory complaints. On the one hand he attacks them as evil. They constitute, in fact, the very source of evilness, inspiring every imaginable vice. In so doing they block the way to honest religion and lead, almost inevitably it would appear, to demon worship, by which Hugh might have in mind idolatry of every sort. To this extent, Hugh's condemnation remains well within the bounds of learned tradition of the preceding centuries. Magic represents a kind of anti-religion, on which grounds it must be absolutely shunned by every Christian. We remain, in short, firmly embedded in the cultural paradigm I have associated with Malinowski. Competitor to religion, magic undermines the basis for real morality and feeds appetites that ought to be contained.

But there is a second arm to Hugh's attack. Moving the focus off morality, this second approach adopts an almost purely epistemic tack. Magic in this instance must be rejected since it cannot claim to be a valid part of philosophy. The magical arts make a pretense at revealing truths about the world. Instead, they yield only falsehoods. At issue here, then, is the question of knowledge. And thus we find ourselves engaged with Frazer's paradigm for analyzing culture. Magic's defect is that it invariably misses the target of being scientific. And with this claim we see the first moves away from the Augustinian parameters that have for so long dominated discourse about magic. For the first time in the west in hundreds of years, the two cultural configurations from which magic could be approached were recognized as different, and they began, in learned discourse, to draw apart.

Yet already in Hugh's day there was emerging a second type of response to magic, expressive of disapproval of a different sort. An example of this kind of reaction to the new magical arts can be found in a brief tale recounted by one of Hugh's contemporaries, again someone familiar with the rapidly expanding world of letters and generally enthusiastic about the opening of intellectual horizons it entailed. The storyteller in this case is Adelard of Bath, an Englishman who, much like his younger compatriot Daniel of Morely, set out for southern Europe – if not Spain, as he claimed, then perhaps Italy – to imbibe the wisdom of the Arabs. His *Natural Questions* (*Quaestiones naturales*), composed in dialogue form most likely a few decades after Hugh's *Didascalicon*, were intended to share what he purports to have discovered about the natural sciences as well as his considerable excitement for them with his contemporaries back home. In them, Adelard provides an account of a visit made with his nephew to the home of an old woman (*anus*) renowned for her skill in producing illusions (*praestigia*). Four hundred years later he almost surely would have labeled her, in Latin, a "*malefica*," a word by then translatable quite simply as "witch." At the time, she was just a wise "old wife." The two men went to see her with the intention of learning something about the art of casting spells (*incantationes*), indication, perhaps, of an unexpected intellectual curiosity on the part of at least some of the learned elite by Adelard's day about the lore of common folk.[86]

According to the nephew – to whom the dialogue relegates the story – time and again in the old woman's house, whenever the company assembled for a meal, a servant would bring to the table a vessel of water for the diners to wash their hands. This vessel had been provided with a number of holes on both its top and bottom. So long as the servant covered the upper holes with his thumb, the water remained inside, but no sooner was the thumb lifted than it sprinkled out from the bottom over the waiting hands. Duly impressed, the nephew at one point confided to his uncle: "No doubt the old woman [really] is a demonic enchantress, given the fact that [even] her servant is able to do such amazing things."[87] But Adelard himself was less struck with awe. He saw in the whole affair nothing more than an illustration of the workings of nature. Returning the dialogue to himself, he patiently laid out before the nephew a naturalist's explanation of the presumed wonder they had witnessed. In his own words: "If that was a marvel (*praestigium*), the enchantment owed more to nature than it did to the water-bearer."[88] What follows in the text is a summary, in accordance with at least one version of the natural science spreading among the learned circles of his day, of the properties of a vacuum and how they restrict movement among the elements. Appended was even a comment that were the vessel solid on the top, water inside would gurgle out of holes in the bottom as air gradually worked its way in around the water, filling the empty space that the water's escape would otherwise produce.[89]

With Adelard, we seem to have left behind the ideological world not just of Latin learning in the central Middle Ages but even that of late Antiquity which Augustine's perspective presupposed. There is in the story of the old woman and Adelard's response no trace of the Malinowskian configuration of culture. In as much as the "wonders" performed in the woman's house can be taken to stand for the magical arts in general, Adelard was disinclined to regard them as indicators of anything remotely like religious belief. Instead, they stood as phenomena in the world that cried out for explanation. And here the alternatives, for the learned observer, were either truth or misunderstanding. An explanation that obscured reality behind enigma was amusing, intriguing, perhaps "magical," but not to be taken seriously. One that set out the regularities of nature by which the happening could be accounted for in concrete terms, with no astonishment, was one to which the intelligent person would give assent. If there was magic in Adelard's firmament, it was magic only of Frazer's sort: the product of knowledge's failure to meet the standards of science. For Adelard, this perspective on the question amounted to the whole of the problem that the claims made for magic introduced. Knowledge that would within decades be habitually referred to as "scientific" was, to Adelard's eyes, just beginning to make its mark. When it had finally won the day, so he seemed to assume, magic would disappear.

The thirteenth century

If we turn to the first half of the thirteenth century, we see more of the same. Magic has found a place in the learning of the literate elite, a place it most often shares with philosophy or science. Yet a difference is also apparent, now that both science and magic have become more vast and more complex. Between 1150 and 1250, many more ancient or Arab disciplines were rediscovered and several brand new fields of inquiry invented. The brave new world of knowledge as an epistemic treasury set in precise language and strictly accounted for by logic had mushroomed in size. Since more will be said about this development in Chapter 3, here I limit myself to a few words. The point to make now is that while the new cultural atmosphere which had installed itself among the learned in the twelfth century expanded its reach and tightened its intellectual grip, one also sees evidence that the debate over science, magic and even religion was acquiring a sharper edge. There were still at least three not always mutually exclusive camps among the educated elite: those who promoted the arts of magic and those who rejected them, on the one hand as evil and irreligious and on the other as false and foolish. But the lines of division had become more deeply drawn.

Let me call upon just two thinkers to serve as examples. The first is Robert Grosseteste, master of theology at Oxford in the 1220s, eminent scholar in both secular and religious studies and bishop of Lincoln – thus ecclesiastical overseer of Oxford – from 1235 to 1253. Robert was especially highly regarded in his own day and among later generations as an expert in natural philosophy, including many of the sciences inserted into western traditions in the twelfth century. It should therefore come as no surprise that as a young man he was an adept of astrology.[90] Later in his career, perhaps under the influence of his increasing pastoral responsibilities, he turned on this old familiar from the world of magical disciplines with considerable acridity. I have even conjectured that William of

Auvergne, Grosseteste's friend and bishop of Paris, who likewise had harsh words for the judicial science of the stars, may have played a role in Grosseteste's change of heart.[91] In any case, toward the end of his years as master and only shortly before he was promoted to the episcopacy, the learned Englishman wrote down in his *Hexaëmeron* his mature thoughts on this venerable but also, by an equally hoary tradition, suspect art.

Grosseteste leveled two principal accusations against astrology, and these two remind us of the two tracks evident in the attacks on the magical arts already in the twelfth century. First of all, he criticized the judgments of the astrologers as deficient – in the end, absolutely valueless – by epistemic standards. Casting a horoscope upon which one could make pronouncements about the future, even given, for argument's sake, that the movement of the heavens actually does determine the course of events in the sublunary world, required a degree of precision far beyond the capabilities of the most talented star-gazer imaginable.

> Predictions drawn from the stars are dependent upon the positions of the heavens and the exact locations of the stars as well as their [positional] interrelations, and from the parts of the planets and their houses and exaltations and other practically innumerable observations, all considered together, and also upon the exact place on earth and the exact moment in which the question is posed concerning a future act or event, or in which a child was born, or at some other designated point in the calendar year. But it is impossible, given the art of astronomy and using astronomical instruments [available to us], to make such observations and to determine the precise timing of the various conditions with a certitude sufficient for the astrologer to say of two babies born in the same house, or perhaps in the same city at one and the same moment in time, or even in two moments following in close succession one upon the another, exactly how the [relevant] configurations of the constellations of the two [actually] differ.[92]

As Grosseteste himself admitted, the argument went back at least to Augustine's *City of God*.[93] It made of astrology not a science impossible to conceive in theory but instead one incapable of being realized by human beings. Here we are, then, back close to the rejection of magic made by Adelard. What astrologers called an art was simply bad science – or, in this case, something not even honestly susceptible to being put into scientific language. Coming as he did when the scholarly lexicon had begun to include the term "science" itself, Grosseteste was even able to articulate the problem with exactitude.

> Thus, two people inquiring about [their horoscope] will stand under configurations of the stars that are entirely indistinguishable, so far as concerns the requirements of scientific investigation, to the eyes of [any] astrologer, no matter how skilled and quick he be – despite the fact that in truth the exact position of the signs and stars differs [for each of the two].[94]

Why should one listen to astrologers, or venerate their learning, when even by their own standards they had nothing informative to say? This is a critique dependent, thus, on the Frazerian paradigm. Magic must be rejected because it amounts to no more than failed science.

But there was a second argument against astrology. In this case, Grosseteste issued an indictment of greater severity. Now, the paradigm I have linked to Malinowski came into play. The competition fell not between magic and science, but rather between magic and morality, ultimately between magic and religion. The charge was old and venerable, but in Grosseteste's mouth it took on an urgency not seen in Latin letters since Augustine. The core difficulty arose from the apparent determinism of the influence of the heavens in face of Christian commitment to freedom of the will. Grosseteste put the Christian position on necessary influence quite eloquently:

> Neither is it true – nor should it be conceded other than for the sake of argument – that the stars have an effect on freedom of the will or on the morals and voluntary acts of human beings. For the free will of a rational mind is, in the natural order of things, subject to no object save God alone. [Most importantly], it is set above all the corporeal [elements] of creation.[95]

He explained most plainly as well the ideological cost he saw if one were to yield on this point and grant to the astrologers their predictive pretensions:

> Those, therefore, who posit for the stars a power over free will, [by that fact] set the nature of the human soul and the dignity of the human condition beneath the nature of bodily [things]. Thus they [render themselves] enemies of human nature, since they make it subject to that which [should] naturally [be] subordinated to it and since they remove from it the image of God... They also [thus reveal themselves as] blasphemers against God, since they detract from God's dignity, positing as they do that the rational mind, which they concede to be God's image, is inferior to bodily objects.[96]

Here, then, no appeal to standards of truth, or to the plausibility of a given construction of the workings of the world. Instead, a threat that if one continues to uphold the claims of the discipline of astrology, one will thereby prove oneself a renegade to God. Both the charge and the motivation for the complaint are moral, not epistemic. At the end of the day, they are religious. With a vehemence in no way less than that of Augustine in the early fifth century, Grosseteste draws the conclusion that accepting or practicing astrology sets one beyond the bounds of Christianity. In Augustinian fashion as well he insists that in the whole business demons or devils are necessarily involved.

To draw to a close, let us issue the following warning. Practitioners of the art of astrology are seduced and [in turn] seducers, their teachings impious and profane, written at the inspiration of the devil. Their books, therefore, should be delivered to the flames, and not only they, but also all who consult them, are lost.[97]

Still, at exactly the same time there were others, themselves also learned and respected for their learning, who saw nothing evil in astrology or in many other new disciplines associated with the magical arts. They make it clear that the novel ideas of those like Gundissalinus or Daniel of Morley had retained their hold despite the criticism. As will become clear in Chapter 3, in some circles they had in fact flourished and ventured onto unprecedented ideological ground. For the moment, I turn merely to the second of my two examples to make my case. Michael Scot, a contemporary of Grosseteste's, had picked up much of his learning in Toledo, that center of cultural ferment and transmission in Castile. He knew Arabic, devoted great effort to translating Arabic works – including Aristotle commentaries of the recent and increasingly celebrated Averroes or Ibn Rushd – and was himself sought out as both physician and astrologer. Though dead already by the time Grosseteste became a bishop, he had made his mark in the intellectual world of Grosseteste's day, supported by popes who relied upon his medical advice and enjoying the patronage of the emperor Frederick II for his original writings and translations.[98] From about 1220 probably up to the end of his life shortly before 1236, he enjoyed the privileged status of principal astrologer at the imperial court. Hardly surprising, then, that Michael entered the lists of scholarly debate as a champion of astrology and a defender of its scientific pretensions.

In the Proemium to his most significant original work, the *Liber introductorius*, Michael set astronomy – which he obviously regarded as constituted in great part by what we would call astrology – not simply among the liberal arts but at the top of them all.

> Since astrology [*astronomia*] is one of the sciences among the seven liberal arts and nobler than [all] the others, located in the seventh [and highest] place by virtue of its truth, it is necessary, useful and desirable to every person wanting to be wise...[It is in fact] necessary and desirable in many [affairs] and for many things, as, for example, to the physician in healing the sick, to kings and barons in executing their agenda, to merchants for the sake of their journeys and business transactions, to sailors because of the variability of the air and the seas, and to alchemists, necromancers and those skilled in the art of images (*ars notoria*) for all the things they do that must be coordinated with the constellations.[99]

Though by the end of this list of applications Michael has come to disciplines that would be viewed with real repugnance by critics of magic such as Hugh of St. Victor, he instead compounds his paean to all learning astrological by going on to claim it as, of all subjects to be studied and mastered, second in rank only to theology itself: "For [astrology] is more worthy than geometry and more elevated than philosophy and every other science…with the exception of theology, which I believe and confess to be the truer among all the arts and sciences and so by its nobility the more useful."[100] Michael even took pains to explain in terms of the general principles of natural science exactly why it was that astrology could play so central a role in our understanding of the realities of the world around us.

> Since it has been proved that there is no mixed substance in nature that is not marked by a configuration in the firmament of the heavens, and that all things here below are due to things above, therefore it is a commonplace among philosophers that there never was nor is nor will be any human or other creature born into this world simply under one sign or one planet without having been already conceived under others or having received [from them] the core of its being…And what is said of human beings is understood to apply [as well] to all things that can be conceived or born.[101]

His only effort to mitigate the determinism of such a scheme of generation in the natural world was to advise the reader that in the end all happenings were traceable back to the will of the Creator, the one God under whose power all phenomena that we witness are not just permitted but in some way even ordained.

> The work of the planets and their significance, as well as that of all the peoples and everything else [in the world], are in the power of the one [true] God, by whom all things are accomplished as he wills [them to be] and under whom every particular thing that [actually] happens is permitted to occur. Whoever thinks otherwise stands outside the true faith and hence can be designated a heretic.[102]

Clearly by Michael's view the Malinowskian paradigm had nothing to say about astrology as a discipline. The ostensibly religious – more correctly, irreligious – aspects of the latter, even if it were labeled a magical art, had nothing intrinsically to do with it but were rather projected onto it by those ignorant enough not to comprehend the reality of the divine dispensation.

Moreover, astrology was not alone among the new arts arousing suspicion in some quarters to attract Michael's attention and his approval. Alchemy, already present in Al-Farabi's and Gundissalinus's listing but even more authentically a novel branch of learning in the late twelfth and early thirteenth centuries than the astral art of judgments, was also a science whose praises Michael sang and to which he dedicated considerable effort at expounding to his literate audience.[103] At least two compositions from Michael's pen were devoted to alchemical matters, an *Art of Alchemy* (*Ars alchemie*) and one of several works circulating under the title *Light of lights* (*Lumen luminum*), both referred to by subsequent writers but not yet sufficiently disentangled from a confusing manuscript tradition to provide the basis for a definitive text.[104] Again in the Proemium to his *Liber introductorius*, Michael spoke of this presumably magical discipline in reverential terms. According to a translation provided by Richard Dales, he said of alchemy that it "as it were, transcends the sky, because by the power of the four spirits it tries to transmute the base metals into gold and silver and to make from them a perfect water."[105]

As the first passage quoted from the *Liber introductorius* reveals, Michael could even mention arts as traditionally considered opposed to Christian teaching as necromancy without giving evidence of disapproval. Further discussion of such aspects of learned magic will have to wait until Chapter 3 in this book. But it is perhaps worth noting here that current scholarship confirms at least as much of Dante's judgment of Michael, which committed him as a sorcerer to the eighth circle of hell, as to concede that he was more than casually familiar with practices of divination and conjuring pouring into learned Latin circles in his day from Arabic and Hebrew sources.[106] Once more, in his approach to the magical art Michael fell under the paradigm provided by Frazer's perspective, whereby magic and science contended for the claim to true knowledge of the workings of the world. Unlike Frazer, of course, Michael regarded the contest as less a competition than a cooperative effort to advance the boundaries of natural philosophy.

Conclusion

So where do we stand as this chapter draws to an end? We began by laying out two paradigms – one drawn from James Frazer, the other from Bronislaw Malinowski – for identifying "magic" and separating it from both "science" and "religion." Then we applied these theoretical templates to the culture of Latin Antiquity, where we discovered that both were relevant. By the fifth century, however, with the great Christian thinker Augustine, the two different paradigms were starting to collapse into one, which increasingly leaned in the Malinowskian direction of regarding magic as primarily a competitor of religion. For the centuries of the early Middle Ages it was this unitary paradigm that held sway, and magic as a rival to science withdrew from the field. Indeed, magic during these early medieval centuries was, from the perspective of the literate elite, almost exclusively a matter of the superstition, the false religion, of the common people.

With the twelfth century, and the commencement of the period about which this book is principally concerned, a dramatic change occurred. As the natural sciences began to flood into the cultural world of the western European learned classes, they brought with them magic once more as a competitor to science, contending for knowledge of the truth. For the first time since Antiquity, magic began to have its champions among the elite. Such a step was necessary for the dynamics which this book will deal with to start to play themselves out. For of course the appearance on the stage of defenders of magic as a vehicle for the truth aroused opposition, expressed not only in the Malinowskian understanding but also the Frazerian. We looked at this contest of perspectives in the twelfth century when it was only getting under way and then in the early thirteenth. The acerbity of the debate seemed slightly more intense in the early thirteenth century. Yet the promoters of magic could still set forth their claims for its epistemic value with relative security. Michael Scot stood as a model of what we might expect.

Yet Michael's untroubled demeanor should not be allowed to obscure for us his concern all the same to mount a defense for his more unorthodox arts or the fact that voices like Grosseteste's were, at least in the schools of theology, growing louder and more strident. Such turbulence at the cultural level of the elites could not, ultimately, but redound upon the populace, more precisely upon the state of relations between populace and elite. The full effect would not be felt for several centuries. But already before the end of the twelfth century we can detect a change in attitude of the elites toward the people, especially toward what could be regarded as their culture. For as magic, after a long, post-Augustinian period of virtual banishment, managed a reentry into the intellectual universe of the lettered, complications arose from the simple fact that for this same elite magic had always existed as a category relevant to the culture of the people. To the eyes of the learned, especially those of the learned clergy, it had existed in a debased form, worthy of occasional reprimand as superstition though hardly serious attention, but it had existed all the same. Inevitably, as the new conception of magic as an element of learned culture matured, it spilled over onto this idea of popular magic

The development restricted itself principally to the ideological world of the literate classes. Yet the results began to express themselves more and more in the form of material action on the life of the populace at large. As learned individuals, initially mostly clerics, took stock anew of the magic of the people, indeed of all aspects of their culture that might be viewed as strange or unorthodox, they started reacting to it in a novel way. For the first time since antiquity, those among the literate elite dared to conceive of a large part of the people's culture as a reservoir of knowledge standing in potential opposition to their own. And this response, I would suggest, effectively demanded that they take it more seriously. One had to examine it more closely. One had to pry more carefully into what it entailed and how it was understood. None of which was likely to bode well for interactions between elite and populace. To understand how, it is necessary to step back and look more broadly at the history of the religious links between elite and people over the whole of the Middle Ages and to explore more fully the connections between superstition and religion or the boundaries between orthodox practice and unsanctioned, potentially condemnable observance.

2

Popular Belief and the Rationalization of Religion, 700–1300

The previous chapter ended with a reminder that the literate elite in western Europe in the early Middle Ages harbored a deep-seated disdain for what we would call the magical beliefs and practices of the populace. It was a contempt so profound that, although it continually aroused formulaic fulminations against straying into such disreputable byways of the culture at large, it, at the same time, stood in the way of any serious effort to examine exactly what such beliefs and practices consisted in or how they were understood by those who purportedly engaged in them. Only from the twelfth century on, as was noted, did attitudes begin to change. Once elite culture had witnessed within itself the emergence of a body of literate and learned magic, then – but not before – did members of the upper ranks of society start taking a slowly building, but eventually quite aggressive, interest in the magic of people who did not read and were not drawing on the sources of the new learning. So far as the earlier lack of curiosity is concerned, it helps to remember that, as the preceding chapter has also made plain, it was completely in conformity with the general posture of the elite toward what it viewed as the populace's superstition, of which magic constituted only a part. In good Augustinian fashion, the learned – particularly the educated clergy – of the early Middle Ages thought of magic and superstition as overlapping categories. They represented either the substance or the inevitable side-effects of false religion, ultimately associable with idolatry and in any event bound up with the influence of devils and demons. Magic by such a construction demanded a reading according to our Malinowskian paradigm. It and all other forms of anti-Christian practice had to be inveighed against. But no more needed to be known about it in the way of detail than was required to recognize the fact of its existence, and that just in order to eradicate it as expeditiously as possible from society.

As the last paragraphs of that chapter also suggested, however, the same approach will not do for us. It is, accordingly, time now to look more closely at this complicated cultural object, indeed at the larger socio-historical reality of which it was a part: the superstition as well as the religion, more broadly speaking, of the common and unlettered folk of the early to central centuries in the medieval west. And the reason is that we shall find here material – cultural artifacts of popular beliefs and practices as well as occasional projections of the literate elite – that will loom large in the subsequent story of the science, magic and social struggle of the late Middle Ages and early modernity I have to tell. We shall then, in the second part of this chapter, have a look at the way the learned elite tried from the twelfth century on to impinge on popular belief, what can be seen as an effort to "rationalize" the religion of the people, as well as attempts on the part of the populace itself to rationalize its own beliefs and institutions. Here, the story shifts for a while to heresy and eventually to the increasingly complex mechanisms of repression that authorities erected to stem the rise of heresy.

So far as the first part of this agenda is concerned, therefore, we must begin with a glance at what might be called popular religion in the medieval west from about the eighth century up through the days when elite attitudes toward the populace had begun dramatically to change, by the early thirteenth century at the latest. In this first instance, our interest will be limited to those aspects of popular religion that might have been expected to – indeed, in most cases did – strike the elite as superstitious, in other words somehow dangerous and false. All this means, of course, that we shall be wading into perilous waters. For among historians of both medieval and early modern Europe, the past 40 years have seen a lively contest over not just the meaning but also even the propriety of the notion of such a thing as "popular religion," as well as more generally "popular culture" itself.

The question of popular religion

For the most part I lean toward accepting the utility of the concepts of popular culture and popular religion for writing the history of Europe, both modern and pre-modern. To that degree, I hark back to an earlier historiographical tradition, represented most eminently by the cultural historians Etienne Delaruelle and Raoul Manselli, that took it as an important task to delineate the boundaries of popular piety as opposed to the religion of the learned and elite. In Delaruelle's eyes, once one had eliminated the priests, monks and nuns, hermits, princes and aristocrats, there remained the "immense and anonymous mass of peasants, either serf or free," whóse religious thoughts and practices constituted a coherent cultural construct proper to themselves and not reducible to the orthodoxy of official Christianity.[1] For Manselli, "la religione popolare" was more the natural product at the level of spiritual sentiment and understanding of the simple events of daily life across the broad expanse of commonplace experience in the medieval world.[2] Manselli was therefore reluctant to associate popular religion with any particular social group or stratum, surely with anything we would want to identify formally as a popular or lower "class."[3] In the case of both scholars' work, however, the religion of the people stood in decisive contrast to learned

Christianity or to anything that might be associated with the subtleties of theological discussion.[4]

Of course, even in Delaruelle's and Manselli's time Peter Laslett had formulated
his argument that before the Industrial Revolution European society, devoid of a
sense of separation of interests, had known only one authentic social class and –
partly as a consequence, partly as a precondition – only one, more or less uniform,
culture. In this bygone "world we have lost," Laslett argued, where the economic
order was based on the domestic unit and economic relationships between high
and low grounded in the ideological image of the family, interactions among
people, even interactions of material production, were effectively, and rigidly,
regulated by – in Laslett's words – the very "content of Christianity itself."[5] How
could there, in such an environment, exist a fundamental divide between the
religion of the people and that of their social superiors? The most eloquent voice
to draw the inescapable conclusion that, before modern times, there was no such
division, outside the fancy of various historians' minds, is surely Eamon Duffy.
His *Stripping of the Altars*, which appeared in 1992, marked a definitive turning
of the tide among scholars against the historiography positing an opposition
between popular and learned religion in medieval and early modern Europe.
Drawing a bead on predecessors of Delaruelle's and Manselli's stripe, Duffy
argued that before the Reformation (and presumably stretching back to the days
of the Germanic conversions or Charlemagne at the very latest) whatever religion
the people of Europe participated in was "a popular religion which extended
from the court downwards, encompassing both clerical and lay devotion."[6] He
had written his book, indeed, expressly to show that in late medieval and early
modern society "no substantial gulf existed between the religion of the clergy
and the educated élite on the one hand and that of the people at large on the
other."[7] Or as he put it in a preface to the second edition of his work in 2005, he
was defending a notion of the "social homogeneity" of late medieval – perhaps
even all medieval – religion. Not that there were no variations of religious belief
and practice in those centuries, but in the final analysis "[t]he division of late
medieval religion" should not be thought "to run along such obvious fault lines
and divides as the distinction between *élite* and *popular*, *clerical* and *lay*."[8]

In the wake of Duffy's monumental work, it has become the norm, even
among those who continue to recognize a divide between the religious practice
and belief of the medieval populace at large and that of a learned, clerical elite,
to refer to the religion participated in and understood by the bulk of the population as drawing on a "common tradition." This latter term makes a nod to Duffy's
own phrase of preference, "traditional religion," which he believed, in contrast to
"popular religion," did justice "to the shared and inherited character of the religious beliefs and practices of the people."[9] The idea goes back at least to another
of Laslett's contemporaries, Peter Burke, whose *Popular Culture in Early Modern
Europe*, published in 1978, argued that before the modern period there existed a
single all-embracing culture in Europe that was open to everyone, even if among
the elite at that time could be discerned a second, higher or "great" tradition that

most people would have been unable to penetrate. As another influential historian of the culture of the people, Gábor Klaniczay, has reminded us, Burke insisted
that only in the modern world did the upper strata turn their back on the broader
cultural construct, sever their ties with "popular culture," and thus relinquish
it to the lower ranks of society alone.[10] In her important *Popular Religion in Late
Saxon England*, Karen Louise Jolly, while allowing for a greater divide than Duffy
between learned approach to religious practice and belief, which she associates
with "formal religion" or what we might think of as the institutionally grounded
fundamentals of orthodoxy, and that of the general population, for the most part
adopts in her analysis Duffy's version of Burke. To Jolly's eyes, for pre-modern
Europe "[p]opular religion... consists of those beliefs and practices common to
the majority of believers" and "encompasses the whole of Christianity, including
the formal aspects... as well as the general religious experience of daily life."[11]

It is not that I stand in no sympathy with the attitude adopted by such as
Duffy and Jolly, and I believe that it sets aright a misguided but not uncommon
earlier notion of how Christianity fit within the broad milieu of religious culture
in high and late medieval times. As Duffy in particular takes pains to make clear,
insofar as the notion of a division between popular and elite religion during the
Middle Ages and before the Reformation reflects the conviction that the popular
tradition was largely "non-Christian" and thus in its foundations ideologically
incompatible with that of the upper strata, which was the Christianity of the
"Church," the historiography of "popular religion" – most definitely popular
religion from about the eleventh century on, the time when Duffy's historical
interest begins – has done us a disservice. Much that has been pointed to among
the religious practices of the populace as evidence for a persistence of paganism
or a pagan residue should instead be regarded as not substantially different
from the broad spirituality promoted by the official church. Such practices – for
example, numerous charms for healing – constituted, in Duffy's words, "not
paganism, but lay Christianity."[12] But to make this point, and most especially
to insist that after the early Middle Ages paganism as "anti-Christianity" existed
hardly anywhere in Europe, so that all of the populace felt in some general sense
under the sway of Christian belief, is not the same thing as to deny that there
were types of religiosity among the lower strata of the populace not to be found
among, indeed sometimes explicitly eschewed by, the social elite, particularly
the learned and the clerical. In this latter regard, I think that Duffy has gone
too far.

Strictly speaking, a view of the medieval religious landscape like that of Ronald
Finucane in *Miracles and Pilgrims*, according to which "[i]t was a long way from
pope or prelate to peasant-priest," is not incommensurate with that of Duffy. It
does not insist that peasant or lower-level religion be considered anti-Christian
or even oppositional to something called the "Church."[13] But unlike Duffy's
perspective it makes plain that throughout the Middle Ages the variations within
religious practice and sentiment did not occur socially at random. There was
in religion a considerable cultural difference between high and low, and that

difference came remarkably close to paralleling the declension of social grada-
tions from the learned and dominant to the unlettered and subordinated. To
pretend therefore that we can excavate a common Christianity shared by all,
even when admitting that the elite had exclusive rights to a rarefied and often
quite differently inflected or intonated set of beliefs and practices, conjures up a
notion of uniformity arrayed around what Jolly called "formal religion" while at
the same time not reducible to it that I find hard to correlate with what we see
from the historical sources. The conviction that the religion of large portions of
the population veered away from, sometimes actually shared little of the temperament of the devotion of the lettered clergy and those who gave them their ideological allegiance is not only a commonplace in the pastoral and confessional
literature from the early Middle Ages on but, I would suggest, to a great extent a
valid representation of the facts. Just because the transition from elite to subordinate cultural traditions presents itself as gradual and almost never marked by
points of sharp discontinuity does not mean that we cannot discern coherent
patterns of real difference, including opposition. Or as Jean-Claude Schmitt has
put it, we historians need a model for our cultural representations that "takes into
account the polar oppositions, the tensions, and the ideological commitments of
a society over the long run or at any precise moment."[14]

Some ambiguities of application

So how does all this bear upon my intention to examine the physiognomy of
popular religion in the early medieval west, most especially those aspects of it
likely to elicit from the standard-bearers of official church orthodoxy accusations
of superstition and perhaps infidelity? Of course, it should be clear that I feel
free to look for elements of culture that can be designated popular in contrast
or opposition to the norms of either clerical learning or official practice. But in
fact the limitations of our historical sources make of this a proposition easier
said than done. For one thing, practically all of what we have to feed our investigation comes from the pens of clerics, often in works intended to oversee the
inculcation of true belief and practice and to exterminate the trace of anything
smacking of heterodoxy or, even worse, paganism, however the latter might be
construed. Such historical sources are likely to amplify the polemical character of
whatever analysis they present, so that authentic ambiguities within what might
be regarded as a common, even elite-sanctioned ritual or confessional tradition
come to be represented as a matter of true religion confronted with its spiritual
opposite. And of course they most definitely cannot be assumed to speak with the
voice of non-clerics or any among the uneducated populace and thus be taken
as unimpeachable representations of whatever we might ultimately conclude
popular belief to be.

At the same time, the subject of our inquiry is in itself elusive. Our sources do
not carefully distinguish between what might be regarded as positively embraced

belief or practice and what we would instead consider more the "literary" treasury of an oral culture. Again, Jean-Claude Schmitt has been especially instructive
in this regard. More than anyone else he has reminded us that in this business
we are dealing with material that must be regarded as belonging to "folklore" as
much as, perhaps more than, to "religion." In that case, familiarity with a belief
or practice, even in a sense acceptance of it as a reality in one or another cultural
or social milieu of the time, says very little about the subject's religious commitment or temperament. Which is not to suggest, as Schmitt makes clear, that there
might not be at any particular time groupings of folkloric themes according to
ideological oppositions, making certain strata of society less receptive to some
elements in the folkloric firmament than others and prepared to regard the mere
cultural conveyance of particular elements as a betrayal of some expected creedal
commitment.[15] Even with folklore one needs to take account of a social topography that would make the very same cultural material resonate quite differently
among different levels of the population.

All of which is to admit, in the end, that when it comes to getting a firm hold
on the elements of popular religion in this period, our reach inevitably exceeds
our grasp. We must read *through* more than *in* the sources, consciously and by
extrapolation, and we must bear with ambiguities of social location, not only
concerning the easily overblown, because polemical, divide between the lay and
clerical sphere, but also with regard to presumed boundaries between dominant
and subordinate, or Christianized, acculturated and non-Christian, semi-pagan
groups. The historian's search for popular religious culture, or popular cultures,
in the early medieval west can therefore never aim for more than approxima-
tion of the historical reality, and it must be satisfied mostly with suggesting lines
of socio-cultural divergence that cannot be inscribed with concrete precision.
Beyond even the specific limitations of the sources just described, there are two
well-nigh irresolvable conceptual or interpretative difficulties standing in the
way of the sharp delineation of cultural fault-lines in this world about which we
will always know so little. These are obstacles to exact description and analysis
we cannot wish away. We must accept them as always lurking beneath or behind
whatever conclusions we draw about the culture of the time.

The first is what I consider the virtual impossibility, even after we have
confronted – and made a decision about how far to allow for – a divide between
lay and clerical sensibilities, especially insofar as the latter are expressed in
learned form, of determining reliably to what extent what I would want to call
the "popular" cultural heritage – in this case, religious or spiritual – that remains
was the preserve of the lower ranks of society or more indiscriminately distributed
among all elements of the laity, from dominant to oppressed. As Peter Brown has
made abundantly clear, the late-Roman habit of projecting onto "the rustics"
whatever aspects of culture the speaker hopes to stigmatize has made it especially
difficult for us to find our way in this regard among our textual sources from the
early Middle Ages.[16] Despite the fact that we know there were profound dispari-
ties in not only status but also wealth and power in the lay world of late Roman

and early medieval Europe, we shall never have the evidential resources permitting us to know how deeply those differences were etched into the cultural map in either the dwindling towns or the vast and thinly populated countryside. The best we can do is to suggest lines of difference and commonalty that accord with the resonances of social animus or disdain we find in our sources over and above the omnipresent expressions of clerical superiority to anything from non-clerical settings.

Second are the exasperating complexities of the conversion from paganism to Christianity. Not only did this conversion begin long before the period we are presently interested in and even outside the geographical area with which we are concerned. It is also true that it was by necessity a gradual process, continuing for over a millennium and constantly given new life by the extension of the boundaries of Romanized European culture through processes of conquest and economically driven acculturation. The inescapable result is that although the conversion was a fact, it is never plain for any specific period or in any designated locale exactly what to make of it, either how far to regard it as having proceeded or in what terms to describe its cultural results. If we confine ourselves just to areas where Christianity had to be introduced to a predominantly Germanic population, as with the Frankish additions to and incursions into Roman Gaul, Swabian and Saxon lands to the east of the Rhine, or Britain of the Anglo-Saxons, we must begin with the currently established opinion among historians that conversion applied to practically the entire population. Bernadette Filotas speaks for the scholarly consensus when she says that "[t]here can be little doubt that after the initial, often traumatic, phases of conversion, the overwhelming majority of the populations of western Europe identified themselves as Christian." But her words reveal as well how little we should think of conversion to Christianity as entailing the absolute eradication of pagan religious behavior or sensibilities: "The conversion of the Franks was inaugurated by the baptism of Clovis (c. 496) but as late as the mid seventh century public signs of pagan cults were being openly displayed in the countryside."[17]

What allows both observations to be valid, as historians have increasingly come to recognize, is the simple reality that the opposition, either behavioral or ideological, between Christianity and what is called paganism, both Roman and Germanic, was in late antiquity and the early Middle Ages not so very stark. Perhaps, as a consequence, there remains the long-recognized willingness of the Christianizers in late Rome and early Middle Ages to adapt and absorb pagan elements as often as to attempt to drive them out, to say nothing of the consequent ambiguity among the converted about what was compatible with Christian belief and what was not.[18] If one strips away the now unfashionable presumption of a determinate Christian norm, one can thus still accept the statement of another of the great lights in the study of medieval popular culture, Jean Delumeau, that "for many centuries the Church spoke thus two languages at once: one strictly correct and directed to a narrow elite, the other more compromising, addressed to the masses."[19]

The strategy of the Christianizing elites was thus most often to absorb traditional patterns of belief and practice but render them unthreatening, indeed supportive of the new establishment, by reinterpreting or imbuing them with a new moral or socio-cultural significance. In the language of earlier scholars like Delaruelle, this process entailed having the Christianizers "accept [much of the mythology of] paganism into the realm of doctrine itself, by reconciling...the myths with the Bible and by accepting pagan versions of the marvelous, in which...demons became the principal actors."[20] Or as more current historical sensibilities would have it, the same phenomenon should be viewed, in words Karen Louise Jolly has used to account for clerical appropriation of English elf charms, "as an ongoing acculturation process occurring in oral culture among rural churches." Along the way, a "more native clergy" adapted to "the needs of a rural population, meeting their day-to-day hardships with the power of Christian ritual and yet still utilizing the familiar folkways."[21]

The practical result is to leave us historians on a cultural terrain of great ambiguity, one might even say ambivalence, for which the drawing of ideological as well as social lines of separation is as much a matter of interpretative preference as it is of faithful distillation of an empirical examination of the sources. If, as I would suggest, Jolly's acculturation model promises to yield the best results, we must be prepared over the long course of the early Middle Ages sometimes to find stages in which absorption and conceptual accommodation to Christian cultural configurations were the rule of the day and other times a more aggressive winnowing of originally alien elements and wholesale refashioning of the interpretative scheme in which they sit. We should also expect to see recurrent cycles of adoption and then reformation. In any case, we need not abandon attempts to identify zones of cultural conformity or coherence distributed along an axis resonant of something like class, status or social dominance, from relatively more popular to relatively more elite.

An example pertinent to the historical materials that will be examined in this chapter is provided by the Anglo-Saxons. Intruding into and then establishing their hegemony over much of Britain in the fifth and sixth centuries, they at first held tight to their Germanic paganism, then gradually through the early seventh century converted to Christianity and made the cultural accommodations necessary to integrate whatever of the earlier traditions they retained, only eventually over the course of the eighth century to give birth to what can be regarded as defining examples of normative Christian culture of the time in the works of monastic scholars of the likes of Bede. But for Anglo-Saxon society as a whole, there would appear to be at least a partial reprise of the same series of cultural occurrences after a hiatus of about a hundred years. Beginning in monastic circles in the tenth century, a sense arose at first of the need for reform in monastic observance but soon for renewal, maybe "re-Christianization," of thought and practice throughout society. Dynamic preachers of the sort of Dunstan, made archbishop of Canterbury in 960, or Aelfric, active in the late tenth and early eleventh centuries, engaged themselves in what looks to be a second phase of cultural accommodation and ideological reconfiguring directed toward bringing the religion of the people still further in line with the intellectuals' vision of the Christian ideal. There follows in the eleventh century another period of learned and mainstream cultural achievement associated with the reign of Edward the Confessor. If we think of these two cycles as not repetitive but rather cumulative, thus indicative of an additive and accelerating process of cultural modification – "acculturation" in short – it is perhaps easier to imagine how something like "popular religion" might be found to manifest itself, sometimes by resistance and sometimes in accommodation, through a slow process of evolution over time.

Popular religion as targeted by the elite

For the purposes of the present essay, I shall focus my investigation on the late ninth, the tenth and the early eleventh centuries. That was, as just indicated, a time when reform was on the agenda, in particular with the intention of modifying the religion and spirituality of the populace at large and inculcating more orthodox patterns of behavior and belief according to learned standards of Christianity. The reform was advanced with special intensity, moreover, both in Anglo-Saxon England and on the continent, especially in cultural borderlands such as the Frankish dominions in the Rhineland and looking eastward into Saxony. Since those two cases provide us with uncommonly plentiful source materials, it is to them that I shall turn in order to seek out the coordinates of popular religion in Latin Europe at the time. In the instance of Rhineland Germany, the richest material has come down to us in the form of penitentials – collections of penances to be assigned to the penitent by a confessor priest to make amends for particular sins revealed in confession – of which the two best known will be drawn upon here. First is the handbook on ecclesiastical discipline winnowing down the decisions of earlier church synods, the *De synodalibus causis et disciplinis ecclesiasticis* of Regino, once abbot of Prüm, who compiled the collection in Trier sometime after 899 and before his death in 915.[22] Second, even more famous, is the more capacious and ultimately more influential work of Bishop Burchard of Worms, most often known by the title *Corrector and Physician* (*Corrector et medicus*).[23] The designation goes back to Burchard himself, who applied it to the nineteenth book of his rambling compilation of extant sources of canonical law called the *Decretum*, which he composed sometime between 1012 and 1023. In fact, chapter 5 constitutes more than half of the whole of book 19, and it is chapters 1 through 5, or alternatively 1 through 9, that were most frequently copied together in the Middle Ages for use as a freestanding penitential and are most commonly intended today whenever the title *Corrector* is used.[24]

For Anglo-Saxon England I rely primarily on works from the pen of the reformer Aelfric. Best known is a sermon that served effectively as a treatise on augury (*De auguriis*) to subsequent readers, along with an addition to the same tacked on slightly later by someone other than Aelfric but consisting nevertheless of excerpts drawn from other genuine sermons of the latter.[25] Since the addition, following a short recounting of a story about St. Macarius, offers a narrative of the tale of Saul and the witch of Endor along with expository commentary on much of the episode's significance, it makes a perfect complement to the earlier sermon to which in two manuscripts it is attached. Notable as well, however, is a sermon on the passion of St. Bartholomew, in which Aelfric deals extensively with matters of paganism and idolatry as well as various heathenish practices he plainly expected to be familiar to, often as not practiced by, his contemporary English audience.[26] Intended as a didactic and cautionary piece, it, like the other two texts, can be expected to give some indication of religious and spiritual beliefs and attitudes thought likely to be found – and we should take as at least possibly present – among the non-Latinate populace of his day. As Aelfric's dates run from c. 955 to c. 1020, we should consider all of this homiletic material as roughly contemporary with Burchard's *Corrector*. Perhaps not surprisingly, records of commonplace medical practices, including healing charms, from generally the same period also open a window onto Anglo-Saxon attitudes, sometimes popular and sometimes literate, toward forms of religion and conceptions of the spiritual world. I thus make use as well of a familiar collection of medical recipes or "Leechbook," unidentified in the manuscript in which it was found but given the title of *Lacnunga* (*Leechings*) by its first modern editor, T.O. Cockayne.[27] Its contents often raise with particular poignancy the problem of determining the relationship between popular beliefs, at various ranks within society, and Christian religion – Christian religion, that is, as adjusted to meet the norms and expectations of the Latin learning of the day.

To make my way through the cultural thickets, or ethnographic complexities and conundrums, of all this material, it has seemed advisable to divide the subject into four pieces, each characterized by a particular social, if often spiritual or ideological, function of the materials involved and each loosely connected to what might be called a different literary source – "literary" taken here as extending to oral traditions. Although the organizing categories for this typology have been chosen with an eye to their historiographical utility, enabling us to impose order on an otherwise bewildering array of practices, beliefs and sometimes just descriptions, they also appear to correspond to semantic distinctions present in the society from which the sources come. In other words, the notion that my four groupings represent separate locations on the cultural landscape – different sorts of action and belief – would not have appeared foreign or bizarre to people in Rhineland Germany or Anglo-Saxon England in the tenth and eleventh centuries. It should be remembered that while the general aim here is to identify aspects of "popular culture," even "popular religion," our precise subject of investigation focuses more narrowly on the elements of belief and practice among the populace that would have struck the learned of the day, particularly clerics, as smacking of superstition in the broad, Augustinian sense of the term. Thus none of the evidence should be taken as meaning that this is all there was to "popular religion" or "popular spirituality" or as indicating that the bearers of the cultural heritage under examination constituted a unitary and distinctively "non-Christian" segment of the population. As for the ever vexatious question of whether "popular" in these instances can in fact be held to refer to subordinate strata of society as opposed to the laity in its entirety, perhaps including some among the clergy, too, the answer of course will remain impervious to definitive resolution. An effort will be made all the same to look for clues to difference in social positioning. In some cases the argument for "popularity" in the sense of association with those of lower and subordinate rank will be stronger than in others.

Witchcraft

The four different cultural objects – my four "pieces" of the culture I am examining – are, briefly put: first, practices and beliefs associated with social actors frequently designated in the English language of the day by one of the cognates of our modern word "witch"; second, measures taken for healing whenever they resonate of assumptions about spiritual or religious reality; third, superstitions in either something like the modern sense of the word or the older notion of "paganizing" practice and belief; and fourth, a number of other peculiar cultural items perhaps best classified under the rubric of folklore. The largest assortment of materials has to do with the first grouping, linked in most cases to the term "witch" or its equivalent. In old English, the word was "*wicca*" in the masculine form, "*wicce*" in the feminine, both associated with a performance and a knowledge-base called "*wiccecraeft*." Most scholars would agree with Audrey Meaney in broadly defining the latter – witchcraft – as "comprising the practice of magic which could be divided between white, or beneficent, and black, or maleficent."[28] Of course, from the perspective of this study, such a definition begs the question of what constituted "magic" in the first place. But it serves nonetheless to locate us more or less where I would like to begin, with something like the semantic domain of "witch" and "witchcraft" as they are commonly employed in modern speech. Meaney reminds us, quoting J. Crawford, that the word for witch was "very likely a contraction of *witega* ['wise-man, prophet'], and certainly cognate with it."[29] It designated, therefore, an individual possessed of an extraordinary, much sought-after and highly practical sort of knowledge, which we shall want now to identify with special care. Again, Meaney is of the common opinion that the persons so designated were, in the mind at least of most Anglo-Saxons, typically – perhaps archetypically – women, even when the gender of the relevant noun employed in a text is either left ambiguous or in some cases given in the masculine.[30] For the moment, I prefer to leave the question of gender unfixed or indeterminate.

Witchcraft as divination

The sort of knowledge – and practice – that was linked to witchcraft in our period appears to embrace a relatively limited spectrum of types. Oldest would seem to be the art of soothsaying or divination, which, as noted in the previous chapter, stood at the origins as well of "*superstitio*" in the classical world.[31] Literally, of course, a derivation of the word "*wicca/wicce*" from "*witega*" would suggest that among the powers or forms of wisdom that witches originally were thought to possess, the prophetic faculty of foretelling the future was particularly salient.[32] And the early, probably eighth-century, Saxon *Indiculus*, written to alert clerics to superstitious practices among their barely converted flock, connects, as Ruth Karras has observed, women associated among the people with the world of enchantment primarily to acts of divination, as opposed to any of the other engagements to which we shall soon turn our attention.[33] The very antiquity of the linguistic and textual link might, however, make us dubious about its relevance to the period with which we are now concerned. In both Regino and Burchard the majority of listings making reference to the practice of divination or recourse to it are lifted from sources dating back to imperial Rome or to late antiquity in the Latin west.

Most striking in this regard is chapter 361 from the second book of Regino's *De synodalibus causis*, which like the entry just preceding it and that immediately following quotes from the Theodosian Code. Drawing upon the lexicon of late imperial Latin, the text takes aim at those who "out of curiosity about the future" have consulted "diviners," also known in Latin as "*harioli*," or perhaps an "inspector of entrails" (*haruspex*), a person in old Rome responsible for delivering the "auguries" (*aurguria*). The terms themselves smack more of Roman usage than that of Regino's own tenth century, not to speak of the punishment to which the alleged offenders stand condemned – that is, execution.[34] Nearly the same, moreover, can be said of Regino, book 2, chapters 354 and 355, taken respectively from decrees of the Council of Ancyra of 314 and a Council of Braga, the results of which were previously reported by St. Martin of Braga in the sixth century.[35] Again, the infraction is to seek out or comply with divinations ("*divinationes*") – as, so read the texts, gentiles or pagans are accustomed to do – or to bring into one's home people who can deliver such pronouncements – chapter 355 calls them "diviners and fortune-tellers" ("*divinos et sortilegos*"). Burchard's *Corrector*, chapter 5, number 60, is surely in large part derivative of both these latter passages in Regino, although it refers to the individuals consulted for their prophetic advice as not just "diviners" or readers of lots ("*sortes*") and deliverers of auguries ("*auguria*") but also – and here it differs – as magicians in the technical sense of the word ("*magos*").[36] It was noted earlier how infrequently this last term was employed with regard to popular practice in the period we are currently examining.

Of course, Dieter Harmening's magisterial *Superstitio* long ago advanced the claim that early medieval penitential and canonical literature was essentially repetitive of what could be found in the homilies of Caesarius of Arles and a few other sixth-century sources. Harmening concluded that almost none among our medieval texts after Caesarius and before Thomas Aquinas in the thirteenth century could reliably be held as witnessing to either belief or practice of the times and societies in which they were composed.[37] Yet not all medievalists have been willing to go so far. Schmitt has made the pertinent observation that repetition of the same sources and the same phrases over the centuries might equally well stand as testament to the continuing and thus real pressure of deviant practices and beliefs among the populace, which church officials felt obligated to respond to and warn against time and time again.[38] Bernadette Filotas dares even to claim that Burchard's *Corrector* deserves special mention as a penitential composed expressly with its contemporary socio-cultural milieu in mind.[39] For my part, I lean in the direction of these latter two.

If anything, the archaizing vocabulary of the cited texts might be more indicative of the social elevation of the cultural target than of any hide-bound or reflexive anachronism among our two author-collectors. Filotas makes the comment, suggestive in this regard, that the ninth-century theologian, Hrabanus Maurus, drew a distinction between "*magi*" and "*arioli*," "known to practice the magical arts," and women, surely of more common status, who made use of charms Hrabanus evidently regarded as belonging to a humbler tradition.[40] The moral infractions of both were equivalent, since their acts were reducible in formal terms to non-Christian behavior of identical – in this case, magical – complexion. Both were therefore subject to the same penance. Yet the precise cultural contents of the practices and beliefs of the magicians and soothsayers, which Hrabanus certainly intended us to recognize as learned, differed from those of the common women, who, so he seems to have been implying, depended upon a distinct and doubtless oral tradition. Perhaps then Regino's and Burchard's invocations of imperial and late antique textual sources were deployed expressly with an eye to a learned and high-status cultural phenomenon, of indeterminate, and perhaps ambiguous, relevance to whatever formally similar cultural patterns might be found among the population farther down the social scale.

Still, there is no reason to believe that all references to soothsaying in the texts of our period constituted either anachronistic evocations of the past or instances where only learned behavior was envisioned. For on other occasions our sources leave the distinct impression that there existed – or at least our authors had in mind – a practice of soothsaying and a belief in its efficacy plainly situated among the common folk and almost surely not traceable back to Latin learning of the Roman world. It would appear, in fact, that divination of this unlearned variety remained up through at least the eleventh century a principal item in the repertory of the stereotypical witch and perhaps even reckoned as commonplace in ordinary life. A case in point is Burchard's *Corrector*, chapter 5, number 62, warning against practices tied to New Year's Day in January. Among this listing's forbidden observances – as so often in these sources characterized as derivative of pagan rites (*ritu paganorum*) – were sitting on the roof of one's house, surrounded by the scratchings of one's sword, in order to intuit what the coming year held in store or taking up a position at a crossroads, seated on an ox skin, with just the same purpose in mind.[41] Or there is the even more curious procedure, easily imagined as performed in the lowliest of households, of that same chapter, number 101. There penance was enjoined for sweeping out the hearth while it was still hot from a fresh fire, and then throwing in grains of barley to see whether they popped up from the heat or simply fell inert. Popping was a sign of imminent peril, lying still of good days to come.[42]

Regino, too, had earlier denounced those who sought out foretellings or omens of various sorts, whether attributed to false holy men and women or drawn from spuriously revered writings. Although the source makes use here of terminology typical of the Late Roman lexicon – "*auguria*," "*sortes*," "*divinationes*" – the context, which goes on to speak about making vows at places like trees or rocks, anywhere other than a church, would seem to indicate as much the circumstances of rural Germany in the tenth century as of the Mediterranean shores of imperial Rome.[43] And almost certainly resonant of observances of his own day – late-tenth- and early-eleventh-century England – are the words of Aelfric in *On Auguries* where he warned of the catastrophic repercussions of running to witches – the term is "*wiccan*" – to learn what should become of one in time of illness. Any prediction a witch might deliver would necessarily arise from the devil and ultimately lead to harm, perhaps even the destruction of one's friends and followers.[44] As Aelfric employs here the feminine pronoun to refer to the witch, he must have had in mind a class of diviners from among the populace at large.

Witchcraft as sorcery

Yet there was a second category of operations or behaviors linked to witchcraft in that same period which, if not of such ancient pedigree as the foregoing instances of divination, is brought to mind perhaps even more readily by the references in our sources. The lexicon employed to designate such practices embraced a wide variety of terms, none of which need be taken as an exact equivalent of any of the others but all of which point generally to a coherent semantic field. In England, as Jolly remarks, writers like Aelfric might refer to the activities I have in mind variously as "*drycraeft*" or "*wiglung*" – the former from the appellative "*dry*," distant relative of the modern word "druid" – either of which was readily associable with our general rubric "*wiccecraeft*."[45] Frequently at issue in similar discussions was recourse to "charms" – in Anglo-Saxon "*galdra/s*" from the singular "*galdor*" – also commonly linked in the texts to "*wiccan*."[46] The Latin of our German disciplinary handbook or penitential speaks of "*carmina*" (verses, songs), or more pointedly "*diabolica carmina*," with precisely the same object in mind.[47] Sometimes the target is implicated by indicating an act of poisoning. The tie between administering harmful potions and performing destructive acts of magic in general went back to classical times, when the Latin "*veneficus/a*" and "*veneficium*" – the former designating a person, the latter an act – made reference as readily to one practice as the other.[48] By the latter days of the empire in the west, the term "*maleficus/a*," literally "evil-doer," had become effectively a synonym.[49] Occasionally in the ninth and tenth centuries a distinction was drawn between "*maleficium*" as the broader rubric and "*veneficium*" as the same type of behavior but specifically reliant on poisons or herbs.[50] More often a difference was apparently not intended, or at least not made clear.[51] The English Egbert penitential refers to women who might kill with their maleficent art ("*arte maleficia*" [sic]), glossing the latter noncommittally as involving either a potion or some other means.[52] As Filotas reminds us, women in any case were stereotypically associated with the commonplace danger poisons were evidently thought to represent.[53]

In all of these cases, the action or operation to which attention was being drawn fell into precisely that category of detestable behaviors to which we have already been introduced in the first part of the so-called Canon Episcopi. As I suggested before, the most appropriate modern word to convey the same referential intent is "sorcery."[54] The text of the canon, which began its long career as quoted by Regino in *De synodalibus causis*, employs of course the phrase "*sortilega et malefica ars*."[55] At the heart of such practice, whether carefully set apart from other doings with which we are concerned in the preceding and following pages or ambiguously left to drift across the boundaries separating one type of work from another, lay the performance of a most often harmful act by means of speaking certain words or manipulating particular objects or carrying out specific rituals. The subject was, in short, "black magic" in what constitutes, according to current common parlance, I believe, its archetypal form.

Although our general topic at present consists in the spiritual or loosely speaking religious culture of the "popular" or subordinate strata of society, sorcery in this primal and foundational sense was neither in practice nor in belief absent from the cultural world of the contemporary medieval elites. There is, for example, the famous case involved in the divorce of the Frankish King Lothar II from his wife Theutberga in the mid-ninth century. Loudly trumpeted in the account written by Hincmar of Rheims, *De divortio Lotharii et Tetbergae*, was the charge that Lothar's mistress, Waldrada, possessed the powers of witchcraft and had used them to promote herself and drive a wedge between the king and queen.[56] All the same, as with the case of divination, specific practice in the lower ranks of society most probably worked differently and looked quite different from any possible correlative among the learned.

Turning exclusively therefore to references that would seem to point in the direction of a lower and broader cultural stratum, we must next inquire what subtypes there were to sorcery or witchcraft of this basic sort. As the frequent mentions in the English texts of charms or *galdra* would suggest, primary among the acts of sorcery stood incantation, in the sense of the actual vocalization of a spell to impose an influence or do harm. Meaney reports how a classic reference by Wulfstan, the great English bishop of the early eleventh century, to the pair *"wiccan oððe wigleras"* is rendered in one manuscript in Latin as *"sortilege vel incantatrices,"* in another as *"incantatores vel incantatrices."*[57] In either case, incantation takes pride of place as an activity that a witch – whether male or female – might engage in. Glosses on the addition to Aelfric's *De auguriis* explain that the key words expressing the subject about which the saint is speaking – *"scincraeft"* and *"drymann"* – should be taken as equivalent respectively to the Latin *"incantatio"* and *"incantator"* – that is, again incantation, followed by spell-caster.[58] And Filotas remarks on how Burchard uses the word *"incantator"* to speak of those who are believed to do such things as raise up storms or addle men's brains.[59] In fact, that precise combination of acts and perpetrators can be traced through Regino all the way back to the Theodosian Code, with enchanters (*incantatores*) and storm-raisers and mind-addlers together labeled as *"malefici."*[60]

Secondary to the vocal casting of spells, witchcraft as we are now using the term was also associated with the manipulation, with evil intent, of particular material objects. Anthony Davies draws attention to the record of a charter making reference to an actual event from mid-tenth-century England, where a woman was drowned by a lynch-mob in the village of Ailsworth because she had allegedly attempted to murder a man by sticking pins into an effigy she had made to represent him. He notes as well the condemnation of precisely this sort of act of evil-doing in the *Old English Penitential*, the penance graduated according to whether the deed resulted in death or not.[61] Burchard, setting his sights again on black magic that women were wont to do, includes among his questions for confessors one relating to what must surely have been a practice drawn from the repertoire of things the German common people believed a witch might do. In this case, the evil act involved women examining the footprints of their neighbors, then taking an appropriate piece of turf from one of them and watching it, maybe performing some operation over it, in the hope of damaging the health of the person who had made the print.[62] Sorcery of this manipulative sort, of course, has constituted a commonplace in numerous cultures.

More specific, but well established as a kind of sorcery with an apparently fearsome reputation among the common folk, was what is usually called "weather magic." The practitioners of such even had their own well attested Latin designation: *"tempestarii."* Surely the most famous reference to evil-doing of this type comes from the letters of the reforming pope Gregory VII. Writing in 1077 to the king of Denmark, Gregory warned against the divine wrath if the monarch did not act decisively to terminate an apparently common practice whereby sometimes priests along with female sorcerers were targeted for "savage punishment" by elements of the populace in the wake of storm-damage to crops.[63] Centuries earlier, Agobard of Lyons had reported that around 820 in his neighborhood concerns about *"tempestarii"* conjuring up damaging storms had occasioned disturbing but widespread panics throughout the countryside.[64] Both Regino and Burchard assess penalties against either trying to operate as or, in Burchard's case, even believing in the existence of what they call "storm-raisers" (*"immissores tempestatum"*).[65]

A further sort of sorcery or witchcraft in this sense was what we may loosely denominate as "love-magic." At least marginally implicated under the latter heading were the "*maleficia et incantationes*" Regino and, following upon him, Burchard attributed to women endeavoring to incite in men's minds either love or hate.[66] The eleventh-century story that Davies draws our attention to from an anonymous twelfth-century compiler of the *Chronicle of the Abbey of Ramsey* provides evidence of an English version of the same stereotype. In that instance, a jealous second wife had a sorceress ("*maleficia*" [sic]) prepare for her a drug that, when given to her husband, completely extinguished the paternal affections that had hitherto bound him to his son.[67] More central to the relevant category of operations was the almost legendary penchant of women who possessed the requisite knowledge to concoct potions increasing the ardor of a male partner or acquaintance, often as not in our sources a husband.[68] Of course, the otherwise generic noun "*venefica*" would apply especially well to evil-doers of this particular variety. Aelfric had perpetrators like this in mind in his *On auguries* when he warned against "witless women" ("*gewitlease wíf*") who prepared their lovers suspicious drinks inducing them to make a proposal of marriage. For Aelfric they belonged along with a number of other wicked female manipulators to the general category of "hags" ("*haetsan*"), often translatable simply as "witches."[69] According to Regino and Burchard, other women drank of their husbands' semen with the intention of arousing in their bed-mates greater love.[70] Or, by Regino's account, they mixed their own menses into the food and drink of their spouses.[71] Whatever the specifics, love-magic seems to have been the one species of sorcery regarded with absolute exclusiveness as women's work.

At the very edge of all these observances was located a practice that serves quite nicely to introduce us to the second piece of the culture we are sifting through among the populace. It involves the combination of incantation with herbal medicine. Curative operations apparently blended easily in the collective imagination of the time – probably among both commoners and elites – with the general conception of sorcerers and what they might do. In the very same entry of Regino's that had cautioned against women drinking their spouses' semen or mixing menstrual fluid with their spouses' food, he also talked about wives giving ashes made from human bones to their husbands to eat in order to ward off sickness.[72] All such operations evidently fell into a common semantic field. Aelfric, too, was prepared to associate witches ("*wiccan, wiccum*") with at least some sorts of healing or the prognostication of an illness's course.[73] This should come as no surprise. Much of medieval curing outside the learned Greek tradition – a tradition that had indeed run quite dry in the west by this central period of the Middle Ages – involved saying certain charms, often over particular herbs. The fact that incantation was also a specialty of sorcerers, particularly, as we have seen, of female witches, ensured that the boundary between some of common medicine and witchcraft should be especially porous.

Measures for healing

We have thus effectively migrated into that second of the cultural pieces I laid out earlier, measures for healing resonant with spiritual or religious connotations. The fact is that we can know only indirectly, through the eyes of clerics – both the censorious and the more accommodating – what little can be gleaned about the medicinal and curative practices of the broad spectrum of the populace in the central medieval centuries. Karen Louise Jolly speaks for the prevailing view among scholars when she reads the evidence as indicating that the providers of healthcare in rural areas in these years – and that would mean for most of the people – were either women steeped in age-old popular traditions or occasionally – and increasingly less often from the late eleventh century on – monks or nuns from a local monastery.[74] It was most likely just such a social configuration that was reflected in Aelfric's association, noted earlier, between witches and healing.

Healing as moral battleground

By and large our sources provide a glimpse of a general perception, at least among an educated clerical elite, of sickness itself, and thereby obliquely healing too, as no less than a moral battleground upon which cosmic forces of good and evil were engaged in combat, the redemptive fortunes of humankind hanging in the balance. Aelfric's sermon on the Passion of St. Bartholomew presents the matter in language as plain as one could hope to find. Recounting the final travails of Bartholomew on his voyage to farthest India, Aelfric explains that the people of that region worshipped as God an idol that they held in high esteem precisely because they perceived themselves to be healed of sickness whenever they made offerings to it. In fact, as Aelfric quickly admonishes his listeners, there was a devil indwelling the idol, who afflicted the people's bodies in the hope that they would turn to him for cure. When they did, he simply withdrew the affliction, satisfied with the knowledge that through their idol-worship they had irretrievably bound their souls to him. Thus no true healing was involved, merely the simulation of illness and remedy.[75]

Presumably the story was to be taken as emblematic of what occurred in instances of idol-worship in all times and other places. Important in the case of Bartholomew, and intended as general edification for his contemporary audience, was Aelfric's additional comment that, in contrast to devils resident in idols, God's saints did in fact possess the authentic power to heal, granted them by the Almighty Himself, and with an intention not much different from that of the devils. In words Aelfric put into Bartholomew's mouth, the saint prayed to God to heal the multitude that they might know Him to be the "one [true] God in heaven, and on the earth, and in the sea."[76] Somewhat muddling the distinction between bona fide healing and false relief from pain, Aelfric went on

to comment that God Himself frequently brought disease upon mankind, sometimes to scourge them for sin, sometimes to try their faith, sometimes to lay open
the way to a miracle.[77] In any case, God was always and alone the genuine healer
of men and women, humankind's "true leech," whether by sickness or cure, ultimately applying the proper therapy to deal with "the sins of his people."[78] Almost
as if to bring us back to the context we are concerned with at present, where it is
not so much the devil that lies under scrutiny as his minions or co-conspirators,
popular healers in the form describable in English as "witches," in two lines from
his *De auguriis* Aelfric lays out the alternatives in no uncertain terms: "Ours is to
seek, if we be afflicted, the remedy from God, not from the cruel witches."[79] There
was, in short, good medicine and bad. The good was practiced under the aegis
of God, the bad under the banner of ungodliness and probably with the help of
demons.

This association of some kinds of healing with ungodliness reached far
back in the Christian tradition and would have been available to the learned
in the central Middle Ages in written form through some of the most venerable of Latin texts. We have already seen Augustine, in his *De doctrina christiana*,
warning against amulets, cures involving incantations or written characters and
certain types of ligatures applied to the body as departures from true medicine
and falling into his category of "superstition," allied thereby with false religion.[80]
Later in the same work he took time to comment on how the natural histories of
his day were filled with lore about the properties of plants, animals and stones,
all of which were worthwhile for the Christian to know so long as they were
not employed medicinally in a way that smacked of superstitious usage. As an
example of the difference he pointed to making a drink from a specific powdered
herb as a cure for stomach-ache in contrast to hanging some of the herb around
the neck to effect the same purpose.[81] The same distinction between genuine
medical recourse to herbs, minerals or animal products, an action completely free
of religious or moral overtones, and use of the same substances in tandem with
suspicious operations and rituals, telltale signs of paganism and irreligion, had
already been advanced among Latin Christians by Tertullian, who had admonished precisely against herbal cures that might derive from paganism – presumably all those not sanctioned by standard medical learning.[82] And shortly after
Augustine, Caesarius of Arles fulminated often against the use of amulets and
ligatures (*phylacteria aut ligaturae*), whether they be simple suspensions of herbs
on the body or the still more ominous wearing of objects inscribed with characters or bearing written texts – all of which Don Skemer places under the rubric
of "textual amulets."[83] Regino was borrowing from this tradition when in his *De
synodalibus causis* he quoted a decree of Gregory the Great anathematizing all
recourse to "*phylacteria*."[84] Among the Germanic populations of early medieval
Europe there was the additional complication introduced by ancient tradition
associating disease with attack by elves, inflicting an often invisible wound by
means of elfin arrows or spears. Even if, by the centuries we are concerned with
now, the Christian clergy had succeeded in linking such elves with demons, the

problem remained of determining whether or to what extent age-old remedies against "*aelfshot*," as these attacks were called, inevitably implicated the practitioner in pagan religiosity.[85]

Standing in the way of any neat separation between proscribed, paganizing curative practice and acceptable, presumably prosaically natural medicine was of course the fact that – as seen in Aelfric's Bartholomew sermon – Christian orthodoxy had its own range of non-natural remedies, among them direct recourse, often through prayer, to the supernatural power of God, frequently mediated through his saints. More complicating still is the emerging scholarly recognition that Christian authorities throughout the Middle Ages, especially in the central medieval centuries, condoned a host of medical practices falling between strictly practical application of herbs and minerals and petitionary recourse to God through prayer, much of which is quite hard to distinguish by either form or apparent intent from the kinds of cures of Augustine's warnings about superstition, not to speak of Caesarius's more wide-ranging attack on paganizing practices. Here a simple admission of how difficult it must have been to disentangle Godly cures procured by visits to the relics of saints, which Ronald Finucane estimates as comprising nine-tenths of the miracles reported at saints' shrines between the twelfth and fifteenth centuries, from ungodly expectations of healing at designated locations, maybe even saints' shrines themselves if connected via popular tradition to old pagan sites of veneration, barely scratches the surface.[86]

Notable was the injunction in both Regino and Burchard against speaking incantations while gathering herbs, except if what was chanted consisted of either the Creed or the Lord's Prayer.[87] The Anglo-Saxon *Lacnunga* offers a prescription for just this latter procedure. As a curative against anal fistula or hemorrhoids, the practitioner was directed to dig up a clump of celandine root or pilewort, choreographing the extraction with a carefully timed chanting of the Lord's Prayer, sung nine times, in order ultimately to prepare from the root a medicinal tincture.[88] More common still in what must certainly have been medicine administered primarily by the clergy was the bare use of incantations – unmistakably Christian, of course – effectively on their own. Again *Lacnunga* presents an extensive Latin text, perhaps taken from lost apocrypha and recounting a story of St. John reciting over poisoned corpses a prayer to God as antidote to poison, which was to be sung into the mouth of a patient too afflicted with a swollen throat to receive an oral potion.[89] Jolly cites another two texts – one from *Lacnunga* and designed to remedy sickness among livestock, another from the margins of an Anglo-Saxon manuscript and directed to the relief of a suffering person – likewise in Latin and intended to be chanted so as to effect a cure.[90] While the first of these works almost as an exorcism to drive an afflicting demon, referred to in the text as a "*diabolus*," from the ailing flock, the second makes a more explicit nod to pre-Christian German ideas of illness by addressing itself to an infecting devil, described as a minion of Satan, himself identified as none other than an elf.[91] For all their openness to non-Christian practice and interpretation, embracing even paganizing descriptives of the etiology of disease, neither charm-remedy presents itself, however, as anything other than fully Christian. Both are offered, in Latin, "in the name of God the Father and the Son and the Holy Spirit."[92]

Perhaps most striking of all instances of Christian concession to curative practices presumably forbidden according to the strict standards of patristic admonitions against superstitious usage are the plentiful references to and instructions for making textual amulets, a surprising number of which have actually survived in material form. Skemer has established beyond a doubt that textual amulets constituted a fully accepted part of learned medicine – in most cases, even medicine of the learned clergy – throughout the Middle Ages.[93] In the Latin of our period such objects were denominated variously by words such as *charta, cedula, littera* and *breve*. Not only were they used widely in monastic and clerical communities, but also monks often served as the source for textual amulets among the laity resident in monastic neighborhoods.[94] In some cases the Christian textual amulets were distinguishable from non-Christian forms and touted in narratives as successful whereas the latter invariably failed.[95] But even clerically sanctioned amulets frequently made use of textual material redolent of non-Christian – and what we would designate as "magical" – traditions. A pectoral cross from the seventh or eighth century, excavated at Lausanne Cathedral from a tomb probably located originally in the cemetery of an early medieval church, is inscribed with the phrases "ABRAXAS" and "ABRACADABRA," magical charms (*"voces magicae"*) that, as Skemer reminds us, go back at least as far as Egyptian gnosticism of the second century.[96] An English medical miscellany written in late Carolingian script and plainly of ecclesiastical origin provides instructions for writing *"characteres"* on ligatures intended to be worn for the purposes of healing. These *"characteres"* include magical script as well as "cryptic series of ordinary letters of the Latin alphabet," some of which Skemer takes to be of runic origin.[97]

Charms and special locations

It is therefore no easy matter to draw the line between medieval medicine – other than the purely herbal or mineral – falling within the bounds of Christian orthodoxy and that which remained unquestionably outside it – this even within the culture of the learned and clerical elite. The problem can only be greater when we attempt to investigate medical practice among the populace at large. Surely directed against unacceptable usage, and one moreover firmly rooted in the non-learned traditions of the people – some ultimately derivative of pre-Christian religion – was the condemnation with which Aelfric concluded his St. Bartholomew sermon. Speaking of "unallowed practices" (*"unalyfedum tilungum"*) resorted to for the sake of healing, two examples of which he identified more specifically as "accursed enchantments" (*"wyrigedum galdrum"*) or "witchcraft of any sort" (*"aenigum wiccecraefte"*), Aelfric warned his listeners that the very fact of turning to such devices and procedures would mark them as no different from the heathens Bartholomew encountered in India, rendering offerings to an idol for the procurement of their health.[98] Presumably it was forbidden charms and recourse to local healers, mostly women, who incorporated charms and spells into their healing, that Aelfric had principally in mind.

Closely connected in Aelfric's mind to these charm- and sorcery-allied medical practices were other sorts of remedies to which he almost immediately addressed himself in that same didactic conclusion to the Bartholomew sermon and which resonated even more plainly of pagan or paganizing tradition. No person who wished to be reckoned a Christian should make a visitation to a stone or a tree – except of course the Godly "tree" of the crucifix – or any particular place other than a church with its sacred altar, in order, as Aelfric put it, "to fetch his health."[99] Burchard prescribed a penance for those who sought healing at springs, stones, trees or crossroads – anywhere, in fact, other than a church or otherwise clerically sanctioned location – in an entry targeting in general all similar ritualizing observances outside the purview of clerical officialdom.[100] The warning was practically a trope in clerical literature of the time. In every case, of course, the practice proscribed was analogous to contemporary church-supported healing at a holy shrine, the near ubiquity of which, as previously noted, Finucane has drawn to our attention. The difference lay in the nature of the "holiness" resorted to, with the forbidden sites most likely all traceable to a topography drawn along lines of pre-Christian habits of worship and veneration.

We thus have, so far, at least two potential categories of commonplace and almost surely unlearned medical practice from our central medieval centuries that deviated from strictly clerical usage and could be said to represent a peculiarly popular and vaguely un-Christian spirituality of healing: particular charms and spells and supplication at locations not sanctified with ecclesiastical approval. And when we look to texts more directly reflective of practice, not simply voicing homiletic and confessor-driven precaution and alarm, we do indeed find evidence not only of such behavior but also of several other types clearly savoring of the common folk and hard to reconcile with learned or clerical norms. Most obvious are simple charms or chants performed to remedy ailments typically linked to popular conceptions of disease and made up of words sometimes imitating Latin but often traceable to the vernacular or representing utter gibberish. A procedure against toothache from *Lacnunga* calls for the healer to sing, just after sunset, the curious phrase "caio laio quaque uoaque ofer saeloficia sleah manna wyrm," mainly pseudo-Latin but ending with the English "strike the worm of men." One must then name the sufferer and his father and follow up with a second line, beginning again in pseudo-Latin, crossing over then into Anglo-Saxon but concluding with the authentic Latin: "finit, amen."[101] Though this prescription might be seen as by implication intended for a literate healer, there is no reason that it could not be performed, perhaps from memory, by a commoner from among the people. Even more suggestive of folk medicine is another remedy which calls for a chant to counter a "penetrating worm." In this case the chant begins with Old Irish for "I wound the animal, I strike the animal, I kill the animal," but then passes into undecipherable Irish- or Anglo-Saxon-like gibberish. To be sung nine times, the charm-cure terminates with a single "Our Father" ("*pater noster*").[102] The whole is to be sung into the wound, on which spittle is then smeared along with ground green cumin and hot cow's urine.[103] Though there is nothing unambiguously non-Christian about these vocalizations, they do strain the bounds of Regino's and Burchard's call for only wordings clearly connected to ecclesiastical ritual.

Expressly against the proscription, found again in both Regino and Burchard, of applying medicinal herbs along with any incantation other than plainly Christian formulas such as the Lord's Prayer or the Creed is a number of still more complicated directives in *Lacnunga*, the origins of which clearly lie in pagan lays and spells.[104] In these cases, where words and herbs are brought together, the healing practice would seem likewise to contravene Aelfric's absolute prohibition of charms ("*galdre*") in herbal medicine. For Aelfric, there was to be no speaking over medicinal herbs unless it was to bless them with the holy word of God.[105] The remedies in question have been examined at some length by Jolly, who singles out these prescriptions in particular as incorporating "native elements" – by which she means not just un-Romanized Anglo-Saxon but also broadly Germanic material of ancient origin – "in a fairly un-Christianized form."[106] Presented by the editors Grattan and Singer under the titles "The Lay of the Nine Herbs," "The Lay of the Nine Twigs" and "The Lay of the Magic Blasts," the three core texts Jolly refers to consist of a set of recipes embodied in incantatory form that by their words alone strike the reader as belonging to neither a learned nor a Christian setting.[107]

Three times the herbs are extolled for their power to stand against the "foe" or "evil one" wandering destructively throughout the land.[108] In each case, the comment is preceded by a reminder of their strength in resisting "onflight" ("*onflyge*"), a peculiarly Germanic notion of evil or venom directed through the air against unwitting victims.[109] Indeed, almost everything about these lays exudes the atmosphere of the un-Christian, the pre-Christian, perhaps the just plain pagan. Among four themes Jolly singles out as characteristic of what she calls "Germanic…medicine transmitted through folklore," three are present throughout the text: flying dangers or poisons, worms or snakes, and the number nine.[110] The god Woden, himself, makes an appearance in the "Lay of the Nine Twigs," portrayed as smiting the infectious viper with nine wonder-working branches in order to cancel its pathogenic effect.[111] Which is not to say that Christian elements are entirely absent. Christ, too, appears toward the end of the "Lay of the Magic Blasts," standing above, and presumably against, the ancient and evil agents of disease.[112] As always, therefore, our written sources – even non-homiletic ones such as these – betray the presence of the clerical elite and cannot be supposed to represent in its purity a popular or resolutely non-Christian cultural tradition. All the same, through them we see cultural sources that at one point were untouched by either Christian or literate influence and which can plausibly be assumed to have remained in practically such purity outside the monastic scriptoria and in the oral resources of the populace.

As for the way these texts, written in Anglo-Saxon, were to be used, the answer comes in the *Lacnunga* entry immediately succeeding them. They are charms to be employed in combination with application of the medicinal herbs to which they refer. That is to say, they are evidence of just the practice Regino, Burchard and Aelfric intended to prohibit. Following directions for exactly how to work the herbs into a salve to be spread directly onto the wound or ailing member, the passage enjoins the healer to "sing the charm" ("*sing þaet galdor*") three times on each herb before preparing the salve and then to sing it again into the patient's mouth and both ears and over the point of application just before laying on the tincture.[113] The contradiction could not be more explicit. Where Aelfric forbade singing charms on medicinal herbs, here that is precisely what the remedy prescribes.[114]

Elves

Then there is the whole body of curative practices directed against the mischief wrought by elves. Harm from elves constituted the fourth of the elements mentioned earlier as associated by Jolly expressly with Germanic, and thus origi-nally non-Christian, folkloric medicine.[115] Medicinal measures to counter elf damage might therefore be thought to implicate the practitioner in a pagan-izing or at least un-Christian spirituality. All the same, it is easy to imagine how the presence of elves and their pathogenic influence could have been absorbed into a Christian point of view, even recalibrated according to Christian expecta-tions of demonic involvement in sickness, and the remedies against both either tacitly accepted as compatible with the norms of catholic behavior or actually transformed to conform to bits of the Christian liturgy. Jolly, for instance, quotes a prescription for a salve against elves and "nightgoers" ("*aelfcynne*" and "*niht-gengan*"), found in a text that matter-of-factly reinterprets the malignant agents in Christianizing fashion as those types of being "with whom the [d]evil has intercourse."[116] Moreover, here the use of the salve is to be accompanied by an unmistakably liturgical censing and signing of the cross.

Whatever meaning we choose to give them, pre-Christian concerns about the noxious effects of all such noisome figures of Germanic folklore emerge frequently in the Anglo-Saxon leechbooks of the time. And in some cases, the counter-elfin medicine we find in the texts comes without any mitigating rein-terpretation or Christianizing additions. On such occasions, we are left on our own to confront historical sources deeply resonant of a pagan spiritual world. An entry in *Lacnunga* presents a lay to be sung against "elfshot," little darts that elves were believed to shoot at their victims and which radiated disease from the point where they embedded themselves in the flesh. From beginning, where the adversaries are described as riding over the hill to confront the sufferer, to end, where the singer of the lay calls upon both elves and their darts to recede, nothings here suggests any other than a paganizing conceptual environment.[117]

Of course, the fact that all the texts we possess were written, and presumably made use of and accepted, in a monastic setting tells us that even in their most unmodified pre-Christian form, these Germanic healing usages had by the tenth and eleventh centuries found their way into educated and clerical sources. They cannot therefore be taken, *ipso facto*, as representing medicine of the populace in contradistinction to that of the elite and of the church. Still, their very presence in monastic manuscripts would have been impossible had not the source for much of what they comprised once existed in solely oral form outside the convent walls. There is, moreover, every reason to think that similar oral conventions circulated contemporaneously among layfolk when these texts were written down, and surely many of these traditions penetrated quite low into the social strata of the time. The further away from Latin learning, and the further down on the social scale, the less likely it is that any Christianizing spiritual resonance would be absorbed, presuming it was even known. Among the people, much curing must have remained quite as it had been before the arrival of Christian missions for centuries even after the time we are concerned with here.

Superstition

All of which brings us quite close to the third of those cultural objects I have designated as the subject of this investigation. It is comprised of the bundle of beliefs and practices among the populace that might best be characterized as superstitions, mostly along lines of the current common meaning of that word but also according to an older understanding of it as "paganizing" convention. Historically speaking, the semantics at either extreme are intimately connected. As Harmening notes, modern scholarly attitudes toward "superstition" can be seen emerging already in the work of early ethnographers of the nineteenth century, most especially Jakob Grimm. He quotes the latter in words expressly laying the basis for the systematic study of mythology in an appreciation of superstition (*"aberglauben"*) as always resting on a more ancient bed of pagan beliefs. What is more, he connects this foundational understanding with the enormously influential formulation of the English anthropologist from later in the same century, E. B. Tylor, whereby *"superstitio"* as designated in the source texts of ecclesiastical literature of the late medieval and early modern periods should be recognized by the enlightened researcher as having consisted precisely in a "cultural survival" of long-since forbidden forms of religion, both their ideological content and their ritual.[118] For his part, Harmening rejects that paradigm as inappropriate for contemporary scholarship. But as Schmitt encourages us to remember, its pedigree goes back at least to Augustine, whose formative notion of "superstition" as equivalent to false religion contains in seed much the same idea.[119]

Regardless of the historical implications of our words, the view of "superstition" that Harmening wants to make obsolete has expressed itself among medieval scholars in a debate over the proper way to characterize the relationship among superstition, paganism and the religion – whether acknowledged as authentically Christian or not – of the people. Raoul Manselli spoke for a viewpoint dominant early in the second half of the twentieth century holding that up through the Carolingians and for several centuries thereafter, the Christianity of the broad base of the populace was constituted of a superficial overlay of orthodox belief and understanding on top of a preponderant base alien to true Christian principles and evocative instead of Germanic tradition.[120] By this perspective, the mentality of the vast majority in the central Middle Ages remained tied to old assumptions about the nature of the world imbued in paganism, so that popular religion was itself superstitious and inherently paganizing.[121] Superstition was hence a facet of popular belief. Alexander Murray represents a more recent approach, consistent with Harmening, insisting that paganism could not survive the conversion to Christianity. Instead, what remained by the days of our central medieval period were bits and pieces derived from pagan antecedents but coalescing into something different from either paganism itself, now truly abandoned, or popular Christian belief – something, that is, much more akin to "superstition" following present-day colloquial usage.[122] Somewhere in between these two positions sits that adopted by Ruth Karras, wherein Germanic paganism did not actually survive but nonetheless left its imprint on Christian practice and belief among the broad populace, even as sanctioned by church officials, or wandered contextless in fragmentary form, each particular fragment targeted by the clergy for criticism as "superstitious."[123] I take it that Jolly is trying to encapsulate both the cultural by-products that Karras had in mind in a single amorphous domain by having recourse to the notion of "folklore," in her understanding an "areligious" vehicle whereby customs and creeds were transmitted into a world where they had been stripped of their original religious context.[124]

Superstition of religious inspiration

When we actually turn to the sources – and that means exclusively the penitentials, in this case from Regino's and Burchard's hand – we find two general sorts of practice or belief picked out for correction that would fall under a category of superstition fashioned broadly enough to accommodate practically all the ideological terrain staked out in the debates just discussed. On the one hand lie patterns of behavior that would appear, at least at first glance, to reflect a religious inspiration, perhaps even a coherent creedal point of view. It is here that claims of cultural survival find their greatest resonance, even if, following Karras, we avoid so vigorous an application of that model as intended by Tylor or found among historians like Manselli. To be honest, the number of entries in the penitentials falling under this first general rubric of superstition is small. And to no surprise, in light of Harmening's warning about a tendency toward archaism and repetition, the specific texts themselves are either quite early in date or draw upon what would appear to be early literary sources. That still does not constitute sufficient reason, in line with Schmitt's observation noted earlier, for rejecting these items out of hand as evidence for practice in the central Middle Ages.[125]

From the Pseudo-Bede penitentials comes a passage in Regino's *De synodalibus causis* excommunicating anyone who has performed a vow or submitted a votive offering at a tree or a rock or indeed any place other than a Christian church.[126] It is interesting that the penance for those seeking forgiveness for such an infraction includes a special provision for those petitioners who also happen to be priests. Even in its earliest form, therefore, this particular intervention could not have had in mind only pagan religious practices entirely independent of Christian worship. A longer entry immediately following, attributed in manuscript to a Council of Nantes but actually of unknown provenance, calls upon the Christian clergy to wage all-out war against religious observances dependent directly upon paganism. Priests and bishops are commanded to cut down pagan holy trees and tear up their roots, so that not so much as a branch is left – and here the clerical-lay divide intrudes – for the common folk (*"vulgus"*) to carry away and venerate. They are to dig up and completely eliminate rocks where, as Regino's words explain, people might be "deceived by demonic games played out in desert places and [deep] in the woods."[127] In this case, church officers are admonished to make it clear that such paganizing behavior cuts people off from God and Christianity, turning them into idolaters. Here, therefore, the divide between prohibited practice and Christianity seems to have been seen as more complete. As before, there follows a prohibition of making a votive offering and, in addition, lighting a candle anywhere other than in a church.[128] In line with Harmening's skeptical expectations, however, the whole text ends with references to condemnations of pagan sacrifice in the biblical Books of Kings.

Lifting again from an early source – this time the *Capitula* of Martin of Braga, active in the sixth century – another text in Regino highlights for condemnation paganizing observances in what is described as a cult of the elements, perhaps also the moon.[129] Attacked as well in this instance is following the course of the stars in order to decide when to build, plant crops or celebrate a wedding. Given that this latter practice smacks more of learned astrology than of the doings of commonplace or popular cult, perhaps this example is not indeed pertinent to practice among the people at large. All the same, despite the archaic provenance, it is worth noting that when Burchard reproduces practically the same text in his own *Corrector*, he prefaces it with an observation that would appear to represent a specific addition of his own. His comment is that some pagan traditions have been passed down from father to son, as if they constituted a precious inheritance transmitted all the way into his own day (*"in hos dies"*).[130] If this is Burchard speaking, he anticipates Schmitt's counter-argument to Harmening by nearly a thousand years.

Superstition more generally

More prevalent than these suggestions of semi-religious behavior, on the other hand, are mentions of a second pattern of practice or belief, one fitting better with the modern colloquial understanding of "superstition" as irrational and odd but not in the end expressly sacral observance. Common in central medieval penitentials are fulminations against New Year's Day rites and celebrations. Burchard alone contains several. One long entry takes aim at a host of practices reserved, "in pagan fashion" ("*ritu paganorum*"), for the first of January, including doing something dramatically different from what would be expected on any other day of the year, setting the table with precious stones and sumptuous dishes, or joining a chorus of singers wending its way through the streets and byways of the town.[131] Two others warn against masquerading as a stag or a calf and expressly choosing the start of the year to begin a project of spinning, weaving or sewing.[132] Kindred in spirit is another entry enjoining penance for, among other things, paying special attention to Thursday, in honor of "Juppiter," presumably Burchard's Latin rendering of "Thor." And then there is the prohibition of wakes for the dead, performed again "in pagan fashion," with songs, dances, drinking, loud laughter and all manner of impious revelry.[133] Or the acid reference to a usage at the funeral of a murder victim, in which an unguent was placed in the cadaver's hand to heal the wound even after death and burial.[134] All of these admonishments would have had pagan antecedents in mind, but the practices envisioned could well by Burchard's day have carried little of the baggage of formal religion.

Likewise redolent of pre-Christian religion, but easily separable in the mind of practitioners or proponents from any particular creedal commitment or even general cosmological orientation was concern for the "three sisters" or the "fates." Once Burchard singled out for opprobrium the mere belief that the fates might designate someone at birth to become what in German was known as a werewolf ("*quod teutonica Werewulff vocatur*"), a man who could, whenever he wished, transform himself into a wolf or other savage creature.[135] He also made special mention of women who, at certain times of the year, would set out food and drink along with three knives on their table, so that if the sisters or fates arrived, they would find refreshment and possibly return the favor.[136] On both occasions, Burchard took time to explain just how the targeted belief or practice was inconsistent with the notion of God's omnipotence. Surely to his mind, at least, there might be many in the populace fully convinced of the fates' reality but with no sense that they thereby put themselves at odds with Christian belief.

Finally, we come upon a number of customs or persuasions that seem far removed from pre- or non-Christian religion in any substantive sense but that reverberate all the same of attitudes about life and death or powers at large within the world for which catholic faith and ritual would appear to have had little relevance. There is, for example, a group of entries in Burchard which all appear related to a curious, and plainly unorthodox, preoccupation with the death of infants.[137] In one, penance is enjoined for women who impale with a stake the corpse of an infant who has died unbaptized, out of fear that otherwise the body would arise from the grave and do harm to the living. Immediately following is prohibition of a similar procedure to be used against both mother and child if they perished in a fatal childbirth. We also have Burchard's instructive account of a disturbing belief that it was unsafe to go about outside the house before daybreak.[138] As he explained it, the belief involved a fear of unclean spirits whose ability to do harm was mitigated only at the cock's crow. Again, for Burchard, the problem was lack of faith in the power of God, transmitted especially through the sign of the cross. For us, more interesting is the convention in itself, reflective of long-standing convictions that we would readily designate superstitious.

Folklore

There remains then only the fourth and final constituent of what I have proposed should be taken as a largely popular, or non-elite, culture in the central Middle Ages, or at least that part of it that might strike learned and clerical contemporaries as suspiciously unorthodox and perhaps even positively non-Christian. For this object of our examination I chose the descriptor "folklore," in what I believe to be a more suitable usage of the term than that attributed earlier to Karen Louise Jolly.[139] "Folklore" as I reserve it for this final cultural element comprises a body of stories and beliefs passed down among the populace from generation to generation but not necessarily attached to any particular practice or behavior and, though loosely carrying spiritual or what one might think of as semi-religious implications, not assigned a fixed place in the ideological firmament of the audience for which it was intended. By the latter I mean to say that it existed in a cultural world where there was something else officially reckoned as "religion" and more or less accepted by the people at large as what "religion" ought to be. But these same stories and beliefs persisted all the same, although they were not easily reconciled, perhaps not even ever asked to be brought into line, with what "religion" had to say. They were, as the word "folklore" implies, more literary than behaviorally prescriptive, more imaginative than descriptive.

Women of the night

The best and most famous example of this sort of cultural item in the period we are concerned with now is found in the second part of that often-cited text, already mentioned twice earlier, referred to by its classic instantiation as the "Canon Episcopi."[140] As we have seen, the first part of this famous item in canon law concerns itself with sorcery, which it takes steps to eradicate by calling upon the clergy to see that known sorcerers are driven from the parish. The second part turns to an entirely different subject and prescribes a completely different remedy for the threat it was thought to pose to Christian order. Almost certainly, this second piece of the "Canon" draws upon a separate source, a synodal act or clerical pronouncement most likely originating in the same general time and milieu as with the source of the first part – that is, the Carolingian church of the ninth century. From its very first words, as recorded in nearly identical versions by both Regino and Burchard, this second part of the "Canon" makes it plain that the subject is no longer sorcery but rather a tale or belief nourished among the common folk. It is the tale of what would often be referred to as the "women of the night," or, as the entry in Regino and Burchard puts it, "an innumerable multitude of women who ride the night sky on various beasts in the train of the goddess Diana, traversing enormous spaces in the dread nocturnal silence while following the goddess's commands as if she were their mistress or lady."[141] The author or authors of the text remark upon the fact that there are actual women among the populace who believe themselves on special nights to join this female multitude and readily confess as much among their neighbors. Learned clerics that they undoubtedly were, however, the same author or authors unequivocally insist that there is absolutely no truth either to these confessions or to the story of the night-riders upon which they draw and to which they give renewed life. Fantasies generated in the minds of wretched women by the devil ("*diabolus*") – indeed, in Regino's version "Satan himself" ("*ipse satanas*") is named as the protagonist – the tales should be resolutely exposed by church authorities for the fictions that they are. Regino calls for lots of public preaching instructing the people in the perversity of such illusions; Burchard prescribes for those who spread the tales two years of penance.[142]

In both Regino and Burchard, shorter references to the same sort of tale add a few details and make some adjustments. A separate entry in Regino's *De synodalibus causis*, frequently alluded to as the "short version" of the "Canon," targets the belief but describes the presumed night-riding multitude as consisting of a host of demons ("*daemonum turba*") who have taken on a female likeness.[143] What is generally regarded as Burchard's own rendition of this same "shorter version" appears in his *Corrector* with an identical explanation that the night-riders are made up of a crowd of demons transformed into womanly shapes. It adds the fascinating observation that the leader of the host is named "Holda" in the vernacular of the people, no mention made of the presumably less authentic, more classicizing "Diana" of the "Canon's" longer version.[144] Finally, earlier on in Burchard's full composition of which the *Corrector* is merely a part, in book 10 of his *Decretum*, a third name for the multitude's leader is offered, this time paired with Diana. Some commoners maintain, this version notes, that Herodias leads the train.[145]

Much ink has been spilled commenting on and interpreting this extraordinary set of passages along with the folkloric base upon which they all presumably rest.[146] Filotas has remarked how already Jakob Grimm identified the leader under the name of "Holda" as reaching back to an ancient German goddess of abundance and fertility.[147] Cohn points to various medieval stories naming Herodias, wife of Herod the Great, and sometimes confused with his daughter Salome, as consigned perpetually to an airy realm from which she commands a considerable following among the people of the world.[148] "Diana" is generally considered a not-inappropriate Romanization reflective of the literary lexicon of the "Canon's" Latinate and clerical recorders. In any case, the association of women, flying at night, a god-like mistress and the assurance of fertility or abundance seems to be essential to the legend or belief, no matter what its precise instantiation. There is no reason not to think that a good bit of this complex of ideas persisted even well beyond the period we are focusing on at present. To the degree that that was so, we are dealing with a bit of folklore independent of and perhaps never happily reconcilable with a Christian point of view.

In this latter regard, it is instructive to turn to a further entry from Burchard's *Corrector*, plainly related to the theme at hand but not included among the passages just examined. On this occasion, Burchard speaks of women who are convinced that on certain nights they secretly and mysteriously escape from their houses, not even having to open the doors, to join together and fly to the very heights of the sky. There, they fight with other presumably similar groups, wounding them insofar as they are able, but also themselves receiving wounds.[149] Although Burchard takes the stories to be nonsense, he makes clear that, to his eyes, anyone even presuming to engage in such activities must be a minion of the devil ("*diaboli membrum*"). What makes this brief mention so interesting is that it links up almost effortlessly with another set of stories, again bits and pieces of folklore, that Carlo Ginzburg has likewise set in the broad context of the legend of the women of the night. In his justly famous *Night Battles*, Ginzburg exhaustively investigates a belief among the populace revealed by inquisitorial proceedings in the sixteenth- and early seventeenth-century Friuli and centering on what would seem to be precisely the same sort of battles in the night sky. Women, and in the Italian case, men as well, go in bands into the sky at night to fight with other similar groups.[150] Those professing this belief said that they fought using fennel stalks, and that their antagonists countered them with stalks of sorghum. The stakes they fought over were no less than the fertility and abundance of the crops and livestock of the surrounding countryside.[151] Those who fought for fertility – for the good – had since time immemorial, so they said, been called "the good-goers," "*i benandanti.*"

To Ginzburg's eyes – and to mine as well – the cases he presents offer evidence of continued familiarity in Europe up to the seventeenth century with practices whose origins must have lain centuries before in what was surely a pagan fertility cult. For Ginzburg, the important point was that this familiarity and these beliefs became mixed up, in the sixteenth and seventeenth centuries, with beliefs about and prosecutions of witches.[152] They were, he explained, signs of a "kernel of truth" in Murray's famous thesis on the historical significance of western witchcraft.[153] For us – momentarily at least – witchcraft itself is of little relevance. Pertinent, on the other hand, is the thought that something very much like shamanism, or at minimum drawing upon shamanistic precedents, was an element up to early modern times in the culture of some of Europe's unlettered populace.[154] The fact that Ginzburg's account heightens the probability that the battles Burchard was talking about had to do in the mind of the common folk with fertility is rendered even more important because of the apparent link between this particular entry and all the other texts more immediately connected to the "Canon Episocopi." They were, it would seem, all part of a broad swath of popular beliefs about the spiritual world and fertility that, once again, sat uneasily in a Christian context.

Yet there are other clues in the stories of the "Canon Episcopi" pointing to still further corners of the culture of the populace that we know flourished in the very same centuries. It is Ginzburg, again, who alerts us to the fact that Holda's counterpart in the south of Germany was another semi-divinity known by the name of "Perchta." This latter, he explains, was not only goddess of vegetation but also commonly taken among the populace as one of the possible leaders of another piece of the folkloric universe relevant to our present concerns, that having to do with stories of the "Wild Hunt" or "Furious Horde."[155] Ginzburg is surely correct in noting that strictly speaking we must maintain a distinction, at least in origin, between the legends of Holda, or some other female leader at the head of her train at night, and those of the army of the dead.[156] For if Claude Lecouteux is right, the "Wild Hunt" or "Furious Horde" was at its most authentic a threatening procession of those who had died but were nonetheless present in bodily form.[157] They would bear little resemblance to the women who rode their beasts behind a mistress a Latinate mind would have wanted to describe as Diana. All the same, some crossover must have occurred, even among the populace, and the process was already well under way by the centuries with which we are now concerned. Again, a notion of fertility might well have been part of the mix. One can do no better than to quote Lecouteux on this very subject: "According to ancestral belief, the dead wander over the earth on certain dates and play an important role for the wellbeing of the living, since they oversee fertility and prosperity."[158]

Strigae

Further distanced from the stories of the ladies of the night riding in the train of Diana, but still recognizable as part of a single vast treasury about frightening night spirits stored in the folkloric memory at varying times and places among the European populace in the central Middle Ages, is another series of legends, brought to our attention from the sources we are examining by just two entries in Burchard's *Corrector*. In his shorter version of the "Canon Episcopi," Burchard had introduced us to the fact that some of the stories about the at-once female and demonic riders of the night named Holda as the mistress that all her consorts followed. A single word alerts us that maybe something further is afoot here than in any of the other versions of the "Canon," for Burchard's text precedes "Holda" with the denomination "*striga*." Precisely put, this text thus stipulates that it is the *striga* whose name is "Holda" that leads the train.[159] Since *striga* is cognate with the modern Italian word for witch, *"strega,"* it is often translated into English as "witch." To my mind, the implied equivalence is misleading with regard to our central medieval period. For that time, I prefer to reserve "witch" to do semantic duty for the Old English *"wicca/wicce,"* which I have consistently rendered as "sorcerer" or "sorceress."[160]

Instead, the word *"striga"* has a venerable classical pedigree of its own. Among the Romans, the Latin *"strix"* (in the plural, *striges*) – literally screech-owl – was thought to designate in addition to the commonplace bird also a bird-like creature that haunts the night skies searching for babies to destroy. Perhaps the two were in fact identical. By Ovid's and Petronius's day, the same amorphous being was further interpreted as an old woman transformed into a bird's shape. She, too, sought out babies, whose entrails she proceeded to eat. In the second century, the grammarian Festus was making use of a new word, *"striga"* (plural: *strigae*), which he defined as a woman addicted to sorcery and who flew at night, and by the fifth century the term had entered the Christian pastoral literature to denominate a female vampire-like creature who prowled the night.[161] Presumably, the parallel semantics of the two words eventually made them synonymous. At any rate, *"striga"* or *"stria"* was being used among Germans as early as the Salic Law of the sixth century to refer to a cannibalistic woman who sometimes gathered with others of her ilk at night. And a Carolingian capitulary of 789 prescribed the death penalty for those among the Saxons who seized women purported to be *strigae*, hence devourers of men, and executed them by setting them afire.[162]

Burchard's second entry reveals that a notion of beings very much the same survived among the populace in the Rhineland of his day. Beginning again with language evocative of the "Canon Episcopi" – specifically "women turned back to Satan" and traversing vast spaces of the earth "in the silence of dread night" – on this occasion the attention suddenly turns to something quite different from the ladies following Diana or Holda. Here, while they or their images lie beside their husbands in bed at night, the targeted women manage, without opening any doors, to go out bodily and with companions of just their sort seize baptized, Christian men, kill them, cook them and eat their flesh.[163] The passage continues that such women also claim that, having killed and devoured the men's flesh, they then stuff straw or wood into the place of their heart and thus bring them back to life, or at least give them the signs of being alive. For all this, which again Burchard apparently takes as completely unfounded in reality, the women confessing such behavior – more precisely, believing that they practiced it – were assigned a fast of bread and water over the subsequent Lent and that of the seven succeeding years. The sin in both cases was to follow one of the commonplaces of folklore so far as to take it for a reality of life. The problem was again that as a reality, the story seemed to infringe upon the power of God and the absoluteness of his order for the world.

So much, then, for the four elements of popular "religion" or spirituality put forward earlier for investigation regarding the central centuries of the Middle Ages. Taken together, they represent an impressive complex of cultural commitments, both beliefs and practices, that can be thought of as belonging most properly to the majority of the population, nearly all of whom were entirely illiterate and most of whom would have to be assigned subordinate status in society. In general, these items in the cultural repertory of the populace were looked at askance by members of the clergy – or at least those learned enough to think of themselves as defenders of catholic orthodoxy – though all of them were likewise subject to some sort of appropriation whereby they could be reconciled with Christian practice, usually being taken as signs of wicked and demon-inspired behavior or erroneous belief. But some of this material had managed to work its way more positively into the intellectual and cultural world of the elite, accepted as at least marginally part of a legitimate Christian inheritance. That was particularly the case with items in the medicinal or therapeutic component, where the mixing of originally Christian elements with those of a decidedly paganizing provenance was more the rule than the exception. In those instances, moreover, it was not just the dominant strata of the laity that were willing to open themselves to more popular influences but also many among the learned, Latinate clergy. All the healing recipes used earlier as evidence were, after all, presumably recorded by monks who were prepared to put them to use. From an historiographical perspective, therefore, all this material not only represents the flesh and bones of the most popular, commonplace and unlearned currents at the margins of officially sanctioned spirituality of the time, but it also must be recognized as continually subject to those processes of acculturation spoken about early on in this chapter. And as noted, such acculturation worked both by accommodation and absorption, in the course of which the cultural raw material would itself undergo modification and sometimes ideological realignment, and by winnowing and selective rejection, in which the culture could be said to be reformed.

The rationalization of religion

Perhaps just because of the obvious ambivalence of this acculturating procedure, some of the classic mid-twentieth-century accounts of medieval culture evaluated the relationship between a large part of the more popular contributions to spirituality and the norms of the official church as by and large mutually sympathetic up through this central period, at least to sometime in the eleventh century. In the words of Delumeau, already quoted earlier, church authorities managed at one and the same time to speak two languages. One was a learned discourse, rigidly orthodox, employed only within the elite. The other was vernacular and more accepting, even "compromised," put to work in communicating with the masses. This double-speak, Delumeau said, allowed the Christian church to draw "rural paganism" within itself, as if by cooptation.[164] Raoul Manselli had much the same in mind when he talked of "Christianization" in the Germanic world before the high Middle Ages as "a superficial Christianization, incomplete, in which there remained elements by nature, one might say, foreign to Christianity."[165] According to this same narrative, however, after the central Middle Ages a dramatic change occurred. For Delumeau the turning point came in the thirteenth century and was manifested by a switch from a "politics of assimilation" to "one of rejection, where [authorities] made an effort to impose on millions of people the religion of just a few."[166] Manselli dated the shift a bit earlier, to the century after the year 1000, but he, too, saw it as calling into question the earlier practices of religious or spiritual accommodation. From the eleventh century on, and starting in the cities and towns, the clergy initiated a process of authentic Christianization that would for the first time profoundly reshape the culture of the populace.[167]

Of course, since we have been viewing the interaction between Christian spirituality as conceived by learned clerics and religious and spiritual conceptions and sentiments as constituted by oral tradition among the common folk as fraught with tension, it won't do for us simply to accept characterizations such as Delumeau's and Manselli's at face value. Christianization could not begin in the high Middle Ages, since it had already been going on for centuries. Recent studies recognize all the same that something changed in cultural relations between the hierarchy of the church and the populace at large in the period of the eleventh and twelfth centuries. Moreover, they tend to embrace so much of the older views of such as Manselli and Delumeau as to agree that the transformation involved, on the part of the learned, the officially clerical and the elite, a hardening of attitudes toward the spiritual culture of the broad populace, a lessening of tolerance even if that tolerance had been disdainful, all manifested in increasing desire to intervene and force that culture to submit to norms imposed from the top down. In the words of Jean-Claude Schmitt, it was an attitude of just this sort among the clerical elite that prompted it at this very time to invent the idea of ("*constituer*") "popular culture," making it an object to be examined, overseen and most importantly put under constraints.[168]

Few would contest the assertion that it is Robert Moore who has of late had most to say about this eleventh- and twelfth-century modulation and exercised one of the most significant influences on how it is generally perceived. Moore's favored ways of talking about the change cast it as either the rise of a persecuting society or as the reappearance in western Europe, for the first time since antiquity, of the problem of popular heresy.[169] As Moore has pointed out, and as is now generally agreed, there were no widespread movements of heresy – nothing that might even remotely be described as "popular heresy" – in western Europe from the conversion of the German Arians, the last of whom reconciled themselves with catholicism in Visigothic Spain of the late sixth century, up until the very final years of the tenth and the beginning of the eleventh century.[170] That is not to say that there was no diversity of belief throughout the European populations. We have in fact been assuming that diversity was endemic in early and central-medieval spirituality in all we have laid out so far in the present chapter. But as Moore has so aptly put it: "Variety of religious opinion exists at many times and places, and becomes heresy when authority declares it intolerable."[171] To Moore's eyes, it was the rise of antipathy to variety, and intolerance of its presence, among clerics and especially ecclesiastical officials, which begins to be noticeable in the years of the late tenth and early eleventh centuries, that explains the simultaneous emergence of popular heresy.[172] Of course, to speak of heresy is apparently to put aside talk of the sorcery, superstition and folklore that have been the subject of our investigation of popular culture up to now. Yet I am prepared to believe that we are in fact dealing with two cultural phenomena whose historical trajectories intersect. Perhaps we are merely shifting from that part of popular religion that was in the eyes of the elite superstitious to that part which had come more closely to imitating the traditional norms of elite Christian practice and belief. Our reason for looking at the latter side of popular religion is that here the intolerant reaction of elites had so much to do with setting up mechanisms of institutional response that would come into play when authorities later on did begin to take an interest in the former sort of popular religion, of the superstitious variety.

What makes Moore's mature assessment of the emergence of radical intolerance among the elite so striking is his conviction that it was at heart political.[173] On the basis of this insight, Moore then devises a chronology for the development of heresy in this period, a process which is for him in the first instance a development in the way heresy was perceived and then pursued by the very elite whose change in attitude had in effect brought it into existence.[174] The heretical movements that first appeared in western Europe at the very end of the tenth century, and which are known to us almost exclusively through accounts of the judicial procedures and trials that they touched off, were for a bit more than a century connected to the political intrigues and conflicts of the court, whether episcopal, royal or baronial. This is to say that the forms of religious and spiritual variety that they represented were identified, focused on and prosecuted just insofar as they could be fitted to factional divisions among the elite and made to serve the purposes of working out factional disputes. Yet beginning already in the early twelfth century, the political resonance of some of the heresy trials and accusations began to change. As the century progressed, this new political tenor was to grow, eventually succeeding in fully replacing the politics of the earlier wave. Here it was not factionalism at court that was targeted but rather a more amorphous resistance located somewhere among the populace at large. Only now, we might say, had "popular heresy" come of age.

All of this, to be sure, implies that "heresy" was little more than a construction of the elite, made to suit its own political goals and aspirations. Moore recognizes that this was not the case.[175] To be exact, he claims that there were even in the early years two threads of heresy, one more properly "elite" in that it arose among literate individuals, and another more genuinely "popular" since it grew up apparently spontaneously among peasants.[176] As an instance of the former he points to the group of people accused at Orleans in 1022, purportedly led by two cathedral canons, Etienne and Lisois, and all burned – the very first heretics to be so treated in the west since the sole previous instance in 383 – by order of King Robert I of France.[177] For the other thread Moore offers us a very early case concerning a peasant, Leutard, from near Châlons-sur-Marne. He was accused by Bishop Gebuin of Châlons of preaching a New Testament literalism to the locals and was driven to drown himself in a well, presumably sometime before Gebuin's departure from the scene in 1008.[178] In all the popular examples, the heretics themselves were humble, yet the accounts of the heretical beliefs all come from the clerical superiors and resonate with Latin learning. For that reason, they appear in Moore's account once more as evidence for the ideas, opinions and actions of members of the elite, and so far as social analysis is concerned, they are still reducible to a matter of the politics of the elite.[179]

For my part, I am more inclined than Moore to make room in the analysis of eleventh-century heresy for both social motivations and ideological substance identifiable with the populace itself. Moore is surely right to contend that much of the fuss about heresy in that first century of its reappearance in the west has to do with elite concerns, often not extending very far beyond the precincts of princely and ecclesiastical courts. Yet there is reason to believe that there existed at the same time an appreciable ideological, spiritual and even religious ferment among the subordinate ranks of the people, as much of the story of which as we are able to reconstruct could be said to constitute a "popular" side to the problem of heresy from that period. Indeed, in the very years in which Aelric was cautioning his Anglo-Saxon flock and Burchard introducing measures into the penitential literature to restrain the tendencies to superstition and paganizing belief among the populace, a novel current was already springing up among those same common folk that bespoke what might be considered a new "popular spirituality."

An example gives an idea of what I have in mind. It concerns what was happening in the English countryside in Aelfric's time, the century before the Norman Conquest. According to Karen Louise Jolly's persuasive presentation, that period of about one hundred years witnessed "a fairly clear pattern of small church building on a rapid and massive scale." Moreover, these were churches "not founded primarily by the church hierarchy or as part of the minster system" but rather set up in what historians have generally come to designate as a system of proprietary churches under the auspices of lay manorial lords. They were, consequently, well distributed throughout the countryside – thus easily available to the peasantry – and, in Jolly's words, reflective of "the pious desires of the laity."[180] Jolly admits that part of the reactive efforts of reforming homilists like Aelric was directed toward just the sort of spiritual currents likely to be introduced into a more officially sanctioned ecclesiastical regimen in these rural chapels and places of worship. Yet more important for us at the moment, she also realizes that out of this environment a new popular religion – that is, a version of Christianity that had to satisfy humble lay needs as well as clerical demands (in these rural cases, rather humble themselves) – would naturally arise.[181] I would suggest that it was just this context and the lay piety emerging from it that came to constitute the common people's contribution to the problem of heresy, which, as noted earlier, even Moore himself is willing to recognize as eventually a self-determining force.[182]

A Weberian analytical scheme

To find our way in such a radically altered cultural and social landscape, we need, I believe, methodological or theoretical assistance. In the first part of this chapter we were talking about currents of what can rightly be called a spirituality of the common folk, all the way up through the central Middle Ages, that preserved strong links to the pre-Christian past but were at the same time gradually subject to a rationalizing pressure, sometimes in the form of a subtle ideological recon-figuration, sometimes in the form of outright criticism, from a learned stratum whose cultural models had at least the nominal support of the ruling elite. Now, as we begin to look at the problem of medieval popular heresy, we gaze upon a spiritual world where the pressures of rationalization arose from both within and without, and where the processes of change were not only accelerated but also radicalized. Here, of great utility are the instruments of social and cultural analysis fashioned over a century ago by Max Weber. Moore has of course anticipated this move by already making use of Weber's ideas. I would like merely to reach a bit further into the same theoretical tool bag.

Doing so requires bringing together two different, but I believe related, theo-retical couplets in Weber's analysis of the process of rationalization in society. For Weber, the concept of rationalization – which he denoted in German by the word "*Rationalisierung*," but sometimes also "*Intellektualisierung*" – brought together an analytical perspective that we historians might think of as belonging to intellectual history with one that would appear more strictly sociological. It thus pointed to a dynamics of social transformation whereby a cognitive schema that we would recognize as somehow peculiarly tied to "reason" and "reasoning" was progressively woven into society so as to provide the rules for its structure, its functioning and ultimately also its legitimacy. But while the notion of "ratio-nalization" appears almost constantly throughout Weber's work, he spoke about this crucial conception of his at different times in different ways. I believe these ways were ultimately harmonious and mutually reinforcing, despite the fact that Weber himself never explicitly said just how they ought to relate.

The single most important way Weber had of approaching his idea of ratio-nalization took form by his dividing it into two sorts or varieties, for which he chose the terms "*Wertrationalität*" and "*Zweckrationalität*." These two crucial but always somewhat elusive ideas can perhaps be best understood by looking at how he applied them to describe what he called two modes of social action. Social action could be said to be "*wertrational*" – which I shall here translate as "oriented with regard to an explicit value" – when the actor consciously chose a course of behavior precisely because that behavior was thought to instantiate a specific value the actor considered worthy entirely for its own sake. Thus action undertaken due to the *Wertrationalität* of its performer was action chosen because of its intrinsic harmony with a value serving for the actor as an absolute goal – in other words, justified by nothing else but its own worth in the actor's eyes. We could thus say that *wertrational* action was action determined by the intrinsic value of the act itself.[183] In contrast, a social action should be designated as *zweckrational* – which I momentarily translate as "oriented towards the achievement of a separate goal" – whenever the actor consciously chose the behavior precisely because she had decided that doing so would bring her closer to achieving a separate and already selected aim or end. On such occasions, therefore, there was no necessity that the performer of the act consider it as in any way reflecting or embodying either the goal itself or an abstract value that the goal represented. Instead, the act was decided upon for what we might call its utility, or in Weber's words, because it was considered an effective means toward the determinate end. Here, then, abstract and absolute value were not so much at play as was careful consideration of causal relations and possible repercussions. *Zweckrational* action, we might thus say, was action determined by consideration of cause and effect and relative benefit.[184]

This latter facet of *Zweckrationalität* is revealed most dramatically in the way Weber characterized the sort of mental process required of the rational actor in such a case. In a separate discussion of how a rational social action might be considered from either a formal perspective or a substantive one, Weber introduced the absolutely critical notion of "calculation." *Substantively*, any rational act could be judged by considering how close it actually came to instantiating an abstract value or proceeding toward a particular goal. *Formally*, however, a rational act had to be examined for the way it worked. Did it involve conceptual clarity, or sharpness in drawing analogies, or logical precision regarding inferences and relationships of cause and effect? Formally speaking, so Weber maintained, a rational act approached most closely to perfection – fulfilled his expectations of "reasonableness" – when it entailed the latter sort of mental operations. And apparently, for Weber, this logical, cause-considering rationality could best be envisioned as the precise making of a calculation.[185] I take it as practically obvious – though Weber never gave explicit confirmation – that this highest, or perfect degree of formal rationality was necessarily, and maybe peculiarly, at work in a system oriented toward achieving a purpose. *Zweckrationalität* at its purest depended upon, indeed reduced to, *calculation*, if possible by means of numbers.

Which brings me to a second way Weber approached his notion of rationalization, one that we find most clearly articulated in another of his works, where nothing is said of how it relates to the theoretical couplet we have just examined. In a lecture, later published as an essay, that Weber originally delivered in 1917, he turned to the notion of rationalization – both in society and in the abstract – but this time brought to the fore a different kind of opposition or difference. This celebrated work, entitled "Wissenschaft als Beruf" ("Science as Profession"), effectively comprises a moral study of the results of "rationalization" as it was adopted in the west. In the space of just a couple of pages, Weber commented that the first step toward full rationalization of society was realized among the ancient Greeks with what he described as the discovery of the "concept" (*Begriff*). He then added that the second step came with the discovery of "experiment" (*Experiment*) – or maybe, "experimental process" – which he dated quite traditionally as occurring in the Renaissance.[186]

These two steps – or more precisely the intellectual object or tool whose discovery they were said to involve – do not bear any express relation to the pair of terms, *Wertrationalität* and *Zweckrationalität*, nor does Weber try to use them to redraw the social analysis laid out earlier. But I think it is legitimate to interpret all four as connected. Discovery of the concept, as Weber plainly had it in mind, was the cognitive step toward the careful distillation of a simple understanding of what in reality was quite complex, comprising a multitude of particulars. It was thus effectively synonymous with the discovery of "the abstract," a purely cognitive object which could be used to analyze reality but did not denote any actual piece of reality itself. As such, discovery of the concept was a necessary, if not of course sufficient, condition for setting an absolute value against which all particular actions could be judged for their compatibility or incompatibility with it. Exercising *Wertrationalität* was itself therefore a function of conceptual thinking. Discovery of experiment is harder to tie with the other member of the preceding pair, *Zweckrationalität*. Still, I do not believe we do much violence to Weber if we attempt the effort. As a rationalist of his time, Weber naturally accepted experiment as the procedural sine qua non of science. The truth of a generalization was determined by testing it experimentally. But if we think more generally about determining truth, about the whole process of verification in the sciences, careful logic, in particular meticulous respect for laws of inference, must be conceded an equally important role. In any event, with "experiment" we are back to cognitive process – to speculating about causation and to weighing alternatives – just as we were when discussing *Zweckrationalität*. I would say that to this degree "experiment" can stand in as a surrogate for Weber's vision of the latter at its purest, for "calculation."

With these two theoretical couplets in hand, I at last hazard to advance an analytic scheme, of simultaneously sociological and historiographical application. Though what I present is admittedly not an authentic product of Weber himself, it might all the same be put forth as "Weberizing" and accepted as faithful to the spirit of his thought. Perhaps it is easiest to conceive of the scheme as designating four modes of rationalization, which might coincidentally be seen to correspond to four stages in the application of "rationality," of a distinctly Weberian sort, to culture and the ordering of society. The first sort of ordering bears primarily on mental constructs or language – on culture, in other words – and consists in the application of concepts to simplify an experiential complexity. Of course, applying concepts requires thinking rigorously about what each concept means and then examining just as carefully objects in reality – either natural or social – to decide how they sort out within the conceptual network. Ordering of the second sort entails moving from cognitive sorting and cultural simplification toward an actual attempt to insure that social actions respect the conceptual cognitive norm. This second step involves therefore aggressive intervention into social relations and sometimes even conflict. It should be clear that while neither of these first two steps is limited to what Weber reserved for *Wertrationalisierung*, nor is the latter itself reducible to just these two, there exists a close connection between tailoring actions to absolute values and being able to manipulate a conceptual scheme.

At the third stage, what I have in mind is a turn to the more complicated cognitive procedures implicated in verification either by applying a strict logic of inferences or speculating about alternatives. In this sense, the new stage presumes the first – the application of conceptual order – but it goes further by manipulating concepts according to complex procedures of mind, even calculation. Again, at this level we are talking about the application of cognitive process primarily to mental constructs and language. But as soon as one progresses very far along this path, it is almost inevitable that one will, as before with conceptual ordering, pass over into active intervention into either social institutions or norms of social activity. At a fourth stage, in short, the procedures Weber would have associated with calculation are themselves turned into principles for construction or refashioning society. Rules of inference, principles of causality, the search for numerical measurements of conceptual qualities and the careful comparison of alternatives by manipulating the numbers according to precise logarithms take on authority in both guiding social behavior and shaping society itself. Rationalization in these two stages thus tilts more decisively toward the side of Weber's dichotomy reserved for *Zweckrationalisierung*.

Rationalization among the populace and the rise of heresy

When we apply these four modes of rationalization to the material we have been examining in this chapter, a pattern of development takes shape. Of course, rationalization of the first sort, involving the imposition of a conceptual framework to simplify as well as perhaps to normalize, was a continually recurring thread in our investigation of the spirituality of the common folk in the early and central Middle Ages. It marked in those instances most typically a product of elite, usually clerically led efforts to intrude on native and more traditional patterns of thought, behavior and ceremonial. The means employed were most often interpretative, as in characterizing age-old taxonomies of spiritual powers as, from a Christian point of view, demonic, or winnowing and suppressive, simply attempting to lift out and erase elements in an older cognitive schema that appeared irreconcilable to a literate and orthodox Christian conceptual grid. In either case, the effects would have remained primarily limiting and negative. For the most part, this early rationalization remained confined to the ideological or cultural sphere. It had to do with a treasury of attitudes and practices yielding a particular understanding of reality, especially those aspects of it touching on spirit and value.

Perhaps that pattern was beginning to change in the early years of what we have identified earlier as the emergence of what would eventually become "popular heresy." The rationalization of popular spiritual attitudes up through the central Middle Ages worked upon a content most of which was rooted in traditional and vernacular culture, and thus found expression principally in warnings and penitential prescriptions of the learned clergy. The rise of religious currents associated with accusations of heresy represented instead the welling up of attitudes and a rhetoric to express them redolent more of learned religion and the Scriptures.[187] Here we start to see signs of a process of transformation and normalization impinging more directly on society's structure. Naturally, the closer we adhere to Moore's assessment of these novel spiritual currents, the less justified we are in retailing them as aspects of a rationalization dependent on social strata below the very elite. But I have already shown how elements of Moore's second thread of early "heresy," manifested for example in Leutard, cannot help but point to a degree of cultural agency at the popular level. At the very least, in these early stirrings we begin to see the contours of a conceptual realignment that betokens at the level of the common people a rationalization of the first of my four sorts. In the response of clerics such as the bishop of Châlons, moreover, we can detect a fear that the populace at large might be taking the business of conceptual reordering and rationalizing beyond merely an intellectual stage toward active engagement in realigning society.

According to the terms of Moore's account in *Formation of a Persecuting Society*, the heretical currents that came to the surface in the early eleventh century – and he meant to include both threads, the more literate and elite as well as the unlearned and subordinate – were absorbed into the raging torrents of what is usually called the Gregorian reform movement of the century's second half.[188] Yet as we move into the twelfth century, even the turbulence of the Gregorian reform cannot hide the fact that there are beginning to be observable differences between currents working for a purified spirituality and institutional realignment that ultimately would reinforce the authority of dominant sectors of society and those that would diffuse control and reduce the weight of hierarchy. Consideration of the social context, therefore, permits the historian again to identify "heretical" pressures for renewal and transformation, separate from superficially similar campaigns which, from the perspective of church history, deserve the designation of "orthodox" reform. These times thus present us in short with the first waves of what can only be called a tide of "popular heresy" in the high Middle Ages.

If before we had to remain somewhat tentative about attributing real agency to the broad populace in the process of rationalizing spiritual culture, from this point on we can proceed with much less reticence. Two striking and remarkably far-reaching examples reveal the receptivity among subordinate groups in these years for a reworking of spirituality on their own terms. Both Peter of Bruys, killed sometime after 1131, and Henry of Le Mans (alternatively identified as from Lausanne), still alive and proselytizing in 1145, spoke a language of spiritual regeneration derived from the Scriptures. Here was thus the application of concepts derived from the cultural heritage of the literate elite. But the audience was anything but high-standing, powerful and learned.

Looking at the phenomenon of Henry alone, we can say that the spiritual – and to elite eyes "heretical" – movements he inspired were without question rational-izing in the first of the four ways I proposed earlier. He drew from his under-standing of church tradition concepts of such qualities as "poor," "chaste," quite likely "apostolic," "sacramental" and "sacrilegious," and wielded them to draw a map of spiritual values and personal behaviors that would define, for him and his vernacular hearers, the genuine culture of Christianity.[189] In his and his followers' consequent challenges to the episcopal, and by implication also comital, lines of authority and legitimacy in Le Mans, it would appear equally clear that the process of rationalization among the "people" at Le Mans in the early twelfth century had passed over into the second of my modes. At stake was a conceptual ordering and reclassification being used to reconfigure society's institutions and change the character of social action and interaction. In fact, there are hints of progress toward the more complicated rationalizing of either the third or fourth sorts. When Henry intervened among the unchaste women, presumably pros-titutes, of what was fast becoming "his flock" to retrieve them from their past, finance a transition to economic independence and then reinsert them through arranged marriage back into a reformed society at a completely new and now honorable locus or station, would he not seem to be making calculations about means and ends and applying an impressively complex social calculus?[190]

The turn to rationalization more in line with Weber's *Zweckrationalität* becomes only more pronounced as the century proceeds. By the turn of the twelfth to thir-teenth centuries, two major networks of popular heresy, known most commonly by the names of Cathars and Waldensians, had established themselves broadly in both French- and Italian-speaking lands and were in the process of taking on genuine institutional attributes as rival churches to the officially sanctioned congregations and clergy associated with the orthodox hierarchy. Of these two, the earlier and up through the first half of the thirteenth century surely more numerous, the Cathars, had made remarkable strides beyond the already impres-sive cultural and social rationalization seen in the movements surrounding Henry and Peter. There can be no doubt that by the third quarter of the twelfth century the Cathars had established a far-flung network of correspondence throughout what now comprises France and Italy – particularly Languedoc, the Milanese terri-tory and Tuscany – and begun to construct a normative institutional hierarchy possessing bishops and a rough division into dioceses. In the late 1160s or early 1170s, these communities were in fact visited by a delegation headed by the Greek Nicetas, bishop of the Bogomil church in Constantinople. Under Nicetas's careful direction, the western heretics' doctrines were reformed and their episcopal orga-nization not only reconsecrated but also meticulously recalibrated to render more explicit the lines of authority and the demarcation of separate spheres of jurisdic-tion.[191] The cognitive and social ramifications of such an enterprise most surely land us in the fourth of my rationalizing modes, whereby complex chains of symbols are manipulated in order to impose an order in society carefully tailored to the specifications of particular cultural and institutional goals.

Yet still more striking instances of sophisticated measures toward rationalizing both culture and social structure can be found if we look only a bit more closely at these Cathar communities of the 1100s and 1200s, not to speak of the Waldensians following only slightly later and an entirely new group of heretics, the English Lollards, of the late fourteenth and early fifteenth centuries. At the purely cultural level, thus bringing us back to rationalization of my first or third variety, we see the introduction of literacy as first of all an ideal and secondly practically an everyday necessity of spiritual life. Already evident among the popular constituencies energized by Henry of Le Mans and Peter of Bruys were the signs of what Moore, drawing from the lexicon of sociology and anthropology, has identified as "passive literacy."[192] In those instances, the common folk had become accustomed to thinking of spiritual and religious norms as necessarily derived from a specific written text, in this case of course the same Scriptures already privileged among the learned elite. Literacy of this passive sort furnished likewise the preconditions for the even more pervasive and culturally unified communities of Cathars. In this instance, moreover, there were other texts besides those championed by the orthodox to which proselytizers could refer. Before the 1170s, at least three items of holy literature borrowed directly from the Bogomils of Bulgaria and Constantinople were circulating in Latin among what we might think of as the incipient priesthood of the Cathar church.[193] The Cathars were consequently permitted to distinguish themselves even more radically from the established authorities and their ideological norms while at the same time staking a claim for yet more firmly rooted legitimacy.

In what has now become a standard model for the analysis of social ordering, including in the first instance that of religious groups, Brian Stock described the forms of social order arising from such conceptual dependency on and legitimating appeal to determined written texts as "textual communities."[194] As he understood, the orientation to a written text as normative source and regulatory ideal might have several results. At the very least, it would, in Stock's words, "[affect] the way people conceptualize...relations" between individual and family on the one hand and the wider community on the other. We might consider this as tantamount to at least a first-order rationalization of the culture, whereby a conceptual grid is applied to reshape understanding. But of course, once textuality has been introduced and made a subject of frequent discussion, it was an easy thing to pass over into more complicated forms of rationalizing reconstruction. Again in Stock's words, these new and increasingly heretical communities "resorted to textual precedents for justifying deviations from what were considered to be merely customary or unwritten ecclesiastical norms."[195] Whether or not Stock had it precisely in mind, I think he is here describing the sort of complex and inferential, cause-and-effect oriented reasoning entailed in my third rationalizing stage. In both cases, of course, the step from rearranging concepts and configurations in the cultural world to influencing interactions in society and the institutions by means of which the interactions were guided and often even performed was almost irresistible. We should not be surprised, therefore, when Cathar communities engaged, as we have already seen in the matter of ecclesiastical organization, in transferring the rationalizing schemes from the merely conceptual or ideological world to that of concrete social structures and interactions.

Most astonishing of all is the fact that the Cathars, as well as most later popular heretical groups, took steps not only to make of literacy and written texts the ideals by which their values would be shaped and according to which their actions and social institutions would be oriented but also to turn literacy into a functioning tool for the heretical community at large. Peter Biller has noted how, especially after 1200, the reality of the Cathar community had begun to challenge the clerical topos of the heretic as illiterate, making room for the grudging recognition of a type of reading heretic.[196] And Lorenzo Paolini has drawn attention to concordances and cross-referencing indices produced and carried about by Italian Cathar propagandists in the early thirteenth century for use primarily as debating aids in their confrontations with establishment clerical opponents.[197] Here we begin to see calculation of practically a Weberian sort. If Paolini is right, it was the heretics who took the most radically innovative steps toward turning reasoning into a form of social interaction or exchange as well as an instrument of transformation.

Rationalization from above

Effectively outmaneuvered by so sophisticated an adversary working among the broader populace and often drawn from it, the ecclesiastical establishment had to play catch-up, in what must have seemed to both prelates and princes a moment of dire crisis, to ensure its dominance in what was plainly becoming an altered social landscape. Its first reaction, generated almost without thinking, was to try and roll back the tides of cultural change that had arisen about it. Most critical here, so it seemed, was to halt the spread of literacy among the laity in the lower social strata and to restrict the capacity of lay folk to exercise, at least for spiritual purposes, whatever literacy they had already attained. Since of written instruments those using the vernacular languages were capable of the quickest assimilation and the most widespread dissemination, it is not surprising to see General Chapter meetings of the Dominican Order already by the 1320s issuing decrees limiting doctrinal communication between the friars and their followers in anything but Latin.[198] And where the clerical and secular elite could not the stanch the flow of literacy out into the towns and countryside and prevent discussion of the faith unsupervised by church-appointed guardians of orthodoxy, it could see to it that there were no texts available to read. From late twelfth century on the high Middle Ages witnessed a surge of efforts to destroy written material propagating heretical beliefs. Anne Hudson is probably right in speculating that, to the clerical elite, "destroying and burning books [was] in some ways even preferable to obtaining the heretic, since the latter could disavow and hide his true beliefs, writing could be obliterated."[199]

Of course, if the populace could not be trusted with the word, and with working out the meaning of the faith on its own, then the clerical hierarchy would have to make a concerted effort to supply what the community could not provide for itself. If any single event epitomized the determination of ecclesiastical authorities to fulfill that obligation it was the Fourth Lateran Council, convened in Rome on the model of the great ecumenical councils of old by Pope Innocent III in 1215. At the head of the decrees issued by the council before it adjourned stood an explicit and precise statement of the faith, putting into words the minimum expected ideologically of a catholic and taking special care to mark critical differences with the heretics.[200] Perhaps even more significant was canon 21 of the conciliar decrees, the famous "Omnis utriusque sexus," which called upon every single one of the faithful to come before her or his parish priest at least once a year to say confession and receive absolution, and presumably in conjunction with that action to take communion at least once a year as well, preferably at Easter.[201] Preaching, too, would constitute an arm of the same campaign for deep acculturation of the European common folk. Efforts to regularize preaching throughout the structure of the established church and to ensure a doctrinally competent and rhetorically adept clergy characterized the policy of forward-looking bishops throughout the century. Notable in this regard was the emergence, first officially promoted by the very Innocent III who had presided over Lateran Council IV, of new orders of regular clerics – semi-monks more properly denominated "mendicant friars" – whose most salient activity soon became wandering through town and country as sermonizers of patently compelling popular appeal. The two most numerous of these orders, the Dominicans and the Franciscans, had assumed by century's end a dominant position in a grand program of homiletic outreach [202]

Coercive measures

Still, learning to manipulate the levers of moral and religious instruction with a degree of mastery unparalleled in earlier European history would not suffice, in the eyes of the ecclesiastical establishment, to ensure its victory over popular cultural resistance and the threat of heretical deviation. Already the twelfth century yields examples of measures much more coercive in nature. A most spectacular instance was the foundation, at the close of that century and the start of the next, of the medieval inquisition.[203] Legists were aware as early as the late eleventh century that Roman law had allowed the court itself to investigate or inquire among the populace whether a crime had been committed and then to enter charges without waiting for the traditional private initiative. They also knew that Roman judges had been permitted to solicit evidence and testimony and make a judgment according to their estimation of the circumstances and their understanding of the law.[204] In the papal bull *Ad abolendam* of 1184, Pope Lucius III directed the bishops of western Europe to adopt such inquisitorial procedure within their dioceses in order to seek out instances of heresy and religious deviance that might not otherwise come to their attention. They were then to prosecute the exposed offenders in their own courts.[205] Innocent III made sure that the same provisions were taken up in the decrees of the Fourth Lateran Council, where they appear in nearly identical language in canon 3.[206] In 1231 Pope Gregory IX took the fateful step, in an official letter to the bishops of Germany, of using Dominicans as inquisitorial agents directly under his control to circumvent episcopal obstacles and inefficiencies and provide for inquiries at papal initiative alone.[207] On the basis of these interventions arose as much of an institutional reality as was ever to attach to the so-called papal inquisition.

If procedurally and institutionally the papal inquisition of the Middle Ages marked only a beginning, it represented all the same a significant intensification of the forces of rationalization working not only on religious ideology but also on behavior and performance. Medieval inquisitors brought the art of using literacy and written documentation as instruments of both acculturation and social regulation to new heights. On this score, it is James Given who has made the crucial observation. While most medieval rulers used written documents primarily for simple tasks, such as providing evidence of title, some medieval inquisitors turned to their meticulously maintained records to provide indications of deviance that would otherwise have been almost impossible to trace. The inquisitor Bernard Gui's *Liber sententiarum* from the early fourteenth century, for instance, bears annotations that show he and his fellows systematically searched through them to identify repeat offenders, build up virtual dossiers on their testimony and behavior and in the end produce a short list of subjects for their measures of ideological control.[208] Here we find the application of complex cognitive procedures to the business of ordering society that take us farther than ever before toward Weberian calculation and orientation of means to ends. Is this not rationalization with a vengeance, even if still on a relatively modest scale?[209]

Beyond procedures, moreover, there was on this coercive side of the balance sheet also a plainly ideological component that was to prove of great significance in the culture wars to which we shall turn later on, during the centuries of the great witch-hunt. Drawing again on Weber, Moore has noted how expansion of governmental control has often throughout history been associated with the promotion of a universal religion, its universality expressed most signally in an abstract system of ethics.[210] For Moore, this ethical component explains the premium put by the early state – and for us, the early papal church – on controlling behavior and persecuting purported deviance. Yet it also provided the language in which the new intrusiveness of officials from an authoritarian center was justified and made to seem almost an urgent need.[211] In an effort to convince the people, down to the lowest social strata, that the authorities represented the community, the standard-bearers of the process of rationalization chose almost predictably to evoke the specter of an enemy at society's core. It had, of course, to be an enemy absolutely antithetical to the newly invigorated ethical norm.[212] In the case of late medieval Europe, where orthodoxy and heresy were principal terms of the debate, it was almost inevitable that the enemy would be stigmatized as not merely religiously different but actually counter-religious. The heat of argument encouraged the most volatile of orthodoxy's champions, but eventually the whole apparatus of inquisition, to see their antagonists as worshippers of evil itself.

For the words with which to express this universalizing calumny of their heretical opponents, some among the established clergy turned back already in the twelfth century to an ancient stereotype of a depraved, orgiastic and sometimes cannibalistic religious sect. We know that early Christians had been subject to accusations from their opponents in the political mainstream of pre-Christian Rome that they practiced together rituals of odious sexuality and unnatural cruelty. Minucius Felix, an educated Roman Christian of perhaps the second or early third century, reports on the rumors circulating around his fellow religionists: that they respected no limits of gender or consanguinity in their sexual activity, worshipped the head of an ass, and initiated converts at a ceremony where an infant was covered in dough, then ritually murdered and devoured both blood and flesh. He also repeats the curious anecdote that at the periodic feasts where they gathered together, a moment came when the lights were extinguished and the whole company gave itself over to unabashed promiscuity in the darkness, each person cohabiting with whoever was nearest at hand.[213] Once Christianity had been adopted by the Roman emperors, clergy with access to the levers of authority directed the same charge against their doctrinal adversaries in what, from Constantine on, became an increasingly high-stakes contest over the designations "catholic" and "heretical." Not the only patristic writer to employ the tactic was Augustine himself.[214]

All these stories fell into oblivion in the early and central Middle Ages. Popular heresy's reappearance, along with the authorities' resort to a universal ethics as rationale for their efforts to seize control, resurrected their utility. In an account of heretics in 1022 at Orleans, the accusations of orgiastic meetings and ritual murder of infants resurface for the first time in hundreds of years. Apparently, the author knew his Augustine. Less than a century later, this initial reemergence of the old calumnies was reenacted in the imagination of Abbot Guibert of Nogent. Asked by the Bishop of Soissons to help with the interrogation of two men accused of preaching heresy in 1114, Guibert, well-read in patristics, instinctively turned to Augustine, in his later recounting of the episode trotting out all the old claims of orgies in the night, murder of infants and the making of bread from their flesh.[215]

For over another century, almost nothing more was made of these accounts. Perhaps it should not surprise us that just as the papal inquisition was getting under way some of those to whom the business of inquiring had been delegated began to draw upon them once again. The same Pope Gregory IX, who in 1231 had opened the door for Dominicans under his protection to bypass the bishops in investigating heresy in their own dioceses, in 1233 issued a decretal letter, "*Vox in Rama*," directed to the archbishop of Mainz, and also the bishop of Hildesheim and a priest whom the archbishop had previously designated as inquisitor, Conrad of Marburg. The inquisitor-priest, most avid of the three in hunting after deviance and eventually murdered by a group of outraged German nobles in July of 1233, had won the ear of the pope. "*Vox in Rama*" represented an effort to strengthen the conviction of church authorities in Germany that heresy was indeed the most evil of conspiracies, ready to strike a mortal blow against Christ's flock. The characterization of the heretics it contained was apparently delivered to the pope directly from Conrad's reports.[216]

Included are the stereotypical accounts of secret rituals and the extinguishing of the light followed by sexual debauchery. Yet now something even more awesome and frightening is introduced. According to Gregory's letter, once the orgiastic escapades were over and light restored, "from a dark corner of the assembly...a certain man emerges, from the loins upward gleaming more brightly than the sun, so they say, whose lower part is shaggy like a cat and whose light illuminates the whole place."[217] The presiding master of ceremonies then offers this shining man a token of clothing from any novices present, the shining figure in turn then commending the novice or novices to the master's custody. There can be little doubt but that the shining figure is Lucifer himself, to whom the decretal letter shortly afterward refers. He is the Devil, the biblical "Satan" as he has come to be understood by twelfth-century homilists and theologians, and personification of Evil.[218] The heretics, moreover, have become his worshippers. Heresy is thus a cult in which not only all pretense of moral behavior is given up but also Satan is substituted for God at the center of religion. The goal of heresy's extermination had at last found its proper ideological voice. Such an ideology, corroborated by papal backing, was capable of unleashing the most ruthless prosecution and driving the rationalization of both culture and society to unimagined lengths.

Conclusion

Again here at the end of the chapter it is worth stepping back to take stock of where we are. After a discussion of historiographical issues relating to the notion of popular religion and some ambiguities attaching to the investigation of it, the chapter began with an extensive examination of those aspects of the religion of the people in western Europe in the central Middle Ages that might have struck the lettered elite in that period as being superstitious. The purpose of this survey was to lay bare some of the processes of acculturation in those central medieval centuries whereby the religion of the populace was partially accommodated to the Christianity of a clerical elite but even importantly to reveal the substance of many such purportedly superstitious beliefs that would reemerge as an issue from the fifteenth century on with the rise of the witch trials, attention to which will be given in Chapter 5. The material related to these beliefs was divided into four groupings: witchcraft or sorcery, measures for healing, superstition in a narrow sense and folklore.

The focus then shifted to the twelfth century up to in some instances as late as the early fourteenth, when the dynamics of the interaction between elite and popular culture, especially with regard to religious matters, started to take on a different complexion. Simply put, the pressures for acculturation ramped up from the twelfth century on so that it becomes possible to speak of the rationalization of popular religion. Here is introduced the notion of popular heresy, which for the rest of the chapter thus replaces popular religion or superstition as the subject of investigation. A short excursus on ways of drawing from Max Weber's ideas about rationalization to produce an analytic schema of use for our purposes was then followed by a survey of the rationalization undergone by popular religion in western Europe in these high medieval centuries.

First a look was given to efforts on the part of the populace itself to rationalize its own religious perspectives. In this endeavor the heretic groups called Cathars and Waldensians played a key role. But then attention turned to a partially reactive move on the part of ecclesiastical elites to counter the religious actions of the people with a rationalization program of their own. The chapter ends with discussion of institutional and ideological measures taken to ensure that the rationalization of popular religion would follow in the direction mandated by this same clerical elite. Once more it is a theme that will bear fruit when picked up again in Chapter 5. But that story can be told only after we return to magic and science in Chapters 3 and 4 in order to chronicle a dramatic deviation among the literate classes toward the demonization of all things magical.

3

Science, Magic and the Demonic, 1200–1400: The Catalyst

When in Chapter 1 we last looked at magic as viewed by the Latinate elite of Europe in the high Middle Ages, we took note of the fact that with the twelfth-century reintroduction of classical traditions of natural philosophy or science, sometimes massively extended by Arab and Jewish thinkers of the central medieval Mediterranean and Middle East, learned circles in the west were compelled, for practically the first time since late Antiquity, once more to confront magical elements within the confines of their own cultural domain. Some welcomed the development as long overdue, while others feared contagion from currents of knowledge and practice calling to mind the dangers of superstitious lore hitherto regarded as restricted to the culture of the populace. Yet while the critics of the new magical arts attacked them for both their falsehood and their evil repute – which is to say, in our terms, from both a Frazerian and a Malinowskian perspective – for the most part no one spoke of legal penalties for attending to such novelties. And the debate focused more on the Frazerian than the Malinowskian side of the divide, seeking to determine whether the new fields of learning were a proper source of truth or wellsprings of error. Meanwhile many learned scholars undertook the defense of magic and proceeded both to study and to practice the new arts without apparent fear of opprobrium. Such were the circumstances in the days of Robert Grosseteste and Michael Scot, put forth earlier as examples for contrasting attitudes in learned circles of the early thirteenth century.

It was just at this moment, however, that there appeared signs of a more disquieting future. Entailed were the early stages of a phenomenon that has attracted increasing attention among historians of late and begun to be almost habitually referred to as the "demonization of magic." The latter notion goes back at least as far as Norman Cohn's work in the early 1970s.[1] But recent scholarship has added enormously to our knowledge of the particulars involved.[2] By my reckoning, this peculiar but important episode in the history of European thought should be counted as simply one among the many effects of the adoption of a "scientific" model for knowledge in the context of the high-medieval university. In this chapter we will deal with the gathering storm clouds. We begin with a substantial figure at the University of Paris who was familiar with at least some of the new magical literature, indeed was himself attracted to parts of it. This is William of Auvergne. With him we see one of the earliest examples of someone at least modestly informed who began to fear elements of the new magic and started to assemble an intellectual apparatus intended to neutralize them. Key to the defense was a more specific association of magic with spirits, demons in particular.

Then we turn to survey four prominent examples of the new literature from the thirteenth to the beginnings of the fourteenth century. These are among the earliest works of this genre we have in Latin from the high Middle Ages. They represent the fleshing out for learned consumption of traditions approached by scholars in the twelfth century in more schematic form. First comes the *Ars notoria*, a work presuming to use a strict regimen of ceremony along with verbalizations and inscribed figures marvelously to advance the learning of the practitioner. Next are two works of varied purpose, the *Liber iuratus Honorii* and *Picatrix*. With them we venture onto magical territory of a more incantatory nature, one moreover where spirits, sometimes nefarious, are conjured up and expected to contribute to the magical act. Finally attention passes to a work more apologetic than any of the others. This, the *Speculum astronomiae*, will serve as an introduction to the kind of astral magic dependent as well on the manipulation of signs. All four constitute a considerable advance in knowledge of magical practice, just the sort of thing feared by William of Auvergne.

Michael Scot

We can pick up the trail of this whole story by returning for a moment to the figure of Michael Scot. Michael seems to have been a leading participant in what appears to have been a ratcheting up of the prominence of what we are accustomed to call the magical arts. A considerable part of the labor for this endeavor was concentrated at the court of that influential patron of the new "scientific" disciplines, the emperor Frederick II.[3] Michael's own *Liber introductorius* has been characterized as the first comprehensive attempt to transpose to a Latinate intellectual idiom the astrological heritage of the many translations from the Arabic produced over the preceding century.[4] His writings on alchemy held a central place among a small corpus of new works, the contents of which we are just getting to know, which served a similar purpose with regard to the art of transmuting metals or producing the elixir.[5] For the first time in the medieval Latin world, it would seem, these branches of learning and practice moved from being primarily objects of reference to actual bodies of knowledge with a tangible literary foundation.

As we have already seen, astrology and alchemy were likely the tamest of the new disciplines to whose diffusion Michael contributed. Mention was made in Chapter 1 of necromancy and an *ars notoria* among the arts he regarded with apparent approval.[6] Yet even they did not exhaust the list. Returning to the passage about the natural sciences from Al-Farabi utilized by Dominicus Gundissalinus and Daniel of Morley in the twelfth century, Michael inserted his own variation on the text into his *Liber introductorius*. Michael's version, like Gundissalinus's, remains strictly faithful to Farabi's original listing, including among fields of knowledge traditionally associated with "magic" the science of judgments – that is, astrology, proper – necromancy (*nigromantica*), the science of images, alchemy and the science of mirrors.[7] Most important for us at the moment are the two, necromancy and the science of images, that would arouse the greatest consternation in the rest of the thirteenth and the fourteenth centuries.[8]

What Michael intended his reader to understand as subsumed under these two disciplines is not entirely evident, but we can reduce the likely candidates to just a few. On the one hand, as we have noted, Michael was familiar with something called the "ars notoria," about which more will be said later. It was a quite specific art, just developing some notoriety in the early thirteenth century, and promising an astonishing and immediate knowledge of all or any of the branches of learning simply by the prescribed manipulation of certain diagrams or figures in conjunction with actions drawing upon astrology and angelology.[9] The diagrams or figures alone make it reasonable to assume that Michael's "science of images" at least overlapped with this particular art. But it is also possible that Michael had in mind a broader array of disciplines and practices connected later in the century with a "science of images," about which we shall also shortly have more to say.

As for necromancy (or nigromancy), we know as well from the *Liber introductorius* that Michael drew a division between sciences to be designated by the Latin word "*mathesis*" and those associated with the only slightly different vocable "*matesis*." The former constituted the standard and unimpeachable seven liberal arts of late Roman tradition. The latter, however, comprised collectively a science of divination ("*scientia divinandi*"), which Michael recognized as being forbidden by catholic Christian teaching but which he nonetheless considered as in itself authentic and productive of true knowledge.[10] Divination might then well be part of what he meant whenever he referred to "*nigromantia*." But there was also a corpus of literature linked to Solomon and prescriptive of other arts and practices, some loosely divinatory but some also overtly devoted to the conjuring of spirits, perhaps even demons, with which Michael was familiar and to which he occasionally directed his reader.[11] More will also be said about this Solomonic and self-described "magical" literature later. One thing for sure, in the form with which Michael was familiar it did, by his own testimony, sometimes involve ceremonies in which actual demons were invoked.[12] Here are practices that plainly spill over into "nigromancy" in the sense of genuinely "black magic." For all their apparent contravention of ecclesiastical norms for intellectual and moral acceptability, these forms of learning and practice were evidently enjoying increased entrée into learned circles and proliferating among Latin written sources. Here was magic of an almost anti-Christian nature that someone like Grosseteste, for all his fulminations against disciplines like astrology, would barely have dreamed of.

William of Auvergne

If we look to another contemporary of Michael's, but one who managed to outlive him by about a decade and a half, we can see in fact how dramatically the body of learned magical lore, including numerous items of potentially suspect moral and religious allegiance, had grown by the middle of the thirteenth century. William of Auvergne, bishop of Paris from 1228 to 1249 and fixture of the ecclesiastical establishment of his day as well as leading light of the increasingly preeminent school of theology at the University of Paris, brought most of his philosophical and theological writings together in a massive and encyclopedic compilation he called *Magisterium divinale ac sapientiale*. From the title alone one can gather its purpose: to serve as a sort of roadmap into wisdom and higher knowledge.[13] Of its seven or eight parts, we shall be interested only in *De legibus*, intended to be paired with a treatise *De fide* and composed probably between 1228 and 1231, and the much longer and more ambitious *De universo*, drawn perhaps from early writings of the 1220s but put into final form in the 1230s, with finishing touches as late as 1240.[14] As is abundantly clear from countless references and sometimes long-winded analyses, William was fully abreast of the new literature involving magical disciplines, often as excited about it as was Michael Scot.

Among the areas associated with Michael's expertise, he claimed to know astrology well – that is, the predictive science he linked to *"astronomici judices"* or *"doctores judiciorum,"* practitioners of the judicial art of the stars and planets.[15] It was an art about which he had grave scholarly as well as moral reservations. Insofar as it implicated any determinism with regard to human acts of will or the particulars of everyday life, he thought it worthy of denunciation, a field of learning to be combated with fire and sword.[16] Alchemy was a science with which he was less familiar. Yet he referred to it from time to time and apparently considered it, unlike astrology, a legitimate part of natural philosophy, capable of wondrous practical applications.[17] Along similar lines, he recognized that parts of medicine, too, contained their own marvels, productive of the kind of surprising effects typically associated with magical learning and its works.[18] Finally, William was conversant with a host of writings bringing to mind elements of the novel magical literature of the twelfth century and that he designated as *"libri experimentorum"* and *"libri naturalium narrationum,"* "books of experiments" and what we might call "books on natural history," taking the latter to refer to curiosities and phenomena of a marvelous kind.[19] He was at home, in short, in the precincts of magical learning expanding among the Latinate elite in the first decades of the thirteenth century.

William on knowledge of higher things

But as we follow William's fascination with learning carrying reverberations of the "magical," we quickly realize that his experience with it was more ambivalent than that of Michael Scot. Though part of the reason was William's own intellectual and ethical commitments as a professional theologian, it is also likely that a wider spectrum of fields associated with magic, as well as increased specificity in the texts available about such matters in Latin, played a role in rendering a straightforward response more problematic. William's scholarly inclinations led him in a direction likely to bring him into contact with some of the most recently revived elements of the learned magical tradition. As he confessed in a treatise whose place in the *Magisterium* remains unclear – the *De anima*, finished probably a few years after *De universo* – he was convinced that the end of the human soul lay in realization within its intellect of the entire panoply of the cognitive habits of science and wisdom.[20] From this conviction arose the whole project of the *Magisterium*, for he visualized human perfection as entailing intimate familiarity with, as he called them, "sublime and hidden things" ("*res sublimes et res occultae*"), matters and subjects he felt equally free to describe as "divine" ("*res divinales*").[21] His collection of treatises was intended to open for its readers the way onto such speculative heights.

Along the journey toward these wise and even godlike truths, William had been prepared throughout his life to employ a variety of means. Many of them we, as well as William's contemporaries, would have connected to magic. He refers, for instance, to the practice of peering into clear or shining bodies ("*corpora* or *instrumenta lucida*"), almost surely including objects such as crystal balls, in order to learn about the higher realities to which the mind is naturally ordained.[22] Apparently related was a procedure he had read about in a work called the *Ars tribilia* or *Ars syntribilia*, which he attributes to a certain Artesius, explicitly graced with the moniker "magician" ("*magus*"). In this case the revelation of higher and hidden truths is obtained by gazing at the reflections on water that has been ceremoniously transfixed by a polished sword.[23] Though in *De legibus* William had revealed his distaste for the impiety of Artesius's writings, in *De universo* he seems all the same to accept as plausible that the water-sword ceremony would produce the intended results.[24]

All of this is consistent with a vision of the human soul as positioned by nature on the border, or as he more often put it, the "horizon" of two worlds, one that of the higher, more spiritual realities above, the other of the less elevating, generally material substances of the sub-lunar world. It was a vision William fully accepted and which he continually set out for the edification of his readers.[25] For William, it served to explain how it was that the human mind could, under the proper conditions, see into those higher realms and gain knowledge of the sublime and divine realities toward which it was ultimately inclined. By William's understanding, the image implied that God, himself, was directly available to the human intellect, once all accidental impediments had been removed, so that in its purest, most natural state, the mind could simply gaze on the higher realities and read the higher truths as God chose directly to reveal them to it.[26] Here lay the foundation for an even more important strategy that William was tempted to employ to obtain the much-desired higher science and wisdom, one that engaged him even more deeply in the new magical currents swirling about him in his day.

The strategy is introduced to the reader by way of a reminiscence drawn from William's own past:

> Thus it is that in the days of my youth it seemed to me that the acquisition of prophetic splendor and great illumination [from above] was easy, precisely because our souls in effect touch both worlds [– that is, the higher and the lower]...I believed that the purgation of our souls from the filth of vice was easy, as was the release of our souls from the snares and chains by which they are bowed down, as if with twisted neck...I thought that little by little through abstinence and tearing my soul away from the cares and delights holding it captive and submerged in [this] lower world, which is the world of sensibles, all those [accretions] that obscure the soul and darken it would be wiped away from it...[so that] the chains and snares would be broken and consumed. Thus my soul would escape, free and capable on its own of bursting forth into that higher region, which is [the world] of light.[27]

Crucially, in the very middle of his account, just after mention of the soul's "twisted neck," he added a brief observation, which immediately clarifies for us all the rest: "[This is all, of course,] just as Mercury has told us in his book, *On the God of Gods (De deo deorum)*."[28]

Nicolas Weill-Parot has reminded us that William's "Mercury" – Latin for the god known in Greek as Hermes – is none other than Hermes Trismegistus, pseudo-author, mystic and magician famous from Late Antiquity through the Renaissance as the source for an abundant body of literature, mostly on astral magic.[29] At times, William himself supplies the longer form by which this figure is known: in his medieval Latin, *Mercurius Trismegistus*.[30] From other indications, as Weill-Parot has pointed out, it is evident that in this particular case William is not referring to the dominant Hermetic tradition, traceable back to the ninth-century Sābians active in Harrān in Mesopotamia.[31] William's citations cast the text he is talking about as a dialogue between Mercury and Asclepius. He is, quite plainly, drawing on the earlier and completely independent Hermetic work, current already in the fourth-century Mediterranean world in original Greek and Latin translation, traditionally known under the title of one of its interlocutors as the *Asclepius* though consistently cited by William as *De deo deorum*.[32] By his own words William has thereby implicated himself in a tradition, associated with its own canonical text, wherein the higher knowledge he believed humankind was destined to seek was revealed through a process of arduous self-discipline and careful adherence to the strictures of an elaborate magical ceremony.

In theory, none of this is surprising given the vision of the human condition mentioned just earlier, nor would William have been obliged to regard it as contradictory to the principles of his own Christian belief. He accepted, after all, that God and the higher regions of reality were naturally available to the human mind. Though few were able to break free into those regions, some did manage to do so, and they accomplished the feat in this world. These were individuals who succeeded in meeting a handful of the most rigorous standards of behavior and mental inclination. William actually lists the standards in *De universo*. Required was that the soul withdraw itself from concern with bodily matters, that it strive with utmost force to set its thoughts on divine concerns, that it pray for the desired reward with vehement devotion and that it throw itself with the most pious ardor on the desire to seize the divinity in all its beauty.[33] To such a soul even Christian law recognized that God would likely grant at least some vision of himself and his divine realities.[34] The fact was, however, as William confessed he slowly came to realize in his maturity, presumably after long efforts at following the prescriptions given in the *Asclepius*, that Hermes Trismegistus was, on one critical point, mistaken. Following a ceremonial regimen and leading even the most pious and ascetic of lives were not themselves sufficient to guarantee the vision and the knowledge so avidly sought. The ultimate purification required for so precious a reward came only by God's grace.[35] It was a technical point, but no less important for that. A magical regime, even one so outwardly noble as that promoted by the *Asclepius*, could not on its own provide the desired end.

William's critique of three types of magic

But William's entanglement with magic went further than his on and off dalliance with ceremonial mysticism. He recognized the existence of a number of other fields of knowledge and practice that were gaining increasing currency among intellectuals in his time. Though these disciplines were not by everyone or in all cases explicitly graced with the description "magical," to no informed observer would there have been any doubt that they opened onto territory with which the notion of "magic" had long been associated. William's reaction to them was sometimes slightly positive, sometimes acidly negative, but in no case simple or unreflective. There is at least one passage where he seems to have expressly brought together for consideration two or three to which he was most ardently opposed. I say "two or three" because only two of the disciplines are expressly named, but the tenor of William's opening remarks and the substance of his succeeding observations suggest that he conceived of his general subject as implicating a third domain of knowing and operating about which he was equally apprehensive.

The discussion I have in mind begins at a point in *De universo* where he had just finished talking about wondrous and foreboding phenomena and purported powers of divination and immediately before he launched into the vast, concluding section of the treatise, effectively about everything one ought to know concerning incorporeal spirits, both good and evil.[36] To steel his readers against efforts to undermine their confidence in his own skepticism regarding the power of distant substances, often celestial, or awe-provoking manipulations here on earth to interfere in the daily order of affairs, he turned for a moment to the theoretical underpinnings to which the promoters of such dubious operations regularly appealed. In his words, the explanation his ideological opponents frequently offered to describe such wondrous works involved a peculiar "mode of operation" ("*modus operationis*") in the real world that he, himself, had just been evoking to account for occurrences in nature that might seem marvelous or contrary to the standard principles of natural philosophy.[37] It bore witness to an aspect of the processes of nature going beyond causation dependent either on interaction between contiguous material bodies or on the transfer of a form from an agent already possessing it onto a receptive subject. Instead, it entailed the conveyance of powers and attributes by a more mysterious and circuitous route, one we shall again find William himself invoking in a discussion of a "natural magic" touched upon later in this chapter.

As William warned his readers, this peculiar mode of operation – itself a perfectly legitimate if somewhat surprising item in nature's toolkit – was disingenuously trotted out at just those awkward moments when a difficulty arose in saying precisely what mechanism was at work in the mysterious operations against which he was to inveigh. It was appealed to, first of all, by astrologers, or those he called, as we have seen, "judicial astronomers" or "doctors of judgments" ("*astronomic[i] judices, hoc est, doctores judiciorum*").[38] Recourse was also had to it by another group of thinkers and practitioners. They were all those who, as William put it, promoted and taught the "learned discipline concerning images" – in his Latin the "*magisterium imaginum*" and which we must take to be either the same as or closely related to the "science of images" we have already encountered among scholars of the twelfth century and in Michael Scot. Finally, he encouraged the reader to look more closely at examples of a presumably parallel operative mechanism at work in various "occult and wondrous operations" they had either read about or observed. Such wonders were, as he reminded his readers, what many physicians and even various natural philosophers meant when they spoke of "*empirica*," or what we might translate as "startling experiments."

With regard to these last operations, it is not hard to see that in fact he regarded many similar marvelous acts as connected to another larger and more loosely defined field of knowledge and practice that, like astrology and the teachings about images, he held in disrepute and believed was erroneously underwritten by much the same explanatory recourse to a special mode of operation. When, in *De legibus*, William had been talking about great social preferments that he knew astrologers were wont illegitimately to attribute to birth under favorable constellations, he noted that these were precisely the claims to be found "in those books which [such men] have written about illusions ("*praestigi[a]*") and images and other evil-doing sacrileges" ("*ali[a] sacrileg[a] malefici[a]*").³⁹ Or, just a bit later in the same treatise, he confessed that the dangerous ideas about which he was then discoursing – conceiving of the celestial bodies as semi-divine and reckoning them up according to the kinds of proclivities they induced in humans born under their ascension in the sky – he, himself, had read about as a young man while perusing the "books of astronomical judgments and…the books of magicians and evildoers" ("*mag[i] atque malefic[i]*").⁴⁰ The recurrent appearance of variants of the word "*maleficium*" – long commonly used, as we know, to refer to sorcery – along with the associated reference to illusions make it plain that William was thinking on these occasions of just the sorts of tricks and wonders we would associate with magic in general.

We are consequently left, at William's own prompting, with what I take to be three fields of learning and even of science that he considered dangerous, all of which rested on an account of natural operations he was determined to expose as inapplicable to the circumstances and covering for what was nothing less than fraud. They were, as I would summarize, astrology, the discipline about images and most of the lore presenting and promoting the marvels associated with learned magic. We can make short work of the first of these, astrology. Important to remember is that what William meant to disparage on this score was the judicial art of drawing prognostications from the positions and movements of celestial bodies, not medieval astronomy as a whole. Like all of his learned contemporaries, moreover, he conceded to the planets and stars an enormous effect on processes and substances in the sub-lunar world. The generation of objects on earth was unquestionably subject to celestial influence, down to matters of such specificity as to be absolutely risible to us today. It was not the assumption that the stars mattered in earthly operations to which he was opposed, but rather the more presumptuous conviction that their power extended all the way into the most particular of events and held sway even over human will.⁴¹ Those who calculated the positions of planets and constellations and drew horoscopes with confidence that they could predict precise events or explain why people ended up doing what they did were wrong. If what they said was true, then all things on earth occurred by absolute necessity.⁴² A more dangerous threat to Christian morality was difficult to imagine. That was the reason astrology had to be fought with fire and sword.⁴³ To William, all such prognostications were simply false, as was the invocation of a special mode by which the stars and earthly substances were operationally interlinked upon which it relied.

William on magical images

Of much greater relevance to our concerns is the second area of knowledge that he had targeted as relying on the assumption about natural operations he intended to discredit. This was the teaching regarding images, objects he at times would identify with even more explicit reference to their dangerous implications as "magical images" (*"imagines magicae"*).[44] Though William spoke of books written about images, at least a few of which it is hard to believe he would not have perused, his knowledge of the field of learning with which they were associated appears to have been superficial, limited mostly to generalities.[45] Indeed it is difficult to draw any definite conclusions about precisely what kind of magical images he had in mind. He claims to have been familiar with various pieces of the magical literature associated with the biblical king and wise man, Solomon. For example, he refers to the four "rings of Solomon" (*"anuli Salomonis"*) and the "Seal of Solomon" (*"sigillum Salomonis"*), as well as to "nine scarabs," which latter must surely be associated with an often cited magical work of the time, the *Novem candariae*.[46] Even more notorious, to his eyes, was an image with which he was familiar that he said was called the "Idea of Solomon" (*"Idea Salomonis"*).[47] And then there was the *"Mandal"* or *"Amandel"* of Solomon, a construction we know about from other sources and which would seem to be ultimately derivative of a true Indian *mandala*, in addition to a figure William refers to merely in passing as the "Pentagon of Solomon," presumably taking it to be well known to his audience.[48] In all these instances, the "image" in question would most certainly have been a geometrical construction or linear design, thus something reproducible in the pages of a book and amenable to being copied by a practitioner of the art. William's term of preference in all these cases of "image" was, not surprisingly, figure or *"figura."*

But he surely also had in mind more literal representations, the most salient example of which was an image tailored to reproduce the features of a human target toward which it was directed. As William noted, recourse to such an instrument of image-magic should technically be designated by the Latin word *"invultuatio,"* for the most common instance involved a little doll or figurine bearing the depicted face (*"vultus"*) of an intended human victim of magical harm or *maleficium*. He thought belief in the use of such representational devices was commonplace among the people, particularly associated with the invariably maligned "old women" of the village, and he was willing to concede that at times it did achieve its anticipated effect.[49] Here, of course, the "image" connected to the magic was something like a model or statuette, and the magical activity almost invariably akin to what we more generally would refer to as sorcery.[50]

Yet there is a third sort of "image" about which William had still more to say. Though in this case his interest would seem to be even more highly engaged than for the other two, and his sense of alarm more vigorously aroused, his understanding of the subject would appear to be if anything less precise. Indeed, his ambiguity about the exact nature of his subject – his tendency when talking about it to trail off into matters that would seem more appropriately assigned to other areas of what he recognized as magical practice – suggests that if he was familiar with a literature concerning magical images of this kind, it was most likely at second hand. "Images" in this third sense were objects employable here on earth whose special powers in fact derived from the stars and constellations under which they were fabricated.[51] They belonged, in short, to a science of images subordinated to astrology. It is a discipline that would emerge with greater specificity and sharper resolution later in the century, when it would likewise be the subject of considerable scrutiny and debate. In William's day it was, to all appearances, only beginning to come into its own.

When speaking most particularly about images of this sort, William returned once more to the Latin term *"figura."* As he explained it, there were four kinds of figures or images involved in this type of magic, and these were seals, rings, characters and – now in a stricter sense than before – images.[52] The first two sorts – seals and rings – evidently linked up with the Solomonic figures already mentioned earlier. Apparently William understood the Solomonic magic he was familiar with as itself requiring astrology's aid. Of greater interest to us now are the last two types – characters and images. To all appearances, William, himself, had difficulty differentiating these two. Speaking of "images" alone, he explained that they were not representational. Instead, they were, as we might put it, more abstract, though for him the only comparison that came to mind was that they were more like "characters."[53] For our purposes, there is probably no great need to separate the two. Important is that these images took shape in nonrepresentational objects that purportedly drew their power in some way from the stars.

Of this latter claim, William was highly skeptical. In his view, there were three primary ways an agent might execute an act in the world of creation – that is, the world of nature, broadly speaking. It could act by intelligence, as did human intellects, purely spiritual substances such as angels or demons, and the divinity itself. It could act by will, again as did the very same three sorts of spiritual entity. Finally, if the agent was a material thing – or, he might have added, resident in a material thing that it controlled, as was the case with the human intellect – it could act by bodily influence, in just the ways that bodies were constrained to work by the rules of nature (*"per virtutem corporalem ad modum naturae"*). Lest there be any doubt about how such natural bodily activity took place, William promptly commented that it proceeded exclusively by contact, either immediate or mediated.[54] William took it to be evident that the sorts of images deployed in the discipline of images under consideration did not operate by either intelligence or will. Such images were, after all, inanimate objects. But it was just as plain that they did not operate corporeally in the way nature would demand. William apparently understood that those resorting to images fabricated under a designated constellation typically made use of them by burying them in the ground and waiting for their effects to be accomplished. Simply put, therefore, none of the ordinary three ways by which action was accomplished in the world was applicable to the images in question.

This fact did not deter his opponents, the image makers and users. As William would complain in the passage further on in *De universo* examined earlier at the introduction to this whole section on his three targeted sorts of disreputable art, the defenders of images crafted with an eye to the stars invoked as foundation for their effectiveness that special "mode of operation" that he, himself, was aware of as at work in an array of bizarre natural phenomena, nature's "occult and wondrous" works.[55] The reasoning was that the images achieved their effects by means of extraordinary powers descending into them from the stars regnant in the heavens at the moment of their fabrication.[56] To William's disapproving eyes, such protestations amounted to nothing but a ruse.[57] If the images actually worked to produce the effects their crafters said they did, then it must be by a mechanism of which the image makers dared not speak.

William was more than prepared to suggest what this unacknowledged mechanism might be. One merely had to look at the repercussions the resort to such images gave rise to in the real world of image users and all those who paid them heed. As William put it, just as anyone who recognized that fire provided heat would turn to fire whenever she or he was seeking warmth, so those who thought that powerful magical images received their potency from the stars would turn to the stars to satisfy their temporal, indeed many of their spiritual, wants.[58] For William, recourse to images confected under carefully selected constellations thus brought to mind the worship of idols.[59] In fact, he considered such image use as related, in the end equivalent, to idolatry itself.[60] And as so often in Christian discourse, when talk of idolatry arose, the subject of demons could not lag far behind. It was demons, so William maintained, who had introduced to humans the practice of fabricating images at astrologically advantageous moments. And they had done so expressly with the intention of leading their gullible followers toward the veneration of the planets, stars and constellations.[61] Indeed, so deeply implicated were demons in this offense to the divinity that in looser terms William was willing to describe it as a version of the cult of demons.[62]

All of which leads to the real mechanism by which William thought the discipline of images worked – whenever it actually managed to accomplish apparent wonders – and which its advocates neither dared to own nor advertised to those credulous enough to be entangled in their snares. At the end of the day, demons were responsible for carrying out whatever actions the magical images were regarded as bringing about.[63] Demons were the natural entities – spiritual beings to be sure and hence able to operate undetected by the senses of image makers, their clients or onlookers to their ceremonial acts – that accomplished whatever it was that image magic could be said to achieve. In return, they thereby rendered the followers of image-magic hateful to God, at the same time, of course, subjecting them to their own power and to themselves as forsaken thralls of the forces of evil.[64]

And what of the images themselves? Anticipating the conclusions of theologians of the later thirteenth century, most notably Thomas Aquinas as shown later, William turned back to Augustine to account for the real function, in the world of nature, these images served. Magical images accomplished their presumed marvels not as simple material things but rather as things exercising an efficacy just insofar as they served as signs, or as William put it technically, "*signa positiva.*"[65] That is to say that magical images, and most expressly the four specific types of "figure" William had pointed out, functioned semantically, conveying a message from the humans who manufactured and manipulated them to the demons who undertook the job of arranging the intended outcomes. Since nothing inherent to the images themselves gave them this semantic value, they had to have been made signs by a voluntary agreement between the parties concerned. And because the images regularly worked if properly crafted, without regard to circumstances such as who was doing the crafting, that agreement must have been tantamount to a legal pact (*"pactum"*).[66] William reminded his readers that Augustine had long before drawn attention to the existence of such a contract, relying upon it to account for what was so ungodly about the use of magic.[67] As both he and Augustine realized, anyone employing the magical images thereby tacitly engaged himself or herself in the pact, becoming as a result co-conspirators with demons, followers of devils.

William on magical marvels

When we turn to the third of William's dangerous disciplines, the connection with demons is plainer still, and the peril of falling into idolatry even harder to avoid. Here we come to the art of producing marvels, part of an even broader set of phenomena William designated as "occult and wondrous operations."[68] Among all such works, those William worried about were more properly referred to as "illusions" (*"praestigia"*), the intentionally misleading proceeds of a strictly ceremonial magic.[69] Trickery of this sort was most typically on display in the practices disseminated in the "books of magicians and sorcerers" (*"libr[i] magorum et maleficorum"*) just beginning to circulate in his day.[70] The latter constituted the stock in trade of those purveyors of a ritualized sorcery he spoke of as "masters of works" (*"magistr[i] operum"*), whom one might expect to find practicing their conjurations from within the confines of a circle sketched out upon the earth or brandishing a sword to strike a designated position on the ground.[71]

As William explained in a well-known passage in *De universo*, the labors these masters carried out should expressly be labeled "works of magic" (*"opera magica"*), properly regarded as "mockery and games" (*"ludificationes"*).[72] They fell into three different types.[73] First there were tricks dependent on the agility of the trickster's hand, sleight of hand operations commonly referred to, William noted, as "handlings" (*"tractationes"*) or "transfers" (*"trajectationes"*). Designed to amuse, such illusions could be easily dispelled merely by calling attention to the quick moves of the perpetrators. In a middle position we find pure appearances, or optical illusions. Here, some kind of apparatus had to be involved. As an example, William pointed to a type of lantern made from wax and the sulfurated skin of a snake, which could make it look as if pieces of straw had turned into writhing serpents. Once more illusion, but nothing very sinister or inexplicable in terms of well-understood processes of nature. Only with the third type did

William tread upon more cautionary ground. In the case of some illusions, an object would seem to present itself, though no causal apparatus was introduced, where in truth no such object was present. On these occasions there was, therefore, no possible explanation according to the normal course of natural operation. Yet even appearances had ultimately to be explicable. All of them, including the most illusory, had to have a cause. In cases like these, only demons (*"maligni spiritus"*) with their secretive actions would fill the bill.[74]

William commented that it was in "books of experiments" (*"libr[i] experimentorum"*) one was likely to find prescriptions for illusions of this third sort.[75] The latter should be stigmatized as, in William's words, a "diabolical fraud."[76] The fraud consisted precisely in the fact that, whatever the machinations of the human operators or the tools employed by them, it was neither tool nor machination that accounted for the illusion. Such objects and actions were merely props, brought into service to satisfy the purposes of the demons, the real agents causing the illusion to occur.[77] And the purpose was to snare human souls. For the using of instruments and working of ceremonies of these so-called *magistri* represented, far from causally effective operations, merely an "offering." The whole performance was an act of service to demons, rightly to be judged as no different from any other cult of demonic spirits.[78] We find ourselves, in short, back at idolatry masquerading again as marvelous intervention into the natural course of affairs.

In the production of illusions, therefore, William was able to discern a specific sub-category of behavior just as detestable as those two other fields of practice he had associated with dangerous magic – astrology and the confection of images – and equally injurious to the moral standing of anyone caught up in it. Associated in his mind with just such evil and illusory operations were, in addition to the general category of "books of experiments," two specific texts (or, in the second case, maybe an item) he expected his readers at least to have heard of, perhaps even seen. They were the "Sworn Book" (*"liber sacratus"*), the name of which hardly ever escaped his lips without addition of the adjective "execrable," and a certain "Mirror" or "Mirror of Apollo" (*"speculum Apollinis"*).[79] William even took the trouble of explaining just how it was that demons were able to pull off the deceptions they did in this art. Whatever the effects produced, and no matter how wondrous they might appear, the demons responsible behind the scenes were limited to proceeding in their operations exclusively by natural means.[80] The fact that demons were usually undetected by human senses made it, of course, especially easy for them to be the agents in such a ruse. Moreover, demons were "spiritual substances," and thus higher beings than the mere mortal "masters of works" who depended on them to execute their magic feats.[81] They had the power to insinuate themselves into the very sensory impressions, perhaps even thoughts, of the human targets of their malicious games.[82] In that manner they could easily induce in the minds of their victims the perception of an experience that in the concrete world of externals had never occurred.

Natural magic

Yet there was still another way demons might be particularly well equipped for the production of marvels. Spiritual beings that they were, demons knew more than most human beings about the workings of nature. And in drawing attention to this fact William was prompted to expound upon a kind of magic that ultimately led out of the world of the demonic and back to the purely benign. For in nature there existed, William was anxious to assert, many secret and wonderful powers (*"virtutes occultae et mirabiles"*), the understanding of which humans could never plumb to their furthest and familiarity with which was extremely difficult to attain.[83] Of course, demons themselves regularly employed these powers to perform their damnable tricks, but it was crucial to recognize that all such operations, as well as all the occult powers upon which they depended, were entirely natural.[84] Only because of their secrecy, and hence their marvelousness, did they constitute a class of phenomena separate from the rest of nature. William, perhaps first in the Latin west, gave to this class the denomination "natural magic" (*"magia naturalis," "magica naturalis"*).[85]

To William's eyes, such a natural magic was wondrous, to be sure, but it was also highly learned and worthy of great praise. He recognized that it had acquired an evil reputation. Pagan thinkers, perhaps even some of the natural philosophers of his own day, were wont to label it "philosophical magic" or, more disturbing still, "necromancy." Yet they were wrong to do so, at least insofar as with those names they meant to imply improbity or fraud. In fact, so William continued, natural magic constituted a legitimate member of the canonical learned disciplines – to be precise, the eleventh part of "natural science."[86] When applied to produce effects that William was willing, without a hint of opprobrium, to call "magical works" (*"opera magica"*), the same discipline resulted in a veritable "art of natural magic" (*"ars magica naturalis"*).[87] To be sure, the potential for the practice of such an art to lead the ignorant to attribute the marvels produced to demonic intervention had prompted the Christian religion prudentially to adopt the habit of branding its practitioners as evil, identifying them as sorcerers or, in the vulgar Latin common already in Augustine's day, *"malefici."*[88] But to those familiar with the occult powers, there was nothing to be taken as evil in such startling manipulations and no necessity to posit in them sorcery of any sort. For the truly learned, they evoked not wonder but instead respect for God's glory, manifest in all the workings of his created world.[89]

Returning to a tack already adopted by the current of Latin scholars dating back to Adelard of Bath and Daniel of Morley in the twelfth century and continuing through Michael Scot in the thirteenth, William even took it upon himself to defend magic of this sort, in his case buttressing the praise with an inventive etymology. Those knowing how to draw upon nature's occult ways were, he conceded, commonly known as magicians, or *"magi."* Yet the name did not fall to them, as Christian tradition might suggest, by virtue of their being "bad" (*"mali"*), thus fairly characterized as "workers of evil," in Latin *"male agentes."*

On the contrary, they had come to be referred to as *"magi"* precisely because the effects that they accomplished were so very grand, rendering them, in Latin terms, *"magna agentes,"* "doers of great things." William added – anticipating Roger Bacon by only a few decades – that if such marvel makers possessed enough skill, and were supplied with an abundance of resources and financial support, they would be capable of deeds more astonishing than anything witnessed before.[90] The fact that some practitioners of the art did turn to demons, employing them as intermediaries manipulating the occult forces on their behalf, meant admittedly that among magicians there were "bad types" (*"mali"*), worthy of designation according to the more commonplace construal of *"magi"* as "doers of evil," in Latin *"mala agentes."*[91] Otherwise, short of turning the instruments of nature – just as would any other criminal – to evil purpose with sinful intent, operating by means of natural magic resulted in no injury to God and did him no offense.[92]

For an idea of the kinds of marvels William thought natural magic was capable of yielding, one need look no farther than his own words, as such prodigious matters plainly fascinated him. In *De legibus*, where natural magic was first introduced, William pointed to the sudden – we might say, spontaneous – generation of frogs, lice, worms and sundry other animals through skillful combination of the seeds for such creatures present throughout the natural world with substances selected to reinforce their potency.[93] By mixing the seeds in novel ways and adding unconventional natural reinforcements, it should be possible even to produce absolutely new species – types of animals, for instance, never yet seen.[94]

Yet much of William's natural magic had to do with occult phenomena at work in nature every day. A favorite case in William's time was provided by the magnet, and there was also the basilisk, capable of killing solely by engaging the direct vision of its victim.[95] The medical literature teemed with instances of operations not easy to explain, what William called the "marvels of medicine."[96] He was especially taken by the case of the peony, about which it was said that if a bunch was hung around the neck of a demoniac, the evil spirits tormenting the poor soul would be driven away.[97] In short, magic, if understood correctly and separated from the sorcery William so greatly feared, permeated nature and constituted for the natural philosopher not just a proper but in fact also an irresistible object of investigation. No louder voice can be found than his for the ambivalence with which the subject had come to be regarded in even the most prestigious – and orthodox – of learned Latin circles toward the mid-point of the thirteenth century.

Ars notoria

At that very moment, however, forces were at work that would tip the scholarly balance, transforming ambivalence, at least among thinkers of authoritative weight, into resolute hostility. William's testimony shows how already in his day Latin works were appearing in circulation offering not just an idea of what wondrous effects traditions of magic might promise but also detailed prescriptions for how to go about producing results. The western literate elite was in possession, for the first time since antiquity, of bona fide manuals of magical operation. They received, from many a scholar or cleric, an enthusiastic reception. But by their very existence they also radically altered the circumstances into which learned magic had to be received. Increasingly over the thirteenth century it became possible not just to talk about magic in sophisticated intellectual circles but also to practice it. For so volatile a subject, the new reality of agency raised the stakes, and hence the acrimony, of the debate.

We are only just now finding ourselves in a position to see precisely what such practice entailed, or at least what it aspired to be. The last three decades have brought us, for the first time, the discovery of authentic medieval texts of learned and explicitly ceremonial Latin magic, some dating from as early as the thirteenth century. A look at four of the most prominent of these to have been made available now in critical editions can give us an idea of exactly what learned magic was about in the heyday of scholastic thought. One of the most recent is the self-proclaimed *Ars notoria*, the name of which has long been familiar to scholars and whose existence we have remarked upon as conceded by Michael Scot.[98]

As a text, the *Ars notoria* was never fixed but consisted rather of a series of versions elaborated over time with respect to a core of literary and diagrammatic materials first cobbled together in northern Italy in the second half of the twelfth century. Though these materials present themselves as part of the Solomonic tradition of which we have seen William of Auvergne make mention, the work as we have it would not appear to be a translation from a Hebrew-language source but rather an original production, in Latin, emerging out of a high-medieval scholarly milieu. The editor of the new edition, Julien Véronèse, has chosen to present the work in three textual instantiations, progressing chronologically from a rather crude amalgamation of foundational bits and pieces to an eventually precise, highly glossed and considerably rationalized rendition of a long and arduous ceremony that began to circulate at the turn of the fourteenth century. For our purposes, the first two versions are, by their date, more pertinent than this third. The very first, which Véronèse designates "Version A," has its earliest manuscript witness from around 1225, while the second, in the edition given the title "*Opus operum*," took shape at the middle of the century.[99]

As Version A announces from the start, the purpose of the *Ars notoria* was to give to the operator following its prescriptions full and expert knowledge of one, if not all, of the "sciences and natural arts" (*eruditio et cognitio omnium scientiarum et naturalium artium*).[100] It could, therefore, be known as the "art of arts" ("*ars artium*") or "science of sciences" ("*scientia scientiarum*").[101] What made it special was that it bypassed the regimen of attendance at school or university and, by means of diligent attention to a scripted ceremonial, provided sudden ("*subitanee*") proficiency in any desired discipline. Version A suggests that for a single art or science one would need, all told, about a month.[102]

The procedure was called the *ars notoria*, as the text makes plain, not just because it was revelatory (*notorius*) of knowledge but also since it depended on a peculiar literary tool called a "note" (*nota*, *notula*). Each "note" was made up of two parts: an "*oratio*," sometimes actually comprised of several *orationes* linked together, and a "*figura*."[103] The "*oratio*" consisted of a string of words to be recited, ranging in character from prayer to what might be called an incantation. The "*figura*" was a complicated image or diagram inscribed on the manuscript page, typically also embellished with written words. It was to be gazed upon at specified moments in the rite. According to the story laid out at the *Ars*'s opening and occasionally referred back to in the text, it was Solomon himself – sometimes somehow also Euclid and, even more oddly, Mani (*Manichaeus*) – who had originally received the "notes" from holy angels. He then passed them along to an Apollonius – most likely identifiable with the legendary magical thinker, Apollonius of Tyana – who converted them into Latin or a Romanized script, whence they ultimately landed in the hands of an anonymous master of arts who produced the core text in the tradition we now have access to.[104]

By its own testimony, the *Ars* had therefore arisen in a Hebrew milieu, and in its Latin instantiation pretended to be entirely compatible with Christianity. Indeed, the ceremonial procedures it advanced could be regarded, in the words of the text, as profound mysteries ("*profunda misteria*"), none of which could be accomplished by anyone lacking the fullness of religious faith ("*non absque fidei magnitudine proferenda*").[105] Some of the *orationes* contain only incomprehensible words or names resonating exotically of ancient Hebrew, Greek and, even more fantastically, Chaldean, the languages in which they were supposed to have been delivered to Solomon.[106] According to the fourteenth-century gloss, such verbalizations consisted of the "sacred names of holy angels," to whom they were delivered in a kind of invocation. The Latin *orationes*, on the other hand, were more authentically prayerful, addressed to God and asking his concession to the angels of the powers to grant the request for knowledge.[107] Moreover, the enterprise required considerable asceticism and an ethical bearing highly inflected to fit Christian norms. Perhaps most salient was the requirement that the performer of the ritual maintain throughout unbroken chastity and stern sobriety.[108] Many of the days of recitation and inspection of the figures had to be spent in fasting, at least till after sundown, often on bread and water alone.[109] It was especially important not to be involved in any crime, which might readily undo the whole procedure.[110]

But precisely what arts and sciences did the notary art promise to render up? In large part the text restricts itself to traditional schematics of the arts. An overview lays them out in groups of seven. There were the seven liberal arts, the seven mechanical arts and seven usually described simply as "*exceptivae*."[111] For the seven liberal arts – the trivium and the quadrivium – it is assumed that no explanation was needed.[112] Though nothing in the thirteenth-century versions makes it clear what was to be included under the rubric "*exceptivae*," the fourteenth-century gloss twice indicates that this category embraced the natural and the moral sciences as well as anything more generally included under "philosophy."[113] Only with the mechanical arts do we venture onto more suspect ground. The text of Version A sets them down as hydromancy, pyromancy, necromancy ("*nigromantia*"), chiromancy, geomancy and two peculiarities: "*geonogia*" and "*neonogia*," this last described as falling "under astrology."[114] The listing hews close to the line of Hugh of St. Victor's divinatory arts of magic, the first five reproducing his total roster except for the replacement of "aeromancy" by "chiromancy."[115] Apparently, "mechanical arts" was thus the *Ars notoria*'s technical term for what Michael Scot intended with his own peculiar usage, "*matesis.*"[116]

Surely anticipating criticism, the text of the *Ars* reveals itself as ambivalent about whether divination was in fact among its intended goals. At the point the mechanical arts are first introduced, it is conceded that of the seven, at least necromancy was highly worrisome. Involved, by the *Ars*'s understanding, was the sacrifice of dead animals, an action – as Version B later put it, sacrifice "to evil spirits" – that was sacrilege at minimum, under no circumstances permissible to a Christian.[117] For all the risk of profanation, however, the same text points out that in ancient times some masters of learning regarded certain ceremonial works accompanied by animal sacrifice as true "mysteries," capable of being performed without sin. Indeed Solomon himself, the text insists, flatly proclaimed that five of seven presumably canonical books of necromancy could be consulted and followed in performance without any moral or religious peril.[118] And in the fourteenth-century gloss, on the two occasions where the prescriptions for operating the ceremonial required to obtain the mechanical arts are specifically indicated, we find absolutely no warning that the reader beware, much less any mention of prohibition.[119]

All this, of course, just with regard to operations designed for the purpose of obtaining knowledge or skill. If one peruses the whole of the *Ars notoria*, one comes upon isolated directives linked to activities sometimes suggestive of outright sorcery. First of all, the user of the *Ars* is several times admonished to keep the proceedings secret and to perform them in isolation.[120] If anyone be allowed to accompany the performer, it should only be an expert supervisor referred to explicitly as a "master of the work," a title immediately evocative of the phrase employed about the same time by William of Auvergne for the operator of wicked illusions, "*magister operum.*"[121] Broaching on sorcery itself would appear to be the observation, offered almost in passing, that one of the most awesome of the *orationes* connected to knowledge of theology had the power as well to incite celestial spirits to accomplish grand and wondrous deeds. The precautionary disclaimer that this would happen only if God permitted hardly masked the otherwise incantatory nature of such pretensions.[122] And with reference to a still more formidable of these theology-linked *orationes*, the text actually dares to propose that if one is seeking an especially compelling power of persuasion, even on a day when one has committed a crime, one can repeat the prayer silently in one's heart, receive the gift and employ it, of all things, to evil effect.[123] On occasions such as these, the *Ars* had definitely passed beyond the bounds of innocent illumination, much less pious mystery.

Liber iuratus Honorii

Even more problematic from the perspective of traditional Christian learning, and more conspicuously implicated in a web of procedures smacking of sorcery and communion with the demonic world, is a second work whose Latin medieval text has likewise been found and made available for modern readers only in the past decade. This is the *Sworn Book of Honorius*, or as it denominates itself in the surviving Latin manuscripts, the *Liber iuratus* or *Liber sacer* (once also *Libellum sacrum*).[124] By its own account the product of a master Honorius of Thebes, himself the son of Euclid, the work explains its name variously as stemming from its sacred contents and output (*sacra*), from the fact that it had been consecrated (*sacratus*) by angels, or from the requirement that its user formally swear (*iurare*) to abide by certain commitments.[125] Given the prominence among the magical writings that William of Auvergne claims to have seen or known of one he calls the *Liber sacratus*, it has been tempting to regard the composition we now possess as the same as that which passed through William's hands.[126] The claim has, in fact, recently been defended in the scholarly literature.[127] Yet the weight of the evidence would now seem to fall on the side of dating the particular *Sworn Book* before us in Gösta Hedegård's edition to the early fourteenth century.[128] The probably apocryphal but arguably still politically meaningful story told in the work's prologue about a meeting of cardinals called by the pope to condemn masters who might resort to procedures like those promoted in the text almost surely dates its origin to the years of the papacy of John XXII, pope from 1316 to 1334.[129]

Whatever the links to the time of John XXII, however, the text as we now have it gives evidence of a longer history of maturation. Even a superficial examination lays bare several organizational layouts that could not have originated simultaneously, pointing to a composition by stages through multiple versions. In all plans, the work is conceived of as divided into pieces, called alternatively treatises (*tractatus*) or works (*opera*), though there is disagreement about their number. Evidence of what is likely the oldest blueprint is found in a listing of 93 chapters distributed among four parts and placed like a table of contents just after the prologue, then repeated part by part, with only minor variations, first at the end but thereafter at the head of each of the respective treatises.[130] Despite the fact that throughout the body of the work reference is made back to these chapters, the content of almost none of them is to be found in the text itself. It would seem that the chapter headings did at some early point lay out the substantive contents of a composition, probably with the name *Liber iuratus*, but that this content was subsequently discarded in what became effectively a new piece. A close look at the chapter titles themselves suggests that there may even have been an earlier stage in which the single volume they sketch out existed instead as two separate works.

Pride of place in the entirety as envisioned in the chapter list goes to the subject of the first two chapters: the fashioning of something – which we learn in the text to be a figure or seal (*sigillum*) – representing the awesome name of God, and the attainment of an end to which this sign could be put, called in the text "*visio divina.*"[131] The latter is effectively the beatific vision, though not in heaven but already here on earth. There follow, rounding out the six chapters of the first treatise, thorough knowledge of the power of the divinity and three quite particular matters concerning absolution from sin and retrieval from purgatory.[132] The second treatise, containing 27 chapters, begins with knowledge of the heavens and of the angels inhabiting them and passes through knowledge of the planets and stars to that of all the spirits of the world. A final chapter of the treatise concerns the consecration ("*sacracio*") of the wonderful book itself.[133] Given the unity of substance in these two treatises – vision of the divinity, of all higher spirits, and access to whatever knowledge they made possible – and the fact that they terminate with formal consecration, it is not far fetched to imagine that the chapters listed convey the outlines of what once comprised a single work on the attainment of such higher insight and awareness.

When we turn to the chapter headings of the third and fourth treatises, the subject matter dramatically shifts. One can almost take as a description of both of these latter two sections put together the titles of the third's first three chapters: "On the binding of spirits, by words...by seals...by figures."[134] If these two treatises once constituted another original and singular whole, as I suggest is plausible, then their subject was the invocation and conjuring of spirits, potentially both angelic and demonic. It would be this book that represents the most likely candidate for whatever *Liber sacratus* William of Auvergne had once perused, if there is a connection between our work and the one that he so stridently condemns. A simple look at the headings themselves reveals why William would have reacted the way he did.[135] From the third treatise, for instance, chapter 64 contains instructions for secretly opening locked doors. In chapters 68 and 69, one learns how to win over women for every pleasure to be desired and how to make it rich. Chapters 70–73 begin with the way to cure any illness, continue with how to bring infirmity upon anyone one chooses, take a step further with the recipe for killing someone and end with instructions for raising storms and wreaking havoc on earth and sea. The fourth treatise is even more stereotypical of the dark arts, and more alarming still. Its first three chapters – 89–91 – concern allowing prisoners to escape, opening locked passageways and prisons, and finding treasures hidden in the ground. But it is the final two – 92 and 93 – that, even for the author of the book, stray beyond the pale. They would have supplied directions for conjuring up the appearance of the dead, along with giving the impression of creating entirely novel animals from the materials of the earth. In the author's words, these two so clearly violate divine prescriptions that they had to be expunged.[136]

Two later initiatives at organizing the original material for the *Liber iuratus* as evinced by the list of 93 chapters have left traces of themselves even more fleetingly in the composition as we now have it. There are vestiges in the text of two concise descriptions of the major parts of the work, its treatises or *opera*.

In each of them the number of treatises is five. The first effectively reproduces the parameters of the work as seen in the chapter listing, the number of treatises being increased by one because what had constituted a single first treatise in the listing is divided into two. As this quick description sketches it out, the *Liber* begins with instructions for fashioning the seal of God – or God's name – turns in a second treatise to the way to employ the seal to receive the vision of the divinity (*"de visione divina"*), and then moves from a third treatise on the vision of all the angels (*"de visione angelorum"*) to a fourth on binding spirits (*"de constriccione spirituum"*), unspecified in the text but presumably higher if no longer angelic, and finally to a fifth on constraining lower spirits, now plainly demonic (*"de ligacione infernorum"*).[137] It is the second summary description in which the vision of the whole has plainly changed. Here the treatises are summarized as comprising an initial one on the divine vision (*"de visione divina"*), a second on good angels (*"de angelis bonis"*), a third on airy spirits (*"de aereis"*), a fourth on earthly spirits (*"de terreis"*) and finally a fifth expounding generally on the entirety (*"de exposicione horum"*).[138] It would appear that what we are witness to on this occasion is an attempt to transform what has so far looked to be disparate and only haphazardly assembled material into an integral and internally consistent whole.

When we turn at last to the body of the text, it is more or less the prospectus of the second of our two short summaries that holds sway. The first and by far the longest treatise concerns itself with construction of the seal of God's name and then with its utilization in a complex ceremonial of *orationes* and ritual acts to arrive at the beatific vision here in this life.[139] The considerably shorter second treatise limits itself to a description of the spirits, angelic and otherwise, assigned to each of the seven planetary spheres, from Saturn at the outermost down to the moon closest to earth, and then rapidly prescribes a ceremonial and a collection of *orationes* and invocations intended to bring these spirits under the operator's control.[140] In the second of the two summaries noted earlier, the spirits are designated the "good angels," but as we see in the actual descriptions devoted to them in the text itself, the various angels of each planet have their subordinate "demons" – *"demones"* in Latin – and whether they are good or bad is not reported. The third treatise advertises itself as having to do with the spirits of the air.[141] It launches into an explanation of how the airy spirits are in actuality those already indicated in the descriptions in the second treatise of spirits subordinate to the angels in charge of each of the planetary spheres, so that the reader is already familiar with their names.[142] The author now makes an effort to clarify their moral complexion. Some of them are good, some are bad, others fall somewhere in between, but in any case they are all associated with the winds, in which they dwell.[143] What follows is again a closer accounting of the various groups of spirits and their natures, succeeded by a quite complicated ceremonial of *orationes*, *invocationes* and *adiurationes*, accompanied eventually by ritual acts, all with the idea of summoning the spirits and compelling their obedient service.

Since the fourth treatise returns to the matters already addressed at the appropriate spot in the original listing of chapter headings, three of which amounted
to plain sorcery and two of which were so nefarious as to have to be – so the
author claims – excised from the text, it is kept tantalizingly brief.[144] By the terms
of the final organizational plan, this treatise engages itself with the earthy spirits
or angels, but the text leaves no doubt that beneath this somewhat neutral rubric
lie in fact, as the first summary description would have it, infernal beings.[145] The
author even specifies them as five in number – a king and four ministers – each
minister commanding a hundred legions, made up in turn of 4,500 demonic
troops. And he excoriates them all as "hellish agents" ("*ministri infernales*").[146] The
orationes and rituals spelled out are kept to a minimum, but they are ominous,
and stereotypically frightening, all the same. Finally there appears in the text, as
promised, a fifth and final treatise, officially dedicated – as the second summary
declared – to an exposition of the whole.[147] It constitutes in fact more supplement
than general commentary, but it is short and to the point, and it nicely clarifies a
few details about *orationes* and rituals left obscure in the preceding text.

Conjuring in the *Liber iuratus*

Yet what are we to make of this complicated work as an indicator of learned and
ceremonial magic in the thirteenth century? Despite the belated attempts to give
the piece a unity, it is probably most useful for our purposes to conceive of it even
in its last instantiation as made up of two separate parts, one directed toward the
beatific vision, the other toward binding of spirits. The former section starts the
work but was presumably pulled together later than the latter. It is of little immediate relevance to us. Worth noting is the fact that, as Hedegård's edition makes
plain, many of the *orationes* and a considerable part of the ceremonial in this
piece of the work are lifted directly from the text of the *Ars notoria*.[148] Indeed, the
entire apparatus of words and acts designed to obtain the beatific vision seems to
be inspired by the practice of the *Ars*. The operator in the *Liber*'s procedures must
be penitent, have confessed to a priest, and maintain a regimen of asceticism
and clean living, particularly by abstaining from sexual activity.[149] Perhaps most
important is the crucial common thread running through both works that all the
operations and any of the interventions of angels, or demons, will be possible
only at the will of God, whose grace and benevolence is fundamental if any of
the ceremonies and angelic responses are to do their work.[150]

The section of the text genuinely pertinent to our concerns consists of treatises three and four, both quite likely concocted from separate manuscript material dating back to the thirteenth century and whose substantive preoccupations
more nicely match those of the *Liber sacratus* commented upon by William
of Auvergne. No matter if we view these two treatises through the lens of the
presumably early chapter headings or take them as they are laid before us in

the actual body of the work, they would look together to comprise an integral, coherent piece on the conjuring of spirits, whether angels or demons, and the performance of wondrous operations at their expense – what William meant whenever he talked about his marvelous *opera*. The demeanor and regimen of activities expected of the operator of these sorts of conjurations and works would become almost stereotypical for much of subsequent learned magic and can be quickly summarized here.

First of all, just as in the case of the preparations for the divine vision outlined in the first treatise, the operator must take care to purify himself, both morally and physically, to remain steady in his devotion to the true God and the catholic faith, and to submit to at least a moderate asceticism emphasizing chastity and fasting. Second, as was in fact also required in the preparation of the original "seal," recourse must be had to proper fumigations. Finally, the celebrant must make the requisite formulaic petitions to the relevant spirits, *orationes* of the sort encountered in the specifications for the beatific vision – to a large degree, indeed, precisely the same ones – with minor modifications necessary to adapt them to a different end.[151] Then too, following the precedent already established with the *orationes* of the first treatise, all the petitions to be delivered to the spirits in these latter parts of the *Liber* have to be reinforced with special supplications to God, without whose consent none of the conjuring operations could ever proceed.[152] And in a truly foreboding ceremonial addition, we see the introduction of the drawing of protective circles around the operator to shield against the terrifying dangers with which the approach of many of the summoned spirits was fraught. The text as we have it even reproduces in diagrammatic form three of these amalgams of circles and signs, one to be sketched on the ground as a site of operations for the conjurer of spirits of the airs or winds in the third treatise, another two – one for the conjurer, a second to contain the presumably more volatile spirits for the fourth treatise's works involving earthy and infernal spirits.[153]

Of course it is of more than passing interest what sort of spirits these might be that are conjured up and so constrained. With regard the third treatise, with its airy spirits, the answer is, as noted earlier, ambiguous.[154] With respect to the fourth treatise, on the other hand, all ambiguity evaporates. Here, the text does not mince words. The earthly agents conjured up in this section of the *Liber* are, so the author readily concedes, "as ugly as can be and full of every sort of depravity."[155] As previously mentioned, they and all their minions must be recognized for what they are: "infernal agents."[156] Whenever they are near, one should fear the worst, for they are destructive beings, prone to inducing such stereotypical misfortunes as the ruination of castles and the uprooting of trees and crops.[157] Even the fumigation employed in the rites for summoning them calls them out. It is the burning of sulfur.[158]

Yet for all the unsavoryness, or at least dubiety, of the invisible agents with which the operator will be implicated in these latter two treatises, even the author who produced the version we now possess wants to retain a place, within the bounds of orthodox Christian behavior, for most, perhaps all, of the conjurations about which we have been speaking. In a fascinating passage set after the prologue and initial chapter headings but before the beginning of the first treatise, we find the only concession that the *Liber* constitutes in fact a work of magic. Speaking of the art passed down by Solomon, the operative prescriptions for which the work sets forth, he refers to it explicitly as "this magical art."[159] But like several of the scholastics examined earlier, he is determined to construe the term "magic" in a positive sense. Contrary to what he expects most his readers will assume, he explains that the name of magician (*"magus"*) need not be associated with evil. For, he continues, the word *"magus"* is properly to be understood as equivalent to the Greek "philosopher," the Hebrew "scribe," or the Latin *"sapiens"* ("wiseman"). Thus "magical art" (*"ars magica"*) must be analyzed etymologically as signifying the "science of the wise" (*"sciencia sapientum"*).[160]

Moreover, though the author recognizes that one might have legitimate qualms about instances in which the magical art is put into practice, he evidently believes that the moral valence of the material presented in his book and the activities it promotes has more to do with the bearing of the operative or performer than with the ceremonies or the implicated enabling spirits in themselves. At the beginning of the first treatise the text lays out three different classes of operatives who might, by following the instructions of the book, attempt to avail themselves of its magic: pagans, Jews and Christians.[161] Pagans would never have access to the sort of spirits involved in the first two treatises but they might well turn their ministrations to the airy and earthy spirits of the third and fourth. Even so, they would never in fact succeed in attaining binding power over the spirits or demons they invoke.[162] Lacking Christian faith, pagans could never produce authentic magical works.[163] Jews wanting to perform the magic of the *Liber* stood in a middle position.[164] Because they lacked the Christian faith, they were not permitted to receive the beatific vision, to have meaningful interactions with angels or spirits, or in the end actually to perform works of magic. But, as the author of the book admits, Jews worshipped the same Creator as the Christians. When Jews performed the ceremonies of the book and delivered the invocations containing the holy names of God, the angels were technically bound to obey the summons and appear. They simply did not have to answer honestly or produce the desired outcomes. For the third class of operators alone were the conditions right. Magic was thus possible, even legitimate, but only when the *orationes* were chanted and the rites performed by Christians, trusting in God and worshipping him according to Christ's new dispensation.[165] In this work's estimation, therefore, conjuring was doable, permissible, perhaps even desirable, and in a fully Christian milieu.

Picatrix

Advancing yet further into the territory of ritual operations that would readily have been looked upon as magical but were even more likely to arouse alarm among those who saw themselves as defenders of Christianity is a third Latin work dating from just a bit later than the first versions of the *Ars notoria* but more or less contemporaneous with the intermediate stages of the *Liber iuratus*. This is the *Picatrix*, Latin translation of an Arabic composition of Spanish origin known under the name *Ghāyat al-hakīm* or *The Aim of the Sage*.[166] Though this work apparently did not circulate throughout the Latin west before the fifteenth century – the first author known to use or even refer to it is the great Florentine Neoplatonist, Marsilio Ficino – it would seem to represent an uninhibited variant of the new ceremonials already hinted at in the warnings of William of Auvergne and exercising a domineering presence well before the thirteenth century had ended.[167] We shall take it here as a stand-in for other works of similar type that circulated more broadly in educated milieus in the latter thirteenth century but the texts of which have not as yet been recovered.

Picatrix, which in the translation purports to take its name from the author of the original Arabic composition, first became available to the west at the court of the illustrious king Alfonso X of Castile.[168] Alfonso's court was unusual in regard to its literary pretensions, which were considerable, in that royal favor inclined to promote letters in the vernacular Castilian language as much as in the more exclusive Latin. Thus it happened that the *Picatrix* was first translated at Alfonso's bidding from Arabic into Spanish, in the year 1256 or slightly thereafter.[169] The Latin version of the book, produced from the Spanish, emerged only after an interval, perhaps of very short duration but possibly of several decades. As for the original Arabic *Ghāya*, although the renowned Arab historian Ibn Khaldun attributed it to the astronomer Maslama ibn Ahmad al-Majrītī, who died in Spain before 1009, the work must in fact have arisen from the hands of an Andalusian Arab scholar, to be sure, but not until the mid-eleventh century.[170] David Pingree convincingly argues that the anonymous eleventh-century compiler drew from a host of Arabic sources produced in the Middle East in the ninth and tenth centuries. Particularly important were Sābian astrological and incantatory texts drawing upon practices established in Harrān, now in modern Turkey, but spilling over into the Islamic cultural sphere after an episode of religious confrontation in the early ninth century.[171]

At first glance, *Picatrix* would appear to belong to a genre of the new learning already testified to by William of Auvergne and evident in the *Ars notoria*. These would be works promising to enable a right-minded reader to participate in, if not arise to, the wisdom of God. Foundational to this program lay an Aristotelianizing presumption, seen in William as well, that the human soul was destined expressly for the purpose of reaching the heights of intellectual fullness.[172] As before with William's aspirations, we find moreover in *Picatrix* an elision between the attainment of the fullness of knowledge pure and simple and a somewhat more charged vision of breaking through to the profoundest depths and most hidden secrets of cognition.[173] The very first lines of Picatrix's Latin prologue announce that the translation – in the first instance, as will be remembered, from Arabic into Castilian – had been ordered by Alfonso for the benefit of his learned associates but, equally importantly, with an eye to the glory of the Divinity, whose wont it was to reveal to his chosen ones the "secrets of the sciences."[174]

Yet for all the quasi-mystical trappings of *Picatrix*'s programmatic, apparent from the start as well is another, considerably more controversial trajectory the author plainly intends to chart out for the recipients of his work. For neither author nor translator mince words about the ultimately ceremonial nature of the operations their course of spiritual advancement will actually entail. As the prologue contends, just after summarizing the charge rendered by King Alfonso: "Here begins the book that Picatrix, the wisest of philosophers, composed about the arts of necromancy."[175] Naturally, given all he has said about attaining proficiency in the sciences, the author contends that necromancy itself constitutes a bona fide science, the "*sciencia nigromancie*."[176] As for what kind of science this is, there can be no doubt from the start that it leads in the direction of the marvelous.[177] Here, moreover, even more important are the qualities of hiddenness and secrecy. First of all, the science of necromancy is hidden to most of humanity because the philosophers expounding it have taken pains to make it so, setting their words behind a veil of figurative speech.[178] On this matter, the telltale language of "occult" emerges into view. *Picatrix* explains that the adepts of necromancy have passed along their teachings to the wise by turning always to linguistic "occultations," speaking "*in occulto*." But second, necromancy amounts to a hidden science by virtue of its subject matter. As the text sets forth, necromancy is a discipline dealing expressly with things concerning which "the greater part of humanity does not understand how they happen or from what causes they arise."[179]

Picatrix's Neoplatonizing rationale

By now it should be clear that a certain disconnect exists between the general terms in which *Picatrix* introduces its subject and goals and the specific description it gives of the content it plans to lay before the reader. In fact, the author made an attempt to bridge the gap by appealing to what can only be called a Neoplatonizing cosmology, or better yet, ontology. David Pingree draws our attention to this maneuver when he remarks that much of the magical contents presented in the *Ghāya* run contrary to the Neoplatonic theoretical justifications in which they are embedded – justifications inserted primarily to defend against charges of demonism.[180] To be absolutely precise, *Picatrix* introduces three different versions of a Neoplatonizing hierarchy, all intended to stand for a general conception of order in the cosmos. It is the last of the three versions presented that depicts in broadest strokes, but thus most simply, the general principles upon which *Picatrix* draws for theoretical justification. It can serve for us as an indicator of what sort of schema the author had in mind.

In a long passage in Book IV, the author says that he will lay before the reader five grades of reality according to which God has disposed his entire creation. If we add in God, himself, and then a final stratum tacked on at the end, we come up with a hierarchy of seven stages.[181] Stages they truly are, for they are offered in authentically Neoplatonic form as emanations, each one descending out of its superior, located directly above it.[182] For the most part, they can also be seen as spheres in the vast apparatus of the world, for the five principle stages are indeed portrayed in astronomical fashion as nested inside each other like the celestial orbs. First there is God, the unique principle productive of all the subsequent stages. In order after the divinity comes next the initial production, given the collective name of "first matter and first form," but which also appears in the text as "first essence" ("*essencia prima*") and once, in a phrase suggestive of alchemy, "first mineral [or ore] for all other things" ("*prima minera omnium*"). Subsequently arise two successive stages, the first, in Latin, "*sensus sive intellectus,*" the second "*spiritus.*" Though it is difficult to say exactly what is meant by these two terms or phrases, which appear repeatedly throughout the whole text but often to somewhat disparate purposes, one can be certain at least that they are evocative, and derivative, of the two classical Neoplatonic emanations out of the One: mind or intellect ($\nu o\tilde{u}\varsigma$) and spirit or soul ($\pi\nu\varepsilon\tilde{u}\mu\alpha$). There follow the "nature of the heavens" ("*natura celorum*"), or sometimes just simply "nature" ("*natura*"), and then, rounding out the five grades promised at the passage's beginning, another collective entity, the "elements and things made from them" ("*elementa et elementata*"). Only at the very end, and almost as an afterthought, do we find mention of a sixth production, this time not linked back to the first emanation, "first form," as were all the others, but just to soul or spirit ("*spiritus*"). In this stratum lie all the "animals and vegetative beings and hard bodies" ("*animalium et vegetabilium atque dura corpora*").[183]

As the passage makes plain, all of the middle five productions or emanations are located or deposited in their own circle or sphere ("*circulus*" but also sometimes "*celum*"), analogous to the arrangement of the heavenly spheres of the classical astronomical cosmos and following a hierarchy not only of descending nobility but also of increasing declension away from purity and toward density ("*grossicies*") or, in a loose sense of the term, matter ("*materies*").[184] The text remarks, too, that soul or spirit ("*spiritus*") occupies a pivotal position, right in the middle of the five stages or grades, and thus right in the middle of the total seven entities as well. Spirit, in short, resides in its own centralizing sphere – the "*celum spiritus*" – with two spheres above it (those of first essence and intellect) and two below (those of nature and of the elements).[185]

Complicating the situation even further is a long comment on the word "matter" ("*materia*").[186] The author explains that matter must be divided into two sorts, spiritual and corporeal ("*spiritualis et corporalis*"), or, alternatively, simple and composite. Spiritual matter, according to the careful indications of the text, is the same as first matter and first form. It constitutes the "higher world" ("*mundus altus*"), an indicator which effectively demands to be read as equivalent to the "first sphere" – that is, the sphere of first matter and first form, the same as first essence – and which functions as a kind of underlying spiritual substance out of which all other spiritual, intellectual and maybe even animated objects are fashioned. Corporeal matter is compounded of the elements – or in some way "is" the elements – and can be found in all the composites scattered throughout the sub-lunar world, such as the animals, vegetative things and, presumably, hard bodies. In light of this additional commentary, it is tempting to conceive of the first sphere (of "essence") and the fifth (of the elements) not so much as authentic cosmic spheres but rather reservoirs of "material" out of which respectively the two spheres of intellect and spirit and the seventh stage of animal, vegetative and hard bodies are constituted. That, of course, leaves the sphere of nature, or the "nature of the heavens," in an ambiguous and awkward position. But there would appear to be nothing in this passage from *Picatrix*'s Book IV to eliminate the difficulty.

Of course, if the cosmological scheme was intended primarily to justify a *modus operandi* and not to be used as a technical instrument of investigation, what should concern us is how *Picatrix* expressly related its Neoplatonizing theory to the concrete recommendations for practice it would urge upon its reader. In this regard, in two short but pithy comments the author would seem most plainly to reveal his hand. The first arises toward the end of a description of the hierarchy slightly different from that presented earlier. What he says, almost predictably, is that those who want to take up the program of operations he is promoting should be aware that they will be asked to pass through the various stages of reality his models present, effectively rising to the top. In precise words: "You must know that he who intends to engage himself in these sciences is expected to follow this course" – which is to say, progress along the pathway through the successive stages the hierarchy has laid down.[187] It hardly needs to be said that what is stated here as prescription is easily converted – if intended mainly to justify behavior – into simply a rationale. The rationalizing, as opposed to truly prescriptive, aspect of the same ideological tack emerges even more evidently in a inspirational coda attached to the version of the hierarchy we have examined: "You who resolve to commit yourself to [the work promoted by] this book, pay heed to how you might [thereby] be enabled to raise your soul to the standing and wisdom of the blessed spirits."[188] No matter that necromancy be the means. The ultimate goal is to be regarded as a form of divine enlightenment and existential transformation.

Necromancy in *Picatrix*

What then about necromancy itself as a particular discipline to be studied and practiced? What about the nuts and bolts of the affairs, both cognitive and operational, to which *Picatrix* actually turns its attention? Early in Book I the text explains that a division must be introduced between necromancy's theoretical and its practical sides.[189] Theoretical necromancy comprised the body of knowledge, the aggregation of abstract scientific truths, upon which necromancy's works would be grounded. As the author hastened to add, the greater part of these truths had to do with the stars and planets. Drawn under this umbrella were the science dealing with the location of the fixed stars, that concerning the ways light rays were projected out from the stars onto the planets, and the science of what the text calls "celestial figures" ("*celestes figure*").[190] It will be remembered that the word "figure" served for William of Auvergne as the preferred way to refer to the images employed most obviously among the Solomonic arts, and it was the term by which the *Ars notoria* denoted the patterns on the page that the user of the art was supposed to gaze at while also delivering his *orationes*.[191] Here in *Picatrix* it would seem to designate an actual configuration in the heavens, as with the constellations, or a more abstract pattern intrinsically linked to a star, a group of stars, probably also a planet.[192] Because the author comments that all of this knowledge ultimately finds its practical relevance in directing the selection of hours and times in which to accomplish the eventually desired operations – one of the standard tasks of judicial astrology – presumably the science of the location of the planets was to be included in the mix as well.[193]

Alongside this almost entirely astronomical and astrological expertise we find mention of another sort of cognition, perhaps constituting a veritable science as well, about which *Picatrix* had much less to say but which apparently occupied a significant position in theoretical necromancy. This knowledge had to do with words. Indeed, words, our author seems to be suggesting, stood parallel to the figures mentioned just earlier, for from the words flowed a power ("*virtus*") comparable in importance for the art's eventual practical operation to that of the celestial figures.[194] It is hard not to regard these "words" as the components of *orationes* and incantations of the sort we have come upon already in the ceremonial arts examined so far.[195] Included under the compass of necromancy's theory must therefore have been a kind of science of relevant ceremonial addresses and incantations.[196]

As for practical necromancy, it came down – in the economical phrase offered in the text – principally to "the compounding of the three natures along with the power of an infusion from the fixed stars."[197] Unspoken here, of course, was the precise end in which the act of composition would result. Yet it had already been made clear in an immediately preceding passage that the mixing of the natures and drawing down of the celestial power constituted the instrumental operations necessary for fashioning an "image" with which to do necromancy's work. In other words, the practical side of necromancy involved the casting of a necromantic "image" founded from the material ingredients of appropriate substances, tuned to the correct proportionalities of the stars, and literally manufactured or minted at the right time – right, of course, according to the dictates of astrology.[198] It is reasonable to surmise that the "proportionalities" in question corresponded to the dimensions of the "celestial figures" already dealt with in necromancy's theoretical branch. And the three natures or ingredients that had to be mixed together almost certainly must be read as signifying the three broad categories of sub-lunar substances: animal, vegetable and mineral.[199] The point was that an object constituted in this way and molded to the prescribed configuration would take within itself an internally resident power derived directly from the stars.

Yet there were still further operations, the details of which would occupy an additional, if subordinate, aspect of practical necromancy.[200] For once the image had been fashioned, the power it had received from the stars needed to be reinforced. First of all, it had to be given what *Picatrix* calls "elemental heat" ("*calor elementaris*"), and that by the performance of proper fumigations.[201] They, and the heat they furnished, were necessary to "complete" the astral power thus far resident in the image with insufficient strength. A second heating was required as well, this time to supply what was called "natural heat" ("*calor naturalis*"). About this heat no more is said than that it served the purpose of rendering possible a "consumption" or "eating" ("*ad comedendum*"). Perhaps heating with a flame was intended, perhaps even the separate preparation of an edible sacrifice. Last but not least, the consummation of the process of reinforcement entailed the intervention of spirit. Of course this might be merely the spirit of the operator himself, although the cooperation of another agent from the spiritual world would surely have occurred to the mind of most contemporary readers.

For present purposes – and in fact for those of the book *Picatrix* as well – it is the practical side of necromancy that is of primary interest. According to our author, this practical science was itself subject to further subdivision into three main parts. Each could be characterized by the particular way in which it mediated between levels of the cosmic hierarchy. The first sort of practical necromancy was directed to operations transpiring exclusively among "spirits" – in exact words, "from spirit to spirit." Added by way of explanation is the comment that by means of such procedures, objects of differing essential nature are somehow rendered similar.[202] With no more to go on than these meager indications, it is possible only to surmise that the kind of necromancy the author had in mind worked by manipulating spirits, maybe resident only at the cosmological sphere of "*spiritus*," and perhaps just by means of incantations or *orationes*, conceivably by means of other ceremonials as well. The goal was possibly a real, more likely an apparent, transformation, whether of spirits alone or of some other more corporeal object is not clear. In any case, nothing that follows in *Picatrix* would seem to fall under this rubric. Prospective followers of necromancy of the first kind would have to seek guidance elsewhere.

Second in line came the practical science whose operations turned upon both spirit and body, somehow combining them instrumentally, but probably with spirit ultimately working an effect on body. In the passage under consideration now, this science is labeled the "composition of images" ("*ymaginum composicio*").[203] At other places in the same chapter it is called the "science of images" ("*sciencia ymaginum*") or alternatively the "*opus ymaginum*."[204] Both of the latter, of course, are denominations for a kind of wondrous or magical discipline we have encountered among preceding authors. By name alone, this second type of practical necromancy would appear to be just the sort of science or discipline fitting the general descriptions sketched out above. Images related

back to figures had seemed, after all, to constitute the identifying mark for practical necromancy in general terms. Moreover, *Picatrix* has an explanation for how
spirits were to be factored in. In the same book and chapter in which this second
of the practical sciences of necromancy is introduced, mention is made of a body
of knowledge familiar to the ancient Greek sages and to which they, too, gave
the designation "science of images."[205] Though at first blush the reference seems
to be to an art of illusion, the text very quickly comes to focus on the drawing
down of celestial spirits, presumably into the images from which the science
took its name. And here we also see the importance for this sort of discipline of
"astrology" or "astronomy." Everything leads to the conclusion that the "science
of images," ostensibly just one of three subdisciplines of practical necromancy,
occupies most of the ground staked out by our author for necromancy under any
guise. This practical art turns out in fact to be what most of *Picatrix* is about.

The third of the practical sciences of necromancy is identified outright as
alchemy – literally, the composition of things that alchemy makes possible
(*"composicio alchimie"*). In this final variety of the discipline the cosmological
connection to be effected is restricted to the bodily levels alone. As the text puts
it, the operations here are of "body in (perhaps equally: on) body."[206] We can, I
think, take this to mean that in this practice bodies are the only entities to serve
an instrumental role. From the comments the author makes, we can see that he
is well acquainted with alchemical traditions. He knows about the "elixir"; he
knows how one might explain the transformations the latter works on corporeal
substances; and he sees a definite parallel between the nature and function of the
"elixir" in this third of necromancy's practical forms and those of the "image" in
its second.[207] As if to concede that alchemy will have little role to play in the work
Picatrix itself, the author adds that he has discovered much about this third of his
sciences in a book entitled the *Book of Orders* (*"Liber de ordinacionibus"*).[208] Pingree
alerts us to the fact that the anonymous author of *Picatrix*'s Arabic instantiation,
the *Ghāyat al-hakīm*, wrote as well a work on alchemy, entitled *Rutbat al-hakīm* or
"Rank of the Sage."[209]

The science of images

Let us return then to the fact that *Picatrix* is ultimately a work about the science
of images. It is worth noting that beside the Neoplatonizing cosmological theory
examined cursorily earlier, there was another more technically explicit, but
equally naturalizing, explanation the author of *Picatrix* advanced for how the
sort of practical necromancy he was interested in might actually work. On several
occasions he put forth a set of functional principles at the level of what we might
think of as natural philosophy that would account for the science of images and
the way it brought powers from the heavens to act here below in the terrestrial
world. By way of a general summation of these principles, it is stated early on in

Book I that the powers of the images produced in the science in question and the effects they exercised on targeted objects in the terrestrial realm derived "from the celestial bodies" and were in fact determined by the motion of such bodies in their celestial regions.[210] Of course, the motions and the positions of these bodies at the precise moment the images were forged were the ones that had to be taken into account.[211] And *Picatrix*'s author believed that he could map out the natural mechanism whereby such bodies, by virtue of their motions, transmitted an influence over so great a distance to the potent image-objects the necromancers produced and manipulated down on earth.[212]

That naturalizing explanation need not concern us here. Indeed, even while it is being advanced, there remain the trappings of a process much less routinized or systematically transparent. On the one hand, we come upon repeated warnings to keep knowledge of the science secret, at least restricted to a very few, and to ensure that its operations are performed away from the light of day or the intrusion of inquiring eyes.[213] It was, after all, a science the author was prepared openly to grace with the volatile name of "necromancy."[214] Perhaps no less audacious, the text continually makes reference to it as a "science of magic" or "magical art."[215] Despite the negative connotations reaching back at least to the days of William of Auvergne, the operations to which the practical art is dedicated are unapologetically associated with the phrase "works of magic" ("*opera magica*").[216] At the end of Book III, in fact, the author speaks favorably of a regimen of training in the art designed with an eye ultimately to making the adept worthy of the title, *magister operum*, special target of vilification in William's writings.[217] This is, therefore, no ordinary part of natural philosophy.

When we turn, moreover, to the specifics of the science's contents and to its operations – which after all occupy the bulk of *Picatrix*'s pages – both Neoplatonizing theory and the technicalities of natural philosophy fast come to appear even more remote from the actualities of the business at hand. Early on in Book II the author presents with evident approval the opinion of an ancient sage that the science with which his book is principally concerned can be divided into three parts.[218] It is almost certain that the discipline he thereby means to be dividing is his "science of images," in strict terms the second of the practical arts falling under the rubric "necromancy." According to this further subdivision, one piece of the art in contention was to be labeled simply "magical science" ("*sciencia magica*"). It comprised a form of learning and practice prominent among what our author calls the "captive slaves of the Chaldeans," who were presumably also to be taken as its principal originators. A second piece consisted in what is here called the "science of the stars" ("*sciencia stellarum*"), and it involved, so the text proceeds, praying to these stars while at the same time performing fumigations, sacrifices, other incantations ("*orationes*") and acts of inscription ("*scripta*"), perhaps on images. The Greeks were particularly adept at this form of the art, which is identified in the text by means of the precise term "astrology" ("*astrologia*"). Third and finally came that part of the science given in this passage no specific label but described as operating by means of fumigations, appropriate incantations and words (*"dicta et scripta"*) in addition to adroit maneuvering of spirits according to their attraction to or repulsion from the spoken formulas. The Indians in particular, the author comments, have proven themselves skillful in this art and were maybe also its founders. It is probably unwise to attempt an unambiguous mapping of each of these three parts of the science of images onto the actual prescriptions and procedures supplied throughout the work. Still, an argument can be made that certain sections fall more under the rubric of one of the three than of the other two.

The first of the parts, labeled simply "magical science," is the hardest to pin down. Ostensibly, the kind of practical necromancy involved here originated among captive subjects of the Chaldeans in southern Mesopotamia. And we do indeed find two sections of the work drawing together materials designated as lifted from a presumably well known *Agriculture of the Chaldeans* (*"Agricultura Caldeorum," "De agricultura Caldea"*).[219] This *Agriculture* is in fact none other than the more correctly entitled *Nabataean Agriculture*, increasingly familiar among specialists on medieval magic.[220] We have, of course, already been alerted by Pingree to the fact that by "Chaldean slaves" the author of *Picatrix* actually meant to designate the Sābians of ancient Harrān.[221] We now see that he did not clearly distinguish between these latter and the Nabataeans from an earlier period in Arabia.

It is currently thought that the *Nabataean Agriculture* arose around the third or fourth century in Syriac from Nabataean roots, but in any case its text was disseminated throughout the Arab world after the ninth century in a translation into Arabic made at that time by the learned Ibn Wahshīyah.[222] This Arabic translation provided the ultimate source for the passages in *Picatrix*. Besides an occasional oration or incantation, most of what our work reports in these sections concerns the application of plant materials – a few times minerals – mixed and prepared in special ways and then used either ritually or as a salve or potion to achieve a specific, often marvelous aim. Examples include the preparation of a substance made from the ground dried berries of the bay-laurel, which, if given as a drink, causes the recipient immediately to be vexed by demons and labeled a demoniac, as well as the use of bay-laurel leaves, subjected to a brief ritual of being thrown in the air and caught, then stuffed behind one's ears, to ward off drunkenness or the hangover often following prolonged imbibing.[223] If this represents the first of the three kinds of the "science of images" it consumes comparatively little of our author's time and effort.

The other two sorts, engaging almost the entirety, I would suggest, of *Picatrix*'s central Books II and III and the first half of Book IV, constitute the author's real preoccupation. Both would appear to be closely connected to the learned and operative traditions stemming this time authentically from the Harrānian Sābians of the ninth and tenth centuries.[224] Precisely labeled "science of the stars" in the summary passage noted earlier, the second kind would seem of the two to be the most directly dependent on astrology and most narrowly focused on the making of images – true talismanic objects. It might be taken as representing the

type itself of "science of images." For this latter I believe we can turn to a definition of "image" offered by the author of *Picatrix* toward the beginning of Book
II. There he states that "an image is nothing other than a power of the celestial
bodies channeled into [one or more] corporeal subjects [here below]."[225] This
same power to produce an effect depends upon what the text sometimes calls a
"nature" embedded in the image-object itself but ultimately impelled into act by
the stars.[226] And the operation that results can be understood as the replacement
of one material form in the target by another, a real transformation of actualities
in the sub-lunar world.[227] To do it right, the operator must juggle several factors
all at once. They are, as laid out in a particularly incisive summary statement in
Book II, chapter 7, the similitude or image itself, linked by its conformity with
a celestial figure to the power of the stars, the actual metallic materials in which
the image will be embodied, and finally strict observance of the requirements of
time and place in which the image-object is to be cast.[228]

Picatrix goes to great lengths to provide the reader with the specifications
needed accommodate these factors in any particular operation. Chapter 10 of
Book II, for instance, could be extracted almost as a handbook laying out some
of the prescriptions a prospective operator would have to follow. In it are listed
for each of the seven planets the appropriate metals or precious and semipre-
cious stones from which an image-object referring back to that planet should be
composed. In addition is given the geometric figure corresponding to the planet
as well as a host of more representational "forms," both of which together can
be taken as providing the "figure" to which the fashioned image must conform.
Finally come the purposes or actions to which the properly fashioned image-object can be put if it has been constructed at the time of a designated astrological
conjunction or moment.[229] With this information in hand, one could begin to
put the practical science of images into effect.

An especially plain example of a concrete application of the science can be
found in a story the author relates in Book II.[230] According to this testimony,
the author had received a report from an expert in the science of images of an
opportunity the latter had had, while studying the science during a stay in Egypt,
to learn from a native of India well versed in the discipline. One day, when the
two of them were confronted with the cries of a person bitten by a venomous
scorpion, the Indian drew out of a pouch a number of image-objects fabricated
out of incense, one of which he said would heal the victim if given to him in a
potion. Putting the claim to the test, the expert took the indicated image and
dissolved it in a drink immediately administered to the sufferer of the bite. He
then watched as the cries abated and the pain disappeared. Before making the
potion, the expert had remarked that on the object the Indian had given him
was represented the form of a scorpion, so he asked just how it was that the
image had been constructed. In reply, the Indian produced a golden signet ring
on which was set a stone inscribed with the figure of a scorpion, explaining that
he had incised this seal at the astrological moment when the moon and the
constellation Scorpio were properly aligned. The author adds that the expert took

the information and followed exactly the prescriptions provided later to engrave his own seal, with which to impress images on bits of incense. The results were just as he had hoped. He was able to use the image-objects to astound onlookers with absolutely marvelous works.

The third of the parts of the science of images in general would appear to have been, if anything, even more wonderful, and more provocative, than this second. It is described as involving fumigations, incantations and the management or exploitation of spirits. And when we look to the contents of *Picatrix*, we do indeed find sections whose subject corresponds well to that description. At times spirits are introduced into a narrative in most other respects indistinguishable from descriptions of the second type of science of images examined just now. It is possible to write off this introduction of "spirits" as merely a figurative way of referring to a non-material power of enacting change, a power driven by the stars but channeled through the images. Yet as one proceeds further into the work, it becomes clear that more is at stake.

First we see unambiguous confirmation that in at least some instances the "spirits" involved, and whose powers must be in some way infused into or conjoined to the corporeal images employed in the operation, are truly spiritual beings. The text speaks explicitly of evoking the powers of the planetary spirits ("*potencie* or *vires spirituum planetarum*"), which can hardly be imagined as much different from the intelligences or angels moving the heavens introduced in an explanatory passage much later on.[231] Moreover it takes pains to clarify that joining these spirits to the images and involving them in the works of the science entail the literal descent of their powers from the heavens where the spirits reside directly to earth.[232] Mention of this descent then introduces the matter of fumigations.[233] Attention must be paid to ensuring that the fumigations arise from the burning of materials specifically suited to the nature of the respective planet.[234] Again, in an effort to provide his reader with a handy resume, the author devotes a whole chapter – Book IV, chapter 2 – to the ceremonials required for appeal to the powers of the moon at each of its twelve stages along the path of the zodiac, carefully specifying for every case the precise fumigation appropriate for a particular operation.[235]

By this point, the factors included in the workings of this science have expanded to include incantations – usually denominated by the term "*orationes*" – and, more than occasionally, sacrifice ("*sacrificia*") as well.[236] One example of a work of this sort, drawn ostensibly from a written source of great repute and unimpeachable fidelity to ancient tradition, goes so far as to characterize the activity as talking to one of the planets, in the process delivering to it a request or petition. The talk, moreover, is expected to follow a predetermined script. In the words of the passage, one must address the planet only by means of its own particular prayers and verbal formulas ("*eius oraciones*").[237] Moreover a short listing of the particulars of ceremonies performed with regard to each of the planets has, on every occasion, the petitioner addressing his request, formulated according to the precise words "I conjure you," not in these instances even to the planet itself but rather to an explicitly designated "angel" belonging to it.[238] As for sacrifice, an especially uninhibited passage in Book III explains how the sages, in doing the works of this science, made stipulated sacrifices in their mosques (*"in moschetis"*) or in their churches (*"in eorum ecclesiis"*), surely in either case a generic designation intended to cover for what we would consider temples. Such sacrifices – in this instance, of animals – varied according to the degree along the ecliptic on which the relevant constellation was at that moment to be found. Here, the authority for the practice is cited as the ancient Hermes, designated not this time in the Latinate "Mercurius," as we saw in William of Auvergne, but in accordance with the Greek with which the tradition of Hermes Trismegistus is most tightly bound.[239] We have hereby arrived at matters which, from many a Christian perspective, would surely be viewed with more than a disapproving eye.

Speculum astronomiae

The fourth and last of the texts to be taken as representative of a new, more substantive foray into the magical arts of the mid-thirteenth century is in nature quite different from the others. So far we have considered works expressly serving to educate the reader in magical operations. Our last composition devotes itself instead to apologetics. Largely defensive in approach, it attempts to convince the reader that much of what might appear as dangerous novelty in the controversial arts is in fact no less useful and benign than the teachings of any of the sciences traditionally accepted in the scholastic curriculum. Its focus falls exclusively on those disciplines bearing on the study of the stars and planets. Although it would appear that the work as originally published and circulated – almost certainly in the mid-1260s – was intentionally left untitled by its author, by the early fourteenth century at the latest it was being copied and attracting increasing attention under the name, *Speculum astronomiae*, or *Mirror of Astronomy*.[240]

As Agostino Paravicini Bagliani has observed, despite the initial anonymity of the work, at least as early as 1340 there emerge manuscript witnesses attributing the *Speculum* explicitly to Albert the Great.[241] Since then, it has been common to accept the piece as a legitimate part of Albert's oeuvre, though some doubt has always lingered about the accuracy of the attribution. Paola Zambelli attempted to end all debate on the matter with her manuscript study of 1992, *The Speculum Astronomiae and its Enigma*, in which she concluded that all signs pointed to Albert as indeed the work's true author. Even so, Zambelli conceded that the latter may have relied upon a few collaborators to help him in the composition.[242] Ironically, it seems that the case of authorship has now been closed for good with a final determination just opposite to what Zambelli proposed. Paravicini Bagliani has advanced what looks to be an unassailable argument – given the sum of the manuscript evidence we are likely to possess any time soon – that it was one of those "collaborators" Zambelli mentioned, the physician and astrologer Campanus of Novarra, who wrote the *Speculum* entirely on his own.[243]

According to Campanus – or as we more prudentially should probably say, the author of the *Speculum* – the writing of the work was prompted by a desire to reestablish the good name of the complete spectrum of scientific disciplines regarding the heavens, the heavenly bodies, and the latter's motions and configurations. Occasioning this desire were aspersions that scholars of repute were casting upon a significant number of works that he considered as having a respectable place among the sciences in question. It was easy to understand how these scholars might have been led to make the accusations they did. For there were still other works circulating at the same time yet propagating techniques for the most reprehensible of operations and arts, works whose subject should properly be recognized as sorcery or, in the author's exact words, "necromancy" (*necromantia*). To hide this ugly truth, these latter works often assumed for themselves the mantle of astronomy (*professio astronomiae*).[244] No surprise, then, that otherwise well intentioned readers might be made suspicious of any work of astronomy, assigning freely the labels "magical" and "dangerous."

To set the record straight, the *Speculum*'s author proposed producing a catalog of all the relevant Latin books he knew, briefly surveying their contents and assigning them either to the camp of licit learned discipline or to that of erroneous, irreligious and maybe even necromantic practice and belief. With this goal in mind the *Speculum* starts out by dividing the whole of astronomy – what has just been referred to earlier as the entire range of scientific disciplines regarding the heavens – into two essential parts. As the text lays down the claim: "There are two great and wise sciences, and both can be designated with the name of astronomy."[245] The task at hand was to establish the attributes of these two sciences and on that basis identify the specific scholarly texts falling under each. Those works of purported astral learning that remained could then be credibly consigned to the body of reprehensible literature that the aforementioned censors presumed to inveigh against.

With regard to the first of the two sorts of astronomy, there was no scholarly dispute about either contents or scientific validity. In the author's words, astronomy of this kind was devoted to describing with precision the figures and motions of the first heaven – presumably the *primum mobile* – and then of all the remaining heavens or spheres nested beneath it, from the sphere of the fixed stars through those of each of the planets.[246] It set itself as well to measuring the magnitude of the spheres, their distance from the earth and the size of the planets and the earth, along with, more significant still, accounting for the exact course of every one of the heavenly bodies. Finally, it took to explaining climate differentials around the world and each region's procession of seasons and cycle of longer or shorter days. Here then was "astronomical science" in a sense more or less analogous to how astronomy is viewed today. No surprise, therefore, that the *Speculum*'s author should anticipate scant controversy about its scholarly credentials. His survey of the constituent literature, proceeding with so renowned a text as Ptolemy's *Almagest* appearing chronologically in second place, included some of the most esteemed titles in the contemporary curriculum of scholastic natural science.[247] Not only was there no hint of untruth in any of them, but our author also dared to add that even the most suspicious of intellectual watch-dogs realized that not a word of their content conflicted with catholic faith.[248]

The same could not be said for the second of astronomy's two grand types. Here difficulties arose regarding not just legitimacy but also acceptability. And here is where the author of the *Speculum* directed the greater part of his attention and all of his argumentation. Astronomy in this second major sense comprised the science of "astral judgments" ("*scientia iudiciorum astrorum*"), meaning the discipline we today would grace with the title of astrology.[249] For our author, this branch of learning was just as valid as astronomy of the first sort.[250] If God had in his wisdom chosen to intervene in his creation at the subcelestial level by employing as instruments the "deaf and mute stars," why would he not have opted as well to grant humanity a science of the regularities according to which motions in the spheres produced corresponding motions in bodies here below?[251] Yet for many of our author's interlocutors the case was not so clear. We have seen the attacks delivered in the thirteenth century by Robert Grosseteste and the cautionary words of his contemporary, William of Auvergne. Despite the initial optimism, the apologetic agenda of the *Speculum*'s author left him therefore with considerable ground to cover.

The journey began in typical scholastic fashion with the drawing of distinctions. First of all, it was necessary to separate this second science of astronomy into two principal parts, one dealing with its theoretical principles and the other laying out the rules for its practice.[252] Within the practical section a further division was required into four sub-parts, each oriented toward a different parameter of the judgment-casting project.[253] First of the sub-parts addressed itself to "revolutions" ("*de revolutionibus*"), the overall rotations of the heavens, including conjunctions or eclipses of the planets. Judgments in this section of the science turned upon major events and catastrophes, as well as more prosaically what to expect from the weather.[254] The second sub-part had to do with nativities ("*de nativitatibus*"), judgments drawn from knowledge of the celestial configurations holding at the moment of an individual's birth. A whole regimen of nurturing and education, along with a schedule of expected life experiences, could be constructed on this basis.[255] Third came the part handling "interrogations" ("*de interrogationibus*"), drawing upon the positioning of the stars to determine the likely outcome of a proposed endeavor.[256] Last in line was the section devoted to the choice of a suitable time ("*de electionibus horarum laudibilium*").[257] One would turn to this portion of astrology to discover the most propitious moment for any particular action.

Having established judicial astrology's component parts, the author then progressed to the task of surveying the relevant literature. Chapters 6 through 10 of the *Speculum* review the titles of Latin works falling under each of the five sectors that had been identified. Together, they constituted a formidable array of renowned books and authors, highly touted within the learned circles of those most interested in the new sciences introduced from the Arab, Greek and Hebrew cultural world. Indeed, no less an authority than Ptolemy appeared again at the head of the list, this time with the *Quadripartitum* presented first among the works having to do with theoretical foundations.[258] Yet now, unlike the case with astronomy's first major part, our author recognized that more would be required to clear the science of astral judgment's name. It was the practice-oriented side of the science that occasioned the most alarm. And so it was to the four sub-parts of applied astrology that the *Speculum*'s author returned in chapters 12 through 15, carefully laying out a reasoned defense for why they should not be taken as inimical to Christian doctrine.

The fundamental issue in these chapters remains the same from beginning to end. Behind all the attacks on the suspect science stood the conviction among its detractors that, no matter what the advice or prediction sought or the procedure involved, adherence to the principles of astrology demanded of its practitioners acceptance of the necessity of the events to which its judgments were held to apply. And that necessity could not, in the eyes of astrology's opponents, but in most cases eliminate the possibility of freedom of the will. The objection was thus universal. The strategy of the *Speculum*'s author was, however, to offer a varied response, tailoring his argument to the specifics of the judgments of each of the four sub-fields of practical astrology in turn.

Sometimes, as with that part of the sub-division addressed to heavenly "revolutions" bearing on changes in the weather, the *Speculum*'s answer was simply to concede necessity while denying any injury to legitimate claims for human freedom to act without predetermination. The weather, so the counter-argument ran, was of course entirely determined by the motions of the heavens, and it would be foolish for any human being so much as to wish to intervene. God himself had established the natural laws by which the motions of the heavens were tied to motions of the atmosphere here in the lower world.[259] The same reasoning applied to the sub-division of revolution astrology concerning planetary conjunctions or eclipses. Though here the astrologer's predictions turned on sometimes terrifying phenomena, such as earthquakes or war and peace, again the predicted event itself was necessary, assuming that the procedures of the science had been properly deployed. Once more, no human should presume it an infringement on his own free will that he did not possess the power to stand in the way.[260]

In other instances, the *Speculum* author's response was not so fully to acquiesce in the necessity of events. The sub-discipline concerning "nativities," upon which the art of horoscopy depended, presented by the author's own admission the thorniest problem for its defenders. If one could predict the course of an individual's life from knowledge of the moment of birth, then what freedom remained to the person in question? Here, our author's answer was that in lieu of resigning oneself to the fact, one could take steps, for instance, to mitigate the ills of an impending misfortune.[261] The matter of a person's moral attributes – we might say personality traits – presented still greater theoretical difficulty. But here, too, the *Speculum* suggests, it was enough to say that the heavenly configuration at birth established merely a behavioral aptitude, against which a resolute will always had the option to rebel.

The *Speculum* on the science of images

It might thus seem that the author of the *Speculum* had achieved his goal: defending astrology from its detractors in the learned circles of his day. Yet there is reason to believe, as most modern scholars of the *Speculum* agree, that we have not as yet penetrated to the heart of the matter for which the work was composed. The real agenda, so the argument runs, touched on an issue of even greater delicacy than any broached thus far. It was, in fact, this delicacy – or danger – that prompted the author, for all his temerity in addressing the issue in public, to choose in the end to remain anonymous. In chapter 4, just at the point of finishing up his introduction of the division of the science of judicial astronomy into its parts, the author adds almost in passing that subsumed under the fourth sub-section, that having to do with choosing the appropriate time to act ("*de electionibus horarum lauda-bilium*"), was to be found a further sub-division distinct enough to stand alone under its own name: the "science of images." Lifting words from a work to which he would later devote considerable attention, he praises this last of his sciences as the very culmination of all astronomical learning ("*sublimitas astronomiae*").[262] Only the lines that follow this tribute alert us to the more troublesome issue he actually has in mind. For as the *Speculum* author continues, it was by virtue of a "science of images" that a host of compositions, all constituting "accursed books of necromancy," had managed to insinuate themselves into the world of astronomical lore. The intention of their promoters was plainly to legitimize such works with the gloss of scientific respectability.[263] The result, the *Speculum* author suggests, was instead to taint the worthy disciplines and the works in which they were expounded.

For the moment nothing more is said of either the science of images or its necromantic simulators. Yet after having surveyed the Latin literature conveying judicial astronomy's theoretical and practical parts, the *Speculum* returns in chapter 11 – which ends up being the longest of the whole work – to that jewel of the art of elections praised earlier as astronomy's highest achievement. Instead of taking up the science's glories right away, however, the chapter begins by focusing on the more nefarious agenda of the works and practices accused of hiding in its shadow. The author explains that fabricated objects of the sort that the authentic science of images applied itself to belonged broadly speaking to a general domain of image-objects divisible into three different sorts, distinguished according to the differing modes by which they were produced.[264] Two of those sorts – the two to which chapter 11 turns first of all – consisted of image-objects to be hated and feared. They represented the sort of object concocted and manipulated in the praiseworthy science of images' false and necromantic cousins. Among these two sorts of condemnable images, moreover, one was worse than the other. In the words of the *Speculum*, the more odious of the confected objects should be labeled as outright "abominable," presumably offensive to Christian faith to the greatest imaginable degree. The manufacture of such images depended on "suffumigation and invocation" (*suffumigatio et invocatio*).[265] Second, and only slightly less offensive but still unacceptable by Christian norms, came a class of image-objects the *Speculum* designated as "detestable." Here, the production of the images required the inscription of characters (*inscriptio characterum*), which were in turn linked to the "exorcism" (*exorcizatio*) – possibly little different from the "invocation" associated with the "abominable" sort of image – of particular names.[266]

There follows in the *Speculum*'s text – just as with the preceding, legitimate sub-fields of judicial astronomy – a quick examination of all the works in Latin laying out the art of image-making with regard to either of the two condemnable sorts. Among those involved with the first kind a prominent place is occupied by texts inscribed under the name of Hermes, while among those connected to the second, more than half are explicitly attributed to Solomon.[267] That general distinction has led David Pingree to suggest classifying the two more precisely as representative, on the one hand, of Hermetic image-magic, and on the other, of Solomonic.[268] By "Hermetic" magic in this case Pingree does not mean the Hermeticism of late Antiquity but rather the subsequent tradition derivative of the literature produced by the so-called Sābians of Harrān, the classic examples of which were dedicated preeminently to the production of talismans imbued with the power of planetary spirits.[269]

Finally, having laid out the two sorts of offensive images and provided a bibliography of two sets of works advocating recourse to each, the author of the *Speculum* gets to the "science of images" as he imagines it ought to be practiced and to which he feels great honor is due. Weill-Parot has argued that the whole of the *Speculum* was composed just to establish that there was such a science of images, free of the corruptions the enemies of all astral magic and most astrology decried with such vehemence and itself a legitimate object of study and practical application.[270] In contrast to the images of the abominable and detestable sort, which the *Speculum* at one point commingles under the single rubric of "necromantic images" ("*imagines necromanticae*"), the images implicated in the science whose praises our author wants to sing should technically be characterized as "astronomical" ("*imagines astronomicae*").[271] By that, the author meant to indicate, as he subsequently explained in no uncertain terms, that the images whose fabrication he advocated relied on no fumigations and invocations, no exorcisms and inscription of suspect characters, all of which suggested supplication of living spirits or reliance on their intervention. Instead, the power of these favored images arose solely from figures in the heavens (*figurae caelestes*) – that is, specific constellations and positions of the stars and planets – brought down to earth at astrologically propitious moments and funneled into an image-object cast or confected at that precise instant.[272]

When it came to listing the Latin works transmitting this science, only two made the grade, among which the utility and perhaps even legitimacy of one stood in some doubt. Alone worthy of full endorsement as an example of what could be found in Latin regarding the praiseworthy science of images – in the lexicon of the *Speculum*, that is, the science of *astronomical* images – was the *Liber de imaginibus* of Thābit ibn Qurra. A second possibility might have been found in the *Opus imaginum* attributed to Ptolemy himself. Yet our author regarded this latter as so devoid of content as to be practically useless.[273] In short, there is but one work that we can take as solid witness to what the *Speculum* author thought would pass under the rubric of acceptable image-science. From this composition our author had in fact lifted the assertion about the "culmination of astronomical learning" with which he had buttressed his initial introduction of the science of images.[274] Whether or not the *De imaginibus* represents the Latin translation of a work actually written by the author to whom it was ascribed – there is no proof that the attribution to Thābit ibn Qurra is historically sound – no doubt exits that its origins reach back directly to the Harrānian traditions of talismanic magic in which Thābit ibn Qurra played so formative a role. These are the very same traditions, moreover, represented in many of the titles listed in the *Speculum*'s survey of works associated with the science of "abominable" images, traditions tributary to no less an example of self-styled necromantic literature of the thirteenth-century than *Picatrix* itself.[275] Odd candidate, therefore, for a work of image-science free of objectionable recourse to the powers of spirits or demons.

By Nicholas Weill-Parot's reckoning, the oddness of the fact is inescapable, and inescapable as well the conclusion that the *Speculum*'s author was engaged in a practically impossible task. He was attracted to the science of images being touted in texts circulating in his day, apparently believed that both the intellectual and operational claims of some of these texts were authentic and perhaps had himself tried out some of their prescriptions, and above all wanted, in Weill-Parot's words, to "leave open a possibility" for this science – a possibility, that is, of its being regarded as legitimate in authoritative circles. The problem was that none of the texts of image-science with which he was familiar could actually escape the charge of relying at some point on the intervention of spiritual beings. Whether these latter were characterized exclusively as celestial or planetary, or conceded at times as having a more demonic pedigree, in no case would recourse to them have been acceptable in the eyes of a purist of Christian orthodoxy. Our author was left, therefore, to create his own category of "science of image" purified of any association with spirits, dependent solely on an impersonal "virtue" found in the figures of the planets and the stars, but in fact represented by nothing in the astrological literature of his day.[276] It was, as Weill-Parot remarks, the job of an apologist.[277] Whether the apology was intended to mask a more spirit-involved reality that our author recognized and tacitly embraced or whether he honestly had hopes that a science of images meeting his specifications was in the process of being devised, is a question we cannot answer. Weill-Parot leans toward thinking that in any case such a science, free of all connections to the invocation of spirits, never came to be.[278]

It may then not be ironic when the author of the *Speculum* takes the opportunity in his very last chapter to abandon his focus on astrology and comment on genres of learning long associated in literate circles with magic pure and simple. Probably not accidental is the fact that of the six specific types of science or art that the author here surveys, five were listed by Hugh of St. Victor under his single category of divination (*mantice*).[279] First among the six stands necromancy, which presumably covers, in addition to the two sorts of reprehensible science of images the *Speculum* had attempted to separate from that devoted to *imagines astronomicae*, a host of other even more overtly sacrilegious practices. For all their disrepute, our author here insists that while writings on such matters should be set aside, it would be unwise physically to destroy them. Occasions might soon arise, he cryptically adds, when recourse might profitably be had even to them.[280] The remaining five genres begin with Hugh's other four in precisely the same order: geomancy, hydromancy, aeromancy and pyromancy, with the addition at the end of chiromancy or palmistry.[281] Again our author reveals his purpose to be rescuing as much from them as possible from the obloquy of anti-Christian disrepute. Hydromancy and pyromancy might sometimes serve as invitations to idolatrous behavior. But geomancy is singled out as worthy of considerable admiration, and even aeromancy and chiromancy are undeserving of blame. All in all, a strange and surprisingly gratuitous conclusion. Little wonder that the *Speculum* succeeded only in further alarming those already worried by the direction learned magic had been taking since the thirteenth century began. In the name of establishing the credentials of a sometimes maligned part of the science of the stars, it might well be taken as the leading edge of a yet another campaign to open the doors to magical practices of the most appalling sort.

Conclusion

All in all, therefore, we have examined works of scholarly literature from the thirteenth to the very early fourteenth century that represent an imposing corpus dealing with actually practicable magic. And we must remember that these are surely only a sample, writings that by good fortune, as well as by enough notoriety in their own day to have been copied in numbers sufficient to survive, have come down to us today. Some promote a magic that is associated with concrete forces embedded in the heart of nature, as with the *Speculum astronomiae*. Others – in fact the majority – either reserve a small place to manipulation of or appeal to actual spirits, or as with the *Liber iuratus*, seem almost entirely devoted to such. Two – *Picatrix* and the *Speculum* – concern that magical art that was taking great strides in the late thirteenth century, the science of images.

The point to be made is that all this literary activity stands as sign of a major advance over the situation in learned Latin circles even so recently as the late twelfth century. Magic need not now be just talked about. It could be studied and even practiced. Moreover, we have reason to believe that the number of its promoters as well as practitioners was growing, especially in the rarefied atmosphere of the university or the courts of prominent princes. No surprise then that in some theological milieus there was soon to be a reaction.

4

Science, Magic and the Demonic, 1200–1400: The Reaction

The previous chapter chronicled the accumulation over the thirteenth century in the Latin west of a body of scholarly works promoting and setting forth the practical details of learned magic, including that of a plainly ceremonial sort and sometimes demonic complexion. Already by the middle of the century the combined weight of such texts had reached a level sufficient to trigger a response. And that response entailed a shift in the balance of scholarly opinion, especially in theological circles, in the direction of resolute opposition to anything magical. It was a turn that would result in the emergence over the next few centuries of a campaign by authorities, both clerical and lay, to exterminate as much of magical practice as was possible and to destroy the textual substratum that continued to nourish it among the literate elite. Along the way would be constructed an understanding of magic that characterized it as always either illusory or perversely deceptive, almost invariably evil, and practically without exception dependent on the agency of demons. This theoretical construct would then establish itself as dominant among the educated and hence normative for all of society, or at least so from the perspective of the bulk of established officialdom.

In this chapter we shall examine the process by which such a momentous transformation occurred. We begin with a thinker, Thomas Aquinas, who by the clarity of his words and the extent of his influence can stand for the intellectual changes in the resolutely anti-magical direction. Once Aquinas's position has been made clear, we then turn to a contemporary of his, Roger Bacon, for an understanding of how those more receptive to magical currents tried to counter the Thomistic attack. Their efforts ultimately failed, and the rest of the chapter tells the story of how a repressive ideological and juridical apparatus was set up among powerful ecclesiastics to go about the business of eradicating learned magic. First, there will be a theoretical aside, drawing on the work of anthropologist Marcel Mauss to sharpen the distinction between magic and either science or religion according to the Frazerian or Malinowskian modes. Then attention shifts to efforts over the early fourteenth century, primarily orchestrated by a series of activist popes, to strengthen the legal case against learned magic. The chapter ends with a look at a pair of inquisitorial handbooks composed in the remainder of the fourteenth century that established the arguments by which the magic that had come of age among scholars in the thirteenth century would be prosecuted at court.

Thomas Aquinas

We begin to see the signs of an overwhelmingly negative conceptualization of the "magical" when we look to the literature of scholastic thinkers from as early as four decades before the turn of the thirteenth to the fourteenth century. The thinker with whom it has habitually been associated in recent scholarship was the theologian and preeminent Dominican master of his day, Thomas Aquinas.[1] Thomas's first extensive examination of magic appears in a work he started composing after he left his chair in the school of theology at Paris in 1259 but surely had completed by the middle of the 1260s, the *Summa contra gentiles*, or *Summa against the Gentiles*.[2] In this self-consciously magisterial composition, Thomas approached the subject of magic by way of considering miracles and the miraculous. From the outset, he made it clear that only God could perform a true miracle, an occurrence fundamentally beyond the ordained workings of things in the created world and thus "supernatural" in the strictest sense of the word.[3] Yet since the cause of many phenomena was unknown to at least a portion of humanity, a much larger set of happenings offered an occasion for wonder and could be described as wonderful, if not actually miraculous. The word Thomas used to describe such an unknown cause was "hidden," or in a form closer to the original Latin, "occult."[4]

Among the wonderful happenings a person might confront in this world beneath the status of miracle, Thomas plainly recognized a category dependent on a power belonging to a natural object, yet a power not understood by most people.[5] These were the sort of operations we have seen introduced before by William of Auvergne as falling under the rubric of his "natural magic," made possible by "occult" but perfectly natural powers (*virtutes occultae*) that some special entities possessed.[6] Two examples referred to by Thomas in the *Summa* were the magnet and a small fish – he was thinking of the torpedo or electric ray – credited with the power of stopping a sailing ship in mid-course.[7] For William of Auvergne, an even more stunning instance had been the spontaneous genera-tion of primitive animals such as worms or lice in decaying materials, and that case, too, was brought forth by Thomas at this spot in his *Summa*.[8] As Thomas explained, spontaneous generation of primitive animals could be attributed to the natural causal powers that the heavens brought to bear on every single case of generation in the terrestrial world. The occurrence could be explained by the rule that less-than-perfect operations, such as the generation of primitive beings, could be initiated in the natural world by the intervention of general or universal causes working solely on their own, in this case without the seed (*semen*) required for the generation of higher animals.[9]

Thomas was indeed interested in probing the causal mechanisms among the whole gamut of wonders below the rank of miracle. From spontaneous generation he moved to considering whether incorporeal beings – spiritual substances such as angels or demons – could also bring about wondrous operations. He agreed that they could, though not by immediately, and expressly as immaterial substances, causing an effect in the corporeal world that we inhabit. Good Aristotelian that he was, Thomas insisted that since change was a species of motion, all change in the material world had ultimately to be traced back to the motion of bodies – that is, back to local motion. Thus, if an immaterial substance like an angel or a demon were to produce an effect here on earth, it would have to do so by acting through the mediation of some bodily object locally moved.[10] A case in point would have been the movement of the human body. The soul, a totally immaterial substance, by its will directly caused its inhabited body, or one of that body's parts, to move. By manipulating moving bodies in the appropriate way, spiritual substances – even separate substances such as angels or demons – could thereby generate any effect naturally producible in the world here below.[11] Thomas might on this occasion have pointed out, as William of Auvergne explicitly had done several decades before, that were an immaterial substance to move a body that itself possessed a hidden or occult power, the resultant effect might appear to bystanders even more wonderful than if one of their embodied human companions had done the same.[12] We can be sure that the idea had at least once occurred to him. In a letter to a knight known by the title, "Concerning the Occult Workings of Nature," written by Thomas between the years 1269 and 1272, he took up the cause of explaining just the sort of operation referred to earlier as typified by the attraction of iron to a magnet.[13] And in that work he specifically considered how superior agents, such as immaterial substances, might with hidden operations move bodies here below to wonderful effect.[14] He even introduced two further examples of occult forces in operation in addition to the magnet: gold, which had the power of lifting the spirits, and sapphire, which worked to stanch the flow of blood.[15]

Yet Thomas wanted to advance beyond speculation simply about interventions in causality here below by separate substances. His attention was still more dramatically engaged by the suggestion that the celestial bodies might operate on earth directly and without the intermediary of local motion typical in the normal generation of plants and animals – in this case, that is, presumably without reliance on the motion either of the stars and planets themselves or of further corporeal intermediaries moving below the lunar sphere. And here is where "magic" for the first time explicitly makes its appearance in the text. As Thomas introduced the subject in his own words: "There have been some who say that the wondrous works of this sort that are accomplished by the magical arts are not brought about by spiritual substances but rather [directly] from a power [residing in] the celestial bodies."[16] To make full sense of Thomas's response to this introduction of magic into his investigation, it is necessary to look further than the *Summa contra gentiles*.

Magic according to Thomas's *Summa theologiae*

Let us therefore turn our sights for a while to Thomas's second extended treatment of the subject of magic. This second examination comes in the Second Section of the Second Part of Thomas's largest work, the *Summa theologiae* – in a piece of the work, that is, composed in Paris with remarkable speed in the interval after 1270 but before Thomas had stepped down from his second regency in theology there in the spring of 1272.[17] In fact, the text in the *Summa theologiae* can be taken as a virtual treatise on magic, its component parts, and on why it should be rejected wholesale as irredeemably evil.

Thomas's discussion begins with general consideration of superstition, the broad category under which "magic" had fallen in the taxonomy Augustine advanced so many centuries before.[18] By Thomas's reckoning, "superstition" ("*superstitio*") constituted the error of excess in religious practice, or as Thomas said, "exceeding the proper bounds of the divine cult."[19] And this excess was manifested by practicing the cult of the divinity either on behalf of a being or object to which it was not really due or in a manner in which it was not to be done.[20] From which it followed that superstition could be divided into two fundamentally different types (*genera*). On the one hand, there was superstition consisting in an attempt to worship the true God but in an unseemly manner. On the other, there was superstition that amounted to offering worship to something that didn't deserve it – in short, not to God but to a creature.[21]

Our interest falls entirely on superstition's second kind: rendering worship where it was not due. Here alone, according to Thomas, was where magic entered. Presuming to draw on Augustine, Thomas recognized three species or types of superstition of this sort.[22] The way he put it, the worship of God could be performed for three quite distinct purposes.[23] When these purposes were perverted by engaging in the worship with an eye to honoring other than the true God, there resulted the three different types of anti-religion or superstition. First and foremost, worshipping God was done with the aim of displaying reverence to him. When the worship was rendered to something other than God, the reverence due God then fell to this other, improper object. The whole could be summed up in a single word, "idolatry."[24] Second, God could be worshipped for the sake of receiving instruction from him. When something other than God was worshipped or petitioned for this purpose, the very act was tainted and the knowledge rendered odious or useless. Superstition of this second type was "divinitive" and constituted the sin of divination. Finally, worship could be performed just for the way it ordered human acts, or rituals, according to rules or norms instituted by God. Such ritual actions, when undertaken while something other than God was being worshipped, amounted to a third type of superstition, which Thomas designated by his own name of the "superstition of observances" or practices. The phrase itself should immediately suggest magic of a ceremonial sort.

As should already be clear, Thomas's second and third sub-types factor most prominently in his investigation of magic and magical operations. Divination, the second sub-type, had to do primarily with the precognition of events that would happen in the future, though strictly speaking there were forms of the practice, such as those directed to the discovery of stolen goods, that bore on past or present happenings.[25] As Thomas conceded, there was nothing wrong with wanting to know what the future would bring nor with actually possessing such knowledge. Knowing the future because one had, by means of human observation and reasoning alone, been able to predict an event that would necessarily come to be from causes already in place, or because via divine revelation one had been allowed to see the course of future contingencies, was no sin.[26] Divination came into play only when the human subject aimed for a knowledge of matters of fact that God had not vouchsafed. In such a case it was, as Thomas put it, as if the person had tried to fabricate the divine gift of knowledge on his or her own.[27]

Of course, we already know that divination as a kind of superstition involved giving divine honors to something other than the true divinity. We should not be surprised therefore to discover that it invariably brought into play those irrepressible counterfeiters of real divinity, evil incorporeal spirits, or more precisely demons. As Thomas said in no uncertain words: "All divination arises from the workings of demons."[28] Demons, after all, not only had the motive for thus implicating human souls in sin but also could at times provide the knowledge the diviners were seeking.[29] The reason why the demonic involvement constituted actual worship, as required by superstition's definition, had already been supplied by Augustine. Time and again quoting the famous assertion from *De doctrina christiana*, Thomas noted that divination worked just because the diviner had engaged with demons in a solemn pact, either expressly or tacitly entered into in return for service due.[30]

As for the substance of divinatory procedure, Thomas admitted that despite the universal reliance on demons, it remained on its surface extraordinarily complicated and varied. At the most general level, divination was to be distributed under three principal headings or kinds (again, "*genera*"). The primary division fell between divinatory types where demonic aid was expressly invoked and those where such assistance was surreptitiously ("*occulte*") insinuated without evident petition on the part of the diviners.[31] In the former case, divination was associated with the magical practices – so Thomas asserted – of necromancers ("*nigromantici*"). Where the assistance of demons was not explicitly petitioned, a further subdivision had to be introduced. First came the kind of divination in which the diviner looked to the disposition or motions of particular objects in the world around him to reveal the future course of events. Within this kind were included all those forms of divining associated in the ancient world with the soothsayers, the "augurs" ("*augures*") as they were known in the days of Rome. Second place fell to divination where the diviner's attention was focused on the outcome of actions or manipulations undertaken by the diviner himself for the express purpose of revealing hidden knowledge. By Thomas's taxonomy, all these last forms of divining could be collected under the single rubric of "lots" ("*sortes*").

Thomas even took care to list the various sorts of divination that were to be brought together within each kind. Beginning with the sort of divination where diviners explicitly called upon demons to aid them in their quest, Thomas divided the genus according to the precise methods the demons used to reveal the knowledge they had to convey. If they employed apparitions ("*praestigiosae apparitiones*"), the divination was called that of "illusion" ("*praestigium*"); if they communicated through dreams, it was "divination by dreams" ("*divinatio somniorum*"); and when they delivered their message by having the dead appear and speak their words for them, the type of divination was "necromancy" ("*nigromantia*") – now, as Thomas took pains to show, in its strict meaning from the original Greek.[32] Demons also sometimes spoke through the mouth of living humans, in which case the type was that relegated to the oracles in the ancient world, whose equivalents at other times or places could be designated by the term "pythons" ("*pythones*").[33] Finally, there came divination characterized by looking for signs of the message in inanimate objects. Here Thomas reproduced the last four of Hugh of St. Victor's five divinatory arts: geomancy ("*geomantia*"), hydromancy ("*hydromantia*"), aeromancy ("*aeromantia*") and pyromancy ("*pyromantia*"), adding as a fifth the ancient practice of examining the viscera of sacrificed animals, in English "haruspicy," in Thomas's Latin "*aruspicium.*"[34]

Proceeding to the first kind of divination in which diviners did not expressly invoke demonic aid, but where they simply examined the disposition of things situated around them, Thomas again divided the genus with regard to the different types of divinatory vehicle. Pride of place belonged to gazing at the stars, the divinatory practice of the astrologers ("*astrologi*"). Thomas also called then "*geneatici*," picking up again on Hugh, this time as echoing Augustine, but corrupting their original term.[35] If the diviner turned instead to the movements or calls of animals, the technical name for the form of divination was "augury" ("*augurium*").[36] Divination dependent on prognostication from the spoken word, when the speaker had no idea of predicting the future, was the type having to do with omens, which Thomas plainly tied to the Roman tradition. To round things off there was divination dependent on the lines and figures visible on certain bodies – particularly bodily parts. Thomas mentioned here palmistry ("*chiromantia*") and prognostication from an animal bone, or "*spatulimantia.*"[37]

Which left the second kind of divination in which demonic assistance was not explicitly called for, and where the evidence consisted in the outcome of actions taken by the diviner. In this case, Thomas did not descend to separate species but merely listed specific instances.[38] Among his examples was a second divinatory art named "geomancy" ("*geomantia*"), which he identified as involving the sketching of points, and which we know to be a practice familiar at least among the learned in the thirteenth century.[39] Others involved operations such as drawing from among scraps of paper or parchment (*"cedulae"*) or drawing straws and throwing dice.

Having paid so much attention to divination, Thomas finally turned to his third sub-type of superstition as rendering worship where it was not due, the "superstition of observances." Perhaps because this sort of practice, with its rituals and ceremonial behavior, so plainly smacked of idolatry, he thought it demanded a less probing analysis. In any case, he made no attempt on this score to sketch out a taxonomy of practices. Instead, he merely commented on a few specific types. First on his list stood the *ars notoria*, which we have noted was already on its way to becoming arguably the most widespread of all the forms of ceremonial magic. Apparently well informed on the details of the art, Thomas characterized it as performed by way of the inspection of peculiar figures (*"inspectio quarundam figurarum"*) and the utterance of certain unintelligible words (*"prolatio quorundam ignotorum verborum"*).[40] To his eyes, such ministrations themselves betrayed the illicit nature of the whole ceremonial. Reliant upon evident signs or signifiers, the prescriptions of the *ars notoria* most certainly constituted communications to unseen demonic forces, from whom its practitioners aspired to receive the gift of knowledge of the science they were seeking. Besides being demonic, the whole procedure was a hoax, utterly inefficacious and performed in vain.[41] But there were also numerous observances that verged on ceremonial and were designed to affect the human body, most often to cure illness or strengthen health. Undoubtedly, a majority in Thomas's day held such practices to be efficacious, thus surely not superstitious, much less illicit, and to a degree he was willing to agree. So long as the procedures drew upon natural processes of cause and effect, they were perfectly acceptable.[42] In addition, there was the practice of writing words (*"divina verba"*) or scriptures on a scrap of parchment and hanging them around the neck. In such cases, two circumstances had to be considered: what the words said and whether or not they contained a character or nonverbal sign (*"aliqui characteres scripti"*). If the words were manifestly religious and Christian, and the sign the mark of the cross, then one should be prepared to accept such practices as commendable and quite likely to succeed. If not, they should be taken as nefarious attempts to invoke demonic aid.[43]

More important for us is the fact that in this context Thomas was led to consider issues of particular significance for his whole attitude toward magic. Regarding ritual observances sometimes used for medicinal purposes, Thomas indicated that among them suspicion fell with special urgency upon the use of characters and the resorting to names.[44] As we have seen, signs of any sort were potentially alarming, since they implied communication, and if not with God then perhaps with unsavory spirits. And having introduced signs, Thomas was immediately led to consider another, related practice. His occasion for turning to this matter was an objection to his own position set at the beginning of article 2, question 96, of the part of the *Summa theologiae* we have been examining. According to the objection, just as natural bodies were subject to the influence of the planets and stars at the moment of their generation, so artificial bodies ("*corpora artificialia*") – artifacts, we might say, produced by an artisan – drew upon influences from the heavens passed along to them at the time of their fabrication. Moreover, since some natural bodies received special and occult powers ("*virtutes occultae*") in the instant of their generation, so some of these artificial objects also took on occult powers when they were made. Those who knew how to effect the artificial constructions could then use the artifacts to perform operations, sometimes to wondrous effect. Surely, so the objection ran, there was nothing superstitious or illicit about their acts.[45]

Thomas rejected the argument entirely. Instead, he rejoined, when such artificial objects were constructed, no power passed to them from the planets and stars. On the contrary, the objects acted as signs or indices to demons, who flocked to attend to them in order to work the wonders that their human fabricators claimed to perform by virtue of a celestially induced capability. These were, in short, magical objects, and their makers magicians.[46] They were worthy of the same condemnation that all other such superstitious confections and their operators deserved. Especially significant, however, is the term that Thomas used to describe these artifacts. He said that the fabricators of such wonder-working objects called them by the name of "astronomical images" ("*imagines astronomicae*").[47] As Weill-Parot has pointed out, it is almost certain that Thomas took this phrase directly from the *Speculum astronomiae*.[48] What is important is that the issue Thomas was addressing here in his *Summa theologiae* was the very one he was attending to in the passage of the *Summa contra gentiles* under consideration when our discussion of that work broke off above. In both cases, Thomas was focusing attention on magical objects whose powers were said to descend directly from the stars and planets. With the help of the *Speculum astronomiae* he now in the *Summa theologiae* had the terminology he needed to specify precisely what sort of object – or talisman – he was concerned with.

A return to the *Summa contra gentiles*

I believe that in the *Summa contra gentiles* Thomas was from the very beginning of his examination of miracles working his way precisely to this sort of magical object. Consideration of it permitted him to make an argument designed to serve as his primary evaluation of magic in general. For after mentioning, in *Contra gentiles*, the claim of some of his contemporaries that the objects they fabricated worked "from a power [residing in] the celestial bodies," he launched into a protracted series of arguments, intended expressly to show not only how this was impossible but also precisely what it was about most of what Thomas would consider ceremonial magic that made it intolerable to him.[49] Yet while the *Summa contra gentiles* lays out the only complete accounting Thomas was ever to give of his attitude toward causality in magic, especially ceremonial, he had not quite seized his target with precision at the time of that work's composition.

Immediately upon introducing the notion of magic working "from a power in the celestial bodies," Thomas turned to the identifying characteristics of the art he had in mind. Its practitioners began by determining the exact position of the stars. Then they applied certain herbs and other materials in order to prepare a substrate to be made into an object receptive of the influence of the heavens.[50] As we know from later in this same chapter, the object – which Thomas at that moment named a "statue" – received in the process a figure ("*figura*") – that is, a shape which converted the matter into a fitting vessel for the forces that would descend from above.[51] We have, of course, seen much the same before. From choosing the proper celestial moment, through applying herbal aids and often fumigations, to molding an object at the right moment into a talisman with a predetermined figure, all this was to be found in the "science of images" promoted by texts such as *Picatrix* and vaguely known already to William of Auvergne.[52] The problem is that when Thomas then proceeded with his arguments about how such magical operations were actually caused, his words seem to imply less a single magical art than two different varieties. Sometimes in this passage he appears to be speaking of the sort of fashioning of animated statues that William called "*dei factitii*" and which a scholar of Thomas's day would have been familiar with from Hermetic treatises such as the *Asclepius*.[53] Yet at other times Thomas talked as if he was concerned more with the manufacture of talismans along the lines of the science of images in the strict sense referred to here. He commented that crucial in these manipulations was the fashioning of not merely figures – which might be no more than another word for the idol's shape – but more importantly "characters."[54] That admission alone would seem to point exclusively in the direction of talismanic magic.

Surely that is why, when he came to writing his overview of magic in his *Summa theologiae*, Thomas seized upon the new term he had found in reading the *Speculum astronomiae*. He must have realized that the category of *imagines astronomicae* made plain the distinction he was groping for in his *Summa contra gentiles*. Here was a division of image-magic that attempted to separate from the type expressly reliant on the invocation of spirits that sort which eschewed all such conjuring and supplication. Exactly the differentiation he stood in need of. For it was just at the point where he spoke about fabricated objects working "from a power [residing in] celestial bodies" that Thomas came to what I think was his real purpose for this part of the *Contra gentiles*: demonstrating exactly how even magicians' most benign explanations for the effectiveness of their operations masked a deeper and more sinister reality. From this perspective, the rationale for what he later knew to call strictly "astronomical images" could be said to be the most insidious, for it came the closest of all to shutting out entirely the operation of spirits. That was a conclusion that we know Thomas was not prepared to abide. And so it was the arguments for the innocence of the causality and ceremonial behind the employ of images of this sort against which Thomas devoted his greatest energies. His comments on this score are consequently those upon which we need, ourselves, to dwell, rather than on those regarding the more Hermetic magic of animated statues.

We can divide Thomas's counter-argumentation regarding the true causation of astrological image-magic into three parts: the first on the extent of natural operation of the celestial bodies, second on the power of words and third on the role of characters and figures. So far as concerns the natural operative power of the stars and planets, Thomas was confronting the contention that in the case of astrological talismans the power of the talisman derived entirely from the stars, working as they normally did in the generation of all things on earth.[55] Thomas's rejoinder asserted the principle that any power derived solely from the influence of the celestial bodies would be capable only of producing a natural effect – one, that is, explainable by the laws of nature and known to be traceable to the natural form of the operating object. Yet as everyone knew, magicians used their image-objects to accomplish all manner of unnatural phenomena, inexplicable by any of nature's regular modes of operation. They opened locks merely by standing before the barred doors; they made people disappear; it was said that they accomplished countless wonderful and completely unexpected things. If accounts of such accomplishments were true, then something other than the celestial bodies had finally to be held to account.[56] Something must have been causally implicated which operated beyond the bounds of the routinely natural – most likely, of course, an intelligence with a will.

As for the words of the magical operator, they were even less capable of inducing a power in the way the defenders of astronomical images claimed. Words or vocables ("*voces*") derived their efficacy solely either from something that could generate them or from something that could grasp their significance – in short, an intellect. No one would dare to claim that a human intellect had so great a potency that solely by speaking words it could directly bring about an effect in the external world. Which meant that any causal power must have come from an intellect to whom the words were directed.[57] Indeed, the very mode of speech that the magicians used should have made it obvious that something like this was taking place. Did they not issue invocations, supplications, even commands? What purpose would these serve unless they were directed to other personal beings in a conversation?[58] Again, what might these receiving intellects be if not invisible spirits?

Finally, there was the shaping of an object into a figure, sometimes even the inscription of characters. Again, Thomas insisted that no mere figure could serve as the effective cause of any act or passion. One need simply consider the case of geometrical figures, immaterial designs that in themselves had no power to accomplish anything but rather proved useful only when manipulated by a calculating mind.[59] In short, where figures were used they were employed as signs (*signa*), whose utility would necessarily depend upon the involvement of intelligent beings able to interpret them.[60] In these latter intelligent beings, the wondrous operations found their cause. Of course, this is precisely the explanation offered earlier by William of Auvergne, and it is hard not to think that Thomas drew his analysis directly from his famous predecessor.[61]

Curiously enough, it was just at this point that Thomas made room for an exception to the rule. He commented that some people might contend that in the case of artifacts of the sort he was talking about, the figure served as a kind of natural or, in Thomas's words, "specific" form. Since the forging or imprinting of the figure provided the occasion by which the image-object became what it was, that very process might be said to be equivalent to the magical object's generation. And because in natural generation, the celestial bodies exercised an influence on the object generated and its natural form, so in this artificial generation, the stars and planets exerted a corresponding influence on the artifact and its artificial form. In this way, the figure might well be the vehicle for what came very close to being a "natural" implantation of a power.[62] It made for an ingenious argument. More important, Thomas took absolutely no steps to refute it. It is well known by now that some readers – Marsilio Ficino among them – took this brief observation by Thomas as constituting a major concession to the pretensions of astronomical image-makers.[63] As for Thomas himself, he evidently later had a change of heart. As already indicated earlier, he took pains in the part of his *Summa theologiae* where he considered magic to introduce the very argument he attributed to unnamed persons in the *Summa contra gentiles* and, in this case, to provide an explicit refutation.[64]

Meanwhile, in the *Summa contra gentiles*, Thomas proceeded to the rest of his argument against the legitimacy of image-magic in its entirety, or nearly so. What was left was to determine exactly what sort of spiritual being it might be that the magicians depended on – and communicated to via their figures or characters – to perform the wonders that they disingenuously attributed to the natural influence of the heavens and the images alone. Of course, the general opinion among learned Christians at least back to the time of Augustine had been that any spiritual beings involved with magic were evil, what in the Christian lexicon already by the time of Augustine had come to be called "demons."[65] But we also know from some of the manuals on magic examined earlier from the thirteenth century that there were those in the Latinate intellectual community of Thomas's day prepared to maintain that in those cases of magical operations they did not already in principle insulate from the intervention spiritual beings altogether, good separate substances, the angels themselves, were often summoned and at work. Especially the Solomonic magical traditions appealed to angelic intervention.[66] Thomas offered a series of arguments to prove them wrong.

Each argument ended with the conclusion that the intellectual being called upon in practically every act of image-magic was not "well disposed" ("*bene dispositus*"). In his first argument, for example, he laid out the supposition that no well-disposed intellect would proffer its aid to any actions contrary to virtue.[67] Yet that was exactly the kind of action that the magic to which he was directing his attention was usually intended to promote. The purposes to which the magical images were put included the furthering of adultery, the abetting of thievery and even the perpetration of murder. Such actions constituted, in the very language which had long been associated with the dangers of sorcery, "*maleficia*." In fact, as Thomas reminded his readers, the operators of the magic by which these deeds were done were labeled in standard Latin usage "*malefici*," a term, as we know, primarily employed since late Antiquity to designate sorcerers. Whatever intellectual substances lent their support to such malevolent people pursuing their malicious aims must have been of comparably evil intent themselves.

We can already surmise what sort of being Thomas thought did involve itself in the operations solicited by the marvel workers and magicians of his day. Indeed, from top to bottom – image-magic to blatantly ceremonial sorcery – magical acts relied upon the agency of beings of a totally intellectual and immaterial nature but of the worst moral disposition. They were, as Thomas added just a bit after making his arguments about their evil intent, those beings whom "in common usage we call demons or devils" ("*daemones vel diabolos*").[68] All magic could trace whatever effectiveness it possessed back to these epitomes of the fall from grace. In Thomas, therefore, we see a universal answer to the question of how magic operated. Out of the ambiguity and debate of the first half of the thirteenth century emerged a position that would in the end win consensus among the defenders of hierarchy and ideological orthodoxy. We might call this a reassertion of the old Augustinian paradigm. It was, however, a reassertion with a difference. For now it arose in a context where magic had for more than a century in the Latin west enjoyed its learned and even Christian promoters. It was thus by necessity a reassertion formulated so as to deal a death-blow to a learned and purportedly pious counter-narrative that those promoters had for some time been offering for how magic worked and the way it should be received.

Roger Bacon

We have ample evidence that magic's supporters were aware of the danger they confronted. Only a few, however, dared speak their mind. Among them is to be found one of the most remarkable figures of late thirteenth-century scholastic thought, Roger Bacon. A master of arts at both Oxford and Paris, who may have studied theology but never incepted as master in the field, Bacon had joined the Franciscan Order around 1257.[69] From then on he spent little of his time in teaching, devoting himself instead intensively to the study of what he considered "wisdom," within which figured prominently the mathematical sciences and some parts of natural philosophy. In the 1260s, Bacon came to the attention of Cardinal Bishop of Santa Sabina Guy of Foulques, who was soon to be elected pope as Clement IV in 1265. A letter of 1266 from Pope Clement to Bacon inquiring about Bacon's forays into new fields of learning prompted a vigorous response. Over the two years 1266 and 1267, Bacon worked feverishly on three works promoting his ideas about learning, all intended for the pope in the hope of gaining his endorsement and patronage for what Bacon conceived as a complete restructuring of the methods of instruction in higher learning of his day. These three compositions, the *Opus maius*, *Opus minus* and *Opus tertium*, comprise surely the most famous pieces of Bacon's considerable body of work. In them we find most of what Bacon had to say about the magical matters of concern to us.

It is clear that at least some parts of the learned traditions of magic as we have been considering them made their way into what Bacon viewed as the legitimate arts and sciences. In a work written around 1262, the *Communia naturalium*, Bacon sketches out for the reader the panoply of disciplines he had either been summarizing in various works written in the preceding years or was preparing to epitomize in others yet to be done.[70] Having begun with the arts of grammar and logic (*grammatica et logicalia*), he had then made his way into the sciences more properly speaking, starting with the mathematical sciences (*partes mathematice*). His intention was eventually to work through a volume devoted to two final disciplines, metaphysics and moral philosophy (*metaphisicalia cum moralibus*). Meanwhile, he was setting his sights on covering what was left, the natural sciences or natural philosophy (*naturalia*). The work in which he was then engaged would present the concepts, principles and conclusions common to all parts of this vast natural field.[71]

Before launching into details on these common elements, Bacon wanted to remind his readers of the specific parts of the natural sciences to which the commonalties would be applied. It is in his listing of these parts – seven in all – that we find the first evidence for how deeply Bacon was caught up in the Greek- and Arabic-influenced vision of the sciences that scholastics had been promoting by his day for nearly a century and a half, in which of course a considerable role was played by magical arts. According to Bacon, the natural sciences consisted of optics (*perspectiva*), astronomy of a judiciary and operative sort (*astronomia judiciaria et operativa*), the science of weights, alchemy (*alkimia*), agriculture, medicine and – in a novel phrase originating with Bacon himself – "experimental science" (*scientia experimentalis*).[72] Right away, of course, judiciary astronomy and alchemy stand out as belonging among the disciplines traditionally seen as a part of magic. If we pay heed to several quick descriptions Bacon subsequently gives, we discover that there is at least one more of the same complexion. It is in fact quite likely that Bacon had in mind the very listing of eight parts of natural science that go back to Farabi and Gundissalinus and which have served us as introduction to magic's emergence among the sciences in high medieval Scholasticism.[73]

Perspectiva or optics constituted for Bacon a critically important science for the understanding of all natural philosophy.[74] But it is not farfetched to conceive of it as an expansion of what in Farabi's and Gundissalinus's listing was contained in the science of mirrors. The phrase "judiciary and operative astronomy" has already betrayed an interest in astrology. What Bacon adds in his quick description serves as further confirmation. As Bacon would have it, "astronomy" in the broadest sense contained three parts. The first part, speculative, concerned itself with the precise geometry of the heavenly bodies, while the second, practical, came down to the canons, tables and instruments by which those bodies and their motions were tracked and measured. Both belonged to the mathematical sciences. Only the third part fit into the natural sciences, and this field had to do with the natural powers of the planets and stars, with their influence on the generation of things below, with judgments about the future and even with marvelous works.[75] Here was at least much of what Farabi and Gundissalinus intended by their "science of judgments." Finally, there is "experimental science." The latter was not quite like any science Bacon's scholastic forebears had known, but it was not entirely distant from what Farabi and Gundissalinus had probably been thinking of with "necromancy according to physics." As we see from Bacon's short description, it not only certified the conclusions of all the other sciences, but it also turned itself to the heavens and made judgments about the future while producing a host of "hidden" works ("*occulta opera*").[76]

In sum, of the eight sciences of Farabi's and Gundissalinus's listing, six were in some way represented in Bacon's scheme of the natural sciences: their medicine, science of judgments, necromancy according to physics, agriculture, science of mirrors and alchemy. As we shall see in this chapter, even the science of images was tacitly folded in, subsidiary to astronomy.[77] It might seem as if we had been transported back to the pro-magical atmosphere of learned circles infatuated with the new sciences of the twelfth century. Yet for all the surface evidence for Bacon's acceptance of much of scientific magic, there is also the counter-fact that in his own general accounting of learned disciplines in the works of 1266 and 1267 he explicitly attacked anything attached to the term "magic" itself.

Bacon's formal position on magic

As Bacon informs his reader, the key to the debate about magic lay in the conflicting claims to truth in an area of disciplinary overlap between what we commonly call astronomy and astrology. Bacon knew that since before the time of Augustine astrologers – judicial astronomers, to be absolutely unambiguous – had been popularly referred to with the often pejorative term "*mathematici.*"[78] We realize, however, that for Bacon "*mathematica*" constituted a category of sciences most important for the entire schema of higher learning. We also have seen that "judicial astronomy" found a place in this same schema among the array of legitimate sciences – natural sciences to be specific.[79] There was thus from Bacon's perspective a dilemma regarding the term "judicial astronomy," and it could be resolved only by determining correctly how this term related to magic. Bacon seized the reins of this dilemma by introducing a distinction between true mathematics ("*mathematicae verae*") and false mathematics ("*mathematicae falsae*").[80] In his view, it was thus the word "*mathematica*" that harbored the primary ambivalence, so the job was to separate the form of it referring to legitimate learning from that referring to unfounded pretenses to knowledge.

To explain how the job was to be accomplished, Bacon turned to the Greek word "*mathesis*" – disciplined learning ("*disciplina*") – from which the term "mathematics" arose. Whether Bacon knew so or not, Michael Scot had already made just the division of this term that Bacon had in mind.[81] Like Scot, Bacon insisted that strictly speaking the form of the term "*mathesis*," with an aspirate linked to the "t," had to be distinguished from the form "*matesis*," where the aspirate was absent. "True mathematics" was the authentic descendant of "*mathesis*," and like its linguistic root it bore the weight of legitimate science and learning. It consisted in the type of astrology – judicial science of the stars – whose findings bore the stamp of veracity. "False mathematics" was the product instead of "*matesis*," without the aspirate. It had lost the property of legitimacy and like its presumed root denoted the more dismal realm of false pretenses.[82] It represented the so-called astrological art that had long been upbraided in educated Christian circles and that could not find an honest place among the sciences. In a word, it was a "magical art" ("*ars magica*"), where the modifier "magic" carried all the weight of opprobrium attached to "superstition" since the time of Augustine.[83]

What betrayed false mathematics' place in the realm of magical lore were certain reprehensible attributes. They can serve as a catalogue for some of the properties that made magic, in Bacon's eyes, the illegitimate pseudo-discipline that it was. First of all, there stood the overwhelming ideological problem that astrology, at least for some of its practitioners, implied an absolute necessity throughout the course of worldly events. Beyond this, there existed a host of other unsavory characteristics. In Bacon's words, false mathematics effectively kidnapped the honest consideration of the stars by deforming it with the addition of various characters, incantations, conjurations, superstitious sacrifices, and ultimately deceitful acts. Besides, as the conjurations and sacrifices revealed, false mathematics or illegitimate astrology appealed to demons for assistance. Finally, as inevitably in cases of demonic intervention, it suffered from the corrosive presence of fraud. This latter trait made it, after all, "false mathematics," or a "*mathematica falsidica*," mendacious to the core. More than anything else, this was what characterized it in Bacon's lexicon as "magical."[84] Its practitioners were rightfully to be condemned as "magicians" ("*magici*"), the works in which its principles and observances were handed down excoriated as "books of magic" ("*libri magici*").[85]

Of course, there were other types of magical art, all sharing some of the foregoing attributes and some mentioned explicitly in this section of Bacon's *Opus maius*. On the one hand was to be found the art of spell-casting or fascination ("*fascinatio*").[86] Bacon also conceded the extraordinary character of an enormous Solomonic literature, in which could be found countless prescriptions for operating outside the common course of natural causation. In itself completely acceptable, this store of practices was on many occasions adopted by magicians (again, "*magici*") in the pursuit of evil ends.[87] Finally, there was to Bacon's eyes a vast territory of the practice of sorcery. Old women ("*vetulae*") from every corner of the earth were known to have their special characters, spells and conjurations, and magicians ("*magici*") everywhere invoked demons, conjured up their presence and offered them petitionary sacrifices.[88] All of this was magical; all of it was to be condemned.

For Bacon, therefore, magic did exist. The "magical" to his eyes constituted a category of learning and operation that would prove in the end to be either fraudulent or demonic and immoral, or both at once. Andrew Molland has suggested that we recognize how Bacon's primary criterion for dividing magic off from the legitimate arts was moral.[89] If we are allowed to add fraud into the mix, then I believe that Molland has it right. Thus, for Bacon, "magic" as a description carried much the weight it had since Augustine.

Yet this did not mean that, in Bacon's eyes, all of what had for a century or more been lodged among the magical arts was properly thus categorized and justifiably repudiated. Indeed, exactly the opposite was the case. Bacon held the deepest conviction that in many instances his colleagues, and some of his predecessors, had extended their condemnation too far. There is, in short, much in Bacon that we would consider magical which escaped his criticism and rejection. Without defending anything to which he would explicitly apply the label "magical," Bacon even confessed as much in his own words. He praised the early church for having separated false, and magical, mathematics off from true mathematics, and for having condemned the former while continuing to turn the latter to the advantage of the faith. The problem was that there had come a time when certain theologians ("*quidam theologi*") – surely including the likes of Thomas Aquinas – who did not really understand magic began to extend the prohibition of it into valid, philosophical forms of knowledge and practice that magic seemed to ape.[90] Bacon pursued his complaint even into the precincts of canon law. No less a figure than Gratian had reproved valuable sciences and arts along with the magical. And just as other specifics of canon law set down in Gratian's *Decretum* had had to be reviewed in more recent times, so much that the *Decretum* said about learning and learned practice needed reexamination and reversal.[91]

Bacon on astrology

Once we realize that despite his rejection of anything he labeled with the word "magical," Bacon actually maintained considerable receptivity to much that fell into what many in his learned circles would have recognized as the magical arts, we can go back to Bacon's own listing of the sciences and consider more deeply his support for those elements we would identify on our terms as part of magic. The ideological basis for his receptivity to them lay in a capacious definition of the category of the "natural." As Bacon made clear at one point in his *Opus maius*, every natural phenomenon or operation that occurred or was performed without demonic aid should be open to human investigation and experimentation. What was consequently determined to be true could without detriment to Christianity be accepted and utilized in practical pursuits, if put to a good purpose.[92]

The judicial astronomy we have already seen Bacon undertake to defend draws our attention right away. What Bacon has to say about it not only reveals his ultimate response to much of the magic of his day but also allows us to understand how his vision of the "natural" differed from that of anti-magicians of the sort of Aquinas. It is in his discussion of the mathematical sciences in the *Opus maius* that Bacon tells us the most about his conception of astronomy, both judicial and otherwise. Picking up on a division that we have already encountered in the *Speculum astronomiae*, Bacon alerts his reader to the fact that there were two great sciences of the heavens. They were speculative astronomy ("*astrologia speculativa*") and practical astronomy ("*astrologia practica*").[93] Speculative astronomy laid out the geometry of the heavens and of the earth, whereas practical astronomy used astronomical apparatus to provide us with a knowledge of the precise position of each heavenly body at every conceivable moment.[94] Of course, all this is exactly what the *Communia naturalium* has prepared us to expect.[95] But in the *Opus maius*, rather than proceed to a third part of astronomy, as in the *Communia naturalium*, Bacon simply continues by ascribing to practical astronomy further obligations. Here, astronomy as practical science went on to make judgments about the past, the present and the future. It also turned to marvelous works, whereby prosperity could be advanced and adversity avoided.[96]

Bacon even endeavored to explain why judicial astronomy was able to make the predictions it did as well as precisely what sort of judgments, and consequently what kind of works, it was capable of.[97] The explanation for the mechanism underlying judicial astronomy – "astrology" in our terms – is not surprising for someone who gave to optics so much explanatory power in the natural sciences. Place at any moment was crucial for determining the character of generation of all natural things. And the reason was that every spot on earth stood at the apex of a discrete cone projecting perpendicularly up into the heavens, different from that associated with any other location. The powers of the heavenly bodies at the base of the cone, proceeding to the ground in straight lines just as did the bodies' light, thus came together in a unique configuration for each spot at each particular time. Knowing the place and time, one could thereby precisely calculate the relevant constellation of forces and make a valid prediction of the consequent effect.

"True *mathematici*" were therefore not implicated in the trappings of false mathematics: conjurings, sacrifices, incantations and characters. They were authentic scientists who plumbed the depths of natural processes to render infallible judgments ("*judicium infallibile*") about necessary happenings ("*rerum necessarius eventus*") here below.[98] In doing so, moreover, they were not, as their critics contended, vying with God for absolute certitude. The predictions put forth by valid astrologers were "general" ("*in universali*") and not particular ("*in particulari*" or "*sufficiens in singulis*"). They did not so much say exactly what would happen as lay out the conditions that would hold.[99] They were indicators of a probable outcome, fully reliable – hence infallible in that restricted sense – so long as one realized that unanticipatable particularities always intervened to modulate the actual result.[100] All this meant, moreover, that those two sorts of events Christian thinkers had always insisted on shielding from astrological judgment escaped the power of the judicial astronomer to determine with precision. The generality of astrological prediction entailed the fact that no human, no matter how learned in the celestial sciences, could infallibly foresee the course of future contingents.[101] Nor would the astrologer's vision into the future ever reach so far as to expunge the freedom of the human will.[102]

Of course, we have seen some of these same points in the works of Thomas Aquinas. Yet Bacon was not merely arguing that a properly conceived astrology was compatible with Christian belief. He was bent on promoting judicial astronomy to the furthest possible degree. Empiricist to the core, Bacon believed that the predictive principles of the astrologer could be affirmed by an historical comparison of the motions of the heavens to events here on earth.[103] The saints, not to speak of the Hebrew patriarchs, realized that this was so, and for so long as the world had existed they had given their firm approval to astrology's responsible use.[104] Indeed, so fundamental was astrology to proper judgment in all other disciplines of knowledge that its outright rejection would have made even theology impossible and done great damage to the church, the commonwealth and the future prospering of the faith.[105] In Bacon's words, "astrology regulates everything else." On this score, it stood preeminent among all disciplines.[106]

Bacon on the science of images

As if that were not enough, there were also those special works which only astrology knew how to bring about.[107] On this point our author comes back to the matter that had so troubled Thomas Aquinas, only to set his feet on just the opposite side of the divide. For there can be no doubt that among the works of judicial astronomy Bacon counted foremost the prodigies of the science of images. If for Thomas they constituted pretended works of "magicians" and cause for alarm, to Bacon they represented the heights to which "true mathematics" could ultimately ascend. Bacon was fully aware of the tradition of the "science of images" stretching back through twelfth-century Latin natural philosophy and into the world of Arabic higher thought. Indeed, knowledge of the "secrets of images" ("*secreta imaginum*"), as he called them, was to be associated with no less an authority than Ptolemy himself.[108] Among its greatest teachers was moreover the very same figure, Thābit ibn Qurra, whose presumed work, *De imaginibus*, the *Speculum astronomiae* had listed as the prime exemplar of the science available in Latin.[109]

Yet Bacon was likewise conscious of the bad odor surrounding such works and their science among his learned colleagues. Few, he admitted, would even speak of their support of the discipline in public, and men like Thābit were labeled by the vast majority of scholars ("*vulgus studentium*") as magicians, though in fact they were the wisest of all humanity.[110] As noted earlier with regard to "true mathematics," Bacon blamed theologians and canon lawyers who, unlearned in such elevated disciplines, condemned them out of ignorance. Seeing magicians use images to do their works of evil, they proffered blanket condemnation of an authentic science.[111] Nearly the same position, of course, was laid out by the author of the *Speculum astronomiae*.[112] But now Bacon takes it up in the most public forum he can find, before the eyes of the pope himself. Immediately he turns to the objective foundations for the science, and as if in response to Thomas himself, he addresses just the three problematic areas of causality focused on in the *Summa contra gentiles*. They were the action of the stars, the power of words, and the suitability of images and characters to serve as agents of change.

For the stars, and the ability of their special powers to operate immediately in this world beyond the standard influence of their local motions, Bacon turned to his theory of the multiplication of species.[113] Every natural agent, both spiritual and corporeal, worked its effect by projecting its power into its surroundings in the form of a similitude ("*similitudo*"), image ("*imago*") or, most precisely, species ("*species*").[114] One version of this effusion of power could be seen in the propagation of light. Yet in the instance of the heavenly bodies there occurred a two-fold multiplication, one univocal, the other equivocal.[115] The multiplication of the species of light acted univocally, so that light at the heavenly source diffused light through the medium, which, when it struck a solid body, brought about illumination. But the sun and stars produced an equivocal species as well, which was not of precisely the luminous nature of its source. When a species of this sort reached its end-point, it imparted not light but rather a special capability for change. This kind of species could thus transfer a power resident in a heavenly body to an object on earth to which it had, by multiplication, advanced.

As for the potency of words, it, too, could be explained by the same theory. According to Bacon, since the rational soul was of greater dignity than the stars, so it should be expected to project its agency even more forcefully by generating species endowed with a special active power.[116] Perhaps not surprisingly, these species were intimately connected with – maybe even identical to – spoken words. Thus, as Bacon explained: "Since the preeminent operation of the rational soul is to use words effectively, formed with [a particular] intention [in mind], the [judicial] astronomer can put forth words at selected moments that will have an almost indescribable power."[117] When the intention was strong and the speaker's confidence high, the resultant words would be more efficacious than any other human act.[118] In combination with the stars, the right words at the right time could have an absolutely astonishing effect: "For where the intention, desire and power of the rational soul – which is of greater dignity than the stars – concur with the power of the heavens, it is inevitable that a word or other work be produced of wondrous power to alter the things of this world."[119] Finally, of course, there were the images themselves. Bacon's explanation of their place in the business he was describing first came to rest on "characters," about whose independent power to act Thomas had had the greatest suspicion of all. For, Bacon asserted, characters were like "images," capable of receiving the power of the stars at the moment of their production.[120] But this meant that for Bacon the paradigmatic case was that of the image alone. And here he returned to a defense of image-making highly reminiscent of the exception concerning artificial objects that Thomas first accepted, and then later rejected, in his own argumentation.[121] In Bacon's words:

> Just as a new-born child, exposed to new air as if to a brand new world, receives the impression of the celestial powers [ascendant at that moment]…so the same holds true for everything newly made, which receives the power of the stars at the very beginning of its existence.[122]

He then proceeded to list the kinds of "newly made" object he was referring to. They were, in addition to charms composed of words strung together, "images" and "characters" forged under a specific constellation. If the time had been correctly determined, they would receive the powers of the aligned stars and retain them, so as to be able to perform works among the things of this world.[123]

All in all, it was a breathtaking defense of the science of images, precisely designed to rebut the sort of arguments advanced in Thomas. Bacon even invented his own phrase to designate the works of this science. While, unlike Thomas, never borrowing from the *Speculum astronomiae* to speak of "astronomical images," he did refer to "works, and words, produced with the help of the stars" ("*opera stellificata*," "*verba et opera stellificanda*").[124] Moreover, let the reader not be mistaken. There was in all this no hint of magic.[125] The works to which Bacon was referring were marvelous, but they were also greatly to be desired and promoted. By their agency, bodies could be healed, dangerous animals caused to flee, the wild brutes tamed, snakes called up from caverns and fish from the depths of the sea. The matter, and matters, of the world could be altered to truly marvelous effect, and all against the machinations of the evil and for the betterment of the human commonwealth.[126]

Bacon's *Scientia Experimentalis*

As if this was not enough, Bacon had yet wilder marvels in his sights. His "experimental science" began with an emphatic theoretical empiricism to end up surpassing in the competition for wonderful productions even the most celebrated achievements imagined for the legendary "masters of works."[127] As Bacon explained it, *scientia experimentalis* contained three great "prerogatives" ("*praerogativae*") or "dignities" ("*dignitates*").[128] By its first prerogative or function, it confirmed by experience – "experiment" in a very general sense – all the conclusions that the other sciences had demonstrated by deduction from principles.[129] The science's second prerogative was to establish truths that fell within the subject matter of other sciences but which they had failed to demonstrate.[130] An example concerned the magnet, whose power to attract iron could not be demonstrated through a necessary cause in natural philosophy but the reality of which could be firmly established by the experimentalist.[131] But it is the third prerogative that truly engages our attention. Bacon made plain that here experimental science passed beyond the bounds of the subjects of other sciences and delved into matters proper to it alone. These matters laid bare the very deepest of nature's secrets.[132]

In fact there were two parts to this final prerogative. The first part, essentially divinatory, had to do with knowledge of the future, past and present. On this score, experimental science proved itself a judicial science, much like astrology, but one attaining to a certitude about the course of events that judicial astronomy could never hope to approach.[133] As for the second part, it tended more toward action than cognition and revealed itself even more marvelous than anything Bacon had broached before. On the one hand, in this second part of its third prerogative experimental science plumbed by experiment ("*experientiae*") the total or complete possibility of all nature and all art.[134] On the other, it yielded an almost infinite number of works, most of which Bacon himself could only dimly imagine. Here we find the production of "works of wonder" ("*opera admiranda*") to which nothing would seem more comparable, from our point of view, than the works of magicians as described from William of Auvergne's day on.[135] Though Bacon hurriedly offered in his *Opus maius* a few examples of what such works might consist in, he conceded to the pope that knowledge of the particulars was something he had to leave to the real wise men ("*sapientes*") of his time, among whom we would certainly want to count Bacon's often-eulogized "experimenter" and expert on the magnet, Peter of Maricourt.[136] As for himself, Bacon confessed, he could only stand in awe at their accounts of works that he could scarcely comprehend.[137] Giving himself over to the rhetoric of magic's promoters in the Scholastic world, he effusively proclaimed that in its last prerogative, experimental science "pried into all the occult works of wisdom."[138] Indeed, everything of wonder and magnificence pertained properly to the domain of this one science.[139] Hidden for the most part from the gaze of the majority of human minds, it offered to the penetrating few the key to human wisdom.[140]

Magic reconsidered

In the end, then, Bacon stood as if an interlocutor with Aquinas, battling over the ground covered by much of what was known as magic in their day. It was not a battle over words, for both agreed that "magic" was something to be excoriated. The combat raged instead over the boundaries for what was to be held as magical in the circles in which both of these thirteenth-century polymaths traveled. Yet this result confronts us with a puzzle. And the puzzle arises from the very fact that Thomas and Bacon did not differ at the level of language or theory in their understanding of and attitude toward magic. No matter which of the two ways of tackling "magic" that I have sketched out one chooses, both thinkers fell on the same side of the divide. If magic is to be taken as concerned with knowledge and contrasted to its competitor, "science," then Thomas and Bacon each argued that magic was false and could muster no rightful claims to being "scientific." If on the other hand magic is a matter of ritual or spiritual orientation, and as such a foil to "religion," again for each of our authors magic was to be condemned and shunned. Yet when all is said and done, there was something about magic that appealed to Bacon and elicited his support. Thus the material appearance within his "science" of much of what we and his contemporaries would recognize as magical.

What was this "something" in, or about, "magic" that held such allure for Bacon? When we pose the question in this way, we see at once how the theoretical scaffolding erected so far for analyzing magic fails us. Neither of our two paradigms can explain what in the magical tradition made Bacon want to embrace parts of it while refusing to recognize them as "magical" in name. To compensate for that failure we need to turn elsewhere. I suggest that an answer lies with the thought of the early-twentieth-century French anthropologist Marcel Mauss. In his now famous essay "Esquisse d'une théorie générale de la magie," Mauss lays out an appreciation of magic that I think allows us to understand the ambiguously opposing stances of Thomas and Bacon.[141] Like both Frazer and Malinowski, Mauss recognized that the idea of magic lay nestled among a cluster of other general concepts, two of the most important of which were "science" and "religion."[142] He agreed with Frazer that magic bore to science at least in part a parental relation, while he conceded à la Malinowski that magic often involved rites laying bare its kinship with religion.[143] Yet for Mauss, the comparison with any of its correlative concepts could not yield a final solution to the question of what made magic what it was.

It was Mauss's signal insight that in the end there was no formal attribute, or even set of attributes, by which magic could be defined. Instead, it had to be accepted that magic was not so much a conceptual matter as it was a social phenomenon.[144] Lacking a formal definition, it had to be pointed to as something associated with specific actions in the social world and the attitudes or emotional responses that they arose from or aroused.[145] The way Mauss put his discovery was to say that "magic" constituted at heart a "collective idea" (*"notion collective," "représentation collective"*).[146] As he explained, it was possible to locate a single, overarching collective idea by which magic was always characterized.[147] He chose to designate this idea with a word that he thought captured its essence best, one drawn from the lexicon of the Melanesian languages, and that word was *"mana."* It was so general a descriptor that it could serve simultaneously as a noun, an adjective and a verb.[148] Complex, it consisted most principally in a convergence of two other, more general considerations. For *mana* was on the one hand a force or a power, associated with what Mauss liked to call the *"potentialité magique."*[149] But it designated as well the precise context in which it was possible for such a power to be exercised.[150]

Yet how was one to identify *mana*? According to Mauss, the most important thing about it was that it was not ordinary, coming into play only insofar as it remained strictly separate from daily life.[151] It was a notion or idea as he insisted "of the same order as the idea of the sacred," and like the "sacred," it constituted just the opposite of the "profane."[152] Indeed, Mauss went so far as to claim that *mana* presented the general category under which the "sacred" fell as a species.[153] Perhaps we should therefore say that *mana* comprised the special forces and the special circumstances that made both the "sacred" and the "magical" the extraordinary phenomena they were.[154] This is, of course, the reason why "magic" and "religion" managed to be both fraternally related and directly opposed. They both reverberated of a world apart from the normal, where emotions were aroused and expectations heightened. But they did so in different ways. "Religion" was evocative of this special force and introduced us to special circumstances under a guise in which society in general – or at least an official class – could have confidence and about which it could feel safe and secure. "Magic" managed exactly the same but in a fashion at which society looked askance and by which society, and not just its official censors, were oddly shaken, sometimes profoundly troubled.

If we take *mana* in Mauss's sense as the identifying attribute of magic, we can, I believe, finally account for those opposing stances of Thomas and Bacon. For we must remember that both thinkers agreed in condemning the word "magic" and anything to which it might be applied, yet they were at the same time fighting over the value of aspects of the treasury of learning that most intellectuals in their day would recognize as firmly entrenched in magical tradition. I see no reason to doubt Bacon's *bona fides* in his denunciations of "magic." He was, I believe, speaking with absolute sincerity when he condemned any magic that sought to compete with Christianity, and he honestly believed that such "magic" would also, of necessity, be untrue, thus not fit for acceptance as scientific knowledge. From the perspective of either of our two paradigms for appreciating "magic" Bacon was thus prepared to turn his back on that category altogether. Yet much of the learning and practice within the currents of magic that had been stirred up among the learned in the Latin west since the beginnings of the twelfth century appealed to Bacon all the same. He could not call these elements, which he in fact integrated into his own category of scientific knowledge, by the name of magic without contradicting his own genuine principles. But still he was attracted to them. He was attracted to them precisely because they had the special quality, which attached to them by dint of learned tradition itself, that Mauss identified as *mana*. It was their *mana* that made them so wonderful, their *mana* that made Bacon want to hide them and to urge the pope to keep them largely to himself, their *mana* finally that convinced Bacon they would do so much to restore and even ennoble humanity.

Of course, by my understanding what appropriated the attribute of *mana* specifically to "magic" was the quality to which Mauss continually alludes by which magic was always also somehow socially suspect, maybe slightly dangerous and at the limit even illicit.[155] Just this quality made anything "magical" so unacceptable to thinkers like Thomas Aquinas. And this very suspiciousness, which took on an almost titillating valence for Bacon when he imagined the powers of these new disciplines to transform the world, drove Thomas to assail anything resonant of it as detrimental to the true faith. Hence Thomas's drive to objectify magic's fatal flaw and which he succeeded in satisfying by making plain that there were no circumstances in which magic did not involve the appeal to demonic assistance. In effect, Thomas turned the limiting case into the rule. And he did that so successfully that even Bacon could not find the courage in his theory of science to delineate a form of "magic," such as William of Auvergne's natural magic, that escaped the censures under which all other forms of magic would have to fall.

The quality of "magic" as fundamentally neither irrevocably anti-religious nor invariably untrue but always somehow *mana*, thus on the far side of the ordinary or profane, is, if Mauss and I are right, universal, and thus it was present as a driving force through all the debates over magic that we have been examining from the very beginning. But it was the circumstances of the thirteenth century – circumstances holding primarily within the university and at court – that brought this quality to the fore and made it more and more the touchstone of all the controversy about magic and its status as beneficent or destructive of society. Key to the whole development was the increasingly open ambivalence of many of those at the very summit of learning about magic's valence – the increasing reluctance of some at the scholarly top to echo the old Augustinian denunciation of everything magical as superstitious. The rise of a literature of magic, technical, precise and adamantly "scientific," was for this ambivalence both symptom and cause. The movement's apparent success, and the depth of its support among the learned and the academically inclined, accounts for the severity of the reaction. The tipping point was reached in the years of Thomas's activity. It is precisely this phenomenon that helps us to explain the subsequent history of magic in the late medieval and early modern west.

Magic demonized at law

To begin to tell this history takes us back to the circumstances examined at the end of Chapter 2. The emergence of dissidence in the form of heresy had led to types of repression with which the high Middle Ages are justly associated. On the one hand, an image of dissident groups, now openly labeled heretical, as complicit with the devil, most likely even devil-worshipping, emerged among the educated elite and made its way into judicial literature. On the other hand, new, more highly rationalized and effective forms of juridical procedure were introduced into law and into regular practice, trial by inquisition marking the most salient manifestation. By 1231, there had even been erected the framework for a papal inquisition, charged with investigation of potential cases of heresy.[156] It would be odd if, once the debate about magic had advanced to open recognition of magic's quality in opposition to the "profane" and to the expression of this recognition in the language of invocation of devils, these same ideological and juridical forces were not unleashed against magic itself.

From the late thirteenth century on, this is precisely the trajectory that we see. Magic as diabolical, and potentially involving devil-worship, had by the early decades of the fourteenth century made its appearance on the juridical stage. The first unambiguous episodes arose at the very top of society, in a series of show trials at both royal and papal courts. The story of these trials is well known and does not need to be rehearsed here in any detail. Both of our most prominent guides to the emergence of a demonizing ideology in the high Middle Ages, Norman Cohn and Alain Boureau, have laid out the particulars for us.[157] Surely the most notorious cases were associated with the court of the French king, Philip IV. An early opportunity for the transition of magic from merely theoretical target of theologians to weapon in legal proceedings presented itself in Philip's confrontation with Pope Boniface VIII. While Boniface was still alive, Philip had charges against him entered at the first meeting of the French Estates General in 1302, including the claim that the pope had a private demon and was prepared to utilize the demonic arts of conjuring magic.[158] After Boniface's death, the king persuaded a new pope, Clement V, to open a posthumous trial at the papal court in 1310, where the charges against Boniface expanded to include the actual practice of ceremonial magic and the worship of demons through veneration of an idol. The whole process came to a halt before a verdict was rendered, but meanwhile Philip had found a second occasion for much the same.

In 1305 Philip's queen, Joan, had died. By 1308 the king had become persuaded that her death was due to the behavior of Bishop Guichard of Troyes, and again Pope Clement was bullied into opening a papal inquiry. Here the charges began with the allegation that the bishop had been caught practicing sorcery back in 1305 in order to kill the queen.[159] Once the inquiry was underway, witnesses added that Guichard had invoked the devil himself, to whom he performed homage, and received in turn instructions for making a wax image, baptizing it in the queen's name and pricking it with pins to do the queen harm. When the trial resumed, after a short stay, in 1309, royal officials managed to have the accusations inflated to include the claim that Guichard was himself the son of an incubus and that he kept a private demon in a flask from which he could produce it to perform all sorts of evil acts. The flagging interest of the king meant that the trial passed through a long period of dormancy, until in 1314 Clement at last declared Guichard innocent and set him free.

Yet if these royal pressures for action established a standard of juridical defamation setting magic and demonic association at the center of well publicized trials, independent undertakings at the papal court were hardly far behind. Two of the Avignonese popes, John XXII, who served from 1316 to 1334, and Benedict XII, 1334–1342, seem to have been nearly as obsessed with such matters as King Philip. John in particular was ridden with fears about attempts on his life by recourse to sorcery, leading him frequently to bring accusations of *maleficium* against perceived opponents.[160] He arrested the bishop of Cahors in 1317 and had him convicted of turning to sorcery and poison to try to kill the pope, while he encouraged his allies in Milan to accuse Matteo Visconti of having fashioned a wax image for the same purpose as well as intervening directly with the devil. In 1318 he opened an inquisitorial investigation that produced evidence of a group of clerics and laymen at Avignon who cast spells, drew magic circles and consecrated images, all ultimately with the intent of calling upon demonic aid. By 1326 two papal inquiries were running simultaneously, turning up evidence of clerical and lay cooperation in using ceremonial magic to wreak havoc and commit murder, again with evoked demonic helpers.

Of course, such prominent legal actions left their mark upon the world of jurisprudence, setting the precedent whereby the practice of ceremonial magic, invariably connected with the involvement of demons, came to be viewed as a prosecutable crime. A link was established as well with the old defamation of devil-worship or at least the veneration of diabolical figures. Less spectacular, but perhaps in the long run even more important, was the development of a legal principle whereby magical practice, especially of the ceremonial sort, was equivalent to professing heresy and thus open to investigation and prosecution by the inquisition, especially in its papally promoted form.

Magical practice as heresy

On this latter front, progress was initially slower, due to the presence of a legal obstacle. For in the 1250s, a number of Italian friars deputized as inquisitors put the question to Pope Alexander IV whether they should proceed as a matter of course against rumor or accusations of magical practices involving divination and sorcery (*"divinationes et sortilegia"*).[161] In response, Alexander issued the bull "Quod super nonnullis," dated 1258. The pope's answer was firm and essentially negative. He reminded the friars that their primary business as inquisitors was defense of the faith. Therefore, unless the cases of magical practice brought to their notice should "manifestly savor of heresy," the friars should in no way involve themselves in them.[162] For Alexander, in short, the papal inquisition did not have a mandate to intervene where magical practices were involved. And this papal reluctance, setting an effective limit on inquisitorial jurisdiction, seems to have lasted up through the pontificate of Boniface VIII.

The first chink in the armor appeared when John XXII was pope. We have already seen how in 1318 John opened an inquiry into practices of ceremonial magic and sorcery at his own court. It is worth looking closely at the language of the letter in which John announced his intention. As John explained, the potential crimes involved several clerics and laymen implicating themselves in "necromancy, geomancy and other undertakings of the magical arts."[163] Among their actions were ritual consecration of mirrors and images, drawing of circles in order to call up evil spirits, and confining of demons in mirrors, circles or rings so as to pose them questions. Here was thus sorcery and divination as Alexander's friars had inquired about sixty years before. In line with Thomas Aquinas's reasoning, John interpreted such behavior as delivering demons the reverence of religious cult. More important is the fact that he said he could not avert his eyes from such behavior precisely because he found it so "plainly suggestive of the blemish of heresy."[164] Ceremonial magic thus easily for John met the test that Alexander had imposed before the inquisition could involve itself in its pursuit.

Sure enough, within only a few years John was calling upon the inquisition to intervene in precisely such matters. In two identical letters dated 1320, one addressed to the inquisitor in Carcassonne, the other to his counterpart in Toulouse, one of the pope's most trusted advisors, William of Peyre Godin, announced that his holiness had decided to take action against "sorcerers" ("*maleficos*") who were found to be infecting God's flock.[165] The means was formally to extend to papal inquisitors in this regard all the power and privileges heretofore delegated to them with respect to the crime of heresy.[166] Especially revealing is William's listing of the sorts of magical activity the pope had in his sights. The inquisitors were to target cases not only where sacrifice had been made to demons or worship given them, but also where magicians had made a pact with demons, or had prepared an image, or even invoked demons to perpetrate an evil act ("*maleficium*"). They should especially be on the lookout for sorcerers ("*sortileg[i] et malefic[i]*") baptizing such images or making use of the consecrated host. All these were stereotypes for the actions of ceremonial magicians, and they were interpreted in just the way theologians of the thirteenth century had made normative, as entailing either worship of or active connivance with demonic spirits. Such activities could now be taken as *ipso facto* evidence of heretical intent. Pope Alexander's scruples should henceforth routinely be set aside.

Still, not all even of the ecclesiastical elite was ready to take the step John intended. According to Alain Boureau, there is reason to believe that the inquisitors of southern France reacted coolly to John's call to action.[167] Hence, John's undertaking, in the very year of Cardinal William's letter, of an opinion survey of noted theologians associated with his court. For in the fall of 1320, John posed five questions to a group of ten distinguished theologians, asking in summary whether a variety of magical practices should be considered in themselves heretical, and why or why not. The practices consisted of baptizing images with intent of maleficent use, baptizing a person solely to cure a case of epilepsy, using the eucharist to practice sorcery, sacrificing to demons in order to bring them to force another person to do what the sacrificer wanted, and finally simply rebaptizing anyone.[168] The alternative to seeing such practices as in themselves heretical was to say that they constituted simply the crime of sorcery, thus outside the inquisition's formal jurisdiction. We have the answers of the theologians, and Boureau has recently provided us with an edition of the text.[169] For the most part, they did not give the pope the answer he wanted. More in line with the inquisitors to whom cardinal William had written in the same year, the theologians consulted hedged in their arguments with careful definitions of heresy as involving only obstinate wrong belief. Little ammunition here for a campaign to turn the inquisition into a scourge of the magicians.

The answers of just a single theologian, Augustine Kažotić, bishop of Zagreb, can stand as a marker for the attitude of the whole group. Kažotić's remarks allow us to see in broad terms how these theologians of the early fourteenth century conceived of ceremonial magic and what they thought of its potential to be viewed as a sign of heresy. To our good fortune, Kažotić took special care to delineate precisely what was meant by the relevant general categories of analysis. "Heresy" he took strictly as a matter of belief. In his words, it consisted in "false opinion concerning any of those things pertaining to the truth of the faith or the excellence of morality." Such false opinion on the part of a presumed Christian fit the definition, but the charge of heresy applied only if the individual was aware of the fact and still pertinaciously held to his wrong belief.[170] "Sorcery" ("sortilegium"), on the other hand, came down primarily to a matter of action. Strictly speaking it consisted in the "illicit investigation of future contingents" – that is, divination or fortune-telling. But more generally speaking Kažotić admitted that one would take sorcery to include the attempt illicitly to procure any effects.[171] Presumably he meant the attempt to use what could be regarded as magical means to perpetrate harm or evil. In either case, if one did in fact succeed, it could only be with the help of malign spirits or demons.[172] All this reaffirmed the now-established view of sorcery as a species of "superstition," apparent already in what we have seen from Aquinas. Still, nothing to contradict the tenets of faith or the beliefs of the church, hence nothing savoring of heresy.

Heresy worked its way into the mix of crimes of action only when Kažotić considered specific cases, and then just when a lapse from the true faith intervened. Invocation of demons, for example, consisted according to our theologian in the act of calling upon evil spirits to do one's will.[173] In most cases the procedure demanded resort to charms and profane rites ("carminibus quibusdam et prophanis ritibus"). These were, therefore, genuine acts of ceremonial magic that Kažotić had in mind, and he specifically called their perpetrators "sorcerers" ("malefici"). Yet if such sorcerers honestly believed that the demons they invoked were compelled to work the acts they did by means of a celestial or hidden natural force ("celesti quadam uel occulta nature ui"), triggered by the charms and rites, then it was the simple crime of sorcery alone into which they fell. If, on the other hand, the sorcerers spoke their charms and performed their rites because they believed that by doing so they would please the demons and thus induce them to provide their services, then they were guilty of a more serious offense. Technically speaking, it was the same as if they had presented the demons with a sacrifice ("*demonibus immolare*"). Here, then, was idolatry. For all that, there still was not a whiff of heresy.

This latter category could be invoked only in yet more serious cases. Here we come to John's first question, involving the baptism of magical images. Kažotić insisted, as had Aquinas, that images in themselves were merely the product of artifice; they had therefore no power to produce wondrous acts.[174] He knew, as well, that there were those in his day – "astrologers," he said – who produced images under a chosen sign and thought thereby to imbue them with special power.[175] If, in addition, such astrological sorcerers – we would know them as practitioners of the science of images – had their images baptized in the belief that the baptism would contribute to their ultimate magical effect, then they would at last be guilty of heresy. After all, their very actions proved that they believed that a sacrament could be turned to pernicious effect. Kažotić claimed all the same that if such magical operators had the baptism performed, not in the belief that it added to the power of the image, but rather with the hope of pleasing demons and thus winning their connivance, then no heresy was incurred. For demons were indeed pleased when Christians turned the sacraments to evil purpose. In such cases, the perpetrators were clearly guilty of sacrilege. Yet they did nothing to stray from the tenets of Christian faith. All of which could not, of course, have pleased the pope. The line between sorcery and heresy remained as firm as ever in our theologian's reasoning. If inquisitors were to act upon accusations of magic, it would have to be in only the smallest fraction of possible cases. For John, looking for allies in his campaign to have inquisitors proceed against magic, the consultation must thus be considered a failure.

Perhaps for this reason John seems to have drawn back from his strategy of enlisting the inquisition in his anti-magical cause. In 1330 he wrote letters to the inquisitors of Carcassonne and Toulouse effectively terminating the processes he had endeavored to get underway back in 1320.[176] Referring to the original letters from William of Peyre Godin, John announced that he understood that the depravities he had been worried about in 1320 continued unabated in southern France. Yet he urged the two inquisitors quickly to bring to a conclusion all the cases they had begun under the earlier papal authority. Moreover, he ordered them not to begin any new inquiries until and unless they received contrary orders from the pope himself. It would seem as if John had lost his confidence in the ecclesiastical courts of southern France to realize his intentions of reining in what he saw as patent magical abuse.

Not that he was prepared to withdraw from prosecuting ceremonial magic on other fronts. In 1326 or 1327 John issued the decretal "Super illius specula."[177] In this document he proceeded as he had plainly wished before, but now without reference either to papal inquisition or directly to the crime of heresy. Bemoaning the fact that numerous Christians were thus in name only, he targeted the many magical practices that he saw as increasingly rampant among the nominal members of God's flock. The list was not that different from what we have found in William of Peyre Godin's letters, with the exception that here there is no mention of that particularly egregious sacrilege, baptizing images to increase their maleficent power. In short, again we are confronted with what had become the papal stereotype of ceremonial magic. This time, instead of addressing himself to inquisitors, the pope turned directly to the Christian people. By his edict he put on warning every member of God's church that no one should teach or learn anything about the exercises of magic he had described, much less make use of a single element of the whole apparatus of maleficent practices. Whoever failed to observe the papal warning would, by that fact alone (*"ipso facto"*), incur a sentence of excommunication.

There was, moreover, no slackening under John's successor, Benedict XII. If anything, Benedict, who had been one of the theologians consulted by John in 1320, had in the interim become more convinced than John that the full power of the inquisition should be unleashed against the perpetrators of ceremonial magic. In 1336 Benedict granted to William Lombardi, canon of Mirepoix and official at the papal court, the power to proceed with the full force of the office of inquisition regarding the crime of heresy (*"iuxta privilegia officii inquisitionis heretice pravitatis"*) against anyone accused in the papal territory of an offense impinging on the faith. Listed together without distinction as fulfilling this criterion were the crimes of heresy, schism, faction, but also sorcery (*"maleficia"*) and "divination (*"sortilegia"*).[178] Apparently, in the pope's own jurisdiction he could forego all scruples about the niceties of the theoretical relationship between ceremonial magic and heretical belief.

Manuals for inquisitors: Bernard Gui

It took decades for ecclesiastics in general, and in particular those involved most immediately with the inquisition, to catch up. But over the course of the fourteenth century they did. As Boureau reminds us, as late as the inquisitor Guido Terreni's treatise on heresy of around 1340, an influential manual for inquisitors could be produced which contained not so much as a mention of sorcery or the charges of adoration of demons.[179] The opening wedge of a first exception had appeared only slightly earlier, sometime after 1324, at the hands of a Dominican friar who had served as papal inquisitor for Toulouse from 1307 until probably the middle of 1324, brother Bernard Gui. Gui's *Treatise on the Practice of the Office of Inquisition Against Heresy* contains five parts, the last of which lays out various heretical teachings and prescribes methods for investigating them and receiving abjuration from presumed or convicted heretics.[180] In this part we find two tiny sections dealing with sorcery, divination and a handful of other magical practices.[181]

The first section was concerned with interrogation procedures. Yet in a short introductory paragraph Gui laid out what he saw as his target. It was the "disease and error of sorceries and divinations and the calling up of demons."[182] According to Gui, the illness was spread widely through the regions of his world due to the "falsehoods and inventions of superstitious men paying heed to the spirits of error and the teachings of demons."[183] From the start, therefore, the connection between sorcery or divination and the active intervention of demonic forces was fundamental to Gui's approach.

When it came to the interrogations themselves, however, Gui's text reveals a wide-ranging sense of what constituted the targeted wicked behavior. The list of matters to be broached begins with a series having to do with magical practices we would associate most readily with the unlearned.[184] Suspects were to be queried about acts taken to promote the harmony or discord of married couples or to induce the impregnation of those whose marriage was barren, and about giving things like hair and fingernails to be eaten. They were to be questioned about what they had announced concerning the state of the souls of the dead or what pronouncements they had made about the outcome of future events. All of these are topics that we have seen before in the early penitentials of Regino and Burchard or in the sermons of Aelfric. We can even speculate that they might have been copied directly from the text of an ancient penitential. Moreover, following these items on sorcery plain and simple, there comes a question about those special women, called popularly the *"bonae res"* ("good things") and said to go about at night.[185] Here then is a piece of folklore, an echo of the women of the night in the second part of the "Canon Episcopi." Again, perhaps evidence of the influence of the old penitentials.

But then the focuses changes. In Gui's words, "inquiry should be made most of all regarding those things smacking of superstition and either irreverence or injury to the sacraments of the church."[186] Most diligently of all the inquisitor must interrogate his suspects about how they have involved themselves with the sacrament of Christ's body. And they should be queried about whether they have made figures of wax and then had them baptized. The list then ends with another piece of image magic: What do you know about "the making of images from lead, and about how they should be fashioned, and to what effect?"[187] By now, of course, we are well into the precincts of the ceremonial magic of the learned, as well as the sorts of sacrilege that seem to have been on the mind of popes like John XXII.

There is in fact reason to believe that it is these final concerns, not the preceding references to popular practices, that truly animated Gui and explain his inclusion of sorcery in a manual for inquisitors. For when he returns to the subject in the second short section, this time listing formulas of abjuration to be imposed, it is only the learned magic that is referred to in the text. The rubric beginning this section makes the point most clearly.

The form for recanting the disease and error of sorceries or divinations and the invocation of demons, especially when they savor of heresy against the truth and piety of the sacrament of the eucharist, or of baptism, or of any of the other sacraments. Or when, in the invocation of demons, sacrifice or offering be made to demons, or any other [act] expressly implicating error against the faith.[188]

Here, too, for the first time we see mention of heresy and a focus on errors of the faith, the very matters that had so vexed John XXII and had led him to consult his ten theologians. And in the formulaic recantations we are presented with we see the very conviction John was looking for in 1320. It is sufficient to quote the first abjuration:

> I, such and such N ... completely abjure all error and heresy pitting itself against the catholic faith of our Lord Jesus Christ, and I especially and expressly abjure all baptism of images or of any other inanimate object and all rebaptizing of persons already baptized by legitimate rite.[189]

If the theologians had been unsure whether baptizing an image amounted to heresy, Gui was not.

Manuals for inquisitors: Nicolau Eymeric

It took the rest of the century for the assumption that sorcery was itself evidence of heretical belief to become ingrained. It did so by way of careful argumentation by trained inquisitors. An important hurdle had been surmounted by 1376, the year of the composition of what was to become a standard handbook on inquisitorial practices up to early modern times. The book is the *Directorium inquisitorum* (*Guidebook for Inquisitors*) of the Dominican friar, Nicolau Eymeric. Eymeric had been inquisitor for Aragon since 1356, and in his *Directorium* he summed up his decades of experience along with much he drew from the writings of previous inquisitors. It is in Eymeric's work that we see the first unambiguous declaration that ceremonial magic in nearly all its forms was to be considered a manifest sign of heresy.[190]

The section that Eymeric devotes to our topic comes in two questions, numbers 42 and 43, from the second of the *Directorium*'s three parts. Question 42 deals expressly with "sorcerers and diviners" ("*sortilegi et divinatores*"), Question 43 with the "invokers of demons" ("*daemones invocantes*").[191] An examination of the text reveals however that Question 42 presents Eymeric's whole thesis on the matter, to which Question 43 adds an important addendum. In that Question 42, Eymeric sets out to determine whether sorcerers and diviners are to be considered as heretics and thus as subject to the judgment of the inquisition.[192] To settle the matter he thought it necessary to divide sorcery and divination into two basic kinds.

There were, on the one hand, sorcerers and diviners pure and simple ("*sortilegi et divinatores meri*").[193] Such magicians practiced their craft by reading their judgments in "natural effects and the routine conditions of human life." From these latter they were able to divine things hidden from the rest of us – that is, predict the future or reveal secrets. Two examples given by Eymeric were palmistry and fortune-telling by drawing straws. He clearly had a category of occult practice in mind akin to what William of Auvergne had more broadly defined as natural magic. On the other hand, however, there were sorcerers and diviners that did not restrict themselves to the *pure* practice of the craft but rather passed over into doing the honor of divine worship (*"latria"*) or at least of veneration (*"dulia"*) to demons to promote their efforts. As he explained, such sorcerers and diviners wanted to peer into the future or penetrate to the secrets of the human heart.

Having introduced his distinction, Eymeric then quickly moved on to answering his question. Practitioners of sorcery and divination of the pure type, or what we might call natural magicians, lay outside the purview of the inquisition of heresy, and inquisitors were not to involve themselves with them. Those diviners, however, who rendered worship or veneration to demons were engaging in activity that manifestly savored of heresy. They should fall directly under the jurisdiction of inquisitors and, if found guilty, should be punished according to the full force of laws pertaining to heretical behavior.[194] It is worth noting that Eymeric added a few examples of what he meant by the sort of divination subject to inquisitorial investigation and punishment, whose practitioners he called "heretical sorcerers" (*"sortilegi haereticales"*).[195] The category embraced predictors of the future who baptized images, rebaptized infants, prescribed the use of holy oil and sometimes even fumigated the heads of the dead. Plainly, our author was concerned with the sort of ceremonial magic that had drawn the attention of John XXII. In his case, however, there is no sign of the scruples revealed in the ten theologians' response to John's consultation of 1320. All such behavior was evidence of heretical belief, and there was no need to quibble further about the perpetrators' intentions.

Question 43 of the *Directorium*, part 2, proceeds to inquire whether those invoking demons should be treated as sorcerers (*"sortilegi"*) – that is, as "pure" sorcerers and thus not subject to inquisitorial investigation – or as heretics or persons suspected of heresy, thus subject to the inquisition's judgment.[196] In fact, this question represents not so much a turn to new material as an opportunity to take a closer look at cases overlapping with what Question 42 had placed under the rubric of heretical sorcery. It serves for us the function of clarifying Eymeric's conception of ceremonial magic. As before in Question 42, so here too our author begins by introducing a division in his subject. There were, he said, three ways demons were wont to be invoked.

By the terms of a first way the invokers plainly rendered the honor of divine worship (*"latria"*) to the demons they called upon.[197] There was, moreover, a multitude of manners in which they managed to do so.[198] Some openly did adoration to the demons; others poured out execrable prayers to them. Some promised them obedience; others swore by the demons' name. Many practiced chastity in reverence to the demons, or entered into long fasts or otherwise macerated their bodies for the demons' sake. Some even performed sacrifices. Most of this we are, of course, familiar with from the magical literature we have examined from the thirteenth and early fourteenth centuries. A second way of invoking demons did not implicate the invokers in worship, but it required that they give to demons the reverence due typically to saints (*"dulia"*).[199] Invokers might, for example, mix the names of demons among those of saints in their prayers to God. Or they might invoke the demons as mediators before the Lord. At the very least, they might light candles to the demons and otherwise attempt to pay glory to God in the demons' name. These, too, include practices seen in the literature examined above. By the third way, the invokers of demons neither worshipped demons nor did them the reverence due to saints. They did invoke them, all the same, and by equally precise and ceremonial means.[200] Again Eymeric offered an example. A sorcerer might draw a circle on the ground, set a youth within its bounds and hand the youth a mirror, sword or vase. The practitioner then would read aloud from a book to draw the attention of the intended demon. It was an art, so Eymeric said, that he had heard reported from many a suspect's mouth.

For each of the three ways Eymeric then returned to answer the question he had posed. And for each, the answer was the same. If someone clearly had been adjudged to have offered to demons the honor of divine worship, no matter what form that worship took, then such a person should be treated juridically as a heretic and rendered up to the justice of the church. If the subject would not repent, then she or he should be turned over to the secular authorities for execution.[201] Among Eymeric's arguments for this conclusion, he claimed that, whether or not sacrifice was offered, any operation of magic in which something was expected from a demon in response to an invocation implicated the perpetrator in apostasy. For such a quid pro quo had necessarily to depend upon a pact, whether explicit or not, and a pact with the devil was conceivable only if one had abandoned God. Since apostasy was equivalent to heresy, such an invoker of demons should be treated as a heretic.[202]

Of course, once this conclusion had been established, the arguments for delivering the other two types of demon-invokers over to the inquisition became considerably easier to make. Indeed, Eymeric hardly needed to lay them out in so many words. He did, however, offer a few, brief comments. First of all, he explicitly made the point that those who invoked demons without giving them divine worship (*"latria"*) but paying them reverence (*"hiperdulia vel dulia"*) all the same were not to be taken as naturalizing or "pure" sorcerers or diviners but rather regarded as heretics and subjected to the jurisdiction of the inquisition.[203] One argument ran that exhibiting the honor of reverence to demons revealed that in one's heart one believed the demon to be holy and a friend of God. But such a thought itself was openly heretical, as was clear from both scripture and the determination of the church. Then Eymeric drew an identical conclusion concerning invokers of demons who did not seem in any way to be worshipping or giving reverence to demons. They, too, should be taken if convicted not as mere sorcerers but as heretics and subjected to the punishments of the inquisition.[204] A simple, global argument was presented in this case. Scripture showed that invoking any spirit was to be considered the same as doing it divine honors. Thus, demon invocation in any form was tantamount to heresy. With Eymeric therefore we see John XXII's hopes realized among judicial theorists perhaps even more greatly than the pope had dreamed possible. Much sorcery involved demons, and any that did, either openly or by subterfuge, should be taken as a sign of heretical belief.

It seems that by the time of Eymeric's treatise the die had thus been cast. Much of learned magic, and certainly all of an explicitly ceremonial sort, now lay open to potential prosecution by the inquisition under the rules and penalties prescribed for heresy. Since the time of late thirteenth-century theologians such as Thomas Aquinas momentum had irreversibly been building toward establishing the rule that learned magic and heresy most often went hand in hand. From this point forth, learned magic would be forced to swim against the tide, not only of much of theological opinion but also of the juridical and punitive powers of the inquisition.

Not that some resistance did not remain. While in papal circles and among some inquisitors the campaign against magic had been fully embraced, there were still those, perhaps in secular government and surely at the episcopal level of the ecclesiastical hierarchy, who proved reluctant to join the fray. In 1374, just two years before Eymeric penned his inquisitorial handbook, Pope Gregory XI wrote to the Dominican James of Morerio, papal inquisitor for France, offering support in the campaign to eradicate the plague of demon invocation from among the nominal Christian flock. Explicitly calling upon the language of John XXII's "Super illius specula," Gregory bemoaned the fact that the invocation of demons and related practices still flourished among many people, including ecclesiastics, within James's judicial purview.[205] More to the point, there were also those from both lay and ecclesiastical spheres who, when James took steps to rein in such diabolical behavior, put themselves in his way, claiming that according to canon law the inquisitorial office did not have authority over such matters. In response, the pope declared that any other papal directives or canonical prescriptions notwithstanding, he by his papal authority was delegating full and free power to the inquisitor to proceed in all such cases. If the pope would have his way, the spirit of John XXII would persist in gathering force. As we shall see, within a century in fact most of the resistance had collapsed. More importantly, however, the campaign had widened to enfold within its embrace much more than ceremonial magic.

Conclusion

Looking back, therefore, we can see how far the reaction to the growth of a body of learned magical literature, most especially that of a ceremonial sort, and to the emergence of what was surely a considerable number of willing practitioners had progressed by the end of the fourteenth century. The critical ideological development had come in the thirteenth century. Thomas Aquinas can stand as an indicator of a new-found conviction that learned magic necessarily entailed reliance on demons and should thus be regarded by Christians with fear and horror. Some resistance to this blanket condemnation was mounted by scholars like Roger Bacon. But their voices were drowned out in the ever amplifying call for censure among members of the ecclesiastical hierarchy. By the early fourteenth century, first royal and then papal juridical procedures against the practice of ceremonial magic had begun to coalesce into a foundation for action against learned magic in court. If inquisitors were to act on these precedents, the argument had to be established that the practice of ceremonial magic was tantamount to heresy. That stage had been reached by the late fourteenth century, as we can see from the evidence in manuals for inquisitors. Let us now look at how upon this foundation was erected the superstructure of the trials of witches.

5

The Witchcraze and the Crisis of Early Modern Europe, 1400–1650

The turn of the fourteenth to fifteenth centuries witnessed a radical shift in the trajectory of the story we have been following so far. From the perspective of the themes of this book, it can be said that the line of development we were following at the end of the preceding chapter, where ceremonial magic had begun in ecclesiastical eyes to be inevitably connected to heresy and thereby open to the judicial oversight of the papal inquisition, reached back and connected to the material investigated in the first half of Chapter 2, the problem of popular beliefs, as well as the subject of the second half of that same chapter, the elite onslaught on popular heresy. Concretely put, what was at stake was the widening of the net of inquisitorial concern about magic from learned and ceremonial forms to the practices and beliefs of the populace at large and then the linkage of this wider set of concerns to an effective crusade against all that smacked of the newly broadened view of a "magical" heresy throughout society. The upshot was nothing less than the emergence of the witchcraze that haunted much of western Europe from the middle of the fifteenth century up through the final decades of the seventeenth.

The rise of the witch trials, some of the story of their persistence across western Europe through the sixteenth and the first half of the seventeenth century, and a broad evaluation of what the trials mean for the history of the early modern period will occupy the present chapter. First, of course, will come a look at the trials' origins. Here the focus falls on a set of four fifteenth-century documents – supplemented by details from a cluster of trials in the diocese of Lausanne – that bear witness to the shift in prosecutorial emphasis from learned magic to popular belief. They testify to the fashioning of a stereotype that will underlie the prosecution of witches in the succeeding centuries. There follows an examination of the spread of the stereotype, particularly as orchestrated by the early modern papacy. The rest of the chapter is then given over to the historiography of the trials, first an overlook at what have been the leading interpretations of their causal foundation, and then consideration of three largely causal factors to which the current study will draw special attention.

Let us then pick up the story with examination of the transition from concern with learned magic to a preoccupation with popular belief. As fate would have it, the shift in direction was initiated at a precise moment and in a clearly delimited geographic space. In the first decades of the fifteenth century, and in an area surrounding the western Alps and their foothills, there emerged a new dynamic, seen both in ideology and in the specifics of judicial procedure, paving the way to the witch trials of subsequent centuries and bringing our story out of the narrow ambits of the learned elite and into the rough and tumble of society at large. A small arc of territories in present-day Italy, Switzerland and France furnished the stage on which the drama played itself out. Beginning in the south with Upper Savoy, extending into the lands of the Swiss dioceses of Sion and Lausanne – the Valais, the Simmental along with the rest of the region under the political control of Bern, and to the west the Pays de Vaud – then curling down to the southwest with the upper Dauphiné, anchored in the important juridical and administrative municipality of Briançon, we can trace a relatively compact area in which the witch trials found their origin.[1]

Though at first sight this arc of territory might seem like an inauspicious location for so dramatic and Europe-wide a phenomenon to get its start, a remote side-way in late medieval and early modern European society, in the end there is reason to believe that there was no spot more likely to generate the change we are about to consider. Historians once attributed the development to the region's marginality and isolation, set on the boundary between civilization and the forbidding mountains where ancient ways and elsewhere long-repressed heresy had maintained a meager existence for several centuries.[2] More prominent now is the view that this was the site of vigorous activity and interaction.[3] Situated along the commercial pathway connecting north and south, this arc of the Suisse romande was particularly sensitive to the economic troubles besetting Europe at the end of the Middle Ages. In addition, the inquisition had recently been especially active there, seeking out the remnants of the heresy of the Waldensians – one of the more organized forms of heretical practice that had grown up in the late twelfth century – which had since the fourteenth century retreated into the relative safety of the Alpine highlands. On top of it all was a surge in this same area of reforming activity within the clerical establishment, spurred on by the two great church councils called in Swiss lands to handle the crisis of the Great Schism, the Councils of Constance and of Basel.[4]

Swiss heresy trials

Triggering the development was a rash of heresy trials in two urban locations in our designated arc, Bern and Fribourg, both located within the diocese of Lausanne and under normal circumstances subject to the jurisdiction of the papal inquisitor based in that city.[5] The target of the trials was a purported Waldensian community in each town. Pierrette Paravy has suggested that the time was ripe. Since the early fourteenth century there had been a papal court situated not far away in Avignon, and the last third of the fourteenth century witnessed a swell of efforts by the Avignonese popes to deal with the Waldensians they understood to be harbored in the mountainous regions lying just to their northeast.[6] In the train of this papal inquisitional fervor, accusations of Waldensian activity were almost bound to arise toward the end of the fourteenth century deep in the Suisse romande.

The first trial seems to have been initiated by Bern's town authorities, though prosecuted under a special inquisitor the city had arranged to have appointed from the Dominican convent in Basel.[7] Over 130 individuals – according to the chronicler Konrad Justinger, our only witness to the trial – hailing from both town and countryside, were brought before the inquisitor in Bern in 1399. Since none of the accused had ever been publicly suspect of heresy before, and since they all abjured their false beliefs and paid a substantial fine, no one was burned. All were eventually released with the requirement that for a duration of time they appear in public only while wearing the yellow cross of heresy on their clothing. Prompted by a denunciation originating out of Bern, and dependent on testimony given in the heresy trial that had just taken place there, a second process against Waldensians was commenced in Fribourg in the fall of the same year. Here the inquisition was directed by the designated authority for such matters in the region, the Dominican papal inquisitor from the convent in Lausanne. In all, 54 residents were accused and tried. The upshot was, however, surely even less to the authorities' liking than had been the case in Bern. Due to disagreement between Bern and Fribourg, which had just gone through a bout of interurban warfare, acceptable evidence could never be presented, so the inquisitor was forced to terminate the process and acquit all accused.

A third trial arose again in Fribourg, this time in 1430. The inquisitor was once more a Dominican from the Lausanne convent, and several of the names of the accused had already appeared on the list of defendants in the same city during the previous trial. Again, the results were meager. Given the fact that the 1399 trial had ended in dismissal, not one of the Fribourg residents could be accused of sliding back into heresy for a second time. They were nearly all released, following the requisite oaths of abjuration. Just one of the accused, who was from Bern and had been among those convicted there of the Waldensian error in 1399, was judged a recidivist and condemned to the flames.

For urban heresy trials in the region, directed against defendants who could in reality be expected to have joined the ranks of a dissident religious group, these incidents amounted to the last hurrah. Kathrin Utz Tremp has suggested that the reason must lie in a learning process among Swiss Waldensians. With the danger of prosecution driven home by three trials within 30 years, heretics picked up the lesson that they must conceal their activities, or if necessary defend themselves with dissimulating denials and abjurations. The fact that Waldensian communities in these areas survived up to the time of the Reformation was most likely due to this technique of adaptation.[8] The inquisitors, however, and those who supported them among the urban authorities, were not to be denied. Stymied within the town walls, they took their efforts out into the countryside.

The beginning of witch trials

It was in trials among the peasant folk that the nature of the target changed. Here, in the rural byways of these mountainous lands, we find the birthpangs of the witchcraze. The whole process took about 40 years, from the first decade of the fifteenth century up through the 1440s. Starting with a hunt for heresy, juridical officials, both lay and ecclesiastical, ended up tracking down and persecuting individuals the charges against whom correspond for the first time in European history to the standard modern stereotype of the activities of a witch.[9] The grinding of the wheels of justice produced the ingredients of this stereotype and refined them for subsequent judges and inquisitors to use. Out of the trials themselves there thus slowly emerged the vision of the early modern witch.

Much of the direct evidence for these trials – actual judicial records of the prosecutions – has disappeared. What remains in the archives of local authorities and jurisdictions has by and large not yet been subjected to scholarly investigation. Only now are studies beginning to appear delving into the appropriate documents and offering us a view into the trials themselves.[10] But we do possess evidence, given to us by contemporary observers, for the ideological transformation the trials underwrote. A few people were actually watching at the time, and they have recorded for us the phenomenon whereby the stereotype, the theoretical grounding for the witchcraze, was shaped and brought into being. It helps to conceive of the whole procedure as in fact marked by two decisive developments. These two were themselves closely related, but they seem to have followed in a slight chronological succession. They can be thought of as comprising two crucial moments in the move from the relatively episodic inquisitorial pursuit of ceremonial magic outlined in the preceding chapter to the sometimes widespread but always socially turbulent juridical chase after a collective heresy of almost unthinkable danger to society, witchcraft in the early modern sense of the word.

In simple terms, the first moment was constituted by the transformation of the inquisitional target we arrived at at the end of Chapter 4 from magic as practiced among a lettered elite to the host of magical and superstitious practices long associated with the culture of the populace at large. For once the hunt after heretics began to take on a popular objective, inquisitors almost by necessity turned to the paradigm of magic as the basis for a type of heretical practice. It was, after all, what we would think of as superstitious practices – sorcery most of all – that came up for judgment in the trials. These popular practices and beliefs were then substituted for – most often, of course, just situated alongside – the learned rituals that had been the juridical target up through the late fourteenth century. Once this first step had been taken, effectively setting a chronically troublesome element of popular culture in the cross-hairs of the inquisition, there followed a second moment in which a whole host of ideological assumptions – defamations more exactly – about the nature of heresy were projected onto popular magic and superstition. In the process, a range of folkloric beliefs touched on in Chapter 2 were swept up into the paradigm for the crime. The end product was the full-fledged stereotype of the witch as a devil-worshipping, sorcery-practicing, night-flying and sabbath-attending arch-heretic and minion of the forces of evil.

Our observers have told the story for us. They need simply to be read with care for the lines of the narrative to emerge. In all they are four individuals, each touched in some way by juridical events of the western Alps in the early fifteenth century and all recording their thoughts probably in the 1430s and 1440s. They need to be supplemented only by what we can gather from a series of trials occurring in the inquisitorial territory under the authority of Lausanne. Except for this latter piece, all the source materials have been brought together in a single volume, published with exquisite care by the scholarly team of Martine Ostorero, Agostino Paravicini Bagliani, Kathrin Utz Tremp and Catherine Chène.[11] Our task is to follow each witness, beginning with the observer of the earliest events and proceeding to the last.

Johannes Nider

Johannes Nider heads the list. He was a Dominican friar, much drawn to the movement of reform in his order getting under way in the early fifteenth century.[12] A student of theology at both Cologne and Vienna, Nider emerged on the Swiss scene as an important figure with his appointment in 1429 as prior of the Dominican convent at Basel, where he was entrusted with the delicate job of introducing the reform. When the Council of Basel convened in 1431, Nider was perfectly placed to play a role, and he did so from the very beginning. It was presumably during the early years of the council that he received much of the information that permitted him to serve as one of our observers of the origins of the witchcraze. In 1434 he was named reader on the *Sentences* at the Dominican convent in Vienna, a post he assumed at the latest in 1435. Though he never returned to Switzerland, it was in Vienna that he wrote down in his *Formicarius* what he had heard about the witch trials. He composed the work between 1436 and the year of his death, 1438.

According to Nider, three direct witnesses provided him the information he shares with us in his *Formicarius* about those early trials. The first was a secular judge identified in the text as from the diocese of Lausanne, more specifically a citizen of Bern who would have served as the Bern-appointed bailiff of the Upper Simmental.[13] This latter territory fell under Lausanne's diocesan jurisdiction, but it had since the early fifteenth century been incorporated into the political dominion of Bern. Joseph Hansen identified this figure as Peter von Greyerz, who is known to have officiated as the bailiff of Upper Simmental from 1392 to 1406, with the exception of a half year in 1397.[14] But in fact, there are two other Peters whom we know to have held the position of bailiff of Upper Simmental between 1392 and the late 1430s, when Nider wrote his work. Contrary to Hansen, either of these could have been the Peter to whom Nider referred. Since the latest was a Peter von Ey, who acted as bailiff from 1413 to 1417, we are left to conclude that Nider's informant was active in the Simmental sometime between 1392 and 1417. The events described must therefore date from those years.

Nider's second informant was, he tells us, an inquisitor from Autun, who was also at some point a resident and reformer in the Dominican convent at Lyons.[15] Though Nider does not provide the details, it would seem that this anonymous inquisitor's reports concern much the same region as that of the bailiff from Bern, or at least territories within the arc described earlier. Since Nider once remarks that he had spoken with this informant the very year he was writing his *Formicarius*, the two must have been in touch at least as late as 1436 or 1437.[16] The inquisitor's testimony thus might have to do with trials and events a decade or so later than those reported by the otherwise unknown Peter, perhaps even the early 1430s. The final informant was not a witness to trials but rather an expert who could speak about magic and sorcery in the Alpine region at the time. Benedict by name, this person was a monk of the Order of St. Benedict who, when Nider knew him, resided in the reformed Benedictine convent in Vienna. As Nider explains it, this informer had as a younger man been an expert in necromancy, and much in demand at the court of secular nobles in his environs.[17] His information was thus that of a true insider.

It is surely from this last source that Nider drew his ideas about necromancy and its relation to magic in general. He understood that by its original meaning the word "*nigromanticus*" referred to someone who, using the pertinent magical rites ("*supersticiosis ritibus*"), could raise the dead to speak of hidden matters. But he also knew that the same term was commonly applied to those who, relying upon demons with whom they had entered into a pact, practiced other ceremonies in which they predicted the future, revealed hidden knowledge and even sometimes harmed their neighbors with maleficent sorcery ("*maleficiis*").[18] That Nider had in mind here primarily the learned magicians of the traditions examined in the preceding chapter is indicated by the fact that his primary example of a practitioner of the art, the monk of Vienna, in his earlier days as magician possessed the "demonic books of necromancy" that make up the stock in trade of the stereotypical ritual magician.[19]

Yet the line between such learned types and more common sorcerers of the popular tradition was easily crossed in Nider's mind. Immediately after his reference to the Viennese monk Nider remarked that the judge Peter had told him about a necromancer, by name of Scavius, stories of whom had emerged in the trials in the territory of Bern, and who might have been practicing as early as 60 years before Nider was writing – that is, perhaps the 1370s. In this case, the individual was associated solely with acts of sorcery, or harmful magic, there being no mention of prediction of the future or raising the dead. Still, his was magic of a learned sort, since he was said to have left commentaries on his fraudulent art ("*sue fraudis commenta*") to a certain disciple, Hoppo, who in turn passed them along to a Scaedelin, in his own right eventually confirmed as a "master in maleficence" (*"in maleficium magist[er]"*).[20] This latter is the one who actually figured in the trials recounted to Nider. With him we begin to see reported acts of magic that spill over into activity of the kind associated with sorcery at the level of the populace, reminiscent of the witchcraft revealed in the sermons and penitentials examined in Chapter 2.

According to the reports written down by Nider, this Scaedelin was wont to perform such tricks as to make a third of the harvest of his neighbors appear miraculously in his own fields, to raise hailstorms and high winds accompanied by thunder, to cause sterility in men and horses, to bring bodily harm to those around him or to hurt them in their property, even to strike them dead with a clap of thunder.[21] Material of this type surely made up the bulk of the accusations in the trials that Nider's two informers reported to him. Presumably drawing on this matter, Nider even offered his readers a definition of sorcerer or witch (*"maleficus"*) that might well serve as the type for the defendants brought before the judges in these trials. *"Maleficus"* came, so Nider claimed, from "evil doing" (*"male faciens"*), or "keeping bad faith" (*"male fidem servans"*), in either case manifested as harming one's neighbor by means of "superstitious" practices.[22] This was, to be sure, the standard understanding of maleficent sorcery or *"maleficium"* among the people.

Nider went so far as to list seven deeds such sorcerers or witches most frequently performed.[23] First there was love sorcery, then hate sorcery, whereby invidious relations were sown between the affected parties. Next came manipulations in which the victims were, in Nider's words, "bewitched" (*"maleficiati"*), so that they became either impotent or infertile. Fourth was making the targets ill in some part of the body, fifth depriving them of life and sixth taking away their rational faculties. Seventh was harming the victims in their material possessions or their livestock. All of these acts had been commonplace in popular renditions of sorcery since before our examples in Chapter 2 from the tenth and eleventh centuries. Yet as Nider explained, and as presumably was laid against the defendants in the trials about which he spoke, the sorcerers or witches did these things not by themselves but solely through the intermediary of demons. Demons were thus the primary actors, and they were induced to be so because of pacts the sorcerers had entered into with them.[24] In Nider's mind, hence also in that of the judges in the trials of which he had been informed, the terms by which the ritual magician had been understood in the inquisitorial literature of the preceding century were beginning to pass over into the conception of the common sorcerer.

But the judicial and ideological net was now being cast even more widely. For there were elements in the reports that Nider recounted bringing us still closer to the full stereotype of the classical witch. According to the bailiff of Upper Simmental, witches (*"malefici"*) of both sexes were often known to eat children in their bestial performances.[25] Old notions of the *strigae* seemed to be seeping into the image of the sorcerer. Indeed, as Nider continued, an apprehended witch confessed to just how it all was done. Having killed infants by their evil ceremonious acts (*"ceremoniis nostris"*) even as they were sleeping by their parents' side, the culprits waited until the children had been buried and retrieved them secretly from the graves.

> We cook them until, free of the bones, most of the flesh is rendered soft enough to chew or be drunk. From the solid matter we make an unguent suitable for our purposes, our arts and our transmutations. With the liquid we fill flasks or wineskins. And he who drinks of this [liquid], once a few ceremonies [of ours] have been performed, is immediately reduced to a co-conspirator of ours and made a master of our sect (*"magister nostre secte"*).[26]

By this point the cannibalism of the *striga* myths has begun to meet the age-old calumnies against heretics, with the term "master" giving a hint of the practice of ceremonial magicians.

At one point Nider's image even seems to embrace the stereotype of heretics as devil-worshippers.[27] For another of the defendants tried by Peter the bailiff purportedly recounted the precise ceremonies by which he was inducted into his company of sorcerers.[28] The pattern was for a potential disciple to enter a church on Sunday in the presence of other witches and there to abjure his faith in Christ. Then he would do homage to the "little master," which Nider explained was the title by which they referred to the devil. Finally he would drink of a potion in a wineskin prepared as described earlier. Immediately, the novice would feel in his innards knowledge of the maleficent art begin to germinate and the rites of the sect take hold. Michael Bailey has suggested that the full-blown version of this stereotype did not emerge in the reports of Nider's earliest witness, the bailiff from Bern, but was rather read back into the earlier accounts by Nider when years later he composed his *Formicarius*.[29] And it is true that the most complete description of the initiation into the rites of a devil-worshipping sect comes in a passage where Nider says he is relating a conversation he had with the inquisitor from Autun the very year in which he was writing.

> The[ir] way of learning such an art was, so he said, for the witches (*"malefici"*) to come together in a special assembly (*"certa concio"*), where by means of their [maleficent] works they saw a demon visibly [present] in the image of a man. To this demon the disciple was required to give his faith, promising to abjure Christianity and [promising] never to venerate the Eucharist and to stomp upon the cross wherever it was secretly possible to do so.[30]

The date of this confession might well have been as late as the 1430s. With it we are very close to the early modern stereotype of the witch.

All the same, Nider held back from mixing in all the elements from popular folklore that would eventually constitute the standard for witches gathering at their sabbath. He knew about the stories of the ladies of the night, traversing the skies in the train of Diana, but he rejected them as hallucinations. Earlier in the *Formicarius* he recounted what he said was a story told to him by his teacher.[31] A

Dominican priest, so the teacher said, had once gone to a village where a woman claimed that she, along with Diana and others of her sex, was transported bodily through the air on numerous occasions. We know of these stories, of course, from as early as the time of Regino of Prüm. In this case, the priest insisted that the woman was mistaken and set about proving his point. He arranged with the woman to have witnesses, including himself, in attendance the next time she planned to undergo one of her marvelous conveyances. On the appointed day, the old woman crawled into a pasta tub, said the requisite words of sorcery and anointed herself with unguent, and immediately went to sleep. While sleeping she began dramatically to whisper and wildly gesticulate, signs to the priest that she was dreaming of her rides with Diana. Her motions became so violent that she upset the tub, banged her head and awoke. As it was plain even to the woman that, though she had been thinking she was out on a night ride, she had in fact never left the room, all present recognized her error. Dreams, and not reality, had made up the stuff of the supposed transportations. Nider realized, moreover, that here he was in line with the "Canon Episcopi," which he cited in support of his interpretation that illusions aroused by demons and not bodily transport lay at the heart of all such stories from the folk.[32]

Witch trials

If we look only slightly later to a series of trials held in the diocese of Lausanne and prosecuted by the papal inquisitor from the Dominican convent in that city, we see virtually the same constellation of transgressions emerging as in Nider's reports. Here, however, since the prosecutor was a member of the clergy, trained in inquisitorial law, there is a shift in perspective. In Nider's trials, most of which were carried out under the supervision of a lay justice, the focus bore upon the crimes of sorcery themselves, traditionally a matter of concern for secular juris-prudence. When, as in these new cases, the driving impetus for the prosecution came from the clergy, greater emphasis was laid on the circumstance that, for all the material emphasis on sorcery, heresy was principally involved. It is worth noting that in all these new trials, the prosecutor was the same person, the ener-getic Dominican, Ulric of Torrenté, papal inquisitor at Lausanne from 1420 to 1440.[33] Ulric, the model of an aggressive inquisitor, seems to have picked up on what we have seen from Nider of the already intensifying juridical emphasis on a mixture of the paradigms of common sorcery, learned magic and heresy, all with an eye to strengthening the authority of the inquisition with regard to this newly emerging criminal target.

As fate would have it, Ulric was the inquisitor presiding over the trial of the Waldensians at Fribourg in 1430, alluded to earlier as providing an entrée to the witch trials.[34] Already even here, there is an indication of seepage of elements of sorcery into the bill of particulars of the accusations. The wife of a certain

Willinus Stucky, for example, was widely accused of "many acts of sorcery and other unspeakable things" ("*diffamata de multis maleficiis et nephandis*"). Her neighbors said additionally that she had a tendency to avenge herself on them as well as other individuals by causing damage both to their persons and their goods. In the judges' estimation she could not have been able to accomplish such deeds "without sorcery and various invocations of demons" ("*sine maleficiis et aliis demonum invocationibus*").[35] Nonetheless, the Fribourg trial concerned itself primarily with authentic Waldensians.

Less than a decade later, the transformation from heresy trial to trial of sorcery as prime indicator of heretical behavior had made remarkable strides. The records summarizing a trial Torrenté directed in the city of Neuchâtel in 1439 make the fact patently clear. Here a certain Enchimandus le Masseller, resident of the surrounding diocese, was accused by a number of presumed co-conspirators of being a heretic. In the end, he was convicted and turned over to the secular branch for punishment.[36] Yet while heresy comprised the accusation and the basis for the conviction, in fact the crime itself specifically drew in elements both from fourteenth-century proceedings against learned magic and from the stock in trade of sorcery among the common folk. As with any heretic, Enchimandus was purported to have denied the true God and forfeited his place in paradise. But he was also said to have promised homage and fealty to the devil, charges that for a century had been typically leveled against the ceremonial magician. Just as striking, however, there arose additional accusations pointing more to the commonplaces of folk sorcery and to material associated in Chapter 2 with folklore. Enchimandus was said to have been a murderer, surely by means of sorcery or poison. He was also reputed, with the help of the devil, duly invoked ("*dyabolica invocatione*"), to have been able to stir up hailstorms. Finally, the accused was reported wolf-like ("*lupino more*") to have devoured human flesh, even that of his own children. By their eclecticism alone these were accusations that rivaled anything seen in Nider and that pointed increasingly in the direction of the classic stereotype of the witch.

A trial presided over by Torrenté in the castellany of Dommartin, just north of Lausanne, only a year before in 1438, generated a similar list of denunciations yet added its own special twist. In this case, a certain Peter de la Prelaz confessed after having been subjected to torture. He had been reported as a heretic, and again was condemned and turned over to the public arm for justice.[37] The crimes entailed once more denying the true God and doing homage to the devil, as well as the more common-folk raising of hailstorms and tempests along with a host of other unnamed sins, all probably consisting in the application of harmful sorcery against his neighbors. But here, the crime of eating human flesh was compounded by that of having presented the flesh, before consumption, as an offering to the devil. Another piece of the stereotype of ceremonial magic had thus managed to work its way into the new accusations. And here, too, there seems to have been greater emphasis on the claim that Peter and his co-defendants made up a definite congregation. Peter is said to have joined a "*consortium*" of followers of the devil along with his co-conspirators and to have remained steadfast as a member of that group – to which the word "sect" is once applied – over a period of time. The notion of a church of heretics surely provided one model for this charge, but we begin to see here as well the outlines of what would soon become the standard for a coven of witches.[38]

A last element comes up in records dealing again with the trials of 1439 in Neuchâtel. Among the defendants there appeared a parishioner named Jaquet dou Plain. The summary of the trial passes quickly over the defendant's alleged crimes, mentioning only abjuration of the faith, swearing homage to the devil and an unspecified array of other detestable actions.[39] It is almost certain that the intention was to implicate Jaquet in the same wrongdoings assigned to Enchimandus in the trial report referred to earlier. What is interesting is that the general label attached to these crimes was not just heresy but also idolatry.[40] A hint of the same was already seen in the offerings to the devil alleged in the trial of 1438 at Dommartin. But to spell out the indictment explicitly bespeaks not only the mindset of a clerical inquisitor, inclined to such normative categorization, but also familiarity with the standard vision of ceremonial magic developed in inquisitorial proceedings of the preceding century. Under Torrenté's aggressive eye the mixture of paradigms was hardening into a crime of real specificity and considerable juridical weight.

Hans Fründ

At about the same time that Torrenté was conducting his inquisitions, and surely earlier than the latest of the trials just surveyed, the new paradigm for a witch was seeing further consolidation in judicial proceedings that took place in the Valais, lands falling under the oversight of the bishopric of Sion and partly within the purview of the inquisitor at Lausanne. In this case, our reporter is the citizen of Lucerne Hans Fründ. It was probably in the early 1430s that he wrote the text of concern to us, a short account of the trials.[41] According to Fründ, they all took place around the year 1428.[42] He heard of them most likely from an official of the bishopric of Sion, a lay bailiff appointed by the bishop.[43] In contrast to the reports of the trials held under the direction of the clerical Torrenté, here a secular perspective obtains.

As Fründ explains, it was in 1428 that evil, murder and heresy made themselves known in the Valais.[44] Thus he starts with the same general category of crime as his ecclesiastical counterpart in the trials with which we have just been concerned. Yet it is immediately apparent that the focus now really lies on sorcery. As Fründ says, the heresy he has in mind is the "heresy of the witches and the sorcerers" ("*die ketzerÿe der hexssen und der zuᵒbrern*") – the former women, the latter men. To make sure his readers understand him, he glosses his words with the comment that these heretics were what in Latin are known as "*sortilegi*" ("*sortileÿ*"). Of the many who were tried and burned for their crime, a considerable number had confessed to having performed many evil acts (*vil boᵉser sachen*"), all of which could be subsumed under the Latin term "*sortilegia*" ("*sortileia*"). We are therefore still in the midst of a frenzy about heresy, but the target has decisively been shifted from suspected Waldensians to the common perpetrators of popular magic.

Fründ lists the activities for which his witches and sorcerers had been brought to trial. Among them are the commonplaces of sorcery. Many confessed to having given poisons, so that their victims either died or became lame or sick. Others, true to the stereotype, admitted that against those for whom they held some resentment, they used their powers to bring about a sudden misfortune, perhaps that the victims became sick or lame, were deprived of their senses or were blinded, or even lost their children to death. Finally there were those who had managed to "bewitch" women of the village ("*vil frowen verzouberten*"), rendering them unfertile.[45] But there were others that Fründ thought apparently guilty of lesser crimes, though still severe enough to warrant condemnation to death. Many, said Fründ, confessed to having used spells to harm the bounty of the land, most especially the harvest of the vineyards and grain. In other cases, the confession was to have taken away milk, or made the victim's cows unable to produce it. Some targeted carts and ploughs, making them useless to their owners.[46] In these latter accusations, the new focus on the sorcery of the countryside could hardly be more evident.

Yet there was more here than just common sorcery of the world of farming and herding. As before, the legends of the *strigae* also made an entrée on the scene. Among the defendants were those who said they killed their own children, then roasted them and ate them.[47] Another version of the same crime was produced in confessions to having attacked either one's own children or those of other parents during the night by approaching them and pressing them against one's own flesh. Such children subsequently were taken ill and died. Once they had been buried, the same suspects came and dug them up so they could eat the flesh.[48] Apparently this particular act of witchcraft was making the rounds in popular culture in our area of the Alps, for an almost exactly identical story had appeared in Nider's *Formicarius*.[49] Yet even more elaborate variants of sorcery were finding their way into the mix, as more elements of folklore were being swept up into the evidence presented at the trials. Some of the accused witches and sorcerers recounted how they were able to become wolves whenever they wanted. They went after sheep and lambs and devoured them as wild beasts would do. But then just as quickly, whenever they so desired, they would turn back into humans. Some others claimed that by their art they could make themselves invisible. They did so by means of the application of particular herbs.[50]

In addition to these ingredients from the common folk, the trials in the Valais also drew upon elements associated with higher magic. Those who wanted to practice the evil arts had to learn them from "the evil spirit" ("*der boᵉse geist*").[51] Surely the latter was Fründ's German phrase for the devil himself. But it was not simply a matter of turning to the devil for knowledge. Pact and homage were required as well. Before one could learn the craft, one had to give oneself over to the same "evil spirit." Moreover, one had formally to foreswear God and to forsake all the saints, Christian baptism and holy church, and, as if in vassal service, promise to make oneself serviceable to the devil. In testament to the homage one owed a yearly payment, a black sheep or lamb or a measure of oats, or perhaps simply after death a limb from one's body. Much of this we have seen before in the other trials. But now another detail from the age-old slander against heretics was incorporated, too. The "evil spirit," so Fründ asserted, most often appeared to his disciples in these encounters not in the form of a man but rather in that of a black animal, sometimes a bear, sometimes a ram, or alternatively some other horrifying form. In such a guise, he would then converse with his followers about the evil they would do.

Not missing from Fründ's accounting was also the important aspect of entering a congregation or sect. Indeed, Fründ gave a description that sounds like a cross between what was to become the witches' sabbath and a meeting of a heretical Bible group.[52] In the text the term for the gathering was a "school" ("schu°le").[53] At night, so the story ran, the witches and sorcerers would come together in a secret place. There, in the guise of a teacher, the "evil spirit" would preach to them against the articles of Christian belief. He would then hear their confessions of misdeeds – in this case, of going to church or doing good – and give them accordingly absolution and penance. As with the old slanders against the heretics, the effect was to recreate the lines of a church service, only in reverse. Bad for good; lies for truth.

There is even hint of a major change in assumptions about what the accused had to say. Nider had his own version of the assembly, but he stoutly rejected the idea of night flight as a means of coming to the meetings. But we know that night-flight had been a commonplace in folklore for centuries. It might well have appeared as an account of transport to the "schools" in the cases Fründ recounts. At least he repeats testimony of night-flights from mountain to mountain or town to town. And unlike Nider, Fründ seems to take them as entirely believable. For he claims that his subjects confessed that the "evil spirit" taught them how to make unguents through which they could accomplish the miraculous feat. They then put the unguents on stools and rode the latter from place to place in the middle of the night.[54] Andenmatten and Utz Tremp think that 1428 is too early for members of the elite to take at face value the reports of night-flight, so they suggest that Fründ wrote down his report many years later than is normally supposed.[55] It is possible that they are right, but it is equally likely that Fründ was precocious in accepting the common tales. There is no reason to think that the stories of night-flight had not been passing around in even the first of these early-fifteenth-century prosecutions.

Fründ says that more than one hundred victims, men and women, were convicted and executed in his trials over about a year and a half.[56] We see in his reporting considerable development toward the mature stereotype of the witch.

Events in the Alps are moving from concern with old-fashioned heresy toward fear of a conspiracy of sorcerers in the populace at large. Our last two witnesses give evidence of the final steps in this regard. With them, the earlier image of heresy and the newer juridical model of learned magic are fully tapped to produce a crime rampant among the superstitious common folk. This dramatic advance is starkly apparent already in the first of these documents. It is an anonymous work entitled *Errores gazariorum* (*Errors of the Gazarii*), more fully: *The Errors of the Gazarii, that is, of those who are said to ride around on brooms or staffs*.[57]

Errores gazariorum

The term "*gazarii*" had been used in northern Italy, particularly Lombardy, in the fourteenth and early fifteenth centuries to refer to Cathar heretics.[58] Here that meaning remains only as an echo, for, as we shall see, the crime in question is something new. Interestingly enough, the word appears only in the title. Perhaps it was added as an afterthought, or by someone other than the original author, once the evil actions in question had already been defined by careful description in the text itself. As for the text, it seems to have arisen in northern Italy, most likely in northern Savoy, around the early years of the Council of Basel – that is, the early 1430s. Two manuscripts of the work remain, and in both, the text is inserted among other documents either from the council or concerning it.[59] Since one of the manuscript witnesses represents an expansion and elaboration on the other, it is clearly posterior to its counterpart. To our good fortune, it contains an entirely new paragraph allowing us to date its redaction with some precision. For there is in this second version a passage about hailmaking from blocks of ice in the Alpine mountains that is so peculiar as certainly to have been lifted from the proceedings of a trial against sorcerer-heretics conducted by none other than Ulric of Torrenté in Lausanne in 1438.[60] It is likely, indeed, that this second version arose in the Dominican convent in Lausanne where Ulric was resident. Perhaps the expanded text is even due to his editorial intervention, or at the very least dependent on marginal additions he made to a copy of the shorter version in his own possession. In any event, it must date to 1438 or after.

The earlier version is the one we shall use in this study. It was almost certainly written closer to the beginning of the decade of the 1430s. Since it is uncontaminated by any of the evidence of our other sources, especially that drawn from Ulric of Torrenté's inquisitorial activity, it suits our purposes better than the longer redaction. There is reason to believe in fact that it arose in the circle of the bishop of Aosta, Georges de Saluces.[61] Bishop at Aosta from 1433 to 1440, Saluces was probably already in those years engaged in hunting for sorcerers in the Savoyard countryside, following the pattern we have seen to the north in the Swiss Alps. We know at least that in 1434 he promulgated synodal statutes calling for curates in his diocese to include in their sermons denunciations of heretics, sorcerers and diviners. In that year he also petitioned the Council of Basel for an inquisitor to be stationed in Aosta, presumably to investigate the same wrongdo-ings. When, in 1440, Saluces was named bishop of Lausanne, he would have been in an ideal position to have introduced the shorter version of the *Errores* to the Dominicans around Ulric of Torrenté.

When we turn to the text of the *Errores* itself, we see that the idea of the heresy it was directed against is not that different from the target in the trials reported on by Fründ. Sorcery among the common folk – maleficent sorcery, that is – constitutes the primary activity that the "*gazarii*" are thought to engage in. Indeed, the author states that one of the major motives people had for associating themselves with the "*gazarii*" and their deeds was a desire to avenge themselves against neighbors with whom they had fallen out.[62] Among the instances alleged is the making of a powder for killing other humans. Concocted from the bodies of dead children and parts of poisonous animals, this powder was, so the author insists, thrown into the air on foggy days, and those who came into contact with it either died or were taken with the gravest of illnesses.[63] Or there is the charge that the adherents of the heresy fabricated an equally maleficent item from the skin of a cat. Having filled the skin with various grains and grapes, they then followed a ceremonial procedure of soaking it for three days, drying it out and pulverizing the remains for easy distribution. When this powder was scattered to the winds from mountain tops, it had – with the devil's assistance – the power to render rich agricultural regions absolutely sterile or otherwise to damage the possessions of inhabitants.[64] Plainly we are in the world of sorcery as conceived by a rural population.

Present as well is the child-killing and cannibalism reminiscent of the legends of the *strigae* as well as the old defamations against heretics. We see in fact a repe-tition of the narrative of such events already found in both Fründ and Nider.[65] According to the *Errores*, the devil committed certain of his followers to enter houses and strangle children even while they were sleeping by their parents' side. These same followers would then appear on burial day at the cemetery to lament the deaths, while at night they would return to excavate the bodies. Taking the flesh that they needed, they would then carry it to their gatherings, where it could be cooked and eaten.[66]

At this point the *Errores* make their dramatic advance. For they draw together the rest of the elements of the crime targeted, and add a few novelties, to produce a full-fledged stereotype of the witches' sabbath. All that is lacking is the name itself.[67] The whole business is laid out in exquisite detail. As the author explains, someone, presumably already a "*gazarius*" working at the instigation of the devil, must approach a likely candidate and persuade him or her to join up with the heretics.[68] There then follows a formal process of initiation, at which the devil himself presides. The event happens at what is presumably a regular gath-ering place for the "*gazarii*." The author refers to it as a "synagogue."[69] Here, the devil appears usually in the form of a black cat, though occasionally in that of another animal or of a part-man, part-animal mix. To start the proceedings, the devil formally inquires of the candidate whether he or she wants to enter into the society of fellow "*gazarii.*" As soon as the entrant has agreed, the devil then extracts a pledge of fidelity ("*iuramentum fidelitatis*"), which itself follows a prescribed formula. First among the list of items pledged is a promise to remain faithful to the presider, as well as to the whole group. Continuing in imitation of the enactment of a feudal bond, the inductee then formally does homage to the devil.[70] Later on the *Errores* explains that at this point the devil draws blood from the entrant's left hand.[71] With the blood he then writes a document ("*carta*"), presumably confirming both the fealty and the homage. This pact the devil is said to keep on his person from then on, a sort of legal hedge against any back-sliding on the part of the inductee.

Yet there is more to the initiation ceremony, and here we see material drawn largely from the old defamatory stereotype of the heretic. Immediately after rendering homage, the entrant is required to kiss the devil directly on the anus.[72] We know that this element of the heresy stereotype was familiar in the region at the time, for mention of it appears in the trial of the Waldensians in Fribourg in 1430.[73] Accompanying the kiss, and serving as a kind of pledge in confirmation of the act of homage, is the consignment of a bodily limb, to be made available to the devil after death.[74] Here is a motif also seen above in Fründ's account.[75] Perhaps more grievous still, the inductee is expected, at the moment of rendering homage, to "adore" ("*adoret*") the devil.[76] Idolatry and devil worship are thus combined and added as a further charge against those implicated in the crime.

Most striking of all is the reappearance of the ancient heretical stereotype of the orgy. For, the *Errores* continues, once fealty and homage have been performed, all in the group celebrate the arrival of the new entrant, eating and drinking and, in particular, devouring the dead infants that have been either roasted or boiled.[77] After everyone has danced his full, the devil, exclaiming the signal word, "*Meschlet,*" extinguishes the light. There immediately follows a bacchanal, men fornicating with women and with other men, fathers with daughters, sons with mothers, brothers with sisters. There are those who even copulate with animals, in the words of the text, "forsaking the order of nature, both diabolically and bestially." Once the frenzy is past, and illumination restored, all drink and eat again. Then each urinates and defecates in a large urn. The text comments that they do so to the contumely of the Eucharist. And the party now over, every participant returns home.

Further details merely round out the picture of what will become the complete paradigm for witchcraft. First of all, among the items promised in the initial oath of fidelity are several activities that will be typically associated with the witch.[78] The novice pledges to do whatever he can to win over new recruits to the group. He or she commits to strangling and killing as many children as possible, especially infants three years and younger, and to bringing the bodies to the synagogue for the group's purposes. Moreover, whenever summoned, the novice agrees to set aside all other business and proceed immediately to the synagogue to join the others. And perhaps as a reminder that evil magic is also involved, there is a promise to impede whatever marriage one can, as the text explains, "by sorcery and other evil ways" ("*per sortilegia et alia maleficia*").

Other provisions of witchcraft are also becoming standard. To the newly initiated entrant the devil is reported as a matter of course to give a phial of unguent and a staff or stick. He then teaches the newcomer how to anoint the staff with the unguent so as to be able to use it to fly to the synagogues he or she will be required to attend. As for the unguent, it has been made, at the direction of the devil, from the fat of infants the group had murdered and other unnamed ingredients.[79] Plainly, night-flight of the participants has come to be fully accepted as real and regular. And closer to the mature stereotype of witchcraft than had been Fründ's account, the *Errores* specifies the flight as precisely to the gatherings at which the evil ceremonies are performed. Regarding the vehicle of conveyance, in the title of the work alone is mentioned as an alternative to the staff the witch's broom ("*scopa*").[80] Paradigmatic to the modern idea of the witch's flight, the broom was, as Martine Ostorero tells us, just beginning to be connected to the witches' sabbath.[81]

Finally, the *Errores* confirms the status of the gathering of sorcerers as a genuine sect. Nider had spoken about an assembly ("*concio*"), and Fründ had said that those with whom he was concerned came together at a school.[82] In Torrenté's trials, as one would expect of proceedings led by an inquisitor for heresy, the word "sect" at last appears.[83] For the author of the *Errores*, his group of sorcerers constituted an "heretical sect" ("*illa secta et heretica*").[84] And the sorcerers themselves true "heretics."[85] The synagogues are thus witness at once to meetings of sorcerers and of heretics. Moreover, the counter-church to which these followers belong was headed up by the devil himself. As had already been suggested in Fründ, the devil was the sect's master or teacher ("*magister*"), referred to explicitly as such by the congregants.[86] The move from targeting Waldensians to seeking out what we would more readily characterize as witches would seem to be complete. From what we can tell, a few contemporaries were even aware of the transition. Ostorero notes that in a 1449 trial at Montjovet in Savoy, as well as in a surely contemporary one at Vevey in the Pays de Vaud, the accused are referred to as "*moderni heretici*."[87] The term itself implies a realization that for all its resemblance to the heresies of immediately preceding experience, the new crime was actually a bird of quite a different feather. Early modern "witchcraft" was coming into its own.

Claude Tholosan

The second of our last two witnesses establishes the fact. It is a short treatise written around 1436 by a secular figure, the high-judge of the Briançonnais, or Upper Dauphiné, Claude Tholosan. Tholosan held his office as high-judge based in Briançon from 1426 to 1449, during which time he was therefore a functionary of the French realm and directly dependant on the Dauphin, who appointed him.[88] His untitled treatise, which begins with a citation from the *Decretum* purportedly originally drawn from Augustine, can conveniently be labeled from its initial lines as "*Ut magorum et malefic[o]rum errores manifesti ignorantibus fiant*" – in English: *So that the errors of magicians and sorcerers can be rendered apparent to the unknowing.*[89] It is, in short, a work on the crime of sorcery, but as will soon be apparent perhaps we can begin to call such a piece a handbook on witchcraft. While the treatise as a whole constitutes a relatively complete juridical and ideological examination of the crime, we are interested primarily in the ideological section at the beginning. In laying out the nature of the crime and elaborating on its particulars, Tholosan was, as he explained, drawing on his own experience in trials held under his jurisdiction in the Dauphiné – ten years' worth if the date of composition is indeed 1436 – in which by his estimate more than one hundred individuals were indicted and most presumably burned.[90]

As Tholosan himself tells us, he held a degree in civil law, so that by both training and office his perspective on our subject was that of a layman.[91] We might suspect that to this degree he would parallel Fründ, and indeed there are striking similarities in approach between the two men's works. But Tholosan was anything but immune to the ecclesiastical approach to the business of sorcery. Indeed, he begins with a clear vision of the target of his inquiry as an item in the criminological catalogue of heresies. In his very first paragraph he declares that he is writing in order to promote the ultimate extinction of the detestable error and sect of the sorcerers ("*secta hujusmodi malefic[o]rum*").[92] It is thus a true sect with which he is concerned, one involved moreover in doctrinal error, and from the start we are tempted to translate his words as concerning the "sect of the witches." Moreover, just as in the *Errores gazariorum*, members of this sect are compelled by the terms of a pact they have all made with the devil to strive to bring in new recruits. According to Tholosan, they are taught to look for likely candidates among those addicted to either revenge or luxury.[93]

The practices of this sect include, to be sure, the resort to evil magic or sorcery – since late antique times, in Latin, *maleficia* – of the sort long associated with the common folk. As one would expect of a lay magistrate, Tholosan was acutely interested in such affairs, and he devotes several passages to laying out a few of the details. Most have to do with the mixing of powders or unguents to impede the workings of things in the world or to influence events. And the targets are just what one would guess. By applying a combination of thistle, devil's piss, an infertile chicken egg and certain other ingredients, members of the sect manage to hinder conception among women or drive men crazy. A mixture including menses works toward the infertility of crops, specifically the drying up of trees. By employing holy oil in a way the devil instructs, they provoke luxurious thoughts and amorous deeds, while, following others of the devil's instructions, they succeed in inhibiting the expected results of matrimony, cooling the fires of carnal desire and rendering men impotent. There is also the use of figurines to torment or bewitch. Drawing on several different traditions at once Tholosan reports that his subjects manufacture a wax from the fat of smothered infants, from which they fashion little images that they then puncture to cause anxieties and illnesses among their intended victims.[94]

Others of the sect's ministrations seem to involve the direct intervention of the operators themselves. By the mere touch of their garments, these sorcerers or witches are able to kill people. With the aid of devils, they can act as divines, revealing secrets. And apparently at will they know how to make their neighbors ill, or just as quickly free them from their maladies.[95] They also make powders from poisons bought in apothecary shops and mixed with devil's piss, and they supply these poisons to those among them who wish to do evil. With the devil's aid, the latter are able to apply the poisons in wondrous ways, especially by administering them while remaining themselves somehow invisible. The effects range, according to the amount of powder used, from sickness and slow wasting away to sudden death, in every case a fate impervious to medical intervention.[96]

Yet Tholosan's primary focus lies on the formal rituals of the sect as a sect. Like the ecclesiastical inquisitors, he is preoccupied with the notion of his targets as subscribers to a heresy. And even more than the author of the *Errores*, he paints an elaborate picture of the ceremony of initiation by which new members are brought in. Prompted by the devil, whom the text names as we have seen in previous sources "the master" ("*magister*"), the novices first of all explicitly renounce God.[97] As a sign of disrespect, they are taught to call this God whom they renounce merely a prophet. They next draw a circle on the earth, and take a vase, into which the devil has urinated and from which they have drunk, turn it over and place it within the circle. They then return the vase to its original position, signifying their total separation from the Christian faith. The initiates promise to the devil, presumably for after their death, a hand or some other bodily part, again denying God and all true faith. In a further act of defiance, they subsequently turn their nude buttocks toward the sky, draw a cross on the ground, spit on it three times and stomp upon it with their feet. The whole performance ends with the entrants three times making an obscene sign against God – the purported "prophet" – all done in the direction of the rising sun.

There is no explicit mention by Tholosan of the ceremony of homage to the devil. But the newly admitted do follow the preceding ceremonies by kneeling before the devil and then rising to kiss him.[98] It is not hard to see in these acts an imitation of the formal rites of feudal commendation. Tholosan comments that the devil appears to them in these instances in the form of either a human being or one of various animals, but unlike our other texts he makes no mention of blackness nor does he specifically speak of the shape of a cat. The kiss, moreover, is on the mouth, not the anal kiss of legendary heretical infamy. Following this act, the initiates commit to the devil both body and soul and promise him one of their children, especially the first born. And here the narrative turns in the direction of the ritual immolations seen in fourteenth-century imaginings of the rites of ceremonial magicians.[99] When the time is right, so the commentary continues, the new members sacrifice the designated child to the flames. Once the sacrifice is done, they then extinguish the flames and bury the remains. Echoing what we have seen in previous accounts, they only later exhume the buried ashes, from which, with the addition of various other ingredients, they make a powder, presumably reserved for their own nefarious purposes.

In only one respect does Tholosan's vision of the ritualistic aspects of his targeted crime appear to be developmentally behind that of the most mature of the other texts. For Tholosan separates much of the ceremonial later incorporated into the full-fledged idea of the witches' sabbath off from the initiatory rites. And regarding this separated ceremonial he falls back on the attitude of the "Canon Episcopi" concerning night-flight, consigning it to the realm of dreams conjured up by the devil. Fründ and the author of the *Errores* took the night-flight of their protagonists as fully corporeal and real. Tholosan does not. Still, the account he gives of what happens at these ceremonial gatherings is even closer to the mature notion of the sabbath than that of either of his other two contemporaries. Moreover, Tholosan explicitly indicates that the account he provides is drawn from the testimony of those indicted in the trials over which he presided. The sabbath remains therefore intact, if manifested only in the wanderings of the participants' minds at night. Presumably it also constituted a part of the crime of which they stood accused.

In Tholosan's words, his subjects believed that they went bodily by night in the company of devils to "synagogues" designated for their particular area or province.[100] At these synagogues the members of the sect gave an accounting of the evils they had committed and presented to the whole body the new initiates they had won. They thought – and claimed – that they flew long distances to such synagogues on staffs spread with the fat of dead children and one of the poisonous powders mentioned in the passages discussed earlier. Alternatively, they traveled there on beasts or brooms. There, they all kissed the devil again. There, too, they brought suffocated children, from whom they extracted the fat and whom they then cooked and ate in common feast. And there, when the devil gave the appropriate sign, they indulged in an orgy of lasciviousness, mixing with demons and with each other even, as Tholosan puts it, against nature. There, as well, appeared a devil higher still in rank than any seen before – prince of the province, as Tholosan calls him – who sat before them "*in cathedra*" and to whom they all paid due and formal reverence. On these occasions, too, they made the powders described before. And then, in an instant, all was done, and everyone returned whence he or she came.

From libelous stereotype of heretical meetings to age-old legends of the *strigae*, every element seen before was drawn upon in Tholosan's recounting. Yet he was prepared to add a finishing touch. Tholosan's gathering of sorcerers, his meeting of witches, not only collected all the lurid imaginings associated for centuries with heretics and combined them with standard assumptions about the content of popular sorcery and magic; it also revealed traces of an authentic religion, a sort of anti-Christianity. For the devil at the head of all these events represented himself to the followers of the sect as not just the "devil of Hell" ("*dyabolus Inferni*") but also the omnipotent God ("*omnipotens et deus*").[101] At one point in his treatise Tholosan actually uses the name "Satan" to refer to this figure, who, he adds, put himself forward as God and succeeded in getting himself to be adored and worshipped as such.[102] This was, moreover, an effectively universal religion. It constituted a sect, in Tholosan's words, "distributed uniformly throughout the whole world."[103]

Spread of the stereotype

By 1440 at the latest, therefore, there had come together what we would consider the stereotype for early modern witchcraft. Present within it was a dual focus on both practices of sorcery, especially the commonplaces associated with popular evil- or love-magic, and the signs of a true sect of believers in a heretical creed. Liberally applied were also borrowings from the old stories of the *strigae*, with cannibalism and the death of infants almost invariably involved. Finally, there was the gathering of the members of the sect at what at this stage was still called a "synagogue," in which the age-old horror stories infamously associated with the image of heresy were now reinforced with elements drawn from the legendary accounts of night-flight in the train of Diana. All that was needed was for this stereotype, incubated in the western Alps, to be picked up by juridical authorities at large and spread throughout Europe. This is precisely what we see if we look to documents emanating from the Papacy in Rome.

Already in 1409, just as the trials were beginning to take hold in the areas about which Nider was informed, Pope Alexander V, of the Pisan adherence, wrote to the Inquisitor of much of southern and eastern France, Ponce Fougeyron, that it had come to his attention how certain Christians and Jews in that jurisdiction were devising new sects in which they secretly practiced and taught rites repugnant to the Christian faith.[104] When it came to declaring exactly who these potential heretics were, the pope described them as "sorcerers, diviners, invokers of demons, enchanters and conjurors" and in general people who had recourse to the "nefarious and prohibited arts."[105] In addition to their own evil practices, such types worked to the perversion of the simple people around them. Clearly, earlier papal concerns about ceremonial magic were opening to the possibility that more broadly popular magic and sorcery might be of interest to the inquisitors of heretical depravity. Using precisely the same wording, the Constance-appointed pope Martin V and his successor Eugene IV both reaffirmed the judicial privileges Alexander had given to Fougeyron to deal with these new sorcerer-heretics.[106]

The hold of the new stereotype on the papal imagination grew rapidly from this point. In 1437 Eugene IV wrote to all inquisitors wherever assigned to encourage them to act against a host of lapsed Christians who had fallen prey to the devil's snares.[107] That he was thinking of a virtual movement defined by the addiction to sorcery and magic is clear from all he said about his target group. As with the presumed magician-heretics signaled for prosecution by the fourteenth-century papacy and its inquisitors, the marks of learned magic were among the first traits assigned to this new and dangerous population. These people, so the pope said, sacrificed to demons, gave them adoration and in return received responses to inquiries, surely about the future and hidden things. Again as had been feared in the fourteenth century, they abused the sacraments and the materials associated with them, turning them to the purposes of their sorcery (*sortilegia et maleficia*). They even baptized wax images which they then used for their nefarious purposes. More in line with what we have seen from the Swiss examples of the early fifteenth century, the charge was made that they did homage to the devil. Pacts were signed by which they confirmed their mutual obligations with the infernal spirits. Most important of all, the evil acts perpetrated on such grounds smacked plainly of magic as performed among the common folk. The new heretics worked foul deeds (*maleficia*), by no more than a sign or a touch, on whomever they wished. They cured infirmities, and they even conjured up storms. All that was missing from the description were night-flight and the witches' sabbath.

As if to confirm the link to the western Alps, Eugene went even further in a bull issued in 1440 from the Council of Florence.[108] Directed against those still sitting in the council at Basel, from which Eugene had fled, this document singled out Duke Amadeus VIII of Savoy, just the year previously elected by the Basel conciliarists as rival pope, Felix V. In its invective against the presumptions of Amadeus, it accused him of being led astray by the tricks and sorcery (*prestigi[a] sortilegi[a] ac fantasmat[a]*) of those men and women whose numbers were reputed to be so massive in the duke's own domain. And now the pope actually characterized the offenders with the names, he said, by which they were known among the populace. The people referred to members of this vicious cabal with variants on the Latin word *striga* – "*stregule vel stregones*" – and they called them "*Waudenses,*" the first textual reference we have to the French "Vaudois" used, not as before to designate authentic Waldensians, but rather with the significance of our modern word "witch."[109]

Succeeding popes continued the interest, though they tended to be more tight-lipped, making reference to magical practitioners in general but with the warning that they appealed to the common folk and seduced them into complicity with their crimes.[110] Only at century's end does the ripe stereotype emerge again. In the infamous bull of 1484, "*Summis desiderantes,*" pope Innocent VIII mines the Swiss material for an all-out attack on witchcraft now clearly in the early-modern sense. A subsequent letter to the archduke Sigismund of Austria had offered praise for the duke's efforts against the heretical sect of witches ("*adversus hereticorum et maleficorum sectam*").[111] With "*Summis desiderantes,*" while arguing for special powers for the crusading inquisitors Heinrich Kramer and Jacob Sprenger, the pope went into a description of the actions of the new heresy he had in mind.[112] True to what had now clearly become standard form, these modern sorcerers began by abnegating their faith, at the instigation of the devil, enemy of the human race. They also indulged in sexually abusive acts with demons, both incubi and succubae. More to the point are the malicious actions such forsakers of religion spread upon the earth. The bull lays out just the sort of attacks on fertility and health that had for centuries been the stock in trade of popular sorcery. These new minions of mankind's foe extinguished childbearing among women, the birthing of animals in rural flocks and the bearing of fruit among the plants of the fields. They tormented men, women and all sorts of domestic animals with excruciating ills. And they intervened generally so that men could not fulfill their conjugal obligations with women, nor women with men. The ferocity of the inquisition was now to be unleashed, in other words, not so much against learned magicians as against anyone in the populace who could be tied to the age-old practices of malefice or witchcraft. As if to set the seal upon the condemnation, in 1500 pope Alexander VI condemned the whole pack: "heretics and witches (*malefic[i]*) who follow their fantasies, the ladies of the night (*Herodiades*) and all the magical arts."[113]

Given this papal imprimatur, it is no surprise that by the end of the fifteenth century the stereotype had been disseminated throughout Europe. It has been noted by historians that the spread of the witchcraft stereotype and interest in prosecuting witches came at a time of increasing concern about reform of the church, and more generally of religion among the people. Michael Bailey has called attention to the reforming interests of Johannes Nider, whose *Formicarius* proved so significant a vector for the encroachment of the new stereotype on other areas of Europe besides the Suisse romande.[114] It is, of course, hardly an accident that this reforming impulse grew at a time when the church community was focused on the issue in the two great councils, Constance and Basel, called to deal with the crisis of the schism in the papacy. More fortuitous might be the fact the two councils – and especially Basel, which turned out to be the more fruitful in the development of the witchcraft stereotype – were convened in precisely the area of Europe where conditions were ripe for the emergence of concern about magic among the populace. Those regions where the Waldensians had retreated offered fertile ground for the rise of an intrusive curiosity of learned elites into the practices, particularly those with religious implications, of the common folk.[115] Add to that the fact that the councils provided an ideal conduit for the insertion of the scholastic analytic spirit into the forums of public debate. Michael Shank is probably right to think of Constance, and by implication Basel as well, as marking the "political 'coming of age' of the European university community."[116] What better location, therefore, and at what better time for the scholastic fear of demon-worshipping and heretical learned magicians, which had fed the inquisitorial concern about magic in the fourteenth century, to be introduced to the public and implanted as the basis for a general attack on magic more broadly among the common populace?

As Andreas Blauert has pointed out, it was immediately from Basel that apprehension about the new heresy, which we have identified with the early modern stereotype of witchcraft, spread into French-speaking lands. Only slightly later, from the 1450s on, did a similar migration take place from Basel toward the east and north, predominantly into the territories of German speech.[117] By the end of the century, the classic witch trials had begun. There was an easing off in the second third of the sixteenth century, perhaps because the outbreak of the Reformation so monopolized the attention of the power elites, leaving practically no energy for juridical enterprises of any other sort. But beginning in the 1560s the pace of witch trials picked up again, with the period from the 1580s to the 1630s witnessing the peak intensity for this phenomenon in the early modern world.[118] The locus of greatest activity was the area corresponding in modern Europe to France, Germany, Switzerland and the Low Countries, with the over-whelming preponderance of prosecutions in the final phase from 1580 to 1640 taking place in Germany alone.[119] In the British Isles, the concentration of cases occurred in the Kingdom of Scotland, a steady docket of litigations happening in England but never any outbreaks to compare with the near hysterical occurrences from time to time and place to place on the continent.[120]

Historical explanations of the craze

Most historians have viewed the expansion of the witch trials from the mid-fifteenth through to the mid-seventeenth centuries – the period during which they animated western Europe – as a calamity. This perspective has sharpened the question of how the expansion occurred, or to put it more precisely, of exactly what general causes underlay its progression. If we look to history, we see a succession of theories that have managed, each for a period of time, to provide the prevailing answer.[121] Among the earliest of the responses laid the blame on clerics, who in their desire to manipulate the populace and dominate society at large made up the crime out of whole cloth and spent centuries persecuting innocents solely for the purpose of forwarding their own interests. They were the ones, then, who orchestrated the developments recounted here and insured that, once the early modern paradigm of witchcraft and the patterns of its prosecu-tion had been established in the Alpine regions, they would spread eventually to all the rest of Europe. Key in this regard was the work of Joseph Hansen, whose textual investigations have served as fodder for much further study of the matter, including this present work.[122] In America, Hansen's ideas were taken up by two highly influential scholars of the same period, Henry Charles Lea and George Lincoln Burr.[123]

Already in the nineteenth century, however, there were efforts to offer a coun-ter-narrative, continuing to view the witch trials as a repressive effort on the part of a power-hungry elite but insisting now that there was a cultural reality of some sort to the target among the populace below. The French historian Jules Michelet saw in the witches peasant rebels to the established order, an interpretation endorsed as late as the mid-twentieth century by then-young Emmanuel Le Roy Ladurie.[124] Much more influential for the twentieth century, on the other hand, was the thesis promoted by Margaret Murray. Drawing on the anthropological model laid out by James Frazer in *The Golden Bough*, Murray insisted, as noted earlier, that the witch trials furnished the opportunity for an onslaught by the elites on an ancient but still-existing pagan religiosity of the peasantry.[125] The witches were thus not truly witches, but they were all the same real adherents to a fertility cult that long preceded Christianity's advance onto the European continent. Rossell Robbins can perhaps be viewed as promoting a peculiar variant on Murray's vision, holding the witches to be authentic according to the early modern paradigm and seeing the efforts to repress them as the justifiable reaction of a vigilant Church.[126]

All of those views had been effectively discredited by the last third of the twentieth century, their attempts to explain the spread of the witch trials supplanted by other theses. For decades three seemed to reign supreme. In the last fifteen years all three have themselves come under criticism, so much so that in many circles they are regarded as insupportable. Perhaps it is better to say that they have been modified, with parts remaining to undergird a full assessment of the causes for the spread of the trials. The first of the three explanations is associated with the name of Norman Cohn. In *Europe's Inner Demons* Cohn argued that necessary for the development of the persecution of witches in the early modern period was the coalescence of the mature stereotype of the witch, key component of which was the link to diabolism whereby all forms of sorcery and many stories arising out of folklore were viewed as symptomatic of a grand conspiracy to worship the devil.[127] Lacking this stereotype or paradigm, nothing more would have been done about claims of sorcery and magic among the populace than had been the case in the past – which is to say, not very much at all. Something like this thesis stands behind much of the narrative of the present book.

Of late voices have been raised against Cohn's thesis. In a recent study of witchcraft prosecution in three Swiss cities, for example, Laura Stokes has taken on the focus on diabolism. Citing the example of Basel, she has argued that demand for action against witches in the fifteenth century arose from the populace in the countryside, where the notion of diabolism was scarcely present, and was forced upon authorities in the town, who would have been the only ones familiar with the new stereotype.[128] Fear of sorcery, and popular notions of the witch, were therefore sufficient to account for the witch trials, charges of diabolism and the new, fuller stereotype being more or less incidental phenomena in the culture of the elite. Yet in her work Stokes manages to reinsert much of Cohn's original claim. Without the stereotype in the minds of the authorities, she admits, the elite in the cities would not have been vulnerable to the pressures from the countryside. As she puts it, "the incipient shift to diabolism in the witch stereotype of the early fifteenth century activated the longstanding but largely latent indigenous fear of the weather witch."[129]

Of course, Cohn's thesis is easy to reconcile with most other explanations for the rise of the witch trials. His argument can be read as merely positing a passive and ideological sine qua non for judicial proceeding against alleged witches. The active force would have to come from outside. And here is where the other two once-standard interpretations enter in. One points to a dominating role for the emergent early modern state. Christina Larner has been the scholar most commonly credited with this interpretation.[130] In part, this second thesis draws in the formulation of the diabolic stereotype, for the state is posited as the actor adopting the stereotype as a formula for prosecution. More central to the entrance of the state as an activating factor, however, are said to be the phenomena of judicial and administrative centralization and a wholesale adoption of new juridical procedures, most salient being the assumption by the state of prosecutorial agency, acceptance of inquisitorial investigation and recourse to torture.[131] For Larner, it was probably the second of these factors that was key. As she has described the crucial elements of the transformation, they were:

> a change from restorative, interpersonal justice, to abstract, rational, bureaucratic justice with repressive sanctions. ... There was also a shift in responsibility from the accuser to the court official, which had the effect of making frivolous or vindictive accusation possible. It also meant that there were those who were responsible, without personal interest, for pursuing the perpetrators of crimes, thus allowing witch-hunting to flourish.[132]

Here, too, however, biting criticism has recently appeared. Scholarship of the last two decades has made it clear that, once the witch trials were underway and especially in the late sixteenth and early seventeenth centuries, the primary pressure for prosecution arose from below. As Stuart Clark has put it, we have seen a wholesale decline of the idea that the witch trials were largely "inspired by government institutions or churches. ... [I]t was [instead] the pressure from the communities to which alleged witches belonged that lay behind a great deal of witch-hunting."[133] Most contested has been the notion that centralization at the national level led to the rash of trials in western Europe.[134] Indeed, as Brian Levack reminds us with reference to the work of Alfred Soman, it was intervention of control from the center – as, for example, the French royal judiciary – that dampened the rage to bring witches to trial and even more importantly to convict them once indicted.[135]

Again, however, new research has not led to the absolute abandonment of the statist argument. If central governments eventually played a moderating role in witchcraft prosecution, local governments were deeply involved in bringing witches to court and punishing them for their crimes. This happened, moreover, just as local governments, particularly those of cities and towns, were extending their jurisdiction out into the countryside around them.[136] It was in the small states, such as those of the bishops and prince-bishops of southern Germany, that the worst of the witch hunts occurred.[137] Laura Stokes, in her study of Swiss cities, notes how trials peaked in number just as city councils were moving to become truly governing bodies, replacing the lordly government that had previously prevailed in rural areas.[138] A new idea of state power and of the centralization of authority, implemented at a local level, thus constituted a necessary precondition for the rash of witch trials to begin.

Third of the more recent standard interpretations was introduced in the 1970s by Alan Macfarlane and Keith Thomas.[139] Drawing upon anthropological models formulated in the study of modern witchcraft, particularly those of Evans-Pritchard, these scholars posited the force driving the prosecution of witches in those signal centuries of early modern Europe to be stress arising within local communities under pressure from mounting social change.[140] As Macfarlane would have it, such stress aroused feelings of guilt and resentment, which could be resolved only when one party to a dispute or awkward encounter projected those feelings onto the adversary by means of an accusation of harmful magic perpetrated with malicious intent. In contrast to statist interpretations, these anthropological explanations located the driving force again among the populace. What was peculiar to them was that they opted to perceive the mechanism through a functionalist lens, whereby the actual workings of accusation, trial and defense were themselves less important than the purpose they served in reestablishing a balance upset by the novelties of social change.

Once more, of course, these theses did not long stand unchallenged. Most immediately critiqued was the particular functionalism of Alan Macfarlane. But eventually the whole functionalist model came under attack. Research began to suggest that community struggles over witchcraft accusations did not need to be interpreted as serving a hidden social purpose but instead could be read as immediately meaningful to the players among whom they arose. James Sharpe and Robin Briggs come to mind as foremost practitioners of this new interpretative enterprise.[141] Perhaps most formative of all was the more generally oriented study of Stuart Clark, focusing not solely on community but also on both elite and popular mentalities.[142] The argument was that the language in which the witchcraft accusations were delivered and the trials proceeded made sense to the people involved at the time, expressing a reality they both understood and lived. It has been a short step from this approach to the most recent endeavors of scholars not just to attend to the sensibility – the reasonableness – of the language of the accusations but to turn to the very events described. In almost all the standard interpretations the common assumption has prevailed that nothing, or almost nothing, approaching the reality of witchcraft ever actually occurred during those two centuries of avid prosecution. That assumption itself has now come under attack. Edward Bever's work on *The Realities of Witchcraft* may go too far for many scholars to accept in its entirety, but his claims that behind the charges of witchcraft lay real acts of malice and often concrete instances of at least psycho-somatic influence will force all historians henceforth to look at the witch trials with a new eye.[143]

Three final concerns

By now it has become established wisdom that no single account of what caused the witch trials will suffice.[144] The causation is multiple, and no one factor can be picked out as dominant over the rest. For the purposes of the present study, however, three sub-currents of causality stand out as particularly relevant to its strongly ideological focus. The first has to do with a process of acculturation, or more forcefully put, a cultural assault by the elites on the world-view and practices of the populace, particularly in the countryside. Robert Muchembled has been most prominently associated with advancing this interpretation. As his work is often understood, he is credited with associating the effort to refashion popular culture with attempts by the state to enlarge its sphere of political control.[145] In fact, however, Muchembled just as often linked acculturation to increasing social upheaval generated by an emerging pre-capitalist economic order, with new commercial and professional elites endeavoring to express their dominance by exercising a cultural hegemony.[146] In any case, the whole interpretative project has come under sometimes scathing criticism in current scholarly literature in the field. Its very top-down orientation would assure as much.

Yet perhaps the reaction has gone too far. The process whereby the stereotype of witchcraft emerged bears the signs of concerns among the elite about aspects of popular culture and a desire to restrain both beliefs and practices that might, from an elite point of view, be considered heretical and possibly outright demonic. And even the most recent studies give reason to believe that, at least for the early decades, acculturation can provide a useful template for evaluating officials and religious elites for their part in stoking the fires of prosecution. In her work on early examples in Switzerland, particularly the Vaudois, Ostorero has drawn attention to the activity of the bishop of Lausanne, Georges de Saluces, already mentioned earlier, who even in his early years in Savoy demonstrated a penchant for disciplining the people of his diocese with regard to the potential heterodoxy of their practices and beliefs. Signal in this regard were Saluces's *Synodal Constitutions* of 1447, probably, as Ostorero suggests, greatly influenced by the reforming spirit incited in the area by the Council of Basel. As Ostorero sees it, the witch trials of this place and period cannot easily be understood outside the context of such a program to "control the practices and beliefs" of the populace at large.[147] Laura Stokes as well, despite her willingness to receive the widespread assumption that Muchembled's ideas have been "largely debunked," still resists the impulse to disconnect the rise of witch hunting from efforts on the part of her urban elites at social control.[148] Separated from a tight association with the rise of the early modern central states, the notion of an acculturating impulse as contributing to the witch hunts is not so far-fetched.

A second causal sub-current has to do with the place of women in the trials. It is a commonplace to say that the attack on witches turned out to be, in fact if not in intention, an attack on women. Although there were pockets, mostly in northern and eastern Europe, where more men than women were brought to trial, for the whole period of the witch prosecutions women made up 75 percent of the accused.[149] Would it not appear that misogyny was an engine driving the whole process? Interestingly enough, most scholars have argued that it was not. Speaking for surely the majority, Stuart Clark has made a most cogent statement of the case.[150] The fact that women, he says, fell into so many of the categories likely to be linked to witchcraft – from the age-old connection of women with popular sorcery to the likelihood that folk healers would be female – meant that as witchcraft moved to center stage as a crime subject to prosecution so women were targeted more frequently by accusations before the courts. Thus the high incidence of women among the accused witches was more a function of the nature of the crime than a causative element in the rise of prosecutions themselves.

Against such a position stands the otherwise curious circumstance that the effective misogyny of the witch trials, the targeting primarily of women, was a factor not tied originally to the story of the attack on magic with which this and the last chapter have been concerned but rather one that developed simultaneously with the emergence of the classic stereotype of the witch. As Bailey, drawing on Kieckhefer, has pointed out, in the trials leading up to the witchcraze, 70 percent of those accused of sorcery in the first half of the fourteenth century were men, 42 percent in the second half, while by the first half of the fifteenth century 60–70 percent were women.[151] As for just the Swiss trials, where the rash of witch prosecutions began, Blauert has noted the high ratio of men to women in the early trials, and Paravy confirms the notable rise in the proportion of women accused steadily throughout the fifteenth and into the sixteenth century.[152] It would seem that something fundamental to the rise of the witch prosecutions entailed an attack predominantly on women, a bias inseparable from the emergence of the crisis itself. Of course, the shift to prosecution of women might be largely the product of the confrontation of an elite juridical apparatus with the witchcraft accusations of the populace, for whom, it can be argued, sorcery always had a gendered, mostly feminine face.[153] That is partly what Clark was arguing earlier. But the fact that it was when this face was uncovered that witchcraft prosecutions truly began to take off surely suggests that misogyny was a part of the dynamic itself.

More important in this regard is an argument about the historical oppression of women put forth by Nancy Caciola. It is still possible to argue that if only the confrontation with popular ideas of sorcery accounts for the overwhelming proportion of women accused of witchcraft in western Europe, then the witchcraze does not represent a new stage in the attack upon women but simply an opening of the floodgates of popular but age-old misogyny once the courts began to welcome witchcraft accusations. Yet Caciola has shown that simultaneous with the rise of the witchcraze occurred the consummation of another process, undeniably associated with the elite, whereby women were being increasingly demonized in the late fourteenth and fifteenth centuries.[154] Exorcism manuals, a new product at just this moment in history, were feeding an impression that

possession among religious women, a factor in the landscape of medieval spirituality since the twelfth century, was largely an indication of demonic intervention. The phenomenon was linked to an ever greater distinction between
somatized religious experience, traditionally typical of female religiosity and now
interpreted as almost invariably of demonic origin, and authentic possession by
the divinity, which was now viewed as intellectual or spiritual, decidedly non-so-
matic, and routinely witnessed in the religiosity of men. In short, feminine spirituality was increasingly being boxed into a demonic corner. In Caciola's words,
from such a paradigm of female emotive behavior "it was but a short step to the
witchcraft stereotype."[155] That the stereotype took off, and prosecution of female
witches began its meteoric rise, just when this preceding misogynistic ideology
had been set firmly in place should make us revaluate the role of the elite in the
misogyny of the witchcraze itself. Were not attitudes about possession now being
displaced onto the eccentric behavior of women throughout the population?

Once this step Caciola predicted had been engaged, the elite began to take
an active role in redefining witchcraft so as to heighten the misogyny it had
already possessed in popular eyes. As has already been indicated, up to the mid-
fifteenth century learned and juridical officials who responded to the new stereotype of the witch had striven mightily to disregard the popular conviction of
the commonfolk that women were the most involved in witchcraft activities.[156]
Bailey has shown that Johannes Nider was out of step as late as the 1440s in
suggesting that more women were likely to be witches than men.[157] By the end of
the fifteenth century, the situation had reversed. Gerhild Scholz Williams argues
that Heinrich Kramer's *Malleus maleficarum* – the *Hammer of Witches* – infamous
for the virulence of its misogyny and often held up as the type for the elite early
modern vision of the witch, intensified the misogyny of the witch paradigm just
in time for the blood-letting of the late sixteenth and early seventeenth centuries.[158] And Sigrid Brauner has noted how the same period of concerted witch
hunting coincides with the time that German "humanist and Protestant thinkers
reinterpreted the social role of the family and of women within the family."[159]
How convenient then to attach the accusation of "witch" to unruly women who
threatened a "new feminine ideal of the submissive housewife."[160]

It thus seems safe to affirm that the dramatic power of the witch trials to
demean women and to terrorize even those who were not accused into projecting
a less assertive profile in society played a role in the two-hundred-year-long hunt
for witches. To put the argument most modestly, as has Robin Briggs, we can
claim that if the "desire to assert masculine dominance" was not a primary cause
of the outbreak of the witchcraze, it was at least a "common secondary factor."[161]
Which is to say that, although the rise of the trials may not have been the
result of a specific choice by males to persecute women and put them in their
place, once the trials had begun the opportunity to use them for misogynist
ends was too much for males to resist. The ferocity of the witchcraze would then
be a true product of these misogynist opportunities.[162] If that is to identify the
causal valence of women-hating and women-controlling in the witch trials as

somewhat functionalist in nature, so be it. As Marianne Hester has reminded us, in the long history of patriarchy in the western world, men have proven remarkably opportunistic in choosing ways to oppress women and keep them down. In Hester's words, "continuity of inequality between men and women relies on changing forms of oppression over time."[163] Indirect causation of this sort is causation all the same, and we should greatly misunderstand the importance of the witch trials in European history were we not to give it the considerable attention it deserves. Granting it such prominence permits us to appreciate, as Anne Barstow has shown, how the phenomenon of the witch trials presented an important moment in early modern European efforts to lower the position of women in society over the long run, to an extent even up to the present day.[164]

Which leaves us with the third of our causal sub-currents. Here, where a question of political ideology is at stake, we find ourselves back in part to the controversial issue of the role of the early modern state. For if a state is to establish its legitimacy, and thus normalize its power over its subjects, it must convincingly advance an ideology of political order to justify its actions. The need holds whether the state be large and highly centralized, like the royal monarchies of early modern Europe, or small and of local jurisdiction, as seems to have been the case with the most virulent episodes of witch hunting in our period. There, as Laura Stokes has noticed among her Swiss towns, an almost persecutory mode of judicial activism can sometimes take hold, as if to teach the citizenry by means of sheer discipline that the state holds ultimate power.[165] In such instances, the ideology justifying the persecution is of critical importance. It is Christina Larner who has pointed most convincingly to the nature of the political ideology at work in the time of the witch trials and to a degree itself necessary or causally implicit in their emergence and elaboration. In Larner's words: "The witchcraft prosecutions in Europe were exactly coterminous with the period during which Christianity was a political ideology."[166]

Larner's observation is generally held to apply mostly to the period of confessionalism following the Protestant Reformation, or as Bailey would have it most precisely to the years 1580–1630, when the witchcraze was at its height.[167] But there is ample evidence that it holds true and perhaps even more firmly for the time when the witch trials were just getting underway in the early 1400s. Here, as current scholarship would lead us to expect, it was smaller states and urban jurisdictions that were principally involved. Andreas Blauert has drawn attention to the simultaneous rise of the classic witch stereotype and a process of state formation and expansion of power into the countryside just in this period in those two crucial areas of Savoy and the Dauphiné.[168] With regard to both, Jacques Chiffoleau has alerted us to the probability that the states involved faced in particularly acute fashion the problem of extending their legitimacy and an expectation of ready obedience out into the territories surrounding their center, where they represented a new authority undermining older, more local allegiances of lordship or community. In such a situation, there was, so Chiffoleau suggests, no better ideology of power than one inherently trumping all others, which is to say the direct mandate from God as a Godly state. No finer expression of the ideology, moreover, than the battle against witches and sorcerers, immediately God's enemies.[169]

The focus on witches and sorcerers is apparent already in Duke of Savoy Amadeus VIII's *Statuta Sabaudie*, or *Statutes of Savoy*, of 1430, where he singled out for special repression "heretics and sorcerers, the invokers of demons."[170] Perhaps this is not surprising in an area where there was a history of authentic Waldensianism and where rumors of witch trials were trickling over the Alps from territory to the north. More telling is the fact that the *Statuta* insisted, contrary to an earlier agreement Amadeus had made with the Savoyard clergy, that sorcery was now to be regarded as reserved exclusively for central state jurisdiction.[171] The rationale, the ideological basis, for such an assumption lay in the notion that the sovereign power – in this case, the Duke – was the sole agent capable of defending the Majesty of the Divinity. Indeed, in a nice elision "lèse majesté" came to be seen as a unitary crime against both the divine and human dignity, the singular representative of which on earth was of course the sovereign himself.[172] In other words, the head of state was the political embodiment of both celestial and human order, God's avenger in a world where God's right constituted legitimacy.

At almost precisely the same time a similar argument was being advanced in the name of the French Dauphin, and ultimately that of the king, in the Dauphiné. Claude Tholosan, witness to and effective chronicler of the witch trials in that small state, which was experiencing the same centralization and encroachment on the countryside as was happening in Savoy, likewise ultimately invokes lèse-majesté as both final sanction for state action against the witches and justification for the severity of the punishment to which they were subjected. Concerning this punishment, Tholosan believed it was apparent that those committing sorcery and witchcraft ("*sortilegia, maleficia*") should be subject to the same penalties – he was thinking about confiscation of their goods – as were heretics. The reason was that such sorcerers and witches had conspired "against the highest majesty" and should be prosecuted precisely as any other indicted for lèse-majesté.[173] Moreover, it was the prince of the territory to whom should fall responsibility for the prosecution. To any prince not recognizing a superior on earth devolved the obligation of vindicating the crime of lèse-majesté. For such a prince was "the immediate vicar of God, and what he does" – as prince – "he does as God, not as a man."[174]

Not that such sentiments were confined to apologists for the smaller states or limited to political ideologies constructed at the beginnings of our trials. Despite the fact the by the late sixteenth century the greater monarchies were more likely to serve as restraining forces for the ravages of the witch hunts than instigators of them, the same ideology prevailed, and well into the seventeenth century. To reduce its impact a new ideology would be required. We see the notion of the royal state as God's defender on earth, for example, in the assignment in 1609 by Henry IV of France of Pierre de Lancre to head the investigation of witches in the southern Labourt region. Though the intensity of these hunts may have been an aberration for France at the time, in would seem that in Lancre's mind he was acting against the witches in the name of the same kind of divine and absolute power of the state as we have just witnessed in the cases above.[175] No one spoke more eloquently of this motivation, in the name of an identical ideology, than the famous adviser to kings and political theorist of the late sixteenth century, Jean Bodin. Fierce advocate for the prosecution of witches, Bodin wrote in his *On the Demon-Mania of the Witches* (*De la démonomanie des sorciers*) words that could have come from those early promoters of the punishment of witches for lèse-majesté such as Tholosan. Though Bodin was speaking presumably for the intervention of a great state like France, which proved in fact relatively reluctant to take up the pursuit of witches, his call, spread widely through the distribution of his *Démonomanie*, reverberated as a rationale for all those smaller authorities and principalities for whom the hunt of witches constituted a major preoccupation.

In defense of the strict punishment of witches, Bodin reached back to an ideology of state juridical authority that perfectly fits the characterization noted from Christina Larner just above. To his eyes, such punishment served one principal purpose.

There are two ways in which states are maintained in their status and greatness: reward and punishment – the former for the good, the latter for the bad. And if there is a lapse in the distribution of these, one must expect nothing but the inevitable ruin of the states… [Moreover], those people greatly delude themselves who think that the penalties are established only to punish the crime. I maintain that this is the least benefit which accrues to the state. For the greatest and the chief one is to appease the anger of God, especially if the crime is directly against the majesty of God, as this one [of witchcraft] is.[176]

Vindication of lèse-majesté against God being the principal function of the state, the attack on witches would seem to be the primary way to put this function into service. A better ideology for taking juridical action against witches – no matter who was calling for their punishment, the people or the elite – could hardly be wished for.

Conclusion

We have thus advanced from concern over learned magic, seen by the thirteenth century as invariably of diabolical origin and hence worthy of stern measures of repression, through a fourteenth-century development whereby evidence of such magic came to be regarded as a sign of heresy and consequently actionable by the papal inquisition, to the period of witch trials from the fifteenth through the seventeenth centuries, when the target shifted to a host of practices and beliefs commonly associated with the populace at large. The end of this chapter accordingly finds us in the first three decades of the seventeenth century, when the witchcraft prosecutions were at their height. Magic has become so volatile an issue that it has triggered a veritable crisis in society. It is time, therefore, for us to look at how Europe escaped from this crisis and emerged into the modern world, where witchcraft was no longer a matter to be feared but rather a curious artifact of primitive beliefs from which the people should be released. Here the story returns us to magic and science as they were elements of learned culture. For part of the story of the decline of the witch trials is also that of the rise of the classical theories of natural philosophy of the Scientific Revolution of the seventeenth century. Here, too, we return to questions of politics, connected to the beginnings of the early modern nation state. These will provide our subject in the following chapter.

6

Desacralized Science and
Social Control, 1500–1700

At the same time the witch prosecutions were heating up in western Europe a curious thing was happening in the cultural world of the learned elite. For toward the end of the fifteenth century and the beginning of the sixteenth we see the emergence once more of efforts by prominent thinkers to undertake the defense of magic.[1] And now, in contrast to the days of Roger Bacon, there was no hesitation to use the word "magic" itself. The standard of magic as a science was raised this time not primarily by members of the university community but rather by a number of scholars outside the Scholastic milieu, mostly of a Platonizing – or Neoplatonizing – bent. Among them, the first able to command the attention of learned circles at large was the great translator and commentator on Plato and Plotinus, client of the Medici at Florence, Marsilio Ficino, born in 1433 and died in 1499. Though his work takes us back over a decade before 1500, it looks forward to the sixteenth century, the period in which it bore fruit among the great defenders of magic of the high Renaissance.

The present chapter begins by examining this newly resurgent learned magic, starting with Ficino and passing through Giambattista Della Porta and Heinrich Cornelius Agrippa. Learned magic here bears on our story as generating some skepticism regarding the witch trials but on the whole, and unlike the learned magic of the thirteenth century, incidental to the dynamics of the witchcraze itself, either its intensification or its diminution. As will be suggested later on, it is more intimately bound up with the rise of classical early modern science. Attention then shifts to themes more relevant to the winding down of the witch trials and more reflective of emergent social norms in early modern Europe. A look is given to the factor that earliest of all applied the brakes to the witchcraze and did the most to lead to its demise. This was the rise of a skepticism among jurists and lawyers about the ability of the trials actually to identify cases of witchcraft and not result in false convictions. The account then turns to a second factor slower to develop but in the end bringing greater ideological finality to the decline in the prosecution of witches, the emergence in natural philosophy of the mechanical hypothesis.

Having introduced consideration of classical early modern science, the chapter next considers how the new paradigm for scientific explanation contributed to what is often called the "disenchantment" of society. But a glance is given as well to how classical natural science, for all its mechanical cast, drew upon some elements of early modern learned magic. Finally, an effort is made to revisit the three causal concerns introduced at the end of the preceding chapter with regard to the emergence of the witchcraze, this time with an eye to explaining its termination. After a brief handling of misogyny and acculturation, more time is devoted to politics and political ideology. And here not simply the decline of the witch trials is at stake but also the establishment of a new social order linked ultimately to the early modern nation state.

Learned magic: Marsilio Ficino

We start with magic's learned defenders. It was in the year 1489 that Ficino finished his most influential piece on magic, the third of his *Three Books on Life* (*De vita libri tres*).[2] This third book was entitled *De vita coelitus comparanda*, or *On the Life to be Obtained from the Heavens*. In an appended "Apology" written shortly after the completion of the book but before its publication in December of 1489, Ficino explained to his readers the difference between the sort of magic he was promoting and the kind about which they might harbor suspicions of opposition to Christian faith. The magic of which he was speaking in his book was, he said, not "profane" but rather "natural," the sort practiced by the Magi who came to adore the infant Christ.[3] According to Ficino, profane magic was bound up in the cult of demons, with whose help its practitioners often foretold the future. It was a magic to be detested and rejected. Natural magic, on the other hand, depended on bringing natural materials together with natural causes, producing wondrous and beneficial effects.[4] It was greatly to be respected and desired. The separation between the two resonated of the division between the sorcerer ("*maleficus et veneficus*") and the sage and priest ("*sapiens et sacerdos*").[5]

Ficino's natural magic was, as might be expected for an avowed Platonist, a magic of a harmonious and even living universe. As he recounted it, the world contained both an intellect and a body, and it was a living soul, the *anima mundi*, that drew these two together, made possible communication between them and thus explained all action in the universe. This soul contained the seminal reasons, thus serving as an intermediary between God and his creation in the coming to be of all worldly things.[6] Once creation had occurred, however, the soul continued to exert its influence on worldly objects, but this time by means of its own intermediary, spirit.[7] Spirit could be thought of as the quintessence, a fifth essence of material type, and thus a "most tenuous" of bodily substances. Or it could be conceived of as the heavens themselves, the place where the quintessence resided.[8] In any event, the world spirit ("*spiritus mundi*") was what connected us to the rest of the universe, even to the stars and the higher intellectual beings, which Ficino called "*daemones*." Insofar as it flowed into our own spirit, it made possible the transference of whatever benefits we could expect from above.[9] It functioned, one might say, as the active principle of all the actions that Ficino would call for in the *De vita coelitus comparanda*.

Such a theoretical context brought Ficino directly into the realm of astrology. That was what this third book of *De vita* was primarily about. As Ficino had alerted his reader in his "Apology," the part of natural magic absolutely necessary to life in this world emerged from the marriage of astrology with medicine.[10] The soul's physician, prepared to work with the stars and planets, could bring benefits to us from the heavens. Of course, spirit played here the crucial role. To the degree that our own personal spirits drank in the spirit of the world, we were provided with the celestial gifts of healthy body and soul. And that degree was greater the more similar we had made ourselves to the heavenly nature.[11] Simply put, the more celestial we became in our mode of living, the more we were open to the world spirit and the more benefits we derived from the heavens and the world soul. Lest anyone think that this was to advance too far in the direction of un-Christian arts, Ficino took refuge behind the authority of Aquinas. Thomas himself, he reminded his reader, had conceded great power to the heavens over our bodies, and through the latter over our mind and sometimes even our fortune.[12]

Within astrology Ficino's primary interest focused on images, or what the medievals would have called the science of images. For he held that within things were inserted occult powers ("*proprietates occultae*") brought to them by the heavens and engrafted, so to speak, by the very rays of the stars.[13] Such forces could be rendered more potent if the simple things containing them were compounded so as to reinforce the strength of each. In this compounding, one should look not just to the properties of the ingredients but also to the exact time in which the compounding occurred.[14] Here is where observation of the heavens entered in, for it was the configuration of the stars and planets that would be crucial to obtaining the greatest potency possible. But that was not all. Because this potency could be further augmented if the compound was at the correct moment shaped into an image, as, so Ficino continued, the astrologers ("*astrologi*") were wont to do with their metals and stones.[15] The natural philosopher who knew how to arrange such things was worthy of the name of "Magician" ("*Magus*"), for he brought heavenly attributes down to earth.[16] A sage ("*sapiens*"), he understood the properties of materials and the proper mixture of them, so that at just the right moment he could collect the celestial influences and generate abundant benefits.[17]

Ficino was aware of the suspicion under which such image-making fell, back to the time of Aquinas and Roger Bacon. So he took pains to declare that anyone was free to reject the whole business of astronomical images ("*imagines astronomicae*") should he so desire. He even added the somewhat unconvincing protestation that he was simply presenting the theory and not personally approving it as legitimate or correct.[18] From the amount of time he spent discussing such images, it is clear, all the same, that he regarded them as of great effectiveness.

The practice of using them rested on the notion he attributed to Ptolemy that images here below were subject to similar celestial images above.[19] By a kind of sympathetic magic, therefore, objects made similar to the heavens (*"inferiora superioribus consentanea"*) at just the right moment should be capable of drawing down to earth heavenly powers in what Ficino described as a "magical moment" (*"illud magicum"*).[20] Such a phenomenon was, to Ficino's eyes, surely probable when it came to mixing simples into compounds. Why not then when adding the additional element of a figure, sculpting the object so as to resemble its heavenly similitude?[21]

In fact, he even advanced a theory of natural philosophy to validate the entire procedure. Just as the rays from heavenly bodies could penetrate the earth to generate marvelous substances, such as gems, so it would be hard to deny that it was possible for them to enter into properly prepared figures and impress upon them special gifts. It made sense to believe that such gifts would be conserved, at least for a length of time.[22] And all the more powerful would they be, since the rays, coming from the heavens, were unlike earthly light. Rays of this sort were living and even sensual, emerging from living bodies.[23] Moreover, the nature of the engraved similitudes themselves could be expanded. In addition to images reproducing the shapes of constellations, such as a scorpion or a lion, astrologers doing image magic might incise the characters designating a certain sign or planet.[24]

By now, of course, Ficino was treading on hazardous ground. He admitted that Aquinas had been skeptical of the power of images, not to speak of that of characters, exposed to the celestial signs. And he anxiously pointed to the place in the *Summa contra gentiles* where Thomas had conceded that perhaps as artificial forms, figures might in some way serve as recipients of a virtue from above.[25] As for himself, Ficino claimed, he gave greater weight to the material out of which the magical objects were to be compounded than to any form or figure impressed upon them. Perhaps in fact in the impression of the image it was not so much the form that made a difference as the concussion of the impressing itself, heating the material and thus rendering it more open to a virtue naturally inserted from above.[26] Yet in less guarded moments, he remained enthusiastic about the role of the image. It was, he said, widely held among astrologers that materials of just the right sort, and impressed with the right image at the right time, take on powers (*"vires, munus"*) from the celestial figures and are able to pass them along to the wearer when used as an amulet.[27]

From time to time, in fact, Ficino was prepared to go even further. Perhaps figure, and maybe character, was not the only ingredients of his celestial magic. Aquinas had held that figure and number, as accidental to the nature of a substantial thing, could hardly be expected to produce any action along the lines of an elemental property or substantial form.[28] When it came to the heavens, Ficino adopted precisely the opposite posture. Among the stars, figure and number were nearly substantial in themselves, and they were capable of acting with a force far greater than any element here below. What surprise should there be then that figure or number engraved on an object should be able to draw upon some of that celestial force?[29] Even inscriptions could be brought into play. Ficino claimed that Albert the Great, whom he took as the author of the *Speculum astronomiae*, did not categorically disapprove of engraving letters or even whole sayings on an object if the intention was solely to attract a power from a celestial body or sign.[30] As for fumigation, Ficino seems at one point to have agreed with the *Speculum* that they were detestable tokens of supplication to demons.[31] Yet only two chapters later he recounted the opinion of the Arabs that fumigations, by affecting the air, the celestial rays, the spirit of the operator and the matter of the image, act mightily to intensify the total effect of an image-making act. Rather than deny the claim, this time Ficino confessed that he felt fumigation worked by bringing the operator more in touch with the celestial influence and able himself to magnify the celestial power.[32]

Concerning incantations – the spoken word – Ficino displayed the same superficial ambivalence. He reported the *Speculum*'s denunciation of "*orationes*," and later, after introducing the Arabs' insistence on using words to direct the powers they were infusing into images, he explained that he thought it likely that any such effect was the result of the work of "*daemones*," either favorable or malicious.[33] His conclusion was that it was imperative to avoid incantations (this time, "*cantiones*") of any sort.[34] And yet at many points he embraced their use. Songs, Ficino thought, were particularly suitable for his astrological magic. He laid out the rules by which appropriate songs should be accommodated to the heavens when celestial gifts were brought to earth.[35] What was critical was not to think of them as worship of the stars but rather attempts to assimilate oneself to the celestial harmonies.[36] Likewise "*orationes*," this time perhaps in the precise sense of prayers though not of a Christian sort, if composed at the right time and with the proper intention, could work to powerful effect.[37] Again, critical was avoiding any impression that in delivering the prayer one was engaging in worship. As Ficino put it: "We are not speaking now of worshipping the gods but rather of a certain natural power of speech and song and words."[38] Roger Bacon would have stood in perfect agreement.

It was only when "*daemones*" were involved that Ficino drew the line. Not that demons could not be elicited while practicing astral magic. But if they were, it was not due to natural effect but rather because they were pleased with the worship they had received.[39] As he always said, such worship was to be absolutely avoided. All the same, some of Ficino's language came close to inviting the participation of celestial beings. He admitted that the word "*spiritus*" could be applied either to a power of the stars or to a being inhabiting a celestial body, a "*daemon*."[40] And when he talked of the human spirit being transformed into the celestial spirit by the love induced by his magical operations, it would not have been clear to any reader exactly what sort of spirit he had in mind.[41] Ficino's idea of astrological images pressed the limits of theological orthodoxy. Here was a magic that under any reading would have tested the patience of a Thomas Aquinas.

Learned magic: Giambattista Della Porta

Once Ficino had opened the door to the defense of magic, other thinkers were glad to pass through. Not all were so interested in the crafting of astrological images. Capturing the attention of many was instead a "natural magic" dependent more on sympathies between materials here in the mundane sphere. The Neapolitan Giambattista Della Porta, born around 1535 and died in 1615, was perhaps the most famous defender of such natural magic in his time. In 1558 he brought out the first edition of his *Natural Magic* (*Magia naturalis*), in four books. The work was soon reprinted several times, and it became celebrated throughout learned circles all over Europe. Revised and greatly augmented to twenty books, the *Natural Magic* was published in a second edition in 1589.[42] By then Della Porta, who gladly took the title of magician, had been brought twice before the Inquisition in Naples, neither time with any negative action taken against him.[43]

Drawing on the precedent established by Ficino, Della Porta opened his work on *Natural Magic* by explaining to his reader that magic was of two kinds. The first was, in Della Porta's words, "infamous and unhappy" and depended on intercourse with what he called "foul spirits." It consisted in "enchantments," or at the very least the exercise of "wicked curiosity." And it was known by the name of "sorcery." Detested by "all learned and good men," this sort of magic did not advance the cause of reason, nor did it lead to the greater understanding of nature.[44] It stood, in short, on the Frazerian scale as a kind of anti-science, clouded further by the illegitimacy that came from involvement with demonic powers. The second sort of magic was anything but detestable. It constituted "natural magic," which "all excellent wise men do admit and embrace." The philosophers of antiquity sought it out, and those who comprehended its depth of meaning, so Della Porta said in a phrase linking him with the medieval tradition harking back at least to Roger Bacon, called it "the very highest point and the perfection of natural sciences." Others – again in a phrase recalling Bacon on "experimental science" – deemed it "the practical part of natural philosophy."[45] Here was a magic on the Frazerian scale as competing with science itself, indeed constituting the very epitome of scientific thought and application.

Of course, magic of the second sort provided the subject of Della Porta's four, or eventually twenty, books. In a nod to Ficino, Della Porta conceded an astral basis to the type of magic he was concerned with. Citing Plotinus, he claimed that his magic was a science "whereby inferiour things are made subject to superiours, earthly are subdued to heavenly."[46] On occasion, he even spoke in Ficino's voice, setting astrology as chief of the arts the natural magician must master: "So the philosopher who is skilful in the stars (for such is properly the magician) works by certain baits, as it were, fitly matching earthly and heavenly things together."[47] But for the most part Della Porta focused on "nature" without distinction between astral and sub-lunar spheres. As he put it at its plainest, natural magic was simply the expository part of natural philosophy as a whole. In his words: "I think that magick is nothing else but the survey of the whole course of nature."[48] Indeed Della Porta's magic anticipated, and in part inspired, the kind of observational natural philosophy we see in the scientific program of Francis Bacon in the seventeenth century.[49] Speaking of his natural magic, but using the term "natural philosophy" as a synonym, Della Porta could not have been clearer on the matter: "For this is to be confirmed in the principles of natural philosophy, that when any new things are to be invented, nature must be searched and followed."[50] Taking his cue from Pico in the *Oration on the Dignity of Man*, he cited Plotinus as authority for the claim that the magician was not so much artificer as minister of the powers of nature, working "by the help of nature only, and not by the help of art."[51]

Given all this, one might almost wonder whether Della Porta had left the Maussian world of "mana" altogether, so that his natural magic had become nothing but standard natural science. Yet in fact he never permitted the vibrant sense of the occult to disappear. At the beginning of his preface to the whole work of *Natural Magic* he announced his pride always to have "laboured earnestly to disclose the secrets of nature."[52] Moreover, in defining natural magic in chapter 2 of Book I, he noted that those philosophers whom he would recognize as magicians were "skilful in dark and hidden points of learning."[53] Tying the notion of secrets to his insistence that natural magic dealt with all of nature, he specifically claimed that "the knowledge of secret things depends upon the contemplation and view of the face of the whole world."[54] In sum, magic was a prying into nature in order to reveal its secrets, and all of nature was thus fair game for its ministrations.

As one would expect, the secrets discovered by the natural magician could be used to produce "wonderful effects."[55] Here a special, and typically magical, principle came into play. As Della Porta saw it, this principle reduced to a matter of sympathies between types of objects in the natural world. The Platonists, he explained, "termed magick to be the attraction or fetching out of one thing from another, by a certain affinity of nature."[56] Or as the Egyptians said, nature had "an alluring power to draw like things by their likes."[57] In his own words, Della Porta chose to call this factor, "which the Greeks call sympathy and antipathy," the consent and disagreement of things by their very nature. It could be described as a kind of love among those things which were alike.[58] Indeed, Della Porta often used the language of love to explain what it was about:

> For by reason that [the parts of this huge world] are linked in one common bond, therefore they have love in common; and by force of this common love, there is amongst them a common attraction, or tilling of one of them to the other. And this indeed is magick.[59]

True to the empirical emphasis of his discipline, Della Porta thought that only experience with nature, and not deductive theorizing, could point to where these affinities and antipathies lay. Indeed, unlike medieval scholastics, he declined to look for any reason, as in the substantial form, for their existence. For such consent and disagreement, he declared, "there can be rendered no probable reason: neither will any wise man seek after any other cause here of but only this, that it is the pleasure of nature to see it should be so."[60]

This power of affinities allowed the magician drawing upon it to perform great works. By what Della Porta called a "compounding" of things that agree or disagree, one could manage "secret and strange operations," or what he once described as "strange works, such as the vulgar sort call miracles."[61] The process depended on the tendency for like to produce like or draw like to it.[62] An excellent example is introduced toward the end of the whole work. To cure sciatica, one should play music on an instrument constructed out of poplar. For the juice of the poplar had an antipathy to diseases such as sciatica, and the musical tone carried the antipathy from the instrument to the patient.[63] Here, then, in the sixteenth century was a form of magic with which William of Auvergne would have felt entirely at home.

Learned magic: Heinrich Cornelius Agrippa

Yet not all sixteenth-century magicians were so benign. The German humanist and self-styled magician, Heinrich Cornelius Agrippa of Nettesheim, ventured freely into more perilous waters. Born in Cologne in 1486 and educated there at the university, Agrippa followed a checkered career of patronage throughout northwestern Europe until his death in 1535 or 1536.[64] A student of the abbot Trithemius, himself a celebrated ceremonial magician, Agrippa revealed an estimation of acceptable magic that took the step Ficino hesitated at and passed over into actual involvement with demonic forces.[65] It was in a work completed in 1510, On the Occult Philosophy (De occulta philosophia), that Agrippa first set down his ideas about the magical sciences. This work remained unpublished for some years, although it circulated in manuscript form. Negative reactions induced Agrippa to issue what amounted to a partial recantation of his support for occult learning, the On the uncertainty and vanity of the sciences (De incertitudine et vanitate scientiarum), yet in 1531 he arranged all the same to publish the first book of his On Occult Philosophy. Then in 1533 all three books came out in an edition produced at Cologne, this time in a form greatly augmented over that of the 1510 version. Agrippa had clearly not abandoned his youthful stance on magic but merely embellished it with learning and interests acquired during the intervening two decades.

Agrippa began his On Occult Philosophy with an encomium of magic. Like Della Porta after him, but referring to all of philosophy rather than just the natural sciences, he echoed Giovanni Pico's Oration on the Dignity of Man by praising the magical disciplines ("magica facultas") as "the absolute consummation of the whole of the noblest philosophy."[66] But unlike either Ficino or Della Porta, Agrippa divided magic into three parts. Just as the world was separated into three regions, the elemental, the celestial and the intellectual – or we might say, super-heavenly – so human sciences were apportioned among three ranks. Lowest were those dealing with earthly affairs, medicine and natural philosophy. They were followed by the disciplines touching on the heavens, the province of astrologers and what Agrippa, obeying medieval usage, called mathematicians. Highest were those that concerned themselves with the powers of the separate intelligences, bound neither to the earth nor to the heavens, and here reigned the study of the sacred ceremonies of religions (*"religionum sacrae ceremoniae"*). Magic, too, yielded to this distribution: there was first natural magic, then celestial, and finally ceremonial. Agrippa announced his intention to devote one of his books to each of the three.[67]

Natural magic, the lowest, came first. As all his predecessors had claimed, so Agrippa insisted that there were in all things, in addition to their elemental attributes, "occult virtues." Like Ficino, following a line back to Aquinas and long before, he linked these occult virtues to the specific form, and he granted them enormous power despite their immateriality.[68] By manipulating them, bringing together the materials that contained them or separating them, the natural magician could accomplish great works. Again like Ficino, Agrippa assumed the hidden forces were subject to an influence emanating from the planets and the stars, so that it was necessary in drawing their substrates together to be aware of the position of the pertinent celestial bodies.[69] He likewise associated the workings of natural magic with the use of appropriate words or incantations. Agrippa conceded to words great power, which was only augmented by the eminence of the subject to which the words referred.[70] Whatever "incantations and prayers" (*"carmines et orationes"*) were used in natural magic, they, too, had to be carefully accommodated to the planets and stars.[71]

When it came to celestial magic, Agrippa revealed even deeper dependence on Ficino. As we have seen, he linked the planets and stars to the powers of things here below. That same principle established the foundation for his celestial magic. Drawing from Ficino, he insisted that the natural virtues of objects are rendered apt to accomplish more marvelous effects when the particular positioning of the heavens is taken into account. In using magic of this sort, one must always choose the moment when the celestial power is strongest for producing the desired effect.[72] Also like Ficino Agrippa maintained that this principle held not just for natural objects but for artificial ones as well. In his words, "artificial things, when they have been exposed to the heavens according to just the right schedule and order," receive from the celestial agent the miraculous celestial virtue to which they have been submitted.[73] This assertion then opened up for him the science of images, of which Ficino of course had been a prime promoter. For Agrippa, images, seals, rings, mirrors and many similar instruments could all be manipulated by the magician working under the correct celestial signs so as to receive wonderful powers.[74] Again, just like Ficino, he held that both the material of the object as well the image itself were important in any such operation, with the stipulation that the figure must be similar to the heavenly configuration from which it should receive its power.[75]

But of course it was with his ceremonial magic that Agrippa took the strides separating him from both Ficino and Della Porta. It has already been indicated earlier how Agrippa associated the ceremonies of this highest type of magic with religion.[76] Indeed, one might almost say that for him ceremonial magic was the general category for all types of sacred ceremonies, including those of Christianity. At the end of his whole work, he even suggested that what he identified with the elements of the religions would have been commonly called among the populace "occult matters" ("*occulta*").[77] For the magician, according to Agrippa, it was above all necessary to know God and to know with what *cultus* he was to be adored.[78] This would provide the foundation for the ceremonial that was to follow. Yet it was not just God that had to be known, and to whom the proper ceremonies had to be directed. First of all there were the highest among what the pagan philosophers called "gods," the Hebrews "numerations," but which the Christian magus would understand to be the divine attributes – things like the divine wisdom, known by the Orphics as "Pallas."[79] They had a place in ceremonial magic. Below them were real spirits, living beings other than the divinity itself, some of which were also referred to as gods by the pagans. Such secondary powers the philosophers had known as the "ministers of God, separate intelligences."[80] Agrippa interchangeably identified them as "*intelligentiae*," "*spiritus*" and most often "*daemones*," specifically noting that when he used the word "daemones" he most often did not mean what people of his time would have referred to as "diaboli" or devils. For him, they were all "intelligible substances" ("*substantiae intelligibiles*"), beings that were pure intellect, containing no matter.[81] They were for him media through which the supreme God often acted, worthy of being called the "cooperators and instruments of God."[82]

Moreover, not all such intelligible beings were good. The Creator so disposed the world as to be governed by various ministers, both beneficent and maleficent ("*ministris beneficis et maleficis*"), creatures identified, Agrippa added, in the *Apocalypse* as "favorable and harmful angels" ("*angeli faventes et nocentes*").[83] Indeed, the magicians understood there to be three ranks of favorable daemones stretching under God, for any of which Agrippa himself could be found using the descriptor "angel." Below them came the subterranean and dark type of demon, which could rightly be called evil demons and vicious spirits ("*mali daemones et spiritus nequam*").[84] For them, it was appropriate to use the word "*diaboli*."[85]

For the most part, the ceremonies by which all such "daemonic" powers were brought into the magicians' operations entailed manipulation of the spirits' names. As Agrippa explained, once all the intelligences had been assigned names and sometimes characters, magicians would then employ those names in "invocations and incantations" ("*invocationes et incantationes*") as well as by incising them into objects, including some presumably very much like the images mentioned before.[86] When evil demons were involved, the names were used in what Agrippa called "conjurations and exorcisms" (*"coniurationes sive exorcismata"*).[87] In either case, chanting of certain formulae was the most common way of applying the names from Agrippa's point of view, and when the chants were performed with a purity of mind, the operator could expect miraculous results (*"mirifica multa"*).[88] As for the names themselves, Agrippa was inclined to draw them from cabbalistic magic, though he sometimes borrowed Hebraic-sounding names from other sources such as *Picatrix*.[89] A curious example of their deployment which he took from his own experience was to write the name of a certain spirit on a piece of parchment at just the right moment under the moon, and then to give the parchment to a river frog to be ingested. After saying a spell over the frog, the magician then returned the frog to the river, and the desired result soon ensued: rain and storm.[90]

As Agrippa understood the workings of his ceremonial magic, good or angelic spirits could not be forced to perform any operation. They did so solely voluntarily, and then only when the worker of the magic performed the ceremony in purity of heart and raised himself thereby almost to the level of the spirit from which he was postulating aid.[91] Evil spirits (*"mali daemones"*) could, on the other hand, be coerced. But that would happen only with the aid of good spirits, a situation that usually demanded moral cleanliness on the part of the performer of the magic.[92] Somewhat incongruously Agrippa admitted, however, that even profane souls could coerce evil demons if they used the right words, so fearsome were the magical formulas to the evil demons' ears.[93] He added only that those who operated under such circumstances did so at the risk of their own damnation.[94]

It might appear obvious that opinions of the sort expressed by these magicians would be unlikely to dampen the fires of the witch trials going on while they were writing. Some, indeed, took these same authors to be apologists for the witches themselves, perhaps even guilty of witchcraft. Not alone was Jean Bodin to fulminate against learned proponents of magic as encouraging the very demonolatry among the common folk that he felt was threatening the world. In Bodin's case, it was Della Porta whom he had first in his sights, although indirectly his criticism would have been intended to implicate Agrippa just as well.[95] In fact, Agrippa revealed a not surprising sympathy for the victims of the witch trials. At Metz, in 1519, he assumed the defense of a woman accused of being a witch, and eventually it was Agrippa's opinion that prevailed in the exoneration of the accused.[96] Agrippa's student, Johann Weyer, would go even further, publishing in 1563 his *De praestigiis daemonum* (*On the Tricks of Demons*), an almost immediately famous attack on the web of presuppositions of demoniacal involvement that lay behind the charges brought against the so-called witches. According to Weyer, one should have pity for deluded old women whose ignorant belief in sorcery exposed them to the fraudulent judicial procedures they faced. Weyer it was whom Bodin had principally in mind, even more than Della Porta, when he wrote his *Démonomanie*.

Yet in the end, neither the skepticism of learned magicians and their sympathizers nor the suspicion aroused against them as witches played much of a role in the witch trials. To this degree, the business of learned magic in the sixteenth century can be seen as marginal to the story of the witchcraft prosecutions. The learned magicians, not arraigned themselves as witches, escaped with little more than censure, and their cautionary word went effectively unheeded both by the populace at large and by officials involved in the witch trials. Meanwhile, the trials continued throughout the sixteenth century and reached a fever pitch shortly after the beginning of the seventeenth. Perhaps nothing shows more clearly the now broadly social character of the witch trials than this irony that learned magic, which had in the fourteenth century done so much to spark the consolidation of a new, demonic paradigm of the witch, should have become so peripheral an issue by the time the witchcraze was actually underway.

Juridical skepticism

It was instead other forces that intervened to alter the course of the trials, and then largely not before the seventeenth century, initially in the very years when the paroxysms of the witch prosecutions reached their height. The alteration in question served first as a restraint on the trials, but eventually led to their extinction altogether. One can argue that at their worst the trials constituted a serious disruption of society, effectively a sort of social dysfunctionalism. Although as Weyer, and Agrippa, have demonstrated, there was already in the sixteenth century a current of skepticism concerning the trials, it would seem that only when this dysfunction reached a critical point did the skepticism escape a small inner-circle of already negatively predisposed elites to embrace a significant proportion in the educated official milieu.[97] As is clear now, the doubts that brought the witch-craze to a close were juridical in nature, and originated not among disbelievers in witchcraft but among jurists and lawyers worried that the trials had become an offense to the precepts of fairness and justice.[98] Perhaps not surprisingly, judicial resistance, sometimes even negative intervention, originating among officials of the larger centralizing states exercised the most profound influence.[99] Social disorder was, after all, most immediately disruptive of the delicate balances necessary to maintain the emergent nation states.

An excellent example of the phenomenon already in the early seventeenth century comes from a country where the centralization of juridical institutions had reached what was for the time almost the degree of perfection. The inquisitor at Logroño in Spain, Alonso de Salazar Frias, decided, shortly after his nomination to a tribunal of the Spanish Inquisition, that he could not place confidence either in the indictments of his juridical co-workers in cases of witchcraft or sorcery or in the testimony received during judicial proceedings. Confessions alone had mounted to more than 500 in the short time since he had arrived on the scene. Shaken by what he had experienced, he became convinced that it would be better to draw the Inquisition completely out of the business of witch trials rather than provide occasion for more of what he believed were unreliable, indeed incredible accusations. In an official protestation from 1610 he wrote, for example:

> [A]ccording to what scholars say of these phenomena, it is demonstrable that the witches go to the sabbaths many times in dreams...even though perhaps at other times they participate bodily...In spite of the great divergence of the methods of participating in the assemblies, to date none of the accused...have been able to distinguish between these two methods; on the contrary they maintain that they always participate personally and bodily. But when they err on such a material point it is extremely probable that they are also in error with regard to those they name as their accomplices.[100]

After four years of similar reports from Salazar's pen, the Suprema, central council of the Spanish Inquisition at Madrid, resolved to adopt in every detail his practical suggestions regarding legal processes against witches or sorcerers. This action effectively withdrew the Spanish Inquisition from the witch hunt.

Gradually, the same reaction saw itself reproduced throughout European centralized judicial institutions. At first – and in many cases over the long run – the response was not so much official, as in the case of Spain, but more simply de facto, a withdrawal of cooperation with accusations or local attempts at prosecution and eventually the silent end of all trials. Beginning in the late seventeenth century, however, several great monarchies took more prescriptive action. By the time they did, the great panic was over, and witch trials had dwindled in western Europe to just a trickle. France took the first step in 1682 with a royal edict forbidding prosecution for magic or witchcraft except in cases where actions were overtly sacrilegious. Great Britain followed in 1736 with a statute repealing the English witchcraft law of 1604 and the even earlier Scottish one of 1563, though again witchcraft was not completely erased from the books. In Great Britain it remained a crime "to pretend to exercise or use any kind of witchcraft, sorcery, enchantment or conjuration." Already by then a ban on witchcraft prosecution had been entered in Prussia in 1714, with similar action subsequently in the Austrian Empire in 1766, Russia in 1770, Poland in 1776 and Sweden in 1779.[101] Before the end of the eighteenth century, most forms of sorcery had ceased to be a crime in all the great European nation states.

The mechanical philosophy

By then, too, the juridical skepticism about fairly proving a case of witchcraft had begun among educated elites to be replaced by the positive disbelief in the existence of sorcery or witchcraft altogether. The phenomenon had begun already in the seventeenth century, the time when juridical skepticism began to be a dominating force, but recent studies have confirmed that it became widely representative of elites, and thus able to exercise a discernible effect, a century later. What is important for us is that this more deeply ideological than simply practical change affected views about not just witchcraft and sorcery but also magic more broadly as well. Here we are brought back to natural philosophy, or again to what we would think of today as natural science. For in natural philosophy there emerged in the seventeenth century a vision of the world of nature that by the end of the century had begun to triumph among the learned and which we associate with the names of René Descartes, Robert Boyle and Thomas Hobbes. Following the terminology of Descartes, one would describe this vision as that of a "corpuscular world," but the more general phrase used even more commonly was that of a "mechanical philosophy."[102]

As with a certain concretizing of natural philosophy we have already witnessed in the work of Thomas Aquinas back in the thirteenth century, this new manner of viewing and analyzing nature demanded precise explications of manifest operations for all that could be credited as scientific in the realm of natural philosophy. But now the "concrete" was reduced exclusively to material entities or to causes explicated in completely material form. No more occult qualities whose causal mechanisms could not be expounded in expressly material terms. And insofar as scientific analysis and exposition was concerned, no more spirits or immaterial beings. That did not mean that there were not immaterial realities, as for example in the case of nearly all the mechanists the human soul. But one must not allow such objects a place in the accounts of natural philosophy. Souls inhabited a universe in which also was to be found God, as well perhaps for Descartes as the primal ideas, and these things were above nature, inexplicable then in the scientific terms of natural philosophy. Everything else must be natural, a part of the world of nature. And in nature there were only two different sorts of reality to be discussed. On the one hand were material things – that is to say, bodies of various size, shape and texture. On the other there were operations in which these bodies were involved, which effectively meant the operations entailed in local motion. Natural reality thus came down to matter in motion, and to nothing else. As Robert Boyle explained in his defense of 1674, "About the Excellency and Grounds of the Mechanical Hypothesis": "[T]here cannot be *fewer* Principles than the two grand ones of Mechanical Philosophy, *Matter* and *Motion*. ... Nor can we conceive any Principles more *primary*, than *Matter* and *Motion*."[103]

Robert Boyle

Indeed, the Anglo-Irish Boyle provides us with one of the clearest statements of the new natural-philosophical vision. For Boyle was one of its greatest promoters, a leading voice in the attempt to bring natural philosophy around to the new materialism and to realign scientific explanation largely to fit this new model. In that same treatise, "About the Excellency and Grounds of the Mechanical

Hypothesis," Boyle undertook to defend in general terms the very perspective about which we are talking. It is worth quoting his words at some length.

> [W]hen I speak of the *Corpuscular* or *Mechanical* Philosophy...I plead onely for such a Philosophy, as reaches but to things purely Corporeal, and distinguishing between the first *original of things*; and the subsequent *course of Nature*, teaches, concerning the *former*, not onely that God gave Motion to Matter, but that in the beginning He so guided the various Motions of the parts of it, as to contrive them into the World he design'd they should compose...and establish'd those *Rules of Motion*, and that order amongst things Corporeal, which we are wont to call the *laws of Nature*. And having told this as to the *former* [i.e., the first original of things], it may be allowed to the *latter* [i.e., the course of Nature] to teach, That the Universe being once fram'd by God, and the Laws of Motion being setled and all upheld by His incessant concourse and general Providence; the Phaenomena of the World thus constituted, are Physically produc'd by the Mechanical affections of the parts of Matter, and what they operate upon one another according to Mechanical Laws.[104]

In short, God created matter, in particulate form, and gave it motion. He then arranged the matter to constitute the universe we now behold, but even more importantly he established the laws by which that arrangement would be preserved. These laws were simply the laws of motion and the laws of mechanics, knowledge of which had greatly progressed in the seventeenth century, beginning with the major steps taken by Galileo. If one knew these laws, then one could explain everything that happened in nature. For all causation, down to that of the minutest phenomena, consisted of particles in motion acting upon each other in accordance with the rules of mechanics.

Not that Boyle did not acknowledge that the mechanical philosophers had not yet managed to explain every phenomenon in the world. He conceded that the alchemists, whom he called "chymists," in their assaying had come up with explanations of the composition and reduction of materials in ways that accorded remarkably well with the phenomena, the real appearances of things. But to his mind, it was only a matter of time before even the alchemists' explanations should be rendered expressible in simpler and more basic terms in the mechanical philosophy:

> For, what ever be the number or qualities of the Chymical Principles, if they be really existent in Nature, it may very possibly be shewn, that they may be made up of insensible Corpuscles of the determinate bulks and shapes; and by the various Coalitions and Contextures of such Corpuscles...many more material Ingredients, may be compos'd or made to result.[105]

Or as he put it only slightly further in the treatise: "[T]here can be no Ingredient assign'd, that has a real existence in Nature, that may not be deriv'd either immediately, or by a row of Decompositions, from the Universal matter, modifi'd by its Mechanical Affections."[106] In the end, matter and motion, coming together under the laws of mechanics, would be seen as the fundamental ingredients of a scientific explanation of any phenomena. As he assured his readers in a recapitulation at the very finish of the work: "These Principles, *Matter, Motion,* (to which *Rest* is related) *Bigness, Shape, Posture, Order, Texture* being so simple, clear and *comprehensive,* are applicable to all the real *Phaenomena* of Nature, which seem not explicable by any other not consistent with ours."[107]

René Descartes

An even more radical version of the same can be discovered in the effective founder of the new perspective on natural philosophy, the great French thinker, René Descartes. The view was more radical in Descartes because he was willing to posit God's intervention in the beginning as the creation of mere matter and motion in a chaos. The order of the universe arose spontaneously and over many years out of the created particles or "corpuscles" operating under the rules of nature – that is, the laws of mechanics. In Descartes's *Discours de la méthode* (*Discourse on Method*), composed probably around 1628–29 but published only in 1637, he described in brief terms the scenario of the workings of the universe he had had the intention of laying out in his up-till-then still unedited *Le monde* (*The World*). With this summary we find ourselves face to face with a vision of both reality and the rules of natural-philosophical thought that certainly provoked, and must be understood as largely in accord with, the more technically phrased explanation we have just seen in Boyle.

> I resolved to leave this entire world here to [the] disputes [of the learned], and to speak only of what would happen in a new world, were God now to create enough matter to compose it, somewhere in imaginary spaces, and were he to agitate in various ways and without order the different parts of this matter, so that he composed from it a chaos as confused as any the poets could concoct and that later he did no more than apply his ordinary concurrence to nature, and let nature act in accordance with the laws he had established. Thus, first, I described this matter and tried to represent it in such a way that there is nothing in the world, it seems to me, clearer and more intelligible, with the exception of what has already been said about God and the soul... Moreover, I showed what the laws of nature were, and... I tried to demonstrate all those laws about which one might have been able to have any doubt and to show that they are such that, even if God had created many worlds, there could not be any of them in which these laws failed to be observed. After that I showed how, as a consequence of these laws, the greater part of the matter of this chaos had to be disposed and arranged in a certain way, which made it similar to our

heavens; how, at the same time, some of its parts had to compose an earth; others, planets and comets; and still others, a sun and fixed stars.[108]

Once more we are left with a world in which, other than God and human souls, there is nothing real other than matter as an entity – with, of course, its dispositions of place, size, shape and so on – and motion as an operation, all acting in accordance with the ineluctable laws of mechanics.

The mechanical philosophy and witchcraft

What did this mechanical philosophy mean for attitudes about witchcraft and magic? We have seen that the rise of scholastic science, while introducing magic to the learned world in western Europe, ultimately led to a hardening of opinion about the fundamental evilness of magic. Upon those foundations was built the ideology – the general stereotype – which led to the hunt of witches from the latter fifteenth through the seventeenth centuries. The emergence of the mechanical hypothesis as standard for natural philosophy entailed the dismantling of precisely this repressive apparatus of ideology. For in a world of only matter and motion, witchcraft, and eventually all magic as well, simply vanished.

On the one hand, the explanations dependent on the occult that the idea of magic had promoted began to seem increasingly irrelevant, if not completely otiose. They started to wither, as much by inattention as by outright assault. On this point it suffices to return to Boyle and his essay "About the Excellency and Grounds of the Mechanical Hypothesis." In talking about the insufficiency of alchemical explanations to account for natural phenomena, Boyle chose the analogy of making a diagnosis of disease by referring to incantation as its cause. To his eyes, no "sober Physician" called to attend to a patient would have been satisfied if, when he inquired of the symptoms, he were "coldly answer'd, That 'tis a Witch or the Devil that produces them." The reason was that "the Curiosity of an Inquisitive Person … seeks not so much to know, what is the *general* Agent, that produces a *Phenomenon*, as, *by what Means*, and after *what Manner*, the *Phenomenon* is produced." According to the mechanical philosophy, the cause of the disease had to be reducible to the operations of matter and motion. To point then to a witch and to bewitchment as the cause was like explicating how a watch worked by pointing to the watch-maker. Instead, the discerning inquirer into the cause of a disease should think "himself bound to search into the Nature of the Morbific Matter, and … not be satisfi'd till he can, probably at least, deduce from that, and the structure of an Humane Body, and other concurring Physical Causes, the *Phaenomena* of the Malady."[109] No wonder then that interest in occult explanation – not to speak of witchcraft itself – should begin to be pushed aside, in the long run reckoned as not just beside the point but also imaginary.

On the other hand, the rise of the mechanical hypothesis tended to lessen any interest in the demonic. In the extreme, it worked to undermine the belief in demonic agency itself. Here one can turn to the English philosopher Thomas Hobbes, himself a promoter of the mechanical hypothesis in an almost purely Cartesian form but even more audacious on the subject of immaterial existents. In his *Leviathan*, published in 1651, Hobbes maintained that all sensory vision was produced by means of motion, more precisely by "the impression made on the organs of sight by lucid bodies."[110] He accepted as well, however, that similar impressions were often introduced by motions that were authentically material, as when one rubbed one's eyes, but that absolutely did not indicate the existence of a lucid body presenting itself to the vision as an object to be seen. Such events – misleading impressions, we might say – offered the occasion for simple folk to believe that they saw objects that in fact they did not see at all, and of which, after having made efforts to locate their presence, they could find no physical trace.

This, according to Hobbes, constituted the historical origin of the notion of spirits – that is, either immaterial beings or invisible bodies.

> Th[e] nature of sight having never been discovered by the ancient pretenders to natural knowledge..., it was hard for men to conceive of those images in the fancy and in the sense otherwise than of things really without us – which some (because they vanish away, they know not whither nor how) will have to be absolutely incorporeal (that is to say, immaterial), forms without matter, colour and figure without any coloured or figured body...and others say are bodies and living creatures, but made of air (or other more subtle and ethereal matter)...But both of them [those who think the images are immaterial and those who think they are material] agree on one general appellation of them: Demons (as if the dead of whom they dreamed were not inhabitants of their own brain but of the air or of heaven or hell...).[111]

Hobbes's conclusion, which he wanted to impose on the understanding of his readers, was that demons, as authentic objects in nature and not images misinterpreted by simple folk, simply did not exist. One can do no better than to cite his own words:

> Nevertheless, the contrary doctrine (namely, that there be incorporeal spirits) hath hitherto so prevailed in the Church that the use of exorcism (that is to say, of ejection of devils by conjuration) is thereupon built, and...is not yet totally given over. That there were many demoniacs in the primitive Church, and few madmen and other such singular diseases (whereas in these times we hear of and see many madmen, and few demoniacs) proceeds not from the change of nature, but of names.[112]

In short, demoniacs, just like demons, did not really – that is, naturally – exist. Where one thought to see them, it was in truth just a case of dementia, both on the part of the demoniac seen but also, in a different sense of the word, on the part of him who did the seeing.

All of which meant that, from Hobbes's point of view, neither was there anything like demoniacal magic. And without demoniacal magic, then there was no legitimate witch-hunt. The "demonomania" that Bodin had claimed to see among the populace was in fact the sign of a kind of insanity among the elite oppressors. Where one claimed to be bringing suit against witches or sorcerers, one was in fact hunting down the demented or, even worse, absolutely innocent and accidentally implicated souls. In Hobbes's day, it was probably a minority of educated members of society who subscribed to his view. By the end of the eighteenth century, the opinion had surely won over the majority. In either case, there finally existed an ideological vessel associated with natural philosophy that could reinforce the skepticism about the witch trials already evidenced on a juridical plane.

The disenchantment of society

One can see at a glance how the ideological boundaries between magic and its opposite – science or religion – had shifted, or perhaps more correctly that the conceptual conventions locating magic itself had begun to disappear. What I have called the Malinowskian perspective, setting magic against religion, had definitely started to disintegrate. To the Hobbesian point of view, magic lost its anti-religious character. In fact, it lost any religious or anti-religious valence altogether. It was instead to be regarded as a kind of sickness, to be dealt with like any other disease by application of the proper remedy. No longer was it something to be dreaded or feared. But as is apparent in Boyles's comments on bewitchment, the Frazerian perspective on magic had likewise been degraded or corrupted. Magic was no longer anti-science, or a competitor to science with even greater claims to be taken as the truth. It had become instead an irrelevancy, a commentary on reality lacking any pretense to being informative. Magic was turning into the joke, or idle game, that it is regarded as being in educated circles in our own day.

Perhaps we can say that in either case – following the language of Marcel Mauss – "mana" had been removed from the equation. There was no longer anything special or forbidden about magic, regarded either as a competitor to religion or as an alternative to normative science. And the reason was that there was, increasingly from the vantage point of the mechanical philosophy, nothing of "mana" left in the world. In such circumstances, was not "magic" bound simply to evaporate? Indeed, that seems to have been the case. And we are not the first to have thought that this was so. Already one hundred years ago Max Weber took note of the phenomenon. In his lexicon, it was associated with a process that he called the "disenchantment" ("*Entzauberung*") of both society and learning, and that has become fashionable today as an explanation of what happened to magic in Europe in the early modern period.

Of course, to say that "disenchantment" explains the disappearance of magic is to say nothing if all we mean by "disenchantment" is the removal of magic. But for Weber, the term meant much more. It was a stage in what he saw as the progressive rationalization of society in Europe over the past several thousand years. It marked for him the moment where reckoning and calculation began to dominate the mental patterns of the social and intellectual elite. Weber's most trenchant statements about disenchantment appear in the lecture he delivered in 1917, "Wissenschaft als Beruf" ("Science as Profession"). There, in talking about the rationalization that came with the rise of modern science, he explained that the reigning idea of scientific progress had truly arrived when a certain intellectual condition prevailed. And that condition was "[t]he knowledge or belief that one could, if one *only wanted to*, make plain how it was that there were fundamentally no secret and incalculable powers playing a role behind the scene – that instead one could, in principle, *through calculation* have mastery over all things."[113] Such an intellectual outlook or demeanor meant, for Weber, just one thing. "It meant," so he said, "the disenchantment of the world."[114] It meant, he added, a commitment to the attitude that one did not need to appeal to or placate secret or hidden powers but that one could domineer in every situation and resolve every problem – at least in theory and with time – by what he called "technical means and calculation." That was the ultimate rationalization that modern society was all about.[115]

No wonder "mana" had disappeared. Calculation had completely squeezed it out. And such calculation was nowhere more plainly epitomized than in the natural philosophy of the new mechanical hypothesis. With the quantities of matter and motion, one could calculate by means of the laws of mechanics the precise circumstances – the actual cause – of every natural phenomenon. If anywhere there was rationalization of the third sort spoken of in Chapter 2, it was here in the mental world of the elites of the seventeenth and eighteenth centuries. Science itself – in fact, soon all sciences – had become desacralized, in the sense not only that they were not themselves "sacral" – allied with "mana" – but also that they no longer even had the ability to entertain a category of the sacred. All reality had been reduced to calculation. And to this degree even natural science, from the seventeenth century on, was more antiseptic, more "desacralized" – less "enchanted" we might say – than the natural science of the scholastics. Small wonder that magic disappeared as either a phenomenon to be reckoned with or a category to be understood.

Magic's bequest to science

Yet there was an historical irony in all this. For at least in learned spheres, the magical tradition had generated knowledge of use to the modern world – even to the modern world of natural science. In part, this circumstance was true substantively, where certain of the magical sciences contained material, sometimes analytical habits, that would prove to be fundamental for what we call modern natural science. Alchemy was the primary "magical" science that served in this way. We have seen how Boyle regarded the alchemists, whom he designated as "chymists," as among the chief competitors to the mechanical philosophy. It was his conviction that if not all the chymists' doctrines could be superseded by different explanations of the mechanists, at least every one would someday be duplicated by what he regarded as the simpler and more basic formulations of pure matter in motion. We now know that his hope was misplaced. Modern chemistry arose much more directly out of the work of the "chymists" than that of the doctrinaire mechanical philosophers. The very notion of elemental properties and of the composition of elements into compounds owed more to the occult qualities and the assaying principles of the alchemists than anyone would have dared to admit even 50 years ago. Boyle himself knew this on an intuitive level and was much more in contact with the alchemists and influenced by their work than his polemics in such pieces as "About the Excellency" would lead one to believe.[116]

Yet more than substance was passed along. Something of the very tenor of magic was retained in parts of the new natural philosophy, even a bit of the occult or unexplained element so akin to the "mana" we have otherwise been seeing edged out of the new intellectual perspectives. Here, Isaac Newton played an important role. If Descartes was the presiding genius of the mechanical philosophy, Newton served as both its ideal champion and its ultimate betrayer. For Newton amended the mechanical hypothesis largely by changing its mechanics, turning the latter, as some say, into a dynamics where force took on a meaning never imagined in the writings of Descartes, or for that matter in the essay we have looked at from Boyle. To do so, once more Newton turned to alchemy, with which he had been associated for most of his life. In the words of Betty Jo Teeter Dobbs:

> Newton concerned himself with the transmutation of the forms of the universal matter for almost all of his long and fruitful life, and he tried to use the techniques of alchemy to probe the internal structures of its particles.... And if his effort met with something less than the success he had once hoped for, still he did succeed in modifying Descartes in just the right direction.[117]

Perhaps Newton was always an ambivalent supporter of the mechanical philosophy in its purity, since he spent his life as an alchemist as well as a mathematician. But on the surface he long remained committed to the idea that the interactions of motion and matter, explained mechanically, could account for all natural phenomena.

Sometime before the publication of his *Philosophiae naturalis principia mathematica* in 1687, he changed his mind. We know that in the years leading up to the writing and publication of this work Newton had begun more and more to consider the possibility that shot through matter from its largest pieces to its tiniest particles were forces other than those imposed by a moving object onto another on impact but rather exerting their pull or push from a distance and even when the forceful object was at rest. Among these forces were many of those occult attractions or antipathies long recorded in the magical sciences, magnetism being the most prominent. Newton's idea was to extend the notion not only to electricity but to gravity as well. Richard Westfall traces the idea – he calls it a "conversion" in Newton's philosophy of nature – back to years 1679–80, and he claims that one of the profoundest influences upon Newton in making it was his alchemy.[118] But of course it was in the *Principia* that the conversion found its greatest application. For the first time in history the motion of the heavens could be explained with reference only to matter and motion, under the laws of mechanics – but only so long as mechanics included the presence of a force like gravity working at a distance. Action at a distance and attractive forces, two notions that had been hallmarks of the traditions of magic, had been swept up in the soon-to-be normative natural philosophy and effectively, in a word, desacralized. In the process, of course, a bit of the wonder of magic had been injected into what would become classical modern natural science.

Causal sub-currents

As the world of the educated elite made its peace with magic – or perhaps more truly said, as magic began to retreat from the intellectual firmament of learned discourse – and as, even earlier, the witch trials wound down, with witchcraft eventually being taken off the books as a crime of demonic proportions, so there had to be commensurate transformations in the workings of the sub-currents of causality mentioned in Chapter 5. Since those sub-currents most typically involved a kind of functionalism, where the virulence of the witch-hunts was fed by a broader social function they served, as the witch trials subsided, either a new mechanism had to emerge to replace the old or society – maybe just the elites – had to find a way to do without the function altogether. In such circumstances, where historical evidence is so hard to come by, one can advance only speculative arguments. Some are stronger than others. But because some such mechanisms almost certainly were at work, it is worth the effort to do the speculating.

One matter about which there can be no doubt is that the terrifying attack on women as potential witches, subject in the courts to prosecution and at worst to execution by hanging or by fire, came to an end. As William Monter has put it, by 1680, "large numbers of old women were no longer being tried and executed as witches anywhere in western, southern and northern Europe."[119] What was left of the witch trials moved east by the late seventeenth and eighteenth centuries, but even there in some places, as in Russia, the majority of the accused began to be male.[120] In the west, in fact, already before the end of the phase of active witch prosecution there had been a shift away from the emphasis on female accused. In central and northern Europe, the focus in the last decades of the craze turned more to youths and children.[121] In short, if witchcraft prosecution had served in the early centuries of the craze as a way of acting out misogyny and putting women in a social position of submission and anxiety about standing out, that function had already started to expire before the period of crisis had come to an end.

Perhaps it can be said that the effort to teach women to restrain their more extrovert public expressions of self had done its work, so that this was a function that no longer needed to be filled once the ravages of the trials were over. More likely, so far as the lower classes were concerned, the disruptions and social dysfunction of the trials had taught the elites that they could tolerate a little behavioral disorder at the lower levels so long as their position of social control did not stand in jeopardy. At the upper levels of society, the same was certainly not the case. Misogyny, in the broad sense of the effort to keep women in a clear position of social inferiority, did not cease. But the means for restraining female behavior were largely transformed, away from the aggressive and largely negative to a perhaps more insidious and positive cultural form. In England, for instance, the late seventeenth century witnessed a move away from the harsh Puritan rhetoric of male control of female behavior toward a formally positive ideal of womanhood as the milder and more benevolent sex, which, as Anthony Fletcher reminds us, in the end worked to encourage the internalization of proscriptions on female activity in the public sphere.[122] The stage was set for a post-Enlightenment idealization of womanhood that trapped women in an ivory tower as restrictive as any of the more overt prohibitions of the crisis periods of the sixteenth and early seventeenth centuries.[123] Again as Fletcher suggests, the key at least in England was the late seventeenth century rise to social and political prominence of the gentry, who combined their class control with gender specifications of "gentle" behavior well-suited to the domination of males.[124] By the nineteenth century, the double assault of sixteenth- and seventeenth-century terror and prohibition and seventeenth- and eighteenth-century idealization had left modern womanhood in a position where liberation was more necessary than ever.

The case of acculturation, or the assault by the elite on the world-view and practices of popular culture, leaves us as historians in greater ambiguity. Indeed, here there is reason to believe that the efforts of the elites to use the trials to change the culture of the lower strata of society spectacularly failed.[125] Most historians agree that among the populace at large, and not just those living in rural districts, concern with witches and witchcraft continued almost unabated after the trials were shut down. In Owen Davies's words, "[T]he masses continued to fear witches."[126] For more than a century after official witch hunts ended in the latter part of the sixteen-hundreds, local communities in western Europe were seen to take their own unofficial action against those who had a reputation for witchcraft.[127] Indeed, Davies has argued that there was a certain collusion between local elites and the popular classes in this regard, so that in England it was only with the rise of a paid civil magistracy in the nineteenth century that repercussions were felt doing away with popular action against witches.[128] All this fits perfectly well with the widely hailed investigations of Judith Devlin among French peasants revealing the continuation well into the nineteenth century of habits of mind and behavior that would appear by elite standards – as well as by our own standards today – remarkably, in Devlin's words, "superstitious."[129]

Of course, this circumstance forces us to pose the question of why it had become acceptable to tolerate a cultural phenomenon that had for more than two centuries seemed completely at odds with social well-being. Short of abandoning the acculturation argument altogether, one can say that there is some evidence of continuing pressures on the popular classes but along slightly different lines. Raisa Maria Toivo has shown that in Scandinavia, indictments on witchcraft charges actually rose in the last quarter of the seventeenth century. But where before the accusations had been serious ones of demonic sorcery or *maleficium*, from the 1670s on they were primarily the more moderate ones of "benevolent" magic, as in curing illness. In such cases, the problem was not connivance with devils but rather religious error or "superstition" in the narrowest sense. Toivo views the effort as part of a campaign on the side of officials to educate the populace.[130] But we have already seen above that the English law repealing the earlier witchcraft statutes continued to make it a crime to practice sorcery – benevolent magic most of all – because of the possibility of defrauding a gullible public. More broadly across western Europe, therefore, sorcery continued to be viewed with alarm by the elites; the issue had simply shifted to delusion, maybe fraud, and otherwise benign practices.[131]

More powerful is the argument that the elites had finally, as Owen Davies has suggested, come to see popular beliefs regarding witchcraft and sorcery as irrelevant. In the fifteenth century, cultural order had seemed threatened by the magical and superstitious practices of the populace. The result was a convulsion of persecution that lasted for over two hundred years. By the late seventeenth century, those in official positions had come to see their cultural – and political – position as inviolate, and so the same magic and superstition could most easily be overlooked. That was especially so since not to overlook it had so disrupted the social fabric. Again, it is Davies who has argued that only in the nineteenth and early twentieth century did elites return to the program of changing popular belief, and this time by means of education. Here, too, religion played a role – in England, for instance, with the rise of Methodism and a new religious agenda capable of being spread among the populace.[132]

Political ideology

In the end, perhaps politics was the crucial piece in the puzzle. The tolerance of the later seventeenth and eighteenth centuries would thus be due primarily to a new-found political security of the elite. Inevitably we are thus led back to the third of our causal sub-currents, that having to do with the role of politics in the late medieval and early modern reaction to witchcraft and to magic. This is not the place to give a history of the rise of the nation state, though it is more than coincidental that the seventeenth and eighteenth centuries were the time when this form of political organization finally emerged triumphant on the European scene. Instead, it is worth our while to take a glance at political ideology. Here we witness a change that stands as a sign for a broad range of phenomena, all pointing to the ascent of a political order in which witchcraft and even the practice of benevolent magic could not be seen as in any way a threat to the foundations of social dominance and power.

Thomas Hobbes

It was suggested earlier – at the instigation of Christina Larner – that an ideology of state dependent on Christianity was conducive to a view of witchcraft, and even sorcery insofar as it implied collaboration with demons, as a capital crime, a form of lèse majesté. Perhaps it is not then surprising that the seventeenth century, the time when the witchcraze died down, saw the introduction of what was to become a dominant model of political ideology that was fully secularized, and thus in which Christianity played no significant role. Instead, the new ideology of state took its foundations from the mechanical philosophy of nature, which was at the same time driving magic out of the intellectual firmament of the learned elite. In England, the early spokesperson for this novel political theory was Thomas Hobbes, confirmed mechanist but also supporter of an absolutist vision of the state. We have already noted Hobbes's mechanistic views on the world of nature as put forth in his *Leviathan*, published in 1651. But of course that same work was more importantly a treatise on political theory, where Hobbes worked out his understanding of the proper theoretical foundation for the state.

Hobbes begins his argument with what can only be called a corpuscular vision of the condition of mankind before – or, in purely speculative terms, without – any institutions of political order. This is the state of nature, into which mankind would naturally fall without the aid of civil institutions. In it, so Hobbes says our reason leads us to recognize, all human beings are effectively equal in power – that is, each has adequate means to obliterate the other under the right circumstances.[133] Furthermore, these corpuscular human beings hit up against each other in a kind of anarchy of might. Each wants whatever he can get, which includes exactly that which each other human being wants. For Hobbes, then, the state of nature is truly a state of chaos of inter-human motion: it is the state of the war of every one against all others.[134] In such a state, no one has any good reason to put his or her industry into any productive endeavor, for it is almost certain that the product will be stolen. It is, therefore, a state of fear – or what

Hobbes calls "diffidence" – in which no gainful activity can reasonably be undertaken. And the "incommodities," as Hobbes calls them, of such a state are plain for all to see.

> In such condition there is no place for industry, because the fruit thereof is uncertain, and consequently, no culture of the earth, no navigation, … no commodious building, … no arts, no letters, no society, and which is worst of all, continual fear and danger of violent death, and the life of man, solitary, poor, nasty, brutish, and short."[135]

Given this reality – or what would be the reality if only nature and not political institutions were to hold – human beings are driven by both their passions and their reason to imagine the conditions that would have to apply to make life livable, to make possible what Hobbes calls "commodious living." And these conditions, because they necessarily involve an end to the natural state of war, Hobbes calls "articles of peace." Since they are also the only conditions that might sustain a commodious life, they can also be seen as the "laws of nature."[136] Which is to say that they are restrictions on human behavior that reason leads all human beings to recognize as necessary for life to be rendered worth living. Of these, the initial two are particularly important. The first is that each person should seek peace with his or her fellow human beings, insofar as it is reasonable to believe that such peace will prevail. This provision means, of course, an end to the state of war. The second law is that each person should be willing to forfeit his original right to possess himself of whatever he wants – which is to say, perhaps, that he or she should respect the peace – if others, too, are willing to abide by the same restriction.[137] Were these two laws to prevail, commodious living might begin.

The problem for humankind is that so long as the state of nature reigns, there is no reason to accept the laws of nature as binding. Anyone doing so would simply expose him- or herself to the predations of one who chose not to recognize the laws. Though the laws of nature exist, they are therefore not obligatory so long as there is no force to punish or prevent infractions. In Hobbes's words, this means that there has to be "a power set up to constrain those that would otherwise violate their faith." The establishment of such a power entails the introduction of civil society, the foundation of a state.[138] In short, the laws of nature as binding laws and the fact of a civil society with a state to enforce the laws must come into existence at precisely the same moment. They are mutually interdependent goals. Here is where Hobbes settles upon the idea of a covenant among human beings. If it is an historical fiction, it constitutes at least a rational necessity for the only kind of human existence worth living. What must happen, so Hobbes explains, is that each person who is to make up civil society must simultaneously agree to establish a power to constrain all to the observance of the laws of nature and to defend the whole against external aggression and must consent to give over all his or her own personal might and right of action to that power so established. Since it is a promise each person makes to all the other prospective members of the society, it is, in Hobbes's words, a covenant – a promise of future action in return for the grant of something from the other party. By means of this covenant is established civil society, which Hobbes now calls the "Commonwealth." And it is guaranteed by the erection of that power upon which all in the society have conferred their own capacity to constrain, which power Hobbes now names as the "Sovereign," whether that be a single person or an assembly.[139]

The "Sovereign" is the eponymous Leviathan of Hobbes's work, a necessary evil for the sake of the only chance for humankind of a commodious life – that is, one worth living. Note that what Hobbes has done is to move from a corpuscular but chaotic state of nature among human beings to a state of the political world such as we see around us in our own time with societies and sovereign states. But he has managed this with nothing more than the ingredients already present in nature. There is no intervention from an external power, God included. Indeed, he is willing to call his Leviathan, the Sovereign of his Commonwealth, a "Mortal God."[140] Here is then, as with the mechanical hypothesis for natural philosophy, an entirely desacralized theory for politics. Moreover from it flow most of the benefits that men and women of the elite in seventeenth-century England could desire. With a Sovereign in place, all the laws of nature follow as binding upon all members of the Commonwealth. The third of these is "that men perform their covenants made," which is to say that all contracts are valid and enforceable – by means, of course, of the sovereign of the state.[141] Implied in this is the recognition of what Hobbes calls "propriety," but which we would think of as private property.[142] We begin to see an ideology of the state, then, well suited to a gentry, inclined toward commerce, that would increasingly dominate English politics from the seventeenth century on. With property and contract secure, and the state independent of Godly intervention, there need be no concern about violation of a Godly compact. Easy to see why witchcraft, already shaken from its status as a major crime by judicial skepticism, should become a progressively distant concern.

John Locke

There was however a problem with Hobbes's theory, especially in an England that had witnessed in the seventeenth century a civil war, the overthrowing of a monarch, and then again a "Glorious Revolution" shifting allegiance from one monarch to another. For Hobbes insisted that the members of a Commonwealth were bound to their sovereign absolutely. "[T]hey that are subjects to a monarch cannot without his leave cast off monarchy and return to the confusion of a disunited multitude, nor transfer their person from him that beareth it to another man, or other assembly of men."[143] Here was a provision that stuck in the craw of many in the English political elite. More to the taste of this elite was the work of another corpuscular in the realm of political theory, one indebted to the Hobbesian model but not thereby inclined to support an absolutist ideology. John Locke composed his major work of political theory, the *Second Treatise of Government*, during the time of the exclusion crisis from 1679 to 1683. It was published, however, only in 1689 – with a publication date of 1690 – after King James II, whose exclusion from the throne had failed, had been driven from power by the assembled might of Parliament and the military strength of the new King William and Queen Mary.[144]

Just like Hobbes, Locke starts by proposing that in the state of nature all humankind stood in a state of complete equality, though he gives the equality a more positive cast by seeing it as the lack of subordination of one to another rather than a kind of physical equipollence of capacity to harm.[145] In that state, too, there exist laws of nature, which can be discovered by using reason to analyze the conditions that such an equality must entail. First of the laws is the obligation of each person to preserve him- or herself as well as to preserve the rest of mankind.[146] It is almost a version, so Locke seems to believe, of the Hobbesian requirement that each person strive to preserve the peace.[147] The second law lays upon each individual the right or power to punish any infraction of the first law – that is, any breach of the peace.[148] Of course, with Hobbes the laws of nature were not binding until the commonwealth had been erected. But for Locke that is not so. Perhaps one should say that Locke has a better opinion of humanity, one that sees human beings as more inclined from the start to respect each other, more filled with mutual benevolence. In any case, Locke insists that the laws are binding upon humankind from the very beginning, and he feels that in the state of nature all of humankind make up what he would recognize as a single society.[149] For Locke, there is thus social life before the institution of the state. For him as well, the state of nature is not a state of war.[150] Attacking one's fellow human beings and disrupting the peace are actions not natural to humankind. They place one unnaturally against one's fellows, and it is to punish them that the second law of nature would come into force.

To Locke's eyes, the state of nature is not therefore completely incommodious, as it was for Hobbes. Nor is it, however, absolutely safe. According to Locke, property arises already in that primitive – and perhaps theoretical – social order. Anything – an object, for instance, or a tract of land – to which someone has added his or her labor – by picking up apples or cultivating the land – is thereby the personal belonging of him or her from whom the labor came. And each person in the state of nature has the sole right to make use of his or her personal property.[151] Yet despite the fact that the state of nature constitutes a sort of society, it is not a society in which one can rest absolutely secure. For there being no power other than individuals to defend property, there are inevitably some who seek to seize the property of others, by force. There is then even in Locke's state of nature something like Hobbes's diffidence. And that slight fear is what drives human beings into civil society pure and simple.

This [uncertainty] makes [the person in the state of nature] willing to quit a condition, which, however free, is full of fears and continual dangers: and it is not without reason, that he seeks out, and is willing to join in society with others, who are already united, or have a mind to unite, for the mutual *preservation* of their lives, liberties and estates, which I call by the general name, *property*.[152]

Civil society, which Locke like Hobbes calls a commonwealth, is established by means of a covenant among the individuals who will make up that society. And by this covenant, the members of the society set up an authority not only to determine the positive laws of the land but also to judge when such laws have been broken and how infractions will be punished.[153] Again, as in Hobbes, each individual member of the society also gives up some of his own liberty under the state of nature. In Locke's case, the individuals consign to the power of the state both privileges of the first two laws of nature – the right to preserve oneself and one's fellows from harm and the right to punish those who break the peace.[154] But for Locke the very conditions of the establishment of the commonwealth set a limit to the sovereign power. For the commonwealth was founded expressly to preserve property. And so for Locke the sovereign cannot deprive any member of the commonwealth of any of his or her property without his or her agreement. In Locke's famous words: "The *supreme power cannot take* from any man any part of his *property* without his own consent."[155] In this case, Locke seems to mean property as possession, despite the fact that, as we have seen above, he had expressly included life and liberty under the category of property as well.

Yet there is an additional condition that Locke sees as bound into the commonwealth as he conceives it. For the covenant by which the commonwealth is established hands over the power of the individuals under those first laws of nature not so much to the sovereign or supreme power as to the community at large. Moreover, this consignment is valid only so long as each individual has the right of appeal in any case against another to an impartial judge.[156] It is in fact the community that selects such judges or magistrates – even if they be the same as the supreme power – and it must ensure their impartiality. For Locke, therefore, an absolute monarchy is ruled out prima facie as a form of legitimate commonwealth. Against an absolute monarch there is no one to whom a mere member of the commonwealth can appeal. And thus an absolute monarch can never be a member of a commonwealth.[157] In fact, the closer any authority in a commonwealth moves toward absolute or arbitrary power, the less secure is its hold on legitimacy. In extreme cases, the people of the commonwealth as a whole have the right – perhaps the obligation – to remove the authority and replace it with another.[158]

Here then was a corpuscular philosophy of politics that could appeal to the English elite of the late seventeenth century. It protected a certain right of rebellion, and it ensured the dominance and inviolate nature of property. By the mid-eighteenth century it had become a political philosophy beginning to appeal to elites in Europe at large. It ensured the propertied classes the position they felt they deserved and that they increasingly held in all the emergent nation states. And it did so without so much as a nod to the sacred or the occult. Mana had been squeezed out of the political arena. But of course by then, concern for matters of witchcraft, and magic, had for over a century been relegated to the margins. Across Europe as a whole, it soon would completely disappear.

Conclusion

By the end of the last chapter we had arrived at a state of equilibrium in western European society. The paroxysms of the witchcraze had been put to rest in a new dispensation that at least temporarily guaranteed serenity at the surface of the social order. If we look to each of the three threads of historical change marked out in the introduction, we see mutually reinforcing resolutions. On the matter of science, which of course for us has also implicated a sizable element of learned magic, we have witnessed two periods of ideological innovation, punctuated by attempts either to reconcile magic with science by seeing them both as legitimate efforts to discover the truth or to turn science against magic as an inveterate source of error and usually a font of evil as well. Here, a tipping point was reached in the thirteenth century, when the accumulation of works laying out the practical details of magic, especially of a ceremonial sort, occasioned a soon to be dominant response on the part of self-styled defenders of scientific truth that magic was meretricious and contingent in its performance on the connivance of demonic powers. Even the resurgence of learned magic in the sixteenth century could not shake the grip of what had become the standard scientific attitude. It was only with the second of the periods of ideological change in the Scientific Revolution of the seventeenth century that this pattern of warfare changed. For the mechanical philosophy not only rendered magic's attempts to explain natural phenomena false, but it also undermined the claim that there actually were such things as magical actions. Driven from the field, magic would soon disappear from the realm of serious learned discourse. Not, however, until after having bequeathed several important insights to early modern natural philosophy.

When it comes to the question of social control, or to the interaction between the elite and the populace, the story line is somewhat different. Here there are not two periods of innovation but rather one long process of continuous development. That development was one of greater rationalization of society. It was an impulse not completely absent from Europe in the early Middle Ages but greatly intensified by the emergence from the twelfth century onward of the medieval scientific current associated with Scholasticism. We have seen that ecclesiastical elites from as far back as the tenth century were concerned about the religious beliefs of the populace, which they saw as superstitious. But in the twelfth century this concern turned to outright alarm, as the populace itself began to draw from the literate culture of Christianity and start to rationalize its own religious observances. The result was an effort by the elites to stifle the rationalizing energies of popular reform. For the first time since late Antiquity, we see an

227

official ecclesiastical condemnation of what can only be called "popular heresy." For the moment at least, concern about what had previously been labeled superstition faded into the background.

Yet so-called superstitious observances were not to be ignored for long. Catalyst in the phenomenon of their reappearance as targets for repressive measures of both lay and ecclesiastical elites was the new attitude toward learned magic noted earlier with regard to science and magic. As the thirteenth century progressed, a standard opposition to learned magic, the literature expounding which had begun to proliferate in both university and courtly circles, established itself among officers of church and state. The operative argument was that learned magic demanded recourse to diabolical forces. And over the fourteenth century ecclesiastic jurists managed to install as a principle that activity in such perilous waters was tantamount to heresy, thus subject to investigation and punishment by the inquisition. Then, in the early fifteenth century, this whole apparatus, both ideological and institutional, was turned upon the populace at large. In a series of trials in the western foothills of the Alps the target of inquisitorial procedures switched from learned magic to popular sorcery and "superstitious" beliefs. By century's end a stereotype had arisen of the classical anti-Christian witch. With that stereotype serving as a template for prosecution, the witchcraze of the sixteenth and seventeenth centuries had begun. Here at last was unleashed the rationalizing impulse with a vengeance.

It is the argument of this book that the witch trials represented a crisis at the level of social control. In their violence, they proved the dysfunctionality of the view that popular fear of witches and belief in a host of other practices that the witch-stereotype embraced constituted a real threat to social order. Juridical skepticism began to restrain the willingness of elites to prosecute accusation of witchcraft. By the time that the mechanical philosophy had won enough adherents among the learned to undermine credence in the fact itself of witchcraft, the witch trials had already ceased to be a major factor on the European scene. There began, instead, a period of relative indifference on the part of elites toward popular belief, especially those areas of it that had been seen to fall under the rubric of "superstition."

The last thread has to do with politics and political ideology. On this count we return to the developmental pattern seen with regard to science and magic. For there is innovation at the commencement of our story, starting in the twelfth century, which innovation builds to a crisis, at which point there appears a new innovation just beginning to be visible in the seventeenth century and leading ultimately to the crisis's resolution. The story gets under way, as we have seen, with the formation of centralizing governments, both lay and ecclesiastical, in the twelfth century. Hand in hand with these governments arise new instruments of control, the most important of which from our perspective were juridical. Inquisitorial procedure was primary on this score, and one of the most notable instances of it was the establishment by the early thirteenth century of a loosely coordinated papal inquisition. At first the inquisition was directed against heresy, represented by the popular efforts for reform of religion mentioned earlier. But for our purposes the weapon of the inquisition was wielded to buttress the authority of state and church to dramatic effect only when it was turned to the hunt for witches.

For witch trials to occur on the scale we see in the sixteenth and seventeenth centuries, there had to have developed the stereotype of the witch mentioned earlier, with demon worship, meeting at covens, night flight, infanticide and, of course, sorcery. This paradigm provided the charges to be leveled against accused witches in court. It constituted a crime so heinous as to be punishable only by death. But it also served to buttress the ideological claims to authority, even hegemony, of the very early modern state. Power as the rightful defender of the Christian church and faith was what the state pretended to, and nothing revealed that role so plainly as the prosecution of witchcraft. Particularly among smaller states or governments, where central command had to compete most directly with local jurisdictions and lordly loyalties, the need for a way to advance the ideological claim to rule was acute. And in those smaller states, particularly in German-speaking lands, the witch trials raged with exceptional ferocity. Such states bought their right to rule at enormous social cost.

An exit from this crisis, the same one as seen with the other narrative threads but now with a distinctly political mien, necessarily entailed at least in part the shedding of the Christian ideology of power so manifest in the trials. By the seventeenth century evidence is beginning to build that an appropriately alter-nate ideology was taking hold. We see it in the theory of the state laid out by Thomas Hobbes, where central authority is established on the grounds that the state is the only institution capable of promoting the peace and making human life worthwhile. But the more influential version of this non-Christian but rather self-styled naturalizing argument for the rights of the civil authority is to be found in the work of John Locke. By natural right and common covenant furnished with the powers of judgment and coercion, the early modern state now emerges as free of the dysfunctional entanglements seen in the witch trials and even more powerful than ever to protect the property rights of an increasingly ascendant commercial elite.

All three of our historical threads thus arrive in the late seventeenth century at a period of relative balance following a time of agitation and crisis. And, of course, as the number of cross-references in these summaries makes clear, they are in very concrete terms greatly intertwined. Developments along the historical line of any one thread have effects in both of the two remaining. In the end it is plain even that a resolution of conflict or tension building in any one of the threads is possible only if there is a comparable resolution of tension in the other two. We have therefore laid bare a period in European history from the twelfth through to the end of the seventeenth century when a complex historical dance was played out at several levels at once – intellectual, cultural, political – leading up to the preconditions for the modern world. The Enlightenment of the eighteenth century has long been held to constitute the dawn of European modernity. This study has attempted to show that if that is so, it is because the social and cultural tensions and contradictions of the preceding 600 years had worked their way to the sort of resolution in which an "enlightened" point of view was possible. Much of the story of those tensions, contradictions and even resolutions must be told in the language of science, magic and belief. From the eighteenth century on, magic drops out of the picture, and even belief becomes a matter of only sporadic concern. Modern times tell their story much more confidently in the rhetoric of science. Whether, after the twentieth century and here in the beginning of the twenty-first, that confidence has begun to wane is a matter I leave to the reader to ponder. Yet for over 250 years the confidence reigned supreme. And the reason can be traced back to the struggles and triumphs with which this book is concerned.

Notes

Introduction

1. Charles Homer Haskins, *Studies in the History of Medieval Science* (Cambridge, MA: Harvard University Press, 1924); and *The Renaissance of the Twelfth Century* (Cambridge, MA: Harvard University Press, 1927).
2. Marie-Dominique Chenu, *La théologie au douzième siècle*, 2nd edn (Paris: J. Vrin, 1966; orig. ed. 1957). See also the work of Tullio Gregory, beginning with his early *Anima mundi. La filosofia di Guglielmo di Conches e la scuola di Chartres* (Florence: Sansoni, 1955).
3. See Andreas Speer, *Die entdeckte Natur. Untersuchungen zu Begründsversuchen einer "scientia naturalis" im 12. Jahrhundert* (Leiden: Brill, 1995).
4. Steven P. Marrone, *William of Auvergne and Robert Grosseteste. New Ideas of Truth in the Early Thirteenth Century* (Princeton: Princeton University Press, 1983).
5. George Sarton, *Six Wings. Men of Science in the Renaissance* (Bloomington: Indiana University Press, 1957); and Alexandre Koyré, *From the Closed World to the Infinite Universe* (Baltimore, MD: Johns Hopkins University Press, 1957).
6. Thomas S. Kuhn, *The Copernican Revolution. Planetary Astronomy in the Development of Western Thought* (Cambridge, MA: Harvard University Press, 1957).
7. Paolo Rossi, *Francesco Bacone. Dalla magia alla scienza*, rev. ed. (Turin: G. Einaudi, 1974; orig. ed. 1957).
8. Charles Webster, *From Paracelsus to Newton. Magic and the Making of Modern Science* (Cambridge: Cambridge University Press, 1982).
9. Betty Jo Teeter Dobbs, *The Foundations of Newton's Alchemy* (Cambridge: Cambridge University Press, 1975).
10. See, most importantly, William R. Newman, *Atoms and Alchemy. Chymistry and the Experimental Origins of the Scientific Revolution* (Chicago, IL: University of Chicago Press, 2006); and Lawrence M. Principe, *The Secrets of Alchemy* (Chicago, IL: University of Chicago Press, 2013).
11. Robert K. Merton, *Science, Technology and Society in Seventeenth-Century England* (Amsterdam: Swets and Zeitlinger: 1938).
12. Steven Shapin and Simon Schaffer, *Leviathan and the Air-Pump. Hobbes, Boyle, and the Experimental Life* (Princeton, NJ: Princeton University Press, 1985). Among other attempts to set the Scientific Revolution into social context,

see the influential Barbara J. Shapiro, *Probability and Certainty in Seventeenth-Century England. A Study of the Relationships between Natural Science, Religion, History, Law and Literature* (Princeton: Princeton University Press, 1983); and Margaret C. Jacob, *The Cultural Meaning of the Scientific Revolution* (New York: A.A. Knopf, 1988).

13. Lynn Thorndike, *A History of Magic and Experimental Science* (New York: Macmillan, 1923–58).

14. D. P. Walker, *Spiritual and Demonic Magic from Ficino to Campanella* (London: Warburg Institute, 1958); and Allen G. Debus, *The English Paracelsians* (London: Oldbourne, 1965).

15. Frances A. Yates, *Giordano Bruno and the Hermetic Tradition* (London: Routledge and Kegan Paul, 1964).

16. For an example of the scholarship on the Middle Ages, see Jean-Patrice Boudet, *Entre science et nigromancie. Astrologie, divination et magie dans l'Occident médiéval, XIIe–XVe siècle* (Paris: Sorbonne, 2006); on medieval to Renaissance magic, see William Eamon, *Science and the Secrets of Nature. Books of Secrets in Medieval and Early Modern Culture* (Princeton, NJ: Princeton University Press, 1994).

17. For a historiographical accounting of approaches to popular religion, see Chapter 2, pp. 33–36. As for witchcraft itself, Chapter 5, pp. 198–93, presents an even more detailed review of the literature than that given here.

18. Margaret A. Murray, *The Witch-Cult in Western Europe* (Oxford: Clarendon Press, 1963; orig. 1921). See also her *The God of the Witches* (Oxford: Oxford University Press, 1931).

19. For more on Murray, see Chapter 1, pp. 1–3.

20. See Norman Cohn, *Europe's Inner Demons* (orig. New York: Basic Books, 1973; revised ed. 1993).

21. See Richard Kieckhefer, *European Witch Trials. Their Foundations in Popular and Learned Culture, 1300–1500* (Berkeley: University of California Press, 1976).

22. Alan Macfarlane, *Witchcraft in Tudor and Stuart England. A Regional and Comparative Study* (London: Routledge and Kegan Paul, 1970; 2nd ed. 1999); and Keith Thomas, *Religion and the Decline of Magic. Studies in Popular Beliefs in Sixteenth- and Seventeenth-Century England* (London: Weidenfield and Nelson, 1971).

23. Christina Larner, *Enemies of God. The Witch Hunt in Scotland* (London: Chatto and Windus, 1981).

24. Stuart Clark, *Thinking with Demons. The Idea of Witchcraft in Early Modern Europe* (Oxford: Oxford University Press, 1997).

25. Euan Cameron, *Enchanted Europe. Superstition, Reason, and Religion, 1250–1750* (Oxford: Oxford University Press, 2010).

26. Robin Briggs, *Witches and Neighbors. The Social and Cultural Context of European Witchcraft* (London: Viking, 1996).

27. Marijke Gijswijt-Hofstra, Brian P. Levack and Roy Porter, *Witchcraft and Magic in Europe. The Eighteenth and Nineteenth Centuries* (London: The Athlone

Press, 1999). See also, more recently, Owen Davies and Willem de Blécourt, ed., *Beyond the Witch Trials. Witchcraft and Magic in Enlightenment Europe* (Manchester: Manchester University Press, 2004).

28. Owen Davies, *Witchcraft, Magic and Culture, 1736–1951* (Manchester: Manchester University Press, 1999); and also Jonathan Barry and Owen Davies, ed., *Palgrave Advances in Witchcraft Historiography* (Basingstoke: Palgrave Macmillan, 2007).

1 Superstition, Science and Magic, 200 BCE–1200 CE

1. Margaret A. Murray, *The Witch-Cult in Western Europe*. As indicated earlier in the introduction (x–xi), Murray's views were entirely discredited among professional historians of witchcraft by the 1970s. But, as suggested here, her influence remains powerful among non-professionals.
2. On Wicca, begin with Michael D. Bailey, *Magic and Superstition in Europe. A Concise History from Antiquity to the Present* (Lanham, MD: Rowman and Littlefield, 2007), 238–40 and 243–46.
3. Murray, *Witch-Cult*, 12.
4. Again, see ibid., 11–12.
5. Ibid., *12*.
6. Margaret A. Murray, *The God of the Witches*, 145.
7. See again, Murray, *Witch-Cult*, 11.
8. See n. 6.
9. See Norman Cohn, *Europe's Inner Demons*, revised edition (Chicago, IL: University of Chicago Press, 2000 [orig. 1993]), 152–53. This revision, subtitled *The Demonization of Christians in Medieval Christendom*, while true to the argument of the work as originally published in 1973 with the subtitle *An Enquiry Inspired by the Great Witch-Hunt* (New York: Basic Books) and taking over practically the entirety of its text, word for word, sometimes radically alters the order of exposition. Chapters, even parts of chapters, of the two versions often do not correspond numerically. Except where noted, the present study will make reference exclusively to the revised edition.
10. Frazer progressively expanded his creation, until the third edition, which appeared between 1911 and 1914, contained 13 volumes. This latter version is taken as standard today, and the quotation given here comes from it: James G. Frazer, *The Golden Bough*, 3rd ed. (New York, 1935), I, 235–36.
11. On this animistic view, see ibid., I, 51; for sympathetic magic, I, 54.
12. See ibid., I, 222.
13. Ibid., I, 226, n. 2.
14. The notion of such an evolution lies behind what Frazer says in ibid., I, 51.
15. Ibid., I, 52–53.
16. Ibid., I, 220–21.

17. Ibid., I, 219.
18. For the latter point, ibid., I, 220.
19. In Frazer's unflinching words: "In both [magic and science] the succession of events is perfectly regular and certain, being determined by immutable laws, the operation of which can be foreseen and calculated precisely" (ibid., I, 221).
20. See ibid., I, 53 and 222.
21. Bronislaw Malinowski, "Magic, Science and Religion," in *Magic, Science and Religion and Other Essays*, ed. Robert Redfield (Boston, 1948; reissued with different pagination, Prospect Heights, IL: Waveland Press, 1992 [cited here]), 89. This article first appeared in 1925.
22. Ibid. 17.
23. Ibid., 34.
24. See note 16.
25. Malinowski, "Magic, Science and Religion," 17–18.
26. Ibid., 86–87.
27. Ibid., 28–29: "[The savage's] experience has taught him also... that in spite of all his forethought and beyond all his efforts there are agencies and forces which... pursue him... and thwart all his most strenuous efforts and his best-founded knowledge. To control these influences and these only he employs magic."
28. Ibid., 87.
29. Ibid.
30. Ibid., 17 and 87.
31. Ibid. Malinowski even gave Frazer credit for having first realized that before belief in animism, there was the early form of magic manipulating forces by charm and spell. See ibid., 19.
32. Ibid., 88.
33. Ibid., 37–38.
34. Appuleius, *De magia*, 25. (Taken from Charlton T. Lewis and Charles Short, *A Latin Dictionary* [Oxford: Clarendon Press, 1966], 1101b.)
35. Matt. 2:1–3.
36. Cicero, *De divinatione,* I: 46. (Taken from Cicero, *Opera philosopha et politica*, ed. J. G. Baiter, VII [Leipzig: Bernhard Tauchnitz, 1863], 139.)
37. For this and the reference to Valens, see Edward Peters, "The Medieval Church and State on Superstition, Magic and Witchcraft: From Augustine to the Sixteenth Century," in *Witchcraft and Magic in Europe: The Middle Ages*, ed. Karen Jolly, Catharine Raudvere, and Edward Peters (London: Athlone Press: 2002), 180.
38. On the reference in the Theodosian Code, see ibid., 180–81. Justinian's *Codex*, 9, 18, 7, refers to "magi qui malefici vulgi consuetudine nuncupantur." (Latter taken from Lewis and Short, *Latin Dictionary*, 1103a.) Peters notes that Isidore of Seville, in his *Etymologies* of the seventh century, repeats the linguistic claim made in the Roman legal texts ("The Medieval Church," 185).

39. Bernadette Filotas, in *Pagan Survivals, Superstition and Popular Cultures in Early Medieval Pastoral Literature* (Toronto: Pontifical Institute of Medieval Studies, 2005), 287–88 and n. 115, claims that *maleficus* in this sense was a Christian invention. She points to Jerome's version of the Vulgate and Augustine's *City of God* for early instances of the term's appearance.

40. Denise Grodzynski, "Superstitio," *Revue des Etudes Anciennes* 76 (1974): 37. See a similar reference to Plautus in Dieter Harmening, *Superstitio. Uberlieferungs- und theoriegeschichtliche Untersuchungen zur kirchlich-theologischen Aberglaubensliteratur des Mittelalters* (Berlin: Erich Schmidt Verlag, 1979), 15.

41. Cicero, *De deorum natura*, 2, 28, 71. (Taken from Lewis and Short, *Latin Dictionary*, 1809c.)

42. See Grodzynski, "Superstitio," 42.

43. Cicero, *De deorum natura*, 1, 42, 117. (Taken from Lewis and Short, *Latin Dictionary*, 1809c.)

44. See Harmening, *Superstitio*, 16–17 and 20; and Grodzynski, "Superstitio," 43.

45. Cited and quoted by Harmening in *Superstitio*, 19–20.

46. Refer to the comments of Jean-Claude Schmitt, "Les 'superstitions,'" in *L'histoire de la France religieuse*, ed. Jacques Le Goff and René Rémond, vol. I: *Des dieux de la Gaulle à la papauté d'Avignon*, 425 (Paris: Seuil, 1988).

47. Grodzynski, "Superstitio," 60.

48. For Grodzynski's words and the reference to Pliny, see ibid., 44 and 47.

49. Ibid., 60.

50. Peters, "The Medieval Church," 179–80.

51. Quoted by Harmening, *Superstitio*, 18, from *Institutiones divinae*, 4, 28, 16.

52. Lactantius, *Institutiones divinae*, 4, 28. (Taken from Lewis and Short, *Latin Dictionary*, 1809c.)

53. Augustine, *De doctrina christiana* 2, 73 [xix 29] (ed. and trans. R.P.H. Green [Oxford: Clarendon Press, 1995], 90). The most recent attempt at a critical edition of *De doctrina christiana* is that by W.M. Green, CSEL 80 (Vienna: Hoelder-Pichler-Tempsky, 1963).

54. Ibid., 2, 74 [xx 30], ed. R.P.H. Green, 90.

55. For this list, see ibid., 2, 74–75 [xx 30], ed. R.P.H. Green, 90–92.

56. Harmening makes this point convincingly in *Superstitio*, 34.

57. Augustine, *De doctrina christiana* 2, 89 [xxxiii 36], ed. R.P.H. Green, 98.

58. Peter Brown, *The World of Late Antiquity AD 150–750* (New York: Harcourt Brace Jovanovich, 1974), 54–55.

59. Marie Theres Fögen, *Die Enteignung der Wahrsager. Studien zum kaiserlichen Wissenschaftsmonopol in der Spätantike* (Frankfurt am Main: Suhrkamp, 1993), demonstrates that this exclusionary attitude, especially as directed against the arts of divination, began at imperial levels of authority before the Christianization of the empire. Her work serves as a reminder not to ignore the political factor in the move toward exclusivity, even as it pertains to Christianity.

60. See Peters, "The Medieval Church," 194.

61. Valerie I.J. Flint, *The Rise of Magic in Early Medieval Europe* (Princeton, NJ: Princeton University Press, 1991), 91.

62. Ibid., 95.

63. See ibid., 93 and 97.

64. Ibid., 94–95.

65. "Magic" under this construction, and "superstition" as well, might thus be regarded as consisting in the surviving elements of pagan practice and belief in an officially Christian society. Schmitt, "Les 'superstititions,'" 428–30, traces such an appreciation of magic as pagan survival back to Augustine. The historical instance in the case of the early Middle Ages would surely have provided grist for the mill of ethnographers from Jakob Grimm on, and anthropologists influenced by E.B. Tylor, both of whom Harmening (*Superstitio*, 11 and 14) criticizes for establishing and entrenching the presupposition of much modern research that superstitions be approached as cultural survivals from a preceding period.

66. Regino of Prüm, *Libri duo de synodalibus causis et disciplinis ecclesiasticis/ Das Sendhandbuch des Regino von Prüm*, ed. Wilfried Hartmann (Darmstadt: Wissenschaftliche Buchgesellschaft, 2004), II, 371 (420): "Episcopi episcoporumque ministri omnibus viribus elaborare studeant, ut perniciosam et a diabolo inventam sortilegam et maleficam artem penitus ex parochiis suis eradant..."

67. See earlier, nn. 38 and 39.

68. Regino, *De synodalibus causis* II, 371 (ed. Hartmann), 420.

69. Ibid. The quotation is from Titus 3: 10–11.

70. For the rest of this paragraph, see ibid.

71. See Marie-Dominique Chenu, *La théologie au douzième siècle*, 2nd ed. (Paris: J. Vrin, 1966), 20–30 and 289–301 (partially translated in *Nature, Man and Society in the Twelfth Century*, trans. Jerome Taylor and Lester K. Little [Toronto: University of Toronto, 1997], 3–18).

72. For an idea of what I mean, see my *The Light of the Countenance*, 2 vols. (Leiden: Brill, 2001), I, 1–18; and perhaps even more plainly, "Medieval Philosophy in Context," in *The Cambridge Companion to Medieval Philosophy*, ed. Arthur S. McGrade (Cambridge: Cambridge University Press, 2003), 16–40.

73. An argument has recently arisen over what exactly was his name. Opinion now seems to be settling down around the old assumption that he was in fact known to his contemporaries as, in Latin, Dominicus Gundissalinus or Dominicus Gundisalvi. Refer to Adeline Rucquoi, "Gundisalvus ou Dominicus Gundisalvi?" *Bulletin de Philosophie Médiévale* 41 (1999): 85–106; and Alexander Fidora and M.J. Soto Bruna, "'Gundisalvus ou Dominicus Gundisalvi?' Algunas observaciones sobre un reciente artículo de Adeline Rucquoi," *Estudios Eclesiastícos* 76 (2001): 467–73.

74. Dominicus Gundissalinus, *De divisione philosophiae/Über die Einteilung der Philosophie*, ed. and trans. Alexander Fidora and Dorothée Werner (Freiburg im Breisgau: Herder, 2007), 76 (reproducing with only minor changes the

Latin text originally edited by Ludwig Baur in Dominicus Gundissalinus *De divisione philosophiae*, Beiträge 4, 2–3 [Münster: Aschendorff, 1903], 20): "Sed quia scientiarum aliae sunt universales, aliae particulares, universales autem dicuntur, sub quibus multae aliae scientiae continentur, tunc scientia naturalis universalis est, quia octo scientiae sub ea continentur: scilicet scientia de medicina, scientia de iudiciis, scientia de nigromantia secundum physicam, scientia de imaginibus, scientia de agricultura, scientia de navigatione, scientia de speculis, scientia de alquimia, quae est scientia de conversione rerum in alias species; et haec octo sunt species naturalis scientiae."

75. Compare Al-Farabi, *Uber den Ursprung der Wissenschaften (De ortu scientiarum). Eine mittelalterliche Einleitungsschrift in die philosophischen Wissenschaften*, ed. Clemens Baeumker, Beiträge 19, 3 (Münster: Aschendorff, 1916), 18–19: "Partes autem huius scientiae [i.e. de naturis], secundum quod dixerunt sapientes primi, octo sunt, scilicet scientia de iudiciis, scientia de medicina, scientia de nigromantia secundum physicam, scientia de imaginibus, scientia de agricultura, scientia de navigando, scientia de alkimia quae est scientia de conversione rerum in alias species, scientia de speculis."

76. Available as Domingo Gundisalvo, *De scientiis*, ed. Manuel A. Alonso (Madrid: Escuelas de Estudios Arabes, 1954).

77. This is an idea promoted by Nicholas Weill-Parot, *Les "images astrologiques" au moyen âge et à la Renaissance* (Paris: Honoré Champion, 2002), 143, drawing upon a comment by Charles Burnett. In fact, Burnett (see Chapter 3, n. 269) seems to have been thinking of a kind of naturalizing talismanic magic akin to one version of the science of images advanced in the thirteenth century.

78. Daniel of Morely, "Philosophia" X, 158, ed. Gregor Maurach, *Mittellateinisches Jahrbuch* 14 (1979), 239. (Text also in edition from one manuscript, entitled "Liber de naturis inferiorum et superiorum," ed. Karl Sudhoff, *Archiv für die Geschichte der Naturwissenschaften und der Technik* 8 [1917]: 34.)

79. Daniel of Morely, "Philosophia" X, 158, ed. Maurach, 239: "De dignitate eius invenitur, quod illius partes, secundum quod dixerunt sapientes primi, octo sunt, scil<icet> scientia de iudiciis, scientia de medicina, scientia de nigromantia secundum phisicam, scientia de agricultura, scientia de prestigiis, scientia de alckimia, que est scientia de transformatione metallorum in alias species, scientia de imaginibus, quam tradit Liber Veneris magnus et universalis, quem edidit Thoz Grecus, scientia de speculis, et hec scientia largior est et latior ceteris, prout Aristotiles manifestat in Libro se speculo adurenti." (Also ed. Sudhoff, 34.)

80. Hugh of St. Victor, *Didascalicon* VI, 15, ed. Charles H. Buttimer (Washington, DC: Catholic University Press, 1939), 132.

81. The following two paragraphs depend precisely on Hugh, *Didascalicon* VI, 15, ed. Buttimer, 132–33.

82. For the reference to Valentinian, see n. 50.

83. As with many of these categories, Hugh took his fanciful etymologies direct
     from Isidore of Seville's famous work of that name, his *Etymologiae*. See
     Isidore, *Etymologiae* VIII, 9, ed. José Oroz Reta and Manuel Marcos Casquero,
     2 vols. (Madrid: Editorial Católica, 1982–83), vol. I, 714.

84. I take the relevant phrase in Hugh, *Didascalicon* VI, 15, 133, l. 18, as reading
     "arte daemoniaca," adopting one variant indicated in Buttimer's critical
     apparatus.

85. Hugh, *Didascalicon* VI, 15, ed. Buttimer, 132.

86. See Adelard, *Die Quastiones naturales* 58, ed. Martin Müller, Beiträge 31, 2
     (Münster: Aschendorff, 1934), 53.

87. Ibid., 53–54.

88. Ibid., 54.

89. Ibid.

90. See James McEvoy, *The Philosophy of Robert Grosseteste* (Oxford: Clarendon
     Press, 1982), 181.

91. Steven P. Marrone, "The Philosophy of Nature in the Early Thirteenth
     Century," in *Albertus Magnus und die Anfänge der Aristoteles-Rezeption im
     lateinischen Mittelalter*, ed. Ludger Honnefelder et al. (Münster: Aschendorff,
     2005), 143.

92. Robert Grosseteste, *Hexaëmeron* V, ix, 1, ed. Richard C. Dales and Servus
     Gieben (London: Oxford University Press, 1982), 165.

93. Augustine, *De civitate Dei* V, 3–9, ed. Emanuel Hofmann, CSEL, 40.1 (Vienna:
     F. Tempsky, 1899–1900), 213–22.

94. Grosseteste, *Hexaëmeron* V, ix, 1, ed. Dales and Gieben, 166.

95. Grosseteste, *Hexaëmeron* V, x, 1, ed. Dales and Gieben, 166.

96. Ibid., 167.

97. Grosseteste, *Hexaëmeron* V, xi, 1, ed. Dales and Gieben, 170.

98. For these meager specifics concerning his life (neither the date nor the place
     of his birth is known), see Charles Burnett, "Michele Scoto e la diffusione della
     cultura scientifica," in *Federico II e le scienze*, ed. Pierre Toubert and Agostino
     Paravicini Bagliani (Palermo: Sellerio, 1994), 371–74 and 378; David Pingree,
     "La magia dotta," in the same volume, 354; and Silke Ackermann, "Empirie
     oder Theorie? Der Fixsternkatalog des Michael Scotus," in *Federico II e le nuove
     culture*, Atti del XXXI Convegno Storico Internazionale, Todi, October 9–12,
     1994 (Spoleto: Centro Italiano di Studi sull'Alto Medioevo, 1995), 287.

99. Quoted in Stefano Caroti, "L'astrologia," in *Federico II e le scienze*, ed. Toubert
     and Paravicini Bagliani, 139.

100. Ibid., n. 5.

101. Ibid., 142.

102. Ibid., 143, n. 19.

103. On alchemy taking root in the west only at this time, see the comments
     of Robert Halleux, "L'alchimia," in *Federico II e le scienze*, ed. Toubert and
     Paravicini Bagliani, 152.

104. Again, see ibid., 153 and 155.

105. Richard C. Dales, *The Scientific Achievement of the Middle Ages* (Philadelphia: University of Pennsylvania, 1973), 158.
106. See Pingree, "La magia dotta," 354–55 and 369. Dante speaks of Michael in his *Inferno* XX, vv. 115–17.

2 Popular Belief and the Rationalization of Religion, 700–1300

1. See Etienne Delaruelle, *La piété populaire au moyen âge* (Turin: Bottega d'Erasmo, 1975), 7 (originally "La pietà popolare nel secolo XI," in *Relazioni del X Congresso internazionale di Scienze storiche*, III, 313 [Florence, 1955]).
2. In Manselli's words from *La religione popolare nel medioevo (sec. VI–XII)* (Turin: G. Giappichelli, 1974), 8: "...una religiosità...aperta...al mondo dei sentimenti immediati...[,] agli eventi semplice della vita..."
3. See Manselli, *Religione popolare*, 5 and 7.
4. See Delaruelle, *Piéte populaire*, 11 (orig. 317); and Manselli, *Religione popolare*, 3–4 and 8.
5. Peter Laslett, *The World We Have Lost*, 2nd ed. (New York: Charles Scribner's Sons, 1971), 4. The first edition of Laslett's work appeared in 1965.
6. Eamon Duffy, *The Stripping of the Altars. Traditional Religion in England c. 1400–c. 1580*, 2nd ed. (New Haven: Yale University Press, 2005; orig. ed. 1992), 279.
7. Ibid., 2,
8. Ibid., xx.
9. For Duffy's words, see ibid., 3. In Karen Louise Jolly's important *Popular Religion in Late Saxon England. Elf Charms in Context* (Chapel Hill: University of North Carolina Press, 1996), 9, she explains that she will employ the words "popular religion," but only to refer to what she thought Duffy would have called "common tradition." Thus, for Jolly, "[p]opular religion, as one facet of a larger, complex culture, consists of those beliefs and practices common to the majority of the believers." Michael D. Bailey, in his equally impressive *Battling Demons. Witchcraft, Heresy, and Reform in the Late Middle Ages* (University Park: Penn State University Press, 2003), 101, comments as well on the dangers of positing a "popular religion" as opposed to a "common tradition," and, while recognizing the exclusivity of much of elite thought, restricts himself to the latter phrase when talking about religious currents among the populace at large.
10. See Gábor Klaniczay, *The Uses of Supernatural Power* (Princeton, NJ: Princeton University Press, 1990), 22–23. Burke, in *Popular Culture in Early Modern Europe* (New York: Harper and Row, 1978), explained that he fashioned his model of two traditions, "great" and "little," with a few modifications on the anthropology of Robert Redfield from the 1930s. To Burke's eyes (see p. 270), the disengagement of the elite from the "little tradition" – that is, popular culture – progressed gradually from 1500 to 1800.

11. Jolly, *Popular Religion*, 9. For her comments on "formal religion" and how it relates to the religion of the whole populace (of which it is, at least technically, a part), see pp. 13 and 18.

12. See Duffy, *Stripping of the Altars*, 283. Also, pp. 278–79: "[A]ny attempt to explain [such a] dimension of late medieval piety in terms of pagan survivalism among the uneducated peasantry is misconceived." And there can be no denying that often among older studies of "popular religion," there hovers the specter of peasant paganism. Manselli himself at times resorted to such language: see his *Relgione popolare*, 39: "...il mancato ottentimento della grazia richiesta, portava, spesso, al desiderio della protezione degli antichi dei pagani..." At the same time, it should be granted that more recent attempts to search for paganism, or paganizing spirituality, in Europe of the Middle Ages, especially of the early medieval period, begin with a less dualistic concept of the opposition between pagan sentiment and Christian and serve well to keep us aware not only of the ways that the official church drew much from paganism into its practices, as indeed had been the case in the Roman world, but also of how long the lower levels of society, particularly the peasantry, retained allegiance to spiritual and even religious forms not welcome in the ambience of the official church. See, for example, Ludo J. R. Milis, ed., *The Pagan Middle Ages*, trans. Tanis Guest (Woodbridge, Suffolk: Boydell and Brewer, 1998), especially the contributions of Milis, Martine De Reu and Christophe Lebbe.

13. Ronald C. Finucane, *Miracles and Pilgrims. Popular Beliefs in Medieval England* (Totowa, NJ: Rowman and Littlefiield, 1977), 11.

14. Jean-Claude Schmitt, "Les traditions folkloriques dans la culture médiévale," *Archives de Sciences Sociales des Religions* 52 (1981), 10.

15. See Schmitt's comments in "Les traditions folkloriques," 6–7. Jolly, in *Popular Religion*, 11, gives a nice statement of the same notion that "folklore" may offer a better conceptual model than "religion" for analyzing the spiritual valence of popular, especially superficially "paganizing," beliefs.

16. See Brown's remarks in *The Cult of the Saints* (Chicago: University of Chicago Press, 1981), 119–24.

17. For the first quotation, see Bernadette Filotas, *Pagan Survivals, Superstitions and Popular Cultures in Early Medieval Pastoral Literature* (Toronto: Pontifical Institute of Medieval Studies, 2005), 20, and for the second, ibid., 40.

18. Ruth Mazo Karras speaks of the church's assimilative tendency, now accepted as a truism, particularly well in her "Pagan Survivals and Syncretism in the Conversion of Saxony," *The Catholic Historical Review* 72 (1986), 553: "As the Church converted new peoples, it both combatted pagan customs and adopted some elements of old belief and practices into the Christian framework." On ambiguity, see the same article (561).

19. Jean Delumeau, "Déchristianisation ou nouvelle modèle de christianisme?" *Archives de Sciences Sociales des Religions* 40 (1975), 10.

20. See Delaruelle, *Piété populaire*, 10 (orig. 316).

21. Jolly, *Popular Religion*, 172–73.
22. See Regino of Prüm, *Libri duo de synodalibus causis et disciplinis ecclesiasticis* (cited earlier in Chapter 1, n. 66), on dating, pp. 1 and 3.
23. See the edition by Herman J. Schmitz, in *Die Bussbücher und das kanonische Bussverfahren* (volume 2 of *Die Bussbücher und die Bussdisciplin der Kirche* 2 vols. [Mainz: Franz Kirchheim, 1883 and 1898/repr. Graz: Akademische Druck- und Verlagsanstalt, 1958]), 403–67.
24. See ibid., I, 762–65.
25. For *De auguriis*, see Walter W. Skeat, ed., *Aelfric's Lives of Saints* 2 vols., Early English Text Society, orig. series 76, 82, 94, 114 (Oxford: Oxford University Press, 1881, 1885, 1890, 1900/rep. in 2 vols, same press, 1966), I, 364–83. The addition is printed in John C. Pope, ed., *Homilies of Aelfric. A Supplementary Collection* 2 vols., Early English Text Society, nn. 259 and 260 (Oxford: Oxford University Press, 1967 and 1968), II, 790–96. On its provenance, refer to Pope's remarks, *Homilies*, II, 786–88.
26. Aelfric, *The Sermones catholici, or Homilies*, ed. Benjamin Thorpe, 2 vols. (London: Aelfric Society, 1844 and 1846/repr. Hildesheim: Georg Olms, 1983), I, 454–77.
27. The version cited here is found in part II of J.H.G. Grattan and Charles Singer, *Anglo-Saxon Magic and Medicine* (London: Oxford University Press, 1952). Cockayne published the work in *Leechdoms, Wortcunning and Starcraft of Early England*, Chronicles and Memorials, 3 (London: Longman, Green, Longman, Roberts and Green, 1866), 1–80.
28. Audrey L. Meaney, "Women, Witchcraft and Magic in Anglo-Saxon England," in *Superstition and Popular Medicine in Anglo-Saxon England*, ed. D.G. Scragg (Manchester: Manchester Center for Anglo-Saxon Studies, 1989), 20.
29. Ibid., 18, citing Jane Crawford, "Evidences for Witchcraft in Anglo-Saxon England," *Medium Aevum* 32 (1963), 108.
30. See Meaney's comments, "Women, Witchcraft and Magic," 18–19.
31. Edward Peters, "The Medieval Church and State on Superstition, Magic and Witchcraft: From Augustine to the Sixteenth Century," in *Witchcraft and Magic in Europe: The Middle Ages*, ed. Karen Jolly, Catharina Raudvere and Edward Peters (London: Athlone Press, 2002), 203, claims that for the Anglo-Saxons, *"wiccaraed"* – the skill that marked a witch – was primarily divination. Also Meaney, "Women, Witchcraft and Magic," 12 and 18.
32. See again n. 29 above.
33. Karras, "Pagan Survivals," 562 and 565.
34. Regino, *De synodalibus causis* II, 361 (ed. Hartmann), 414: "Quicunque pro curiositate futurorum…vel divinos, quos ariolos appellant, vel aruspicem, qui auguria colligit, consuluerit, capite puniatur." Valerie I.J. Flint, *The Rise of Magic in Early Medieval Europe* (Princeton, NJ: Princeton University Press, 1991), 50, 53 and 91, has shown how for medieval writers such as Regino or Burchard, a classic listing of such late Roman terms along with their definition would have been supplied by the seventh-century Isidore's *Etymologies*

VIII, 9, sometimes mediated through other works – for instance, the eighth-century canons attributed to Pope Gregory III.

35. Regino, *De synodalibus causis* II, 354 and 355 (ed. Hartmann), 412.
36. Burchard, *Corrector* 5, 60 (*Decretum* 19, 5, 60), in *Die Bussbücher und die Bussdisciplin*, ed. Schmitz, 2, 422–23.
37. See Harmening, *Superstito*, 44, 50–51, 72, 75 and 318.
38. Jean-Claude Schmitt, "Les 'superstitions,'" in *Histoire de la France religieuse*, 1, 451.
39. Filotas, *Pagan Survivals*, 56.
40. See ibid., 286.
41. Burchard, *Corrector* 5, 62 (*Decretum* 19, 5, 62), in *Die Bussbücher und die Bussdisciplin*, ed. Schmitz, 2, 423.
42. Ibid. 5, 101 (*Decretum* II, 5, 101), 2, 431.
43. Regino, *De synodalibus causis* II, 365 (ed. Hartmann), 416.
44. Aelfric, *De auguriis* (ed. Skeat), I, 372, ll. 124–26.
45. Jolly, *Popular Religion*, 87, and more specifically on "*dry*," p. 6. See, for example, Aelfric, in *Homilies of Aelfric* (ed. Pope), II, 796, ll. 124–25: "Deofolgild and drycraeft, wiccecraeft and wiglunga/synd swyðe andsaete urum Haelende Criste..."
46. Anthony Daves, "Witches in Anglo-Saxon England. Five Case Histories," in *Superstition and Popular Medicine in Anglo-Saxon England*, ed. Scragg, 41, points to Dunstan preaching to King Edward at his coronation in 975, that one of his jobs was to suppress "wiccan and galdra" (see the quotation, p. 52, n. 4). Also again, Jolly, *Popular Religion*, 87.
47. Regino, *De synodalibus causis* II, 5, 44 (ed. Hartmann), 244, condemns the practice of herdsmen or hunters who chant "*diabolica carmina*" over bread or herbs, which they then place in a tree or at a crossroads in order to protect their own herds or injure someone else's. Burchard's *Corrector* 5, 63 (*Decretum* 19, 5, 63), in *Die Bussbücher und die Bussdisciplin*, ed. Schmitz, 2, 423–24, reproduces much of the same text, practically verbatim.
48. See Filotas, *Pagan Survivals*, 287, and her citations on 293, n. 144.
49. See Chapter 1, p. 10, esp. nn. 38 and 39.
50. Again, Filotas, *Pagan Survivals*, 293, n. 143.
51. Ibid., 281, provides examples from the "canons of Gregory III" in the eighth century and Hrabanus Maurus in the ninth.
52. Meaney, "Women, Witchcraft and Magic," 29.
53. Filotas, *Pagan Survivals*, 301. Burchard, *Corrector* 5, 165 (*Decretum* 19, 5, 165), in *Die Bussbücher und die Bussdisciplin*, ed. Schmitz, 2, 445, includes among a list of questions specifically to be asked of women an inquiry about dispensing a deadly potion.
54. See Chapter 1, pp. 16–17.
55. Regino, *De synodalibus causis* II, 371 (ed. Hartmann), 420. See the quotation earlier, Chapter 1, n. 66.

56. Flint, *The Rise of Magic*, 56, gives a useful summary of Hincmar's claims. See also her mention of Paschasius Radbertus's denunciations of witchcraft as rife at the court of Louis the Pious earlier in the same century (ibid., 63).

57. Meaney, "Women, Witchcraft and Magic," 18.

58. See the critical apparatus to Aelfric, in *Homilies of Aelfric* (ed. Pope), II, 790, ll. 2 and 3.

59. Filotas, *Pagan Survivals*, 281, referring to Burchard, *Corrector* 5, 68 (*Decretum* 19, 5, 68), in *Die Bussbücher und die Bussdisciplin*, ed. Schmitz, 2, 425.

60. Regino, *De synodalibus causis* II, 360 (ed. Hartmann), 414: "Malefici vel incantatores vel immissores tempestatum vel qui...mentes hominum turbant..."

61. For both citations, see Davies, "Witches in Anglo-Saxon England," 49–50.

62. Burchard, *Corrector* 5, 175 (*Decretum* 19, 5, 175), in *Die Bussbücher und die Bussdisciplin*, ed. Schmitz, 2, 447.

63. See the comments on Gregory VII, *Registrum* 7, 27, ed. E. Caspar (MGH, Epistolae, ii, pts. 1-2), 498, in Alexander Murray, "Missionaries and Magic in Dark-Age Europe," *Past and Present*, no. 136 (Aug. 1992): 196; and Raoul Manselli, *Religione Populare*, 97.

64. Michael D. Bailey, *Magic and Superstition in Europe* (Lanham, Md.: Rowman and Littlefield, 2007), 69.

65. Regino, *De synodalibus causis* II, 363 (ed. Hartmann), 416; and Burchard, *Corrector* 5, 68 (*Decretum* 19, 5, 68), in *Die Bussbücher und die Bussdisciplin*, ed. Schmitz, 2, 425.

66. Regino, *De synodalibus causis* II, 5, 45 (ed. Hartmann), 244. The heart of the text is reproduced almost verbatim by Burchard, *Corrector* 5, 69 (*Decretum* 19, 5, 69), in *Die Bussbücher und die Bussdisciplin*, ed. Schmitz, 2, 425.

67. Davies, "Witches in Anglo-Saxon England," 45–47.

68. Refer to Filotas's comments, *Pagan Survivals*, 292–93 and 296.

69. See Aelfric, *De auguriis*, in Skeat, ed., *Aelfric's Lives of Saints*, I, 374 (ll. 148 and 157–58) and 376 (l. 164).

70. Regino, *De synodalibus causis* II, 369 (ed. Hartmann), 418; and Burchard, *Corrector* 5, 166 (*Decretum* 19, 5, 166), in *Die Bussbücher und die Bussdisciplin*, ed. Schmitz, 2, 445. The passage in Regino, which in fact originated in a penitential brought together in the ninth century by Hrabanus Maurus, does not specifically say the purpose was to arouse love. Davies, "Witches in Anglo-Saxon England," 46, remarks that the penitential of Theodore stipulated the procedure as entailing women mixing semen into their husbands' food.

71. See the passage from Regino cited in the preceding note, which again, of course, does not explicitly tie the procedure to love magic.

72. Refer to nn. 70 and 71. Again, Regino had lifted the text from Hrabanus Maurus.

73. Aelfric, *De auguriis*, in Skeat, ed., *Aelfric's Lives of Saints*, I, 372 (ll. 124–26) and 376 (ll. 181–82).

74. Jolly, *Popular Religion*, 103.

75. Aelfric, *The Sermones catholici, or Homilies* (ed. Thorpe), I, 454. Even more pointed statements about devils using illness and false healing to instigate idolatry occur in the same work, I, 460 and 462.

76. Ibid., I, 464–66.

77. Ibid., I, 470.

78. Ibid., I, 472: "God is se soða laece, þe ðurh mislice swingla his folces synna gehaelð."

79. Aelfric, *De auguriis*, in Skeat, ed., *Aelfric's Lives of Saints*, I,376, ll. 181–81.

80. See Chapter 1, at n. 55.

81. Augustine, *De doctrina christiana* 2, 110 [xxix 45] (ed. R.P.H. Green), 106–108.

82. See the reference in Bailey, *Magic and Superstition*, 50.

83. Don C. Skemer, *Binding Words. Textual Amulets in the Middle Ages* (University Park: Pennsylvania State University Press, 2006), 41, with quotations in n. 59. On pp. 6–9, Skemer explains how his terminology differs from that of scholars such as Brian Copenhaver, who reserve "amulet" for uninscribed objects, using "talisman" for those with inscriptions. (See Brian P. Copenhaver, "Scholastic Philosophy and Renaissance Magic in the *De vita* of Marsilio Ficino," *Renaissance Quarterly* 37 [1984]: 530–31.) Skemer instead distinguishes between "textual amulets" – that is, ligatures bearing words – and talismans – limited to astrological seals and figures. My usage will follow Skemer's.

84. Regino, *De synodalibus causis* II, 336 (ed. Hartmann), 412.

85. Jolly introduces this issue in *Popular Religion*, 134, and the term *aelfshot* on 139.

86. Ronald C. Finucane, *Miracles and Pilgrims. Popular Beliefs in Medieval England* (Totowa, NJ: Rowman and Littlefield, 1977), 60. In n. 43, we have seen clerical concern about resorting to certain sites to learn about the future.

87. Regino, *De synodalibus causis* II, 374 (ed. Hartmann), 424: and Burchard, *Corrector* 5, 65 (*Decretum* 19, 5, 65), in *Die Bussbücher und die Bussdisciplin*, ed. Schmitz, 2, 424.

88. "Lacnunga," LXXXIII, in Grattan and Singer, *Anglo-Saxon Magic and Medicine*, 156–57. The directions indicate that the Lord's Prayer was expected to be recited in Latin.

89. "Lacnunga," LXVII, in Grattan and Singer, *Anglo-Saxon Magic*, 128–31.

90. Jolly, *Popular Religion*, 143–45.

91. Ibid., 145: "Adiuro te satanae diabulus aelfae." Jolly translates this nicely as: "I adjure you Devil of Satan, Elf."

92. Indeed, the second (ibid.) ends thus: "In nomine dei Patris et Filii et Spiritus Sancti."

93. See Skemer's explicit general comments, *Binding Words*, 3–5.

94. Ibid,, 79.

95. See the example Skemer presents (ibid., 48) from a Merovingian life of St. Eugendus of Saint-Claude.

96. Ibid., 49–50.

97. Ibid., 81.
98. Aelfric, *Sermones catholici* (ed. Thorpe), I, 474. Jolly quotes this passage in her own translation in *Popular Religion*, 92.
99. Again, Aelfric, *Sermones catholici* (ed. Thorpe), I, 474.
100. Burchard, *Corrector* 5, 66 (*Decretum* 19, 5, 66), in *Die Bussbücher und die Bussdisciplin*, ed. Schmitz, 2, 424.
101. "Lacnunga," XXII, in Grattan and Singer, *Anglo-Saxon Magic*, 104–105.
102. "Lacnunga," XXVI, in Grattan and Singer, *Anglo-Saxon Magic*, 106–107.
103. "Lacnunga," XXVII, in Grattan and Singer, *Anglo-Saxon Magic*, 106–108.
104. For the proscriptions in Regino and Burchard, see Regino, *De synodalibus causis* II, 374 (ed. Hartmann), 424; and Burchard, *Corrector* 5, 65 (*Decretum* 19, 5, 65), in *Die Bussbücher und die Bussdisciplin*, ed. Schmitz, 2, 424.
105. Aelfric, *Sermones catholici* (ed. Thorpe), I, 476
106. Jolly, *Popular Religion*, 124–25.
107. The three basic texts are numbers LXXIX to LXXXII of "Lacnunga," in Grattan and Singer, *Anglo-Saxon Magic*, 150–56.
108. See Lacnunga," LXXIX, in Grattan and Singer, *Anglo-Saxon Magic*, 150–52, ll. 6, 13, 20.
109. "Lacnunga," LXXIX, in Grattan and Singer, *Anglo-Saxon Magic*, 150–52, ll. 5, 12, and 19
110. Jolly, *Popular Religion*, 124.
111. "Lacnunga," LXXX, in Grattan and Singer, *Anglo-Saxon Magic*, 152, l. 32–33.
112. "Lacnunga," LXXXI, in Grattan and Singer, *Anglo-Saxon Magic*, 156, l 58.
113. "Lacnunga," LXXXII, in Grattan and Singer, *Anglo-Saxon Magic*, 156.
114. On Aelfric, see the passage cited earlier, n. 105.
115. Jolly, *Popular Religion*, 124.
116. Ibid., 159.
117. "Lacnunga," CXXXV, in Grattan and Singer, *Anglo-Saxon Magic*, 174–76.
118. Harmening, *Superstitio*, 11 and 14. Filotas, *Pagan Survivals*, confirms the link between Tylor and the notion of such "survivals."
119. Schmitt, "Superstitions," 428–30. See also the reference to both Harmening and Schmitt earlier in Chapter 1, n. 65, as well as the discussion in that chapter of both Augustine (12–14) and some of his Christian and non-Christian predecessors (11–12).
120. Manselli, *Religione popolare*, 81
121. Raoul Manselli, "Simbolismo e magia nell'alto medioevo," in *Simboli e simbologia nell'alto medioevo*, Settimane di Studio del Centro Italiano di Studi sull'alto Medioevo, 23 (Spoleto: Centro Italiano di Studi sull'alto Medioevo, 1976), 313. A similar view was presented by Jean Delumeau, "Déchristianisation ou nouvell modèle du christianisme?" *Archives de Sciences Sociales des Religions* 40 (1975), 10: "Le christianisme [adapté aux masses] acceptait ainsi d'intégrer le paganisme rural..."
122. Alexander Murray, "Missionaries and Magic in Dark-Age Europe," *Past and Present* no. 136 (August 1992), 200.

123. Karras, "Pagan Survivals," 553.

124. See Jolly, *Popular Religion*, 10–11.

125. See this discussion of Harmening's and Schmitt's views at nn. 37 and 38.

126. Regino, *De synodalibus causis* II, 365 (ed. Hartmann), 416. This passage is referred to above in connection with divination, n. 43.

127. Regino, *De synodalibus causis* II, 366 (ed. Hartmann), 416–18.

128. Much the same ground is covered in an entry of Burchard's cited earlier, n. 100, where the issue is supplication for bodily health. Burchard's text makes plain that at issue may just as well be the health of the soul – that is, its salvation.

129. Regino, *De synodalibus causis* II, 373 (ed. Hartmann), 424.

130. Burchard, *Corrector* 5, 61 (*Decretum* 19, 5, 61), in *Die Bussbücher und die Bussdisciplin*, ed. Schmitz, 2, 423.

131. Burchard, *Corrector* 5, 62 (*Decretum* 19, 5, 62), in *Die Bussbücher und die Bussdisciplin*, ed. Schmitz, 2, 423.

132. Burchard, *Corrector* 5, 99 and 104 (*Decretum* 19, 5, 99 and 104), in *Die Bussbücher und die Bussdisciplin*, ed. Schmitz, 2, 431 and 432.

133. Burchard, *Corrector* 5, 92 (*Decretum* 19, 5, 92), in *Die Bussbücher und die Bussdisciplin*, ed. Schmitz, 2, 429.

134. Burchard, *Corrector* 5, 97 (*Decretum* 19, 5, 97), in *Die Bussbücher und die Bussdisciplin*, ed. Schmitz, 2, 431.

135. Burchard, *Corrector* 5,151 (*Decretum* 19, 5, 151), in *Die Bussbücher und die Bussdisciplin*, ed. Schmitz, 2, 442.

136. Burchard, *Corrector* 5, 153 (*Decretum* 19, 5, 153), in *Die Bussbücher und die Bussdisciplin*, ed. Schmitz, 2, 443. Burchard referred to these objects of solicitude in classicizing Latin as "*parcae*," or in this particular instance as "*illae sorores.*" As Filotas reminds us in *Pagan Survivals* (37), in Nordic literature they were called the "Norns."

137. Burchard, *Corrector* 5, 180 and 181 (*Decretum* 19, 5, 180 and 181), in *Die Bussbücher und die Bussdisciplin*, ed. Schmitz, 2, 448.

138. Burchard, *Corrector* 5, 150 (*Decretum* 19, 5, 150), in *Die Bussbücher und die Bussdisciplin*, ed. Schmitz, 2, 442.

139. See n. 124.

140. See Chapter 1, pp. 16–17, and Chapter 2, p. 46, at nn. 54 and 55.

141. Regino, *De synodalibus causis* II, 371 (ed. Hartmann), 420, referring to women who "profitentur [se] nocturnis horis cum Diana paganorum Dea et innumera multitudine mulierum equitare super quasdam bestias, et multa terrarum spatia intempestae noctis silentio pertransire, eiusque iussionibus velut dominae obedire…" Only trivial differences mark the version of these words found in Burchard, *Corrector* 5, 90 (*Decretum* 19, 5, 90), in *Die Bussbücher und die Bussdisciplin*, ed. Schmitz, 2, 429.

142. Regino, *De synodalibus causis* II, 371 (ed. Hartmann), 420; and Burchard, *Corrector* 5, 90 (*Decretum* 19, 5, 90), in *Die Bussbücher und die Bussdisciplin*, ed. Schmitz, 2, 429.

143. Regino, *De synodalibus causis* II, 5, 45 (ed. Hartmann), 244.
144. Burchard, *Corrector* 5, 70 (*Decretum* 19, 5, 70), in *Die Bussbücher und die Bussdisciplin*, ed. Schmitz, 2, 425. In Burchard's words, the women say that they ride "cum daemonum turba in similitudinem mulierum transformatam, quam vulgaris stultitia hic strigam holdam vocat . . " The grammar is faulty, but the point seems clear: "Holda" substitutes for the "Diana" of the longer version.
145. See the references in Carlo Ginzburg, *Storia notturna. Una decifrazione del sabba* (Turin: Einaudi, 1989 and 1995), 66 (at n. 5); and in Filotas, *Pagan Survivals*, 75, particularly the citations given in n. 50; and 314, n. 266.
146. A good entrée to this literature is provided by Norman Cohn, *Europe's Inner Demons*, rev. ed. (Chicago: University of Chicago [orig. London: Pimlico], 1993), 166–75; and Ginzburg, *Storia notturna*, 65–70.
147. Filotas, *Pagan Survivals*, 76. Refer to the scholarly literature cited by Cohn, *Europe's Inner Demons*, rev. ed., 255, n. 25.
148. See Cohn, *Europe's Inner Demons*, 168–69.
149. Burchard, *Corrector* 5, 171 (*Decretum* 19, 5, 171), in *Die Bussbücher und die Bussdisciplin*, ed. Schmitz, 2, 447.
150. See the whole of Carlo Ginzburg's *The Night Battles. Witchcraft and Agrarian Cults in the Sixteenth and Seventeenth Centuries*, trans. John and Anne Tedeschi (Baltimore, MD: Johns Hopkins University Press, 1983/orig. Italian *I Benandanti*, Turin: Einaudi, 1966), but for a first description of the testimony, esp. p. 3.
151. For details on the days and the stakes, see, for instance, ibid., 1 and 6.
152. Ibid., xx–xxi.
153. Ginzburg said so explicitly in his preface to the English translation of his work: ibid., xiii.
154. Ginzburg brought up the notion of shamanism early in his work: ibid., xxi.
155. Ibid., 40, 187, n. 21, of the same work, offers a bibliographical introduction to the scholarship on the subject.
156. See his comments in *Storia notturna*, 78–79. Similar remarks on a distinction between an "agrarian" and a "funereal" version of the old ideas of a horde of wanderers at night can be found in Ginzburg, *Night Battles*, 58–59.
157. Claude Lecouteux, *Chasses fantastiques et cohortes de la nuit au moyen âge* (Paris: Imago, 1999), 8.
158. Ibid., 202.
159. See the quotation earlier, n. 144. Filotas, *Pagan Survivals*, 76, has interesting comments on variants in the manuscript tradition, including sometimes the word "*friga*" – another fertility goddess – instead of "*striga*."
160. Regarding this distinction it is worth commenting that it bears on a differentiation between two typologies of witchcraft Kieckhefer argues we can trace to two different fourteenth-century source locations – one the Swiss Pays de Vaud and the other Italy. It is the latter stereotype that fits best with the Italian word "*strega*." See Richard Kieckhefer, "Mythologies of

Witchcraft in the Fifteenth Century," *Magic, Ritual, and Witchcraft* (Summer 2006), esp. 80–81 and 95–96.

161. For most of the foregoing on the etymology of *"striga,"* see Cohn, *Europe's Inner Demons*, 162–63; on pastoral mention, see Filotas, *Pagan Survivals*, 310.
162. On these Germanic usages, again see Cohn, *Europe's Inner Demons*, 164; and Filotas, *Pagan Survivals*, 311.
163. Burchard, *Corrector* 5, 170 (*Decretum* 19, 5, 170), in *Die Bussbücher und die Bussdisciplin*, ed. Schmitz, 2, 446. It may be worth noting that this entry immediately precedes that given earlier, n. 149, where targeted women likewise left their houses at night without opening any doors. It is hard not to think that there existed a connection between these two cases, at least in Burchard's mind.
164. See the passage cited earlier, n. 19.
165. Manselli, *La religione popolare*, 81.
166. On the same page as the passage recalled in n. 19. For Delumeau, this new turn constituted "acculturation" in the authentic sense. See his "Déchristianisation," 12.
167. Manselli, *La religione popolare*, 91 and 93.
168. See Schmitt, "Les traditions folkloriques," 14.
169. Moore laid out his views in early form in *The Origins of European Dissent* first published in 1977 (London: Penguin), but issued in a second edition in 1985 (Oxford: Oxford University Press). They were revised and presented in what is surely now their best-known form in *The Formation of a Persecuting Society* (Oxford: Blackwell, 1st ed. 1987; 2nd ed. 2007).
170. Moore, *Formation of a Persecuting Society*, 12–13.
171. Ibid., 64.
172. See the whole discussion, ibid., 64–66.
173. Moore, *Formation of a Persecuting Society*, 64: "Heresy…can arise only in the context of the assertion of authority, which the heretic resists, and is therefore by definition a political matter."
174. Moore lays out the schema that follows most succinctly in *Formation of a Persecuting Society*, 134–37.
175. As he says in *Formation*, 21: "[A] background of widespread, discreet but often determined lay piety…is an essential context for the growing appeal of the heretical movements." Or as he put it in "Literacy and the Making of Heresy, c. 1000–c. 1150," in *Heresy and Literacy, 1000–1350*, ed. Peter Biller and Anne Hudson (Cambridge: Cambridge University Press, 1994), 25, popular heresy was at one and the same time a "social construction" and a social reality and force in itself.
176. See Moore's statements, *Formation*, 13.
177. Ibid., 14–15.
178. Ibid., 16.
179. Moore makes this especially clear with his words in ibid., 17.
180. For the foregoing quotations, see Jolly, *Popular Religion*, 48 and 52.

181. Ibid., 70: "The development of local churches in large numbers throughout England in the tenth and eleventh centuries created an entirely new environment...from that of the minsters.... Popular religion was a product of this local environment."
182. See the passage quoted earlier, n. 175.
183. For the preceding analysis, see Max Weber, *The Theory of Social and Economic Organization*, trans. A.M. Henderson and Talcott Parsons (New York: Free Press, 1964/orig. Oxford: Oxford University Press, 1947), 115. This is the translation of Part 1 of a large endeavor Weber was engaged in writing at the time of his death in 1920, *Wirtschaft und Gesellschaft* or *Economy and Society*, which in turn was published as volume 3 of the even larger *Grundriss der Sozialoekonomik* (*Foundation of Social Economies*), on which Weber was working collaboratively with others.
184. For this analysis, see Weber, *Theory of Social and Economic Organization*, 117.
185. Ibid., 184–85.
186. Max Weber, "Wissenschaft als Beruf," in *Max Weber Gesamtausgabe*, ed. Wolfgang J. Mommsen and Wolfgang Schluchter, I, 17 (Tübingen: J.C.B. Mohr, 1992/orig. ed. 1919), 89–90.
187. Refer again to what I have said earlier, pp. 67–68.
188. See Moore, *Persecuting Society*, 17–18. The idea had in fact been advanced early on by Arno Borst, *Die Katharer* (Stuttgart: Hiersemann, 1953), 71–80.
189. All these words or their grammatical roots appear in the account given by an anonymous monastic chronicler of Le Mans, and in some cases the implication is that they were drawn from the speeches of Henry. See the passage translated from a chronicle of deeds of the bishops of Le Mans in Walter L. Wakefield and Austin P. Evans, ed. and trans., *Heresies of the High Middle Ages* (New York: Columbia University Press, 1969), 108–114, the Latin text of which is available in G. Busson and A. Ledru, ed., *Actus pontificum Cenomannis in urbe degentium*, Archives Historiques du Maine, 2 (Le Mans: Société Historique de la Province du Mans, 1901), 407–15.
190. Ibid.
191. On the reorganization and Nicetas's visit, see Malcolm Barber, *The Cathars* (Harlow, England: Pearson Education, 2000), 7–8, with an important historiographical note 3, and 71–72. As Barber indicates, the most authoritative recent survey and evaluation of the scholarship on the Cathars is Malcolm D. Lambert, *The Cathars* (Oxford: Oxford University Press, 1998).
192. Robert I. Moore, "Literacy and the Making of Heresy," in *Heresy and Literacy*, ed. Biller and Hudson, 31–32. See also William A. Graham, *Beyond the Written Word. Oral Aspects of Scripture in the History of Religion* (Cambridge: Cambridge University Press, 1987), 29, 37–38 and 40–41, on how literacy and orality could co-exist and functionally interact in late medieval and even much of early modern Europe.
193. Barber, *Cathars*, 33.

194. See the exceptionally clear statements in Brian Stock, *The Implications of Literacy* (Princeton, NJ: Princeton University Press, 1983), 90 and 522.
195. For both quotations, see Stock, *Implications of Literacy*, 88.
196. Peter Biller, "Heresy and Literacy: Earlier History of the Theme," in *Heresy and Literacy*, ed. Biller and Hudson, 5 and 6.
197. Lorenzo Paolini, "Italian Catharism and Written Culture," in *Heresy and Literacy*, ed. Biller and Hudson, 92.
198. Klaus Schreiner, "Laienfrömmigkeit," in *Laienfrömmigkeiit im späten Mittelalter*, ed. Schreiner, 19.
199. Anne Hudson, "'Laicus litteratus,'" in *Heresy and Literacy*, ed. Biller and Hudson, 232.
200. See H. J. Schroeder, *Disciplinary Decrees of the General Councils. Texts, Translation and Commentary* (St. Louis, MO: B. Herder Book Co., 1937), 237–39 and 560–61.
201. Ibid., 259–63 and 570.
202. On the foundation of the two main mendicant orders, see John Moorman, *A History of the Franciscan Order from its Origins to the Year 1517* (Oxford: Clarendon Press, 1968); and William A. Hinnebusch, *The History of the Dominican Order* 2 vols. (New York: Alba House, 1975).
203. The best introduction to the medieval inquisition is Edward Peters, *Inquisition* (New York: Free Press, 1988).
204. On the transition from ordeal to inquest and official judgment, see the excellent discussion by Moore in *Formations of a Persecuting Society*, 117–27. James B. Given, *Inquisition and Medieval Society. Power, Discipline and Resistance in Langudoc* (Ithaca, NY: Cornell University Press, 1997), 20–21, comments convincingly on what this transition meant for the nature of governance.
205. Refer again to Moore, *Persecuting Society*, 1184; and Given, *Inquisition and Medieval Society*, 13.
206. Schroeder, *Disciplinary Decrees*, 244 and 563.
207. See the letter in Edward Peters, *Heresy and Authority in Medieval Europe. Documents in Translation* (Philadelphia: University of Pennsylvania Press, 1980), 196–98.
208. Given, *Inquisition and Medieval Society*, 27, 29 and 41–42.
209. Moore, *Formation of a Persecuting Society*, 125–26 and 128, has interesting comments on further manifestations of this sort of professionally under-written and clerk- (or in Weberian terms, bureaucrat-) implemented rationalization over the period of the rise of the early modern state.
210. Ibid., 105–106.
211. Ibid., 83–85.
212. On the turn to constructing the image of an "enemy of society" and a source of "contamination," see Moore, *Persecuting Society*, 92–93.
213. Minucius Felix, *Octavius* 9, ed. Jean Beaujeu (Paris: Société "Les Belles Lettres," 1964), 12–14.

214. See Cohn, *Europe's Inner Demons*, 36, with its quotation (at n. 6) from Augustine's *De moribus Ecclesiae Catholicae et de moribus Manichaeorum*, 2, 7.
215. On these two seminal twelfth-century episodes and their chroniclers' accounts, see Moore, *Origins of a Persecuting Society*, 14, 60 and 114–15.
216. See the account of Conrad's activity in Cohn, *Europe's Inner Demons*, 43–50.
217. See the text as translated in Alan C. Kors and Edward Peters, ed., *Witchcraft in Europe 400–1700. A Documentary History*, 2nd ed. (Philadelphia: University of Pennsylvania Press, 2001), 116. For the Latin text of the letter, see Carl Rodenberg, ed., *Epistolae saeculi XIII e regestis pontificum Romanorum*, Monumenta Germaniae Historica, Epistolae (Berlin: Weidmann, 1883), I, 432–34.
218. For the history and historiography of the idea of Satan, begin with Henry A. Kelly, *Satan. A Biography* (Cambridge: Cambridge University Press, 2006).

3 Science, Magic and the Demonic, 1200–1400: The Catalyst

1. What must be considered the classic statement is presented in what have become chapters 6 and 7 of the revised edition of Cohn's *Europe's Inner Demons*, 102–43.
2. Alain Boureau has proven exceptionally fruitful on this score, the threads of his previous efforts pulled together in the spectacular *Satan hérétique. Naissance de la démonologie dans l'Occident médiéval, 1280–1330*. (Paris: Odile Jacob, 2004), translated into English as *Satan the Heretic*, trans. Teresa L. Fagan (Chicago: University of Chicago Press, 2006).
3. See the comments of Robert Halleux, "L'alchimia," in *Federico II e le scienze*, 152; and Silke Ackermann, "Empirie oder Theorie?" in *Federico II e le nuove culture*, 287.
4. See Charles Burnett's comments in "Michele Scoto e la diffusione della cultura scientifica," in *Federico II e le scienze*, 385.
5. Robert Halleux draws our attention to this fact and lists the other works in "L'alchimia," in the same volume, 153 and 155.
6. See Chapter 1, pp. 28 (at n. 99) and 30.
7. As quoted by Caroti in "L'astrologia," in *Federico II e le scienze*, 149, n. 39: "Et partes huius scientie secundum scientiam quorundam naturalium sunt octo ad minus, videlicet scientia de iudiciis, de medicina, de nigromantica, de ydeis (sic), de agricultura, de navigatione, de alchimia, que est scientia de conversione rerum in alias species...et scientia de speculis." Given the readings in both Farabi and Gundissalinus, the word "ydeis" must surely be taken – as Caroti suggests – as a scribal error for "imaginibus."

8. Jean-Pratice Boudet, *Entre science et nigromance. Astrologie, divination et magie dans l'Occident médiéval (XIIe–XVe siècle)* (Paris: Publications de la Sorbonne, 2006), 92–94, has shown that by Michael's day "necromantia" and "nigromantia," originally simply orthographic variants on the same word, were increasingly assuming the contours of different terms. In some circles, a clear distinction was being made between "necromancy," centering on seeking information from the dead, and "nigromancy," a more unambiguously demoniacal pursuit associated etymologically with the word "nigra" or "black" and resonant of "sorcery" in the most pejorative sense.

9. See, for instance, the definition give by Boudet, "Magie théurgique, angélologie et vision béatifique dans le *Liber sacratus sive juratus* attribué a Honorius de Thèbes," *Mélanges de l'Ecole Française de Rome. Moyen Age* 114 (2002): 858, n. 2.

10. For this again, see the passage quoted by Caroti, "L'astrologia," 148–49 (at n. 37).

11. See the comments on Michael's knowledge of Solomonic treatises, and speculation about where he might have come into contact with them, in David Pingree, "Learned Magic in the Time of Frederick II," *Micrologus. Natura, scienze e società medievali* 2 (1994): 54.

12. Note the example from the *Liber introductorius* referred to by David Pingree in "La magia dotta," 369, in which the services of a virgin girl of five–seven years were employed to conjure up the demon.

13. On William's biography and the chronology of his literary production, see the comments and references in my *William of Auvergne and Robert Grosseteste. New Ideas of Truth in the Early Thirteenth Century* (Princeton, NJ: Princeton University Press, 1983), 27–28; and my *The Light of Thy Countenance. Science and Knowledge of God in the Thirteenth Century* (Leiden: Brill, 2001), I, 30–33 and 36–37. Roland Teske comments on the meaning of William's title for his compilation in "William of Auvergne on Philosophy as *divinalis* and *sapientialis*," in *Was ist Philosophie im Mittelalter?*, ed. Jan A. Aertsen and Andreas Speer, Miscellanea Mediaevalia, 26 (Berlin: De Gruyter, 1998), 475–81.

14. References to these treatises will be made to the two-volume (plus a supplement) *Opera omnia* (Orleans: F. Hotot, 1674; reproduced Frankfurt am Main: Minerva, 1963), henceforth cited as *Mag. div.*

15. William, *De universo* 2, 2, 76 (*Mag. div.* I, 929bA).

16. *De universo* 1, 3, 20 (*Mag. div.* I, 785aC-785bB).

17. See, for instance, William's remarks in *De universo* 2, 3, 21 [marked as 20 in the text] (*Mag. div.* I, 1058bF).

18. For example, William, *De universo* 2, 3, 22 (*Mag. div.* I, 1060aH).

19. See William, *De universo* 2, 3, 22 (*Mag. div.* I, 1060bF). Several times in the same chapter (1059a–b) William refers to those conversant in such matters as *"experimentatores"* ("experimentors").

20. William, *De anima* 7, 9 (*Mag. div.* II, suppl., 216b).

21. In *De universo* 2, 3, 20 (*Mag. div.* I, 1054aF [incorrectly printed as 1044]), he bemoaned the obstacles often preventing the soul from reaching the intended *"[perfectio] rerum sublimium et rerum occultarum,"* which objects he plainly referred to in the succeeding column (*Mag. div.* I, 1054bF) as *"res divinales."*

22. In *De universo* 2, 3, 20 (*Mag. div.* I, 1053bC), William explains how "divinationes per inspectionem lucidorum instrumentorum fiant secundum nonnullos philosophos, et absque ministerio daemonum et per naturam tantum instrumentis huiusmodi ... adiutam." In the same chapter (*Mag. div.* I, 1054aD) and the following (*De universo* 2, 3, 21 [marked 20 in the text] [*Mag. div.* I, 1057bC]) he adds his own opinion that such knowledge-acquiring operations are "surely possible" (*"possibile indubitanter"*), though in the latter passage he worries about the ease with which they might be corrupted by demons involving themselves in them on the sly.

23. William, *De universo* 2, 3, 21 [20 in the text] (*Mag. div.* I, 1057bC). Nicolas Weill-Parot, *Les "images astrologiques" au Moyen Âge et à la Renaissance* (Paris: Honoré Champion, 2002), 179, n. 75, notes that Lynn Thorndike identified this "Artesius" with an "Artephius" talked about by Roger Bacon and to whom were attributed several alchemical works. See also the remarks of David Pingree, "Learned Magic in the Time of Frederick II," 41.

24. See William's comments in *De legibus* 27 (*Mag. div.* I, 91aD-bA), where the author is identified as "Arthesius," magician and philosopher (*"mag[us] simul et philosoph[us]"*).

25. Refer to my exposition of this view of the human condition in *William of Auvergne and Robert Grosseteste*, 34–37.

26. In fact it was just such a reading William used to account for the presumed access to higher realities provided by a crystal ball. By the wondrous operations of nature, the ball opened the human mind directly to the light of God himself. See his words shortly after the first passage quoted above in n. 22 (*De universo* 2, 3, 20 [*Mag. div.* I, 1053D).

27. William, *De universo* 2, 3, 20 (*Mag. div.* I, 1056aH-bE).

28. Ibid.: "sicut dixit Mercurius in libro suo de Deo deorum."

29. Weill-Parot, *Les "images astrologiques,"* 188–89.

30. For example, in *De legibus* 23 (*Mag. div.* I, 66bF): "Et hanc adinventionem extollit Mercurius Trismegistus in libro quem scripsit *De helera*, hoc est, *De deo deorum* ..."

31. On this dominant Hermetic tradition, see David Pingree, "Learned Magic in the Time of Frederick II," 42.

32. See again n. 29, and William, *De legibus* 23 (*Mag. div.* I, 66b[G-H]).

33. William, *De universo* 2, 3, 20 (*Mag. div.* I, 1054bE [erroneously in the text as 1044]).

34. William, *De universo* 2, 3, 20 (*Mag. div.* I, 1054bG [erroneously in the text as 1044]).

35. See William, *De universo* 2, 3 20 (*Mag. div.* I, 1056bF), following immediately upon the passage cited in n. 27.
36. In *De universo* 2, 2, 77 (*Mag. div.* I, 930b[F-G]), William introduced this last section with a summary of the subjects it would cover.
37. See n. 38.
38. The passage upon which this paragraph depends is found in *De universo* 2, 2, 76 (*Mag. div.* I, 929bA).
39. William, *De legibus* 23 (*Mag. div.* I, 67aA).
40. *De legibus* 25 (*Mag. div.* I, 78aF): "Et haec omnia in libris judiciorum astronomiae et in libris magorum atque maleficorum tempore adolescentiae nostrae nos meminimus inspexisse."
41. See the passage cited in n. 38.
42. See the overview of the problem given in *De universo* 1, 3, 19 (*Mag. div.* I, 785a[B-C]).
43. Refer to the passage cited in n. l6, from the chapter immediately following the overview referred to in n. 42.
44. See the passage cited in n. 38, as well as the revealing phrase, "*imagines magicae*," in *De universo* 1, 1, 46 (*Mag. div.* I, 663aA).
45. See the reference to books about images in the passage cited in n. 39.
46. William, *De legibus* 27 (*Mag. div.* I, 89bD). For a clear résumé of all William's references to the literature of magic, see Weill-Parot, *Les "images astrologiques,"* 177–79.
47. Again, *De legibus* 27 (*Mag. div.* I, 89bD). The early-fourteenth-century version of the *Ars notoria* (Véronèse's "version B") refers to a Solomonic work of learning-acquisition called the "*Ydea Salomonis*, possibly related to what William was talking about. See *Ars notoria*, ed. Véronèse, 147.
48. For the "Mandal," *De legibus* 27 (*Mag. div.* I, 89bD), and for the "Pentagon," the same chapter (88bH). On the medieval "*Almandal* of Solomon" and its Indian roots, see Pingree, "Learned Magic in the Time of Frederick II," 42.
49. On "*invultuationes*," see William's remarks in *De universo* 1, 1, 46 (*Mag. div.* I, 663aC and 663bD).
50. William also took note of images of this more literal and representational sort that seem to fall somewhere between this category of sorcerers' figurines and the third type of image to be discussed in the next few paragraphs. They were little statuary representations, most often of animals chosen with an eye to embodying the targets to which the image magic would apply – a housefly, for instance – but sometimes also probably symbolically linked to a constellation, such as the scorpion. What ties these statuettes to the third sort of image is the insistence that they be fabricated under a particular astrological configuration. See William, *De legibus* 23 (*Mag. div. I*, 67aA).
51. A loosely sketched picture of images of this sort can be found in *De legibus* 23 (*Mag. div.* I, 66bH-67aA).
52. William, *De legibus* 27 (*Mag. div.* I, 89bC): "Debes autem scire, quia quatuor genera figurarum posuerunt idolatrae stellarum in planetis, videlicet: sigilla,

anulos, characteres et imagines." The same four are quickly laid out in *De legibus* 23 (*Mag. div.* I, 67aB).

53. See William's words immediately following the passage quoted in the preceding note.

54. For the matter of this paragraph, see *De universo* 1, 1, 46 (*Mag. div.* I, 663a[A-B]).

55. See above, at nn. 37 and 38.

56. *De universo* 1, 1, 46 (*Mag. div.* I, 663aB).

57. William laid out several counterarguments to his opponents' claim in *De universo* 1, 1, 46 (*Mag. div.* I, 663a[B-C]).

58. William, *De universo* 1, 1, 46 (*Mag. div.* I, 663aD-bA).

59. Note the sudden appearance of the words "idolatry" and "idolator" in *De universo* I, 1, 46 (*Mag. div.* I, 663aD-bA), the context for the passage cited in the preceding note.

60. In the middle of a discussion in *De legibus* about idols, William listed as fifth and sixth of ten types of idolatry the cult of images and the cult of figures. See *De* legibus 23 (*Mag. div.* I, 67a[B-C]).

61. William, *De universo* 1, 1, 46 (*Mag. div.* I, 663bD).

62. William, *De legibus* 27 (*Mag. div.* I, 89bD): "[H]aec idolatria, quatuor scilicet illorum [generum figurarum], hoc est per quatuor ista exercebatur, et intus erat idolatria daemonum."

63. William, *De universo* 1, 1, 46 (*Mag. div.* I, 663bD).

64. See William, *De universo* 1, 1, 46 (*Mag. div.* I, 663aD).

65. William, *De legibus* 27 (*Mag. div.* I, 89aD).

66. Ibid.

67. William, *De legibus* 27 (*Mag. div.* I, 89bC). For Augustine's words about such a pact, see Chapter 1, nn. 54, 56 and 57.

68. Refer back to the passage cited in n. 38.

69. See the reference cited in n. 39.

70. See William's confession about his own early inclinations in this direction, quoted in n. 40.

71. In *De universo* 2, 3, 12 (*Mag. div.* I, 1039aC), William made acid remarks about apparitions that were visible only to those ("his") "qui intra circulum sunt – vel magistro operum et sociis ejus," and commented how another such master ("hujusmodi magister") might "strike the earth stretching before him to the east with extended sword." Lest there be any misunderstanding on the part of the uninitiated, he made plain only a few sentences later (*Mag. div.* I, 1039aD) that such doers of works were also known as "sorcerers" ("hujus-modi malefic[i]").

72. *De universo* 2, 3, 22 (*Mag. div.* I, 1059aA).

73. On these three types, see *De universo* 2, 3, 22 (*Mag. div.* I, 1059aA-bA). Pingree, "Learned Magic," 40, somewhat misleadingly takes this whole passage as setting forth William's concept of the taxonomy of magic as a whole, rather than just of that part of magic involving "*praestigia.*"

74. Ibid. (*Mag. div.* I, 1059bA).
75. Ibid.
76. Ibid. (*Mag. div.* I, 1059bB): "Haec igitur est fraus diabolica in huiusmodi operibus.
77. See the passage cited in n. 74.
78. In the same place (*Mag. div.* I, 1059b[A-B]), William commented on the sort of operation he was talking about – such as the shooting of a special bow and arrow – with the words: "[H]oc ipsum oblatio est. Oblatio autem non potest hic intelligi, nisi diabolicae servitutis et culturae, sive servitii." In a parallel passage in *De universo* 2, 3, 12 (*Mag. div.* I, 1039aB), William observed that the operations and use of special tools in such instances were equivalent to "sacrificia nefaria oblationesque et observantia[e] sacrilega[e]."
79. William, *De legibus* 24 (*Mag. div.* I, 70aF). See also *De universo* 2, 3, 21 (erroneously in text: 22) (*Mag. div.* I, 1058aG-bE), for the full name, "speculum Apollinis."
80. William, *De legibus* 24 (*Mag. div.* I, 69bC); and also *De universo* 2, 3, 12 (*Mag. div.* I, 1039aB): "Et intendo facere te scire in sequentibus causas hujusmodi fantasiarum, viasque et modos quibus naturaliter fiunt. [N]am et ipsi maligni spiritus per res naturales haec omnia faciunt…"
81. William, *De universo* 2, 2, 76 (*Mag. div.* I, 930b[E-F]).
82. See the discussion in *De universo* 2, 3, 23 (*Mag. div.* I, 1061b[B-D]). William made similar remarks about demons' power over the imagination, especially in dream states, in *De universo* 1, 1, 46 (*Mag. div.* I, 663bC).
83. William, *De universo* 2, 3, 22 (*Mag. div.* I, 1060aE).
84. Refer back to the first of the passages cited in n. 80, which serves for William as the occasion immediately to launch into an exposition of occult powers and the "natural magic" they made possible: "Et de operibus hujusmodi est magia naturalis…"
85. For example, see, n. 84 and n. 86.
86. Starting with the quotation given at the end of n. 84, William's words were: "Et de operibus hujusmodi est magia naturalis, quam necromantiam seu philosophicam philosophi vocant, licet multum improprie, et est totius <sci>entiae naturalis pars undecima." For the form "*magica naturalis*," see *De universo* 1, 1, 43 (*Mag. div.* I, 648aG), as well as *De universo* 1, 1, 46 (*Mag. div.* I, 663bD), quoted in n. 92.
87. William, *De universo* 2, 3, 22 (*Mag. div.* I, 1060bF).
88. See William's discussion, *De legibus* 24 (*Mag. div.* I, 69bD-70aE).
89. Ibid. (*Mag. div.* I, 70aE).
90. William lays out the whole argument in *De universo* 2, 3, 21 (marked in text as 22) (*Mag. div.* I, 1058bH).
91. Ibid.
92. William, *De universo* 1, 1, 46 (*Mag. div.* I, 663bD): "De his autem quae fiunt per magicam naturalem, scito quod nullam habent creatoris offensam vel injuriam, nisi quis ex ea arte vel nimis curiose vel malum operetur."

93. See *De legibus* 24 (*Mag. div.* I, 69bD).

94. *De legibus* 24 (*Mag. div.* I, 70aE).

95. On the magnet, see William, *De universo* 2, 3, 22 (*Mag. div.* I, 1059b[B-C]); for the basilisk, *De universo* 1, 1, 43 (*Mag. div.* I, 648aF).

96. *De universo* 2, 3, 22 (*Mag. div.* I, 1060aH).

97. For William on the peony, see ibid. (*Mag. div.* I, 1060aF and 1060b[F-G]).

98. See the recent edition by Julien Véronèse, *L'Ars notoria au Moyen Age. Introduction et édition critique*, Micrologus's Library (Florence: SISMEL/Edizioni del Galluzzo, 2007). The references by Michael are mentioned at nn. 6 and 9.

99. On the production of the work and the chronology of its versions, see Véronèse's comments in *Ars notoria*, 18–21 and 25–26.

100. *Ars notoria* (Version A, 1), ed. Véronèse, 34.

101. As the text points out: *Ars notoria* (Version A, 32a), 44–45.

102. The "suddenness" of the effect is commented on in *Ars notoria* (Version A, 5), ed. Véronèse, 35, while the estimation of a month's total effort is produced at Version A, 14, p. 38.

103. *Ars notoria* (Version A, 21), ed. Véronèse, 41: "Nota est quedam cognitio per orationem et figuram superpositam...." The clearest exposition of the *nota* and its parts has to wait until the fourteenth-century gloss: *Ars notoria* (Version B, gloss to variation 1), ed. Véronèse, 142.

104. See the earliest recital of the story in *Ars notoria* (Version A, 1, 2 and 8), ed. Véronèse, 34 and 35–36.

105. *Ars notoria* (Version A, 8), ed. Véronèse, 36.

106. See *Ars notoria* (Version A, 15), ed. Véronèse, 38. By the early-fourteenth-century Version B, the story ran that an angel named Pamphilus had delivered Solomon the "notes" in the form of gold tablets bearing the names of holy angels and *orationes* written in the three tongues: Greek, Chaldean and Hebrew.

107. *Ars notoria* (Version B, gloss to 25), ed. Véronèse, 165.

108. For example: *Ars notoria* (Version A, 86), ed. Véronèse, 65: "sciendum est quod quando ipsas [notas] pronuntiaveris caste vivendum est et sobrie diebus earum."

109. See, for example, *Ars notoria* (Version A, 79), ed. Véronèse, 63.

110. *Ars notoria* (Version A, 81), ed. Véronèse, 64.

111. See *Ars notoria* (Version A, 71), ed. Véronèse, 58.

112. It is worth noting that at least by Version B, the *Ars* has substituted "*phisica*" – that is, medicine – for geometry among the quadrivial arts. See, for example, *Ars notoria* (Version B, gloss to Var. 1), ed. Véronèse, 143.

113. *Ars notoria* (Version B, gloss to 87), ed. Véronèse, 203. Virtually the same words appear in Version B at the *figura* for the seventh note of philosophy (ed. Véronèse, 283).

114. *Ars notoria* (Version A, 71), ed. Véronèse, 58: "Mechanice autem septem sunt iste: ydromantia, pyromantia, nigromantia, cyromantia, geomantia, geonogia, sub astrologia neonegia."

115. See Chapter 1, at n. 81.

116. See n. 10.

117. For the first mention, see *Ars notoria* (Version A, 71), ed. Véronèse, 58–59; for the reference to "sacrificando *malignis spiritibus*," Version B, gloss to 71, p. 186.

118. See the remarkable testimonial in *Ars notoria* (Version A, 71), ed. Véronèse, 59.

119. See *Ars notoria* (Version B, gloss to 88 and gloss to 126f), ed. Véronèse, 204–205 and 230.

120. On secrecy, see *Ars notoria* (Version A, 40), ed. Véronèse, 48; and Version A, 103, p. 71. On solitude, see *Ars notoria* ("Opus operum," D[b]), ed. Véronèse, 102; or "Opus operum," E, p. 104.

121. *Ars notoria* ("Opus operum," E), ed. Véronèse, 104. In Version B (gloss to 147), ed. Véronèse, 193, the operator himself is once referred to as "*magister operans.*"

122. *Ars notoria* (Version A, 42), ed. Véronèse, 48.

123. *Ars notoria* (Version A, 63), ed. Véronèse, 55.

124. See the critical edition by Gösta Hedegård, *Liber iuratus Honorii. A Critical Edition of the Latin Version of the Sworn Book of Honourius*, Studia Latina Stockhomiensia 18 (Stockholm: Almqvist & Wiksell International, 2002). The work names itself in the Prologue, 18 (61), and chapter CXLI, 1 (150). An early English translation of the work as the "Sworne Booke of Honoryus" is found in one sixteenth-century manuscript and has been published in an uncritical transcription: Daniel J. Driscoll, ed., *The Sworn Book of Honorius the Magician, As Composed by Honourius through Counsel with the Angel Hocroell* (Gillette, NJ: Heptangle Press, 1977; repr. 1983).

125. *Liber iuratus* Prol, 15, and CXLI, 1, ed. Hedegård, 60 and 150. The rationales for the name are given in *Liber iuratus* Prol, 18 and 29, ed. Hedegård, 61.

126. See n. 79. In addition to the two citations recorded there, William refers to the work a third time in *De legibus* 24 (*Mag. div.* I, 89bD).

127. Robert Mathiesen, "A Thirteenth-Century Ritual to Attain the Beatific Vision from the *Sworn Book* of Honorius of Thebes," in *Conjuring Spirits. Texts and Traditions of Medieval Ritual Magic*, ed. Claire Fanger (University Park: Pennsylvania State University Press, 1998), 146–47.

128. See the arguments of Richard Kieckhefer, "The Devil's Contemplatives: The *Liber iuratus*, the *Liber visionum* and Christian Appropriation of Jewish Occultism," in *Conjuring Spirits*, ed. Fanger, 253–54; Gösta Hedegård, in his edition, *Liber iuratus Honorii*, 11–12; and Jean-Patrice Boudet, "Magie théurgique," 859–61. Their persuasive judgments are reflected in the following paragraph.

129. See *Liber iuratus* I, ed. Hedegård, 60–61.

130. *Liber iuratus* II; and CII, 1; CLIII, 2–10; CXVI, 1–12; and CXXXIV, 1–2, ed. Hedegård, 62–65, 115, 116, 124–25 and 142.

131. *Liber iuratus* II, 2–3, ed. Hedegård, 62.

132. Ibid., II, 3, p. 62.
133. Ibid., II, 4–14, pp. 62–63. In this first listing, the chapter on airy spirits precedes that on fiery ones, but in the reiteration of them all at the head of the second treatise in the text, the order has been corrected to represent more logically the locational descent of the four elements, with fiery before airy: *Liber iuratus* CIII, 6, ed. Hedegård, 116.
134. *Liber iuratus* II, 15, ed. Hedegård, 63.
135. The chapter headings that follow are to be found in *Liber iuratus* II, 19–28, ed. Hedegård, 64–65.
136. *Liber iuratus* II, 28, ed. Hedegård, 65: "Set ista duo capitula subtraximus, quoniam erant contra Domini voluntatem."
137. Ibid. III, 7–8, ed. Hedegård, 65.
138. *Liber iuratus* CXXXVI, 1–2, ed. Hedegård, 144.
139. This treatise consumes, in the edition, *Liber iuratus* IV–CII, ed. Hedegård, 67–116.
140. In the edition, *Liber iuratus* CIII–CXV, ed. Hedegård, 116–24.
141. In the edition, *Liber iuratus* CXVI–CXXXIII, ed. Hedegård, 124–42.
142. *Liber iuratus* CXVII, 1–2, ed. Hedegård, 125.
143. Ibid., CXVIII, 1–4, ed. Hedegård, 126.
144. In the edition, *Liber iuratus* CXXXIV–CXXXV, ed. Hedegård, 142–44.
145. See n. 137.
146. *Liber iuratus* CXXXV, 8–9, ed. Hedegård, 143: "Sunt autem 5....Et quilibet [quattuor minstrorum] habet legiones centum, et in qualibet sunt demones 4500...et sunt ministri infernales."
147. In the edition, *Liber iuratus* CXXXVI–CXL; ed. Hedegård, 144–50.
148. Hedegård, ed., *Liber iuratus* (Introduction), 45–48.
149. See, for instance, *Liber iuratus* V, 1–4, ed. Hedegård, 71.
150. For just one example, see the passage from an *oratio* from the first treatise, directed to God (*Liber iuratus* CI, 42–43, ed. Hedegård, 114): "...respice super me et exaudi preces meas, ut per graciam tuam et virtutem sanctorum nominum tuorum animam meam a tenebris mei corpusculi suscitare...digneris..."
151. *Liber iuratus* IV, 56–59, ed. Hedegård, 70–71, sets out these three primary requirements – at this moment in the text, of course, as intended for the consecration of the "seal" (see also n. 149) – but it makes a special point of alerting the reader that precisely these same methods as directed toward attaining the divine vision will have to be repeated in the cases dealt with later in the book having to do with the conjuring of spirits and angels, the form of the petitions altered to suit the new circumstances.
152. See the exemplary instructions from the middle of the third treatise regarding conjuring the spirits of the winds (*Liber iuratus* CXXVIII, 26–28, ed. Hedegård, 133).
153. See *Liber iuratus* CXXVII, 6–15; and CXXXV, 18–19, ed. Hedegård, 130 and 143–44, for the instructions; *Liber iuratus*, ed. Hedegård, 131 and 143–44,

for the diagrams. It should be noted that the text also calls for a conjurer's circle in the operations of the second treatise. See *Liber iuratus*, CXII, 1–6, ed. Hedegård, 119. No diagram is provided on this occasion.

154. See n. 143.
155. *Liber iuratus* CXXXV, 2, ed. Hedegård, 142.
156. See n. 146.
157. *Liber iuratus* CXXXV, 11, ed. Hedegård, 143.
158. Ibid. CXXXV, 12 (143).
159. *Liber iuratus* III, 27, ed. Hedegård, 66, where he comments that those following the book's instructions will be operating "per hanc artem magicam."
160. Ibid., III, 27–29, ed. Hedegård, 66.
161. Ibid., III, 16, ed. Hedegård, 66.
162. Ibid., III, 16–17, ed. Hedegård, 66.
163. *Liber iuratus* III, 18, ed. Hedegård, 66: "Et quia [operantes pagani] fidem malam habent, opera eorum nulla."
164. On Jews and the *Liber's* magic, see *Liber iuratus* III, 20–25, ed. Hedegård, 66.
165. Ibid., III, 26, ed. Hedegård, 66: "Solus igitur Christianus potest in hac visione et in omnibus aliis [in hoc libro descriptis] operari."
166. See the recent edition by David Pingree, *Picatrix. The Latin Version of the Ghāyat Al-Hakīm* (London: The Warburg Institute, 1986).
167. Consult the references in Weill-Parot, *Les "images astrologiques,"* 126–27, nn. 121–25.
168. See *Picatrix* prol., ed. Pingree, 1.
169. *Picatrix* prol., ed. Pingree, 1.
170. David Pingree, "Some of the Sources of the *Ghāyat al-hakīm*," *Journal of the Warbourg and Courtauld Institutes* 43 (1980): 1.
171. Again Pingree, "Some of the Sources," 2 and 15. See also n. 31.
172. *Picatrix* II, v, ed. Pingree, 50. For William on this matter, see n. 20.
173. The connection is abundantly evident in the speedy transition, over the course of just a few lines, from *Picatrix's* invocation of the "ways by which human beings might attain the sciences and wisdom of God" (*Picatrix* prol., ed. Pingree, 1, ll. 25–26), to its imprecations to the reader who "wants to know the sciences of the philosophers and look into their secrets" (ibid., 1, ll. 29–30).
174. *Picatrix* prol., ed. Pingree, 1, ll. 1–6.
175. *Picatrix* prol., ed. Pingree, 1: "Incipit liber quem sapientissimus philosophus Picatrix in nigromanticis artibus... composuit."
176. *Picatrix* prol., ed. Pingree, 1, l. 31; as well as I, ii, 5.
177. The first citation given in the preceding note refers to the "marvels" of necromancy, the "*mirabilia sciencie nigromancie*."
178. *Picatrix* prol., ed. Pingree, 1–2.
179. *Picatrix* I, ii, ed. Pingree, 5.
180. Pingree, "Some of the Sources," 14–15, as well as the first sentence of the first full paragraph on p. 5.

181. The key elements of this first version are sketched out in *Picatrix* IV, i, ed. Pingree, 174, l. 4–175, l. 7, but pertinent comments continue along in the text through p. 176, l. 5.

182. See *Picatrix* IV, i, ed. Pingree, 174 for repeated use of the verbs *"emanare," "descendere"* and *"procedere"* to describe the process by which the stages come to be.

183. For this last stage, see the comments in *Picatrix* IV, i, ed. Pingree, 175, ll. 1–6. I have interpreted the odd Latin phrase reproduced here in the text as implying the word *"corpora"* to serve as ground for the two genetives, *"animalium"* and *"vegetabilium,"* in addition to its role as subject for the adjective *"dura."*

184. See the remarkable observations in *Picatrix* IV, i, ed. Pingree, 174, ll. 19–29.

185. Refer to *Picatrix* IV, i, ed. Pingree, 174, ll. 29–34.

186. *Picatrix* IV, i, ed. Pingree, 175, l. 28–176, l. 5.

187. *Picatrix* I, vii, ed. Pingree, 29.

188. *Picatrix* IV, i, ed. Pingree, 176.

189. *Picatrix* I, ii, ed. Pingree, 6.

190. Ibid., p. 6, ll. 7–10.

191. For the case of William, see just after n. 18 on p. 91, for the *Ars notoria*, the citation given in n. 103.

192. For example, *Picatrix* I, ii, ed. Pingree, 6, ll. 7–8: "quia ex [locis stellarum fixarum] componuntur celestes figure et forme celi ... "

193. See *Picatrix* I, ii, ed. Pingree, 6, ll. 10–12.

194. Ibid., p. 6, ll. 15–16: "Et eciam verba sunt in una parcium nigromancie quia verba in se habent nigromancie virtutem."

195. *Picatrix* I, v, ed. Pingree, 24, in fact explicitly links the words (*"verba"*) to *"oraciones."*

196. I take this to be the implication of the passage in *Picatrix* I, v, ed. Pingree, 24, ll. 10–14.

197. *Picatrix* I, ii, ed. Pingree, 6.

198. See *Picatrix* I, ii, ed. Pingree, 5.

199. See the mention of the three for similar composites like the elixir of alchemy in *Picatrix* I, ii, ed. Pingree, 5, ll. 35–36, or more pertinently in the case of the science of images itself in *Picatrix* III, v, ed. Pingree, 103, ll. 7–9; and IV, viii, p. 218, ll. 14–15.

200. On these, see *Picatrix* I, ii, ed. Pingree, 6, ll. 23–28.

201. The need for fumigations is confirmed shortly before in the same Book, same chapter (*Picatrix* I, ii, ed. Pingree, 5, ll. 19–20), and here the additional comment is offered that they "draw certain spirits" (*"attrahuntur spiritus"*) to the images.

202. *Picatrix* I, ii, ed. Pingree, 5: "Et pars istius sciencie est in practica propter quod sua opera sunt de spiritu in spiritum, et hoc est in faciendo res similes que non sunt essencia."

203. Following immediately after the quotation in n. 202: "Et ymaginum composicio est spiritus in corpore…"
204. See *Picatrix* I, ii, ed. Pingree, p. 6, ll. 39 and 11, respectively.
205. See the full discussion, *Picatrix* I, ii, ed. Pingree, 6, l. 37–7, l. 16.
206. Following immediately after what is quoted in n. 203: "et composicio alchimie est corpus in corpore."
207. Refer to *Picatrix* I, ii, ed. Pingree, 5, l. 20–26, l. 4.
208. Ibid., p. 6, ll. 4–5.
209. Pingree, "Some of the Sources," 1.
210. *Picatrix*, I, v, ed. Pingree, 22.
211. As is made clear in the same passage referred to in n. 210, the relevant observations of celestial place and motion were those of the very moment in which the images were cast (*"in fundendo ymagines"*).
212. In the eyes of our author, the effect of the celestial motions on the images was effected by the mediation of light rays emitted by the bodies in the heavens. For Latin scholars in the thirteenth century, the classic source for a systematic explanation of action in the world by means of "rays" – emitted from all things, including celestial bodies and bodies here below – was the ninth-century Arab Al-Kindi's *De radiis*. Its Latin translation is edited by Marie-Thérèse d'Alverny and Françoise Hudry in "Al-Kindi, *De radiis*," *Archives d'Histoire Doctrinale et Littéraire du Moyen Age* 41 (1974): 139–260. See also Pinella Travaglia, *Magic, Causality and Intentionality. The Doctrine of the Rays of al-Kindi* (Florence: SISMEL/ Edizioni del Galluzzo, 1999).
213. For example, *Picatrix* I, v, ed. Pingree, 23; or see n. 178, on the insistence that it be treated as an "occult" art.
214. Refer to nn. 175 and 176.
215. For *"sciencia magice,"* *Picatrix* I, vi, ed. Pingree, 27, ll. 33–34; for *"ars magica"* or *"magica ars,"* *Picatrix* I, iv (p. 14, l. 17); I, vii (p. 30, ll. 11–12); and II, vi (p. 55, ll. 33–34).
216. See *Picatrix* IV, vii, ed. Pingree, 206, ll. 18–24.
217. *Picatrix* III, xii, ed. Pingree, 172, ll. 18–19. For William's usage, see n. 71.
218. See *Picatrix* II, v, ed. Pingree, 46, ll. 3–16.
219. *Picatrix* III, viii; and IV, vii, ed. Pingree, pp. 138–40 and 205–209.
220. The *Agriculture* has been edited in Arabic: Ibn Wahshīyah, *Kitāb al-Filāhah al-Nabatīyah. L'Agriculture nabatéenne*, ed. Tawfīq Fahd, 3 vol. (Damascus: Al-Maʿhad al-ʿIlmī al-Faransī, 1993–98).
221. Refer to Pingree, "Some of the Sources," p. 3, n. 14, as well as here to n. 171.
222. For its history, see Pinella Travaglia, "Considerazaioni sulla magia nel medioevo. Il libro dell'agricultura nabatea," in Alessandro Musco et al., ed., *Universalità della ragione. Pluralità delle filosofie nel Medioevo*, XII Congresso Internazionale di Filosofia Medievale (Palermo: Officina di Studi Medievali, 2012), vol. 3, 153–64; and the comments of Pingree in "Some of the Sources," 3 and 12.

223. *Picatrix* IV, vii, ed. Pingree, 205, l. 28–206, l. 3.
224. Refer again to n. 171 and to additional remarks by Pingree in "Some of the Sources," 12 and 15.
225. *Picatrix* II, vi, ed. Pingree, 51, ll. 16–17: "ymago nihil aliud est quam vis corporum celestium in corporibus influencium."
226. The duality of an active nature somehow present in the image-object working in conjunction with motive forces of the stars and planets is rendered in particularly plain language in *Picatrix* II, vi, ed. Pingree, 51, ll. 37–39; and even more poignantly a few lines later (p. 52, ll. 7–8).
227. See ibid., p. 52, ll. 32–38.
228. *Picatrix* II, vii, ed. Pingree, 58: "propter quod opus ymaginis indiget similitudine effectuum stellarum et opere metalli ex quo ymago componitur tempore in quo fit ipsa et loco in quo talis ymago funditur et paratur." These are effectively the same parameters or factors as had been assigned previously in the text to "practical alchemy" in general – see n. 198.
229. Refer to the whole compilaton in *Picatrix* II, x, ed. Pingree, 64–74.
230. *Picatrix* II, I, ed. Pingree, 32.
231. For two variant references to these powers, see *Picatrix* III, v, ed. Pingree, p. 107, ll. 17–18 and 29–30. In *Picatrix* IV, 1, ed. Pingree, 177, l. 7–8, on the occasion of a discussion of possible referents for the words "*sensus*" and "*spiritus*," we find open acknowledgment of the "*spiritus intelligenciarum vel angelorum movencium celos.*"
232. *Picatrix* III, v, ed. Pingree, 108, ll. 13–15.
233. Consult the whole passage at ibid., p. 108, ll. 5–15.
234. Ibid., p. 108, ll. 5–7.
235. *Picatrix* IV, ii, ed. Pingree, p. 178, ll. 33–34 for the summary heading, pp. 179–87 for the full listing of details.
236. See the explicit mention of both at the beginning of the chapter indicated in the preceding note (p. 178, l. 37–179, l. 1), and refer again to the subsequent catalogue of ceremonnial particulars.
237. *Picatrix* III, vii, ed. Pingree, 112.
238. *Picatrix* IV, ii, ed. Pingree, 187–88. For instance, on. p. 187, ll. 9–10: "[D]icas: In nomine Anzil, qui cum Saturno positus est. Tu, Anzil, qui es Saturni angelus! Coniuro te … ut meam peticionem … adimpleas."
239. *Picatrix* III, vii, ed. Pingree, p. 135, ll. 25–30.
240. Paola Zambelli, *The Speculum Astronomiae and its Enigma* (Dordrecht/ Boston: Kluwer Academic Publishers, 1992), 3, has established the dating now generally accepted by other scholars. Agostino Paravicini Bagliani, *Le Speculum Astronomiae, une énigme? Enquête sur les manuscrits* (Florence: Edizioni del Galluzzo, 2001) argues convincingly that in its original form the work was intentionally left untitled and unattributed to any author. The text has received a semi-critical edition in *Speculum astronomiae*, ed. Stefano Caroti, Michela Pereira and Stefano Zamponi, under the direction of Paola Zambelli (Pisa: Domus Galilaeana, 1977), which edition is reproduced

without emendation at the end of Zambelli's *Speculum Astronomiae and its Enigma*. All references to the *Speculum* in the present work will follow the pagination of the 1992 publication.

241. Paravicini Bagliani, *Le Speculum Astronomiae, une énigme?*, 153. On pp. 155 and 161, he argues that the attribution to Albert was primarily at first a Parisian phenomenon, linked to the academic politics in Paris at just that time.

242. See Zambelli, *The Speculum Astronomiae and its Enigma*, 121–22, 124, and on collaboration, 111 and 125.

243. Paravicini Bagliani, *Le Speculum Astronomiae, une énigme?*, 162.

244. See *Speculum astronomiae*, Prooemium, ed. Caroti et al. (in Zambelli, *The Speculum Astronomiae*), 208.

245. *Speculum astronomiae* 1, ed. Caroti et al., 208, ll. 2–3.

246. For the topics laid out in this paragraph, see *Speculum astronomiae* 1, ed. Caroti et al., 208–12.

247. See *Speculum astronomiae* 2, ed. Caroti et al., 212–18.

248. Ibid., 218, ll. 80–83.

249. *Speculum astronomiae*, 3, ed. Caroti et al., 218–20, ll. 2–4.

250. It is worth noting that the division of "astronomy" into two main parts, which we would designate by our terms "astronomy" and "astrology," was standard among thirteenth-century scholastics and among them was typically traced back to Ptolemy himself. Zambelli – *The Speculum Astronomiae and its Enigma*, 22 – quotes an emblematic assertion of the bifurcation by Albert himself in his *De fato*.

251. *Speculum astronomiae* 3, ed. Caroti et al., 220, ll. 4–13.

252. *Speculum astronomiae* 4, ed. Caroti et al., 222, ll. 2–4.

253. *Speculum astronomiae* 4, ed. Caroti et al., 222, ll. 5–6.

254. On the sub-science "*de revolutionibus*," refer to *Speculum astronomiae* 7, ed. Caroti et al., 228–32.

255. *Speculum astronomiae* 8, ed. Caroti et al., 232–34.

256. *Speculum astronomiae* 9, ed. Caroti et al., 234–36.

257. For the "*pars electionum*," see *Speculum astronomiae* 10, ed. Caroti et al., 238.

258. *Speculum astronomiae* 6, ed. Caroti et al., 226, ll. 2–6.

259. See *Speculum astronomiae* 12, ed. Caroti et al., 250, ll. 9–24.

260. *Speculum astronomiae* 13, ed. Caroti et al., 256, ll. 2–11.

261. *Speculum astronomiae* 13, ed. Caroti et al., 258, ll. 29–43.

262. *Speculum astronomiae* 4, ed. Caroti et al., 222, ll. 7–8. As indicated in n. 8 of the original printing of the edition published in 1977 at Pisa (p. 15), the work is the *De imaginibus* attributed in the Latin manuscript tradition to Thābit ibn Qurra.

263. *Speculum astronomiae* 4, ed. Caroti et al., 222, ll. 8–12.

264. *Speculum astronomiae* 11, ed. Caroti et al., 240, ll. 2–4.

265. For the summary description of the mode of manufacturing these "abominable" images, see *Speculum astronomiae* 11, ed. Caroti et al., 240, ll. 4–20.

266. On manufacturing this class of images, see *Speculum astronomiae* 11, ed. Caroti et al., 240, ll. 21–33.
267. The listing of works concerning the "abominable" images appears in *Speculum* 11, ed. Caroti et al., 242–44, ll. 45–75, as well as a few more on 246, ll. 89–98; the listing of works on the "destestable" images in *Speculum* 11, 244–46, ll. 76–89. Weill-Parot, *Les "images astrologiques,"* 41, n. 37, points to the two foundational works on the content of this double listing: Lynn Thorndike, "Traditional Medieval Tracts Concerning Engraved Astrological Images," in *Mélanges Auguste Pelzer* (Leuven: Bibliothèque de l'Université, 1947), 217–74; and David Pingree's "Learned Magic" (see n. 11). His own exposition in *Les "images astrologiques,"* 42–58, draws on those beginnings to present an updated and exhaustive summary.
268. See Pingree, "Learned Magic," 41–42 and 48.
269. Again ibid., 42. See the earlier reference to the tradition in n. 31. Charles Burnett, "Talismans: Magic as Science? Necromancy among the Seven Liberal Arts," in *Magic and Divination in the Middle Ages* (Aldershot: Variorum, 1996), article 1, 4–6, simply lumps together both of the odious types of image described in the *Speculum*'s first two image "sciences" as "exorcising," in contrast to what some twelfth-century texts describe as "pure" talismanic magic, working "*secundum phisicam.*"
270. Weill-Parot, *Les "images astrologiques,"* 84.
271. For the phrase "*imagines necromanticae,*" see *Speculum astronomiae* 11, ed. Caroti et al., 240–42, ll. 34–35; and also 248, l. 134. The term "*imagines astronomicae*" comes in the passage at the very start of chapter 11, cited here in n. 264. See the same form, chapter 11, p. 246, l. 103; and chapter 16, p. 270, l. 2; but chapter 11, p. 248, ll. 133–34: "*imagines astronomiae.*"
272. *Speculum astronomiae* 11, ed. Caroti et al., 246, ll. 103–106: "Tertius enim modus est imaginum astronomicarum, qui eliminat istas spurcitias, suffumigationes et invocationes non habet, neque exorcizationes aut characterum inscriptiones admittit, sed virtutem nanciscitur solummodo a figura caelesti…" The final words in this passage are repeated to the same effect in chapter 16, p. 270, ll. 4–5.
273. For mention of these two, see *Speculum astronomiae* 11, ed. Caroti et al., 248–50, ll. 129–39.
274. See n. 262. Weill-Parot, *Les "images astrologiques,"* 64–65, remarks upon this signal instance of tribute by the *Speculum* author to the general ideology of *De imaginibus*.
275. As Pingree remarks, "Sources of the *Ghāyat al-hakīm,*" 5, the works of Thābit ibn Qurra had to do with the "talismanic" category of image-science he characterized as one of two types found in *Picatrix*.
276. For this argument in full, see Weill-Parot, *Les "images astrologiques,"* 84–85.
277. Ibid., 85: "le vrai dessein – apologétique – du Magister Speculi…"
278. Weill-Parot, *Les "images astrologiques,"* 385–86.
279. Refer to the account given in Chapter 1, at n. 81.

280. For these comments on *"libri necromantici,"* see *Speculum astronomiae* 17, ed. Caroti et al., 270–72, ll. 2–6.
281. On these five, see *Speculum astronomiae* 17, ed. Caroti et al., 272, ll. 6–21.

4 Science, Magic and the Demonic, 1200–1400: The Reaction

1. As early as the work of Henry Charles Lea, and shortly thereafter that of Rossell Robbins, a finger was pointed to Thomas Aquinas as critical in the establishment of all magic as demonic – foundational, according to these early views, for the rise of the witch hunts of early modern Europe – though an early attempt to separate Thomas from the ideology behind the witch-craze is Charles Edward Hopkin, *The Share of Thomas Aquinas in the Growth of the Witchcraft Delusion* (Philadelphia: University of Pennsylvania, 1940; rprt. New York, 1982). A spate of recent works on Thomas and magic eschew the misleading direct connection to the witch trials but greatly advance the case for his having been instrumental in the ideological demonization of the magical arts. Among the very best of these are Thomas Linsenmann, *Die Magie bei Thomas von Aquin* (Berlin: Akademie Verlag, 2000), and chapter 4 of Alain Boureau's *Satan Hérétique*.
2. Refer to the exceptional overview of Thomas's life and writings, Simon Tugwell's introduction to Thomas in the volume he edited, *Albert and Thomas. Selected Writings* (Mahwah, NJ: Paulist Press, 1988), in this case, pp. 251–52.
3. Thomas Aquinas, *Summa contra gentiles* III, 101 (Turin: Marietti, 1935), 342b: "Illa igitur simpliciter miracula dicenda sunt quae divinitus fiunt praeter ordinem communiter servatum in rebus."
4. Ibid.: "Illud ergo simpliciter mirum est quod habet causam simpliciter occultam..."
5. Thomas, *Summa contra gentiles* III, 102, Marietti edition, 343a.
6. See Chapter 3, pp. 96–97.
7. See the passage in n. 5.
8. For William, see Chapter 3, at n. 93, and for Thomas, *Summa contra gentiles* III, 102, p. 343b.
9. The preceding discussion of generation of less and more perfect beings depends on Thomas, *Summa contra gentiles* III, 102, p. 343b.
10. Ibid., III, 102, p. 343b–44a. On Thomas's emphasis on the priority of local motion as a cause of change in the sublunar world, see also Steven P. Marrone, "Magic and the Physical World in Thirteenth-Century Scholasticism," *Early Science and Medicine* 14 (209), esp. 174–79.
11. Thomas, *Contra gentiles* III, 103, p. 345a.
12. For William on this, see Chapter 3, p. 96, esp. at nn. 83 and 84.

13. See Thomas, "De operationibus occultis naturae ad quendam militem ultramontanum," in *Opera Omnia* (Leonine edition) 43 (Rome: Editori di San Tommaso, 1976), 183a. The editors confirm the dating of the work to 1269–72 in their introduction to the text (163–64).

14. See specifically "De operationibus occultis," in *Opera Omnia* 43, p. 183b, ll. 58–64.

15. Ibid., p. 185b, ll. 214–22. William of Auvergne had likewise pointed to the sapphire to similar effect. See Marrone, "Magic and the Physical World," 172–73. For consideration of the Galenic origins of the notion of causality behind such occult operations, begin with Brian P. Copenhaver's "Natural Magic, Hermetism and Early Modern Science," in *Reappraisals of the Scientific Revolution*, ed. David C. Lindberg and Robert S. Westman, 272–73 (Cambridge: Cambridge University, 1990); and "Scholastic Philosophy and Renaissance Magic in the *De vita* of Marsilio Ficino," *Renaissance Quarterly* 37 (1984): 540–41 [rpt. in Brian P. Levack, ed., *Renaissance Magic*, Articles on Witchcraft, Magic and Demonology, 11 (New York: Garland Publishing Co., 1992)] .

16. Thomas, *Contra gentiles* III, 104, 345b.

17. Again, on dating, see Tugwell, *Albert and Thomas*, 256.

18. See Chapter 1, pp. 12–13

19. Thomas Aquinas, *Summa theologiae* IIa IIae, 92, 1, in *Opera Omnia* (Leonine edition) 9 (Rome: Typographia Polyglotta, 1897), 298b; and also IIa IIae, 94, 1, p. 304b.

20. See the first passage cited in the preceding note.

21. Thomas, *Summa theologiae* IIa IIae, 92, 2 (Leonine edition), 299a.

22. In *Summa theologiae* IIa IIae, 92, 2, p. 299b, Thomas expressly referred his own position back to that of Augustine in *De doctrina christiana*.

23. In *Summa theologiae* IIa IIae, 92, 2, p. 299a, Thomas called them "diversi fines divini cultus."

24. For the three types, see ibid., 299a–b.

25. See the nominal definition in *Summa theologiae* IIa IIae, 95, 1, p. 311a: "[D]icendum quod in nomine divinationis intelligitur quaedam praenuntiatio futurorum."

26. *Summa theologiae* IIa IIae, 95, 1, p. 312a.

27. See *Summa theologiae* IIa IIae, 95, 1, p. 311b.

28. *Summa theologiae* IIa IIae, 95, 2, p. 313a: "Omnis autem divinatio ex operatione daemonum provenit...."

29. Such seems to be the implication of the assertion that concludes the sentence begun in the passage quoted in the preceding note.

30. See, for instance, ibid., ad 2. (p. 313b). For Augustine's words, consult Chapter 1, p. 13 (at n. 54), and also p. 14 (at n. 57).

31. For the rest of this paragraph, see *Summa theologiae* IIa IIae, 95, 3, pp. 315a–16b.

32. For these three types, see *Summa theologiae* IIa IIae, 95, 3, p. 315a. On the gradual divergence in the thirteenth century between "necromancy" as having to do with the dead and "nigromancy" as more general sorcery, see the comments in Chapter 3, n. 8.
33. *Summa theologiae* IIa IIae, 95, 3, p. 315a–b.
34. Ibid., p. 315b. For Hugh's listing, see Chapter 1, p. 22.
35. Ibid., p. 315b. See Chapter 1, pp. 22 and 13, for Hugh and Augustine on "*genethliaci*."
36. *Summa theologiae* IIa IIae, 95, 3, p. 315b.
37. Ibid., pp. 315b–16a.
38. For them all, refer to ibid., p. 316a.
39. On "geomancy" in this sense, see Jean-Patrice Boudet, *Entre science et nigromance. Astrologie, divination et magie dans l'Occident médiéval (XIIe–XVe siècle)* (Paris: Publications de la Sorbonne, 2006), 108–112.
40. *Summa theologiae* IIa IIae, 96, 1, p. 330a–b. Thomas makes an apparent reference to the *ars notoria* – on this occasion unnamed – also in his *Summa contra gentiles* III, 94, p. 346b.
41. See the discussion in ibid., p. 330b.
42. *Summa theologiae* IIa IIae, 96, 2, p. 331a–b.
43. *Summa theologiae* IIa IIae, 96, 4, pp. 334a–35a.
44. We see this in the responses to initial arguments in the article referred to in n. 42. See at first *Summa theologiae* IIa IIae, 96, 2, ad 1., pp. 331b–32a.
45. See *Summa theologiae* IIa IIae, 96, 2, obj. 2, p. 331a.
46. *Summa theologiae* IIa IIae, 96, 2, ad 2., p. 332a–b.
47. *Summa theologiae* IIa IIae, 96, 2, ad 2., p. 332b: "Unde etiam imagines quas astronomicas vocant, ex operatione daemonum habent effectum."
48. Weill-Parot, *Les "images astrologiques,"* 38–39.
49. For the passage launching the discussion, partly quoted here, see n. 16.
50. *Summa contra gentiles* III, 104, p. 345b (almost immediately after the lines cited in n. 16).
51. Ibid., p. 346b.
52. See Chapter 3, on *Picatrix*, pp. 111–12 and 112–13, and for William, pp. 91–92, at nn. 51 and 52.
53. See the evidenced scattered throughout *Contra gentiles* III, 104, pp. 345b–47a.
54. *Summa contra gentiles* III, 105, p. 347b.
55. See the relevant passage from *Contra gentiles*, quoted at n. 16, and referred to in n. 49.
56. For the foregoing argument, see *Summa contra gentiles* III, 104, p. 346a.
57. For this argument, see *Summa contra gentiles* III, 105, p. 347a–b.
58. Ibid., p. 346b.
59. *Summa contra gentiles* III, 105, 347b–48a: "Figura autem nullius actionis principium est neque passionis; alias mathematica corpora essent activa et passiva." The first six words of this passage were repeated nearly verbatim in the later *Summa theologiae* IIa IIae, 96, 2, ad 2., p. 332b.

60. See *Summa contra gentiles* III, 105, p. 348b.
61. On William, see Chapter 3, pp. 93–94.
62. *Summa contra gentiles* III, 105, p. 348b.
63. See Chapter 6, at n. 25, and most importantly Brian Copenhaver, "Scholastic Philosophy and Renaissance Magic," 533–39; and in a more generalized but, to my eyes, less well-founded statement of the case, "Natural Magic, Hermetism and Early Modern Science," 273–74.
64. For both the objection and Thomas's rebuttal, see *Summa theologiae* IIa IIae, 96, 2, arg. 2 and ad 2. (pp. 331a and 332a–b). These passages have been addressed at nn. 45 and 46.
65. Refer, for example, to the passages quoted from Augustine's *De doctrina christiana* in Chapter 1, nn. 54 and 57.
66. On Solomonic magic, see Chapter 3, pp. 91 and 99.
67. *Summa contra gentiles* III, 106, p. 348b.
68. See *Summa contra gentiles* III, 107, p. 351a.
69. On Bacon's chronology, see Andrew G. Little, "Introduction: On Roger Bcon's Life and Works," in *Roger Bacon Essays*, ed. Andrew G. Little (Oxford: Oxford University Press, 1914), 1–31; "Rogerus Bacon O.F.M.," in Charles H. Lohr, "Medieval Latin Aristotle Commentarires. Authors: Robertus-Wilgelmus," *Traditio* 29 (1973): 115–21; but most importantly and reliably Jeremiah M.G. Hackett, "The Meaning of Experimental Science (*Scientia Experimentalis*) in the Philosophy of Roger Bacon," PhD thesis, University of Toronto, 1983, pp. 40–47.
70. Refer to Bacon, *Liber primus communium naturalium*, I, 1, c. 1, ed. Robert Steele, in *Opera hactenus inedita Rogeri Baconi*, fasc. II (Oxford: Clarendon Press, 1913), 1. On the date of the *Communia naturalium*, see Thomas S. Maloney, "The Extreme Realism of Roger Bacon," *The Review of Metaphysics* 38 (1985): 823.
71. *Communia naturalium* I, 1, c. 2, p. 3.
72. Ibid., p. 5: "... preter scienciam communem naturalibus sunt septem speciales: videlicet, Perspectiva[;] Astronomia, judiciaria et operativa[;] Sciencia ponderum de gravibus et levibus[;] Alkimia[;] Agricultura[;] Medicina[;] Sciencia Experimentalis."
73. On Gundissalinus's listing, see Chapter 1, p. 19, esp. at n. 74; on Farabi, Chapter 1, p. 19, n. 75.
74. As a mathematically and optically oriented "scientist" consciously self-fashioned in the mode of Robert Grosseteste, Bacon considered optics to be the intellectual foundation necessary for all the other sciences. See his comments in *Opus maius* V, 1, 1, c. 1 (in *The "Opus majus" of Roger Bacon*, ed. John Henry Bridges, 2 vol. and supplement (Oxford: Clarendon Press, 1897, and London: Williams and Norgate, 1900), vol. 2, p. 3.
75. For the foregoing description, see Bacon, *Communia Naturalium* I, 1, c. 2, Steele ed., p. 6.
76. Bacon gives his quick description in *Communia naturalium* I, 1, c. 2, p. 9. In his *Opus tertium*, c. 13, ed. J.S. Brewer, in *Opera quaedam hactenus inedita* I

(London: Longman, Green, Longman, and Roberts, 1859), 44, Bacon says much the same.

77. See below, pp. 144–46.
78. Refer Chapter 1, p. 13.
79. See n. 72.
80. See *Opus maius* IV, section on judicial astronomy, ed Bridges, vol. 1, 238–39.
81. See Chapter 3, p. 84 (at n. 10).
82. See the long discussion in *Opus maius* IV, section on judicial astronomy, ed. Bridges, vol. 1, 239, where – as the editor notes – Bacon has in fact confused his explication by implying that the aspirate had disappeared from the instance where he actually intended it to be present. As Bridges's note also indicates, there are other places in unedited works where Bacon gets the explanation perfectly right.
83. Ibid., 240: "...falsa mathematica est ars magica."
84. For the foregoing assertions, see ibid., 240.
85. Ibid., 246. On p. 240, Bacon noted that all the attributes he was attacking "expresse asseruntur in libris magicis," by the latter phrase clearly intending to target specifically false juridical astronomy.
86. See ibid., treatise on astrology, 398.
87. See ibid., 392.
88. Ibid., 395–96.
89. See Andrew G. Molland, "Roger Bacon as Magician," *Traditio* 30 (1974): 459.
90. Bacon lays out this argument in detail in *Opus maius* IV, section on judicial astrology, ed. Bridges, vol. 1, 248.
91. Refer to *Opus maius* IV, treatise on astrology, ed. Bridges, vol. 1, 396. In his *Opus tertium*, c. 13, ed. Brewer, I, 45, Bacon accused Gratian and others of having made their overextended condemnation out of ignorance about the subject of which they were speaking
92. *Opus maius* IV, treatise on astrology, ed. Bridges, vol. 1, 398.
93. *Opus maius* IV, 2, c. 1, ed Bridges, vol. 1, 109. Bridges observes in his edition, p. 242, n. 1, that in this Part IV of the *Opus maius*, Bacon tends to reserve the word "*astronomia*" for the practical science of the stars alone. "*Astrologia*" for Bacon should thus be taken as closer to our general category of astronomy thought of as including all learning about the heavens, including our "astrology" only as a part. On the *Speculum*'s two sorts of celestial science, see Chapter 3, pp. 119–20, esp. at n. 245, and the comment in n. 250 about how some such division was standard in the thirteenth century.
94. See *Opus maius* IV, 2, c. 1, ed. Bridges, vol. 1, 109.
95. Consult, pp. 139–40, and the citation in n. 75.
96. *Opus maius* IV, 2, c. 1, ed. Bridges, vol. 1, 109–110.
97. For the following paragraph, see *Opus maius*, IV, 4, c. 5, ed. Bridges, vol. 1, 138.
98. See Bacon's comments to this effect in *Opus maius* IV, section on judicial astronomy, ed. Bridges, vol. 1, 242.

99. See Ibid., 242 and 245.
100. Ibid., 246.
101. Ibid.
102. As Bacon insisted, ibid., 249, all astrological predictions were made "salva tamen in omnibus arbitrii libertate." See also his comments on the ultimate power even of a weak will, ibid., 139.
103. *Opus maius* IV, treatise on astrology, ed. Bridges, vol. 1, 389.
104. Ibid., 388.
105. Ibid., 248.
106. See the comments, ibid., 390, where Bacon declares: "[A]stronomia regulat omnia, propter hoc quod omne opus magnificum debet fieri in temporibus electis. Et ideo...praeest omnibus scientiis in hac parte..."
107. Ibid. These were, of course, the marvelous works ("*opera miranda*") that Bacon had always listed as the last of practical astronomy's contributions – see p. 143, n. 96.
108. *Opus maius* IV, treatise on astrology, ed. Bridges, vol. 1, 394.
109. Ibid. For the reference in the *Speculum*, see Chapter 3, p. 124, at nn. 273 and 274.
110. *Opus maius* IV, treatise on astrology, ed. Bridges, vol. 1, 394.
111. See the citations given in nn. 91 and 92.
112. Refer Chapter 3, p. 119, at n. 244.
113. For the best introduction to Bacon on this score, see the discussion of Bacon in David Lindberg, *Theories of Vision from Al Kindi to Kepler* (Chicago: University of Chicago Press, 1976), as well as Lindberg's introduction to his edition of Bacon's *De multiplicatione specierum*, published under the title *Roger Bacon's Philosophy of Nature* (Oxford: Oxford University Press, 1983). In technical terms, it is important to remember that Bacon held that species spread their influence not by means of local motion, as was the case in most Aristotelianizing visions of action in the corporeal world below the moon, but rather by generation through a medium. See his comments in *Opus maius* V, 1, 9, c. 4, ed. Bridges, vol. 2, 72; as also IV, 4, c. 1, ed. Bridges, vol. 1, 127.
114. See *Opus maius* IV, 2, c. 1, ed. Bridges, vol. 1, 111, as well as the summary reference in IV, appendix, p. 396. Bacon lays out a more general defense of this theory beginning (in the part of his work devoted to the science of optics) in *Opus maius* V, 1, 5, c. 1, ed. Bridges, vol. 2, 31.
115. The following analysis depends upon Bacon's *Opus maius* IV, 3, c. 1, ed. Bridges, vol. 1, 119–20.
116. *Opus maius* IV, treatise on astrology, ed. Bridges, vol. 1, 396.
117. Ibid., 395.
118. See ibid., 399.
119. Ibid., 395.
120. *Opus maius* IV, treatise on astrology, ed. Bridges, vol. 1, 395.
121. On Thomas, see pp. 133–34 and 17.

122. Bacon, *Opus maius* IV, treatise on astrology, ed. Bridges, vol. 1, 396. The same apparent acceptance of the argument about "artificialia" would seem to be at work in a similar discussion, just a bit later, on p. 397, where Bacon was arguing against an objection not differentiating between already existing objects and newly confected ones.
123. Ibid., 396.
124. For the former phrase, see ibid., 395; for the latter, 399.
125. Ibid., 399: "Et si hujusmodi multiplicatio speciei et verbi prolatio fiant in constellatione debita, necesse est quod operatio valida consequatur; et in his omnibus nihil est magicum vel insanum."
126. For all these wonders, see ibid., 395.
127. Still the best single assessment of Bacon's "scientia experimentalis" is Jeremiah Hackett's "The Meaning of Experimental Science." Useful comments can also, however, be found in Stewart C. Easton, *Roger Bacon and his Search for a Universal Science* (New York: Columbia University Press, 1952). Less reliable by now is the classic work of Alistair C. Crombie, *Robert Grosseteste and the Origins of Experimental Science 1100–1700* (Oxford: Oxford University, 1953). There are also interesting remarks in N.W. Fisher and Sabetai Unguru, "Experimental Science and Mathematics in Roger Bacon's Thought," *Traditio* 27 (1971), esp. 367–69.
128. *Opus maius* VI, c. 2, ed. Bridges, vol. 2, 172. The references to these three in the *Opus tertium* variously name them as "*praerogativae*" and as "*dignitates*" – see, for example, *Opus tertium*, c. 13, ed. Brewer, I, 43–44.
129. *Opus maius* VI, c. 2, ed. Bridges, vol. 2, 172–73. The same point is made in *Opus tertium*, c. 13, ed. Brewer, I, 43. On the epistemic radicality of this emphasis on experience, see my comments in "Metaphysics and Science in the Thirteenth Century: William of Auvergne, Robert Grosseteste and Roger Bacon," in *Medieval Philosophy*, ed. John Marenbon, Routledge History of Philosophy, 3 (London/New York: Routledge, 1998), pp. 219–20.
130. See *Opus maius* VI, c. unnumbered, ed. Bridges, vol. 2, 202; and *Opus tertium* c. 13, ed. Brewer, I, 43.
131. *Opus maius* VI, c. unnumbered, ed. Bridges, vol. 2, 202.
132. Ibid., 215. *Opus tertium* c. 13, ed. Brewer, I, 44, explains by saying that for this part of the discipline, the subject terms of the other sciences are left behind.
133. *Opus maius* VI, c. unnumbered, ed. Bridges, vol. 2, 215. The same estimation is mentioned in passsing in *Opus maius* IV, section on judicial astronomy, ed. Bridges, vol. 1, 246; and pointedly emphasized in *Communia naturalium* I, 1, 2, ed. Steele, II, 9.
134. *Opus tertium* c. 13, ed. Brewer, I, 44.
135. For this term, "*opera miranda*," refer to *Opus maius* VI, c. unnumbered, ed. Bridges, vol. 2, 215.
136. Bacon was probably also referring to Peter in *Opus tertium*, c. 13, ed. Brewer, 46–47, where he lauded an unnamed expert in experimental science. The

only two extant works of Peter have been edited by Loris Sturlese and Ron B. Thomson as Petrus Peregrinus de Maricourt, *Opera* (Pisa: Scuola Normale Superiore, 1995). On Bacon's probable references to him, see François Picavet, "Nos vieux maîtres: Pierre de Maricourt, le Picard, et son influence sur Roger Bacon," *Revue Internationale de l'Enseignement* 54 (1907): 289–315.

137. *Opus maius* VI, c. unnumbered, ed. Bridges, vol. 2, 219.

138. See *Communia naturalium* I, 1, 2, ed. Steele, II, 9: "Sciencia Experimentalis… opera sapiencie occulta rimatur."

139. *Opus tertium* c. 13, ed. Brewer, I, 45.

140. In *Opus maius* VI, c. unnumbered, ed. Bridges, vol. 2, 216, Bacon noted, for example, that in its judicative part this last prerogative consisted of four "secret sciences" ("*scienti[ae] secret[ae]*").

141. Marcel Mauss and Henri Hubert, "Esquisse d'une théorie génèrale de la magie," originally in *Année Sociologique* (1902–1903), reprinted in *Sociologie et Anthropologie*, 1–141 (Paris: Presses Universitaires de France, 1960 [1st ed. 1950]). Despite the fact that Hubert is listed as co-author, the work is generally credited to Mauss on his own. *Sociologie et Anthropologie* has by now gone through ten editions, the latest from 2003. The following citations are taken from the 1960 edition, which retains the pagination of the 1950 first edition, as do all the others, including the tenth.

142. Mauss, "Esquisse," 134.

143. On science, see "Esquisse," 136–37, while on religion, see p. 15. At times, Mauss even seems willing to grant magic a certain parental role with regard to religion, running parallel to its relation to "science" – see ibid., 5: "La religion est sortie des échecs et des erreurs de la magie."

144. Mauss stated so explicitly at the end of his ibid., 134: "La magie est donc un phénomène social."

145. Ibid.,16.

146. For these two forms, see, for example, ibid., pp. 115 and 137, respectively.

147. Mauss announces his conviction that such a notion exists – he calls it a "*nouvel element*" in his analysis as well as, more exactly, a "*notion supérieure*" – in ibid., 100.

148. Ibid., 101.

149. See ibid., 100: "Complexe, [cette notion] comprend d'abord l'idée de pouvoir ou encore mieux, comme on l'a appelée, de 'potentialité magique.'"

150. Ibid.: "Cette notion comprend, en outre, l'idée d'un milieu où s'exercent les pouvoirs en question."

151. See "Esquisse," 105.

152. Ibid., 112.

153. Ibid.

154. Strictly speaking, this is my language, not that of Mauss. Mauss wanted to see *mana*, and thus "magic," as both the source for religion and something different from it. I prefer simply to consider "magic" and "religion" as two

complementary but different manifestations of the same special kind of force and set of circumstances.

155. The latter is exactly what Mauss, himself, says in his ibid., 16, when he avers that magic always comes down to a "rite privé, secret, mystérieux et tendant comme limite vers le rite prohibé."

156. Refer to the discussion in Chapter 2, pp. 77–80.

157. See Norman Cohn, *Europe's Inner Demons*, esp. chapters 5 and 7; and Alain Boureau, *Satan hérétique*, esp. chapters 1 and 2.

158. On the charges against and trial of Boniface (a trial that ended before a determination had been made), see Cohn, *Europe's Inner Demons*, 120–23.

159. For the trial of Guichard, see ibid., 125–30.

160. On John's judicial enterprises, see ibid., 130–34; and Boureau, *Satan hérétique*, 34–38.

161. Refer to the citation given in the following note. Of course, we have these words only as reported by the pope in his response. Since *sortilegia* might well refer just to another form of divination and not more broadly to sorcery, it is possible that the friars were concerned only with the rather narrow category of magic intended to predict the future. Almost certainly, however, they would have had in mind ceremonial forms, especially those which might be interpreted as invoking demonic aid.

162. The text is found in Joseph Hansen, *Quellen und Untersuchungen zur Geschichte des Hexenwahns und der Hexenverfolgung im Mittelalter* (Bonn: Carl Georgi, 1901), 1. It is worth quoting the relevant lines: "[I]nquisitores ipsi de [aliquibus denunciatis de divinationibus et sortilegiis], nisi manifeste haeresim saperent, ratione huiusmodi officii sibi commissi se nullatenus intromittant, sed eos relinquant suis iudicibus pena debita castigandos."

163. The text of the letter is given in Hansen, *Quellen*, 2–4. Here, see pp. 2–3.

164. Ibid., p. 3.

165. See the text in Hansen, *Quellen*, 4–5.

166. Ibid., 5.

167. See Boureau, *Le pape et les sorciers. Une consultation de Jean XXII sur la magie en 1320 (Manuscrit B.A.V. Borghese 348)* (Rome: Ecole Française de Rome, 2004), xviii.

168. Ibid., ix–x.

169. The Latin text, drawn from a single manuscript witness, appears in ibid., 3–138.

170. Ibid., 3.

171. Ibid.

172. Ibid., 3–4.

173. The analysis of invocation of demons follows Kažotić's discussion, ibid., 4.

174. Ibid., 5.

175. For this and the following discussion of baptism of images, see ibid., 5–6.

176. Refer to the text in Hansen, *Quellen*, 6–7.

177. For the analysis that follows, see the text in ibid., 5–6. As Boureau, *Satan hérétique*, 24 (and esp. n. 20 on p. 271), reminds us, there are those who doubt the authenticity of this bull. It cannot be found among the papal registers and is first explicitly mentioned by other texts only later in the century.
178. See the text, Hansen, *Quellen*, 8.
179. See Boureau, *Satan hérétique*, 23.
180. A modern edition of the last of five parts of this treatise can be found in Bernard Gui, *Manuel de l'inquisiteur*, ed. Guillaume Mollat and Georges Drioux, 2 vols. (Paris: Champion, 1926; reprinted as bound together in Les Classiques de l'Histoire de France au Moyen Age, 44 [Paris: Les Belles Lettres, 2006]). In the introduction (v. 1, p. viii), Mollat notes that the full title of the work in Latin is: *Tractatus de practica officii inquisitionis heretice pravitatis.*
181. The title Gui gave to this fifth part (see Gui, *Manuel*, ed. Mollat and Drioux [Paris, 2006], vol. 1, p. 2) is: "De modo, arte et ingenio inquirendi et examinandi hereticos credentes et complices eorumdem." Mollat notes (v. 1, pp. xxiv–xxv), that these sections were derived in part from an earlier manual for inquisitors, which we have in a manuscript of French origin from the thirteenth century. Thus, Gui is not absolutely novel in including sorcery and magic among the topics discussed in a practical handbook for inquisitors.
182. Ibid., 2, 20: "Sortilegiorum et divinationum et invocationum demonum pestis et error..."
183. Ibid.
184. Ibid., 20–22.
185. Ibid., 22.
186. For this and the following two questions, see ibid., 22.
187. Ibid., 23.
188. Ibid., 2, 50–52.
189. Ibid., 52.
190. This latter conclusion has already been put forth by Cohn in *Europe's Inner Demons*, 115–16, and reaffirmed by Michael D. Bailey, "From Sorcery to Witchcraft. Clerical Conceptions of Magic in the Later Middle Ages," *Speculum* 76 (2001), 971. On Eymeric, see the aforementioned pages by Cohn as well as the summary mention in Alan C. Kors and Edward Peters, ed., *Witchcraft in Europe, 400–1700. A Documentary History*, 2nd ed. (Philadelphia: University of Pennsylvania Press, 2001), 121–22.
191. Nicolau Eymeric, *Directorium inquisitorum* (Venice: Simone Vasalini, 1595), 335b and 338a. The text of this Venice edition is effectively identical with that of the Roman edition of 1587, down even to pagination. My references to the 1595 edition can therefore be easily tracked down in that of 1587. The 1595 edition is electronically available through Google Books.
192. Eymeric, *Directorium*, 335b.
193. On these two kinds of sorcery and divination, see ibid., 336a.

194. Ibid.
195. As Eymeric said (ibid.), such diviners were to be treated and punished as heretics "non quia sortilegi vel divinatores meri sint, sed quia haereticalia in talibus sortilegiis and divinationibus admiscentes, dicuntur sortilegi haereticales." In Part 3 of the *Directorium*, 443a, he called such persons *"magi haereticantes"* – hereticizing magicians.
196. Ibid., 338a.
197. Ibid.
198. See the listing, ibid., 338a–b.
199. Ibid., 338b.
200. Ibid.
201. For this conclusion regarding the first instance, see ibid., 338b–39a.
202. For the foregoing argument, see ibid., 339b.
203. Ibid., 342a–b.
204. For this conclusion and the argument, see the paragraph, ibid., 342b–43a.
205. Hansen, *Quellen*, 16–17.

5   The Witchcraze and the Crisis of Early Modern Europe, 1400–1650

1. Arno Borst, "Anfänge des Hexenwahns in den Alpen," in *Barbaren, Ketzer und Artisten. Welten des Mittelalters*, 284 (Munich/Zurich: Piper, 1988), was one of the first to point to the critical role in the witchcraze of the tiny territory surrounding the western Alps. More recently the same theme has been picked up by Bernard Andenmatten and Kathrin Utz Tremp, "De l'hérésie à la sorcellerie: l'inquisiteur Ulric de Torronté OP (vers 1420–1445) et l'affermissement de l'inquisition en Suisse romande," *Revue d'Histoire Ecclésiastique Suisse* 86 (1992), 98; and Martine Ostorero, *"Folâtrer avec les démons." Sabbat et chasse aux sorciers à Vevey (1448)*, 7 (Lausanne: Université de Lausanne, 1998). Andreas Blauert, in his magisterial *Frühe Hexenverfogungen. Ketzer-, Zauberei- und Hexenprozesse des 15. Jahrhunderts* (Hamburg: Junius Verlag, 1989), 8, delineated the area of origin as the territorial triangle formed by the cities of Lucerne, Lausanne and Neuchâtel.
2. See, for example, Blauert's reference, in *Frühe Hexenverfolgungen*, 51, to Joseph Hansen's impression that the witch-hunt resulted when Alpine heresy trials stumbled upon the widespread superstition of the populace in such cultural backwaters.
3. See the especially suggestive comments of Pierrette Paravy, *De la chrétienté romaine à la Réforme en Dauphine*, 2 vols. (Rome: Ecole Française de Rome, 1993), vol. 2, 785 and 903.
4. Michael D. Bailey, *Battling Demons. Witchcraft, Heresy, and Reform in the Late Middle Ages* (University Park: Pennsylvania State University Press, 2003), has done the most to stress the importance of church reforming circles in the initial stages of the witch trials.

5. See Blauert's comments on the importance of Waldensian trials in these two cities between 1400 and 1430, in *Frühe Hexenverfolgungen*, 37 and 41; as well as the introduction to Catherine Chène, Martine Ostorero, Agostino Paravicini Bagliani and Kathrin Utz Tremp, *L'imaginaire du sabbat. Edition critique des textes les plus anciens (1430 c.–1440 c.)* (Lausanne: Université de Lausanne, 1999), 11.

6. Paravy, *De la chrétienté*, 789.

7. The following account is drawn from Kathrin Utz Tremp, "Der Freiburger Waldenzerprozess von 1399 und seine Bernische Vorgeschichte," *Freiburger Geschichtsblätter* 68 (1991): 57–85.

8. See the remarks of Utz Tremp, "Der Freiburger Waldenzerprozess," 85.

9. For one of the best résumés of the whole stereotype, see the description in Cohn, *Europe's Inner Demons*, rev. ed., 144–47.

10. Pierrette Paravay's *De la chrétienté romaine*, in n. 3, constitutes a ground-breaking and paradigmatic early example. The University of Lausanne has undertaken a series of publications dealing with just this previously unexamined material.

11. This is the work referred to in n. 5.

12. The details of Nider's life have been drawn from Catherine Chène's introduction to selections from the *Formicarius*, found in Ostorero et al., *L'imaginaire*, 102–103 and 107. Much fuller information on this interesting figure can be found in Bailey's *Battling Demons* (see n. 4).

13. See Nider, *Formicarius* V, 3 (ed. Catherine Chène), in Ostorero et al., *L'imaginaire*, 150.

14. See the commentary by Catherine Chène, in *L'imaginaire*, 201 and 224.

15. Nider, *Formicarius* V, 3, in Ostorero et al., *L'imaginaire*, 150.

16. Ibid., 154.

17. Same as n. 15.

18. Nider, *Formicarius* V, 4, in Ostorero et al., *L'imaginaire*, 164.

19. Ibid., 166.

20. Ibid., 168.

21. See ibid., 170.

22. Nider, *Formicarius* V, 3, in Ostorero et al., *L'imaginaire*, 146.

23. Ibid., 148.

24. Ibid.

25. Ibid., 150–52.

26. Ibid., 154.

27. Michael Bailey, "From Sorcery to Witchcraft: Clerical Conceptions of Magic in the Later Middle Ages," *Speculum* 76 (2001): 979, has commented on how close Nider came to passing ideologically from earlier conceptions of sorcery to "full-fledged witchcraft."

28. Nider, *Formicarius* V, 3, in Ostorero et al., *L'imaginaire*, 156.

29. Bailey, *Battling Demons*, 43.

30. Nider, *Formicarius* V, 3, in Ostorero et al., *L'imaginaire*, 154.

31. Nider, *Formicarius* II, 4, in Ostorero et al., *L'imaginaire*, 134–36.
32. Ibid., 138. On this part of the "Canon Episcopi," see Chapter 2, pp. 60–62.
33. On Ulric and the territory of the Lausanne inquisition, see Andenmatten and Utz Tremp, "De l'hérésie à la sorcellerie," 70–73.
34. See the mention above, p. 165.
35. For the details of this example, consult Andenmatten and Utz Tremp, "De l'hèrèsie à la sorcellerie," 88–89.
36. See the summary of the trial in ibid., 116–17.
37. On the charges and the condemnation, see ibid., 110 and 112–13.
38. For the specific listing, see ibid., 111.
39. See ibid., 114.
40. Ibid. The text speaks of "Iaquetum douz Plain…accusatum…de heresi, ydolatria et criminibus pluribus aliis enormibus."
41. See the introduction to the text by Kathrin Utz Tremp, in *L'imaginaire*, 25–26.
42. See Fründ, ["Rapports sur la chasse aux sorciers et aux sorcières"], ed. Kathrin Utz Tremp, in *L'imaginaire*, 30.
43. See Kathrin Utz Tremp's explanation in *L'imaginaire*, 43, n. 18.
44. Fründ, ["Rapports"], ed. Utz Tremp, in *L'imaginaire*, 30–32.
45. Ibid., 34.
46. For these latter charges, see Fründ, ["Rapports"], in *L'imaginaire*, 38.
47. Ibid., 36.
48. Ibid., 36–38.
49. See pp. 169–70.
50. For these last two, see Fründ, ["Rapports"], in *L'imaginaire*, 36.
51. For this paragraph, see ibid., 32.
52. See ibid., 36.
53. In *L'imaginaire*, 37, n. 9, Utz Tremp notes that the same term emerged in the Waldensian trials at Fribourg in 1430 as a description for the assemblies of heretics.
54. On these night-flights, see Fründ, ["Rapports"], in *L'imaginaire*, 34.
55. See Andenmatten and Utz Tremp, "De l'hérésie à la sorcellerie," 81.
56. Fründ, ["Rapports"], in *L'imaginaire*, 40.
57. See *Errores gazariorum*, ed. Kathrin Utz Tremp and Martine Ostorero, in *L'imaginiaire*, 278.
58. See the "Commentaire" by Martine Ostorero, in *L'imaginaire*, 301–303.
59. See "Introduction" by Utz Tremp and Ostorero, in *L'imaginaire*, 269–70.
60. See Utz Tremp's and Ostorero's "Introduction," 271–72; and Ostorero's "Commentaire," 328–29.
61. For this speculation about Georges de Saluces and the details of his career, see Ostorero in her "Commentaire," in *L'imaginaire*, 332–34.
62. See *Errores* 10, ed. Utz Tremp and Ostorero, in *L'imaginaire*, 284.
63. *Errores* 6, ed. Utz Tremp and Ostorero, in *L'imaginaire*, 280–82.
64. *Errores* 8, ed. Utz Tremp and Ostorero, in *L'imaginaire*, 282.
65. See nn. 48, 49 and 26.

66. *Errores* 16, ed. Utz Tremp and Ostorero, in *L'imaginaire*, 286.
67. As Michael Bailey notes, *Magic and Superstition in Europe*, 135, Nicholas Jacquier's *Flagellum haereticorum fascinariorum* of 1458 is possibly the first text to use the word "sabbath" in reference to the gathering of witches.
68. On the following procedure, see *Errores* 1 and 2, in *L'imaginaire*, 278.
69. On the anti-Semitic background to the use of this word, and "sabbath" as well, to refer to the gatherings of witches, see the comments of Carlo Ginzburg, *Storia notturna. Una decifrazione del sabba* (Turin: Einaudi, 1989), 45–46 and 54–55 (in English as *Ecstasies. Deciphering the Witches' Sabbath*, trans. R. Rosenthal [New York: Pantheon, 1991], 71–72 and 80).
70. *Errores* 2–3, ed. Utz Tremp and Ostorero, in *L'imaginaire*, 278.
71. Ibid., 15, in *L'imaginaire*, 286.
72. Ibid., 3, in *L'imaginaire*, 278–80
73. Utz Tremp, "Der Freiburger Waldenserprozess," 82. On this trial, p. 165.
74. *Errores* 3, ed. Utz Tremp and Ostorero, in *L'imaginaire*, 280.
75. See p. 175.
76. *Errores* 2, ed. Utz Tremp and Ostorero, in *L'imaginaire*, 278.
77. For the details of this description, consult *Errores* 3, in *L'imaginaire*, 280.
78. For this listing, see *Errores* 2, in *L'imaginaire*, 278.
79. Ibid., 4, in *L'imaginaire*, 280.
80. See n. 57.
81. Refer to Ostorero's "Commentaire," in *L'imaginaire*, 304.
82. See p. 170, at n. 30; and p. 175, at n. 53.
83. See p. 173, at n. 38.
84. *Errores* 10, in *L'imaginaire*, 284.
85. In the description of the bacchanal cited in n. 76, the text says that the initiation having been performed, members of the group "celebrate the admission of a new heretic."
86. *Errores* 14, in *L'imaginaire*, 286, the text comments that the members of the sect call the devil presiding over them their master (*"eorum magistrum"*). There is a similar reference to *"magister presidens,"* in ibid., 2, in *L'imaginaire*, 278. For the reference in Fründ to a school, see p. 175, at n. 53.
87. Ostorero, "Commentaire," in *L'imaginaire*, 332, referring back to her own *Folâtrer*, 174 and 274.
88. See Pierrette Paravy's Introduction to the text, in *L'imaginaire*, 357.
89. Claude Tholosan, *Ut magorum et maleficiorum errores...*, ed. Pierrette Paravy, in *L'imaginaire*, 362. As Paravy explains in her Introduction (*L'imaginaire*, 359) and her commentary (*L'imaginaire*, 417), Tholosan's treatise is found as an insert in the *Quintus liber fachureriorum* (*Fifth Book on Sorcerers*), the only extant volume of the series comprising one among the registers of the Chamber of Accounts of the *baillage* or bailiwick of the Dauphiné. As high judge, Tholosan himself would have been the source of almost all the activity accounted for in the register, so it is hardly surprising to see him intruding his piece into the larger work.

90. See Tholosan, *Ut magorum* 12, ed. Paravy, in *L'imaginaire*, 374. Pierrette Paravy's *De la chrétienté romaine à la Réforme en Dauphiné*, 2 vols. (Rome: Ecole Française de Rome, 1993), book III (vol. 2: 770–905) presents an exhaustive study of the entire span of trials for sorcery, or witchcraft, in the Dauphiné in the fifteenth century, including the period when they were directed by Tholosan.

91. Tholosan, *Ut magorum* 35, in *L'imaginaire*, 414.

92. Ibid., 1, in *L'imaginaire*, 362.

93. See Tholosan, *Ut magorum* 2, in *L'imaginaire*, 362–64.

94. For all of the preceding manipulations, see *Ut magorum* 8, in *L'imaginaire*, 370.

95. On the foregoing, see *Ut magorum* 9, in *L'imaginaire*, 370.

96. See *Ut magorum* 7, in *L'imaginaire*, 368.

97. The ceremony is described in *Ut magorum* 3, in *L'imaginaire*, 364.

98. On this part of the ritual, see *Ut magorum* 4, in *L'imaginaire*, 364.

99. Ibid., 364–66.

100. The whole account of night-flight to the synagogue and the activities enacted there comes in *Ut magorum* 6, in *L'imaginaire*, 368.

101. See *Ut magorum* 5, in *L'imaginaire*, 366.

102. *Ut magorum* 14, in *L'imaginaire*, 376.

103. Tholosan, *Ut magorum* 28, in *L'imaginaire*, 402.

104. Hansen, *Quellen* (n. 24), 16–17.

105. Ibid., 17: "…sortilegi, divini, demonum invocatores, carminatores, coniuratores…utentes artibus nefariis et prohibitis…"

106. Hansen, *Quellen* (nn. 25 and 26), 17.

107. Ibid. (n. 27), 17–18.

108. Ibid. (n. 28), 18.

109. Ibid., 18. Martine Ostorero, *"Folâtrer avec les démons*, 176–78, points to this example as the first case in a text, but she notes that it is reflective of contemporary Francophone usage of the term "vaudois" in the area around Lake Leman. She draws upon her experience with inquisitional documents emerging from the trials in the 1440s in the town of Vevey.

110. See, for example, Hansen, *Quellen* (nn. 31 and 32), 19–20.

111. Ibid. (n. 38), 28.

112. For the following description, see Hansen, *Quellen* (n. 36), 25.

113. See the letter of January 31, 1500 (in Hansen, *Quellen* [n. 41], 30).

114. Bailey, *Battling Demons*, as cited in n. 4, and especially his chapter 6 (pp. 119–38).

115. See the comments of Pierrette Paravy, *De la chrétienté romaine*, 785.

116. Michael Shank, "Academic Consulting in Fifteenth-Century Vienna: The Case of Astrology," in Edith Sylla and Michael McVaugh, ed., *Texts and Contexts in Ancient and Medieval Science. Studies on the Occasion of John E. Murdoch's Seventieth Birthday*, 250–51 (Leiden/New York: Brill, 1997).

117. See Blauert's comments, in *Frühe Hexenverfolgungen*, 30 and 51.

118. For a quick survey of the dates of the European witch craze, see Brian P. Levack, *The Witch-Hunt in Early Modern Europe*, 3rd ed. (Harlow: Pearson Education Limited, 2006), 204–209.

119. Again, Levack, *Witch-Hunt*, 211–12 and 217–18; as well as the comments by William Monter, "Witch Trials in Continental Europe 1560–1660," in Bengt Ankarloo, Stuart Clark and William Monter, *Witchcraft and Magic in Europe. The Period of the Witch Trials*, 13 and 15 (London: Athlone Press, 2002).

120. See again Monter, "Witch Trials in Continental Europe," 13.

121. The quick historical overview presented in the succeeding paragraphs draws heavily upon Malcolm Gaskill, "The Pursuit of Reality: Recent Research into the History of Witchcraft," *The Historical Journal* 51 (2008), especially pp. 1069–72, though it is not completely congruent with it.

122. See especially Joseph Hansen, *Zauberwahn, Inquisition, und Hexenprozessen im Mittelalter und die Entstehung der grossen Hexenverfolgung* (Munich: R. Oldenbourg, 1900), and his collection of sources, used frequently in the present work: *Quellen*.

123. Henry Charles Lea, *Materials toward a History of Witchcraft*, ed. Arthur C. Howland (Philadelphia: University of Pennsylvania, 1939); and George Lincoln Burr, "The Literature of Witchcraft," in *Selected Writings*, ed. L. O. Gibbons, 166–89 (Ithaca: Cornell University Press, 1943) [original date: 1889], and Burr, ed., *Narratives of the Witchcraft Cases, 1648–1706* (New York: C. Scribner's Sons, 1914).

124. Jules Michelet, *La sorcière* (Paris: A. Lacroix, Verboeckhoven, 1865) (translated as *Satanism and Witchcraft. A Study in Medieval Superstition*, trans. A.R. Allinson [Seacaucus, NJ: Citadel, 1939]), and Emmanuel Le Roy Ladurie, *Les paysans de Languedoc* (Paris: Mouton, 1966), pp. 239–47.

125. See the references given in Chapter 1, nn. 1 and 6.

126. Rossell Robbins, *The Encyclopedia of Witchcraft and Demonology* (New York: Crown Publishers, 1959).

127. Cohn, *Europe's Inner Demons*, as cited on many occasions earlier.

128. Laura Stokes, *Demons of Urban Reform. Early European Witch Trials and Criminal Justice, 1430–1530* (Basingstoke: Palgrave Macmillan, 2011), 17–18, and on Basel, 47–49.

129. Stokes, *Demons of Urban Reform*, 33. On p. 178, Stokes confesses that she has relegated the influence of an "idea of diabolic witchcraft" to "secondary status."

130. Christina Larner, *Enemies of God. The Witch Hunt in Scotland*.

131. For a fuller construal of this statist argument, along with excellent bibliographical references, see Brian P. Levack, "State-Building and Witch Hunting in Early Modern Europe," in Jonathan Barry, Marianne Hester and Gareth Roberts, ed., *Witchcraft in Early Modern Europe. Studies in Culture and Belief*, 96–98 (Cambridge: Cambridge University Press, 1996).

132. Christina Larner, " '*Crimen Exceptum*'? The Crime of Witchcraft in Europe," in *Witchcraft and Religion. The Politics of Popular Belief*, 59–60 (Oxford: Basil Blackwell, 1984).

133. Stuart Clark, "Witchcraft and Magic in Early Modern Culture," in Bengt Ankarloo, Stuart Clark and William Monter, *Witchcraft and Magic in Europe. The Period of the Witch Trials*, 113 (London: Athlone Press, 2002). See also the even sharper comments of Brian Levack in "State-Building and Witch Hunting," 99 and 103; as well as in "Crime and the Law," in Jonathan Barry and Owen Davies, ed., *Palgrave Advances in Witchcraft Historiography*, 158–59.

134. See Levack, "State-Building," 99.

135. Levack, "Crime and the Law," 152–53, where he refers to Soman, "Decriminalizing Witchcraft. Does the French Experience Furnish a European Model?" *Criminal Justice History* 10 (1989): 1–22.

136. While arguing against prosecutorial pressure from the center, Levack makes just this point about the local authorities in "The Decline and End of Witchcraft Prosecutions," in Marijke Gijswijt-Hofstra, Brian P. Levack and Roy Porter, *Witchcraft and Magic in Europe. The Eighteenth and Nineteenth Centuries*, 13; as does William Monter, "Witch Trials in Continental Europe 1560–1660," in Ankarloo, Clark and Monter, *Witchcraft and Magic in Europe. The Period of the Witch Trials*, 9.

137. See Michael D. Bailey, *Magic and Superstition in Europe. A Concise History from Antiquity to the Present*, 159 and 162–69 (Lanham, MD: Rowman and Littlefield, 2007).

138. Stokes, *Demons of Reform*, 125.

139. Alan Macfarlane, *Witchcraft in Tudor and Stuart England. A Regional and Comparative Study*; and Keith Thomas, *Religion and the Decline of Magic. Studies in Popular Beliefs in Sixteenth- and Seventeenth-Century England*.

140. Especially important was Edward E. Evans-Pritchard, *Witchcraft, Oracles and Magic among the Azande* (Oxford: The Clarendon Press, 1937).

141. James Sharpe, *Instruments of Darkness. Witchcraft in England, 1550–1750* (London: Hamish Hamilton, 1996); and Robin Briggs, *Witches and Neighbors. The Social and Cultural Context of European Witchcraft*.

142. Stuart Clark, *Thinking with Demons. The Idea of Witchcraft in Early Modern Europe*.

143. Edward Bever, *The Realities of Witchcraft and Popular Magic in Early Modern Europe. Culture, Cognition, and Everyday Life* (Basingstoke: Palgrave Macmillan, 2008).

144. For a nice statement of the fact, see Robin Briggs, " 'Many Reasons Why': Witchcraft and the Problem of Multiple Explanation," in Barry, Hester and Roberts, ed., *Witchcraft in Early Modern Europe*, 49–63.

145. See, for example, Andreas Blauert on Muchembled in *Frühe Hexenverfolgungen*, 12–13, a position which, as can be seen on pp. 51 and 53–54, Blauert effectively takes up as his own.

146. See, for instance, Robert Muchembled, "The Witches of Cambrésis," in James Obelkevich, ed., *Religion and the People, 800–1700*, 222, 255–56 and 259 (Chapel Hill: University of North Carolina, 1979); and more classically in *La sorcière au village (XVe–XVIIIe siècle)*, 19, 69 and 206 (Mesnil-sur-l'Estrée: Gallimard, 1979).
147. Ostorero, *Folâtrer avec les démons*, 61–62, and also 63, where she speaks of efforts like those of Saluces as a "stratégie de contrôle des moeurs." See also Ostorero's comments on Saluces's earlier actions in Savoy, in her commentary on the *Errores gazariorum* in Ostorero, Paravicini Bagliani and Utz Tremp, ed., *L'imaginaire du sabbat*, 333.
148. Stokes, *Demons of Urban Reform*, 153.
149. Michael D. Bailey, *Magic and Superstition*, 148–49.
150. Stuart Clark, "The 'Gendering' of Witchcraft in French Demonology: Misogyny or Polarity?" *French History* 5 (1991): 426–37.
151. Michael D. Bailey, *Battling Demons*, 49–50.
152. Blauert, *Frühe Hexenverfolgungen*, 48–49; and Paravy, *De la chrétienté romaine à la Reforme*, 780.
153. Bailey draws this conclusion in *Magic and Superstition*, 148. Gerhild Scholz Williams, *Defining Dominion. The Discourses of Magic and Witchcraft in Early Modern France and Germany* 10 (Ann Arbor: University of Michigan Press, 1995), reminds us that high magic in Europe was always read as male, popular magic and sorcery generally as feminine.
154. Nancy Caciola, *Discerning Spirits. Divine and Demonic Possession in the Middle Ages* (Ithaca, NY: Cornell University Press, 2003), especially pp. 272–73 and 275–76. Caciola's findings run parallel to those, very closely related, of Dyan Elliott, *Proving Woman. Female Spirituality and Inquisitional Culture in the Later Middle Ages* (Princeton, NJ: Princeton University Press, 2004).
155. Caciola, *Discerning Spirits*, 277.
156. See the comments of Paravy, *De la chrétienté romaine*, 800–801.
157. Bailey, *Battling Demons*, 49; and also "From Sorcery to Witchcraft. Clerical Conceptions of Magic in the Later Middle Ages," *Speculum* 76 (2001): 987.
158. Williams, *Defining Dominion*, 1–2. See similar reflections by Sigrid Brauner, *Fearless Wives and Frightened Shrews. The Construction of the Witch in Early Modern Germany*, 3 and 48 (Amherst : University of Massachusetts Press, 1995).
159. Brauner, *Fearless Wives*, 5.
160. Ibid., 116. See also in the same work pp. 24, 27 and 118.
161. Robin Briggs, "'Many Reasons Why,'" 51–52.
162. Lyndal Roper puts the point well when, in *Witch Craze. Terror and Fantasy in Baroque Germany*, 121 (New Haven: Yale University Press, 2004), she remarks how the stereotypes of the witch touched a deeper nerve when they were applied to women rather than men.
163. Marianne Hester, "Patriarchal Reconstruction and Witch Hunting," in Barry, Hester and Roberts, ed., *Witchcraft in Early Modern Europe*, 293. See also

Hester's powerful *Lewd Women and Wicked Witches. A Study of the Dynamics of Male Domination* (London: Routledge, 1992).

164. Anne Llewellyn Barstow, *Witchcraze. A New History of the European Witch Hunts*, 12–13, 160 and 165 (San Francisco: Pandora, 1994).

165. See Stokes, *Demons of Urban Reform*, 178; and also the complementary analysis of R. Po-Chia Hsia, *Social Discipline in the Reformation. Central Europe 1550–1750*, 123 and 129 (New York: Routledge, 1989).

166. Christina Larner, "Witchcraft Past and Present," in *Witchcraft and Religion*, 90. See also similar comments in her *"Crimen Exceptum?"* in the same work, 66.

167. Bailey, *Magic and Superstition*, 156.

168. Blauert, *Frühe Hexenverfogungen*, 29, and his even sharper comments about the rise of the witch stereotype and an increasing monopoly of judgment and law on p. 116.

169. Jacques Chiffoleau, "Amédée VIII ou la Majesté impossible?" in Bernard Andenmatten and Agostino Paravicini Baglioni, ed., *Amédée VIII-Felix V Premier Duc de Savoie et Pape (1383–1451)*, 27–28 and 43 (Lausanne: Presses Centrales Lausanne, 1992).

170. See Ostorero, *Folâtrer avec les démons*, 28 and 30. The words in the *Statuta* are: "heretici sortilegi demonum invocatores."

171. Chiffoleau, "Amédée VIII," 43.

172. Ibid., 42 and 43. Ostorero, *"Folâtrer avec les démons"*, 57–58, makes it clear that not just princes but the lay elites in general, as in the city-states of Switzerland, were prepared to assert this power to punish the *crimen majestatis*, whether against Godly or human sovereignty.

173. Tholosan, "Ut magorum," in *L'imaginaire*, 408.

174. Ibid.

175. See Williams, *Defining Dominion*, 90 and 95.

176. Jean Bodin, *De la démonomanie des sorciers* IV, 5, 4th ed. (Lyon: Antoine de Harsy, 1598), 426. The translation is, with minor changes, taken from Randy Scott, trans., *On the Demon-Mania of Witches* (Toronto: Centre for Reformation and Renaissance Studies, 1995), as quoted in Alan C. Kors and Edward Peters, ed., *Witchcraft in Europe, 400-1700. A Documentary History*, 290–91 (Philadelphia: University of Pennsylvania Press, 2001).

6 Desacralized Science and Social Control, 1500–1700

1. See the comments of Weill-Parot, *Les "images astrologiques,"* 592 and 756.

2. See Brian P. Copenhaver, "Scholastic Philosophy and Renaissance Magic," 523.

3. Marsilio Ficino, *Three Books on Life*, ed. and trans. Carol V. Kaske and John R. Clark, Apologia (Binghamton, NY: Medieval and Renaissance Texts and Studies, 1989), p. 396, ll. 58–61 and 63–65.

4. Ficino, *Three Books*, Apologia, p. 398, ll. 75–79. On beneficial effects, see the passage cited in n. 3.
5. Ficino, *Three Books*, Apologia, p. 396, ll. 65–66.
6. On the world soul, see *Three Books* III, c. 1, p. 242.
7. For this spirit of the world, see *Three Books* III, cc. 1 and 3, pp. 246, ll. 75–79, and 254, ll. 4–7.
8. See *Three Books* III, c. 3, p. 256, ll. 24–26, on the spirit as both quintessence and heavens (*coelum*); ll. 31–33 on it as a *"corpus tenuissimum."*
9. *Three Books* III, c. 4, p. 258, ll. 1–8.
10. Ficino, *Three Books*, Apologia, p. 398, ll 86–87.
11. *Three Books* III, c. 4, p. 258, ll. 8–12.
12. Ibid., III, c. 8, p. 280, ll. 66–76. The reference to Thomas was specifically to his *Summa contra Gentiles* III, 92.
13. *Three Books* III, cc. 12 and 16, pp. 298–300, ll. 27–35, and 322, ll. 37–40.
14. Ibid., III, c. 12, p. 302, ll. 98–100.
15. Ibid., III, c. 12, p. 304, ll. 113–16.
16. *Three Books* III, c. 16, p. 386, ll. 53–55.
17. Ibid., p. 388, ll. 68-72; as well as Apologia, p. 398, ll. 70–71.
18. *Three Books*, Ad lectorem, p. 238, ll. 20–24. See the even more emphatic statement that he did not use images: ibid., III, c. 15, p. 320, ll. 109–13.
19. *Three Books* III, c 13, p. 304, ll. 1–4.
20. Ibid., III, c. 15, p. 318, ll. 85–87.
21. Ibid., p. 318, ll. 90–91, and the discussion, ll. 96–106.
22. See *Three Books* III, c. 16, p. 322, ll. 15–19 and 24–28.
23. Ibid., p. 322, ll. 40–45.
24. *Three Books* III, c. 18, p. 332, ll. 1–4 and 8–10.
25. Ibid., pp. 340–42, ll. 141–155. For Thomas on artificial forms, see Chapter 4, p. 137. See also the comments of Copenhaver, "Astrology and Magic," in Charles B. Schmitt et al., ed., *The Cambridge History of Renaissance Philosophy*, 282–83 (Cambridge: Cambridge University Press, 1988).
26. *Three Books* III, c. 16, p. 326, ll. 84–94; as well a c. 18, p. 342, ll. 164–72.
27. Ibid., III, c. 17, pp. 330–32, ll. 50–54 and 61–64.
28. On Thomas, see Chapter 4, p. 136.
29. Refer to the discussion in *Three Books* III, c. 17, pp. 328–30, ll. 1–23.
30. Ibid., III, c. 18, p. 340, ll. 135–37.
31. Ibid., p. 340, ll. 134–35.
32. *Three Books* III, c. 20, p. 352, ll. 42–53. The editors of the *Three Books*, Kaske and Clark, see here the influence upon Ficino of *Picatrix* (*Three Books*, p. 452, n. 5).
33. See the passage cited in n. 31, as well as *Three Books* III, c. 21, p. 354, ll. 1–3 and 7–9.
34. Ibid., p. 354, l. 21. See also ibid., c. 13, p. 306, ll. 22–23.
35. In *Three Books* III, c. 21, p. 356, ll. 61–62, he prefaced a long discussion of the use of songs with the words: "Sed iam ad regulas cantum sideribus accommodaturas perveniamus."

36. Ibid., p. 356, ll. 54–56.
37. Ibid., p. 362, ll. 144–45.
38. Ibid., p. 362, ll. 148–49.
39. *Three Books* III, c. 20, p. 350, ll. 30–35.
40. Ibid., ll. 23–24.
41. See ibid., p. 352, ll. 65–67. D.P. Walker, *Spiritual and Demonic Magic from Ficino to Campanella* (London: Warburg Institute, 1958), 53 and 75, asserted that in *De vita* Ficino kept to a spiritual magic of the sort where spirit itself was not a living being, but he felt that in other works he ventured into the territory of demonic magic.
42. On the publication of this work, see William Eamon, *Science and the Secrets of Nature. Books of Secrets in Medieval and Early Modern Culture* (Princeton, NJ: Princeton University Press, 1994), 199 and 203. Eamon (p. 221) notes that the fame of the work was greatly spread by the widely disseminated Antwerp edition of 1560.
43. Ibid., 202.
44. Della Porta (Porta, John Baptista), *Natural Magick in Twenty Books* (London: Thomas Young and Samuel Speed, 1658; rptd. New York: Basic Books, 1957), I, ch. 2, p. 1.
45. Ibid., p. 2.
46. Ibid.
47. *Natural Magick*, I, ch. 9, p. 14.
48. Ibid., I, ch. 2, p. 2.
49. See, for instance, Paolo Rossi, *Francesco Bacone. Dalla magia alla scienza*, rev. ed. (Turin: G. Einaudi, 1974; orig. ed. 1957), pp. 18–19 and 343–44.
50. Della Porta, *Natural Magick*, XX, ch. 5, p. 400.
51. Ibid., I, ch. 2, p. 2. Paola Zambelli, *L'ambigua natura della magia. Filosofi, streghe, riti nel Rinascimento*, 2nd ed. (Venice: Marsilio, 1996 [1st ed. Milan: Mondadori, 1991]), pp. 27–28 and 141–42, pointed out how this claim was drawn almost verbatim from Pico's *Oration*.
52. Della Porta, *Natural Magick*, Preface, p. i.
53. Ibid., I, ch. 2, p. 2.
54. Ibid., I, ch. 10, p. 15.
55. Ibid., I, title, p. 1.
56. Ibid., I, ch. 9, p. 13.
57. Ibid., I, ch. 2, p. 2.
58. Ibid., I, ch. 7, p. 8.
59. Ibid., I, ch. 9, p. 13.
60. Ibid., I, ch. 7, p. 8.
61. On compounding to produce secret operations, see *Natural Magick* I, ch. 12, p. 17; on "strange works," ibid., I, ch. 2, p. 2.
62. Ibid., I, ch. 12, p. 18. It is worth noting that Della Porta was at least aware of a sort of compounding that mixed simple substances together to aggregate their various powers. At least in theory he was willing to admit that

such mixtures drew down their ingredient virtues from the heavens, and he understood that magicians sometimes formed their compounds into images. To that degree, Della Porta seems to have countenanced a sort of astro-medical science of images of the sort that Ficino promoted. See *Natural Magick* I, ch. 18, p. 23.

63. See *Natural Magick*, XX, ch. 7, p. 404.
64. See V. Perrone Compagni, "Introduction," to Cornelius Agrippa, *De occulta philosophia libri tres* (Leiden: Brill, 1992), pp. 1–10.
65. Zambelli, *L'ambigua natura*, 148, singles out Trithemius as a promoter of ceremonial magic in the sixteenth century. Walker, *Spiritual and Demonic Magic*, 75, claimed that Agrippa picked up the trail of Ficino's second and rejected type of magic, the "profane" or demonic.
66. Agrippa, *De occulta philosophia*, ed. V. Perrone Compagni, I, ch. 2, p. 86. The textual apparatus on this page makes reference to Pico's *Oration*.
67. Agrippa, *De occulta philosophia*, I, ch. 1, p. 85.
68. Ibid., I, ch. 10, pp. 104–105.
69. See, for example, *De occulta philosophia* I, ch. 46, p. 173, ll. 15–18.
70. Ibid., I, ch. 69, p. 232, ll. 11–23.
71. Ibid., I, ch. 71, p. 235, ll. 14–17.
72. Agrippa, *De occulta philosophia*, II, ch. 29, p. 341, ll. 17–20.
73. Ibid., II, ch. 35, p. 351, ll. 20–23. Just like Ficino, Agrippa also turns to Thomas Aquinas for theoretical support in this assertion, though he cites only the *De fato*, falsely attributed to Aquinas, and not the passage from the *Summa contra gentiles*.
74. *De occulta philosophia* II, ch. 35, p. 351, l. 26–352, l. 1.
75. Ibid., p. 352, ll. 8–13.
76. See n. 67.
77. *De occulta philosophia* III, ch. 43, p. 564, ll. 20–21.
78. Ibid., III, ch. 7, p. 415, ll. 15–19.
79. Ibid., III, ch. 10, p. 423, ll. 9–17.
80. Ibid., III, ch. 7, p. 418, ll. 9–14.
81. See ibid., III, ch. 16, p. 445, ll. 11–18.
82. Ibid., III, ch. 58, p. 575, l. 22–576, l. 1.
83. Ibid., III, ch. 12, p. 435, ll. 8–10.
84. See Ibid., III, ch. 16, p. 445, ll. 18–19; and 450, ll. 13–17.
85. Ibid., III, ch. 18, p. 454, ll. 12–14.
86. Ibid., III, ch. 16, p. 446, l. 26–447, l. 2.
87. Ibid., III, ch. 32, p. 498, l. 27–499, l. 3.
88. Ibid., III, ch. 11, p. 431, ll. 10–12.
89. See the names and charts of names given, for example, in *De occulta philosophia* III, ch. 24-25, pp. 468–81.
90. Ibid., III, 24, p. 469, ll. 11–15.
91. Ibid., III, 30, p. 495, ll. 5–18.
92. Ibid., III, 32, p. 498, ll. 25–27.

93. Ibid., p. 499, ll. 3–5.

94. Ibid., p. 501, ll. 15–18.

95. See Zambelli, *L'ambigua natura*, 36.

96. Perrone Compagni, Introduction to Agrippa, *De occulta philosophia*, 5.

97. This chronological phenomenon – early doubts in the sixteenth century but practically effective skepticism only in the seventeenth – has been pointed to by Brian Levack, "The Decline and End of Witchcraft Prosecutions," in Gijswijt-Hofstra, Levack and Porter, *Witchcraft and Magic in Europe. The Eighteenth and Nineteenth Centuries*, 26.

98. See the comments of Brian P. Levack, "Crime and Law," in Barry and Davies, ed., *Palgrave Advances in Witchcraft Historiography*, 153; Edward Bever, "Witchcraft Prosecutions and the Decline of Magic," *Journal of Interdisciplinary History* 40 (2009): 269; and Stuart Clark, "Witchcraft and Magic in Early Modern Culture," in Bengt Ankarloo, Stuart Clark and William Monter, *Witchcraft and Magic in Europe. The Period of the Witch Trials* (London: Athlone Press, 2002), pp. 130–31.

99. See Brian P. Levack, "State-Building and Witch Hunting in Early Modern Europe," in Jonathan Barry, Marianne Hester and Gareth Roberts, ed., *Witchcraft in Early Modern Europe. Studies in Culture and Belief* (Cambridge: Cambridge University Press, 1996), p. 108, as well as his "Decline and End," 13.

100. Quoted here according to the translated version of the passage furnished by Gustav Henningsen, *The Witches' Advocate* (Reno : University of Nevada, 1980), pp. 178–79.

101. On these laws removing most witchcraft from the lawbooks, see Levack, "Decline and End," 75-77.

102. For an introduction to the mechanical philosophy, see Richard S. Westfall, *The Construction of Modern Science. Mechanisms and Mechanics* (New York: John Wiley and Sons, 1971), chapter 2 (pp. 25–42).

103. Robert Boyle, "About the Excellency and Grounds of the Mechanical Hypothesis," in Michael Hunter and Edward B. Davis, ed., *The Works of Robert Boyle*, vol. 8 (London: Pickering and Chatto, 2000), 105. See also, in the same work, pp. 104 and 115.

104. Boyle, "About the Excellency and Grounds," in Hunter and Davis, ed., *Works*, vol. 8, pp. 103–104.

105. Ibid., 112.

106. Ibid., 113.

107. Ibid., 116.

108. René Descartes, *Discours de la méthode* V, Etienne Gilson, introduction and notes (Paris: J. Vrin, 1964), pp. 104–105. The translation is taken from Donald A. Cress, trans., Descartes, *Discourse on the Method for Conducting One's Reason Well and for Seeking Truth in the Sciences*, 3rd ed. (Indianapolis: Hackett, 1998), p. 24.

109. For this entire discussion of disease by incantation, see Boyle, "About the Excellency and Grounds," in Hunter and Davis, ed., *Works*, vol. 8, p. 108.

110. Thomas Hobbes, *Leviathan* III, 45, ed. Edwin Curley (Indianapolis: Hackett, 1994), p. 435.

111. Ibid., p. 436.

112. Hobbes, *Leviathan* III, 45, ed. Curley, p. 441.

113. Max Weber, "Wissenschaft als Beruf," 87. Weber's first comments on "disenchantment" appeared in *The Protestant Ethic and the Spirit of Capitalism*, originally published 1904-5 as *Die protestantische Ethik und der Geist des Kapitalismus* in *Archiv für Sozialwissenschaft und Sozialpolitik*. But he worked out the full implications of the idea only in his later "Wissenschaft als Beruf."

114. Weber, "Wissenschaft als Beruf," 87.

115. Ibid., where Weber spoke of "technische Mittel und Berechnung." And he added: "Dies vor allem bedeutet die Intellektualisierung als solche."

116. The clearest statement of the importance for the new science of the alchemical traditions is William R. Newman, *Atoms and Alchemy. Chymistry and the Experimental Origins of the Scientific Revolution* (Chicago: University of Chicago, 2006). See also by Newman and Lawrence M. Principe, *Alchemy Tried in the Fire. Starkey, Boyle and the Fate of Helmontian Chemistry* (Chicago, IL: University of Chicago, 2002). The origins of an idea of a connection between alchemy and the new natural science go back several decades, to work such as that of Keith Hutchison, "What Happened to Occult Qualities in the Scientific Revolution?" *Isis* 73 (1982): 233–53; and John Henry, "Occult Qualities and the Experimental Philosophy: Active Principles in Pre-Newtonian Matter Theory," *History of Science* 24 (1986): 335–81.

117. Betty Jo Teeter Dobbs, *The Foundations of Newton's Alchemy* (Cambridge: Cambridge University, 1975), 233.

118. On these forces, the "conversion," and Newton's debt to alchemy, see Richard S. Westfall, *Never at Rest. A Biography of Isaac Newton* (Cambridge: Cambridge University, 1980), 388–90, with nearly the whole passage reproduced in Westfall's condensation of the former work, *The Life of Isaac Newton* (Cambridge: Cambridge University, 1993), 153–54. Again, the notion was not new. Refer to Westfall, "Newton and the Hermetic Tradition," in Allen G. Debus, ed., *Science, Medicine and Society in the Renaissance. Essays to Honor Walter Pagel* (New York: Neale Watson Academic Publications, 1972), 185.

119. William Monter, "Witch Trials in Continental Europe 1560–1660," in Ankarloo, Clard and Monter, *Witchcraft and Magic in Europe. The Period of the Witch Trials*, 51.

120. See Brian Levack, *The Witch-Hunt in Early Modern Europe*, 141–42 and 235.

121. Lyndal Roper, *Witch Craze. Terror and Fantasy in Baroque Germany* (New Haven, CT: Yale University, 2004), 181.

122. Anthony Fletcher, *Gender, Sex and Subordination in England 1500–1800* (New Haven, CT: Yale University, 1995), 377–78.
123. See the suggestive comments of Lyndal Roper, *Witch Craze*, 256.
124. Fletcher, *Gender, Sex and Subordination*, 283.
125. Edward Bever, in fascinating recent work, has argued to the contrary that the witch trials succeeded in drastically reducing the actual practice of witchcraft on the popular level, which he sees as more extensive than perhaps any other historian would be willing to admit. See his "Witchcraft Prosecutions and the Decline of Magic," *Journal of Interdisciplinary History* 40 (2009): 291; and even more importantly *The Realities of Witchcraft*, 413 and throughout.
126. Owen Davies, *Witchcraft, Magic and Culture 1736–1951*, 6.
127. Brian Levack, "Decline and End," 46.
128. Davies, *Witchcraft*, 119.
129. See Judith Devlin, *The Superstitious Mind. French Peasants and the Supernatural in the Nineteenth Century* (New Haven, Conn.: Yale University, 1987), esp. chapter 2 on "Traditional Medicine."
130. See Raisa Maria Toivo, "Marking (dis)order: Witchcraft and the Symbolics of Hierarchy in Late Seventeenth- and Early Eighteenth-Century Finland," in Davies and de Blécourt, ed., *Beyond the Witch Trials. Witchcraft and Magic in Enlightenment Europe*, 9–10.
131. See the comments of Owen Davies and Willem de Blécourt about current scholarship in "Introduction," to Davies and de Blécourt, ed., *Beyond the Witch Trials*, 7.
132. Davies, *Witchcraft, Magic and Culture*, 76.
133. Hobbes, *Leviathan* I, 13, 1, ed. Curley, p. 74.
134. Ibid., I, 13, 3 and 8, pp. 75–76.
135. Ibid., I, 13, 9, p. 76.
136. Ibid., I, 13, 14, p. 78.
137. Hobbes, *Leviathan* I, 14, 4 and 5, ed. Curley, p. 80.
138. Ibid., I, 14, 18–19, pp. 84–85.
139. For the establishment of the Commonwealth and the erection of the Sovereign, see the important passage, *Leviathan* II, 17, 13 and 14, ed. Curley, p. 109.
140. Ibid.
141. Hobbes, *Leviathan* I, 15, 1, ed. Curley, p. 89.
142. Ibid., I, 15, 3, p. 89.
143. Hobbes, *Leviathan* II, 18, 3, ed. Curley, p. 111.
144. See Peter Laslett in the Introduction to his edition of John Locke, *Two Treatises of Government. A Critical Edition with an Introduction and Apparatus Criticus* (Cambridge: Cambridge University, 1960), pp. 33–37 and 45–66.
145. John Locke, *Second Treatise of Government* II, 4, ed. C.B. Macpherson (Indianapolis: Hackett, 1980), p. 8.
146. Locke, *Second Treatise* II, 6, p. 9.

147. As Locke says in the *Second Treatise* II, 7, p. 9, this second law arises from a nature "which willeth the peace and *preservation of all mankind.*"
148. Locke, *Second Treatise* II, 8, p. 10.
149. *Second Treatise* IX, 128, p. 67.
150. See Locke's comments, *Second Treatise* III, 19, ed. Macpherson, p. 15.
151. Locke, *Second Treatise* V, 27, p. 19.
152. *Second Treatise* IX, 123, p. 66.
153. *Second Treatise* VII, 89, p. 48.
154. *Second Treatise* IX, 129–30, p. 67.
155. *Second Treatise* XI, 138, p. 73.
156. *Second Treatise* VII, 87, pp. 46–47.
157. Ibid., VII, 90–91, pp. 48–49.
158. See Locke's comments on the legislative power when it acts to deprive members of the community of their property: *Second Treatise* XIX, 222, p. 111.

Bibliography

Primary sources

Adelard of Bath. *Die Quaestiones naturales*. Ed. Martin Müller. Beiträge 31, 2. Münster: Aschendorff, 1934.

Aelfric. *De auguriis*. In Walter W. Skeat, ed. *Aelfric's Lives of Saints*, vol. 2 (Early English Text Society 82), 364–83. Oxford: Oxford University Press, 1885/repr. same press, 1966.

——. *The Sermones catholici, or Homilies*. Ed. Benjamin Thorpe. 2 vols. London: Aelfric Society, 1844 and 1846/repr. Hildesheim: Georg Olms, 1983.

Agrippa of Nettesheim, Heinrich Cornelius. *De occulta philosophia libri tres*. Ed. V. Perrone Compagni. Leiden: Brill, 1992.

Al-Farabi. *Uber den Ursprung der Wissenschaften (De ortu scientarum). Eine mittelalterliche Einleitungsschrift in die philosophischen Wissenschaften*. Ed. Clemens Baeumker. Beiträge 19, 3. Münster: Aschendorff, 1916.

Al-Kindi. *De radiis*. Ed. Marie-Thérèse d'Alverny and Françoise Hudry. In "Al-Kindi, *De radiis*," *Archives d'Histoire Doctrinale et Littéraire du Moyen Age* 41 (1974): 139–260.

Augustine. *De civitate Dei*. Ed. Emanuel Hofmann. CSEL, 40.1. Vienna: F. Tempsky, 1899–1900.

——. *De doctrina christiana*. Ed. and trans. R.P.H. Green. Oxford: Clarendon Press, 1995.

Bacon, Roger. *Communia naturalium*. In *Opera hactenus inedita Rogeri Baconi*, ed. Robert Steele, fasc. II–IV. Oxford: Clarendon Press, n.d., 1911, 1913.

——. *The "Opus majus" of Roger Bacon*. Ed. John Henry Bridges. 2 vols. and supplement. Oxford: Clarendon Press, 1897, and London: Williams and Norgate, 1900.

——. *Opus tertium*. In *Opera quaedam hactenus inedita*, ed. J.S. Brewer, I, 3–310. London: Longman, Green, Longman, and Roberts, 1859.

Bodin, Jean. *De la démonomanie des sorciers*. Lyon: Antoine de Harsy, 1598.

——. *On the Demon-Mania of Witches*. Trans. Randy Scott. Toronto: Centre for Reformation and Renaissance Studies, 1995.

Boureau, Alain, ed. *Le pape et les sorciers. Une consultation de Jean XXII sur la magie en 1320 (Manuscrit B.A.V. Borghese 348)*. Rome: Ecole Française de Rome, 2004.

Boyle, Robert. "About the Excellency and Grounds of the Mechanical Hypothesis." In *The Works of Robert Boyle*, ed. Michael Hunter and Edward B. Davis, 8, 99–116. London: Pickering and Chatto, 2000.

Burchard of Worms. *Poenitentiale Ecclesiarum Germaniae* (*Corrector et medicus*). In *Die Bussbücher und das kanonische Bussverfahren*, ed. Herman J. Schmitz (vol. 2 of *Die Bussbücher und die Bussdisciplin der Kirche*), 403–67. Mainz: Franz Kirchheim, 1898; repr. Graz: Akademische Druck- und Verlagsanstalt, 1958.

Busson, J., and A. Ledru, ed. *Actus pontificum Cenomannis in urbe degentium*, Archives Historiques du Maine, 2. Le Mans: Société Historique de la Province du Mans, 1901.

Chène, Catherine, Martine Ostorero, Agostino Paravicini Bagliani and Kathrin Utz Tremp, ed. *L'imaginaire du sabbat. Edition critique des textes les plus anciens (1430 c.-1440 c.)*. Lausanne: Université de Lausanne, 1999.

Cicero. *Opera philosopha et politica*. Ed. J.G. Baiter. Vol. 8. Leipzig: Bernhard Tauchnitz, 1863.

Cockayne, T.O. *Leechdoms, Wortcunning and Starcraft of Early England*. Chronicles and Memorials, 3. London: Longman, Green, Longman, Roberts and Green, 1866.

Daniel of Morley. "Liber de naturis inferiorum et superiorum." Ed. Karl Sudhoff. *Archiv für die Geschichte der Naturwissenschaften und der Technik* 8 (1917): 1–40.

——. "Philosophia." Ed. Gregor Maurach. *Mittellateinisches Jahrbuch* 14 (1979): 204–55.

Della Porta, Giambattista (Porta, John Baptista). *Natural Magick in Twenty Books*. London: Thomas Young and Samuel Speed, 1658; repr. New York: Basic Books, 1957.

Descartes, René. *Discours de la méthode*. Intro. and notes by Etienne Gilson. Paris: J. Vrin, 1964.

——. *Discourse on the Method for Conducting One's Reason Well and for Seeking Truth in the Sciences*. Trans. Donald A. Cress. 3rd ed. Indianapolis: Hackett, 1998.

Driscoll, Daniel J., ed. *The Sworn Book of Honourius the Magician, As Composed by Honourius through Counsel with the Angel Hocroell*. Gillette, NJ: Heptangle Press, 1977; repr. 1983.

Eymeric, Nicolau. *Directorium inquisitorum*. Venice: Simone Vasalini, 1595.

Ficino, Marsilio. *Three Books on Life*. Ed. and trans. Carol V. Kaske and John R. Clark. Binghamton, NY: Medieval and Renaissance Texts and Studies, 1989.

Grosseteste, Robert. *Hexaëmeron*. Ed. Richard C. Dales and Servus Gieben. London: Oxford University Press, 1982.

Gui, Bernard. *Manuel de l'inquisiteur*. Ed. Guillaume Mollat and Georges Drioux. 2 vols. Paris: Champion, 1926; repr. in Les Classiques de l'Histoire de France au Moyen Age, 44, Paris: Les Belles Lettres, 2006.

Gundissalinus, Dominicus. *De divisione philosophiae*. Ed. Ludwig Baur. Beiträge 4, 2-3. Münster: Aschendordff, 1903.

——. *De divisione philosophiae/Uber die Einteilung der Philosophie*. Ed. and trans. Alexander Fidora and Dorothée Werner. Freiburg im Breisgau: Herder, 2007.

——. *De scientiis*. Ed. Manuel A. Alonso. Madrid: Escuelas de Estudios Arabes, 1954.

Hansen, Joseph. *Quellen und Untersuchungen zur Geschichte des Hexenwahns und der Hexenverfolgung im Mittelalter*. Bonn: Carl Georgi, 1901.

Hedegård, Gösta, ed. *Liber iuratus Honorii. A Critical Edition of the Latin Version of the Sworn Book of Honorius*, Studia Latina Stockholmiensia, 18. Stockholm: Almqvist and Wiksell International, 2002.

Hobbes, Thomas. *Leviathan*. Ed. Edwin Curley. Indianapolis: Hackett, 1994.

Hugh of St. Victor. *Didascalicon*. Ed. Charles H. Buttimer. Washington, DC: Catholic University Press, 1939.

Ibn Wahshīyah. *Kitāb al-Filāhah al-Nabatīyah. L'Agriculture nabatéenne*. Ed Tawfīq Fahd. 3 vols. Damascus: Al-Ma'had al-'llmī al Faransī, 1993–1998.

Isidore of Seville. *Etymologiae*. Ed. José Oroz Reta and Manuel Marcos Casquero. 2 vols. Madrid: Editorial Católica, 1982–83.

Kors, Alan C., and Edward Peters, ed. *Witchcraft in Europe 400–1700. A Documentary History*. 2nd ed. Philadelphia: University of Pennsylvania Press, 2001.

Lacnunga. In *Anglo-Saxon Magic and Medicine*, ed. J.H.G. Gratton and Charles Singer, Part II. London: Oxford University Press, 1952.

Lewis, Charlton T., and Charles Short. *A Latin Dictionary*. Oxford: Clarendon Press, 1966.

Locke, John. *Second Treatise of Government*. Ed. C.B. Macpherson. Indianapolis: Hackett, 1980.

Minucius Felix. *Octavius*. Ed. Jean Beaujeu. Paris: Société "Les Belles Lettres," 1964.

Peter Peregrinus of Maricourt. *Opera*. Ed. Loris Sturlese and Ron B. Thomson. Pisa: Scuola Normale Superiore, 1995.

Peters, Edward. *Heresy and Authority in Medieval Europe. Documents in Translation*. Philadelphia: University of Pennsylvania Press, 1980.

Pingree, David, ed. *Picatrix. The Latin Version of the Ghāyat Al-Hakīm*. London: The Warburg Institute, 1986.

Pope, John C., ed. *Homilies of Aelfric. A Supplementary Collection*, 2 vols. Early English Text Society, 259 and 260. Oxford: Oxford University Press, 1967 and 1968.

Regino of Prüm. *Libri duo de synodalibus causis et disciplinis ecclesiasticis/Das Sendhandbuch des Regino von Prüm*. Ed. Wilfried Hartmann. Darmstadt: Wissenschaftliche Buchgesellschaft, 2004.

Rodenberg, Carl, ed. *Epistolae saeculi XIII e regestis pontificum Romanorum*, Monumenta Germaniae Historica, Epistolae. Berlin: Weidmann, 1883.

Schroeder, H.J. *Disciplinary Decrees of the General Councils. Texts, Translation and Commentary*. St. Louis, MO: B. Herder Book Co., 1937.

Speculum astronomiae. Ed. Stefano Caroti, Michela Pereira and Stefano Zamponi, under the direction of Paola Zambelli. Pisa: Domus Galilaeana, 1977.

Thomas Aquinas. "De operationibus occultis naturae ad quendam militem ultramontanum." In *Opera Omnia* (Leonine edition), 43, 181–86. Rome: Editori di San Tommaso, 1976.

——. *Summa contra gentiles*. Turin: Marietti, 1935.

——. *Summa theologiae*. In *Opera Omnia* (Leonine edition), 4–12. Rome: Typographia Polyglotta, 1888–1906.

Véronèse, Julien, ed. *L'Ars notoria au Moyen Age. Introduction et édition critique*, Micrologus's Library. Florence: SISMEL/Edizioni del Galluzzo, 2007.

Wakefield, Walter L., and Austin P. Evans, ed. and trans. *Heresies of the High Middle Ages*. New York: Columbia University Press, 1969.

William of Auvergne. *De anima*. In *Opera omnia*, II, supp., 65-228. Orleans: F. Hotot, 1674; repr. Frankfurt am Main, 1963.

——. *De legibus*. In *Opera omnia*, I, 18-102. Orleans: F. Hotot, 1674; repr. Frankfurt am Main: Minerva, 1963.

——. *De universo*. In *Opera omnia*, I, 593-1074. Orleans: F. Hotot, 1674; Frankfurt am Main: Minerva, 1963.

Secondary sources

Ackermann, Silke. "Empirie oder Theorie? Der Fixsternkatalog des Michael Scotus." In *Federico II e le nuove culture*, Atti del XXXI Convegno Storico Internazionale, Todi, 9–12 October 1994, 287–302. Spoleto: Centro Italiano di Studi sull'Alto Medioevo, 1995.

Andenmatten, Bernard, and Kathrin Utz Tremp. "De l'hérésie à la sorcellerie: l'inquisiteur Ulric de Torronté OP (vers 1420–1445) et l'affermissment de l'inquisition en Suisse romande." *Revue d'Histoire Ecclésiastique Suisse* 86 (1992): 98.

Bailey, Michael D. *Battling Demons. Witchcraft, Heresy, and Reform in the Late Middle Ages*. University Park: Pennsylvania State University Press, 2003.

——. "From Sorcery to Witchcraft. Clerical Conceptions of Magic in the Later Middle Ages." *Speculum* 76 (2001): 960–90.

——. *Magic and Superstition in Europe. A Concise History from Antiquity to the Present*. Lanham, MD: Rowman and Littlefield, 2007.

Barber, Malcolm. *The Cathars*. Harlow, England: Pearson Education, 2000.

Barry, Jonathan, and Owen Davies, ed. *Palgrave Advances in Witchcraft Historiography*. Basingstoke: Palgrave Macmillan, 2007.

Barstow, Anne Llewellyn. *Witchcraze. A New History of the European Witch Hunts*. San Francisco: Pandora, 1994.

Bever, Edward. *The Realities of Witchcraft and Popular Magic in Early Modern Europe. Culture, Cognition, and Everyday Life*. Basingstoke: Palgrave Macmillan, 2008.

——. "Witchcraft Prosecutions and the Decline of Magic." *Journal of Interdisciplinary History* 40 (2009): 263–93.

Biller, Peter. "Heresy and Literacy: Earlier History of the Theme." In *Heresy and Literacy, 1000–1350*, ed. Peter Biller and Anne Hudson, 1–18. Cambridge: Cambridge University Press, 1994.

Blauert, Andreas. *Frühe Hexenverfolgungen. Ketzer-, Zauberei- und Hexenprozesse des 15. Jahrhunderts.* Hamburg: Junius Verlag, 1989.

Borst, Arno. "Anfänge des Hexenwahns in den Alpen." In *Barbaren, Ketzer und Artisten. Welten des Mittelalters,* 262–86. Munich/Zurich: Piper, 1988.

——. *Die Katharer.* Stuttgart: Hiersemann, 1953.

Boudet, Jean-Patrice. *Entre science et nigromance. Astrologie, divination et magie dans l'Occident médiéval (XIIe–Xve siècle).* Paris: Publications de la Sorbonne, 2006.

——. "Magie théurgique, angélologie et vision béatifique dans le *Liber sacratus sive juratus* attribué a Honorius de Thèbes." *Mélanges de l'Ecole Française de Rome. Moyen Age* 114 (2002): 851–90.

Boureau, Alain. *Satan hérétique. Naissance de la démonologie dans l'Occident mediéval, 1280–1330.* Paris: Odile Jacob, 2004.

——. *Satan the Heretic.* Trans. Teresa L. Fagan. Chicago, IL: University of Chicago Press, 2006.

Brauner, Sigrid. *Fearless Wives and Frightened Shrews. The Construction of the Witch in Early Modern Germany.* Amherst: University of Massachusetts Press, 1995.

Briggs, Robin. "'Many Reasons Why': Witchcraft and the Problem of Multiple Explanation." In *Witchcraft in Early Modern Europe. Studies in Culture and Belief,* ed. Jonathan Barry, Marianne Hester and Gareth Roberts, 49–63. Cambridge: Cambridge University Press, 1996.

——. *Witches and Neighbors. The Social and Cultural Context of European Witchcraft.* London: Viking, 1996.

Brown, Peter. *The Cult of the Saints.* Chicago, IL: University of Chicago Press, 1981.

——. *The World of Late Antiquity AD 150–750.* New York: Harcourt Brace Jovanovich, 1974.

Burke, Peter. *Popular Culture in Early Modern Europe.* New York: Harper and Row, 1978.

Burnett, Charles. "Michele Scoto e la diffusione della cultura scientifica." In *Federico II e le scienze,* ed. Pierre Toubert and Agostino Paravicini Bagliani, 371–94. Palermo: Sallerio, 1994.

——. "Talismans: Magic as Science? Necromancy among the Seven Liberal Arts." In *Magic and Divination in the Middle Ages,* article 1. Aldershot: Variorum, 1996.

Burr, George Lincoln. "The Literature of Witchcraft." In *Selected Writings,* ed. L.O. Gibbons, 166–89. Ithaca, NY: Cornell University Press, 1943.

——, ed. *Narratives of the Witchcraft Cases, 1648–1706.* New York: C. Scribner's Sons: 1914.

Caciola, Nancy. *Discerning Spirits. Divine and Demonic Possession in the Middle Ages.* Ithaca, NY: Cornell University Press, 2003.

Cameron, Euan. *Enchanted Europe. Superstition, Reason, and Religion, 1250–1750.* Oxford: Oxford University Press, 2010.

Caroti, Stefano. "L'astrologia." In *Federico e le scienze,* ed. Pierre Toubert and Agostino Paravicini Bagliani, 138–51. Palermo: Sallerio, 1994.

Chenu, Marie-Dominique. *Nature, Man and Society in the Twelfth Century.* Trans. Jerome Taylor and Lester K. Little. Toronto: University of Toronto, 1997.

——. *La théologie au douzième siècle.* 2nd ed. Paris: J. Vrin, 1966.

Chiffoleau, Jacques. "Amédée VIII ou la Majesté impossible?" In *Amédée VIII-Félix V Premier Duc de Savoie et Pape (1383–1451),* ed. Bernard Andenmatten and Agostino Paravicini Baglioni, 19–49. Lausanne: Presses Centrales Lausanne, 1992.

Clark, Stuart. "The 'Gendering' of Witchcraft in French Demonology: Misogyny or Polarity?" *French History* 5 (1991): 426–37.

——. *Thinking with Demons. The Idea of Witchcraft in Early Modern Europe.* Oxford: Oxford University Press, 1997.

——. "Witchcraft and Magic in Early Modern Culture." In *Witchcraft and Magic in Europe. The Period of the Witch Trials,* ed. Bengt Ankarloo, Stuart Clark and William Monter, 97–169. London: Athlone Press, 2002.

Cohn, Norman. *Europe's Inner Demons.* New York: Basic Books, 1973; rev. ed. Chicago, IL: University of Chicago Press, 1993.

Copenhaver, Brian P. "Astrology and Magic." In *The Cambridge History of Renaissance Magic,* ed. Charles B. Schmitt et al., 264–300. Cambridge: Cambridge University Press, 1988.

——. "Natural Magic, Hermetism and Early Modern Science: The 'Yates Thesis'" In *Reappraisals of the Scientific Revolution,* ed. David C. Lindberg and Robert S. Westman, 261–301. Cambridge: Cambridge University Press, 1990. [Repr. in Brian P. Levack, ed., *Renaissance Magic,* Articles on Witchcraft, Magic and Demonology. New York: Garland Publishing Co., 1992.]

——. "Scholastic Philosophy and Renaissance Magic in the *De vita* of Marsilio Ficino." *Renaissance Quarterly* 37 (1984): 523–54.

Crawford, Jane. "Evidences for Witchcraft in Anglo-Saxon England." *Medium Aevum* 32 (1963), 99–116

Crombie, Alistair C. *Robert Grosseteste and the Origins of Experimental Science 1100–1700.* Oxford: Oxford University Press, 1953.

Dales, Richard C. *The Scientific Achievement of the Middle Ages.* Philadelphia: University of Pennsylvania Press, 1973.

Davies, Anthony. "Witches in Anglo-Saxon England. Five Case Histories." In *Superstition and Popular Medicine in Anglo-Saxon England,* ed. D.G. Scragg, 41–56. Manchester: Manchester Centre for Anglo-Saxon Studies, 1989.

Davies, Owen. *Witchcraft, Magic and Culture, 1736–1951.* Manchester: Manchester University Press, 1999.

Davies, Owen, and Willem de Blécourt, ed. *Beyond the Witch Trials. Witchcraft and Magic in Enlightenment Europe.* Manchester: Manchester University Press, 2004.

Debus, Allen G. *The English Paracelsians.* London: Oldbourne, 1965.

Delaruelle, Etienne. "La pietà popolare nel secolo XI." In *Relazioni del X Congresso internazionale di scienze storiche,* vol. III, 309–32. Florence: Sansoni, 1955.

——. *La pieté populaire au moyen âge.* Turin: Bottega d'Erasmo, 1975.

Delumeau, Jean. "Déchristianisation ou nouvelle modèle de christianisme?" *Archives de Sciences Sociales des Religions* 40 (1975): 3–20.

Devlin, Judith. *The Superstitious Mind. French Peasants and the Supernatural in the Nineteenth Century*. New Haven, CT: Yale University Press, 1987.

Dobbs, Betty Jo Teeter. *The Foundations of Newton's Alchemy*. Cambridge: Cambridge University Press, 1975.

Duffy, Eamon. *The Stripping of the Altars. Traditional Religion in England c. 1400–c. 1580*. 2nd ed. New Haven, CT: Yale University Press, 2005.

Eamon, William. *Science and the Secrets of Nature. Books of Secrets in Medieval and Early Modern Culture*. Princeton, NJ: Princeton University Press, 1994.

Easton, Stewart C. *Roger Bacon and his Search for a Universal Science*. New York: Columbia University Press, 1952.

Elliott, Dyan. *Proving Woman. Female Spirituality and Inquisitional Culture in the Later Middle Ages*. Princeton, NJ: Princeton University Press, 2004.

Evans-Pritchard, Edward E. *Witchcraft, Oracles and Magic among the Azande*. Oxford: Clarendon Press, 1937.

Fidora, Alexander, and M.J. Soto Bruna. " 'Gundisalvus ou Dominicus Gundisalvi?' Algunas observaciones sobre un reciente artículo de Adeline Rucquoi." *Estudios Eclesiásticos* 76 (2001): 467–73.

Filotas, Bernadette. *Pagan Survivals, Superstitions and Popular Cultures in Early Medieval Pastoral Literature*. Toronto: Pontifical Institute of Medieval Studies, 2005.

Finucane, Ronald C. *Miracles and Pilgrims. Popular Beliefs in Medieval England*. Totowa, NJ: Rowman and Littlefield, 1977.

Fisher, N.W., and Sabetai Unguru. "Experimental Science and Mathematics in Roger Bacon's Thought." *Traditio* 27 (1971): 353–78.

Fletcher, Anthony. *Gender, Sex and Subordination in England 1500-1800*. New Haven, CT: Yale University Press, 2004.

Flint, Valerie I.J. *The Rise of Magic in Early Medieval Europe*. Princeton, NJ: Princeton University Press, 1991.

Fögen, Marie Theres. *Die Enteignung der Wahrsager. Studien zum kaiserlichen Wissenschaftsmonopol in der Spätantike*. Frankfurt am Main: Suhrkamp, 1993.

Frazer, James G. *The Golden Bough*. 3rd ed. 13 vols. New York: Macmillan, 1935.

Gaskill, Malcolm. "The Pursuit of Reality: Recent Research into the History of Witchcraft." *The Historical Journal* 51 (2008): 1069–88.

Gijswijt-Hofstra, Marijke, Brian P. Levack and Roy Porter. *Witchcraft and Magic in Europe. The Eighteenth and Nineteenth Centuries*. London: The Athlone Press, 1999.

Ginzburg, Carlo. *Ecstasies. Deciphering the Witches' Sabbath*. Trans. R. Rosenthal. New York: Pantheon, 1991.

———. *The Night Battles. Witchcraft and Agrarian Cults in the Sixteenth and Seventeenth Centuries*. Trans. John and Anne Tedeschi. Baltimore, MD: Johns Hopkins University Press, 1983.

———. *Storia notturna. Una decifrazione del sabba*. Turin: Einaudi, 1989/1995.

Given, James. *Inquisition and Medieval Society. Power, Discipline and Resistance in Languedoc*. Ithaca, NY: Cornell University Press, 1997.

Graham, William A. *Beyond the Written Word. Oral Aspects of Scripture in the History of Religion*. Cambridge: Cambridge University Press, 1987.

Gregory, Tullio. *Anima mundi. La filosofia di Guglielmo di Conches e la scuola di Chartres*. Florence: Sansoni, 1955.

Grodzynski, Denise. "Superstitio." *Revue des Etudes Anciennes* 76 (1974): 36–60.

Hackett, Jeremiah M.G. "The Meaning of Experimental Science (*Scientia Experimentalis*) in the Philosophy of Roger Bacon." PhD thesis, University of Toronto, 1983.

Halleux, Robert. "L'alchemia." In *Federico II e le scienze*, ed. Pierre Toubert and Agostino Paravicini Bagliani, 152–61. Palermo: Sollerio, 1994.

Hansen, Joseph. *Zauberwahn, Inquisition, und Hexenprozessen im Mittelalter und die Entstehung der grossen Hexenverfolgung*. Munich: R. Oldenbourg, 1900.

Harmening, Dieter. *Superstitio. Uberlieferungs- und theoriegeschichtliche Untersuchungen zur kirchlich-theologischen Aberglaubensliteratur des Mittelalters*. Berlin: Erich Schmidt Verlag, 1979.

Haskins, Charles Homer. *The Renaissance of the Twelfth Century*. Cambridge, MA: Harvard University Press, 1927.

——. *Studies in the History of Medieval Science*. Cambridge, MA: Harvard University Press, 1924.

Henningsen, Gustav. *The Witches' Advocate*. Reno: University of Nevada Press, 1980.

Henry, John. "Occult Qualities and the Experimental Philosophy: Active Principles in Pre-Newtonian Matter Theory." *History of Science* 24 (1986): 335–81.

Hester, Marianne. *Lewd Women and Wicked Witches. A Study of the Dynamics of Male Domination*. London: Routledge, 1992.

——. "Patriarchal Reconstruction and Witch Hunting." In *Witchcraft in Early Modern Europe. Studies in Culture and Belief*, ed. Jonathan Barry, Marianne Hester and Gareth Roberts, 288–306. Cambridge: Cambridge University Press, 1996.

Hinnebusch, William A. *The History of the Domincan Order*. 2 vols. New York: Alba House, 1975.

Hopkin, Charles Edward. *The Share of Thomas Aquinas in the Growth of the Witchcraft Delusion*. Philadelphia: University of Pennsylvania Press, 1940; repr. New York, 1982.

Hsia, R. Po-Chia. *Social Discipline in the Reformation. Central Europe 1550–1750*. New York: Routledge, 1989.

Hudson, Anne. "'Laicus litteratus': The Paradox of Lollardy." In *Heresy and Literacy, 1000–1350*, ed. Peter Biller and Anne Hudson, 222–36. Cambridge: Cambridge University Press, 1994.

Hutchison, Keith. "What Happened to Occult Qualities in the Scientific Revolution?" *Isis* 73 (1982): 233–53.

Jacob, Margaret C. *The Cultural Meaning of the Scientific Revolution*. New York: A.A. Knopf, 1988.

Jolly, Karen Louise. *Popular Religion in Late Saxon England. Elf Charms in Context.* Chapel Hill: University of North Carolina Press, 1996.

Karras, Ruth Mazo. "Pagan Survivals and Syncretism in the Conversion of Saxony." *The Catholic Historical Review* 72 (1986): 553–72.

Kelly, Henry A. *Satan. A Biography.* Cambridge: Cambridge University Press, 2006.

Kieckhefer, Richard. "The Devil's Contemplatives: The *Liber iuratus*, the *Liber visionum* and Christian Appropriation of Jewish Occultism." In *Conjuring Spirits. Texts and Traditions of Medieval Ritual Magic*, ed. Claire Fanger, 250–65. University Park: Pennsylvania State University Press, 1998.

——. *European Witch Trials. Their Foundations in Popular and Learned Culture, 1300–1500.* Berkeley: University of California Press, 1976.

——. "Mythologies of Witchcraft in the Fifteenth Century." *Magic, Ritual, and Witchcraft* (Summer 2006): 79–107.

Klaniczay, Gábor. *The Uses of Supernatural Power.* Princeton, NJ: Princeton University Press, 1990.

Koyré, Alexandre. *From the Closed World to the Infinite Universe.* Baltimore, MD: Johns Hopkins University Press, 1957.

Kuhn, Thomas S. *The Copernican Revolution. Planetary Astronomy in the Development of Western Thought.* Cambridge, MA: Harvard University Press, 1957.

Lambert, Malcolm D. *The Cathars.* Oxford: Oxford University Press, 1998.

Larner, Christina. "'Crimen Exceptum'? The Crime of Witchcraft in Europe." In *Witchcraft and Religion. The Politics of Popular Belief*, 35–67. Oxford: Basil Blackwell, 1984.

——. *Enemies of God. The Witch Hunt in Scotland.* London: Chatto and Windus, 1981.

——. "Witchcraft Past and Present." In *Witchcraft and Religion. The Politics of Popular Belief*, 79–91. Oxford: Basil Blackwell, 1984.

Laslett, Peter. "Introduction." In John Locke, *Two Treatises of Government. A Critical Edition with an Introduction and Apparatus Criticus*, ed. Peter Laslett, 1–145. Cambridge: Cambridge University Press, 1960.

——. *The World We Have Lost.* 2nd ed. New York: Charles Scribner's Sons, 1971.

Le Roy Ladurie, Emmanuel. *Les paysans de Languedoc.* Paris: Mouton, 1966.

Lea, Henry Charles. *Materials toward a History of Witchcraft.* Ed. Arthur C. Howland. Philadelphia: University of Pennsylvania, 1939.

Lecouteux, Claude. *Chasses fantastiques et cohortes de la nuit au moyen âge.* Paris: Imago, 1999.

Levack, Brian P. "Crime and the Law." In *Palgrave Advances in Witchcraft Historiography*, ed. Jonathan Barry and Owen Davies, 146–63. Basingstoke: Palgrave Macmillan, 2007.

——. "The Decline and End of Witchcraft Prosecutions." In Marijke Gijswijt-Hofstra, Brian P. Levack and Roy Porter, *Witchcraft and Magic in Europe. The Eighteenth and Nineteenth Centuries*, 1–93. London: Athlone Press, 1999.

——. "State-Building and Witch Hunting in Early Modern Europe." In *Witchcraft in Early Modern Europe. Studies in Culture and Belief*, ed. Jonathan Barry, Marianne

Hester and Gareth Roberts, 96–115. Cambridge: Cambridge University Press, 1996.

——. *The Witch-Hunt in Early Modern Europe*. 3rd ed. Harlow: Pearson Education Limited, 2006.

Lindberg, David, ed. *Roger Bacon's Philosophy of Nature*. Oxford: Oxford University Press, 1983.

——. *Theories of Vision from Al Kindi to Kepler*. Chicago: University of Chicago Press, 1976.

Linsenmann, Thomas. *Die Magie bei Thomas von Aquin*. Berlin: Akademie Verlag, 2000.

Little, Andrew G. "Introduction: On Roger Bacon's Life and Works." In *Roger Bacon Essays*, ed. Andrew G. Little, 1–31. Oxford: Oxford University Press, 1914.

——. "Rogerus Bacon O.F.M." In Charles H. Lohr, "Medieval Latin Aristotle Commentaries. Authors: Robertus-Wilgelmus," *Traditio* 29 (1973): 115–21.

Macfarlane, Alan. *Witchcraft in Tudor and Stuart England. A Regional and Comparative Study*. London: Routledge and Kegan Paul, 1970; 2nd ed. 1999.

Malinowski, Bronislaw. *Magic, Science and Religion and Other Essays*. Ed. Robert Redfield. Prospect Heights, IL: Waveland Press, 1992.

Maloney, Thomas S. "The Extreme Realism of Roger Bacon." *The Review of Metaphysics* 38 (1985): 807–37.

Manselli, Raoul. *La religione popolare nel medioevo (sec. VI–XII)*. Turin: G. Giappichelli, 1974.

——. "Simbolismo e magia nell'alto medioevo." In *Simboli e simbologia nell'alto medioevo*, Settimane di Studio del Centro Italiano di Studi sull'alto Medioevo, 23, 293–329. Spoleto: Centro Italiano di Studi sull'alto Medioevo, 1976.

Marrone, Steven P. *The Light of Thy Countenance. Science and Knowledge of God in the Thirteenth Century*. 2 vols. Leiden: Brill, 2001.

——. "Magic and the Physical World in Thirteenth Century Scholasticism." *Early Science and Medicine* 14 (2009): 158–85.

——. "Medieval Philosophy in Context." In *The Cambridge Companion to Medieval Philosophy*, ed. Arthur S. McGrade, 16–40. Cambridge: Cambridge University Press, 2003.

——. "Metaphysics and Science in the Thirteenth Century: William of Auvergne, Robert Grosseteste and Roger Bacon." In *Medieval Philosophy*, ed. John Marenbon, Routledge History of Philosophy, 3. London/New York: Routledge, 1998.

——. "The Philosophy of Nature in the Early Thirteenth Century." In *Albertus Magnus und die Anfänge der Aristoteles-Rezeption im lateinischen Mittelalter*, ed. Ludger Honnefelder et al., 115–57. Münster: Aschendorff, 2005.

——. *William of Auvergne and Robert Grosseteste. New Ideas of Truth in the Early Thirteenth Century*. Princeton, NJ: Princeton University Press, 1983.

Mathiesen, Robert. "A Thirteenth-Century Ritual to Attain the Beatific Vision from the *Sworn Book* of Honorius of Thebes." In *Conjuring Spirits. Texts and Traditions of Medieval Ritual Magic*, ed. Claire Fanger, 143–62. University Park: Pennsylvania State University Press, 1998.

Mauss, Marcel, and Henri Hubert. "Esquisse d'une théorie générale de la magie." In *Sociologie et Anthropologie*, 1–141. Paris: Presses Universitaires de France, 1960.

McEvoy, James. *The Philosophy of Robert Grosseteste*. Oxford: Clarendon Press, 1982.

Meaney, Audrey L. "Women, Witchcraft and Magic in Anglo-Saxon England." In *Superstition and Popular Medicine in Anglo-Saxon England*, ed. D.G. Scragg, 9–40. Manchester: Manchester Centre for Anglo-Saxon Studies, 1989.

Merton, Robert K. *Science, Technology and Society in Seventeenth-Century England*. Amsterdam: Swets and Zeitlinger, 1938.

Michelet, Jules. *La sorcière*. Paris: A. Lacroix: Verboeckhoven, 1865.

——. *Satanism and Witchcraft. A Study in Medieval Superstition*. Trans. A.R. Allinson. Seacaucus, NJ: Citadel,1939.

Milis, Ludo J.R., ed. *The Pagan Middle Ages*. Trans. Tanis Guest. Woodbridge, Suffolk: Boydell and Brewer, 1998.

Molland, Andrew G. "Roger Bacon as Magician." *Traditio* 30 (1974): 445–60.

Monter, William. "Witch Trials in Continental Europe 1560-1660." In Bengt Ankarloo, Stuart Clark and William Monter, *Witchcraft and Magic in Europe. The Period of the Witch Trials*, 1–52. London: Athlone Press, 2002.

Moore, Robert I. *The Formation of a Persecuting Society*. Oxford: Blackwell, 1987; 2nd ed. 2007.

——. "Literacy and the Making of Heresy, c. 1000–c. 1150." In *Heresy and Literacy, 1000–1350*, ed. Peter Biller and Anne Hudson, 19–37. Cambridge: Cambridge University Press, 1994.

——. *The Origins of European Dissent*. London: Penguin, 1977; 2nd ed. Oxford: Oxford University Press, 1985.

Moorman, John. *A History of the Franciscan Order from its Origins to the Year 1517*. Oxford: Clarendon Press, 1968.

Muchembled, Robert. *La sorcière au village (XVe–XVIIIe siècle)*. Mesnil-sur-l'Estrée: Gallimard, 1979.

——. "The Witches of Cambrésis," In *Religion and the People, 800–1700*, ed. James Obelkevich, 221–76. Chapel Hill: University of North Carolina Press, 1979.

Murray, Alexander. "Missionaries and Magic in Dark-Age Europe." *Past and Present*, no. 136 (August 1992): 186–205.

Murray, Margaret A. *The God of the Witches*. Oxford: Oxford University Press, 1931.

——. *The Witch-Cult in Western Europe*. Oxford: Clarendon Press, 1963.

Newman, William R. *Atoms and Alchemy. Chymistry and the Experimental Origins of the Scientific Revolution*. Chicago: University of Chicago Press, 2006.

Newman, William R., and Lawrence M. Principe. *Alchemy Tried in the Fire. Starkey, Boyle and the Fate of Helmontian Chemistry*. Chicago, IL: University of Chicago Press, 2002.

Ostorero, Martine. *"Folâtrer avec les démons." Sabbat et chasse aux sorciers à Vevey (1448)*. Lausanne: Université de Lausanne, 1998.

Paolini, Lorenzo. "Italian Catharism and Written Culture." In *Heresy and Literacy, 1000–1350*, ed. Peter Biller and Anne Hudson, 83–103. Cambridge: Cambridge University Press, 1994.

Paravy, Pierrette. *De la chrétienté romaine à la Réforme en Dauphiné*. 2 vols. Rome: Ecole Française de Rome, 1993.

Paravicini Bagliani, Agostino. *Le Speculum Astronomiae, une énigme? Enquête sur les manuscrits*. Florence: Edizioni del Galluzzo, 2001.

Peters, Edward. *Inquisition*. New York: Free Press, 1988.

——. "The Medieval Church and State on Supersition, Magic and Witchcraft: From Augustine to the Sixteenth Century." In *Witchcraft and Magic in Europe: The Middle Ages*, ed. Karen Jolly, Catharine Raudvere and Edward Peters, 174–245. London: Athlone Press, 2002.

Picavet, François. "Nos vieux maîtres: Pierre De Maricourt, le Picard, et son influence sur Roger Bacon." *Revue Internationale de l'Enseignement* 54 (1907): 289–315.

Pingree, David. "La magia dotta." In *Federico II e le scienze*, ed. Pierre Toubert and Agostino Paravicini Bagliani, 354–70. Palermo: Sellerio, 1994.

——. "Learned Magic in the Time of Frederick II." *Micrologus. Natura, scienze e società medievali* 2 (1994): 39–56.

——. "Some of the Sources of the *Ghāyat al-hakīm*." *Journal of the Warburg and Courtauld Institutes* 43 (1980): 1–15.

Principe, Lawrence M. *The Secrets of Alchemy*. Chicago, IL: University of Chicago Press, 2013.

Robbins, Rossell. *The Encyclopedia of Witchcraft and Demonology*. New York: Crown Publishers, 1959.

Roper, Lyndal. *Witch Craze. Terror and Fantasy in Baroque Germany*. New Haven, CT: Yale University Press, 2004.

Rossi, Paolo. *Francesco Bacone. Dalla magia alla scienza*. Rev. ed. Turin: G. Einaudi, 1974.

Rucquoi, Adeline. "Gundisalvus ou Dominicus Gundisalvi?" *Bulletin de Philosophie Médiévale* 41 (1999): 85–106.

Sarton, George. *Six Wings. Men of Science in the Renaissance*. Bloomington: Indiana University Press, 1957.

Schmitt, Jean-Claude. "Les 'superstitions.'" In *L'histoire de la France religieuse*, ed. Jacques Le Goff and René Rémond, vol. I: *Des dieux de la Gaule à la papauté d'Avignon*, 417–551. Paris: Seuil, 1988.

——. "Les traditions folkloriques dans la culture médiévale." *Archives de Sciences Sociales des Religions* 52 (1981): 5–20.

Schreiner, Klaus. "Laienfrömmigkeit—Frömmigkeit von Eliten oder Frömmigkeit des Volkes? Zur sozialen Verfasstheit laikaler Frömmigkeitspraxis im späten Mittelalter." In *Laienfrömmigkeit im späten Mittelalter. Formen, Funktionen, politisch-soziale Zusammenhänge*, ed. Klaus Schreiner, 1–78. Munich: R. Oldenbourg Verlag, 1992.

Shank, Michael. "Academic Consulting in Fifteenth-Century Vienna: The Case of Astrology." In *Texts and Contexts in Ancient and Medieval Science: Studies on the Occasion of John E. Murdoch's Seventieth Birthday*, ed. Edith Sylla and Michael McVaugh, 245–70. Leiden/New York: Brill, 1997.

Shapin, Steven, and Simon Schaffer. *Leviathan and the Air-Pump. Hobbes, Boyle, and the Experimental Life*. Princeton, NJ: Princeton University Press, 1985.

Shapiro, Barbara J. *Probability and Certainty in Seventeenth-Century England. A Study of the Relationships between Natural Science, Religion, History, Law and Literature*. Princeton, NJ: Princeton University Press, 1983.

Sharpe, James. *Instruments of Darkness. Witchcraft in England, 1550–1750*. London: Hamish Hamilton, 1996.

Skemer, Don C. *Binding Words. Textual Amulets in the Middle Ages*. University Park: Pennsylvania State University Press, 2006.

Soman, Alfred. "Decriminalizing Witchcraft. Does the French Experience Furnish a European Model?" *Criminal Justice History* 10 (1989): 1–22.

Speer, Andreas. *Die entdeckte Natur. Untersuchungen zu Begründsversuchen einer "scientia naturalis" im 12. Jahrhundert*. Leiden: Brill, 1995.

Stock, Brian. *The Implications of Literacy*. Princeton, NJ: Princeton University Press, 1983.

Stokes, Laura. *Demons of Urban Reform. Early European Witch Trials and Criminal Justice, 1430–1530*. Basingstoke: Palgrave Macmillan, 2011.

Teske, Roland. "William of Auvergne on Philosophy as *divinalis* and *sapientialis*." In *Was ist Philosophie im Mittelalter?*, ed. Jan A.A. Aertsen and Andreas Speer, Miscellanea Mediaevalia, 26, 475–81. Berlin: De Gruyter, 1998.

Thomas, Keith. *Religion and the Decline of Magic. Studies in Popular Beliefs in Sixteenth- and Seventeenth-Century England*. London: Weidenfield and Nelson, 1971.

Thorndike, Lynn. *A Hisory of Magic and Experimental Science*. 8 vols. New York: Macmillan, 1923–58.

——. "Traditional Medieval Tracts concerning Engraved Astrological Images." In *Mélanges Auguste Pelzer*, 217–74. Leuven: Bibliothèque de l'Université, 1947.

Toivo, Raisa Maria. "Marking (dis)order: Witchcraft and the Symbolics of Hierarchy in Late Seventeenth- and Early Eighteenth-Century Finland." In *Beyond the Witch Trials. Witchcraft and Magic in Enlightenment Europe*, ed. Owen Davies and Willem de Blécourt, 8–25. Manchester: Manchester University Press, 2004.

Travaglia, Pinella. "Considerazioni sulla magia nel medioevo. Il libro dell'agricultura nabatea." In *Universalità della ragione. Pluralità delle filosofie nel Medioevo*, ed. Alessandro Musco et al., XII Congresso Internazionale di Filosofia Medievale, 3, 153–64. Palermo: Officina di Studi Medievali, 2012.

——. *Magic, Causality and Intentionality. The Doctrine of the Rays of al-Kindi*. Florence: SISMEL/Edizioni del Galluzzo, 1999.

Tugwell, Simon. "Introduction" to Aquinas. In *Albert and Thomas. Selected Writings*, ed. Simon Tugwell, 201–351. Mahwah, NJ: Paulist Press, 1988.

Utz Tremp, Kathrin. "Der Freiburger Waldenzerprozess von 1399 und seine Bernische Vorgeschichte." *Freiburger Geschichtesblätter* 68 (1991): 57–85.

Walker, D.P. *Spiritual and Demonic Magic from Ficino to Campanella*. London: Warburg Institute, 1958.

Weber, Max. *The Protestant Ethic and the Spirit of Capitalism*. Trans. Talcott Parsons. New York: Charles Scribner's Sons, 1958.

——. *The Theory of Social and Economic Organization*. Trans. A.M. Henderson and Talcott Parsons. Oxford: Oxford University Press, 1947; New York: Free Press, 1964.

——. "Wissenschaft als Beruf." In *Max Weber Gesamtausgabe*, ed. Wolfgang J. Mommsen and Wolfgang Schluchter, I, 17, 71–111. Tübingen: J.C.B. Mohr, 1992.

Webster, Charles. *From Paracelsus to Newton. Magic and the Making of Modern Science*. Cambridge: Cambridge University Press, 1982.

Weill-Parot, Nicholas. *Les "images astrologiques" au moyen âge et à la Renaissance*. Paris: Honoré Champion, 2002.

Westfall, Richard S. *The Construction of Modern Science. Mechanisms and Mechanics*. New York: John Wiley and Sons, 1971.

——. *The Life of Isaac Newton*. Cambridge: Cambridge University Press, 1993.

——. *Never at Rest. A Biography of Isaac Newton*. Cambridge: Cambridge University Press, 1980.

——. "Newton and the Hermetic Tradition." In *Science, Medicine and Society in the Renaissance. Essays to Honor Walter Pagel*, ed. Allen G. Debus, 183–98. New York: Neale Watson Academic Publications, 1972.

Williams, Gerhild Scholz. *Defining Dominion. The Discourses of Magic and Witchcraft in Early Modern France and Germany*. Ann Arbor: University of Michigan Press, 1995.

Yates, Frances A. *Giordano Bruno and the Hermetic Tradition*. London: Routledge and Kegan Paul, 1964.

Zambelli, Paola. *L'ambigua natura della magia. Filosofi, streghe, riti nel Rinascimento*. 2nd ed. Venice: Marsilio, 1996.

——. *The Speculum Astronomiae and its Enigma*. Dordrecht/Boston: Kluwer Academic Publishers, 1992.

Index

Abracadabra, 52
acculturation, 38–40, 65, 78, 80–1, 190, 219
Ackermann, Silke, 251
action at a distance, 218
  compare causation by contiguity
Adelard of Bath, 24–6
Aelfric, 39–41, 45, 47–50, 53, 68, 157, 241–5
aeromancy, 22, 125, 132
Agobard of Lyons, 47
Agrippa, Heinrich Cornelius, xvi, 197, 204–7, 287–8
Albert the Great, 118, 201, 264
alchemy, xi, 19–20, 28–30, 83–5, 109, 113, 139–40, 211, 217–18, 289
Aldhelm, 15
Alexander IV, pope, 152–3
Alexander V, pope, 183
Alexander VI, pope, 185
Al-Farabi, 19, 21, 84, 139–40, 237, 251, 269
Alfonso X, king, 107
Al-Kindi, 262
Alps, foothills of, xv, 164, 186, 228, 276
Amadeus VIII, duke of Savoy, 184, 194
amulet, 13, 15, 22, 50, 133, 244
  textual, 52
Andenmatten, Bernard, 175, 276, 278
angelology, 84
angels, 117–18, 129, 137, 206–7
animism, 4–5, 7
Apollo, Mirror of, 95
Apollonius of Tyre, 99
Appuleius, 9–10, 234

Aquinas, Thomas, *see* Thomas Aquinas
Aristotle, 21
ars notoria, 28, 83–4, 133
  see also Ars notoria
Ars notoria, 83, 97–100, 104, 107, 111, 254, 257–8, 261
Ars syntribilia, 86
artes exceptivae, 99
Artesius, 86, 253
artificial object, 133–4, 137, 146, 200, 205
arts
  liberal, 99
  mechanical, 99–100
Asclepius, 87–8, 135
astrology, 13, 15, 19–20, 22, 25–9, 58, 83–5, 89, 90, 92–4, 113–15, 120–4, 132, 139–41, 143–4, 155, 199, 202, 205, 270
  see also images, science of
astronomy, 26, 119–20, 139–40, 143, 270
Augustine, xiv, 12–15, 17, 21, 23, 26–7, 30, 50, 79, 93, 130–1, 137–8, 141–2, 150, 235, 238, 244, 267–9
Aulus Gellius, 11
Averroes, 28
Avignon, 164–5

Bacon, Francis, 203
Bacon, Roger, xv, 97, 127, 138–50, 162, 197, 199, 201–2, 253, 269–73
Bailey, Michael, 185, 191–3, 233, 239, 243–4, 275–7, 279–80, 282–4
baptism of images, 153, 155–9, 184

Hangman

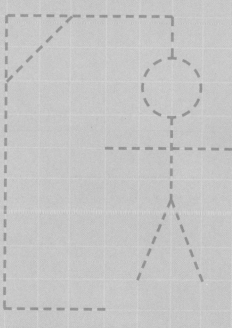
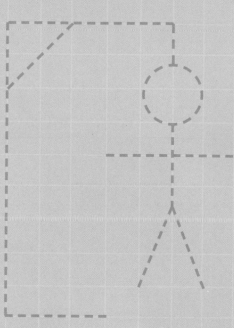

Your subject is MONSTERS.
Use the space below for your word.

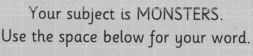

Hangman

Your subject is ANIMALS.
Use the space below for your word.

a	b	c	d	e	f	g	h	i	j	k	l	m
n	o	p	q	r	s	t	u	v	w	x	y	z

Hangman

Your subject is SPACE.
Use the space below for your word.

a	b	c	d	e	f	g	h	i	j	k	l	m
n	o	p	q	r	s	t	u	v	w	x	y	z

Hangman

Your subject is FOOD AND DRINK.
Use the space below for your word.

| a | b | c | d | e | f | g | h | i | j | k | l | m |
| n | o | p | q | r | s | t | u | v | w | x | y | z |

Hangman

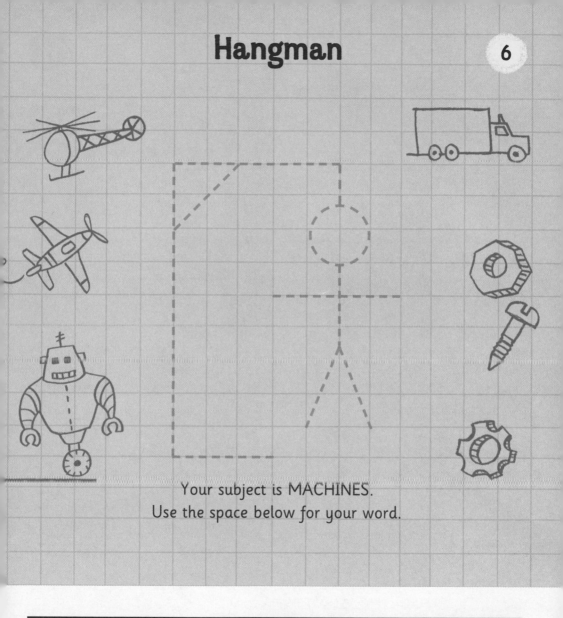

Your subject is MACHINES.
Use the space below for your word.

a	b	c	d	e	f	g	h	i	j	k	l	m
n	o	p	q	r	s	t	u	v	w	x	y	z

Hangman

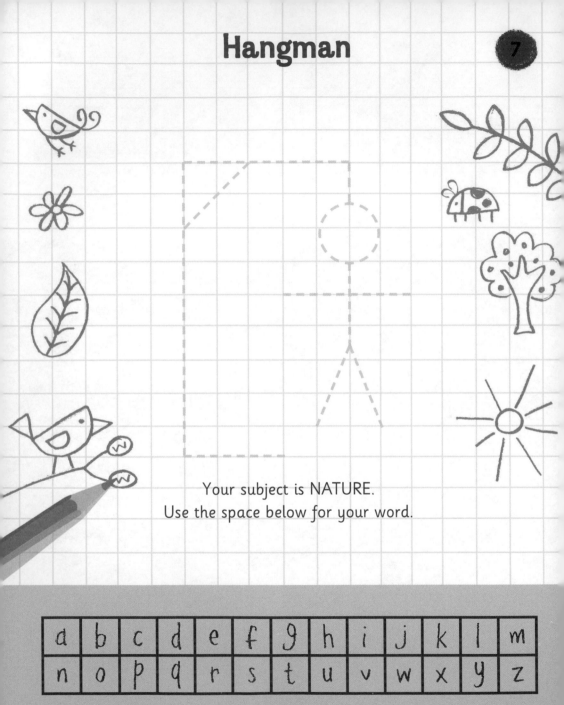

Your subject is NATURE.
Use the space below for your word.

a	b	c	d	e	f	g	h	i	j	k	l	m
n	o	p	q	r	s	t	u	v	w	x	y	z

Hangman

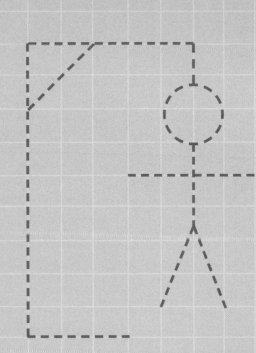

Your subject is AROUND THE WORLD.
Use the space below for your word.

a	b	c	d	e	f	g	h	i	j	k	l	m
n	o	p	q	r	s	t	u	v	w	x	y	z

Hangman

9

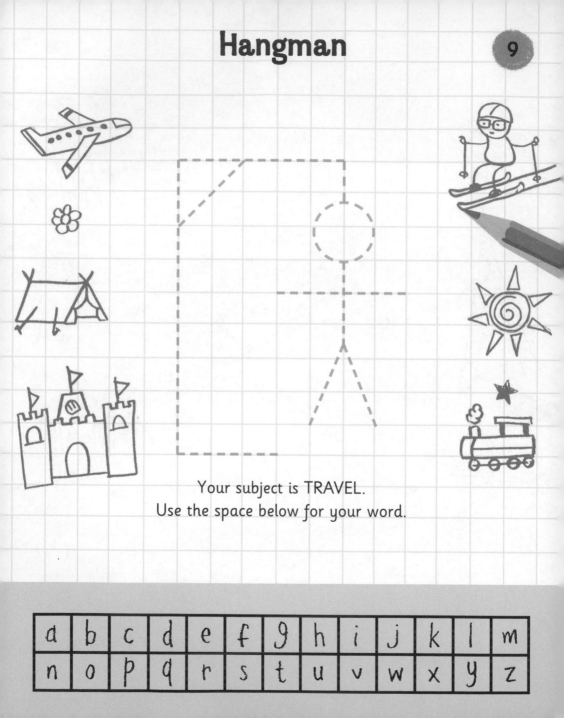

Your subject is TRAVEL.
Use the space below for your word.

a	b	c	d	e	f	g	h	i	j	k	l	m
n	o	p	q	r	s	t	u	v	w	x	y	z

Hangman

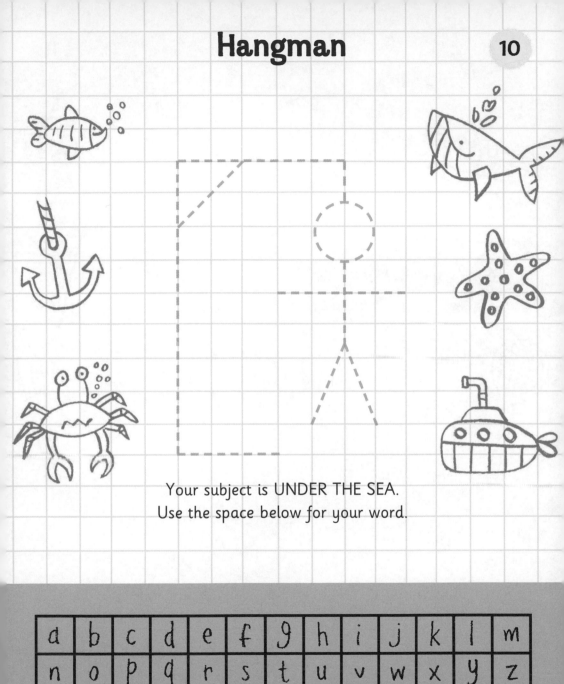

Your subject is UNDER THE SEA.
Use the space below for your word.

a	b	c	d	e	f	g	h	i	j	k	l	m
n	o	p	q	r	s	t	u	v	w	x	y	z

Hangman

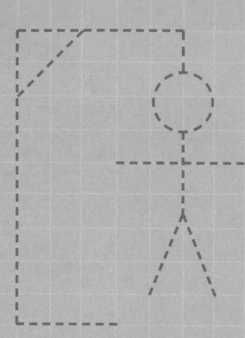

Your subject is SPORTS.
Use the space below for your word.

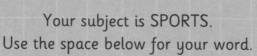

Stepping stones instructions 12

1 Player 1 starts by connecting two of the purple dots together using a horizontal or vertical straight line.

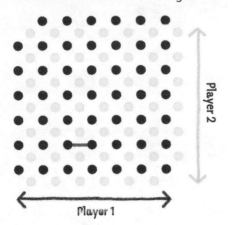

2 Player 2 then connects two of the yellow dots together using a horizontal or vertical straight line.

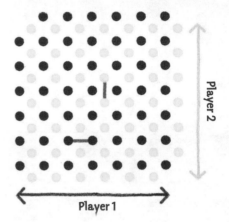

3 Taking turns, connect two of your dots anywhere on the grid. But you can't cross a line that's already been made.

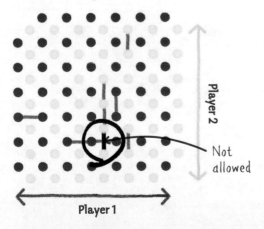

Not allowed

4 The first player to cross the grid is the winner. Player 1's chain must cross from side to side, and Player 2's from top to bottom.

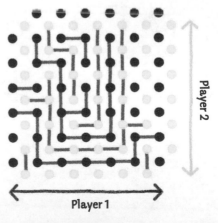

(Player 1 won this game.)

Stepping stones

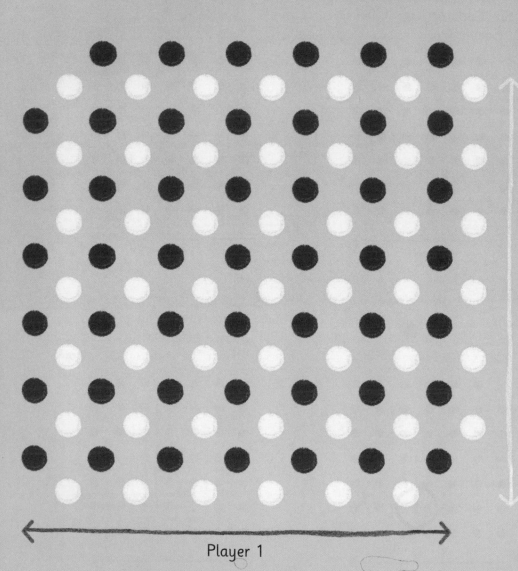

Player 1

Player 2

Stepping stones

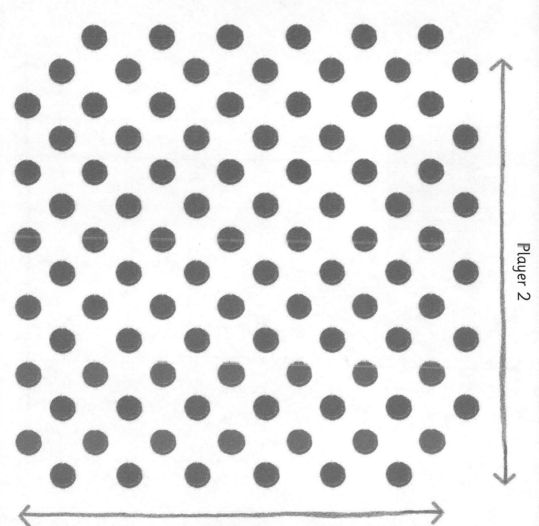

Player 2

Player 1

Stepping stones

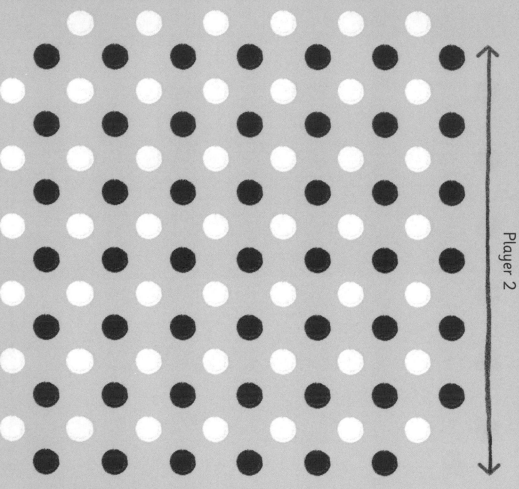

Player 2

Player 1

Stepping stones

16

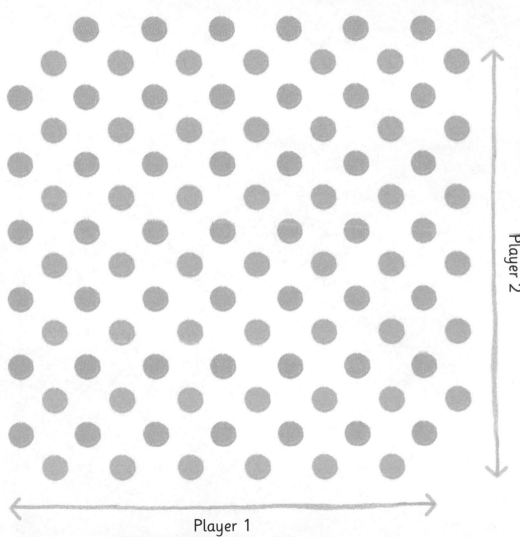

Player 2

Player 1

Stepping stones

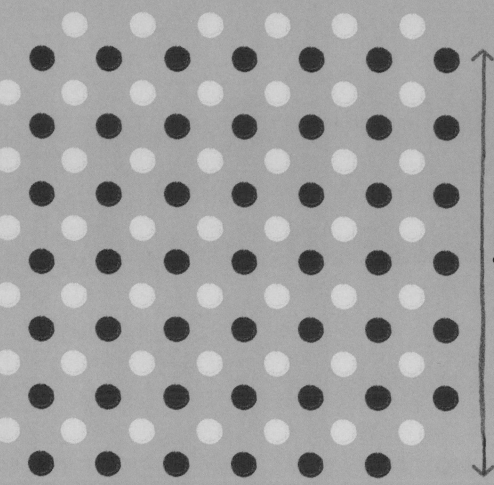

Player 2

Player 1

Stepping stones

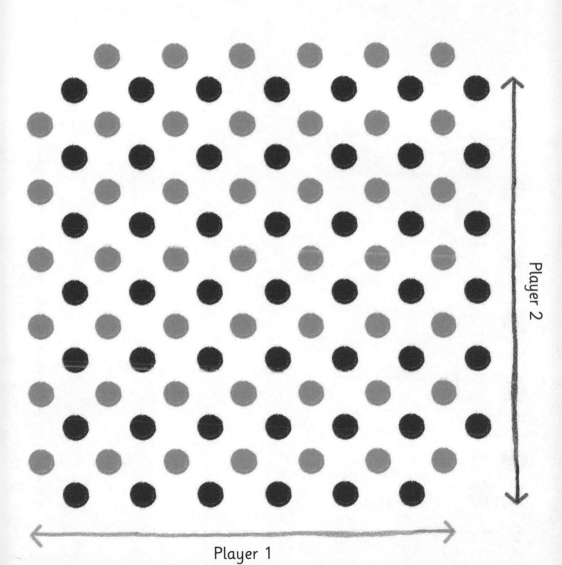

18

Player 2

Player 1

Stepping stones

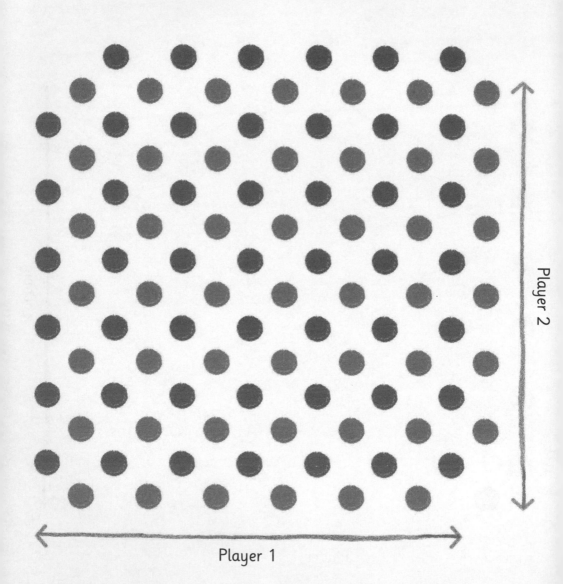

Player 2

Player 1

Player 2

Player 1

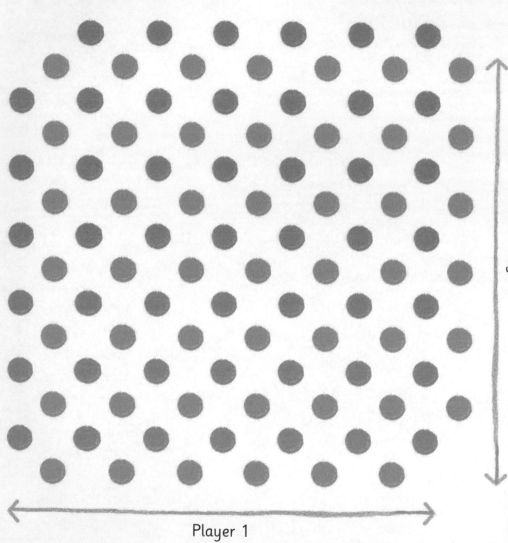

Player 1

Player 2

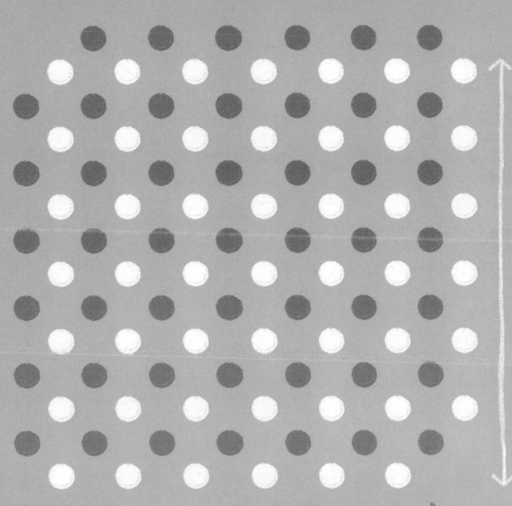

Player 2

Player 1

Stepping stones

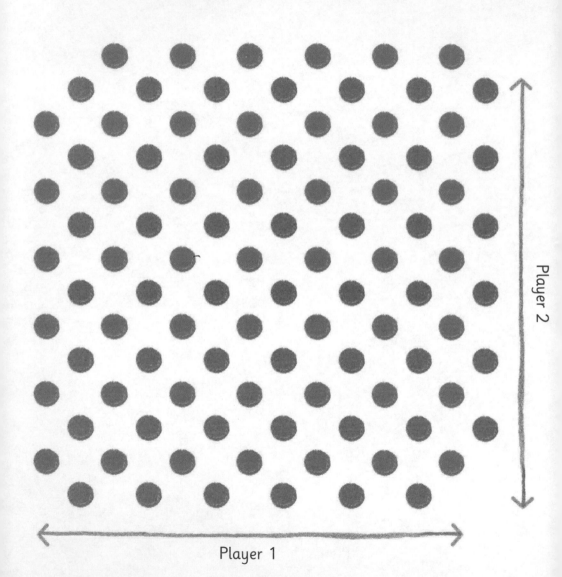

Player 2

Player 1

Four in a row instructions

1 Player 1 starts by drawing an X in any box on the bottom row.

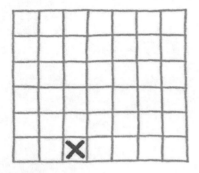

2 Player 2 then draws an O in any of the other squares on the bottom row, or in the square above the X.

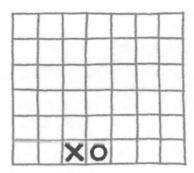

3 You can draw your symbol in any column you like, but you must always draw it in the column's lowest empty square.

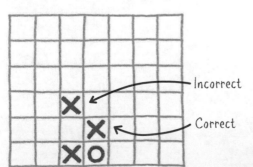

Incorrect

Correct

4 The first player to make a straight line of four is the winner. The line can be horizontal, vertical or diagonal. Player 1 won this game.

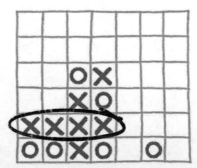

Four in a row

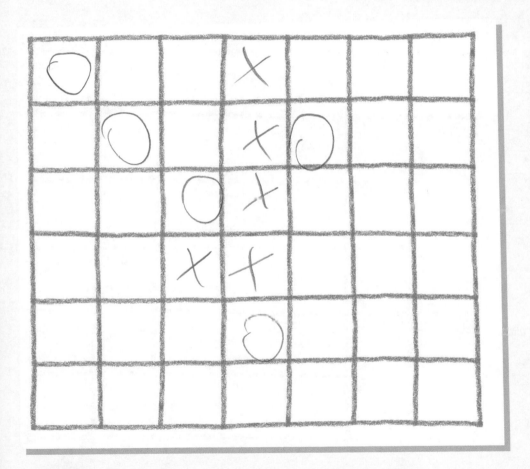

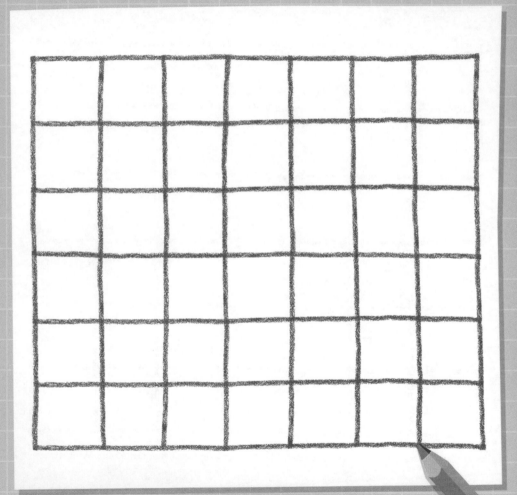

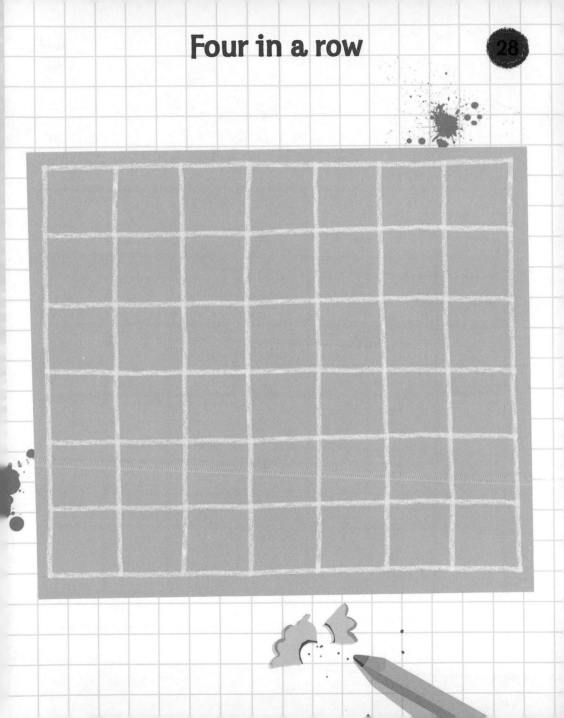

Four in a row

29

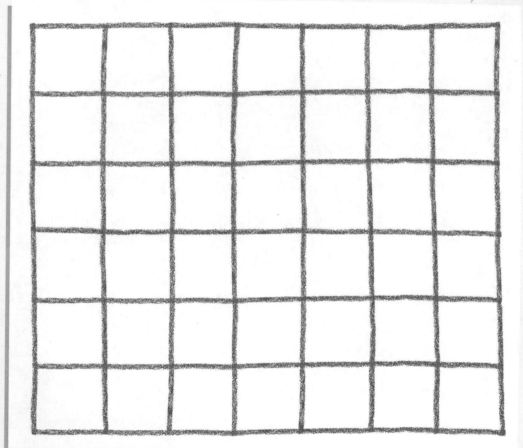

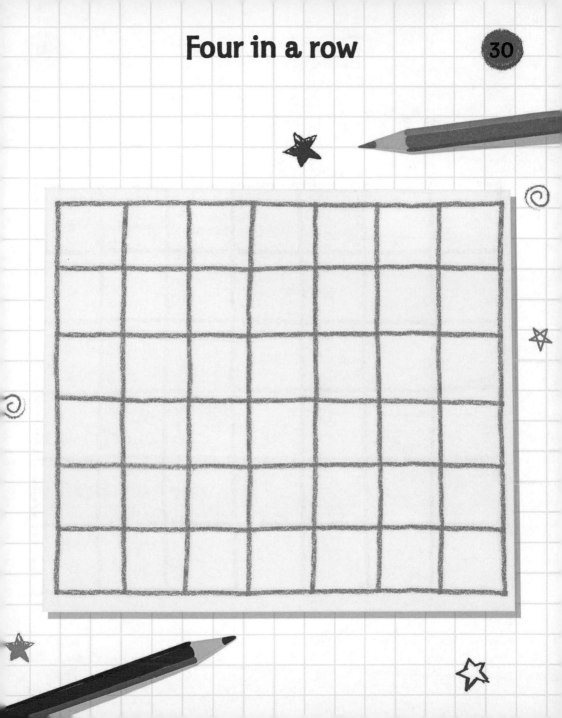

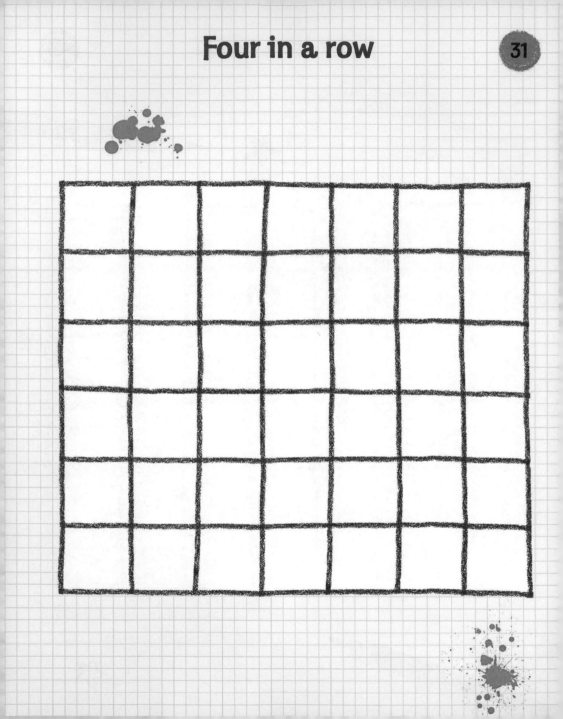

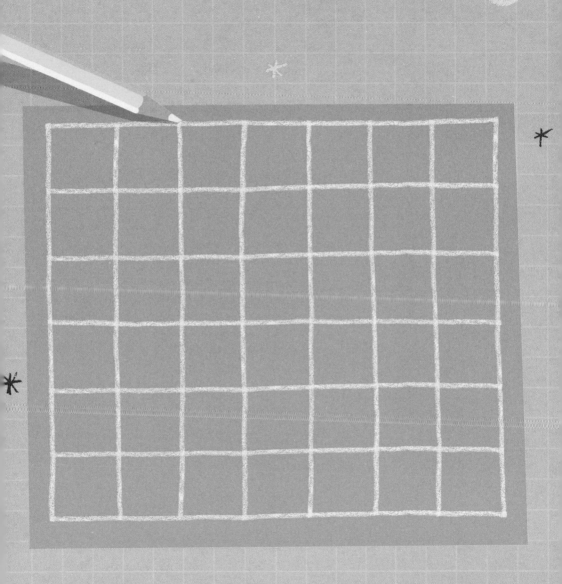

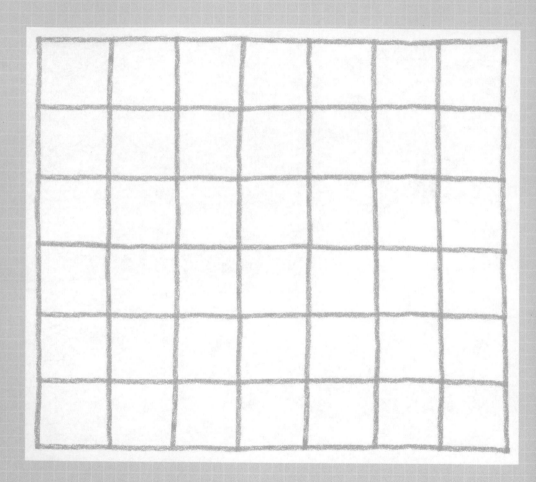

Four in a row

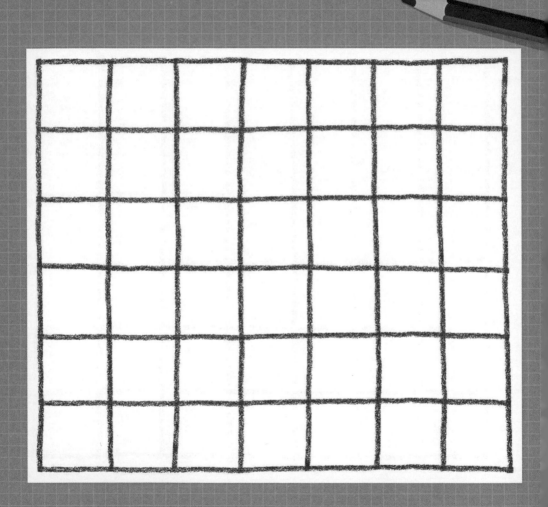

Minefield instructions

Before you begin, cut or tear along the dotted line so that each player has their own pair of grids.

1. Each player draws ten mines on the crosspoints of their minefield, and keeps them hidden from the other player. You can't have more than two mines on the same horizontal or vertical line.

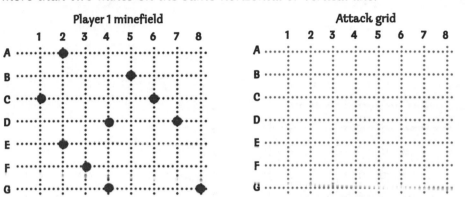

Player 1 minefield · Attack grid

2. The aim is to move from left to right across your opponent's minefield. Starting anywhere on line 1, take turns calling out your moves. Mark your own moves on your attack grid, and your opponent's moves on your minefield.

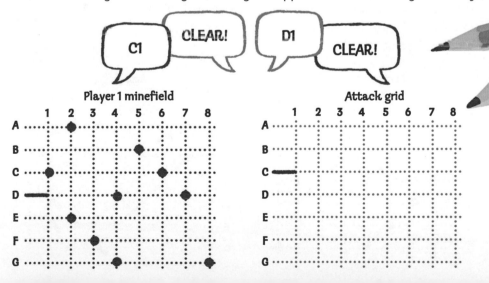

CLEAR! · C1 · D1 · CLEAR!

Player 1 minefield · Attack grid

3 You can move one square at a time, either vertically, horizontally or diagonally. If you find a mine, don't move onto it, but mark it on your grid. On your next turn, find a route around the mine.

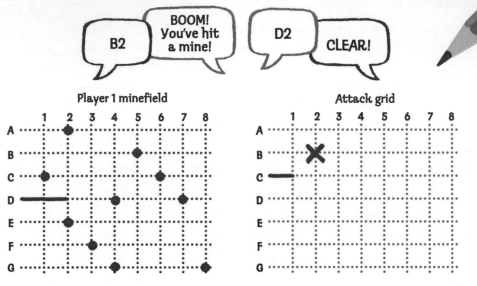

4 The first player to make it safely to the right side of the grid is the winner. The game is a tie if both players make it across in the same number of turns. Player 2 won this game.

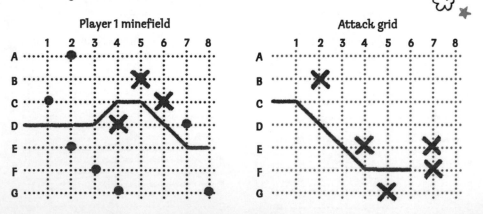

Minefield

Player 1 minefield:

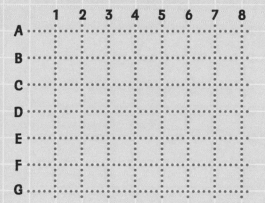

Attack grid:

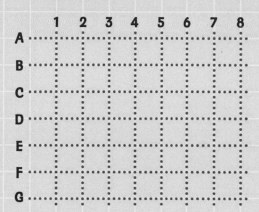

Cut or tear along the dotted line.

Player 2 minefield:

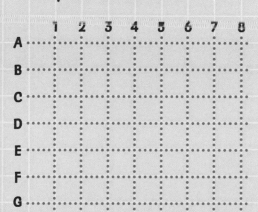

Attack grid:

Minefield

Player 1 minefield:

	1	2	3	4	5	6	7	8
A								
B								
C								
D								
E								
F								
G								

Attack grid:

BOOM!

	1	2	3	4	5	6	7	8
A								
B								
C								
D								
E								
F								
G								

Cut or tear along the dotted line.

Player 2 minefield:

	1	2	3	4	5	6	7	8
A								
B								
C								
D								
E								
F								
G								

Attack grid:

	1	2	3	4	5	6	7	8
A								
B								
C								
D								
E								
F								
G								

Minefield

Player 1 minefield:

Attack grid:

Cut or tear along the dotted line.

Player 2 minefield:

Attack grid:

Minefield

Player 1 minefield:

	1	2	3	4	5	6	7	8
A								
B								
C								
D								
E								
F								
G								

Attack grid:

	1	2	3	4	5	6	7	8
A								
B								
C								
D								
E								
F								
G								

Cut or tear along the dotted line.

Player 2 minefield:

	1	2	3	4	5	6	7	8
A								
B								
C								
D								
E								
F								
G								

Attack grid:

	1	2	3	4	5	6	7	8
A								
B								
C								
D								
E								
F								
G								

Minefield

BOOM!

Player 1 minefield:

Attack grid:

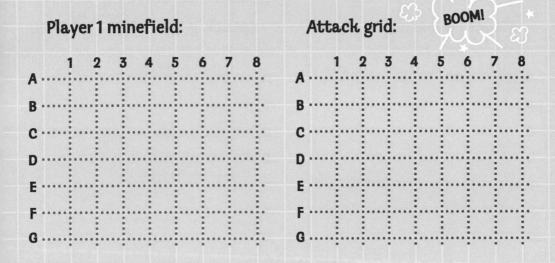

	1	2	3	4	5	6	7	8
A								
B								
C								
D								
E								
F								
G								

Cut or tear along the dotted line.

Player 2 minefield:

Attack grid:

	1	2	3	4	5	6	7	8
A								
B								
C								
D								
E								
F								
G								

Minefield

BOOM!

Player 1 minefield:

	1	2	3	4	5	6	7	8
A								
B								
C								
D								
E								
F								
G								

Attack grid:

	1	2	3	4	5	6	7	8
A								
B								
C								
D								
E								
F								
G								

Cut or tear along the dotted line.

Player 2 minefield:

	1	2	3	4	5	6	7	8
A								
B								
C								
D								
E								
F								
G								

Attack grid:

	1	2	3	4	5	6	7	8
A								
B								
C								
D								
E								
F								
G								

Minefield

Player 1 minefield:

	1	2	3	4	5	6	7	8
A								
B								
C								
D								
E								
F								
G								

Attack grid:

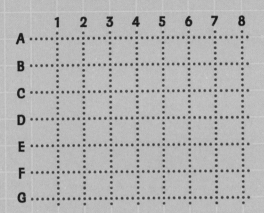

Cut or tear along the dotted line.

Player 2 minefield:

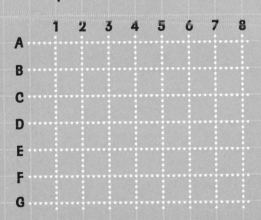

Attack grid:

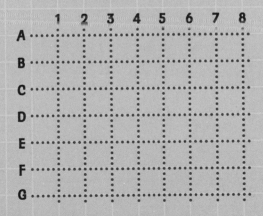

Minefield

Player 1 minefield:

Attack grid:

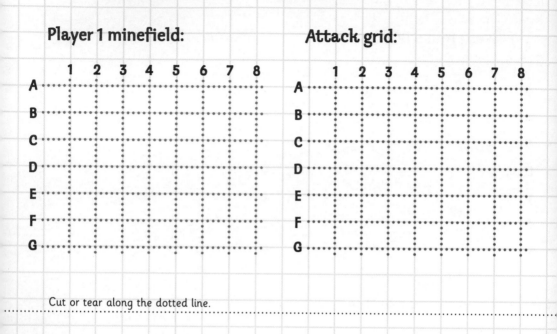

Cut or tear along the dotted line.

Player 2 minefield:

Attack grid:

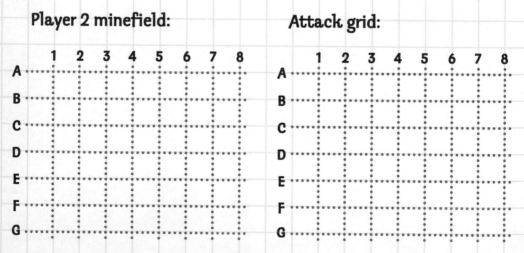

Minefield

Player 1 minefield:

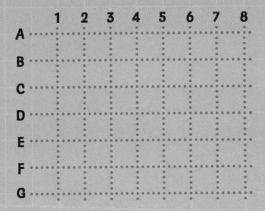

Attack grid:

Cut or tear along the dotted line.

Player 2 minefield:

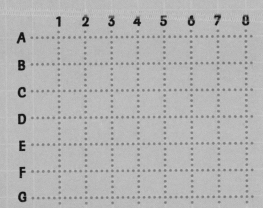

Attack grid:

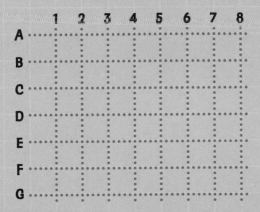

Minefield

Player 1 minefield:

	1	2	3	4	5	6	7	8
A								
B								
C								
D								
E								
F								
G								

Attack grid:

	1	2	3	4	5	6	7	8
A								
B								
C								
D								
E								
F								
G								

Cut or tear along the dotted line.

Player 2 minefield:

	1	2	3	4	5	6	7	8
A								
B								
C								
D								
E								
F								
G								

Attack grid:

	1	2	3	4	5	6	7	8
A								
B								
C								
D								
E								
F								
G								

Os and Xs instructions

1 Player 1 marks an O in any of the spaces in the grid.

2 Player 2 marks an X in any of the other spaces.

3 Taking turns, try to make a straight line of three in a row. The line can be horizontal, vertical or diagonal.

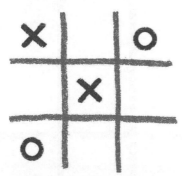

4 The winner is the first player to make a line of three in a row. If no one makes a line, the game is a tie.

Os and Xs

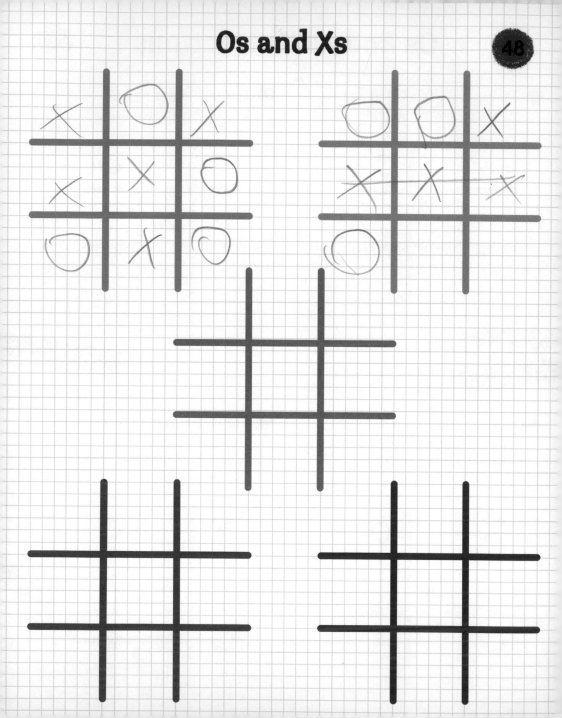

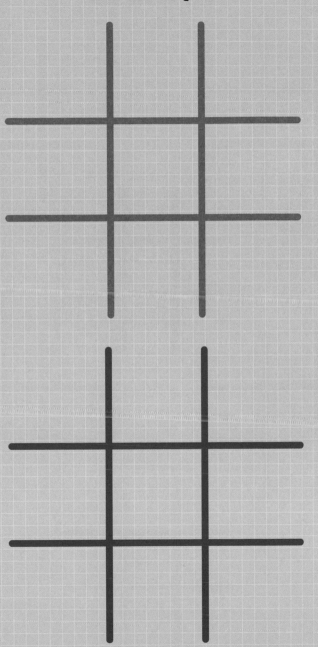

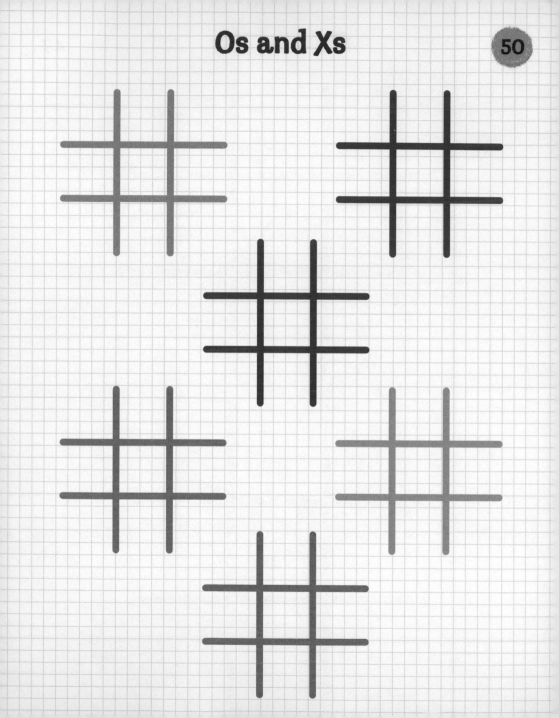

Os and Xs

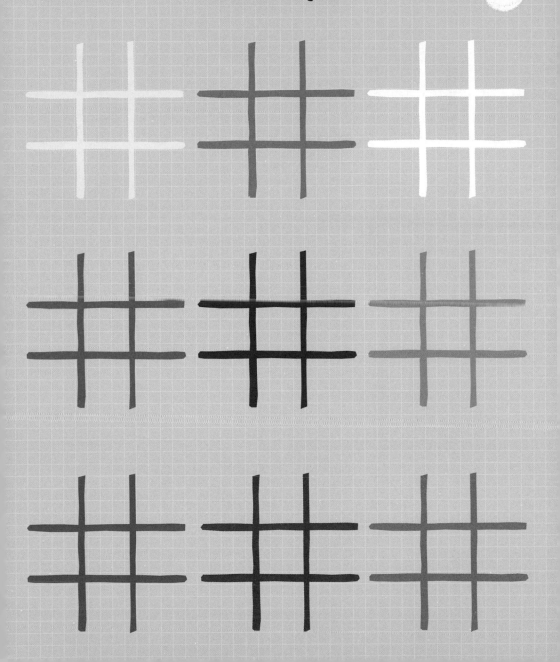

Os and Xs

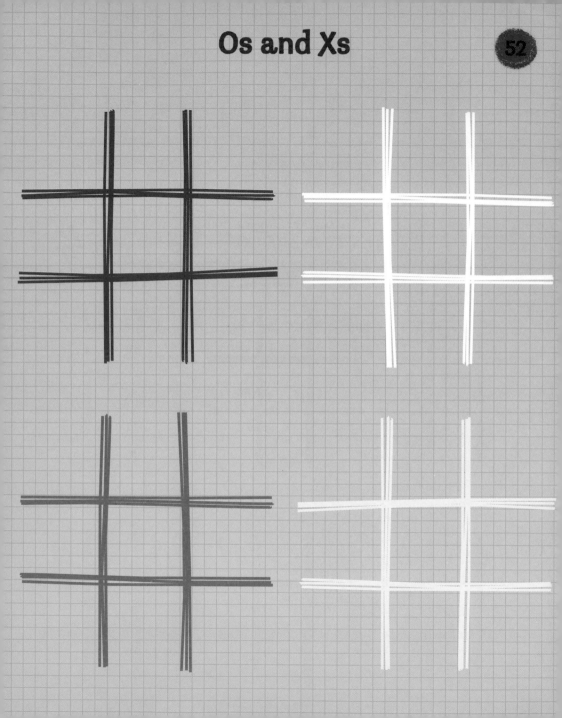

Os and Xs

Os and Xs

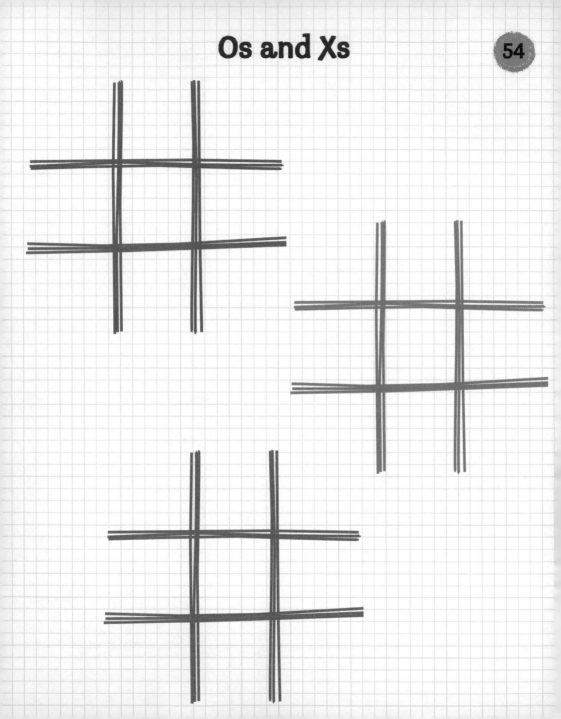

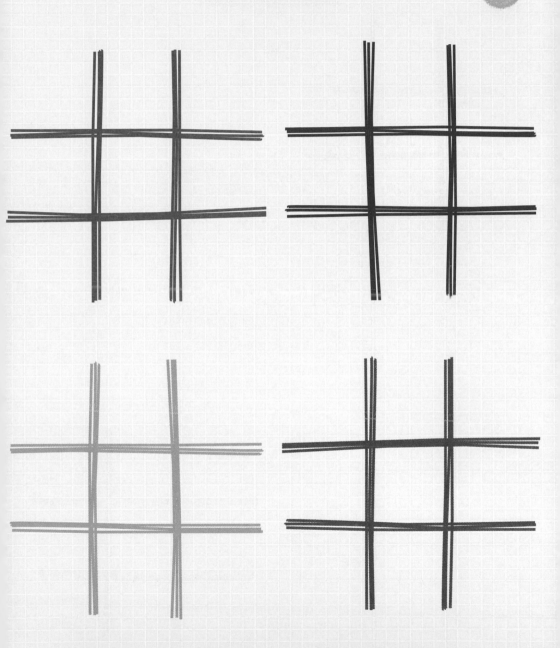

Hive instructions

1 Player 1 (blue) fills in one
of the hexagons on the grid.

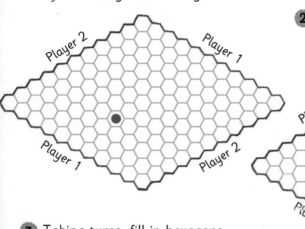

2 Player 2 (red) then
fills in any of the other
hexagons on the grid.

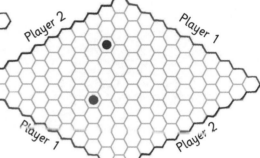

3 Taking turns, fill in hexagons
anywhere on the grid. The goal
is to make a chain that connects
your two sides of the grid.

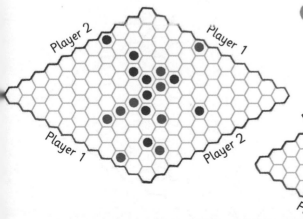

4 The winner is the first player
to make a complete chain.
Player 1 won this game.

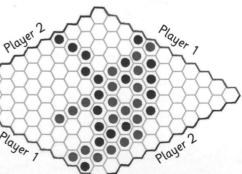

Hive

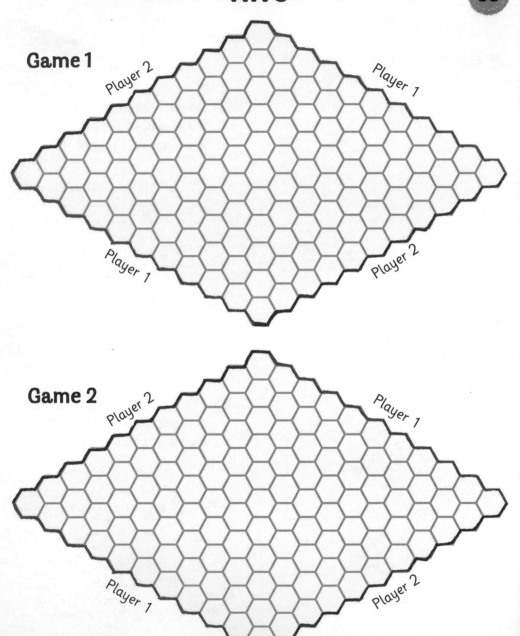

Game 1

Player 2

Player 1

Player 1

Player 2

Game 2

Player 2

Player 1

Player 1

Player 2

Hive

Game 1

Player 2

Player 1

Player 1

Player 2

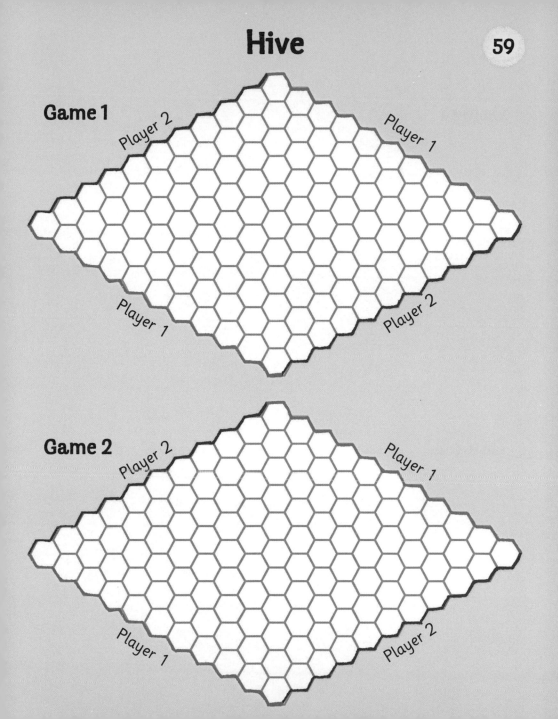

Game 2

Player 2

Player 1

Player 1

Player 2

Hive

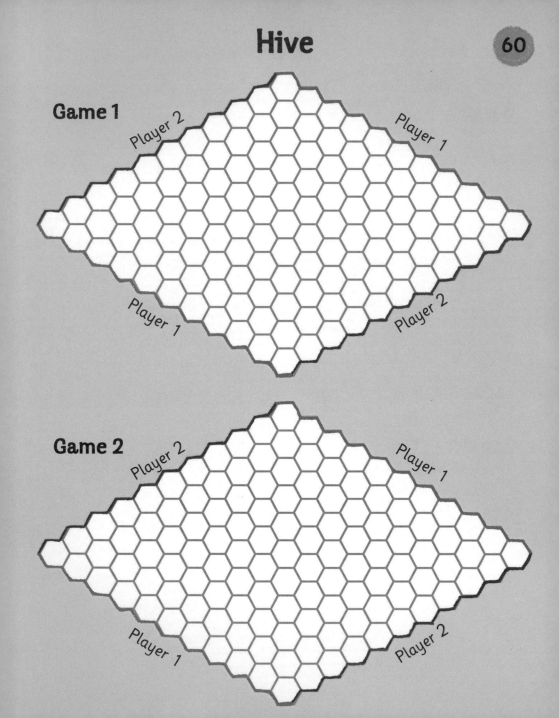

Game 1

Player 2

Player 1

Player 1

Player 2

Game 2

Player 2

Player 1

Player 1

Player 2

Hive

Game 1

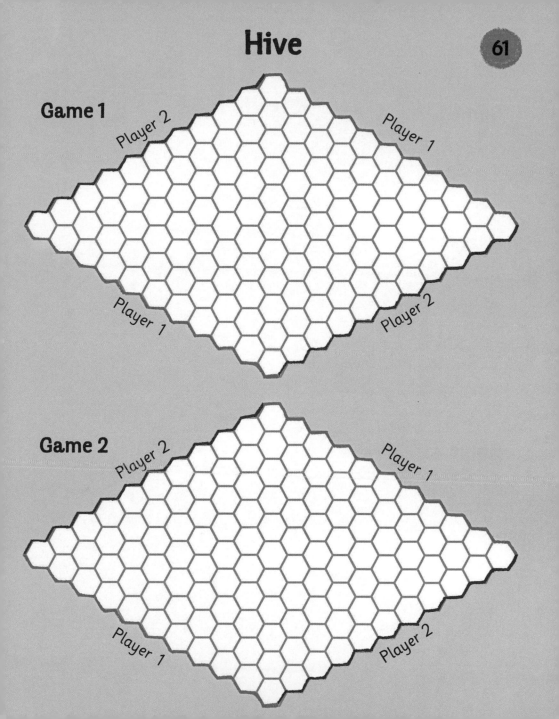

Player 2

Player 1

Player 1

Player 2

Game 2

Player 2

Player 1

Player 1

Player 2

Hive

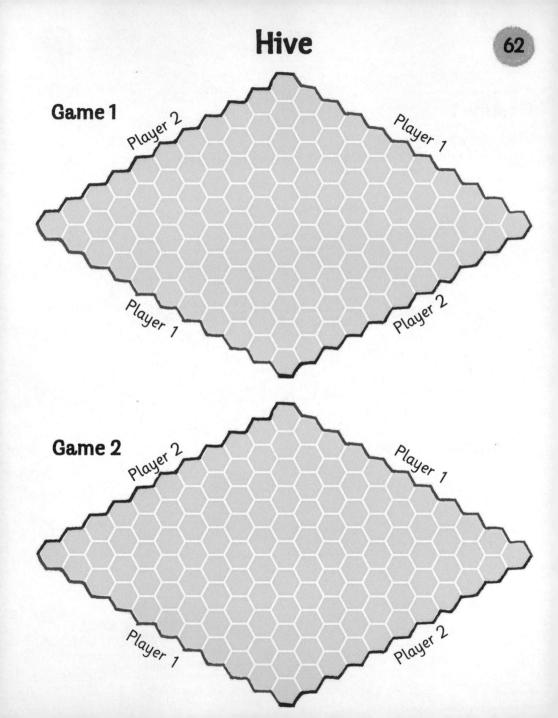

Game 1

Player 2

Player 1

Player 1

Player 2

Game 2

Player 2

Player 1

Player 1

Player 2

Hive

Game 1

Player 2

Player 1

Player 1

Player 2

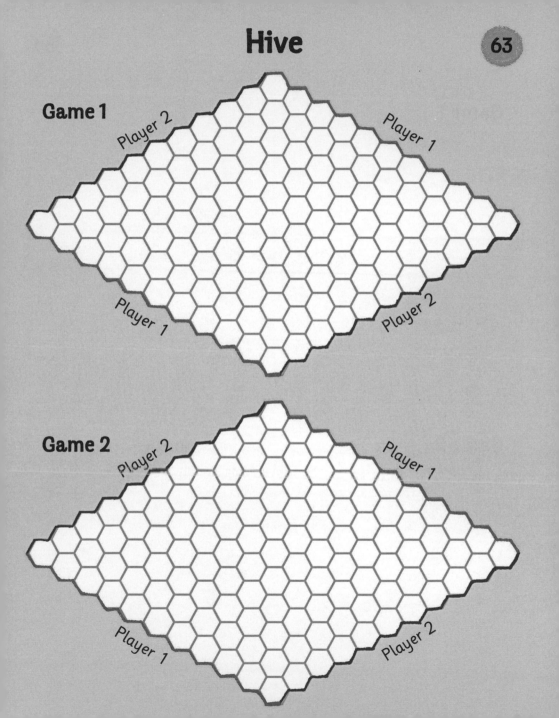

Game 2

Player 2

Player 1

Player 1

Player 2

Hive

Game 1

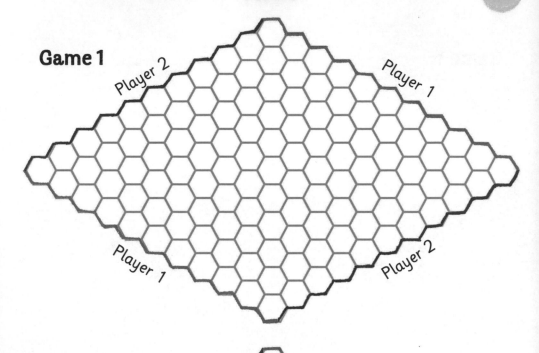

Player 2

Player 1

Player 1

Player 2

Game 2

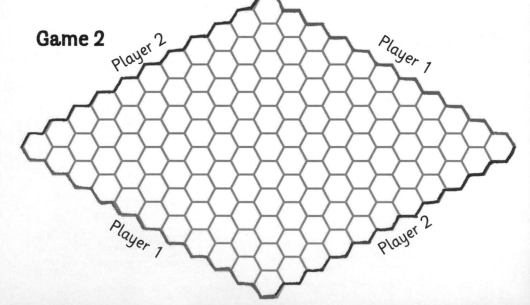

Player 2

Player 1

Player 1

Player 2

Hive

Game 1

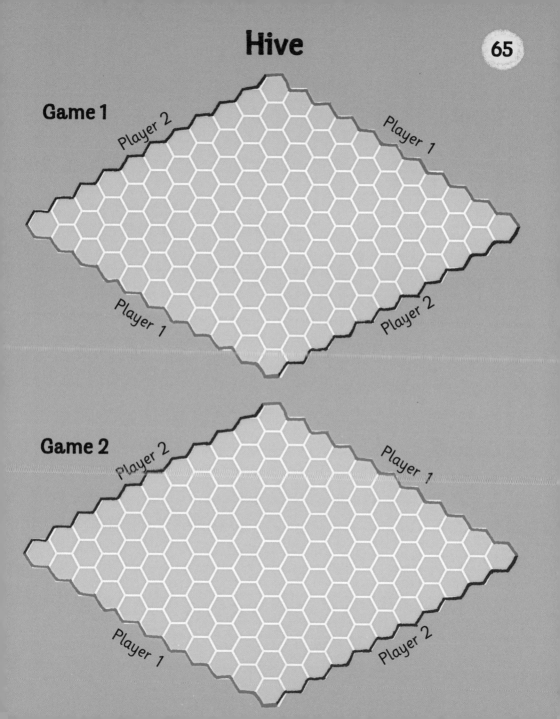

Player 2

Player 1

Player 1

Player 2

Game 2

Player 2

Player 1

Player 1

Player 2

Hive

Game 1

Player 2

Player 1

Player 1

Player 2

Game 2

Player 2

Player 1

Player 1

Player 2

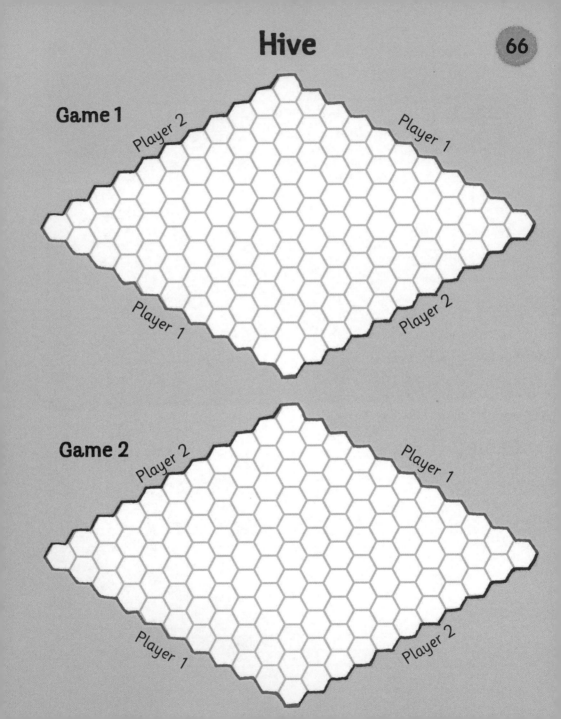

Strike out instructions

1 Player 1 (red) chooses a row, and crosses out some of its lines. You can cross out as many lines as you want, but only from that row.

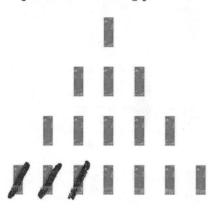

2 Player 2 (blue) then chooses a row and crosses out some of its lines. You can choose the same row as Player 1, or a different row.

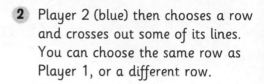

3 The winner is the player who crosses out the last line.

4 Player 2 won this game.

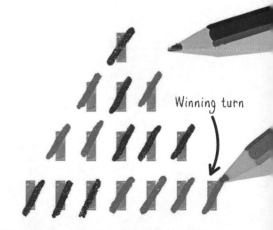

Winning turn

Strike out

Game 1

Game 2

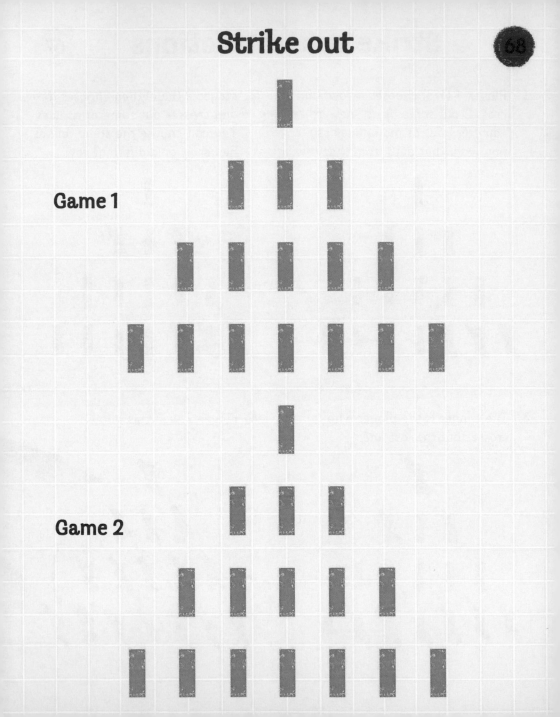

Game 1

Game 2

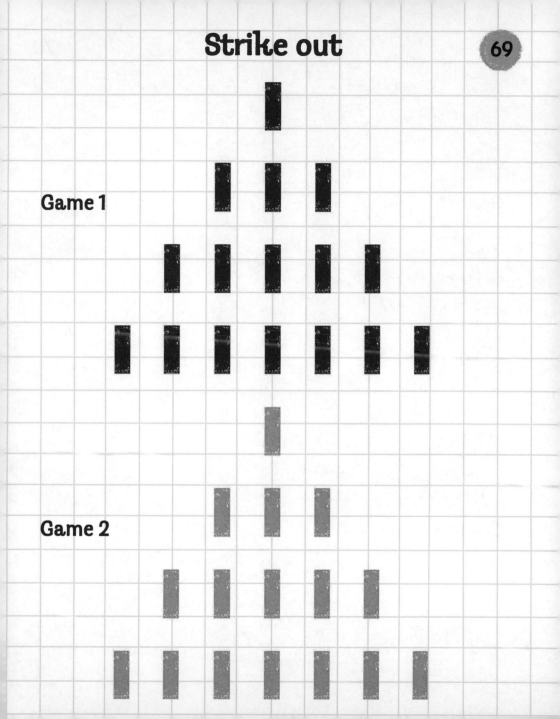

Strike out

Game 1

Game 2

Strike out

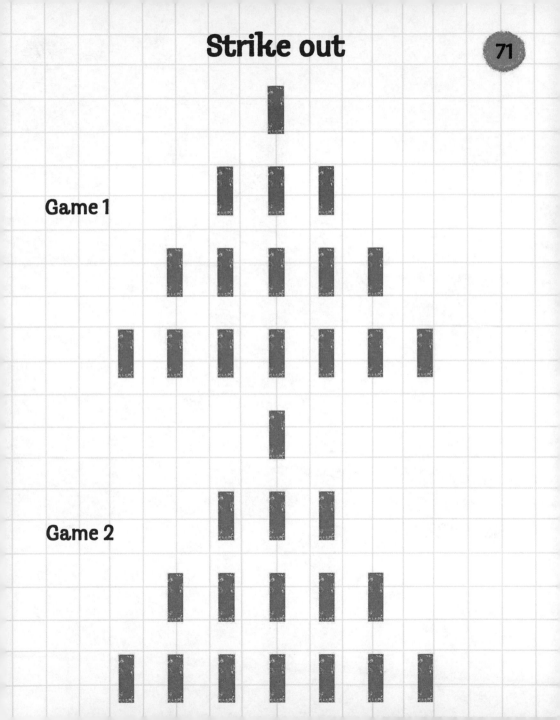

Game 1

Game 2

Strike out

Game 1

Game 2

Strike out

Game 1

Game 2

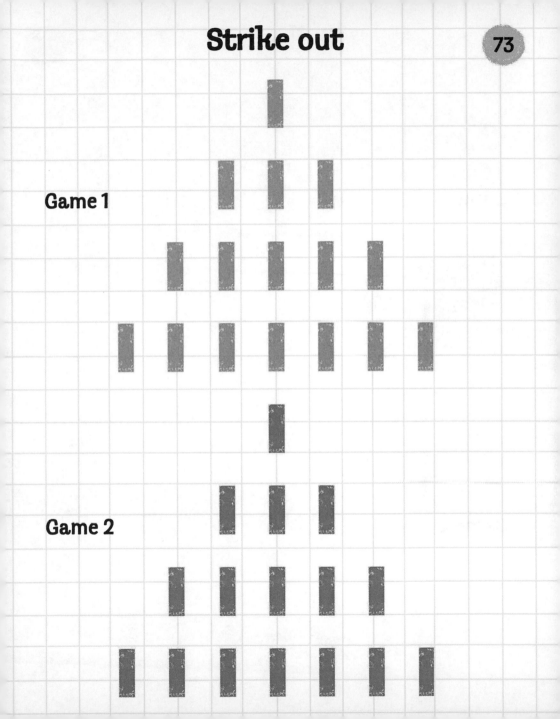

Strike out

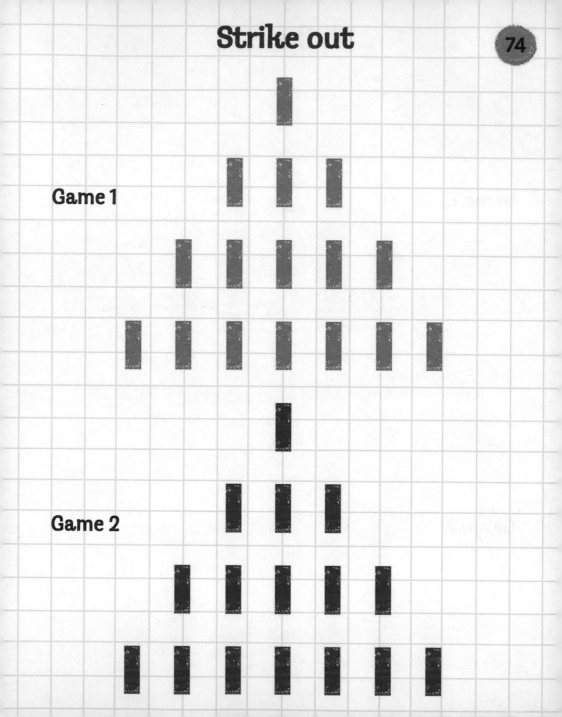

Game 1

Game 2

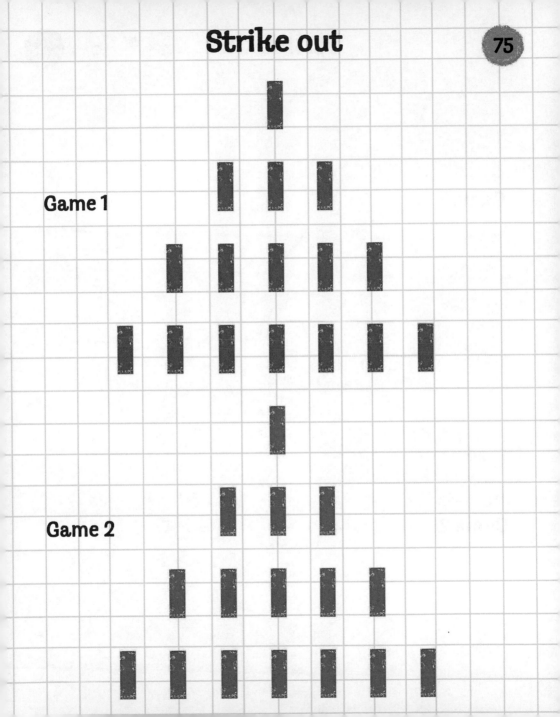

Game 1

Game 2

Strike out

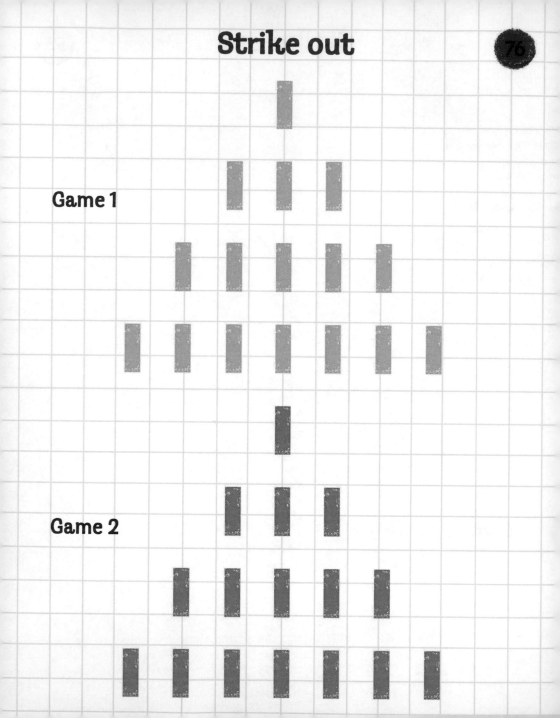

Game 1

Game 2

Code breaker instructions

Before you begin, cut or tear the page in two along the dotted line.

1 Player 1 takes the top part of the page and writes a secret four-digit code in the boxes. You must choose numbers between one and six, and you can't use the same number more than once.

2 Player 2 has their first try at guessing the code. Player 1 then puts a mark under the green circle for a number that's correct and in the right position, and a mark under the orange circle for a number that's correct but in the wrong position.

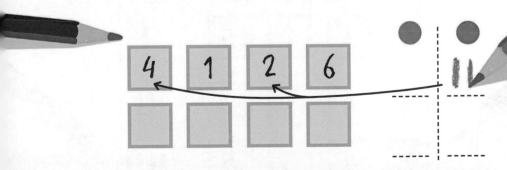

Player 2 has another guess, using the marks as clues. This time there are more correct numbers, but still none in the right place...

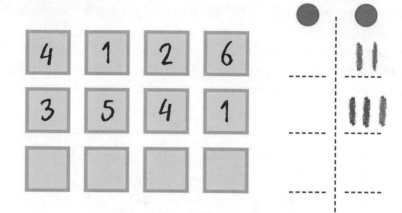

The goal is to crack the code in seven turns or less. Player 2 took five turns in this game.

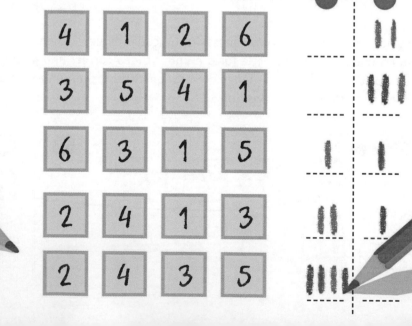

Code breaker

Cut or tear along the dotted line.

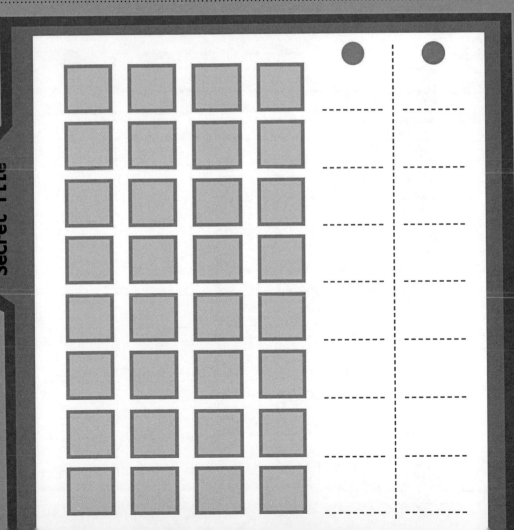

Secret file

Code breaker

Cut or tear along the dotted line.

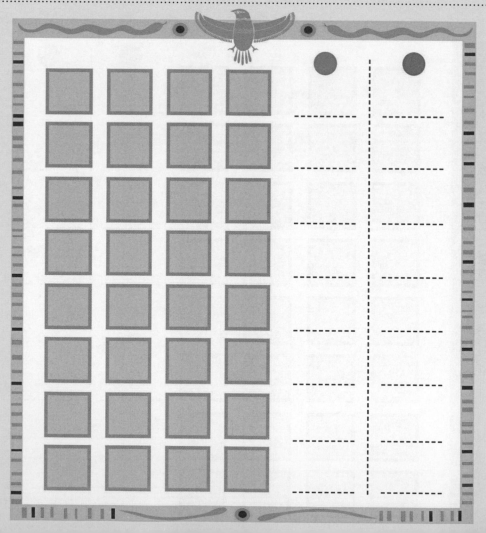

Code breaker

Cut or tear along the dotted line.

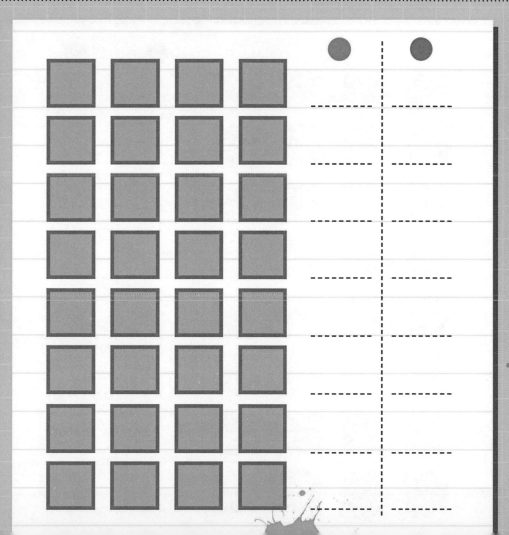

Code breaker

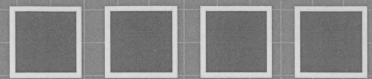

Cut or tear along the dotted line.

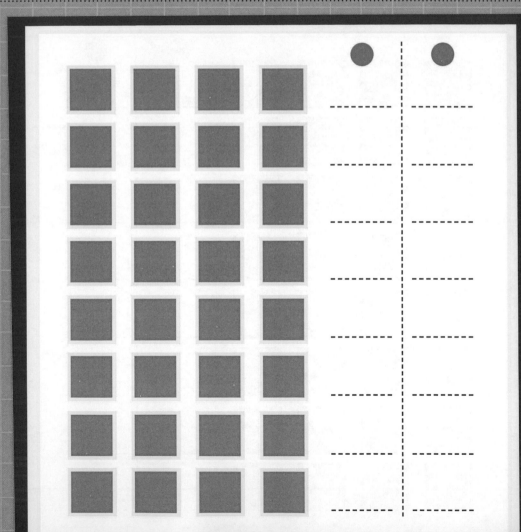

Code breaker

Cut or tear along the dotted line.

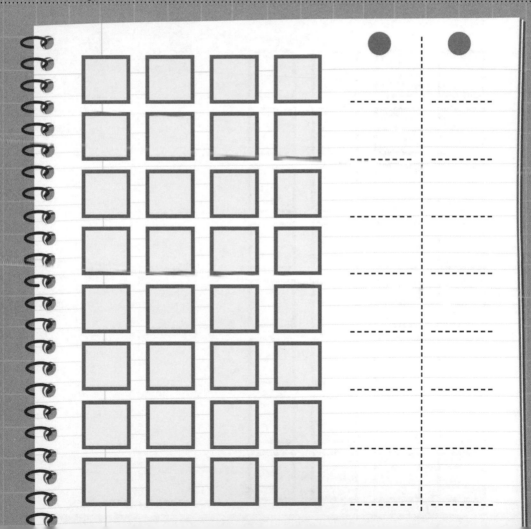

Code breaker

Cut or tear along the dotted line.

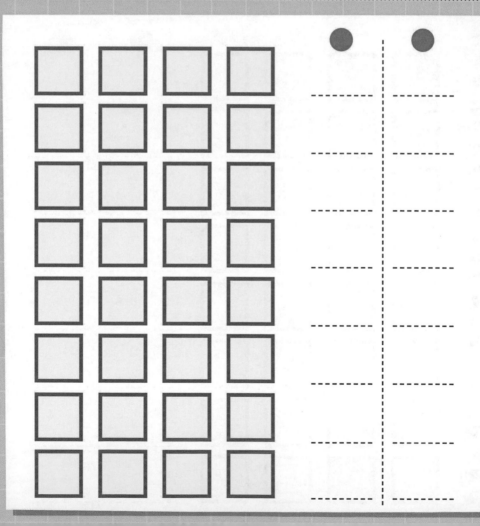

Code breaker

Cut or tear along the dotted line.

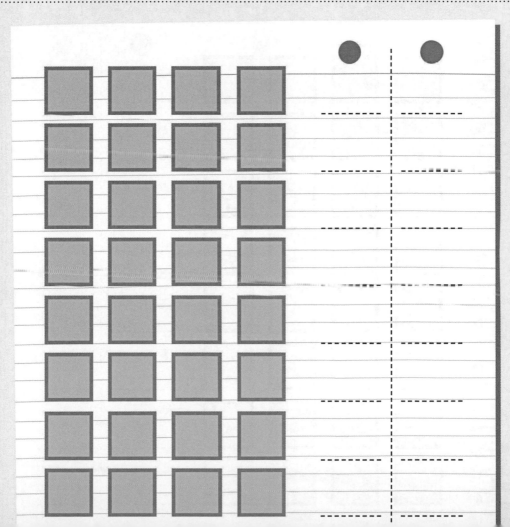

Cut or tear along the dotted line.

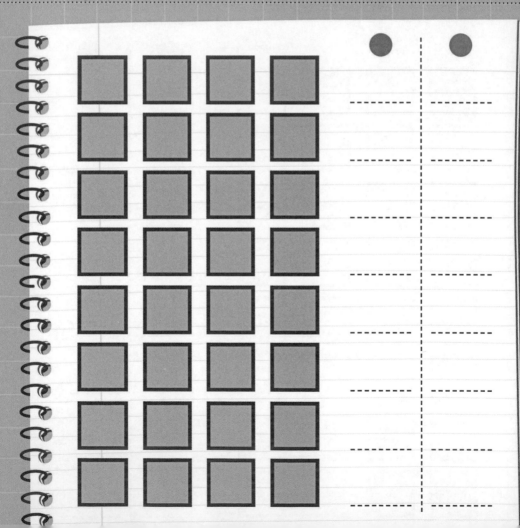

Sharp shooter instructions

1 Before the game begins, both players mark an 'X' anywhere along the borderline of their zone. This is your starting position.

2 The goal is to draw a line in one quick swipe from your starting position straight through your opponent's zone.

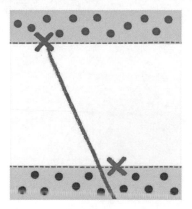

3 To score a point, your line must reach the back edge of your opponent's zone and not touch any dots on the way.

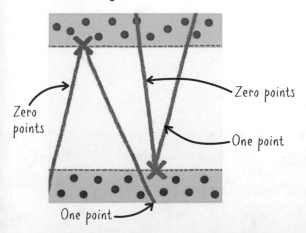

Zero points

Zero points

One point

Zero points

One point

4 The first player to score five points is the winner. If both players reach five points in the same number of turns, the game is a tie.

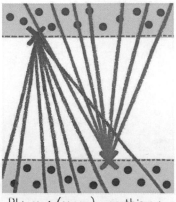

Player 1 (green) won this game.

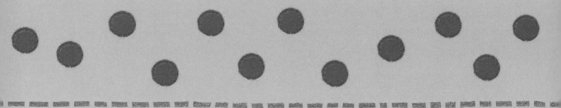

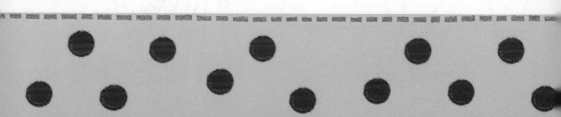

Sharp shooter

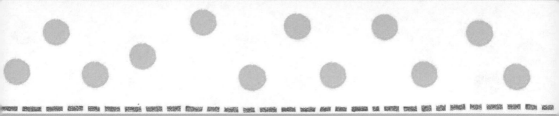

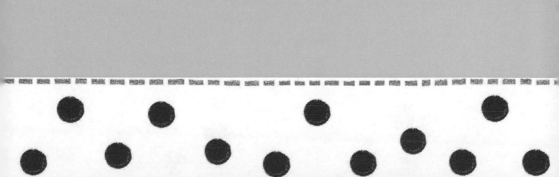

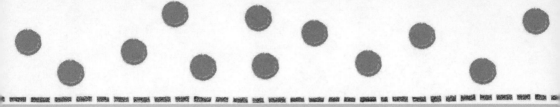

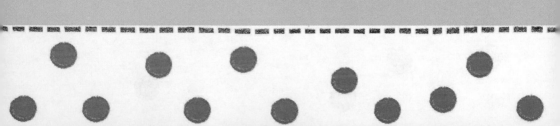

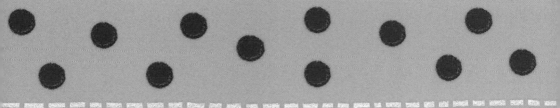

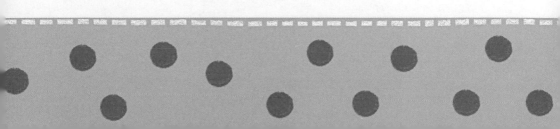

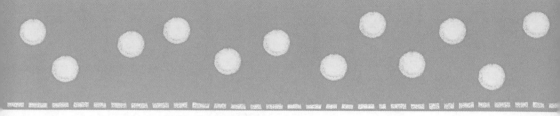

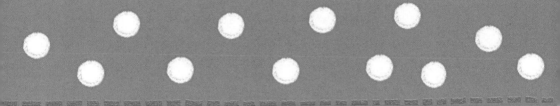

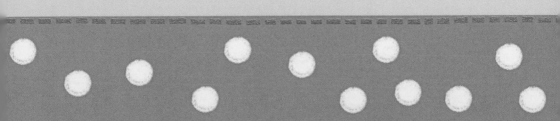

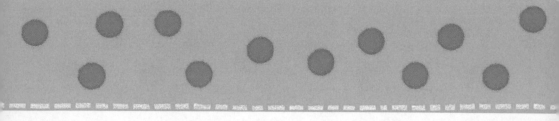

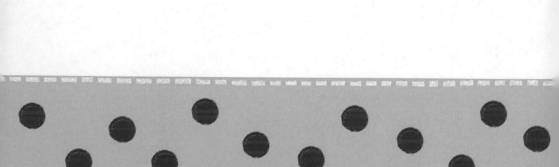

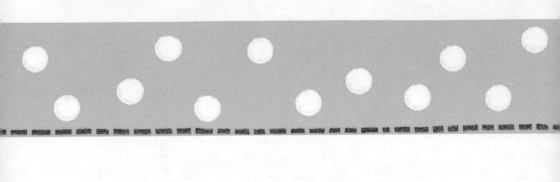

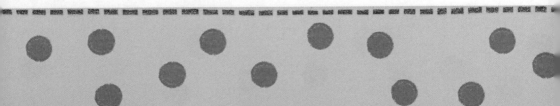

Battleships instructions

Before you begin, cut or tear along the dotted line so that each player has their own pair of grids.

1 Draw three ships on your fleet grid without letting your opponent see them. The ships go horizontally or vertically in lines of 3, 4 and 5 squares.

Player 1 fleet

	1	2	3	4	5	6	7	8
A								
B			Cruiser					
C								
D								
E		Destroyer				Battleship		
F								
G								
H								

Target grid

	1	2	3	4	5	6	7	8
A								
B								
C								
D								
E								
F								
G								
H								

2 Take turns firing at each other. Mark your own shots on your target grid, and your opponent's shots on your fleet grid. Use X for a miss and O for a hit.

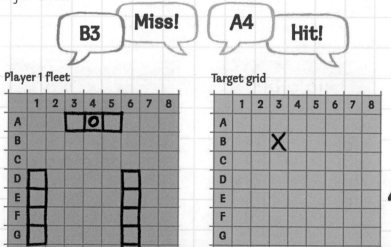

B3 Miss! **A4** Hit!

Player 1 fleet

	1	2	3	4	5	6	7	8
A				O				
B								
C								
D								
E								
F								
G								
H								

Target grid

	1	2	3	4	5	6	7	8
A								
B			X					
C								
D								
E								
F								
G								
H								

3 A ship is sunk when all its squares are hit. Tell your opponent which ship they've sunk.

A5

Hit! You've sunk my cruiser.

Player 1 fleet

	1	2	3	4	5	6	7	8
A		X	O	O	O			
B								
C								
D								
E								
F								
G								
H								

Target grid

	1	2	3	4	5	6	7	8
A								
B			X					
C								
D								
E						O	O	X
F								
G								
H								

4 The first player to sink all of their opponent's ships is the winner. Player 2 won this game.

Player 1 fleet

	1	2	3	4	5	6	7	8
A		X	O	O	O			
B			X					
C								
D	O					O		
E	O			X		O		
F	O					O	X	
G	O					O		
H					X	O		

Target grid

	1	2	3	4	5	6	7	8
A					X	O	X	
B			X			O		
C						O		
D						X		
E			O	O	O	O	O	X
F								
G					X			
H	X	O					X	

Battleships

Player 1 fleet

◎	1	2	3	4	5	6	7	8
A								
B								
C								
D								
E								
F								
G								
H								

Target grid

◎	1	2	3	4	5	6	7	8
A								
B								
C								
D								
E								
F								
G								
H								

Hit!

Cut or tear along the dotted line.

Player 2 fleet

Target grid

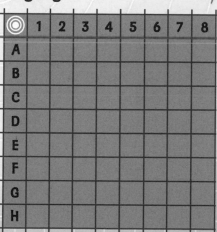

Battleships

Player 1 fleet

	1	2	3	4	5	6	7	8
A								
B								
C								
D								
E								
F								
G								
H								

Target grid

	1	2	3	4	5	6	7	8
A								
B								
C								
D								
E								
F								
G								
H								

Cut or tear along the dotted line.

Player 2 fleet

	1	2	3	4	5	6	7	8
A								
B								
C								
D								
E								
F								
G								
H								

Miss! Hit!

Target grid

	1	2	3	4	5	6	7	8
A								
B								
C								
D								
E								
F								
G								
H								

Battleships

Player 1 fleet

	1	2	3	4	5	6	7	8
A								
B								
C								
D								
E								
F								
G								
H								

Target grid

	1	2	3	4	5	6	7	8
A								
B								
C								
D								
E								
F								
G								
H								

Cut or tear along the dotted line.

Player 2 fleet

	1	2	3	4	5	6	7	8
A								
B								
C								
D								
E								
F								
G								
H								

Target grid

	1	2	3	4	5	6	7	8
A								
B								
C								
D								
E								
F								
G								
H								

Battleships

Player 1 fleet

◎	1	2	3	4	5	6	7	8
A								
B								
C								
D								
E								
F								
G								
H								

Target grid

◎	1	2	3	4	5	6	7	8
A								
B								
C								
D								
E								
F								
G								
H								

Hit!

Cut or tear along the dotted line.

Miss!

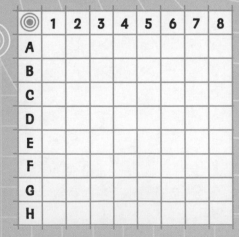

Player 2 fleet

◎	1	2	3	4	5	6	7	8
A								
B								
C								
D								
E								
F								
G								
H								

Target grid

◎	1	2	3	4	5	6	7	8
A								
B								
C								
D								
E								
F								
G								
H								

Battleships

Player 1 fleet

	1	2	3	4	5	6	7	8
A								
B								
C								
D								
E								
F								
G								
H								

Target grid

	1	2	3	4	5	6	7	8
A								
B								
C								
D								
E								
F								
G								
H								

Cut or tear along the dotted line.

Player 2 fleet

	1	2	3	4	5	6	7	8
A								
B								
C								
D								
E								
F								
G								
H								

Target grid

	1	2	3	4	5	6	7	8
A								
B								
C								
D								
E								
F								
G								
H								

Battleships

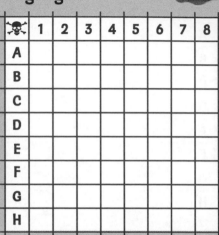

Player 1 fleet

☠	1	2	3	4	5	6	7	8
A								
B								
C								
D								
E								
F								
G								
H								

Target grid

☠	1	2	3	4	5	6	7	8
A								
B								
C								
D								
E								
F								
G								
H								

Cut or tear along the dotted line.

Player 2 fleet

☠	1	2	3	4	5	6	7	8
A								
B								
C								
D								
E								
F								
G								
H								

Target grid

☠	1	2	3	4	5	6	7	8
A								
B								
C								
D								
E								
F								
G								
H								

Battleships

Miss!

Player 1 fleet

⊚	1	2	3	4	5	6	7	8
A								
B								
C								
D								
E								
F								
G								
H								

Target grid

⊚	1	2	3	4	5	6	7	8
A								
B								
C								
D								
E								
F								
G								
H								

Hit!

Cut or tear along the dotted line.

Player 2 fleet

⊚	1	2	3	4	5	6	7	8
A								
B								
C								
D								
E								
F								
G								
H								

Target grid

⊚	1	2	3	4	5	6	7	8
A								
B								
C								
D								
E								
F								
G								
H								

Battleships

Player 1 fleet

	1	2	3	4	5	6	7	8
A								
B								
C								
D								
E								
F								
G								
H								

Target grid

	1	2	3	4	5	6	7	8
A								
B								
C								
D								
E								
F								
G								
H								

Cut or tear along the dotted line.

Player 2 fleet

	1	2	3	4	5	6	7	8
A								
B								
C								
D								
E								
F								
G								
H								

Target grid

	1	2	3	4	5	6	7	8
A								
B								
C								
D								
E								
F								
G								
H								

Battleships

Player 1 fleet

	1	2	3	4	5	6	7	8
A								
B								
C								
D								
E								
F								
G								
H								

Target grid

	1	2	3	4	5	6	7	8
A								
B								
C								
D								
E								
F								
G								
H								

Cut or tear along the dotted line.

Player 2 fleet

	1	2	3	4	5	6	7	8
A								
B								
C								
D								
E								
F								
G								
H								

Target grid

	1	2	3	4	5	6	7	8
A								
B								
C								
D								
E								
F								
G								
H								

Battleships

Player 1 fleet

	1	2	3	4	5	6	7	8
A								
B								
C								
D								
E								
F								
G								
H								

Target grid

	1	2	3	4	5	6	7	8
A								
B								
C								
D								
E								
F								
G								
H								

Cut or tear along the dotted line.

Player 2 fleet

	1	2	3	4	5	6	7	8
A								
B								
C								
D								
E								
F								
G								
H								

Target grid

	1	2	3	4	5	6	7	8
A								
B								
C								
D								
E								
F								
G								
H								

Caterpillar instructions

1 Player 1 (red) starts by drawing a line between two dots. The line can be vertical or horizontal.

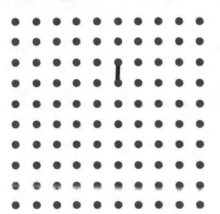

2 Player 2 (green) then joins one end of the line to another dot.

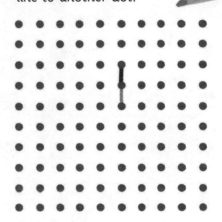

3 Take turns until one of you can't join either end of the line to a dot that hasn't been used. This player loses the game.

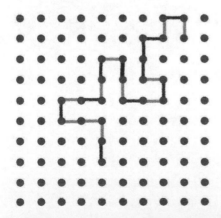

4 Player 1 wins the game below, because Player 2 can't connect to a dot that hasn't been used at either end of the line.

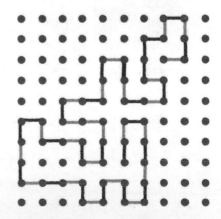

Caterpillar

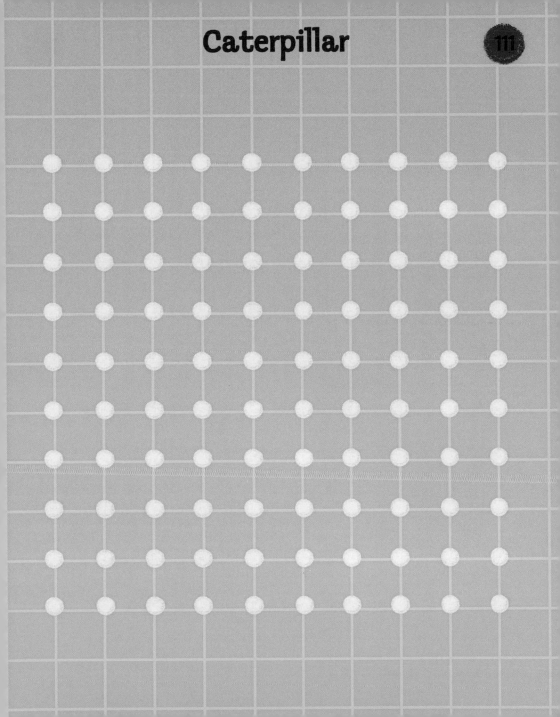

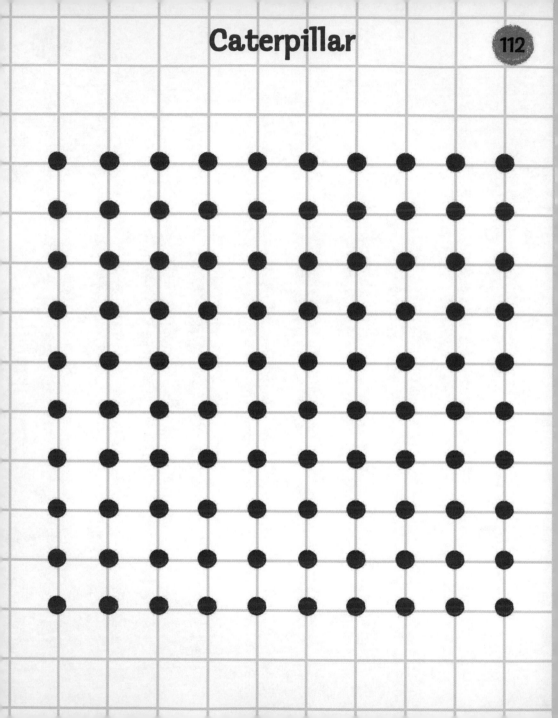

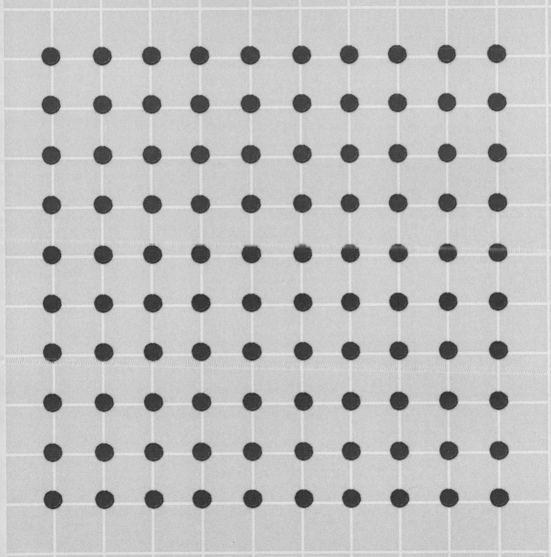

Caterpillar

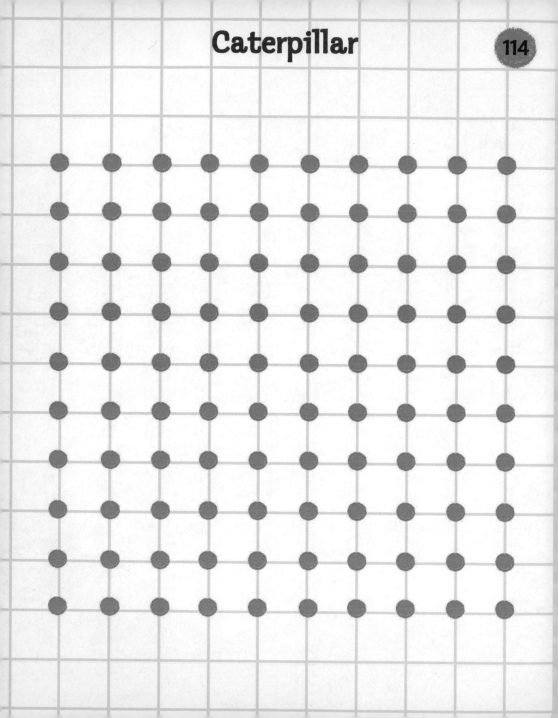

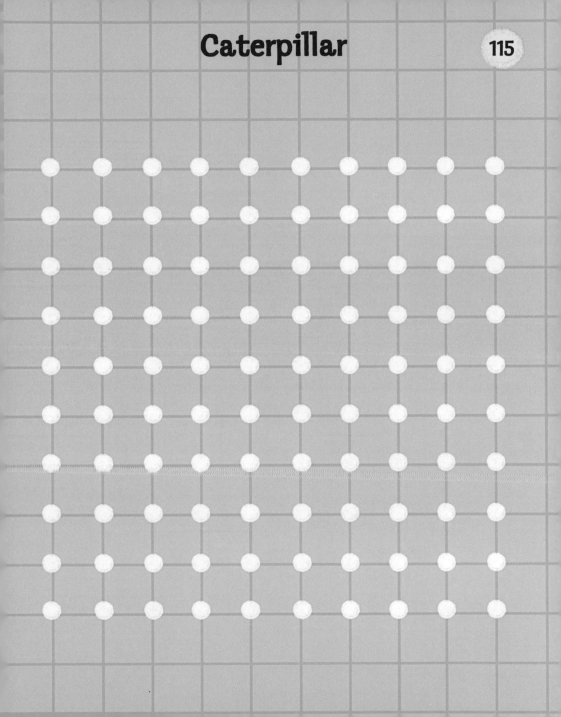

Caterpillar

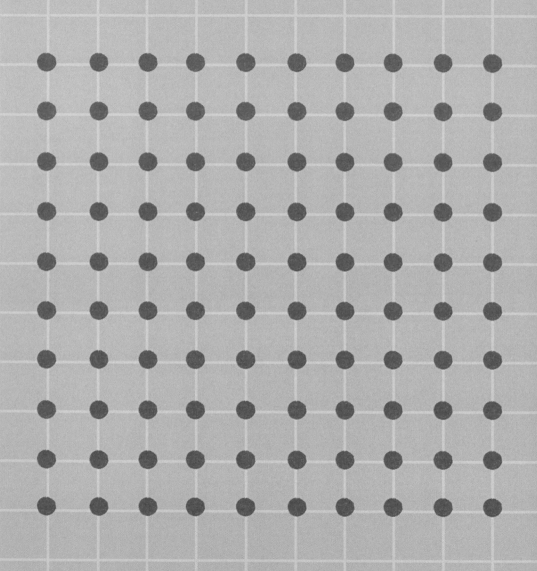

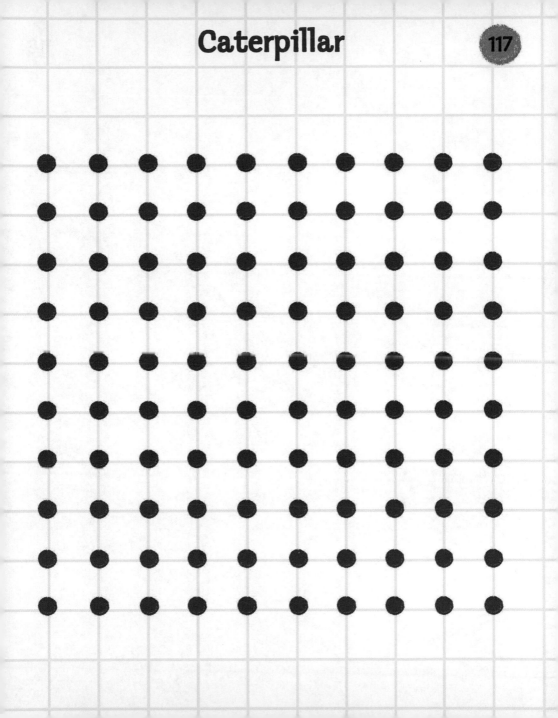

Caterpillar

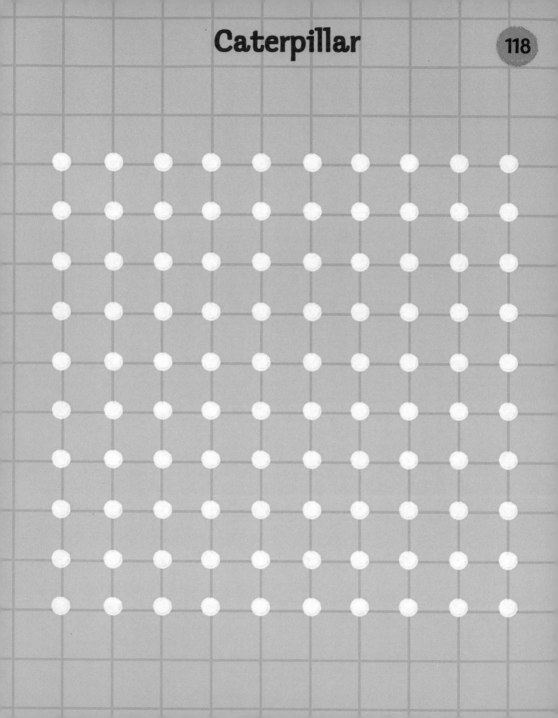

Shooting stars instructions

1 Before the game begins, each player draws a small circle anywhere along the start line. This is your starting position.

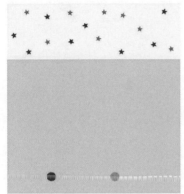

Player 1   Player 2

2 The goal is to hit a star by drawing a straight line in one quick swipe. In this game, Player 1 aims at the purple stars, Player 2 at the blue.

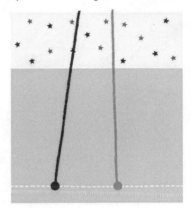

3 Score a point for each star you hit. But if you also hit your opponent's star with the same line, score zero points. If you hit two of your own stars, score two points.

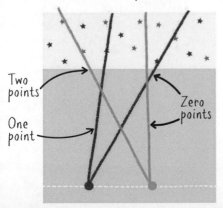

Two points

One point

Zero points

4 The first player to score three points is the winner. If both players reach three points in the same number of turns, the game is a tie. Player 2 won this game.

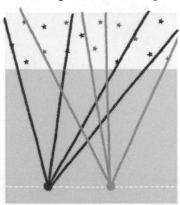

Shooting stars

Shooting stars

Shooting stars

Shooting stars

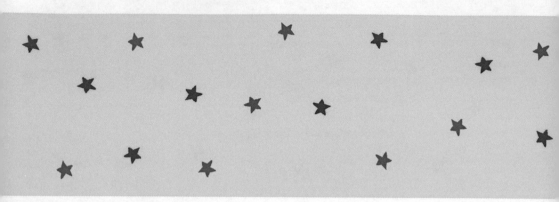

Shooting stars

Super Os and Xs instructions

1 Player 1 marks an X in any of the spaces on the grid.

2 Player 2 then marks an O in any of the other spaces.

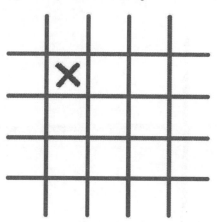 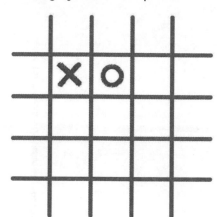

3 The goal is to make horizontal, vertical or diagonal lines of three in a row. You can't reuse one of your symbols to make another line.

4 The winner is the player who makes the most lines of three in a row. Player 1 won this game.

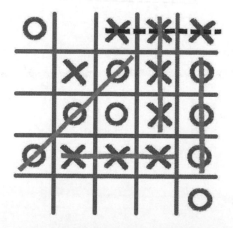

Super Os and Xs

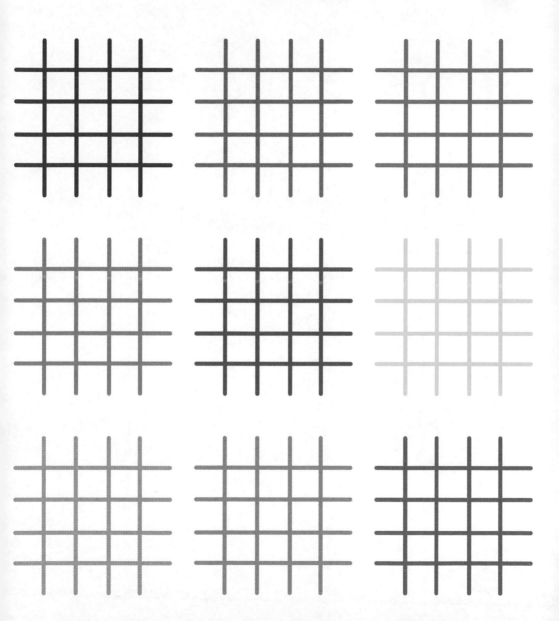

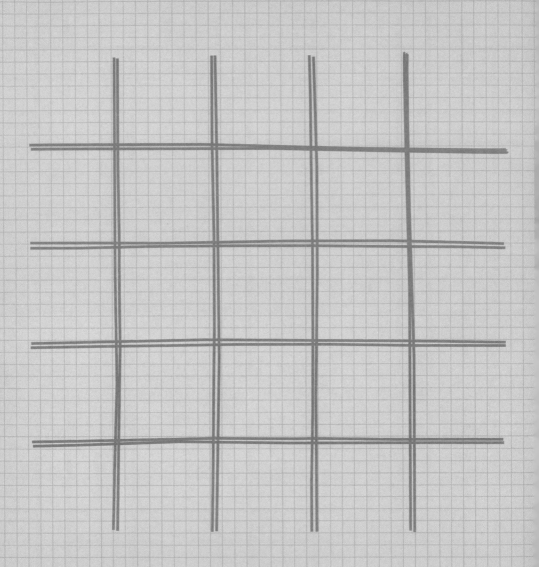

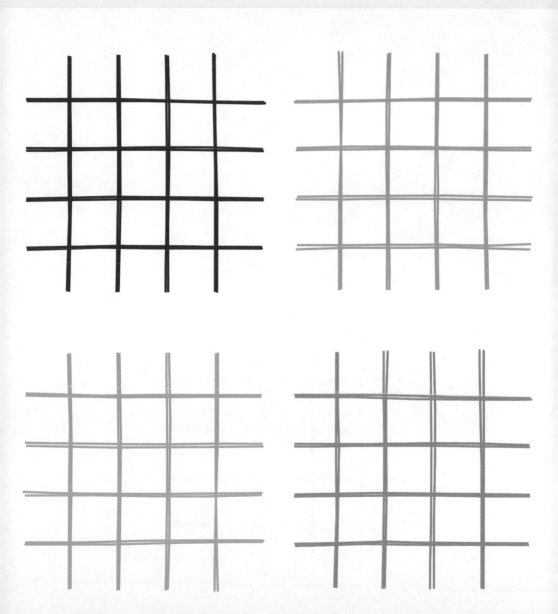

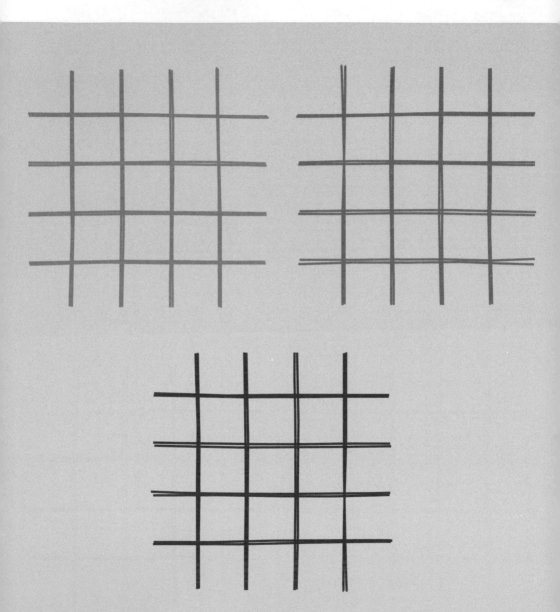

Super Os and Xs

Super Os and Xs

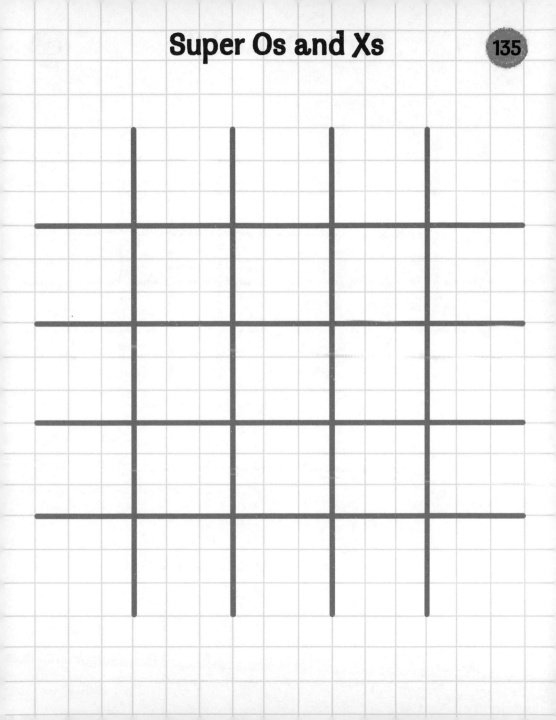

135

Super Os and Xs

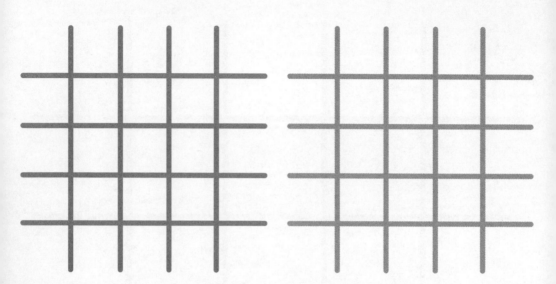

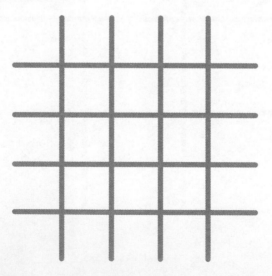

Crossed words instructions

1 Player 1 thinks of a word, then writes it down and crosses out all those letters from the top alphabet.

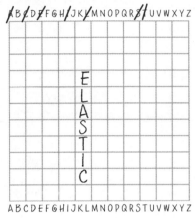

2 Player 2 joins a word to the first word and crosses out all those letters from the bottom alphabet (except for the one used in the first word).

3 You can't play a letter more than once, and words can't go side by side unless each pair of letters makes a new word.

4 The game ends when neither player can use any more letters. The player who's used the most letters is the winner. Player 2 won this game.

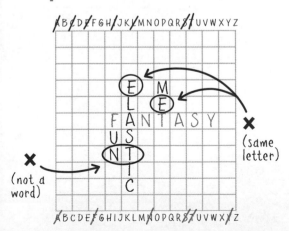

Crossed words

a b c d e f g h i j k l m n o p q r s t u v w x y z

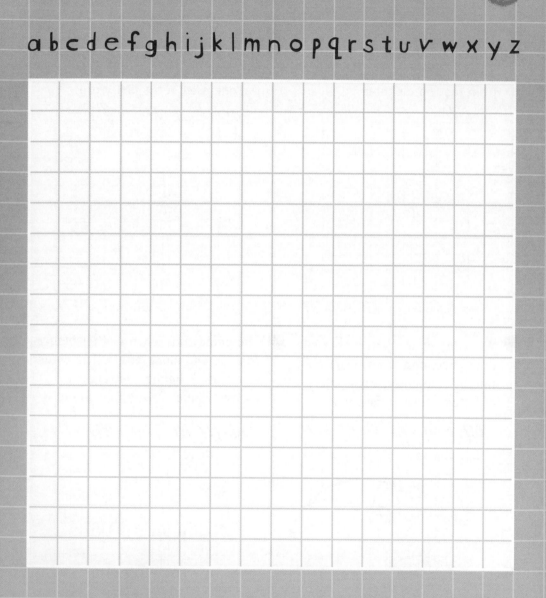

a b c d e f g h i j k l m n o p q r s t u v w x y z

Crossed words

a b c d e f g h i j k l m n o p q r s t u v w x y z

a b c d e f g h i j k l m n o p q r s t u v w x y z

Crossed words

abcdefghijklmnopqrstuvwxyz

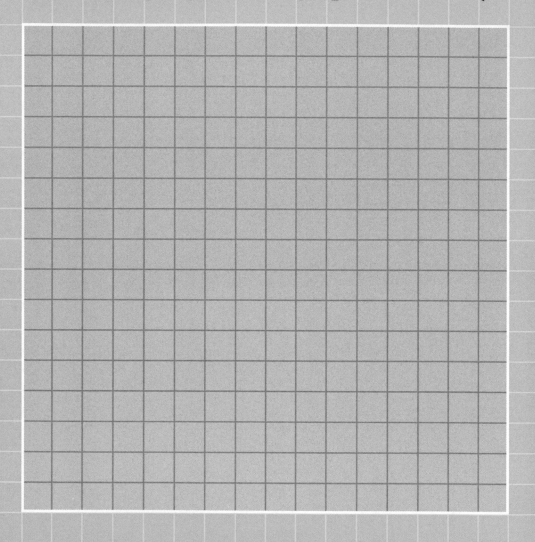

abcdefghijklmnopqrstuvwxyz

Crossed words

A B C D E F G H I J K L M N O P Q R S T U V W X Y Z

A B C D E F G H I J K L M N O P Q R S T U V W X Y Z

Crossed words

a b c d e f g h i j k l m n o p q r s t u v w x y z

a b c d e f g h i j k l m n o p q r s t u v w x y z

ABCDEFGHIJKLMNOPQRSTUVWXYZ

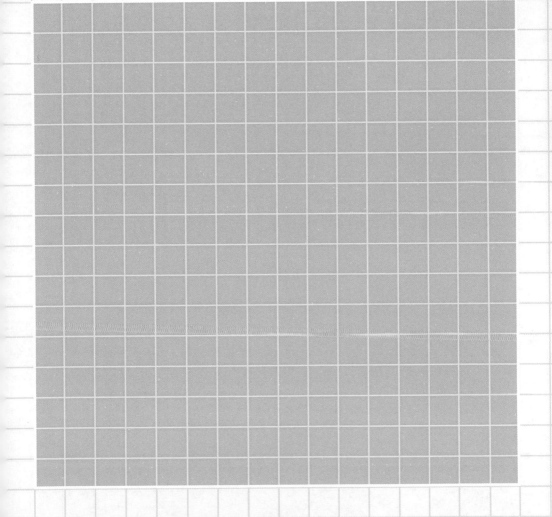

ABCDEFGHIJKLMNOPQRSTUVWXYZ

Crossed words

144

A B C D E F G H I J K L M N O P Q R S T U V W X Y Z

A B C D E F G H I J K L M N O P Q R S T U V W X Y Z

Crossed words

abcdefghijklmnopqrstuvwxyz

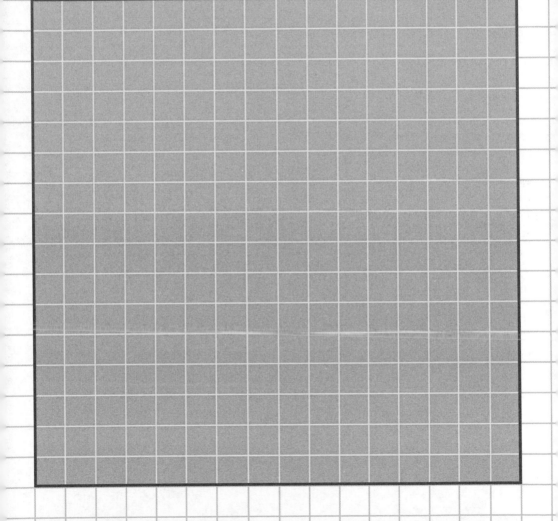

abcdefghijklmnopqrstuvwxyz

a b c d e f g h i j k l m n o p q r s t u v w x y z

a b c d e f g h i j k l m n o p q r s t u v w x y z

Crossed words

a b c d e f g h i j k l m n o p q r s t u v w x y z

a b c d e f g h i j k l m n o p q r s t u v w x y z

a b c d e f g h i j k l m n o p q r s t u v w x y z

a b c d e f g h i j k l m n o p q r s t u v w x y z

Boxes instructions

1 Player 1 (green) joins any two dots with a horizontal or vertical straight line.

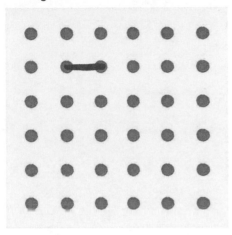

2 Player 2 (orange) then makes another horizontal or vertical straight line.

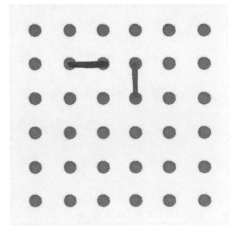

3 The goal is to be the player that completes a box. When you complete a box, write your initial inside and take an extra turn.

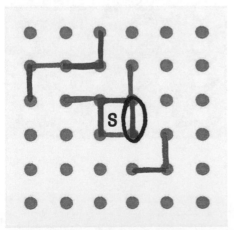

4 When no more lines can be added, the winner is the player who's made the most boxes. Player 1 won this game.

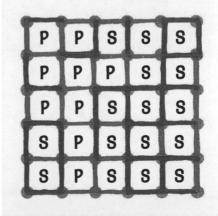

Boxes

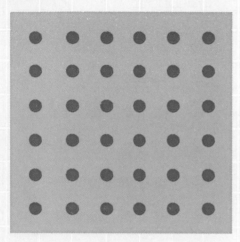

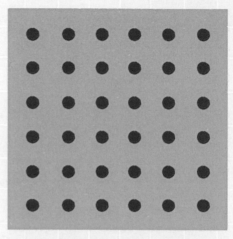

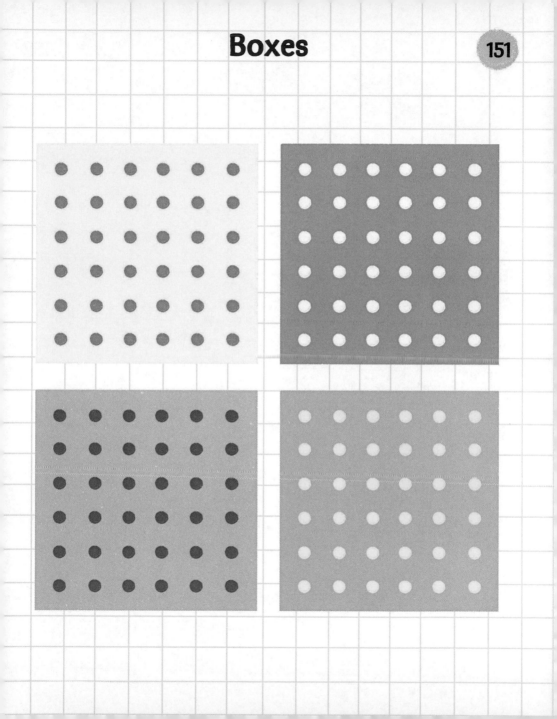

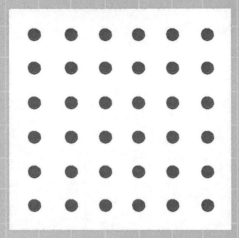

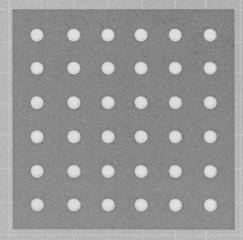
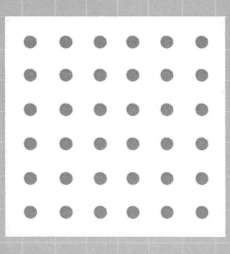

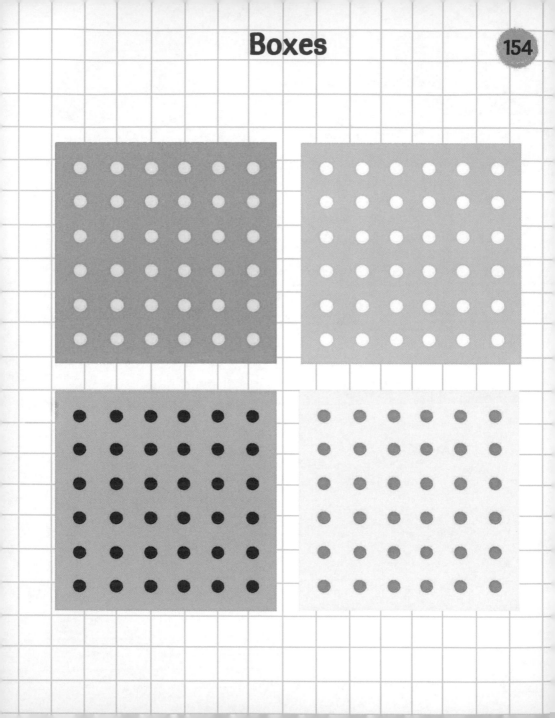

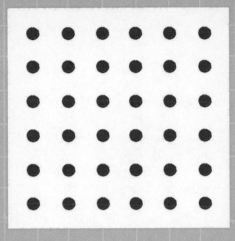

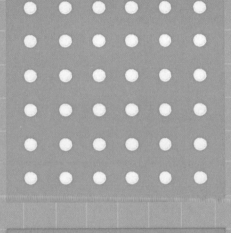

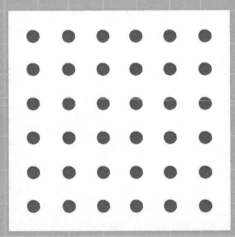

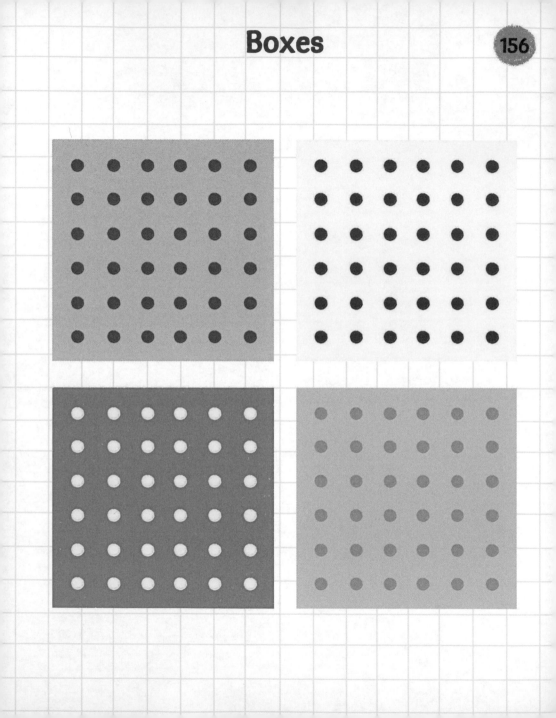

Triangles instructions

1 Player 1 (red) chooses one of the 'crosspoints' between the triangles, and draws a dot.

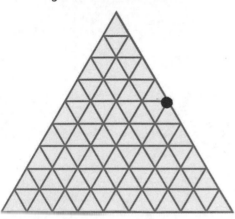

2 Player 2 (blue) then chooses one of the other crosspoints and draws a dot.

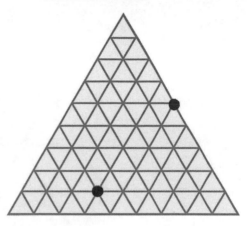

3 Take turns to mark crosspoints anywhere on the grid. Your goal is to make a chain that connects all three sides of the grid.

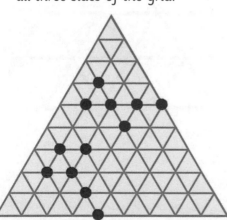

4 The winner is the first player to complete their chain. Player 1 won this game.

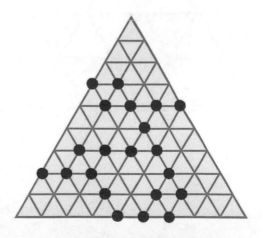

Triangles

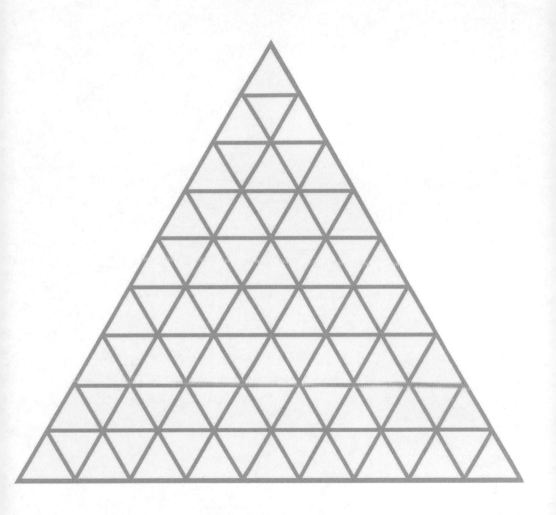

Triangles

Triangles

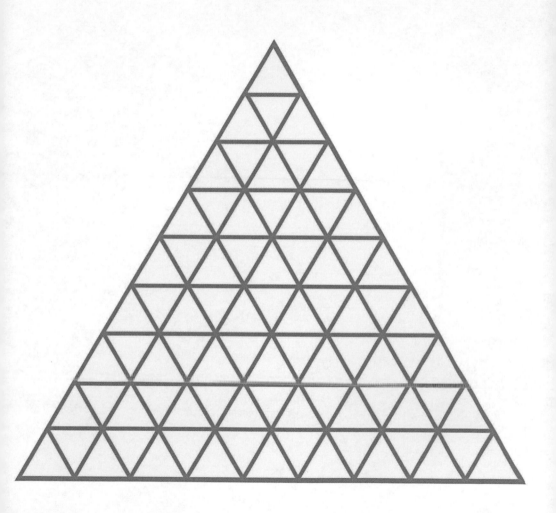

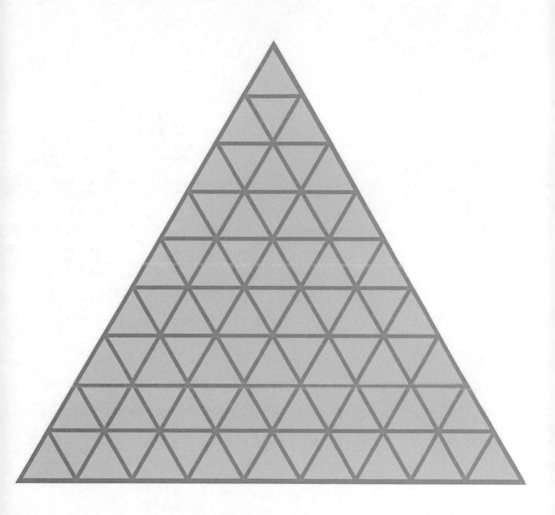

Triangles

Treasure hunter instructions

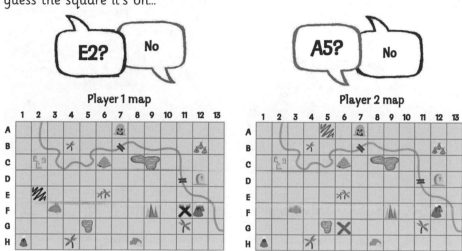 167

Before you start, cut or tear along the dotted line so you both have a map. Then secretly mark your treasure in one of the squares with an X.

1. Now take turns searching for your opponent's treasure. You can either guess the square it's on...

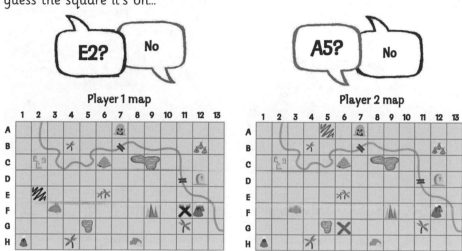

2. ...or ask a yes/no question to narrow the search.

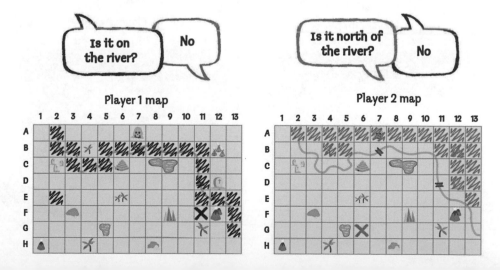

3 You can also use features on the map to help you in your search.

4 The first player to find their opponent's treasure is the winner.

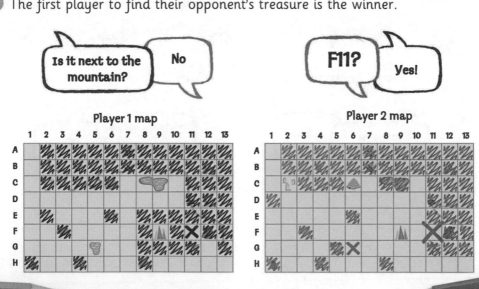

Treasure hunter

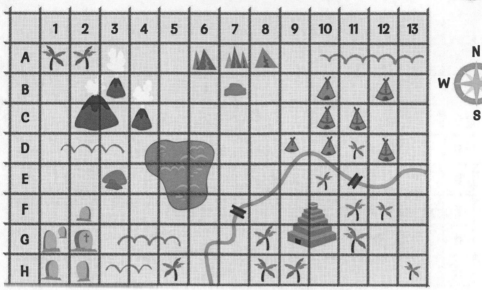

Cut or tear along the dotted line.

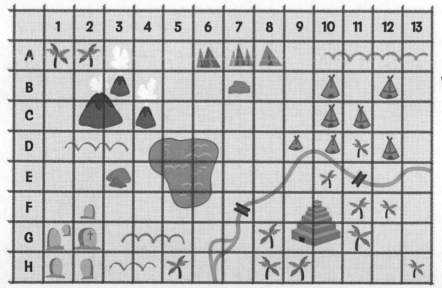

Treasure hunter

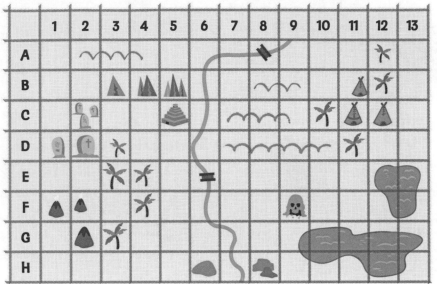

. . . .

Cut or tear along the dotted line.

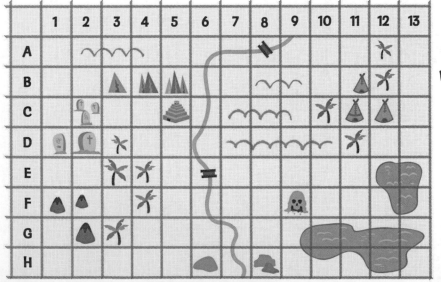

Treasure hunter

Cut or tear along the dotted line.

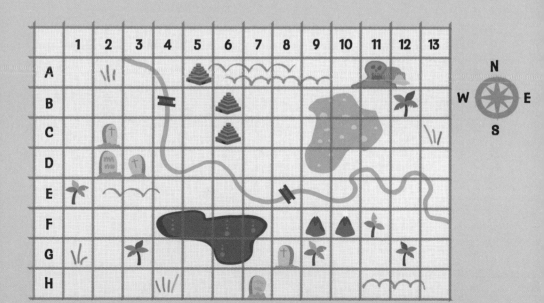

Treasure hunter

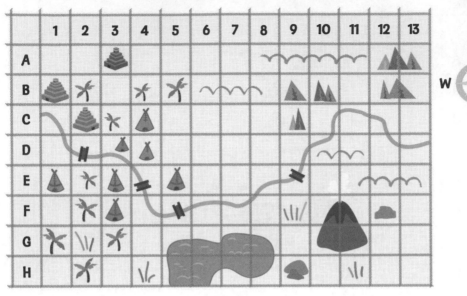

Cut or tear along the dotted line.

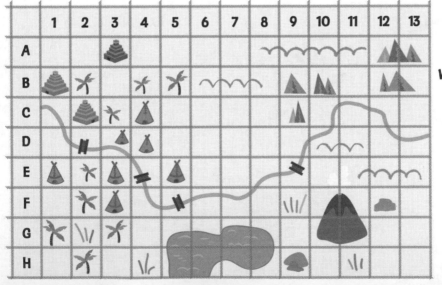

Treasure hunter

Cut or tear along the dotted line.

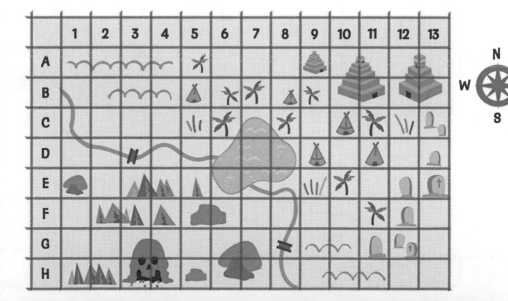

Treasure hunter

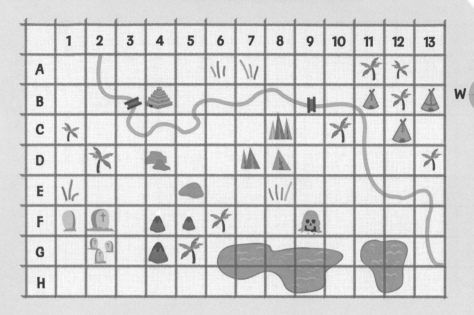

Cut or tear along the dotted line.

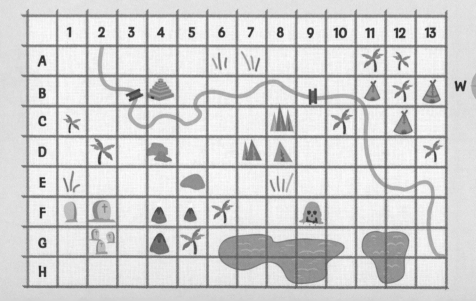

Treasure hunter

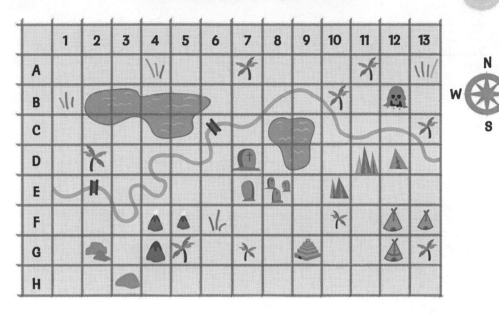

Cut or tear along the dotted line.

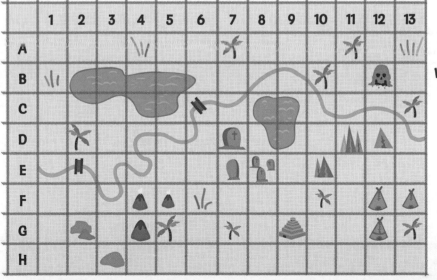

Treasure hunter

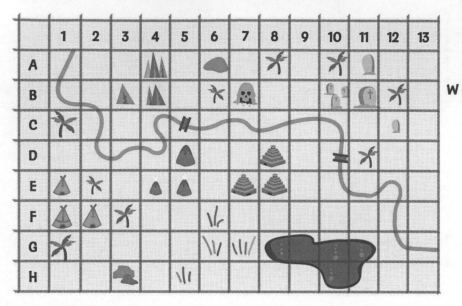

Cut or tear along the dotted line.

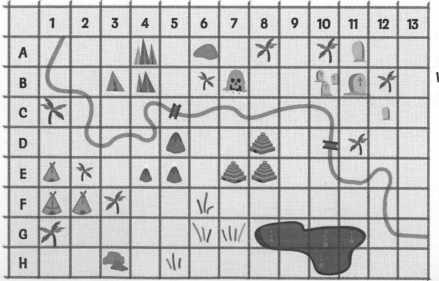

Sprouts instructions

1 Player 1 (blue): connect two of the dots, or draw a loop to connect a dot to itself, then add a new dot somewhere along the new line.

2 Player 2 (green): do the same. You can use the original dots, and also the new dot added by Player 1.

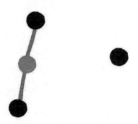

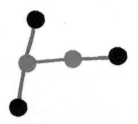

3 There are two things to remember: a dot can only have three lines coming out of it, and none of the lines can cross each other.

4 The loser is the first player who can't make a move. Player 1 won this game as Player 2 has nowhere to go.

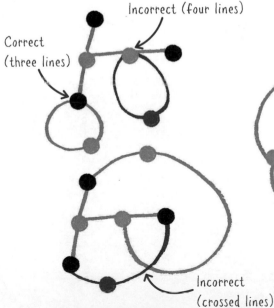

Incorrect (four lines)

Correct (three lines)

Incorrect (crossed lines)

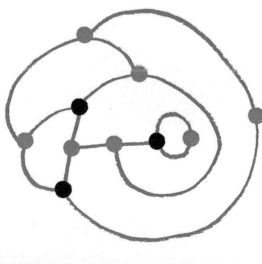

Sprouts

Sprouts

Sprouts

Sprouts

Sprouts

Sprouts

Sprouts

Sprouts

Sprouts

OXO instructions

1 Player 1 (black) and Player 2 take turns to mark an O or an X in empty squares on the grid. Both players can use either letter.

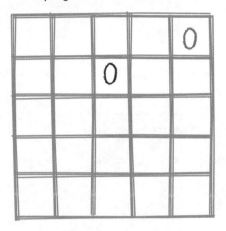

2 The goal is to complete lines that read 'OXO'. Player 1 has just completed a line by marking an O in the space below.

O	X	X		O
		O		
X		X		
	X	⊙	O	
		X		

3 If you complete two lines with one letter, you get an extra turn. Player 2 has just completed two lines below.

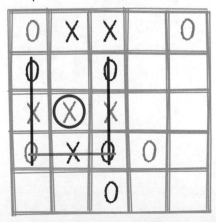

4 When all the spaces have been filled, the player who has completed the most lines is the winner. This game was a tie.

O	X	X	X	O
O	X	O	O	X
X		X	O	O
O	X	O	O	O
X	O	O	X	X

OXO

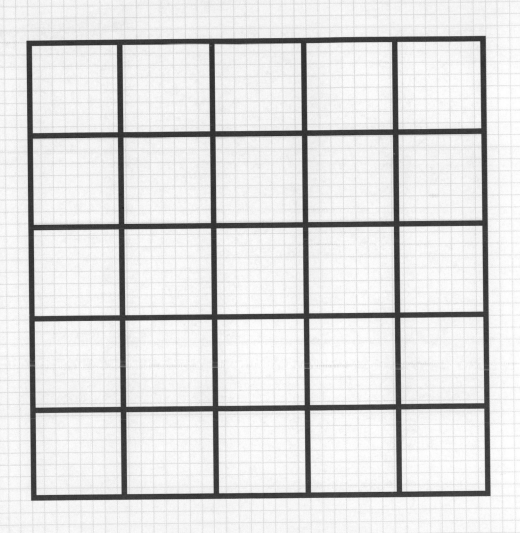

Pair them up instructions

1 Player 1 (blue) draws a line between any matching pair.

2 Player 2 (green) then draws a line between any other matching pair.

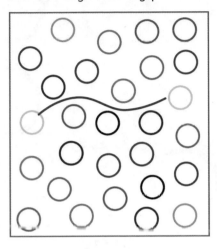

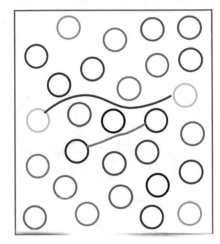

3 You must draw your line without taking your pen off the page. If it touches a circle from a different pair, or another line, you lose the game.

4 Player 2 won this game, because Player 1 touched another line while trying to join the two dark blue circles.

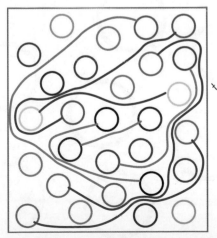

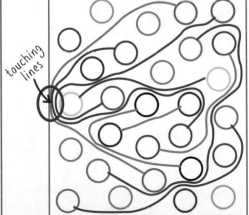

touching lines

Pair them up

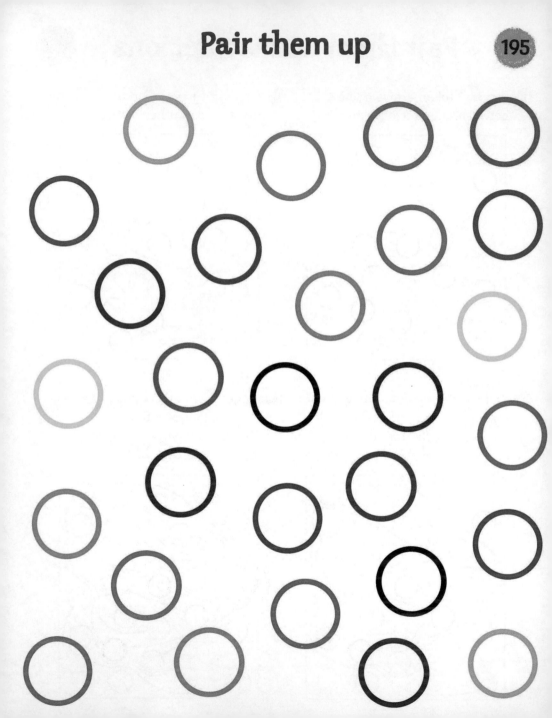

Pair them up

Pair them up

Pair them up

Pair them up

Pair them up

200

Pair them up

201

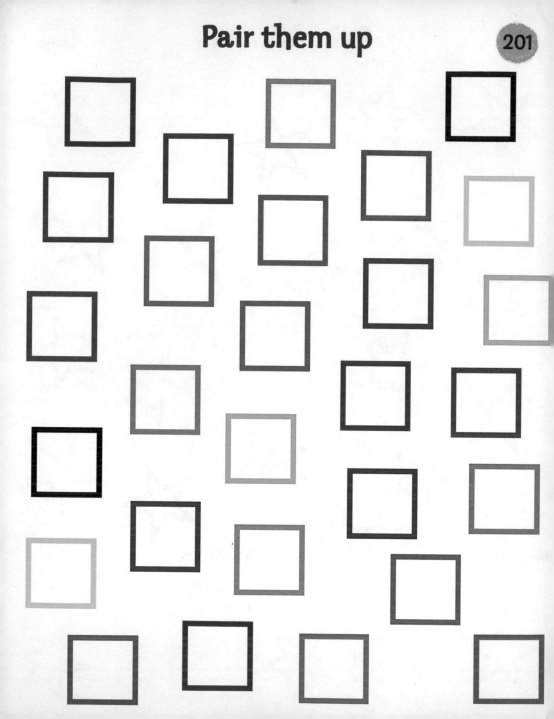